HIDDEN®
Tahiti

HIDDEN ®
Tahiti

Including Moorea, Bora Bora,
and the Society, Austral, Gambier,
Tuamotu and Marquesas Islands

Robert F. Kay

Jad Davenport
Update Author

FIFTH EDITION

color insert by Jad Davenport

Ulysses Press ®
BERKELEY, CALIFORNIA

Published by:
ULYSSES PRESS
P.O. Box 3440
Berkeley, CA 94703
www.ulyssespress.com

ISSN 1098-8998
ISBN 1-56975-426-8

Printed in Canada by Transcontinental Printing

20 19 18 17 16 15 14 13 12 11 10 9

MANAGING EDITOR: Claire Chun
COPY EDITOR: Lily Chou
EDITORIAL ASSOCIATES: Leona Benten, Jay Chung
TYPESETTERS: Lisa Kester, James Meetze
CARTOGRAPHY: Stellar Cartography
HIDDEN BOOKS DESIGN: Sarah Levin
COVER DESIGN: Sarah Levin, Leslie Henriques
INDEXER: Sayre Van Young
FRONT COVER PHOTOGRAPHY: Douglas Peebles
ILLUSTRATOR: Glenn Kim

Distributed in the United States by Publishers
Group West and in Canada by Raincoast Books

I'd like to dedicate this book to my dear friends,
Philippe and Rosalie Guesdon of Papeete,
and to the memory of Rebecca Bruns.

Write to us!

If in your travels you discover a spot that captures the spirit of Tahiti, or if you live in the region and have a favorite place to share, or if you just feel like expressing your views, write to us and we'll pass your note along to the author.

We can't guarantee that the author will add your personal find to the next edition, but if the writer does use the suggestion, we'll acknowledge you in the credits and send you a free copy of the new edition.

ULYSSES PRESS
P.O. Box 3440
Berkeley, CA 94703
E-mail: readermail@ulyssespress.com

What's Hidden?

At different points throughout this book, you'll find special listings marked with a hidden symbol:

◄ HIDDEN

This means that you have come upon a place off the beaten tourist track, a spot that will carry you a step closer to the local people and natural environment of Tahiti.

The goal of this guide is to lead you beyond the realm of everyday tourist facilities. While we include traditional sightseeing listings and popular attractions, we also offer alternative sights and adventure activities. Instead of filling this guide with reviews of standard hotels and chain restaurants, we concentrate on one-of-a-kind places and locally owned establishments.

Our authors seek out locales that are popular with residents but usually overlooked by visitors. Some are more hidden than others (and are marked accordingly), but all the listings in this book are intended to help you discover the true nature of Tahiti and put you on the path of adventure.

Contents

Maps

OUTDOOR ADVENTURE SYMBOLS

The following symbols accompany national, state and regional park listings, as well as beach descriptions throughout the text.

Symbol	Activity	Symbol	Activity
	Swimming		Waterskiing
	Snorkeling or Scuba Diving		Windsurfing
	Surfing		Canoeing or Kayaking

Foreword

Tahiti is not easy to describe because there are, in fact, many Tahitis: the ancient Tahiti, still visible in the overgrown ruins which dot the coastal plains and valleys; the historical Tahiti, which emerges in all its sensual brilliance and violence from the journals of Captain Cook and other early voyagers; the modern Tahiti, embodied by bustling, traffic-choked Papeete, deluxe tourist hotels and the dazzling *Heiva* festival, and the Tahiti of the remote quiet "districts," where life goes on as it did nearly 50 years ago.

In this *tour de force*, veteran South Pacific travel author Rob Kay has provided a remarkably comprehensive, objective and utilitarian guide to the many-faceted realities of what must still be considered the world's most alluring island. He does not limit himself to Tahiti or even to the Society Islands alone. Instead, he applies his acute powers of observation and his wealth of background knowledge to guide the more adventuresome tourist far off the beaten pathways of tourism, to the exotic "outer islands" of the Tuamotu, Austral and Gambier archipelagos, and even the still mysterious Marquesas. Rob's coverage of this vast area is truly amazing: for example, few Americans have ever heard of the Mata Iva, a small atoll at the northwest end of the Tuamotu chain. Rob has not only been there, he's seen more of this fascinating spot than I have and gives a very balanced view of its tourist potential, a service he performs for many other islands in the Tuamotus and other archipelagos.

Hidden Tahiti is much more than a tourist guide, however; it's actually a good introductory text to the natural history, archeology, history, sociology and politics of the entire area. Within one set of covers, it provides answers to a host of questions commonly asked by visitors on a wide variety of subjects. Rob deftly summarizes all the major events in Eastern Polynesian geologic, prehistoric and historic time, from the geological origins of the Pacific island world to the recent anti-nuclear demonstrations and their aftermath. He combines this breadth and depth of coverage with insightful and practical notes about such highly diverse matters as the pervasive Tahitian *fiu* attitude (a national characteristic which has probably hurt

French Polynesian tourist revenues), negative local attitudes toward European surfers, the transsexual population of Tahiti and its history, the hazards of tattooing and many other current topics. This is no small achievement! For each island or island group, material on archeology, history, etc., is neatly meshed with carefully arranged descriptions of tourist accommodations, restaurants, recreational opportunities, nightlife and transportation—aimed at the full range of pocketbooks—and all well-seasoned with good tips and warnings. There are good biographical summaries for leading South Pacific authors and artists such as Herman Melville, Jack London, Somerset Maugham and the perennial Paul Gauguin, the not-so-noble savage of Tahiti, as well as an annotated bibliography which will prove quite useful.

Rob has demonstrated his familiarity with tourists' needs by assembling information which is difficult to obtain but nonetheless absolutely necessary for efficient travel in these far-flung outposts of France. He includes an excellent guide to French Polynesia's colorful but strangely assorted interisland transportation industry (with often pungent evaluations of the quality of service and accommodations), as well as explains the so-called PK mailing address system. He also presents lists of normal store hours, banking procedures and legal holidays.

Finally, as one who might be called an "old Polynesian hand," it was a pleasure to find so many old friends and acquaintances and familiar places so accurately portrayed in Rob's book. For me, this volume is more than a reminder of bright days of the past: it is an essential guide to equally bright days of the future under the tropical sun. I hope that it will be the same for you!

Robert C. Suggs, Ph.D.
Alexandria, Virginia
September, 1996

ONE

History and Culture

The origins of the Polynesians are shrouded in mystery. Despite advances in technology and recent archaeological discoveries, we know very little of the roots of the Polynesian race, much less how they discovered and populated some of the most remote islands on the planet. The most widely accepted theory is that the Polynesians are a blend of peoples originally from various parts of Asia as far north as Taiwan. Indications are that this amalgamation took place in the area extending from the Malay Peninsula through the islands of Indonesia. After an undetermined length of time, these people journeyed across the Pacific, possibly between 3000 and 1000 B.C.

Archaeologists tell us that the human history of Tahiti and its neighboring islands dates back about 2000 years to when the Marquesas Islands were first settled by migrating Polynesians from the Samoan and Tongan regions. From the Marquesas, ancient Polynesian mariners continued their migration, settling in New Zealand, the Society Islands (to which Tahiti belongs), Hawaii, and Easter Island.

Perhaps the most well-known alternative theory, advanced by the adventurer Thor Heyerdahl, is that Polynesians migrated from South America. His theory was given at least some credence by the successful crossing of his *Kon Tiki* expedition from Peru to French Polynesia in 1947, but it is not popular today in academic circles. Most data (linguistics, genetics and archaeological evidence) support a movement of people eastward across the Pacific, rather than westward. That Polynesians may have visited South America, or that some minor exchange occurred between South America and Polynesia, is less disputed.

Wherever they came from, there's no disputing the ancient Polynesians were among the finest sailors in the world. They used the sun, stars, currents, wave motion and flight patterns of birds to navigate the vast reaches of the Pacific. When for some reason, whether it was tribal warfare or overpopulation, Polynesians chose to settle elsewhere, they put their families, worldly goods, plant cuttings, animals and several months' supply of food into their huge, double-hulled canoes and set sail to find new homes.

POLYNESIAN ARRIVAL   According to the most widely held beliefs, the people of Southern China and Taiwan began to migrate south and east some 6000 years ago. Their languages, culture and genes can be found in the Polynesians of today.

The first archaeological evidence of any migration is from the Lapita culture, so named for a pottery called Lapita ware discovered in New Caledonia. The "Lapita people" established themselves in Melanesia about 1600 B.C., and during the next 600 years began the migration eastward to Fiji, Tonga and Samoa.

The latest theory suggests the Marquesas were settled in a subsequent migration, at about 500 B.C., as was Mangaia in the Cook Islands. The proximity of Mangaia to the Society Islands gives fuel to speculation that Tahiti was settled much earlier than empirical evidence indicates.

Using radiocarbon dating techniques and comparative studies of artifacts, scientists have pinpointed the earliest settlement of Tahiti and its neighboring islands at around A.D. 850. The most intensive research in this area is being undertaken by Dr. Y. H. Sinoto of the Bishop Museum in Honolulu, Hawaii. In 1973, Dr. Sinoto began excavation of the Vaito'otia/Fa'ahia site (on the grounds of the former Bali Hai Hotel) on Huahine and found it to be the oldest settlement yet discovered in the Society Islands. The implements that were excavated closely match those found in the Marquesas Islands, strengthening the theory that the Society Islands were settled by Polynesians migrating from the Marquesas. Why were the journeys undertaken? No one knows for sure, but war, banishment and overcrowding may have been factors.

The most important *marae* is Taputapuatea on Raiatea, which was the most prominent political and religious center in the Society Islands.

Pre-contact religion remains an enigma to archaeologists. It is known that Polynesians believed that the human race descended from gods and spirits. There was no distinction between the world humans inhabited and the supernatural universe. Because spirits and humans occupied the same turf, parts of that world were *tapu* or restricted. It is thus from Polynesia that we get the concept of taboo.

Ancient Polynesia was a hierarchical society and chiefs, the nearest thing to gods on earth, were afforded the privilege of declaring things *tapu*. Naturally, they used this concept to their advantage by restricting consumption of anything they deemed valuable—pigs, fruit, water or any other item necessary for survival. A *tapu* that was disobeyed meant swift and sometimes deadly consequences. In this manner, the ancestral spirits, through their divine offspring, ran society. However, everyone—regardless of their rank—lived in fear of spiritual retribution.

SURVIVAL OF THE FITTEST The navigational talents of the ancient Polynesians are legendary, but one must admire their superb survival skills as well. How were the first colonizers of Polynesia able to survive in their new island homes? After enduring a blue-water crossing to settle a new island, Polynesian voyagers arrived on their canoes like South Pacific Noahs, fully provisioned with breeding stocks of pigs, chickens and dogs, as well as stowaway rats, lizards and, no doubt, insects. In addition to animals, seeds, and vegetable cuttings, cultivated plants were taken onboard. They also brought along tools such as lines made from coconut fiber and seashell hooks to catch fish. These tools and the precious cargo of animals, vegetables and plants were essential for sustaining life. Of the indigenous flora that already grew on or near the islands, there were only a few varieties such as seaweed, *pandanus* nuts and coconuts that could provide any real sustenance.

Although wild coconuts were waiting for them in abundance on the new islands, the settlers would most certainly have brought them along on the voyage. And with good reason. It's almost impossible to imagine how life on an island could be supported without this humble nut. Of all the tropical plants found on the islands, none had a wider number of applications than the coconut. The timber was used to construct homes; coconut fiber was plaited into cord or sandals; the leaves were woven into baskets, thatch and walls; and the shells were used as cups or containers. Coconut water was drunk when there was no fresh water. The flesh was eaten raw, grated and strained for milk, or dried and its oil extracted for use as *monoi* or salve. The sap was fermented and used as an alcoholic beverage or boiled down to a syrup that when dried and rolled in grated coconut flesh was made into a nutritious candy.

Other plants carried onboard included breadfruit, bananas, taro, yams, arrowroot, sugarcane and a woody-stemmed lily known as *ti*. Rich in sugar, *ti* was used to make candy, and is still used by modern-day Polynesians to wrap food in underground ovens for cooking.

The mythic vision of the noble savage living in harmony with the environment has little validity. However, like all humans, Polynesians forever changed the face of the land they inhabited. As an island was populated, varieties of indigenous plants and animals declined or disappeared altogether. For example, several species of pigeons and rails reached nearly every Pacific island long before man. However, today there is only a fraction of the bird population that once existed and many are threatened with extinction. Other rail and pigeon species were part of the pre-contact Polynesian cuisine and were no doubt hunted to oblivion. So much for the environmentally correct "noble savage."

Text continued on page 6.

French Polynesia

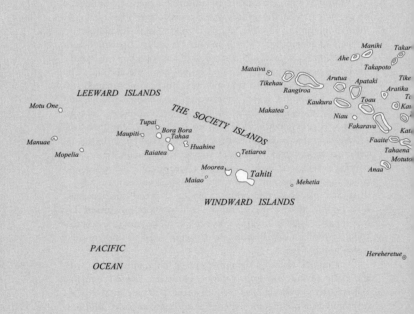

PACIFIC

OCEAN

Manihi   Takar
Ahe   Takapoto
Mataiva   Arutua   Tike
Tikehau   Rangiroa   Apataki   Aratika
LEEWARD ISLANDS   Kaukura   Toau   Te
Motu One   THE SOCIETY ISLANDS   Makatea   Niau   Kav
Tupai   Fakarava
Maupiti   Bora Bora   Kata
Manuae   Tahaa   Faaite
Raiatea   Huahine   Tahaena
Mopelia   Tetiaroa   Motuto
Moorea   Anaa
Maiao   Tahiti
Mehetia
WINDWARD ISLANDS

PACIFIC

OCEAN   Hereheretue

Maria

Rurutu
Rimatara
THE AUSTRALS   Tubuai

Raivavae

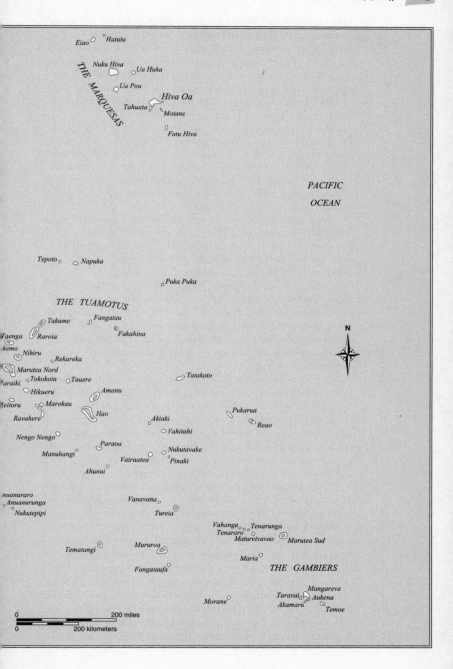

FIRST EUROPEAN CONTACT—BIRTH OF "THE MYTH"   It would be close to 250 years after Ferdinand Magellan sailed to the East Indies, and after more than 20 explorers sailed the vast waters of the Pacific, that the first Europeans would set foot on Tahiti. But as the islands were few and far between and navigational aids were often inaccurate, explorers often had no idea where they were. In 1767, British Captain Samuel Wallis, commander of the HMS *Dolphin*, laid claim to Tahiti for King George III.

The initial contact between the crew of the HMS *Dolphin* and the Tahitians was of a mixed nature. The crew bartered beads, mirrors and knives for food and sex. Nails quickly became the most sought-after item by the Tahitians, who used them to make fish hooks. To the horror of those responsible for the seaworthiness of the *Dolphin*, nails became the chief medium of exchange for sexual favors and rapidly disappeared from the vessel.

Not all the meetings between the British and Polynesians were amicable. On one occasion the English were pelted with stones and in savage reprisal the *Dolphin* opened fire with cannon and muskets. The Tahitians set about making amends by giving lavish gifts, which included the favors of women.

Although Captain Samuel Wallis and his crew "discovered" Tahiti, the first English explorers learned very little about the Tahitians. Wallis, who was ill most of the time, never had the opportunity to investigate the new land and, although the crew found the natives hospitable and carefree, they learned little about the island's government, religion or laws. These remained for later explorers to uncover.

In April 1768, while Wallis was on his way back to England, Louis de Bougainville, commanding the *Boudeuse* and the *Etoile*, found his way to Tahiti. Not realizing the English had beaten him to the task, Bougainville took possession of the island for France. The Frenchman was met by a flotilla of canoes bearing bananas, coconuts, green boughs and fowl as gifts. In return Bougainville gave them nails and earrings.

This is how Bougainville described the scene:

"They pressed us to choose a woman and come on shore with her; and their gestures, which were not ambiguous, denoted in what manner we should form an acquaintance with her."

Once ashore the French were treated with kindness and quickly learned the obvious qualities about their guests—the Tahitians were friendly, generous, sexually uninhibited—and they stole. To their credit, the French were philosophical about the latter characteristic, realizing that the islanders simply did not have the same sense of private property that Europeans did. Bougainville, unlike his English counterpart, was a distinguished scholar and perhaps a better observer. Because of his good health during the visit, he had the opportunity to mix more freely with the Tahitians. In just

The Tahitian Temple

Ancient Polynesians worshiped their gods in open-air sanctuaries known as *marae*. These rock formations were a place of worship consecrated to a particular god, as well as a meeting place tied to a family organization.

The size of the *marae* marked the importance and social rank of the owner, and the social implications were of more importance than the god associated with the *marae*. Thus, a man's position was linked to where he would sit within the enclosure. His position in society was determined by the genealogies chanted during the religious ceremonies.

What little that is known about the ancient religion was compiled by Teuria Henry, the daughter of one of the first missionaries to Tahiti. Her book, *Ancient Tahiti*, is considered a classic on the subject. Henry tells us that there were several categories of *marae*, ranging from a simple cluster of stones a few square feet in area to elaborate structures covering hundreds of thousands of square feet. The simplest *marae* were known as *marae tupuna* or "*marae* of the ancestor." Here the ordinary Tahitian would fulfill his (they were strictly for men) religious duties.

The *marae* consisted of a paved area surrounded by a small wall that had a stone platform or *ahu*. Inside the confines of the structure was a wooden platform, *fata tupap'au*, protected by a roof of leaves. (This is where the dead lay in state before their burial.) Various sacred objects such as consecrated feathers or relics belonging to the ancestors were placed in a box hidden under a paving stone. Close to the *marae* a pit was dug to hide cult objects, fingernail clippings, hair clippings, the umbilical cord of the newly born and anything else that could be considered dangerous for the family if some evildoer were to confiscate it and use it for black magic. (Enemies or mischief makers could use personal objects and effects to place a hex or spell on the individual.)

a few days the French captain had acquired a skeletal working knowledge of the island's government and customs. But Bougainville's stay was cut short by anchorage problems among the dangerous coral heads.

CAPTAIN COOK In 1769, Captain James Cook, perhaps the greatest English navigator ever, arrived in Tahiti on the HMS *Endeavour*. The purpose of his visit had relatively little to do with Tahiti or its residents. Cook had come to study the transit of Venus across the sun, which would enable scientists to precisely measure the distance between the sun and the earth. This determination would be an invaluable navigational aid for future explorers. For the voyage, an impressive group of scientists, scholars and artists was assembled to study Tahiti as well as the transit. However, their 18th-century instruments weren't accurate enough to gather the data needed, and in terms of observing the transit, the voyage was a failure.

On the other hand, Cook's three-month Tahitian sojourn did provide a wealth of information about the island and its people. His experience was generally a good one, but there were problems. Cook was a tolerant man but he simply could not deal with one aspect of Tahitian character—their thievery. Tahitians found it amusing to confound their visitors by devising ways of relieving them of their property. For the natives it was a game to outwit the English, and they usually gave back what was taken. For Cook the matter was deadly serious. At one point he impounded Tahitian canoes in order to get equipment back. In another instance he unfairly imprisoned five chiefs and held them for ransom until two of his sailors (who had deserted ship to be with their Tahitian girlfriends) were returned to his custody.

Cook cared about his crew and their behavior toward the Tahitians. He was particularly bothered by a shooting incident that left a Tahitian dead. He was also concerned about the spread of venereal disease (which the English later blamed on the French), and about the internment of the chiefs. Two days before the *Endeavour* lifted anchor he wrote, "We are likely to leave these people in disgust at our behavior." Perhaps Cook was too sensitive because one of the Tahitians' greatest qualities was their forgiving nature. When Cook left, the Tahitians genuinely wept. He was to return to Tahiti two more times before his death in Hawaii.

BLIGH AND THE BOUNTY The year 1788 marked the arrival of the HMS *Bounty*, a name forever associated with legendary Tahiti. It also marked the end of the era of exploration and the beginning of exploitation.

The *Bounty*'s mission was to retrieve breadfruit plants needed as a cheap source of food for the numerous slaves working on West Indies plantations. The voyage was led by Lt. William Bligh, a former sailing master who had accompanied Cook on a previous visit to Tahiti. Bligh, who may have been unfairly maligned in the annals of history because of his reputation as a ruthless taskmaster, spent six months in Tahiti supervising his crew as they transplanted the valuable plants onto a makeshift greenhouse aboard the ship.

The crew made the most of their time here, befriending the fun-loving Tahitians and living like sultans. Not surprisingly, some of the crew did not wish to depart when it was time to set sail. Three weeks after leaving Tahiti, a mutinous band of men led by Fletcher Christian coldly turned Bligh and 18 other crew members adrift in a 23-foot cutter with minimal provisions. Bligh and his followers faced what seemed like certain death through uncharted waters, tempestuous weather and islands teeming with cannibals. Miraculously, they survived 41 days in an open craft, traveling 3609 miles to the Dutch-held island of Timor in Indonesia.

Meanwhile, under orders from Christian, who wished to avoid returning to Tahiti, the *Bounty* sailed for the island of Tubuai in the Austral Group, where the mutineers briefly attempted to settle. Finding the natives unfriendly, Christian returned to Tahiti to pick up pigs for food and female consorts for companionship on Tubuai. Not all of his crew wished to return with him to the forlorn island, so Christian allowed seven loyalists and nine mutineers to remain behind on Tahiti.

The attempt to establish a community on Tubuai soon failed. The Tubuaians were particularly hostile to the visitors because the *Bounty* mutineers repeatedly attempted to take land and women. The *Bounty*'s final destination was lonely Pitcairn Island, where Fletcher Christian and his men soon quarreled with their erstwhile Tahitian comrades. Only one European survived the butchering

A MATTER OF DEBATE

The cause of the celebrated mutiny on the *Bounty* is still a matter of debate. Some historians believe that the real reason for the uprising may have been the sailors' longing to return to their Tahitian *vahines* rather than Captain Bligh's cruelty. For the most part, novels and films have portrayed Bligh as a monster, when in fact the real villain may have been the unstable and perhaps emotionally disturbed Fletcher Christian. In his book *Pitcairn: Children of Mutiny*, Australian journalist Ian M. Ball tells us that if anything, Bligh, a former officer under the legendary Captain Cook, was a tolerant man who treated his men better than did the average English captain of his day. After the *Bounty* affair was over, Bligh was promoted to admiral and eventually became the governor of New South Wales in Australia.

that ensued during the following months. (The mutinous crew's descendants still live on Pitcairn Island today and are quite proud of their English/Polynesian roots.)

After recovering from his mutiny, Bligh returned to Tahiti for the breadfruit—this time with a contingent of 19 marines aboard. He did not want to take chances on another uprising. In the interim, the survivors of the crew that Christian had left behind on Tahiti had been rounded up by another British ship, the *Pandora*, put in shackles and taken back to England to stand trial before Bligh returned. Several perished when the *Pandora* later sank off Australia.

A MISSION FROM GOD As always, in the wake of explorers came the men of the cloth. In 1797, 30 members of the London Missionary Society arrived in Tahiti. Although previous visitors had been appalled by many of the local customs (such as human sacrifice), the Society seemed more distraught over the overt sexual proclivities of Tahitians. They attempted to dissuade the population from this "immoral" behavior by converting the king to Christianity.

The Polynesians cultivated 16 different varieties of coconuts and gave them names based on their uses.

Anthropologist Bengt Danielsson writes that they also persuaded the natives to drink tea, eat with a knife and fork, wear bonnets and coats, sleep in beds, sit on chairs and live in stone houses—in short, to emulate the English lower middle-class manner of Society members. Within a few years, the missionaries succeeded in converting the entire population and managed to rid them of such customs as infanticide and human sacrifice. However, they never quite convinced the natives to give up their hedonistic ways. (Even after his conversion to Christianity, Tahitian King Pomare II continued his relationship with his two sisters—one of whom he was married to—and eventually died from the effects of alcoholism.)

THE FRENCH In 1836, a French naval vessel under the command of Admiral Dupetit-Thouars arrived in Papeete and demanded indemnity for a previous expulsion of Catholic missionaries from Tahiti. Queen Pomare IV, the current ruler, paid the money under threat of naval bombardment and later was forced to sign an agreement that would allow French missionaries to spread Catholicism.

Admiral Dupetit-Thouars returned to Polynesia in 1842 and annexed the Marquesas Islands with the idea of turning them into a penal colony. In the process of procuring land, he decided to annex Tahiti as well. This move outraged the London Missionary Society and almost whipped up enough anti-French sentiment in England to send the two nations to war. In 1843, the French returned to Tahiti with three ships to take formal possession of the island. This marked the beginning of European colonization in the South Pacific.

After the Tahitians realized the French were there to stay, they took up arms (bush knives and a few muzzle-loaders) and waged a three-year guerrilla war on French garrisons, settlements and missionary stations. In the end, the Tahitians were crushed and Queen Pomare came out of hiding to become a rubber-stamp monarch. Likewise, the Missionary Society, seeing the futility of resisting French influence, ceded their holdings to a French Protestant group and headed for greener pastures.

The colonial period marked the gradual erosion of the Tahitian culture. By the time Paul Gauguin arrived in the late 19th century, what remained of pre-contact Tahitian society and religion were gone. The colony of Tahiti was a quiet, unassuming place and the lack of natural resources meant there was little to plunder or extract from the earth. There was no inducement for change or ferment, and for many years French Polynesia remained a distant outpost in the empire. It wasn't until the mid-20th century that life would be drastically transformed for the Tahitians.

MID-20TH-CENTURY POLYNESIA   French Polynesia remained a backwater colony until the 1960s, when three events triggered drastic changes in the island chain. These were the building of an international airport in Tahiti, the beginning of nuclear weapons testing in the nearby Tuamotu Islands and the making of the MGM film *Mutiny on the Bounty* starring Marlon Brando and Trevor Howard. As tourists—lured no doubt by Hollywood's version of the islands—and military personnel flooded Tahiti in increasing numbers, the character of the once-sleepy island changed dramatically. Money was pumped into the economy, new businesses sprang up to accommodate the influx of arrivals, and thousands of Polynesians left their far-flung island homes to look for work in Papeete. Suddenly, Tahiti found itself very much in the 20th century.

The topics of the day were dissent over nuclear testing, brawls between soldiers and Tahitians, inflation and a shift from a subsistence economy to one based completely on money.

The increased French presence was not without its positive effects: new roads, schools, hospitals, agriculture and aquaculture projects, many new airstrips and eventually the highest standard of living in the South Pacific. Accompanying economic growth was a greater political awareness and a demand by the Polynesians for more voice in the government, which was controlled more or less by France. In 1977, French Polynesia was finally granted a much greater degree of autonomy under the auspices of a new constitution. The new arrangement provided Polynesians with a larger voice in internal affairs, which included managing their own budget.

In 1984, a statute passed by the French parliament in Paris created yet another incarnation of the French Polynesian constitution, giving Tahiti even more autonomy. For the first time, the legislative body was allowed to elect the Territorial government's own president. (Prior to this, the highest position a Tahitian could hold was Vice-President of the Territorial Government Council.) Thus, instead of sharing power with the Paris-appointed High Commissioner, which the vice-president had to do, the president was given the power to run the Council of Ministers alone.

The 1984 statute did not create complete autonomy for Tahiti's local government. However, in areas that remain in the hands of the French, such as defense or foreign affairs, the Tahitian government has been granted the right to participate in negotiations regarding matters that may have a bearing on French Polynesia's future.

French Polynesia Today

GEOGRAPHY

French Polynesia lies in the South Pacific, halfway between Australia and California, and approximately halfway between Japan and Chile. The term *French Polynesia* refers to the five archipelagoes that comprise this entity, each of them being culturally, ethnically and climatically distinct. They include the Marquesas, the Tuamotus, the Society Islands, the Australs and the Gambiers. Although French Polynesia is spread over an expanse of water the size of Western Europe (2,000,000 square miles or approximately 5,000,000 square kilometers), the total land mass of its 118 islands only adds up to about 1544 square miles (4000 square kilometers).

Tahiti is the largest and best known of the Society Islands. The Society Islands are divided into the Windwards or *Iles du Vent* (Tahiti, Moorea, Maiao and Tetiaroa) and the Leeward Islands or *Iles sous le Vent* (Bora Bora, Maupiti, Huahine and Raiatea). The Leeward Islands lie 100 miles (160 kilometers) to the northwest of Tahiti and are so named because of their position in relation to the prevailing wind.

For the most part, the Society Group consists of high islands—volcanic peaks surrounded by a barrier coral reef that protects them from the full force of the pounding surf. All have similar terrain and vegetation.

Tetiaroa, an atoll that lies 26 miles (42 kilometers) north of Tahiti, is classified geographically as part of the Windward Islands, but is geologically much older than Tahiti and the other members of the Society Group. It consists of 12 small islets grouped in a circular configuration surrounding a lagoon about 4.3 miles (7 kilometers) in diameter. This circular or oblong contour is characteristic of an atoll or low island.

The other member of the Society Group that does not conform to the typical high island classification is Maiao, located 43 miles (70 kilometers) southwest of Moorea. It is also a low-lying coral island, but with the unusual characteristic of having a 154-yard-high hill at its center, flanked on two sides by a brackish lake. Inhabited by about 250 individuals, this island is infested with mosquitoes and is rarely visited by outsiders.

This is in sharp contrast to Bora Bora, which has been inundated with visitors since the 1960s and is best known as the seductive Bali Hai of the Broadway musical *South Pacific*. Bora Bora derives its natural beauty from the erosion of a volcano that erupted at least three million years ago. Since then, its central core has split and eroded, leaving sheared peaks created by volcanic chimneys. The surrounding lagoon, which is proportionally much larger than the core of the island, is vast.

The Tuamotu Archipelago, a giant arc of coral atolls located between the Society and Marquesas islands, consists of two parallel island chains 740 miles (1200 kilometers) long. It is the largest collection of atolls in the world. One of the islands in the Tuamotu Group, Rangiroa, is the second-largest atoll in the world. Indeed, it is so large, the lagoon could accommodate the entire island of Tahiti within its perimeter. The island is so wide—17.5 miles (28 kilometers)—that a sea level–based observer looking across the lagoon would be unable to see the opposite side of the atoll.

Though atolls are what readers of *Robinson Crusoe* may consider paradise, they are actually not well suited for sustaining life, whether plant, animal or human. The absence of precipitous peaks shrouded by clouds means there is less rainfall and almost perennially dry soil. Not only is the soil arid, it is primarily derived from coral (which created the atoll) and thus lacks many of the nutrients otherwise found on a more biologically diverse high island. Consequently, it's very difficult, if not impossible, to grow such crops as taro, bananas and the like. What does sustain the inhabitants are the nearby reef systems, which are rich in sea life.

At the far eastern end of the Tuamotu Archipelago, almost on the Tropic of Capricorn, are the Gambier Islands, located 1031 miles (1650 kilometers) southeast of Tahiti. Often linked geographically with the Tuamotus because they appear to be the east-

MOTUS AND ATOLLS

What exactly are those *motus* and atolls that everyone seems to be talking about? **Motus** are the sandy (often palm-covered) barrier islands that have built up around reefs protecting a lagoon. They make for great beachcombing and romantic getaways. **Atolls** are actually islands created as coral reefs rise around a sinking island. When the island in the middle has completely vanished into the lagoon, all that is left is the donut-like atoll. The lagoon is usually connected to the outside sea by one or more passes that flush and fill the lagoon with the tides. Rangiroa is the second-largest atoll in the world.

ern terminus of the archipelago, the Gambiers are in reality a different class of islands. The Gambiers are a cluster of ten rocky islands surrounded by a barrier reef on three sides. The largest and most northerly is Mangareva.

The Australs are the southernmost island chain in French Polynesia and are geologically related to the Cook Islands. Lying 375 miles (600 kilometers) south of Tahiti, they are actually an extension of the same submerged mountain chain as the southern Cooks, and share similar geologic aspects. For example, Rurutu in the Australs and Mangaia in the Cooks are both upthrust islands, with extremely rugged terrain and numerous limestone caves.

Roughly 1000 kilometers north of Papeete are the rugged Marquesas Islands. Rocky, precipitous and volcanic in origin, these six islands are as distinct culturally from the rest of French Polynesia as they are in topography. The Marquesan population was devastated by diseases carried by whalers and other early visitors.

PEOPLE   French Polynesia's annual population growth is 1.72 percent, and the current population is around 253,500, of which 30 percent is under age 15. Approximately 75 percent of the population of French Polynesia lives on the island of Tahiti. The population is an amalgam of Polynesians (78 percent), Chinese (12 percent) and Europeans (10 percent). Among these racial categories exists every conceivable mixture. It would not be unusual for a Tahitian named Pierre Jamison to have Chinese, American, Polynesian and French ancestors.

The social structure of French Polynesia is a complicated study in politics, economics and intermarriage. Economically, the Chinese are the most powerful group, while *demis* (half-castes) of Polynesian and Caucasian blood make up a class of Europeanized Tahitians that controls the political sphere. The *demi* population maintains an interesting mixture of Tahitian and European values. While some have adopted French culture and eschew speaking Tahitian, others identify with both cultures. The majority of the population—those whose ancestry is primarily Polynesian (with perhaps a splash of Chinese or European blood)—are known as *kaina* (pronounced kai-na) and are at the lowest rung of the socioeconomic ladder.

Due to their lack of economic clout, the Polynesians have the least amount of political power, even though they are the majority of the population. They make up the blue-collar segment of society—the dock workers, the laborers, etc. Not surprisingly, it is the *kaina* who harbor a particular discontent with the status quo, especially in the sometimes harsh, urban setting of Papeete. And who can blame them? They have the smallest share of the economic pie.

The Chinese first came to Tahiti as plantation workers during the 1860s, the time of the U.S. Civil War. They were the labor force in a scheme hatched by two Scottish businessmen to produce

Nuclear Fallout

In 1995, Tahiti made international headlines as protests mounted over France's plans to resume nuclear testing in the region. Riots broke out on September 5 in Papeete and lasted 36 hours. During the rampage, which involved hundreds of participants, the International Airport in Faa'a was severely damaged. The airport was closed from September 5 to September 8. During this period, several buildings in Papeete were burned, storefront windows at the Vaima Center and another tony shopping area nearby were smashed and, in some instances, looted. The rioting was brought to a halt when Foreign Legionnaires and para-military troops arrived.

So, what caused the riots? The resumption of nuclear testing on Mururoa clearly was the catalyst for the riot. But there were other issues as well. A pro-independence, Tahitian-language radio station was allegedly urging Tahitians to take to the streets and wreak havoc. Reports were that many of the rioters were disenfranchised Tahitians venting their rage.

After all, nuclear tests were nothing new to French Polynesia. Since 1960, there have been 45 atmospheric and 134 underground tests. However, in this case, the countdown in Tahiti to the September 5 detonation was a media circus. The presence of Greenpeace off Mururoa was highly publicized by a gaggle of international journalists in Papeete, reporting to news bureaus in New York, Sydney, Paris, Auckland and around the world. From the French point of view, the media whipped up a frenzy of propaganda aimed at Paris. While many Tahitians were never big fans of nuclear testing, many had good-paying jobs related to the experiments. The resulting drop in tourism meant the loss of a great deal of revenue by small hoteliers, not to mention job cuts for Tahitian hotel workers. Ironically, many of the Papeete area hotels were kept afloat during the time of the tests by the 800 *gendarmes* brought in from France. Due to a shortage of housing, virtually all of the visiting policemen were billeted at local hotels until the tests ended in March 1996. The airport has been repaired and things are calm once again. The tourism fallout of the experiments has already faded into memory.

Because the end of testing also meant the end of the millions of dollars the military pumped into the local economy, France has committed to subsidizing the Tahitian economy through 2006.

cotton, then unavailable in the northern U.S. When the Civil War ended, the venture went bankrupt but the Chinese indentured laborers remained in Tahiti. Through the years, Chinese have continued to migrate to Tahiti, while keeping their culture. Many have married Polynesians or Europeans. Through hard work and their mercantile tradition, the Chinese gained prominence as merchants and traders to become the wealthiest class in Tahitian Society.

GOVERN-MENT

Today, French Polynesia is governed by a 49-member Territorial Assembly, elected by popular vote every five years. The members select ten among them to form a Council of Ministers *(Conseil des Ministres)*, the most powerful ruling body. The assembly also elects the president.

French Polynesia's official status is "POM" (Pays d'Outre-Mer), which roughly means it is a semiautonomous colony, much like the U.S. territories of Puerto Rico and Guam. However, unlike the residents of the United States territories, French Polynesians are permitted to vote in national elections and elect representatives (two deputies and a senator) to the metropolitan French National Assembly and Senate in Paris.

The metropolitan French government runs French Polynesia's foreign affairs, defense, police, justice system and secondary education. In addition to local rule, a French High Commissioner is charged with administrative duties, especially regarding the observance of French law.

ECONOMY

Although French Polynesians cling to traditional values, the face of Tahiti has changed considerably in the past 30 years. The influx of money from both continuing tourism and a large military presence during the 1990s has transformed the region's economy from agriculturally based subsistence level to that of a modern consumer society. Money, not essential to an islander years ago, is now necessary for buying outboard motors, stereos, color televisions, video decks, cars, motorcycles, gasoline and—when one can afford them—the latest fashions. The younger generation has become enamored with the things money can buy and their ability to consume is tempered only by the high price of imported goods.

Lured by the promise of a better life, French Polynesians from the outer islands have moved to Tahiti in ever greater numbers. Life in Papeete, however, often is not easy for those who have left their outlying homes. In the capital the cost of living is high, and life for the new inhabitants is fraught with such basic problems as finding housing and employment. In Papeete, it is simply not possible to fish for an evening meal or gather fruits and vegetables from the land. Thus, for those who have migrated, traditional life has been exchanged for an urban existence and all its woes. To counter this trend, the Tahitian government promotes economic development of the outer islands. Through aquaculture, tourism and commercial pearl ventures, the authorities hope to encourage the rural population to stay put.

Indeed, agriculture still plays an important role in supporting the rural population. The leading product is copra (dried coconut), produced by drying coconut meat in the sun, after which it is processed into oil for copra cakes (cattle feed), soap, cosmetics, margarine and other items. Processed coconut oil known as *monoi* is scented with flower blossoms and used locally for skin care. Copra is a vital source of income to families on remote islands where a shortage of resources and/or lack of accessibility to distant markets make it difficult to eke out a living. The government buys the dried coconut at inflated prices to subsidize French Polynesians caught in this situation. Other agricultural and aquacultural products include vanilla, coffee, fruit, cultured black pearls, pearl shell, fish, shrimp and oysters.

The two main sources of hard currency for French Polynesia are tourism—which accounts for a quarter of the gross national product—and the money generated by the metropolitan French government.

The black pearl industry remains one of the few bright spots in the Tahitian economy. Black pearl cultivation and its related activities now take place on approximately 30 islands in the Tuamotu Group and have largely replaced copra and commercial fishing as a source of revenue. Prior to the commercial exploitation of pearl shell in French Polynesia (where mother-of-pearl was used primarily in buttons) early in the 19th century, locals used it for religious and decorative ornamentation and for implements such as fishhooks and lures.

Harvesting oysters for pearls gained importance in the Tuamotu Islands during the 1850s, but it wasn't until the early 1960s that scientists began cultivation experiments with the indigenous black pearl oyster *Pinctada margaritifera*. Today the pearls are cultivated in the Gambier Islands as well.

In recent years, pearl cultivation has become an increasingly important source of income for French Polynesia, particularly as consumers in the international marketplace have become more aware of the black pearl.

Making pearls is an intriguing process: three- to five-year-old oysters are collected by divers and selected for pearl cultivation. A nucleus, or tiny mother-of-pearl sphere fashioned from the shell of a Mississippi River mussel (or similar species), is then attached to a graft of tissue from the oyster and placed inside the animal's gonad. If all goes well, the tiny graft grows around the nucleus and acts as an irritant, which causes the slow formation of layer upon layer of black pearl. After a donor nucleus has been added to each oyster, they are placed inside cages to protect them from predators. Under ideal growing conditions, they are left to recuperate from the operation for 18 months to three years before harvesting. During that time, the shells are repeatedly inspected and hauled to the surface for cleaning. Water conditions are scrupulously checked for salinity, temperature and possible pollutants.

Only 20 percent of the oysters implanted with a nucleus ever bear salable pearls, and only 5 percent of the crop harvested bear perfect pearls—specimens that meet exacting industry standards. Value is determined by size, luster, sheen, color and lack of defects such as bumps, dents or scratches. Prices range from US$100 for a small pearl of average quality to US$10,000 for a perfectly round pearl with an 18 mm diameter.

LANGUAGE The official languages of French Polynesia are Tahitian and French, but numerous other tongues are spoken as well. Paumotu (the language of the Tuamotu Islands), Mangarevan (spoken in the Gambiers) and Marquesan (the language of the Marquesas Islands) are all native tongues. These languages belong to the great Austronesian or Malayo-European language family. This widely scattered family includes the languages of Micronesia and Melanesia as well as Bahasa Malay (the language of Malaysia and Indonesia), Malagasy (the language of Madagascar) and the original languages of Taiwan. The origins of the Tahitian languages date back some 5000 years to the ancient languages of Indonesia, which later spread to Fiji, then to Samoa and Tonga.

The first explorers to set foot on Tahiti thought the Tahitian language childishly simple. Cook recorded 157 words and Bougainville estimated the entire vocabulary to be approximately 500 words. Tahiti was chosen as a fertile ground for evangelical groups such as the London Missionary Society in part because the Tahitian language appeared easy to learn (the famous Captain Bligh of the HMS *Bounty* is often cited as a source of this misperception). As the missionaries soon discovered, however, the Tahitian language was not as easy to learn as earlier explorers assumed. As each day passed, the missionaries encountered baffling subtleties, foreign idioms and confusing sounds. The slightest change in pronunciation, barely discernible to an untrained ear, could impart a very different meaning (there are several sounds, such as glottal stops and long vowels, that are not common to many other tongues). As one reader astutely pointed out, the missionaries most likely also had difficulty learning word order as well as complicated inclusive and exclusive pronouns. Furthermore, there were not words to express Western ideas about the arts, sciences or business, but there were words describing the natural environment such as the weather, the ocean, the stars, animal behavior, and the like.

Once exclusively the language of Tahiti and its neighbors, Tahitian is now spoken on about 100 islands of French Polynesia. The language gained prominence because Tahiti was the most pop-

Why Is Life So Expensive in Tahiti?

There are several reasons for the high prices in Tahiti. Perhaps the pivotal one is the high tariffs the government tacks on to almost everything that is imported. Only certain foodstuffs such as sugar, rice and flour are exempt from import duties. When you combine high tariffs, the price of transporting goods to Tahiti and the added profit (often a large margin) that merchants tack on, it's easy to see why prices are so high.

Despite the high tariffs, the revenue raised by these duties covers only 70 percent or so of the government's operating budget. A yearly infusion of capital from France covers the deficit. France's largess probably encourages a "France-will-take-care-of-it" attitude.

To complicate things even more, the tremendous outflow of capital overseas to pay for imports goes against every sane economic tenet. After all, the classic definition of a solvent economy is one that exports more than it imports—not the other way around. However, if a government depends almost totally on import duties for its revenue, it will have difficulty surviving without encouraging spending on imported goods. And spending money on imported goods is something Tahitians do a lot of.

Papeete is a wonderland of tropical consumerism. Walking through the capital it's almost impossible not to notice that many of the people drive late model cars, sport flashy watches, drip with jewelry and wear the latest Paris fashions. Often the most humble Tahitian shack will have a stereo, VCR and TV—all costing double what you would pay in a developed country.

Even those high in government acknowledge that there are some serious problems for a nation that spends a lot on imports. There is little, however, that can be done to alleviate Tahiti's economic woes and high prices. Though French Polynesia exports fruit juice, pineapples, black pearls, mother-of-pearl, vanilla and fish, the islands have practically no export crops or minerals to provide substantial amounts of hard currency. No one in Tahiti knows what the future will bring given these circumstances.

ulous island and the primary island chosen for missionary work. As the written word and Christianity were spread by native pastors, the printed Tahitian word more or less superseded other local dialects and languages.

Like all languages, Tahitian was influenced by foreigners, mostly early missionaries and seafarers who mingled with the local population. Many languages, including Hebrew, Greek, Latin, English and French, contributed words that have become part of modern-day Tahitian. The translation of the Bible into Tahitian introduced such words as *Sabati* (Sabbath); but the English connection provided many loan words such as baby, butter, money, tea, pineapple and frying pan, which became *pepe, pata, moni, ti, painapo* and *faraipani* in Tahitian.

PRONUNCIATION

There are five vowels in Tahitian:
   a as in "far"
   e as in "day"
   i as in "machine"
   o as in "gold"
   u as in "flute"
There are eight consonant sounds in Tahitian:
   f as in "fried"
   h as in "house"; pronounced "sh" as in "shark" when preceded by "i" and followed by o, as in *iho* (only, just)
   m as in "man"
   n as in "noted"
   p as in "spark"—shorter than the "p" of "pan"
   r as in "run"—sometimes trilled like a Scottish "r"
   t as in "stark"—softer than the "t" of "tar"
   v as in "victory"
Aside from the eight consonants, a glottal stop is used in many words. For example, the word for "pig" is *pua'a*; "person" is *ta'ata*; "beer" is *pia* and "coconut" is *ha'ari*. A U.S. English equivalent, as D. T. Tryon points out in his excellent Tahitian primer *Say It in Tahitian*, is "co'n" for "cotton."

Although many shopkeepers, hotel personnel and students speak English, it helps to have some command of French. If you really want to talk with the people and acquire knowledge of the culture, learn Tahitian.

PLACE NAMES
   Ahe (Ah-hay)
   Faa'a (Fah-ah-ah)
   Gambier (Gahm-bee-aye)
   Huahine (Who-ah-hee-nay)
   Mangareva (Mahng-ah-rave-ah)
   Manihi (Mahn-nee-hee)
   Maupiti (Mau-pee-tee)

Nuku Hiva (New-kew-hee-vah)
Papeete (Pa-pee-ay-tay)
Raiatea (Rye-ah-tay-ah)
Rangiroa (Rang-ghee-row-ah)
Tahaa (Tah-ha-ah)
Tuamotu (Too-ah-mow-too)
Tubuai (Toop-oo-eye)

SOME USEFUL WORDS AND PHRASES

Those who spend any time in the islands are sure to run into catch phrases containing important concepts that are useful in trying to understand the Tahitian character.

Fiu is an expression that encompasses varying shades of boredom, despair, hopelessness and frustration. Put yourself in the place of a person who has spent his or her life on a small island, perhaps only a bit of coral in the midst of a blue expanse of ocean. The only stimuli are the ceaseless trade winds, the sound of the waves crashing on the reef, the sight of the sun bleaching the coral white and the sweltering heat. You can always go fishing or turn on Radio Tahiti, but this can get boring after a while. Life can be an endless monotone, and when someone mutters, "I'm *fiu*" with husband or with job, very little explanation is necessary. The essence of *fiu* is in the languorous tropical air.

> The word *taboo* is derived from the Tahitian *tapu*.

Aita pe'ape'a' is another often-used expression; it translates literally as "no problem." It means take things the way they are and don't worry about them. It is basically the Tahitian equivalent of *mañana*. At best, it implies a fatalistic and easy-going acceptance of the here and now. At worst, it is a kind of intellectual lethargy and lack of concern.

Following is an abbreviated vocabulary list with Tahitian and French translations:

American—*marite* mah-ree-tay (*Américain*)
ancient temple—*marae* marah-ayee (*marae*)
Cheers! Down the hatch—*manuia* mah-noo-yah (*a votre santé*)
crazy—*taravana* tar-ah-vah-nah (*fou, folle*)
finish, finished—*oti* woh-tee (*fini*)
friend—*e hoa* ay-oh-ah (*ami, amie*)
good—*maita'i* my-tye (*bon*)
goodbye—*nana* nah-nah (*au revoir*)
good morning; good day—*ia ora na* your-rah-nah (*bonjour*)
house—*fare* fah-ray (*maison*)
I'm bored; disgusted—*fiu* phew (*Je suis dégoûté*)
man—*tane* tah-nay (*homme*)
no—*aita* eye-tah (*non*)
no good—*aita maita'i* eye-tah-my-tye (*pas bien*)

no problem; don't worry—*aita pe'ape'a*
  eye-tah-pay-ah-pay-ah (*pas de problème*)
pretty, beautiful—*nehenehe* nay-he-nay-he (*joli, jolie*)
thank you—*mauru'uru* mah-rhu-rhu (*merci*)
traditional dance—*tamurei* tah-mu-ray (*danse traditionelle*)
very good—*maita'i roa* my-tye-row-ah (*très bien*)
woman—*vahine* vah-hee-nay (*femme*)

CUISINE

The blend of Polynesian and French cultures has proved a fertile environment for cuisine. There is a wide array of excellent food available in Tahiti ranging from traditional Tahitian fare to fine French cuisine. One can also find any number of Italian, Vietnamese and Chinese restaurants of various price categories and quality. Fast food–starved Americans will find outlets serving steak and fries, hamburgers and other similar fare throughout Papeete and on some of the outer islands. Although food in French Polynesia is generally expensive, one need not pay a king's ransom for a tasty meal. The price of a decent, inexpensive meal starts as low as US$15.

Access to a kitchen facility can make eating here more relaxing and less expensive. Families with children and people on special diets (vegetarian, low fat, food allergies, etc.) will find their dining choices very limited. Restaurants are not as accommodating as people from North America may expect. Fortunately, most destinations have at least some lodging options with kitchen facilities.

Tahitian fare is more or less the same as in the rest of Polynesia —fish, shellfish, breadfruit, taro, cassava (manioc), pork, yams, chicken, rice and coconut. Beef, very popular, is rare on most of the outer islands. Vegetables such as tomatoes and onions are grown on Tahiti and some of the outer islands, but are nonexistent on the atolls. On most of the high islands, tubers such as manioc and taro are staples for the locals. Visitors soon find them bland and heavy. In the Tuamotus, where taro and manioc cannot be grown, rice, breadfruit and white bread are the main starches.

The dish most likely to grace a French Polynesian table is *poisson cru*. This consists of chunks of raw fish marinated in lime juice or vinegar and salt and is usually topped with coconut cream, oil and onions. When prepared properly, the bite-sized pieces of fish melt in your mouth.

Chevrettes, found on most high islands, are freshwater shrimp. *Salade russe* is a potato salad with tiny pieces of beet. Manioc and taro are usually boiled and eaten as the main starch. Taro, which is served in large slices, contains significant quantities of fluoride and keeps teeth healthy. Young taro leaves, boiled and topped with coconut cream, resemble and taste like spinach. Finally, poi is a heavy, sweet pudding usually made with taro, bananas or papayas. It is served warm and topped with coconut milk. (Those who have sampled Hawaiian poi will find the Tahitian variety entirely different.)

A local fruit that no visitor should miss is the *pamplemousse*, a huge variety of grapefruit, which was most likely brought from Asia. Unusually sweet and tasty, the *pamplemousse* is available fresh in markets or you can buy the juice in liter-sized cartons. Occasionally, you can find it fresh-squeezed in restaurants or cafés. Likewise the *rambutan*, a soft, spiny, red fruit (also from Asia) related to the lychee, can be found at roadside stands or in local markets in season. Don't leave Tahiti without trying both of them.

The Polynesians who originally settled the islands brought with them bananas, breadfruit, taro, yams and, strangely enough, the South American sweet potato. How the Polynesians got this last item is a mystery, but Dr. Y. H. Sinoto of the Bishop Museum conjectures that Polynesian mariners traveled to South America, perhaps traded with the locals and made their way back to Polynesia with the sweet potato.

The missionaries later introduced sugarcane, cotton, corn, oranges, limes, guavas, pineapple, coffee and numerous other fruits and vegetables.

Depending on their degree of assimilation, many Tahitians have adopted French cuisine, including coffee, French bread, butter and canned goods. Unfortunately, it is a sign of the times to see them opening cans of Japanese tuna instead of fishing for the real thing.

Shoppers will discover that the best bargain in the store is French bread, which sells for about 40 CFP per loaf or baguette. Note that on the larger islands it is delivered daily in boxes along the roadside where one might think mail would be placed. Fruit is the next least expensive food in the islands, with the exception of watermelons—which cost 1000 CFP and up.

EAT ON THE CHEAP

Sandwiches are a food bargain in French Polynesia. They typically cost 125 to 175 CFP in snack bars or takeaways, 250 to 300 CFP in small eateries where you can sit down to enjoy them. The tasty local bread (made from subsidized flour) makes a fine sandwich or *casse-croûte*. Note that snacks (as snack bars are known locally) are ubiquitous in the communities of French Polynesia. Many are small grocery stores or shops with a counter, usually with a handful of stools at a bar. While mixed alcoholic drinks are expensive, a good bottle of French wine can be had for under US$20.

▼▼▼▼▼▼▼▼▼▼▼▼

Art and Culture

Upper-class Tahitians have adopted Western pop culture with a vengeance. French Polynesians wear the most chic fashions, listen to the latest pop music and, if they can afford it, drive the latest German cars and Japanese motorcycles. Yet they still have their own language and customs despite 200 years of foreign influence.

Tahiti has captured the imagination of European intellectuals and artists since Rousseau waxed about the "Noble Savage" and Melville penned *Typee*, the first novel about a romance between a white man and a Polynesian native. However, perhaps the most famous and influential (and troubled) artist to ever set foot on Tahiti's shores was Paul Gauguin. (See "Tahiti's Literati" at the end of the book.)

MUSIC & DANCE

Perhaps the most resilient aspects of Polynesian culture are music and dance. To hear the thunder of their drumming for the first time is a stirring experience. Traditional percussionists, who always accompany dance troupes, offer one of the purest expressions of Polynesian music and are as much a part of the music scene today as are electric guitarists. Traditional music is performed both for the entertainment of visitors and local audiences. Drumming, unless part of the reenactment of a religious ceremony, is never performed without accompaniment of dancers.

The modern *tamure* is a bastardized form of the traditional dance performed by troupes acting out a legend or event depicting warriors, kings, fishermen, heroes, priests—a far cry from today's slick, often showbiz-style productions.

As in all cultures, modern Tahitian music and dance owe quite a bit to outside influences. Popular Tahitian music (as opposed to the chants and traditional songs performed during a *tamure*) is an admixture of various derivations. This includes melodies and rhythms acquired from American pop or rock and roll, reggae, French *chansons* and even hymns borrowed from the missionaries. Like musicians anywhere else in the world, Tahitian bands equipped with the most modern Fender guitars and Yamaha amplifiers crank out endless songs about love, romance and betrayal.

Perhaps the most familiar aspect of Tahitian culture is its dance, in particular the hip-shaking and often erotic *tamure*, a step that every Tahitian is taught at an early age. The *tamure* resembles the Hawaiian hula from the waist down, but is more forceful, suggestive and sometimes more violent than the Hawaiian dance. Tahitian dancers have amazingly flexible and controlled hip movements—an art that has to be seen to be appreciated.

CRAFTS

Traditional mat or basket weaving and carving have all but disappeared in Tahiti, Bora Bora and Moorea, the most visited islands. I have never seen a French Polynesian woman of any age weave a mat, a skill that is ubiquitous in other parts of the Pacific. That is not to say it is not done anymore, but the closest thing a visitor is likely to see is hats being woven at the Papeete municipal market.

In the more remote areas, such as the Marquesas, Tuamotu and Austral islands, traditional crafts are still practiced. The Australs, in particular, are famous for the quality of mats and hats woven from *pandanus*, a tree that grows throughout the South Pacific. Carving or wood sculpture is strictly a product of artisans in the Marquesas Islands. The most popular items are reproductions of tiki, exquisite bowls and coconut shells with intricately etched Marquesan motifs.

Hats, mats, weavings and wood sculpture can be purchased at the municipal market in Papeete, and at several private shops or boutiques. It's also possible to buy art directly from the artisans in the outer islands. The closer you are to Papeete, the higher the prices. A foot-high wooden *tiki* in the Marquesas might sell for $60. That same *tiki* in Papeete could well sell for US$300. On some of the outer islands, such as Huahine, it is also possible to purchase *tifaifai* (Tahitian quilting). A traditional skill that is still very much in vogue throughout French Polynesia is the weaving of flowered leis (*hei*), crowns (*hei upo'o*) and shell necklaces (*hei pupu*). Several different varieties of flowers are used in making leis, including *tiare* (the national flower), hibiscus and frangipani.

TATTOOS

Polynesia is the birthplace of the tattoo, where it has been an integral part of the culture since ancient times. During the current era of Polynesian cultural revivalism, the tattoo has experienced a resurgence. And if you haven't noticed, this ancient art form is undergoing a renaissance in North America and Europe. In fact, it's difficult to walk down a busy street in Papeete or a quiet country lane in Moorea without seeing men or women with tattoos on any body part where there is skin.

The word tattoo is derived from the Tahitian term *tatau* and was first recorded by Captain James Cook in 1769, who described in great detail how it was done and what type of designs were used.

Although in former times all adult men and women were tattooed, the design and area decorated were restricted by social, political and economic factors. Certain motifs were suitable only for the chiefly class. Since the artists were paid with mats, pigs and other goods, wealthier men were the only people extensively tattooed. Unfortunately, there are gaps of knowledge of the ancient art of tattooing. Since the canvas used had a limited life expectancy and few photos of this art were ever taken, little is known. The practice was abandoned at an early date because the missionaries (naturally) condemned it as, in Bengt Danielsson's words, "a morally dangerous glorification of the sinful body."

The missionaries no doubt understood that Polynesians found tattoos to be erotic. People who were not tattooed were less desired by the opposite sex. This explains why so many European sailors and beachcombers gladly submitted to the excruciating experience of getting a tattoo.

At the turn of the century, when British anthropologist H. Ling Roth proposed a study of tattooing, there were no living specimens in the Society Islands. However, he was fortunate enough to find a preserved specimen close at hand, that of a Tahitian who had signed on as a sailor on a European ship and died in England in 1816. Prior to burial, a doctor who admired the tattoo skinned the sailor and donated the specimen to the Royal College of Surgeons. Using the preserved skin along with observations of early explorers and missionaries, Roth determined that women had fewer tattoos than men, but for both sexes the bare minimum was having one's thighs, hands and feet adorned. In general, geometric designs were the most popular motifs, along with plants, leaves, fish and birds. Some of the designs were particular to geographic areas so that one could tell if an individual was from the Australs, Tuamotus or elsewhere.

Nowhere was the art of tattooing as developed as in the Marquesas, where both men and women covered their faces and bodies with intricate geometric designs. When German anthropologist Von Steinen arrived in 1897 he found a number of fully decorated men and women. His photos were reproduced in the first volume of his classic work *Die Markesaner und Ihre Kunst* (*The Marquesans and Their Art*). Twenty-three years later, when American anthropologist Willowdean Handy visited the same islands, she found only 125 partially tattooed men and women. In 1951 when Bengt Danielsson did an acculturation study on Hiva Oa, he found only one man with traditional tattooing.

Today young Tahitians are reinventing their ancestors' artistry, freed from the constraints of the missionaries. Created with modern tattoo irons and sterilized equipment, neo-traditional tattoos are common on both men and women of all ages throughout the

FLOWERS IN THEIR HAIR

You will never see a race of people so enamored with putting flowers in their hair as the French Polynesians. Fresh *tiare* or hibiscus blossoms are always worn behind the ear or braided with palm fronds and other greenery into floral crowns. Tradition has it that if a woman or man tucks the flower behind the left ear she or he is taken; a flower placed behind the right ear means the person is available. Tahitians joke that if someone waves a flower behind their head it means "follow me." I have never witnessed this, but will report the outcome of such an invitation if fortunate enough to experience it.

islands. Some people choose a more radical path—adopting full- or half-body designs as a way to reclaim the narrative of their family history. Although the traditional tattoo method—tapping a block of bone or shell needles with a stick to insert the pigment—was banned in 1986 by the Ministry of Health, one can still find practitioners far afield in the Solomon Islands.

As with other Third World peoples, Tahitians experienced a cultural blossoming and reawakening in the 1970s, manifested through the *Maohi* or neo-Polynesian artistic movement. Artists explored traditional Polynesian motifs, while writers and playwrights went digging into their own mythology for themes. According to the late Bobby Holcomb, a respected Hawaiian artist who lived in Tahiti until his death in 1991, neo-Polynesian painters like himself use the Polynesian color scale (earthy browns, reds, yellows) in traditional Polynesian historical and mythical themes. Neo-Polynesian art is often more abstract than traditional Pacific art and may incorporate eroticism, sensuality, local flora and fauna, as well as the classic Polynesian geometric patterns as displayed in tattoos and tapa cloth.

Politically, the movement produced nationalist stirrings, calling for greater autonomy and even independence from France. Today, the nationalist maelstrom and a "back-to-the-roots" sentiment have taken hold over a greater portion of society. Teaching the Tahitian language in schools, once illegal, is now part of the curriculum. Politicians of every stripe espouse traditional Tahitian culture, and artists enjoy the support of the state. In the last few years, the French Polynesian government has nurtured the talents of young artists by displaying their works in exhibitions and providing cash prizes. Displays of Tahitian art and re-enactments of ancient ceremonies—such as the crowning of a king—can readily be seen during *Heiva*, which takes place in July as part of Bastille Day celebrations.

One of the most novel groups to appear on the cultural scene is *Pupu Arioi*, a small but dedicated organization that specializes in teaching children about their Polynesian heritage. Named for an ancient Polynesian society that allowed members to criticize their leaders and rise in an otherwise rigid social structure, *Pupu Arioi* began in 1977 as a theater troupe. Later, the group's emphasis shifted to education. Members now travel from school to school, teaching teachers and pupils relaxation techniques, which calm children and put them into a receptive state, and then introduce them to theater, dance, music and costuming. Children are not pushed, but nudged into thinking about their culture and traditions. *Pupu Arioi* members also discuss Polynesian mythology and philosophy with the idea of educating children in the oral traditions that were once the backbone of Tahitian culture. Perhaps they will be successful in reinfusing values into a society that for many reasons has lost a number of its old traditions.

**SEX & THE
TAHITIAN
MYTH**

"There is a scale in dissolute sensuality, which these people have ascended, and which no imagination could possibly conceive."
—Captain Cook

When discussing Tahiti, inevitably the beauty and (the real or imagined) sexual proclivities of the natives arise. Since the time of Wallis and Cook, the myth of Tahiti as the "Isle of Love" has flourished—and is still used as a major selling point by the travel industry. As a result of books such as *Typee* and *The Marriage of Loti* and movies such as *Mutiny on the Bounty*, countless men have traveled to Tahiti's shores in search of its beguilements.

From the earliest accounts, Tahitian women genuinely relished lovemaking, and sailors arriving in the islands were greeted by boatloads of willing maidens. According to those narratives, the arrival of a ship was like a circus visiting a small town. Days and nights were filled with wild abandon, rum drinking and the comic sight of pale white men in strange costume. Amorous flings had the benefit of material rewards as well, usually a trinket of some sort. In Cook's day, nails were often given as gifts. This sometimes reached a hazardous stage as eager sailors began to wrench nails from the very ships themselves.

Today, things are quite different. Tahitians have by no means lost their joyful abandon, but male visitors are mistaken if they think Tahitian women are just waiting to fulfill their fantasies. Male tourists are advised not to adopt the attitude that they are God's gift to *vahines*. More often than not, they will feel that they are on the outside, looking into a totally different world.

And what a different world it is. I for one do not profess to understand much about the psycho-sexual nature of the Tahitian. One can only assume that Tahitian customs and traditions, which are so foreign to the Judeo-Christian ethic, existed long before the white visitor appeared on the scene. I also think it is wrong to assume that Tahitians are totally uninhibited and free from neuroses. As with people everywhere, they have their share of hang-ups and sexual difficulties.

For those going to Tahiti seeking pleasures of the flesh, some final words on the subject: for those lucky in love, Tahiti will be just like anywhere else, only warmer.

**TAHITI'S
THIRD SEX**

Homosexuality has been a culturally accepted lifestyle in Polynesia for centuries. When the Europeans came, they were shocked and puzzled at the behavior of male transvestites who did striptease acts for the crews and unabashedly had sexual relations with other men. Commenting on this behavior, Lt. Bligh said:

"It is strange that in so prolific a country as this men should be led into such sensual and beastly acts of gratification, but perhaps no place in the world are they so common or extraordinary as in this island."

In the years that followed, the brethren from the London Missionary Society did their best to convert the Tahitians into upright Protestants, but with little success. The cultural heritage of the *mahu* (transvestites or men that take on female roles) continues to play an important role in Polynesian culture. According to anthropologist Bengt Danielsson, the *mahu* is "a popular and honored member of every village throughout the Society Islands."

Anthropologist Robert I. Levy writes that one becomes a *mahu* by choice or by being coaxed into the role, or both, at an early age. The boy associates primarily with females and learns to perform the traditionally feminine household tasks. After puberty, the *mahu* may assume a woman's role by cooking, cleaning, looking after children and wearing feminine clothing. He may dance what are normally the women's parts during festivals, often with greater skill than the women around him. Despite their proclivity to take on female roles, *mahus* are not necessarily homosexual in their preferences. In the villages he may work as a maid, and in Papeete can often find employment as a waiter, bartender or professional dancer. (Some male visitors may find out belatedly that the attractive Tahitian dancer who had been looking their way is actually a man.)

Although Tahitians may poke fun at *mahus* there is none of the deep-seated hostility that exists towards homosexuals in the West. Young adolescents may seek out *mahus* for sexual favors, but generally only if there are no girls available. If a young man does have sex with a *mahu*, there is little stigma attached to the act. In Papeete there are several nightclubs that feature male striptease acts and cater to a varied sexual spectrum.

Anthropologist Danielsson fears that the *mahu* tradition is in danger of disappearing because of what he calls the "brutal mod-

RELIGION

The church is an important institution throughout the Pacific island nations and French Polynesia is no exception. On the outer islands the local priest or minister often wields a powerful hand in community affairs. In most areas, church attendance is high. Most French Polynesians (about 55 percent) are Protestants, followed by Roman Catholics (30 percent), Mormons (6 percent) and Seventh-Day Adventists (2 percent). Buddhists, Confucianists and Jehovah's Witnesses make up about 2 percent of the population.

ernization process." He has already noticed the trend of *mahus* turning to Western-style homosexual prostitution as a way of making a living in a modern society incompatible with the traditional *mahu* way of life.

MYTH &
LOCAL
BELIEFS

Though we shall never fully understand the religious beliefs of the ancient Tahitians, it is known that the creator was *Te Atua*, who was rarely seen on earth. A pantheon of lesser gods, however, were often encountered in one manifestation or another. These included *Ta'aroa* (god of the sea), *Oro* (god of war), *Rongo* (god of agriculture) and *Tane* (god of sex and procreation). Spirits were forever intruding in the lives of man and communicated with people in a number of ways. Trees were often a medium and the rustling of the wind was a sure sign that the gods were present. Tiki figures, carved of wood or stone, were a medium through which spirits or gods interacted with mortals.

Although Christianity has spread throughout the islands, there is still a strong belief in vestiges of Polynesia's pre-Christian religion. In the outlying areas especially, myths of gods, giants and supernatural creatures are spoken of as fact and it is not unusual for a person to have had encounters with *tupa'pau* (ghosts).

One man in Maupiti matter-of-factly described to me the occasion on which he had seen a dozen ghosts floating down a moonlit road outside his village. These ghosts, he said, were the spirits of passengers who had perished in a shipwreck several weeks earlier. The spirits were those of native Maupitans, returning home as the dead always do.

Accepting the locals' belief that the supernatural is a normal part of life often makes Westerners question their own beliefs. In the Tuamotus, I met a young Frenchman by the name of Patrick who had spent several years living on the atoll of Ahe. He said that one evening he and an old villager were fishing in a skiff inside the atoll's lagoon. The Frenchman spotted an object resembling a ball of fire that rose from a spit of land on the lagoon's far edge and floated in the direction of the village. Awestruck by the sight, he pointed it out to the old man who sat contentedly fishing. The Tahitian glanced at the luminous ball and nonchalantly remarked that it was only the spirits returning to the village and really nothing to get excited about.

TWO

Traveling in French Polynesia

Choosing where to go in French Polynesia is akin to perusing the menu at a five-star restaurant. There are so many places to visit, it's really a tough call. Each of the five major island groups has its own distinctive attractions. The main thing is to get *out* of Papeete and either spend time in one of Tahiti's outer districts or visit one of the outer islands. Only in Tahiti's countryside or on an outer island are you likely to experience the pace and hospitality of genuine French Polynesia.

My personal favorites in the Society Group (which includes the Windward and Leeward islands) are Moorea, Huahine and Maupiti. If you can, you should also make a point of visiting at least one island in the Tuamotu Group so that you can experience an atoll, which is entirely different from a high island. Among these islands you might consider one of the less-visited atolls such as Tikehau, Takaroa, Mataiva or Fakarava. If you have the time and the budget, at least one of the Marquesas Islands should also be on your itinerary. Remote and seldom visited by tourists, their precipitous terrain is absolutely spectacular. Fatu Hiva is considered by many to be the most beautiful island in the group.

SOCIETY GROUP Tahiti, French Polynesia's largest and most populous island, is home to the international airport and the capital, Papeete. Papeete has a charming waterfront, fine restaurants and the *marché* (public market), but the capital is only one part of the equation. To really get a handle on Tahiti it's best to get out of town. I would suggest renting a car and spending at least one day exploring the countryside, or *district*, as the locals call it. Outside Papeete's urban jungle, people are friendlier, and chances are you'll see a glimpse of old Tahiti. My favorite corner of Tahiti is *Tahiti Iti* or (Little Tahiti), the smaller appendage of the island connected to the main body by the Isthmus of Taravao. There are some restaurants in the tiny hamlet of Taravao and a multitude of stunning vistas. The Tautira Village area in particular has a spooky edge-of-the world feeling about it that stays with you. Here the coastal road traces the steep terrain. The mountains are thick with foliage and rise precipitously into the mist. On Tahiti Iti one senses that progress has yet to encroach on this corner of French Polynesia.

31

Because of its proximity to Tahiti, **Moorea** has become a "suburb" of Papeete. Despite this moniker, the island is dramatically beautiful, with sharp serrated peaks that command deep cleft valleys. The pace is slower than Tahiti, it's less congested with cars, and it has an abundance of good beaches—many more than Tahiti. Tourism development on the island has increased considerably over the past few years—more than I'd like to see—but the island still retains its charm and friendliness. It's very easy to get to Moorea from Tahiti The fast ferry takes only 30 minutes. I'd consider staying at one of the smaller pensions rather than a large hotel. You'll find the service more personal and the feeling more intimate. Once there, rent a car and take the time to drive around the island. Be sure to visit the interior for the vistas and the archaeological sites. The jeep tours are a terrific way to see hidden Moorea.

When James Michener called **Bora Bora** the most beautiful island in the world, he may have been right. Once a sleepy outpost, the island is dominated by two towering volcanic peaks that overlook a stunning translucent blue lagoon. There are terrific white-sand beaches and wonderful places to eat. The luxury hotels along the Matira Beach are world class. The island also offers scuba divers some once-in-a-lifetime opportunities such as swimming with giant manta rays. My personal feelings about the island are, however, ambivalent. Though the name Bora Bora evokes magic, its fame has brought in multitudes of visitors. It has become too popular, too crowded and out of the range of mid-range and budget visitors. That's the bad news. The good news is, a fair number of reasonably priced restaurants and lodgings have sprung up like mushrooms in the past few years. If you do plan to visit and don't have a king's ransom to pay, there is hope!

Huahine is a diamond in the rough, and a stronghold of Polynesian culture. One of the most picturesque and geographically diverse islands in the Society Group, the tourism market has happily not yet discovered this verdant isle. There are numerous white-sand beaches, the best and most consistent surfing in all of French Polynesia, and a variety of lodging for every budget. Restaurants in Fare, the main community, are diverse and reasonably priced. Those who come to Huahine for cultural tourism will not be disappointed. Huahine's resilient people prefer to speak Tahitian rather than French and regard their traditions as sacred. There are also more ancient temples (many of which have been reconstructed) per square foot than anywhere else in the South Pacific. The only thing it doesn't have are swarms of visitors—one of the best reasons to come here.

The sister islands of **Raiatea** and **Tahaa** are unreservedly off the beaten track. Uturoa, the main community of Raiatea, is a government administrative center, while Tahaa is still an undeveloped backwater. Both islands have recommended budget and mid-range accommodations. There is also one superb *motu* resort, Vahine Island, located off Tahaa, that ranks as one of the best in French Polynesia. There are a number of good restaurants in the Uturoa area. Those with an interest in archaeology will want to visit Raiatea, which has the largest and most important Polynesian temple in the South Pacific—Marae Taputapuatea. There are no beach resorts on either island, but you can find them on the off-shore *motu*. Diving is first rate in the lagoon shared by Raiatea and Tahaa. Like Huahine, few visitors find their way to Raiatea and fewer yet to Tahaa.

The smallest of the Society Islands, **Maupiti** is a hidden gem. Mountainous and verdant, it's so small you can walk around it in several hours. There is also a superb white-sand beach and lovely beaches on the *motu*, as well. Locals have spurned the advances of major hoteliers so there are no major resorts or hotels here. To prevent exploitation of its natural resources, Maupiti forbids the export of food, fish, timber and other products. In terms of tourism it is perhaps the least developed of any in the Society Group, but has a fine selection of pension-style accommodations in the main village and on the offshore *motu*. Despite Maupiti's location (it's the most far-flung of the Society Islands), there is daily air service. Visitors who want a taste of traditional Polynesia would do well to visit this stunning island.

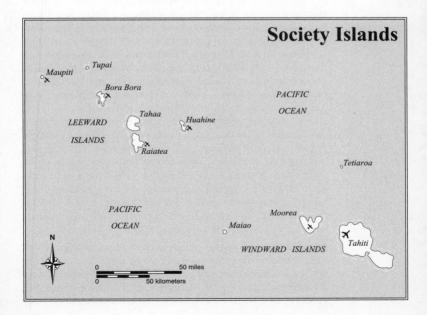

TUAMOTU GROUP   The Tuamotus (also known as the Paumotu Islands) differ from the Society Islands both geographically and culturally. Unlike the high islands that characterize most of French Polynesia, the Tuamotus are flat rings of coral surrounding lagoons. Culturally and linguistically, they are also distinct from the rest of French Polynesia. If you believe, as I do, that geography influences human behavior, you will agree that the Tuamotu experience is unique. It is my belief that anyone who takes the time and effort to explore French Polynesia should spend several days on an atoll. Why? Unlike a high island, there is no place to hide (physically or psychologically) on an atoll. You naturally turn inward on a flat island surrounded by only a few square yards of soil and an endless ocean. You are laid bare before the elements—the hot sun, the pounding surf and unceasing trade winds that whistle through the palm fronds. Don't expect the lap of luxury in the Tuamotus. With the exception of Rangiroa or Manihi, the accommodations are modest. Lodging is pension-style and there are no restaurants, no stores, no amenities. However, you will be cared for. Tuamotu hospitality is unforgettable. The Tuamotus generally have excellent beaches and arguably the best and wildest diving in the entire territory. And the traditional Paumotu music is hauntingly beautiful.

> That chirping sound you hear at night isn't an insect, or even a bird—it's a gecko, the adorable little lizard that is ubiquitous in the South Pacific.

MARQUESAS ISLANDS   Physically, the Marquesas Islands are nothing short of phenomenal. Volcanic in origin, they have few reefs and rise like jagged spires from the sea. Rocky and precipitous, these isolated outposts have deep, lush trench-like valleys and remote beaches. Of the six that are inhabited—Nuku Hiva, Ua Huka, Ua Pou, Hiva Oa, Tahuata and Fatu Hiva—three are accessible by air, the others by sea. All the Marquesas Islands have pension-style or mid-range accommodations, and Hiva Oa and Nuku Hiva each have a small yet luxurious Pearl Lodge. Marquesan culture (quite distinct in language and custom from Tahiti) and breathtaking scenery are the draws here. There are numerous archaeological sites, and an otherworldly ambience straight out of *Raiders of the Lost Ark*. Unlike the Society Group, you can still find traditional woodcarvers and craftspeople plying their trades. Visitors to the Marquesas Group need to be independent travelers, patient and able to rough it. Overland travel is nearly always by four-wheel-drive vehicle (or via horseback) as the roads are horrendous. If you have the time and money, I would strongly recommend a sojourn to these isolated rocks.

THE AUSTRAL ISLANDS   The Australs seldom get outside visitors. Perhaps that is the best reason to go there. You can be virtually guaranteed there will be few, if any, guests from outside of French Polynesia. Like the Marquesas, they are quite remote and very expensive to get to. The latitude here offers a milder climate than you'll find in the other Polynesian island groups. There are few beaches in the Australs. Tubuai, the largest of the Austral Group, is best known for the way its people sing—their purposefully atonal sound is perhaps one of the last vestiges of pre-contact religion and culture left in French Polynesia. A journey by private yacht, or the passenger freighter *Aranui III* (which stops at all six inhabited islands), are the best ways to explore these isles.

THE GAMBIER GROUP   The Gambier Islands are another remote and seldom-visited island group. Like the Australs, their southerly latitude makes them slightly cooler than the Society Group. The largest and most accessible of the inhabited islands is Mangareva. Rikitea, the main community in Mangareva, has a number of ruins from its days as a missionary center. The mostly tumbledown ruins have an eerie, dark feel about them, testament, perhaps, to the islands' iron-handed Christian legacy. The main industry in the island group is black pearl cultivation. There are few beaches here, but there are several excellent pensions on Mangareva.

When to Go

SEASONS

November through May are the hot and humid months, while June through October brings a cooler and drier climate. It may rain any time of the year, and tropical downpours can be quite heavy. In June, July and sometimes August a gusty trade wind called the *mara'amu* bears down on the islands, bringing wind, rain and sometimes nasty weather from the south. If your resort is located on a southern coast of the Society Islands, chances are you will experience the *mara'amu*. Nothing to worry about, just don't forget to bring an extra windbreaker. If you are a diver, for visibility you're better off going in the drier months, when muddy rivers don't obscure visibility along the coasts.

If you are interested in dance and music, the best time to visit is during July when the country is in the midst of *Heiva*, the month-long Tahitian holiday that melds into traditional French Bastille Day celebrations. Unfortunately, that is the time most other visitors come to French Polynesia as well. If you choose to go at this time of year, book early.

Another seasonal wild card that affects the visitor, especially the budget traveler who needs low-cost pensions or hotel rooms, is the timing of local school holidays. It may be a good idea to orchestrate your vacation around school holidays so that you don't end up fighting for a bed with a Tahitian student. If you think this may be an issue, check with the Tahiti Tourist Board.

CALENDAR OF EVENTS

JANUARY

January 1   **New Year's Day** is a time for friends and families to gather for merrymaking. The long-standing tradition is to spend

New Year's Day driving around visiting friends and relatives. Children's games are held in town halls on most islands.

Late January to February **Chinese New Year** is celebrated on Tahiti during a four-day *fête* that includes dances, martial arts demonstrations, calligraphy, painting and fireworks. Local beer-maker Hinano sponsors the **Hinano Surf Tour** competition at the world-renowned Teahupoo break on Tahiti, as well as the **Hinano Cup Va'a** canoe race.

FEBRUARY

Mid-February The **Tahiti Nui International Sunrise Marathon** is held on Moorea. This is a 26-mile (42-kilometer) marathon starting in Maatea on the island's south coast and finishing in Pao-pao on the northern coast. The race draws more than 600 partici-pants from around the world. A six-kilometer mini-marathon is also offered. A traditional feast is held that evening in Tiki Village.

Late February to early March The **Polynesian Cultural Fair**, part of the Heritage Days celebration, is held at the Place Vaiete, a public square adjacent to the Port of Papeete on Tahiti. The fair showcases ancient cultural traditions such as tattooing, basket weaving and Ra'au Tahiti—traditional medicine. **Tahiti Pearl Regatta**, an international sailing competition, is held in the Leeward Isles, departing from Raiatea.

MARCH

March 5 Protestant parishes throughout the islands celebrate the **Arrival of the First Missionaries** (Arrivée de l'Evangile) in 1797. The celebrations feature re-enactments of the missionaries' arrival. Many of the activities are held at the Willy Bambridge Sta-dium complex in Papeete, Tahiti, and on Afareaitu in Moorea.

Early March The **International Billfish Tournament**, a deep-sea fishing contest (held every other year) takes place on Bora Bora. Every two years, Bora Bora hosts the **World Va'a Speed Champ-ionship**, a canoe-sprinting competition.

Mid-March The **Austral Inter-Island Games** are held on Rurutu. Competitions feature traditional Polynesian sporting events.

BEST BEACHES

Popular belief aside, finding the perfect beach in Tahiti isn't always easy. The key to finding a good beach in the oft-visited Society Islands is a quick trip to an offshore *motu*. Tahiti and Moorea have nice mainland beaches, while Bora Bora and Huahine have the best *motu* beaches. If what you really need are miles of endless strands, then head to the Tuamotus. These cir-cular atolls are nothing more than two beaches separated by a stand of coconut palm trees. One beach fronts the open ocean (large waves and sharp coral ledges can make swimming risky here), while the other beach slopes into the tranquil waters of the lagoon.

April Heineken Beer hosts the **Heineken Kayak Contest** on Huahine, Raiatea and Bora Bora.

Mid-April The **Miss Bora Bora Beauty Contest** is held in one of the hotels followed by a Tahitian feast and dance on Bora Bora.

Late April On Tahiti, the **Polynesian Sports Festival** features traditional activities such as javelin throwing, outrigger canoe racing and fruit carrying races.

May As part of the World Competition Tour, the **Gotcha Tahiti Pro surfing contest** highlights the world's top surfers at Tahiti's
infamous Teahupoo break.

Mid-May Miss Tahiti is selected to represent the country in international beauty pageants at a Tahiti venue. **Miss Heiva i Tahiti** is also chosen to reign over the Bastille Day celebrations or *Heiva*. A contest for **Miss Moorea** is held on Moorea also. Not forgetting the other half of the human race, contests for **Mr. Muscles**, **Mr. Heiva i Tahiti** and **Mr. Tahiti** are held on Tahiti.

May 23–25 Every two years, Tubuai residents commemorate the 1778 **Arrival of the Bounty** by re-enacting the event.

Late June Golfers from around the Pacific compete for prize
money in the **International Golf Open,** held at the 18-hole, par-72 Oliver Breaud International Golf Course on Tahiti. Although there is no fixed schedule, a variety of small **surfing and canoeing competitions** are also typically held during June. June 29 is **Autonomy Day,** when citizens celebrate winning a degree of home rule.

July 1–21 Centered around France's **Bastille Day** (July 14), *La*
Fête, known as *Tiurai* or *Heiva* in Tahitian, is French Polynesia's biggest celebration. The festivities last around three weeks and begin at the tail end of June or the start of July. They are celebrated with dance competitions, singing, *pirogue* races and other sporting events. A large **exhibition of arts and crafts** is scheduled as part of the *Heiva* at the Aorai Tinihau Exposition Hall in the Pirae district of Tahiti.

Late July The annual **pro-am surfing competition** held in Tahiti features some of the best amateurs and pros from around the world. The **Te Aito Marathon Outrigger Canoe Races** held in Tahiti is one of the islands' more important competitions.

July through August The **Cultural Heiva** gets well under way as people from all the islands—and around the world—converge on Tahiti for the festivities. Polynesian arts and crafts, song, food and live entertainment are all featured at the new *Heiva* grounds at the Tahua To'ata waterfront complex in Papeete.

Late August Local musicians compete in Papeete's **Night of the**
Guitar and Ute performing *ute,* which are satirical improvisational songs as old as the Tahitian culture.

SEPTEMBER   **Late September**   **World Tourism Day** is celebrated by employees of travel-related industries donning festive clothing. The Public Market in Papeete is the venue for singing and dancing.

OCTOBER   **Early October**   In Papeete, the **Tipanier Ball**, organized by the Women's Liberation Council of Tahiti, is a traditional dinner dance where prizes are awarded for the loveliest woven floral crowns.
October 19–26   The Papeete waterfront is transformed by the **Tahiti Carnival**, which draws some 15,000 participants for food, fun and games.
Late October   The **stone-fishing ceremony** held on the island of Tahaa in late October or early November features traditional activities include copra-cutting contests, canoe racing and a fire-walking ceremony. The stone-fishing ceremony is held on the last day and is followed by a Tahitian feast.
October to November   The **Hawaikinui Va'a canoe race,** with over 100 canoes, is the event of the year in the islands. The annual race between Huahine, Raiatea, Tahaa and Bora Bora is held over a three-day period and is the culminating event of *Heiva*.

NOVEMBER   **November 1**   On **All Saints Day** families throughout the islands visit cemeteries and illuminate the graves with candles. In the evening hymns are sung in memory of the dead.

DECEMBER   **Early December**   Tahitians pay homage to the Tiare Tahiti by celebrating **National Flower Day**. Post office bureaus, banks and other businesses compete for the best floral decorations and Tiare Tahiti blossoms are handed out throughout the town.
December 25   **Christmas Day** in Tahiti is a time for families and friends to congregate.

▼▼▼▼▼▼▼▼▼▼
How to Go

AIR

All incoming international flights to French Polynesia touch down at the Faa'a Airport near Papeete, Tahiti. Tahiti is generally a stopover destination between Australia or New Zealand and the United States. There are also connections between Tahiti and Chile via Easter Island, as well as connections from other Pacific islands.

Airlines that fly into Tahiti include Air France, Air New Zealand, Air Tahiti Nui, Aircalin, Corsair, Hawaiian Airlines, Lan Chile and Qantas Airways. Needless to say, the best fares can be found by calling several travel agents and checking out the ads in newspaper travel sections for discounted air tickets.

TO/FROM THE USA   Los Angeles has the most nonstop flights from mainland U.S., although Air Tahiti Nui will start direct New York to Papeete flights in 2005. Carriers that service the

LAX/Papeete route include Air France, Air New Zealand and Air Tahiti Nui. Corsair, a French charter service, flies nonstop out of L.A. and Oakland. Flight time is approximately seven hours and 50 minutes for LAX flights. Hawaiian Airlines services Tahiti out of Los Angeles, San Francisco and Seattle, but layovers in Hawaii can be as long as seven hours. Air Tahiti Nui is an international carrier actually based in French Polynesia, with scheduled service from LAX and, soon, New York City.

> Get to the airport early! There is no departure tax charged to visitors leaving French Polynesia, but there *can* be an inordinate amount of time waiting at the airport in order to pass through airport security, immigration and the like.

During low season—December 25 to June 15—roundtrip fares from Los Angeles to Tahiti start at around US$700 on Corsair. Corsair flies once a week out of LAX and Oakland, twice a week in July and August. ~ 800-677-0720; www.nouvelles-fron tieres.fr, e-mail nouvellesfrontieres@mail.pf. Air France has three flights weekly out of Los Angeles, with additional flights during the summer. ~ 800-237-2747; www.airfrance.com.

Air Tahiti Nui has service from Papeete to Los Angeles three times weekly. Prices for roundtrip service out of LAX begin in the US$800 range during low season. The airline also flies between Tokyo and Papeete twice weekly and will soon begin flights between New York and Papeete. ~ 877-824-4846; www.airtahitinui-usa.com, e-mail info@airtahitinui.pf. Likewise, Air New Zealand, which has service out of LAX, flies to Papeete four times per week. ~ 800-262-1234; www.airnz.co.nz.

Hawaiian Airlines has a weekly service out of any West Coast gateway; this entails a stopover in Honolulu. ~ 800-367-5320; www.hawaiianair.com. Circle-Pacific fares to New Zealand or to Australia can be routed via Tahiti, and discounted roundtrip tickets to Tahiti can be found if you are prepared to shop around. Look at the advertisements in the Sunday newspaper travel sections in major West Coast cities.

If you go strictly by price, the airline of choice would have to be a charter carrier. However, charters may lack the flexibility you want. All of the scheduled carriers cluster their Tahiti service on the weekends. (The only exception is Air Lib, which has mid-week departures.) Another consideration is what time of day your airline arrives—you don't want to miss most of a day of vacation. Air France flights arrive at around 5 a.m., so you can hit the ground running—if you get some sleep on the way over.

FROM AUSTRALIA AND NEW ZEALAND Despite Australia's and New Zealand's relative short distance from French Polynesia, there are no significant discounts on direct flights to Tahiti. In fact, you could probably get a return ticket to Los Angeles via Tahiti for the same price as a return ticket to Tahiti only (unless

Text continued on page 42.

Heiva—
Bacchanal in the Islands

*H*eiva or *Tiurai* combines France's Bastille Day (which commemorates the storming of the Bastille Prison during the French Revolution) with traditional Tahitian festivities. It begins on or around June 29, and lasts for approximately three to four weeks. During this period business grinds to a halt, hotels are booked solid and everyone enjoys an orgy of food, drink and dance. It is the islands' most important festivity—a combination of Mardi Gras, 4th of July and Walpurgis Night rolled into one.

Many island communities put on their own *fête* consisting of traditional dance competitions, rock-and-roll bands, foot and canoe races, javelin throwing, spearfishing and other sports activities. The largest celebration occurs in Papeete, where the waterfront is turned into a fairground crowded with booths, bars and restaurants, a Ferris wheel and a grandstand for viewing the all-important dance competitions.

Though the biggest celebration takes place in Papeete, there are other *Heiva* activities going on simultaneously at various locales around the country.

Along with dance competition, the most interesting event is the "Crowning of the King" re-enactment at the Marae Arahurahu, held 22.5 kilometers outside of Papeete. A gala outdoor theatrical event that re-creates the glory of Tahiti's pagan heritage, it is taken very seriously by locals who observe the celebration in hushed tones. If you have the opportunity, the festival is well worth seeing.

The event in Papeete opens with a parade featuring beauty contestants, sports association members, folkloric and *tamure* groups and flower-studded floats. On Bastille Day (July 14) there is a military parade that begins with a salvo of canons, followed by a sea of uniforms, brass bands playing military marches, and baton-twirling troupes of majorettes. The grand finale in the evening is the ball held at the mayor's residence.

The three weeks of celebration are also crowded with numerous activities such as horse races, speedboat races, bicycle races, parachuting displays, motorcycle competition, an international golf tournament and waterskiing. There is even room for the traditional Polynesian sports of fruit-carrying races and archery contests, as well as displays of tattoos, basket weaving, tapa cloth, copra cutting and Polynesian arts and crafts.

During this period French Polynesians converge on Tahiti to watch the dancing and partake in the good times. It is not unusual for Tahitians to stay up all night and frolic, sleep through the day, start chugalugging Hinano beer and begin the cycle again. *Tiurai* is above all a time to socialize, forget your troubles, and perhaps mend fences with a neighbor.

One criticism that long-time residents of Papeete have about *Tiurai* is that it has become too commercialized. During the holiday, prices shoot up and merchants make windfall profits. Commercialized or not, *Tiurai* in Papeete is packed shoulder-to-shoulder with people shoving their way along the carnival row. In one section, a crowd gathers in front of madly gesticulating Chinese shills, who spin the wheels of fortune in their gambling booths and attempt to out-bark each other on bullhorns. Meanwhile, locals try their luck at the shooting galleries, vendors hawk kewpie dolls and cowboy hats, and young children tug their parents' arms in the direction of the merry-go-round. The temporary outdoor cafés selling beer, barbecued chicken and steak swell with inebriated tourists and Tahitians alike.

Outside the grandstand entrance, the scene is a mob of performers and gawkers. Troupes of tasseled, straw-skirted dancers mill around awaiting their turn to go on stage. They are the *crème de la crème* of French Polynesian dancers. The air is thick with nervous energy and the scent of *Tiare Tahiti* blossoms. Nearly everyone is adorned with a crown of flowers or a single blossom behind the ear.

Tiurai is more than a carnival. For local entrepreneurs of the smaller island communities the festival is economically important. Not only is it a big affair for the established merchants but ordinary families set up small concessions and sell food and liquor as well. The celebration also performs an important educational function. It provides French Polynesian youth with an outlet for traditional cultural expression, which is in increasing danger of being lost due to the encroaching influence of Western culture.

you used a package plan that would most likely include accommodations in the price). Keep in mind that there are three pricing seasons for flights out of Australia—low, shoulder and high. Shop around: prices vary enormously. From New Zealand, Air France and Air New Zealand sell 45-day roundtrip tickets from Auckland to Papeete.

Another option is to make Tahiti a stopover on a Round-the-World (RTW) ticket. The available combinations on an RTW ticket are almost endless. You can fly via Tahiti to the United States or Canada, for example, then to Europe, and the same on return, or come back via Asia. Continental/KLM offer a one-year RTW ticket with unlimited stops, returning via Asia.

FROM THE U.K. AND EUROPEAN CONTINENT Few travelers fly all the way to the South Pacific just to visit Tahiti. Air Tahiti Nui serves Charles de Gaulle Airport in Paris.

Tahiti can also be easily visited en route to Australia or on a RTW ticket. Air-line ticket discounters (bucket shops) in London offer RTW tickets that include Tahiti in their itinerary.

A typical round-the-world route from London is Los Angeles, Tahiti, Sydney, Fiji, Rarotonga, then back to London via Los Angeles. Or, you could fly to Bangkok, Cairns, Sydney, Tahiti, and once again back to London via Los Angeles. As with flights out of Asia, Air France is generally the airline carrier servicing Tahiti, though Air New Zealand flights may also be used from London (via Los Angeles).

Trailfinders in west London produces a lavishly illustrated brochure that includes air-fare details. STA Travel also has branches in the United Kingdom. Look in magazines such as *Time Out*, the Sunday papers, and *Exchange & Mart* for ads.

Most British travel agents are registered with the ABTA (Association of British Travel Agents). If you have paid for your flight

FINDING A GOOD TRAVEL CONSULTANT

A competent travel agent should be able to tailor an itinerary around your special interests, such as golf or snorkeling. In most cases South Pacific specialists have toll-free phone numbers and can advise you of the current airfare bargains and seasonal discounts. They should also have fares for interisland travel. Most importantly, a reputable agency can save you money. For U.S. residents, I recommend Manuia Tours in San Francisco. It is owned by a Tahitian family, and they know their destination. They offer a variety of package tours that cater to divers, sailors, honeymooners, cruises and those interested in condo rentals or home stays. ~ 59 New Montgomery Street, San Francisco, CA 94105; 415-495-4500, 866-682-4484, fax 415-495-2000; e-mail manuiatravel@yahoo.com.

to an ABTA-registered agent that then goes out of business, ABTA will guarantee a refund or an alternative. Unregistered bucket shops are sometimes cheaper, but are also riskier.

Getting to and from French Polynesia from the Continent is straightforward. You go through Paris on Air France, Air Tahiti Nui or Corsair, all via Los Angeles. (Note: 95 percent of European travelers go to Tahiti with package deals.)

FROM OTHER PACIFIC ISLANDS There are surprisingly few connections between Tahiti and other Pacific islands. The ones that exist are not inexpensive. Aircalin (310-670-7302; www.air calin.com) flies between Noumea (New Caledonia) and Tahiti. They also have a connection from Fiji, via Noumea, to Tahiti.

There are also various excursion fares that span the South Pacific. For example, Air New Zealand has a fare from Los Angeles to New Zealand (with three stopovers) that takes you to Tahiti, Fiji and the Cook Islands. A similar ticket is available to Australia. If you want to stop in more than in three places along the route, the price goes up accordingly.

FROM ASIA Air Tahiti Nui operates two direct flights to Tokyo and one to Osaka each week; they also offer a triangular Papeete –Tokyo–Osaka–Papeete route once a week.

FROM SOUTH AMERICA Lan Chile connects Tahiti with Latin America via Easter Island twice a week.

Unfortunately, the romantic days of catching a tramp steamer and working your way across the Pacific no longer exist. Unless money is no object, the prohibitive cost of taking ships long distances makes it much more inviting to fly. However, once you are in the islands it is still possible (although difficult) to take freighters from one South Seas port to another.

SEA

Booking passage on a freighter between French Polynesia and other Pacific Islands entails going down to the dock and talking the vessel's skipper into giving you a berth. If there is room aboard, and the captain likes you, you are in luck. (On U.S.-registered ships, hitching a ride is impossible unless you have sailor's papers.) The schedule of international cargo vessels coming into Papeete is posted at the waterfront branch of the immigration police adjacent to the tourist office.

An affordable compromise is the passenger freighter *Aranui III*, which makes regular monthly voyages from Papeete up through the Tuamotus to the Marquesas. See "Travel between Islands: Ferries and Other Interisland Vessels: Marquesas Islands" below for details.

YACHTS For people with time on their hands and adventure in their hearts, traveling to Tahiti by yacht can be a reality. To become a crew member, go to Honolulu or one of the larger ports on the West Coast—preferably Los Angeles, San Diego or San Francisco—that are departure points for most Tahiti-bound yachts.

To find the boats headed to the South Pacific you must do some sleuthing down on the docks of the local yacht club. Usually notices are placed on yacht-club bulletin boards by skippers needing crew members, or by potential sailors looking for a yacht. The best thing to do is ask around the docks or marine supply shops.

Because exchange rates fluctuate, some yachties do not change their bond into Pacific Francs, ensuring that their refund is worth the same as their deposit. This is possible at Banque de Polynesie, which charges a US$20 handling fee plus 1 percent of the total amount.

Naturally, someone who has previous sailing experience, or is a gourmet chef or a doctor, will have a better chance to get on as a crew member. The six-week sailing season starts during the last half of September, with a secondary window opening in January and continuing through March.

If you are serious about getting on a yacht, it's best to start doing your research at least six months ahead of time. Get to know the people you are going to sail with and help them rig the boat.

Sailing time from the West Coast of the U.S. to French Polynesia takes about a month, with nowhere to get off in the middle of the Pacific. Papeete is one of the major transit points for yachts in the South Pacific, and once there it is generally no problem for an experienced sailor to hitch a ride from Papeete to any point east or west.

ENTRY PERMITS—YACHTS   For stays of less than 30 days, only passports are required for citizens of the United States, Canada, Australia, Japan and several other countries. Citizens of the European Union can stay three months without a visa. Anyone wishing to stay longer than their status permits must arrange for a tourist visa ahead of time. If coming from a country that does not have a French consulate, the visitor must, after five days, secure a valid visa from the Immigration Service—good for three months for all of French Polynesia.

Each crew member must also have a deposit in a special account at a local bank or at the Trésorerie Générale equal to the one-way fare from Tahiti back to the country of origin. Citizens of European Union countries are no longer required to post bond when arriving by yacht.

Papeete is the main port of entry and all yachts must obtain clearance there. However, the outer islands are also informal ports of entry. When landing on an outer island, yachts must identify themselves to the local police. The *gendarme* (police) in the first port of arrival will issue papers to present to officials in every other island visited on the way to Tahiti. U.S. and Canadian passport holders are given a 30-day grace period to clear into Papeete and complete the formalities. The bond is normally refunded the day before leaving Tahiti. Yachts staying less than a month may be able to waive the bond requirement.

During the yacht's stay in French Polynesia the crew list must correspond with the list of passengers made at the time of arrival. Any changes must be accounted for with the Chief of Immigration. Crew changes can only be made in harbors or anchorages where there are *gendarmes*. Disembarkation of crew members can only be authorized if the person in question has a bond deposit or an airline ticket with a confirmed reservation. Yachts may not stay longer than one year during a two-year period without paying duty. There is a branch of the Immigration Office near the Fare Manihini (Visitors' Bureau) on the waterfront.

TRAVEL BETWEEN ISLANDS

Traveling between the islands of French Polynesia served by Air Tahiti or scheduled ferry service is not usually a difficult affair. Thanks to French largess the transportation infrastructure is quite sophisticated. There are modern airstrips, well-paved highways, numerous boats and ferries, and a bus system that works. Visitors will find that most transportation is reasonably priced, and despite the general *mañana* attitude, things generally run on time. Americans, now used to tight security, will find Tahitian airports a relaxing affair.

The two means of transportation to the outer islands are by air and interisland vessels. Traveling by air is the fastest and most efficient method, but not necessarily the most economical. Although the local carrier, Air Tahiti, flies to quite a few destinations, it does not go to all the islands.

Interisland vessels, on the other hand, do go to every inhabited island but take more time, and overall are a much cheaper form of transportation than planes. On shorter routes they can be a great bargain and, at the same time, give you the chance to meet some locals.

A third possibility is to combine air and sea transportation. For example, if you want to visit Ahe, which has no air service, it is possible to book a flight to Manihi and then catch a speedboat from there to Ahe.

LOCAL AIR SERVICES The major interisland carrier, Air Tahiti, provides service to every island group. The island hoppers are well-maintained first-class ATR equipment. However, Air Tahiti's virtual monopoly means fares are high and service is inconsistent. Air Tahiti reservations agents tend to be very professional in Papeete, but not necessarily on the outer islands, where a change of plan means reservations are apt to disappear. Confirm your Air Tahiti flights if you skip or change any portion of an itinerary. Air Tahiti offers unadvertised discounts of up to 50 percent (depending on class of service) for people under 25 or over 60 years of age and for families traveling together. Applications for discounts can only be made once you arrive; they take three days to process. Travel can commence on the fourth day. My suggestion is to look into this immediately after arrival in Papeete. ~ Papeete; 86-42-42.

There are a plethora of other discounts available on Air Tahiti if you do a little digging. For example, "Pass Bleu" will allow you to visit Huahine, Bora Bora, Raiatea and Moorea for less than individual tickets to each island.

Air Tahiti also has several "Air Tahiti Passes" that are good for 28 days and allow one stopover for each island on a circular route.

Those interested in visiting the outer islands can use the *Extension Marquises* or *Extension Australes* to add these distant destinations to any Air Tahiti Pass.

The basic options are:

1. Pass Decouverte: Moorea/Huahine/Raiatea; 28,500 CFP.

2. Leeward Islands Pass: Moorea/Huahine/Raiatea/Bora Bora/Maupiti; 40,700 CFP.

3. Pass Lagons: Moorea/Rangiroa/Tikehau/Manihi/Fakarava; 45,600 CFP.

4. Pass Bora–Tuamotu: Moorea/Huahine/Raiatea/Bora Bora/Maupiti/Rangiroa/Tikehau/Manihi/Fakarava; 59,300 CFP.

5. Extension Marquises: Nuku Hiva, Atuona; 57,500 CFP.

6. Extension Australes: Rurutu, Tubuai; 25,600 CFP.

If you hold a ticket to Tahiti from an international destination, two bags weighing up to 20 kilos (twice the normal allowance) are permitted. Bags are routinely weighed at check-in; however, cabin baggage (one piece) is not weighed as part of the allowance.

In some cases, flights to and from the outer islands are direct, while in others they are routed via Papeete. For example, you can fly directly from Huahine to Raiatea but to fly from Huahine to Rangiroa you must pass through Faa'a Airport in Papeete. The types of aircraft used on most flights are the ATR 42 (hi-tech, twin-prop, 46-seat) and ATR 72 (66 seats). Nineteen-seat Twin Otters and smaller Britten-Norman Islanders are used on shorter routes. Seat assignments are not made on domestic flights, so if you want a particular seat (like the popular left-hand window seat on the hop from Tahiti to Bora Bora), make sure you board at the head of the queue.

For information on Air Tahiti in the U.S. contact Tahiti Vacations. ~ 800-553-3477.

Several other small airlines charter planes or helicopters for visitors. If flights are full, standby service is often available. Baggage allowance on interisland flights is only 22 pounds (10 kilo-

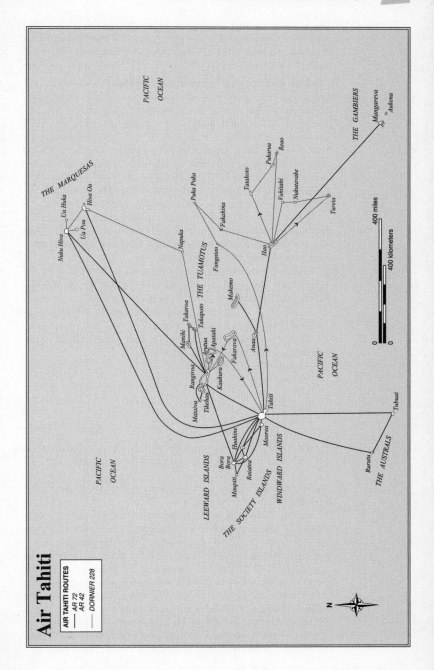

Air Tahiti

AIR TAHITI ROUTES
— AR 72
— AR 42
- - DORNIER 228

PACIFIC
OCEAN

THE GAMBIERS

Mangareva
Aukena

Pakarua
Reao

Tauaboto
Vahitahi
Nukutavake

Puka Puka

Fakahina

Turcia

Hao

THE MARQUESAS

Ua Huka
Hiva Oa
Ua Pou
Nuku Hiva

Napuka

THE TUAMOTUS

Fangatau

Mamiti
Takaroa
Takapoto
Apataki
Arutua
Makemo

Rangiroa
Kaukura
Fakarava

Matarea
Tikehau

Anaa

Tahiti

Huahine
Bora Bora
Raiatea
Maupiti

Moorea

PACIFIC
OCEAN

WINDWARD ISLANDS

LEEWARD ISLANDS

THE SOCIETY ISLANDS

Tubuai

Rurutu

THE AUSTRALS

PACIFIC
OCEAN

400 miles

400 kilometers

0

0

N

grams). Airlines will charge you without hesitation if your baggage is overweight. One of the more reliable charter companies is **Wan Air** of Tahiti. ~ Faa'a, Tahiti; 86-61-61, fax 86-61-72; e-mail liparo@wanair.pf.

FERRIES AND OTHER INTERISLAND VESSELS   Despite the increase in air transportation, interisland vessels remain a vital transportation link for travelers and cargo to the outer islands. In many instances, interisland steamers or much smaller skiffs are the only way to reach isolated communities. If you don't mind roughing it and take sensible sea-sickness precautions, interisland boats are a wonderful way to travel and meet local people. Make sure you allow plenty of time for this type of voyaging. Trips may range from a few hours to a few weeks. They are also usually inexpensive. Check the itineraries carefully before setting sail.

If you decide to travel by a conventional interisland boat, the best reported conditions were on the *Vaeanu*, which is the cleanest, and has marginally better accommodations. You will, however, not confuse it with the *QE II*.

Unlike the interisland boats, the ferries to Moorea generally leave on the hour, and you can purchase a ticket literally minutes before the boat departs. Some of the boats speed across the channel in less than 30 minutes, while others, like the 300-passenger *Moorea Ferry*, take an hour or longer.

All of the Moorea-bound ferries depart from the dock opposite the Royal Papeete Hotel. They include:

Aremiti Catamaran IV ~ 42-85-85
Aremiti Ferry ~ 42-85-85
Moorea Jet ~ 42-37-42
Moorea Ferry ~ 42-34-34
Ono Ono ~ 42-35-35

The following is a description of ferry itineraries and operator addresses for ferries serving each of the island groups.

Society Islands   There are four vessels that regularly serve these islands.

Taporo VII is one of the larger interisland boats, but it only takes 12 passengers because it is a freighter. During the day, when the tickets are purchased at the wharf, the 12-passenger rule is strictly enforced. In the evening, when the ticketing becomes the responsibility of the captain, the rule is stretched, especially if the boat is not on its way to Papeete where an official may check the number of passengers on arrival. The vessel has fewer passenger amenities than ferries and is not as clean or comfortable. When the seas are rough, the *Taporo VII* is *the* vessel of choice if you are prone to seasickness because it is doesn't pitch and roll as much as a smaller vessel. *Taporo VII* departs Monday, Wednesday and

Friday at 4 p.m. ~ *Compagnie Francaise Maritime de Tahiti Maritime de Tahiti*, BP 368, Papeete (Fare Ute), Tahiti; 42-63-93, 43-79-72, fax 42-06-17.

Taporo VII Route	Voyage time
Papeete/Huahine	9 hours
Huahine/Raiatea	2 hours
Raiatea/Bora Bora	3 hours
Bora Bora/Tahaa	2 hours
Tahaa/Raiatea	1 hour

The *Aremiti III* departs Papeete and serves Huahine and Raiatea twice a week, offering deck passage for up to 350 passengers. Snacks are available onboard. Offices are open Wednesday, Thursday and Saturday from 8 a.m. to noon and 2:30 p.m. to 5 p.m. ~ Gallieni Wharf, Papeete; 42-88-88, fax 42-83-83; e-mail aremiti@ netcourrier.com.

AREMITI III DEPARTURE AND ARRIVAL TIMES

Monday and Friday

Departs	at	Arrives	at
Papeete	7:00 a.m.	Huahine	10:45 a.m.
Huahine	11:00 a.m.	Raiatea	12:00 p.m.
Raiatea	12:20 p.m.	Huahine	1:30 p.m.
Huahine	1:45 p.m.	Papeete	6:00 p.m.

The *Hawaikinui*, a massive 350-foot freighter, visits all of the Society Islands (except Maupiti) twice a week. Because of its size, the ship is very stable in the water, making it a good choice for

ARRIVING EARLY

Most international flights into French Polynesia arrive in the middle of the night, but interisland air services do not start before 6 a.m. Since many travelers visiting the outer islands do not want the hassle and cost of a late-night return taxi and hotel room for only a few hours' wait, Faa'a Airport has a fair number of people either attempting to sleep on the molded plastic chairs or sprawled on the floor in sleeping bags. No one seems to mind, and if you're feeling social, the airport snack bar is open all night. However, it can still be a long night. If you really need to sleep for a few hours, there are a few very modest pensions directly across the street (and up a side street) from the airport. These have cheap dorm beds and private rooms under US$60. Try calling **Tahiti Airport Lodge** (82-23-68) or **Chez FiFi** (82-63-30) to see if there's a vacancy.

those who get seasick. Deck passage is available, as are five double cabins (with communal bathrooms). Given the boat's size, the 12-passenger maximum is routinely ignored. There are comfortable viewing chairs on deck as well as a small dining room below. A hearty meal is available at a reasonable price from the ship's mess when there's enough to go around. Office hours are Monday through Friday, 7:30 a.m. to 4 p.m. *Note:* The initial departure times in the charts below leave the afternoon or morning before the listed day. However, check with the office on arrival in Tahiti since times are subject to change. ~ Motu Uta, Papeete; 45-23-24, fax 45-24-44; e-mail sarlstim@mail.pf.

HAWAIKINUI DEPARTURE AND ARRIVAL TIMES

Wednesday

Departs	at	Arrives	at
Papeete	4:00 p.m.*	Huahine	2:00 a.m.
Huahine	3:00 a.m.	Raiatea	5:30 a.m.
Raiatea	8:00 a.m.	Bora Bora	11:00 a.m.
Bora Bora	1:00 p.m.	Tahaa	3:30 p.m.

Papeete departure is Tuesday afternoon

Thursday

Departs	at	Arrives	at
Tahaa	4:00 p.m.*	Papeete	4:00 a.m.

Tahaa departure is Wednesday afternoon

Friday

Departs	at	Arrives	at
Papeete	4:00 p.m.*	Huahine	5:00 p.m.
Huahine	6:00 p.m.	Tahaa	11:00 a.m.
Tahaa	11:30 a.m.	Raiatea	12:30 p.m.
Raiatea	2:00 p.m.	Bora Bora	6:45 a.m.
Bora Bora	8:00 a.m.	Tahaa	11:00 a.m.

Papeete departure is Thursday afternoon

Saturday

Departs	at	Arrives	at
Tahaa	11:30 a.m.*	Papeete	4:00 a.m.

Tahaa departure is Friday morning

Vaeanu is my favorite of the boats because it is filled with Tahitians who cover the decks wall-to-wall with their sleeping mats. For the long, overnight trip from an outer island to Papeete, sleeping on the deck covered with mats and pillows is quite com-

Interisland
Vessel Booking

To book passage on an interisland vessel, walk down to where the boats are moored (past the naval yard in Fare Ute in Papeete) and see which ones are in port. You can also obtain a list of all the copra boats and their destinations at the government tourist office. Chat with the skippers on the dock, double-check the current prices and determine where they are going and when they are departing.

Boat schedules are not reliable. Like so many things in the South Pacific, they are subject to change. Departure and arrival times listed are only approximate. If you absolutely, positively *must* catch a vessel, especially on a remote island where communication is minimal, take a tip from the locals and camp on or near the dock.

You often have the option of either bringing your own food for the journey or eating the ship's fare—the difference in price can be substantial. Sometimes only deck passage is available, which means just that—sleeping, eating and drinking on deck with others who have chosen this economical route.

It is recommended that you purchase tickets at least a half-day before the scheduled departure date. In the outer islands tickets can be bought on the dock. Although old-fashioned ferries are a cheap alternative to air transportation to the outer islands, they are by no means comfortable. The toilet facilities are usually appalling, and seasick passengers can add to their unpleasantness. If you add that odor to the acrid smell of diesel fumes you begin to get the true flavor of ferry travel in the romantic South Seas (at least during foul weather). If you're not willing to put up with these inconveniences, I suggest you book a ticket on Air Tahiti.

Keep in mind that a roundtrip voyage may last a month or more, so jumping ship on an island that has no air service may turn out to be a long-term commitment—at least until another ship comes along.

A sea cruise on a copra boat is appealing as long as you can contend with the occasional storm, seasickness, diesel fumes, engine noise, claustrophobia and cockroaches. The camaraderie, adventure, salt air, guitar playing and drinking of Hinano beer by moonlight, on the other hand, are hard to beat.

fortable and lots of fun. Inexpensive mats can be purchased at any Chinese store in any town. There is no snack bar so BYO food (ditto for toilet paper). Another note: *Vaeanu* prohibits alcohol and the crew will unceremoniously pour your Hinano overboard if they catch you imbibing. Tickets can be purchased ahead of time at the wharf. The one-way fare for deck passage between any of the islands is 825 CFP. Cabins are variously priced depending on the leg of the journey and whether it includes a private bathroom. The vessel departs Papeete on Monday, Wednesday and Friday at 5 p.m. ~ *Société Coopérative Ouvriere de Production IHITI NUI*, BP 9062, Papeete (Motu Uta); 41-25-35, fax 41-24-34; e-mail torhiatetu@mail.pf.

Other boats that make the circuit of the Society Islands include the *Tahiti Nui, Meherio II, Meherio III* and *Te Aratai*. Departures for these boats are irregular and are determined by the needs of local service providers. Although these boats offer only deck passage, meals are available. Offices are open Monday through Thursday, 7:30 a.m. to 3:30 p.m. and Friday from 7:30 a.m. to 2:30 p.m. Contact Mr. Leonard Puputouki. ~ Motu Uta, Papeete; 50-66-71, fax 43-32-70.

Tuamotu Islands   The *Cobia II* operates between Papeete/Kaukura/Arutua/Apataki/Aratika/Toau. No meals are served and no cabins are available. There is one voyage weekly, which departs from Papeete on Monday and returns to Papeete on Thursday. The cost is 3120 CFP per person. ~ *SNC Degage & Cie*, BP 9274, Papeete, Tahiti; 43-36-43.

The *Dory* has weekly journeys to Tikehau, Rangiroa, Manihi, Ahe, Apataki, Arutua and Kaukura. The entire voyage lasts four days. The vessel departs from Papeete on Monday at 2 p.m. and returns Friday at noon. Meals are served. The cost is 3640 CFP per person for deck passage. ~ *SNC Agnieray*, BP 9274, Papeete; 42-30-55.

- -

WORKING IN PARADISE

Who hasn't thought about chucking it all and moving to paradise? But the cold facts run contrary to the dreams. To live and work in Tahiti is not easy for nonresidents. A work permit is tied to a residence permit and is issued two months following the request for a work contract. The permit is issued care of the employer, who is responsible for the employee's return to his or her homeland. A local is always given priority in filling a job so you have to be able to provide a special skill not found in Tahiti. U.S. citizens skilled in the hotel/restaurant business may have the best chance because some of the hotels in Tahiti are owned or operated by Americans.

The *Kura Ora II* and *III* visit the eastern Tuamotus. Their itinerary includes Anaa, Faaite, Katiu, Makemo, Taenga, Nihiru, Hikueru, Marokau, Tauere, Amanu, Hao, Vairaatea, Nukutavake, Vahitahi, Reao, Pukarua, Tatakoto, Puka Puka, Tepoto North, Napuka, Fakahina, Fangatau, Takume, Raroia, Anaa and Hara-iki. The boats, which depart from Papeete, make one voyage every three weeks but the entire trip lasts 18 days. Food is served and prices begin at 6500 CFP per person. ~ *CTMIT,* BP 9779, Papeete; 45-55-45.

The *Mareva Nui* visits the western Tuamotu Group, which includes the islands of Makatea, Mataiva, Tikehau, Rangiroa, Ahe, Manihi, Takaroa, Takapoto, Raraka, Kauehi, Aratika, Taiaro, Fakarava, Arutua, Apataki, Niau, Toau and Kaukura. The *Mareva Nui,* which departs from Papeete, has one journey every 15 days; the duration of the voyage is 8 days. Meals are served and prices begin at 6500 CFP per person for deck passage. ~ *TMTO,* BP 1816, Papeete; 42-25-53, fax 42-25-57.

The *Nuku Hau* is a smallish vessel that visits the far-flung islands of Hao, Nego Nego, Tureia, Vanavana, Marutea, Rikitea, Tematangi, Anuanuraro, Nukutepipi and Hereheretau. Voyages last 15 to 18 days and one voyage departs from Papeete every 25 days. Prices begin at 8250 CFP per person and meals are served. ~ *STIM*, BP 635, Papeete; 45-23-24, fax 45-24-44.

The *Rairoa Nui* visits Rangiroa, Arutua, Apataki and Kaukura once a week. The four-day voyage departs out of Papeete on Monday at 10 a.m. Prices are 3000 CFP per person for deck passage. ~ Contact Didier Makiroto, BP 1801, Papeete; 48-35-78, fax 48-22-86.

The *Vai Aito* visits the western Tuamotu Group exclusively. Its itinerary includes Tikehau, Rangiroa, Ahe, Manihi, Aratika, Kauehi, Toau and Fakarava. Duration of the journey is seven to eight days and there are two to three trips per month out of Papeete. Meals are served. Prices begin at 4040 CFP for deck passage. ~ *Transport Maritime inter-Insulaire*, BP 9777, Papeete; 43-99-96, fax 43-53-04.

The *Saint-Xavier Maris Stella* has six routes that visit the Tuamotus, and which also include Rangiroa, Ahe, Manihi, Takaroa, Arutua, Apataki, Kaukura, Niau, Kauehi, Raraka, Tikehau and Mataiva. The average length of a voyage is ten days—two voyages per month. (There is no set schedule.) Roundtrip fare is about 20,000 CFP for deck passage, including three meals per day. ~ *Société de Navigation des Tuamotu SARL,* BP 14160, Arue, Tahiti; 42-23-58, fax 43-03-73.

Marquesas Islands   The *Aranui III* is the newest incarnation of   ◀ HIDDEN
French Polynesia's largest and most storied interisland freighter. The vessel, which made its maiden voyage in summer 2002, accommodates up to 200 passengers for regularly scheduled serv-

ice to the Marquesas Islands. The 343-foot *Aranui* offers three classes of air-conditioned cabins as well as dormitory beds. Public areas include a dining room, a business and conference center, a bar, a fitness room, a video room and a small swimming pool. The itinerary consists of two days in the Tuamotu Islands (Takapoto and Rangiroa) and a ten-day swing through the Marquesas Islands (Ua Pou, Nuku Hiva, Hiva Oa, Fatu Hiva, Tahuata, Ua Huka). Activities include visits to a pearl farm and a botanical garden, jeep tours, horseback riding, visits to the major archaeological sites, handicraft lessons, lectures on board and ashore, swimming and snorkeling, and fishing. The *Aranui* is still a working cargo boat and offers you an opportunity to visit the islands in comfort while seeing a slice of outer island life. The ship is also known for its easy-going shipboard ambience. The voyage lasts 15 days and 16 nights. The schedule varies each month—call for information. The price includes three meals a day and all shore excursions. For more information in the United States, call 800-972-7268; www.aranui. com, e-mail cptm@aranui.com.

Austral Islands The *Tuhaa Pae II* is reportedly unreliable and changes its schedule rather often, which makes it impossible to plan a visit if one has a scheduled return flight home. The trip to the Australs is rather rough but the islands, especially incredibly remote Rapa, are worth a visit. The route includes Tubuai, Rurutu, Rimatara and Raivavae and takes about 15 days. A trip is made to Rapa every two months. The boat departs from Papeete and can accommodate 44 passengers on deck and another 44 in cabins. ~ *Société Anonyme d'Economie Mixte de Navigation des Australes*, BP 1890, Papeete, Tahiti; 42-93-67, fax 42-06-09; e-mail snathp@mail.pf.

The *Vaeanu II* visits Rimatara, Rurutu, Tubuai and Raivavae three times a month and makes a trip to Rapa every two months. There is room for 12 passengers on deck and 8 more in cabins. One-way deck passage costs 3970 CFP and a berth is 7642 CFP. Meals are available. ~ *Societe Coopérative Ouvrière*, BP 9062, Motu Uta, Tahiti; 41-25-35, fax 41-24-34; e-mail torehiatetu@mail.pf.

Gambier Group The *Nuku Hau* visits the far-flung islands of Hao, Nego Nego, Tureia, Vanavana, Marutea, Rikitea, Tematangi, Anuanuraro, Nukutepipi and Hereheretau. Voyages last 15 to 18 days and one voyage leaves Papeete every 25 days. Prices begin at 7670 CFP and meals are served. ~ *STIM*, BP 635, Papeete; 45-23-24, fax 45-24-44.

CRUISES Cruising the islands has a distinct advantage for travelers who want to be taken care of *and* desire a "structured" tour package. The disadvantage is that you are at the mercy of the ship's schedule.

The *Haumana* ("Magical Spirit") is a 110-foot, 147-ton, luxury catamaran based in Bora Bora. Equipped with two 1000-

Cruising the South Pacific

The sharks were not as frightening as the manta rays. There were only six or so black-tipped reef sharks, but at least fifty rays with five-foot wingspans thrashing around us. Some brushed against my legs and I could feel the smooth, oily surface of their backs and the sandpaper ridges at the edge of their wings. The ship seemed an impossible distance away. We had ventured out along the reef in a small boat with "Shark Boy," who has become famous for taking visitors snorkeling along Bora Bora's coastline and then inviting every shark and manta ray for miles around to a free meal (of chum, that is, not snorkelers).

The only cruise ship to sail in Tahitian waters year-round, the *Paul Gaughin* is a 500-foot-long vessel with seven decks that carry 320 passengers. We had boarded a few days before in Papeete on Tahiti. As we set sail that night for Raiatea, it seemed like we had entered a dreamscape with room service. On board, we sat down to the first in a week-long succession of gourmet dinners presided by waiters in white jackets.

That memory seemed as far off as the *Paul Gaughin* as sharks streaked through the water, devouring chum like so many vacuum cleaners with teeth. Later, of course, when we settled into the plate-glass La Palette lounge for afternoon tea, our fears seemed rather silly. But it made us realize that a romantic vacation meant not only our relationship but our relation to the place we were visiting. That second aspect of our romantic vacation was going to mean hiking the archipelago and swimming among its razor-toothed denizens. Radisson Seven Seas Cruises had arranged an array of day trips to explore French Polynesia: an anthropologist led us through Moorea's interior valleys, we paddled a kayak beneath Raiatea's adze-like volcanic cliffs to the palm-thatched *motus* that encircle the island like planets.

During our week in the islands, the *Paul Gaughin* proved almost too comfortable. Waking up each morning in a stateroom furnished in mahogany and cherry wood, our most taxing responsibility was deciding whether to have breakfast in the cabin or on deck and determining which of the three dining rooms to reserve for dinner. On board there was a swimming pool, bar, spa, fitness center and reading room. Several times we convinced ourselves to catch a ship's launch and explore an island, but as the days passed we succumbed to the lure of shipboard life and began hanging up the "Do Not Disturb" sign, realizing that as enticing as that world outside might be, romance begins at home. For details on the *Paul Gaughin*, contact **Radisson Seven Seas Cruises** at 877-505-5370; www.rssc.com.

horsepower engines, it can cruise 14 knots. The vessel offers six different cruises, ranging from three to seven nights. Trips include visits to Bora Bora, Huahine, Raiatea and Tahaa. The *Haumana* has 21 air-conditioned cabins; various configurations offer one queen-size bed or two single beds, porthole, minibar, television and VCR. The main deck features a panoramic restaurant; the upper deck offers a lounge for 40 and an outdoor terrace. ~ 43-43-03, fax 45-10-65; www.boraborapearlcruises.com, e-mail hau mana@mail.pf.

The 18,800-ton motor sailor *Paul Gauguin* made its inaugural voyage in early 1998. It is the newest addition to the Radisson Seven Seas fleet. The 320-passenger luxury vessel, flying the French flag, makes weekly seven-night voyages out of Papeete, visiting the islands of Rangiroa, Raiatea, Bora Bora and Moorea all year round. The ship boasts one crew member to every 1.5 guests, ensuring a high level of service for its well-heeled passengers. There is a comprehensive recreational program, a casino, a Carita of Paris spa, two French restaurants, a Polynesian cultural center, optional land excursion and transfer packages, and almost anything else you could dream of. This pampering comes at a high price (fares start at US$2605 per person for the seven-night cruise) but in Polynesian tradition, it's inclusive of gratuities. In the United States contact Radisson Seven Seas (800-333-3333; www.rssc.com).

> Keep in mind that virtually everything is frightfully expensive here so purchase film, sunblock and other such items before you leave home (see the "Medical Info" section later in this chapter for suggestions). You'll thank yourself later for being so clever.

The most luxurious cruises in the islands are the one-week voyages through the Leeward Islands aboard **Bora Bora Cruises'** *Tia Moana* or *Tu Moana*, a pair of 37-cabin luxury yachts. The cruises take you into the heart of the lagoons at Bora Bora, Raiatea, Tahaa and Huahine, where much larger vessels cannot venture. This is private yachting at its best. You'll pay $4695 per person for the pleasure, or $3988 with a 90-day advance purchase. ~ 800-780-4014 in the U.S.; www.boraboracruises.com.

Before You Go

PASSPORTS & VISAS

Visitors need passports. Citizens of the U.S., Canada and Japan can stay for up to 30 days without a visa. Guests from EC countries have even greater latitude—they can visit for three months or less without a visa. If you are from the United States, Canada, Japan, Australia, New Zealand, South Korea or most European nations, it is *not* necessary to obtain a visa.

Visitors from a host of nations from South America, Africa and Asia are obligated to apply for a visa before entering, but don't need the approval of the local French High Commissioner. However, visitors from some nations need the approval of the French High Commissioner before visiting the country.

In most cases, visitors will automatically be granted visas of up to three months without the High Commissioner's approval. Upon expiration, tourist visas may be extended for another three months, with a possibility of renewal for an additional six months. No foreigner can stay for more than a year with a tourist visa.

For visitors who wish to apply for a visa, the best bet is to go back to the airport immigration office and make your arrangements there, instead of going to the government offices in town. (The immigration people in Papeete will eventually send you to the airport anyway.) After filling out the necessary forms, the airport people will then send you to the post office to purchase a 3000 CFP stamp. To avoid the hassle and spending the 3000 CFP, if you know before leaving for Tahiti that you will stay for more than 30 days, it's much better to arrange things with the nearest French consulate.

The airport immigration office is open Monday through Friday, 9 a.m. to noon and 2 p.m. to 5 p.m. In addition to completing the necessary form (which will require the name of a local guarantor and a disclosure of your financial resources), you will need to bring a 3000 CFP stamp (available from the post office) and a passport-size photograph (QSS film stores offer instant pictures). Allow several weeks prior to the expiration of your visa to process the application. Backpackers have reported police visits to check guests' documents at some of the hostels.

TOURIST BOARDS

The main Tahiti Tourisme office is in Paofai Building D in the Paofai section of Papeete; 50-57-00, fax 43-66-19; www.tahiti-tourisme.com, e-mail tahiti-tourisme@mail.pf.

Overseas addresses of Tahiti Tourisme are:

ASIA Pacific Leisure Group ~ 8/F Maneeya Center, 518/5 Ploenchit Road, Bangkok 10 330, Thailand; (66) 26-52-05-07, fax (66) 26-52-05-09; e-mail eckard@plgroup.com

AUSTRALIA 12 Ann Street, Surry Hills NSW 2010, Sydney; (61) 2-9281-6020, fax (61) 2-9211-6589; www.tahiti-tourisme.com.au, e-mail info@tahiti-tourisme.com.au

CHILE Ave. 11 de Septiembre 2214, Of. 116, Casilla 16057–Santiago 9; (56) 2-251-2826, fax (56) 2-233-1787; www.en tahiti.cl, e-mail tahiti@cmet.net

ENGLAND BGB & Associates ~ 7 Westminster Palace Gardens, Artillery Row, London SW1P 1RL; (0) 20-7233-2300, fax (0) 20-7233-2301; e-mail virginia@bgb.co.uk

FRANCE, BELGIUM, SWITZERLAND, LUXEMBOURG, THE NETHERLANDS, EASTERN AND CENTRAL EUROPE Tahiti Tourisme Paris ~ 28 Blvd. Saint-Germain, 75005, Paris; (33) 1-55-42-64-34, fax (33) 1-55-42-61-20; www.tahiti-tourisme.fr, e-mail tahititourisme@tahiti-tourisme.fr

GERMANY www.tahititourisme.de

ITALY   Aigo ~ Piazza Caiazzo 3, 20 124 Milano; (39) 02-66-980-317, fax (39) 02-66-92-648; www.tahiti-tourisme.com, e-mail tahiti@tahiti-tourisme.it

JAPAN   TCAT 42-1 Nihonbashi Hakozakicho, Chuou-ku, Tokyo 103-0015; (81) 3-3639-0468, fax (81) 3-3665-0581; www.tahiti-tourisme.jp, e-mail info@tahiti-tourisme.jp

NEW ZEALAND   200 Victoria West Street, Suite 2A, P.O. Box 106192, Auckland Downtown; (64) 9-368-5262, fax (64) 9-368-5263; www.tahiti-tourisme.co.nz, e-mail info@tahiti-tourisme.co.nz

NORTHERN EUROPE   3, Larsbjørnsstraede DK-1454 Copenhagen K; (45) 33-37-71-12, fax (45) 33-32-43-70; www.tahiti-tourisme.dk, e-mail info@tahiti-tourisme.dk

SPAIN/PORTUGAL   Orense, 85, Edificio Lexington, 28 020 Madrid; (34) 915-678-415, fax (34) 915-714-244; www.tahiti ysusislas.com, e-mail info@tahitiysusislas.com

UNITED STATES   300 Continental Boulevard, Suite 160, El Segundo, CA 90245; 310-414-8484, fax 310-414-8490; www. tahiti-tourisme.com, e-mail info@tahiti-tourisme.com

SHOTS   Tahiti is malaria-free and inoculations are not required except for those arriving from an area infected with smallpox, cholera or yellow fever, which exempts 99.9 percent of visitors. (For more information on the general topic of health, please see the "Medical Info" section later in this chapter.)

INSURANCE   You might consider purchasing a travel insurance policy to cover theft, loss and medical problems. There are a number of policies available and your travel agent will have recommendations. Check the small print. Some policies specifically exclude "dangerous activities," which can include scuba diving, motorcycling or even trekking. You may prefer a policy that pays doctors or hospitals for claims later rather than you paying on the spot. If you have a claim make sure you keep all documentation. Some policies ask you to call back (reverse charges) to a center in your home country where your problem can immediately be assessed. Be sure to check if the policy covers ambulances or an emergency flight home. If you have to stretch out you will need two seats and somebody has to pay for them! Emergency Evacuation Insurance may be a good idea if you are planning to visit a very remote area such as the Marquesas or the Tuamotu Group.

> Make sure to bring toilet paper with you as you travel around the islands. Many restaurants and lodgings, especially in the budget category, do not provide it.

Divers should consider purchasing Diver Alert Network (DAN) insurance. Depending on the level of coverage selected, a policy can cover both diving and non-diving accidents. ~ 800-446-2671; www.diversalertnetwork.org.

Dress in Tahiti is almost always casual and because of the warm **PACKING**
climate it is easy to subscribe to the adage "travel light." Unless you
are planning to travel to the outer fringes of French Polynesia,
such as the Austral Islands, you can be certain it will be warm,
even at night. Clothing should be lightweight. Bathing suit and
shorts (for both men and women) are always practical and fashionable. Cotton shirts and dresses are also necessary, as are sandals, a light plastic raincoat or windbreaker for the odd tropical
downpour, a light sweater, a hat to shield you from the intense
rays of the sun, sunscreen, insect repellent, a first-aid kit, and perhaps some small souvenirs or toys for Tahitian children. If you
plan to walk on the reef, reef shoes are an absolute necessity. Nike
makes a good model and Speedo's brand also works.

In addition to personal effects, the following are allowed into **CUSTOMS**
Tahiti duty-free: 200 cigarettes or 100 cigarillos or 50 cigars or
250 grams of smoking tobacco, 50 grams of perfume, .25 liter of
lotion, 500 grams of coffee, 100 grams of tea and 2 liters of spirits. Cultured pearls of non–French Polynesian origin are prohibited outright.

Costs   French Polynesia is not a budget holiday spot. While some **MONEY**
of the pensions, particularly on the outer islands, are reasonably **MATTERS**
priced, nothing is inexpensive. You should not even consider visiting French Polynesia without realizing that "sticker shock" will be
your constant companion. Expect to spend more money than you
planned on food, accommodation, film, liquor and virtually everything else—except bread.

Currency   The currency used in French Polynesia is the French
Pacific franc or CFP. Notes come in denominations of 500, 1000,
5000 and 10,000, and coins in denominations of 1, 2, 5, 10, 20,
50 and 100.

Exchange rates in mid-2004 were:
1 euro = 119 CFP
1 U.S. dollar = 97 CFP
1 yen = .88 CFP

Banks and Exchange Centers   There is a currency exchange center at the Faa'a Airport, where all international flights to French
Polynesia arrive. The center is open 7:45 a.m. to 3:30 p.m., one
hour before departing flights and whenever there is an arriving
flight. The rates are typically less that what the hotels charge.

In a building adjacent to the Tahiti Manava Visitor's Bureau on
the waterfront in Papeete, there is a money exchange center called
MG Finances. They don't take any commission, but their exchange rates are lower than the banks'. Closed Sunday. ~ Boulevard Pomare at Fare Manihini, Papeete; 43-22-77.

There are several other small exchange centers in downtown Papeete, and you can exchange currency at any bank as well. Major banks include New Caledonie, Tahiti Societe Generale, Banque de Polynesie, Banque Socredo and Banque de Tahiti.

Credit Cards and ATMs   Visa credit cards are accepted (banks will give you a cash advance), as are (less frequently) American Express and, in some places, MasterCard. (On many of the smaller islands, credit cards are not accepted.) ATMs are rapidly making inroads in Tahiti and American ATM cards will work here. Travelers report having difficulty, however, with ATM cards that bear the Cirrus logo. Although many machines include Cirrus in the list of cards they honor, Cirrus cards do not always work reliably in French Polynesia. It is wise to check whether your card is part of the Cirrus system before you come. ATMs permit a maximum withdrawal of 35,000 to 40,000 CFP.

Traveler's Checks   While seemingly old-fashioned, traveler's checks are easily cashed at banks and hotels. Traveler's checks combined with a major credit card are the best way to travel in French Polynesia. All banks charge a 350 to 400 CFP commission on a traveler's check transaction, particularly if you are changing from one currency to another.

Tipping   Tipping is a vexing topic for most travelers to French Polynesia. It is officially discouraged but Tahitians have been introduced to this practice and are not averse to receiving tips. Though some "experts" discourage tipping, I believe it should be done at your discretion.

LODGING   Room prices for conventional hotels in Papeete and in much of the rest of French Polynesia fall into two general categories—expensive and very expensive. Aside from air conditioning, beach-frontage, discos, restaurants and bars, upscale resorts may provide swimming pools, tennis courts, bicycles and free snorkeling gear. Prices for this type of hotel range from US$180 to US$275 for double occupancy.

On the other end of the scale are lodging options for budget-minded travelers. Your choices may include older hotels that lost their luster when the more modern resorts opened up, smaller family-operated pensions, or boarding arrangements with families. Some facilities also offer campgrounds or dorm facilities with spartan accommodations (usually small bunks, primitive kitchen areas and shared bathroom). Somewhat better and in the budget-to-moderate spectrum are the local-style *fares,* or thatch-roofed bungalows. Indigenous to French Polynesia, these units offer modest but comfortable lodging that usually includes a kitchenette, one or two bedrooms and a sitting area. Depending on the tariff, it may or may not have hot water, but it will always sport fans instead of air conditioning. Budget accommodations may not afford all the luxuries, but nevertheless many people do find them acceptable.

Throughout this book, hotels are described according to price category. *Budget* hotels have rooms starting from US$30 to US$ 100 per night for two people. *Moderate* facilities begin between US$100 and US$150. The smaller, budget-to-moderate hotels may have air conditioning, a pool and not much else in the way of extras. *Deluxe* hotels offer rates starting from US$150 to US$200. *Ultra-deluxe* establishments rent rooms at prices above US$200.

These prices do not include a 5 percent room tax and—like all things in this world—are subject to change.

Eating out in French Polynesia generally requires copious amounts of cash. However, an important step in reducing hotel food costs was implemented by the local government, which reduced import tariffs on liquor and encouraged hoteliers to lower prices on food. This dramatically reduced prices on MAP (Modified American Plan—three meals per day) and AP (American Plan—breakfast and dinner) plans at various hotels as well as tabs at hotel bars. Although it varies from hotel to hotel, the law has resulted in a 15 to 40 percent reduction in food bills. Though the government has made a valiant attempt to bring prices down by slashing import duties on liquor, these reduced prices apply only to special tourist menus featured at some hotels and some restaurants that have volunteered to go along with the revised pricing scheme. Most à la carte items retain their normal (usually expensive) price. The government is encouraging all restaurants to provide discounts in the future.

DINING

An easy and tasty snack can be made with breadfruit by peeling it, slicing it into thin strips and frying it in a skillet with vegetable oil. A little salt completes the perfect breadfruit *pommes frites*.

If the high price of restaurants has you spooked, there are plenty of modern grocery stores and supermarkets on the islands with major population centers. The selection of cheese, produce, wine and meat is first class, as you might expect of a French colony. Naturally, the stores and fine restaurants are frequented by Polynesians who have adopted the French science of appreciating fine food. This very civilized quality separates even the most humble French Polynesians from their island neighbors, and from most North Americans. You may not know a good Bordeaux from a bad Burgundy but middle-class Tahitians will. What this also means is that stores are incredibly well stocked with every conceivable cheese, wine, olive oil and fresh produce. Rest assured that people who like to cook for themselves will not want for quality food.

A few guidelines will help you chart a course through French Polynesia's restaurants. Within each chapter, restaurants are placed geographically and categorized as budget, moderate, deluxe or ultra-deluxe in price. Dinner entrées at *budget* restaurants cost US$12 or less. The ambience is informal café style and the crowd is often a local one. *Moderately* priced restaurants range between US$12 and US$20 for dinner entrées and offer pleasant surroundings, a more varied menu and a slower pace. *Deluxe* establishments tab their entrées around US$20 to US$30, featuring a more sophisticated cuisine and more personalized service. *Ultra-deluxe* are entrées priced above US$30.

Breakfast and lunch menus vary less in price from restaurant to restaurant. Even deluxe-priced kitchens usually offer breakfast and lunch buffets, which place them within a few dollars of their budget-minded competitors.

Beyond the bright lights of Papeete and other large population centers dining is an entirely different proposition. The outer islands frequented regularly by visitors (such as Moorea, Bora Bora and Huahine) offer a good selection of restaurants and *roulottes* (vans that sell simple meals) as well as supermarkets where ample and varied food supplies may be obtained. However, the remote areas of the Tuamotu Group, the Australs and the Gambiers are generally devoid of restaurants and large markets. Visitors must rely on their pension or hotel to provide food. Incidentally, virtually all the islands have small mom-and-pop stores, but these establishments sell only a limited selection of canned goods (such as sardines or tinned beef) and other staples, and often have erratic hours. The availability of food and manufactured goods on the remote islands is almost always dependent upon when the last interisland boat visited.

A visit to French Polynesia gives a child a great opportunity to meet youngsters from other countries and to glimpse how other cultures live.

NIGHTLIFE   French Polynesia offers a variety of nightlife ranging from tony private clubs, dance halls, casinos and discos to seedy bars. Papeete, one of the genuine fleshpots of the South Pacific, is where the nightlife is centered. However, most urban areas on the outer islands also have nightclubs or offer entertainment at hotels.

In Papeete, the clubs that are situated along the waterfront or in the Vaima Center area don't open up until 9 p.m., and the action doesn't start until 11 p.m. Closing time is usually 2 or 3 a.m. (or later), and most of the nightclubs are closed on Sunday. Expect to pay a 1000 CFP to 1500 CFP cover charge, which also includes the first drink. Beer is around 500 CFP and mixed drinks range from 1000 CFP to 1500 CFP.

"Making the scene" at the clubs is a big thing for locals, as there just isn't much else to do on a weekend, especially on the outer islands. Another cultural observation is that everyone in Tahiti dances, sings, plays guitar or does it all. Thus going to a club to dance, especially for young single people, is part of growing up in the islands. Those who want to experience an important part of local culture would miss a great deal by not at least spending one evening at a nightclub that features a traditional Tahitian band. But, be prepared to spend money. Being tight-fisted won't get you too far with the locals.

**TRAVELING
WITH
CHILDREN**

French Polynesia is an ideal place to take youngsters—the warm sea, friendly inhabitants and the excitement of new, exotic surroundings stir their imaginations. Polynesians in general are terrific with kids, and anthropologists tell us that in many ways they care for them better than so-called developed societies.

Use a travel agent to help with arrangements; they can reserve spacious bulkhead seats on airlines and determine which flights are least crowded. They can also seek out the best deals on inexpensive lodging, saving you money on both room and board.

Planning the trip with your kids stimulates their imagination. Books about travel, airplane rides, beaches, and Polynesian culture help prepare even a two-year-old for an adventure. This preparation makes the "getting there" part of the trip more exciting for children of all ages.

And "getting there" means a long-distance flight. Plan to bring everything you need on board the plane—diapers, food, toys, books and extra clothing for kids and parents alike.

Allow extra time to get places. Book reservations in advance and make sure that the hotel or pension has the extra crib, cot or bed you require. And when reserving a rental car, inquire to see if they provide car seats and if there is an added charge.

Besides the car seat you may have to bring along, also pack shorts and T-shirts, a sweater, swimsuit, waterproof sandals and a sun hat. A stroller with sunshade for little ones helps on sightseeing sojourns; a shovel and pail are essential for sandcastle building. Most importantly, remember to bring a good sunblock. The quickest way to ruin a family vacation is with a bad sunburn. Also plan to bring indoor activities such as books and games for evenings and rainy days.

Many supermarkets carry diapers, food and other essentials— though at very steep prices. If your child is very young, to economize you might consider bringing a separate suitcase with diapers, wipes, food, toys and the like.

Among the basics you should pack is a first-aid kit. Check also with your physician about taking along a treatment for diarrhea.

If your child becomes sick or injured in Tahiti, first-class medical care is available from French doctors. Look for island-specific contact information at the end of each chapter.

The only caveat about taking children is that it might prevent you from staying in some of the luxury hotels. Many have "no children" policies. However, hotels that welcome kids generally have no problem arranging babysitters.

WOMEN TRAVELING ALONE

It is a sad commentary on life today, but women traveling alone must take precautions. Be aware of your surroundings and always lock your door at night, no matter where you are. Sadly, lodgings on many of the islands—even those in the far-flung atolls—have occasional problems with local men entering at night to fondle female visitors and steal belongings.

Rape in French Polynesia is common among the local population, but as far as I know it is a rare occurrence for visitors. If you are by yourself late at night in downtown Papeete, be extra cautious. In Tahiti, when a man asks you out, chances are he expects more than a good night kiss—even on the first date. Likewise, an invitation to a midnight stroll on the beach implies more than gazing at the stars and holding hands. Dating in the Pacific tends to mean sex may be in the offing or expected sooner rather than later. This is especially true for Europeans or North Americans, who, for better or worse, are perceived as sexually liberated in the eyes of locals.

It's unwise to hitchhike alone. At night, even in rural areas, if you are alone keep the doors and windows shut. There are many uninvited lotharios attempting the classic climb-through-the-window-at-midnight routine. I say classic because this seems to be rather a common practice in the Pacific.

Should a woman traveling solo accept an invitation from a family to stay with them? Absolutely. That is, if you feel good about the invitation. More often than not it will be a great experience, especially in an outerisland setting with a traditional family. Being invited to spend time in a local home has become a rarity in French Polynesia when compared to other South Pacific destinations, so count yourself lucky if you have been invited.

Finally, I've had letters from several women, including a Peace Corps volunteer with years of experience, who suggested that I bring up the subject of "Peeping Toms." My Peace Corps reader tells me that this behavior is relatively common throughout the South Pacific. Without probing the sociocultural aspects of this practice or judging whether or not it is innocuous, just be forewarned that "they" are out there and visitors are fair game.

SENIOR TRAVELERS

French Polynesia gets more than its share of well-heeled older travelers. Given the expensive nature of travel in this area, it takes a great deal of disposable income to afford a first-class vacation in this part of the world. Unfortunately, I am not aware of any senior discounts in French Polynesia except those given by Air Tahiti (see the "Air Travel" section).

The **American Association of Retired Persons** (AARP) offers membership to anyone over 50. AARP's benefits include travel discounts with a number of firms. ~ The **American Association of Retired Persons** (AARP) offers membership to anyone over 50. AARP's benefits include travel discounts with a number of firms. ~ 601 E Street NW, Washington, DC 20049; 800-424-3410; www.aarp.com.

Those with fragile health should take into consideration the intense tropical heat and humidity when planning a trip to the tropics. Visitors who have never experienced this type of climate should not overextend themselves. Fortunately, first-rate doctors and health care facilities are available in Tahiti. While the other islands have less sophisticated amenities, excellent health practitioners are available. Consider carrying a medical record with you—including your medical history and current medical status as well as your doctor's name, phone number and address. Make sure your insurance covers you while you are away from home.

Canadian and U.S. residents should note that there are no honorary consuls to represent them.

GAY & LESBIAN TRAVELERS

The good news for gay and lesbian travelers is that people in French Polynesia do not discriminate against homosexuals. French society has traditionally been tolerant toward same-sex relationships, and Polynesians are even more tolerant. Indeed, Polynesia has its own cultural heritage of a "third sex"—the *mahu*, male transvestites who take on traditional female roles. (For more information about *mahu* and how they fit into contemporary Polynesian society, see the section covering "Tahiti's Third Sex" in Chapter One.) Simply put, in French Polynesia one's sexual preferences are not an issue. Two people of the same gender booking a room will scarcely evoke a second thought, much less a second glance. Gays are treated with respect, or disrespect, like other tourists. Due, perhaps, to the lack of discrimination, gay-exclusive facilities do not tend to form. The closest thing to gay gathering places I could find are the bars in Papeete that feature female impersonators. (See the "Nightlife" section for Papeete in Chapter Four.)

DISABLED TRAVELERS

Tahiti is not very accessible to travelers with disabilities. Unlike the United States and other more enlightened destinations, French Polynesia has no laws that stipulate wheelchair access to public buildings or similar policies that consider the needs of persons with disabilities. Hotel facilities in the more remote areas of French Polynesia have marginal infrastructure with regard to this issue. Some hotels and facilities are more helpful than others. If there is a question about your particular situation, be sure and check in advance.

The **Society for Accessible Travel & Hospitality** (SATH) offers information for travelers with disabilities. ~ 347 5th Avenue, Suite 610, New York, NY 10016; 212-447-7284; www.sath.org, e-mail sathtravel@aol.com.

Travelin' Talk, a network of people and organizations, also provides assistance. ~ P.O. Box 1796, Wheat Ridge, CO 80034; 303-232-2979, fax 303-239-8486; www.travelintalk.net, e-mail travelin@travelintalk.net.

Access-Able Travel Source has worldwide information online. ~ 303-232-2979; www.access-able.com.

Once You Arrive

VISITORS CENTERS

The main tourist information center, the **Manava Visitor's Bureau**, is on the quay nearly opposite the Vaima Shopping Center. It is situated in a cluster of brown buildings constructed to resemble traditional Tahitian dwellings (*fares*). The knowledgeable and friendly staff speaks English and can answer your questions as well as give you a variety of useful pamphlets, schedules and maps. ~ Boulevard Pomare at Fare Manihini; BP 65, Papeete, Tahiti, French Polynesia; 50-57-00.

Some of the outer islands do have tourist offices and information centers but hours and availability of the locally run tourism bureaus vary a great deal. In some locales, professionalism is very high, while on other islands you're lucky if a staff member is actually in the office.

On some of the outer islands the tourist board information office is also a tour booking office. Despite this seeming conflict of interest, I found the information to be quite accurate. The Faa'a International Airport branch of the Tahiti Tourist Board is open for the arrival of all international flights—including those in the middle of the night.

FOREIGN CONSULS

AUSTRALIA/CANADA Nick McGlynn, P.O. Box 9 068-98 715 Motu Uta, Papeete; 46-88-88, fax 43-39-26

BELGIUM Honorary Consul ~ P.O. Box 20 169-98 713, Papeete; 42-94-89, fax 43-90-05; e-mail raynalp@yahoo.com

DENMARK Honorary Consul Claude Girard ~ BP 548, Papeete; 54-04-54, home 43-68-30; e-mail groupavocats@mail.pf

FINLAND Honorary Consul Jean-Pierre Fourcade ~ BP 25, Papeete; 54-24-54, home 53-43-50

ISRAEL P.O. Box 37 98-713, Papeete; 77-39-99, fax 42-41-00; e-mail israelconsultahiti@yahoo.fr

ITALY Honorary Consul Lucia Grolli ~ BP 380412, Punaauia; 43-45-01, fax 43-45-07, home 58-32-91; e-mail mariolucia@hotmail.com

JAPAN BP 342, Papeete; 45-45-45, fax 43-12-60

KOREA Bernard Baudry ~ 43-64-75, fax 45-45-74, home 43-76-22; e-mail baudry@mail.pf

NETHERLANDS Honorary Consul Engelbertus Den Breejen ~ Tahiti-Holland Trading, BP 2804, Papeete; 42-49-37, fax 43-56-92, home 43-06-86; e-mail htt@mail.pf

NEW ZEALAND Honorary Consul Christian Destrieux ~ BP 73, Papeete; 54-07-40, fax 42-45-44

NORWAY Honorary Consul ~ BP 368, Papeete; 42-63-93, fax 42-06-17; e-mail taporo@mail.pf

SWEDEN Michel Solari ~ BP 2, Papeete; 47-54-75, home 41-99-89; e-mail jacques.solari@sopadep.pf

UNITED KINGDOM Honorary Consul Robert James Withers ~ BP 1064, Papeete; 81-98-41, fax 85-58-76, home 42-43-55; e-mail withers@mail.pf

UNITED STATES P.O. Box 10 765 98-711 Paea, Tamanu Iti Center (1st floor) Punaauia; 42-65-35, 50-80-95, cell 77-76-54, fax 50-80-96, or 917-464-7457 in the U.S.; e-mail usconsul @mail.pf or ckozely@mail.pf

TIME

French Polynesia is ten hours behind Greenwich Mean Time (GMT), two hours behind U.S. Pacific Standard Time and twenty hours behind Australian Eastern Standard Time. Thus, when it is noon Sunday in Tahiti, it is 2 p.m. Sunday in Los Angeles, 5 p.m. Sunday in New York, 10 p.m. Sunday in London, 11 p.m. Sunday in Paris and 8 a.m. Monday in Sydney. The Marquesas Islands are half an hour ahead of the rest of French Polynesia, so when it's noon in Tahiti, it's 12:30 p.m. in the Marquesas. The Gambier Islands are one hour ahead of Tahiti.

BUSINESS HOURS

Most businesses open their doors between 8 and 10 a.m. on weekdays and close at 5 p.m. Some larger stores stay open until 7 p.m.; small, family-run corner stores may not close until 10 p.m. There is usually a very long lunch hour (noon to 2 p.m.), but many banks are open at this time (whereas banks in Moorea

THE "PK" SYSTEM

On larger islands like Tahiti and Moorea, you can pinpoint your position on the map from the red-topped "PK" (kilometer) markers along the inland, or mountain side, of the road. Thus to find someone's home you must rely on the PK system, which means watching the kilometerage and knowing what side of the road (ocean or mountain) you are headed. For example, a PK address in Tahiti might be PK 3.3 *cote mer* (ocean side) in Arue (the district). There are no street names on the majority of the islands and most people receive mail at a P.O. box.

are closed during lunch). On Saturdays, shops close for the day at 11 a.m. Most businesses are closed on Sundays.

Legal Holidays   Legal holidays, where government services are shut down, include New Year's Day, *Arrivée de l'Evangile* (March 5), Good Friday, Easter, Easter Monday, May Day (May 1), Victory Day 1945 (May 8), Ascension (the last Thursday in May), Pentecost and Pentecost Monday (the first Sunday and Monday in June), Internal Autonomy Day (June 29), Bastille Day (July 14), Assumption (August 15), All Saints Day (November 1), Armistice Day (November 11) and Christmas Day.

Government employees are off on these days, but the observance by store owners varies.

Banking Hours   Regular banking hours vary slightly. The Bank of Tahiti opens at 7:45 a.m. and closes for lunch from 11:45 a.m. to 2 p.m. It re-opens at 2 p.m. and closes at 4 p.m. The Bank of Polynesia has the same hours, except that it opens at 7:30 a.m. The Bank of Socredo is open from 7:30 a.m. to 3:30 p.m. Some banks (e.g., the Bank of Tahiti) are open from 7:45 to 11:30 a.m. on Saturday mornings.

If you need to get to a bank on Saturday, your hotel can tell you where the nearest open one is. Exchange counters are available at Faa'a International Airport at arrival and departure times.

WEIGHTS & MEASURES   Whether you're getting gas, checking the thermometer or looking at road signs, you'll notice the difference: everything is metric. French Polynesia is on the metric system, which measures temperature in degrees Celsius, distances in meters, and most substances in liters, kilos and grams.

To convert from Celsius to Fahrenheit, multiply by 9, divide by 5 and add 32. For example, 23°C equals [(23 x 9)/5] + 32, or

WRAPAROUND WEAR

If you stay long enough in the islands you will undoubtedly adopt the local article of clothing called a pareu (par-ay-you), a rectangular piece of cloth about five to six feet long. This practical item is a brightly colored wraparound cotton cloth worn by men and women and is sold in every store. It makes a terrific and inexpensive gift. It can be tied a number of ways but is usually wrapped skirt-like around the waist and worn with a T-shirt. Although Western men might at first cringe at the idea of wearing a skirt, they soon find that in Tahiti's often sweltering climate, a pareu is a practical item of clothing to wear around the hotel. Get hooked and you will find yourself bringing a few pareus back home. They come in a variety of colors and patterns, as well as several grades of quality. Accepted attire in even the most luxurious hotels, pareus can be dressed up with accessories and fancy sandals for evening wear.

(207/5) + 32, or 41.4 + 32, or about 73°F. If you don't have a pocket calculator along (but you probably should), just remember that 0°C is 32°F and that each Celsius degree is roughly two Fahrenheit degrees. Here are other useful conversion equations:

1 mile = 1.6 kilometers	1 kilometer = 3/5 mile
1 foot = 0.3 meter	1 meter = 3 1/3 feet
1 pound = 0.45 kilo	1 kilo = 2 1/5 pounds
1 gallon = 3.8 liters	1 liter = 1/4 gallon (about a quart)

ELECTRIC VOLTAGE

The current is 220 volts AC in the more modern hotels and 110 volts in the older facilities. All modern units have power outlets for electric shavers, hair dryers and other appliances. If you have any doubts, don't plug in a thing until you check with the facility. You may want to examine the light bulbs for any hints of what voltage is utilized. Many hotels also have converters for appliances. If you use a computer or any other appliance that utilizes a three-pronged plug, you may have to purchase a two-pronged adapter at a local hardware store for several hundred CFP. (Or bring one with you!) Most computer and camera chargers these days have built-in adapters. Check for voltage information on the charger or contact the manufacturer.

DRIVING

Those interested in renting a car may use a driver's license from their own country (or state) or an international license.

The roads that follow the perimeters of Tahiti, Bora Bora and Moorea are almost fully paved. This is not the case with the more remote communities where auto traffic is less frequent or, as in the Tuamotus, virtually nonexistent. The roads that do exist, especially in more populated areas, are modern and well maintained.

Car and Motorcycle Rentals   For the visitor spending any appreciable time in Tahiti, or someone wishing to do an around-the-island tour solo, renting a car, motorcycle or scooter is a necessity. Aside from the big names like Budget, Hertz and Avis, there are small, locally-owned, good-quality rentals—but consumers should be wary. Scrutinize the vehicle before you drive it away, lest you find nonexistent brakes or flat tires. Allow plenty of time when collecting and returning your car; this may happen on island time. Depending on your choice of model, prices range from US$50 to US$120 per day or more. Rates are generally based on time plus distance and there is an insurance charge of 600 to 1500 CFP. Gasoline (petrol) is not included and it isn't cheap—figure on paying around 140 CFP per liter!

Bicycle Rentals   Bicycle rentals are available on most islands, generally at hotels. If the traffic is not too congested, a bike is a great way to get around an island. I don't recommend bicycles for Tahiti because of the sheer numbers of automobiles on that island. Bora Bora used to be a great place to explore by bicycle but growing numbers of vehicles make it more precarious. Expect to pay at least 1000 CFP per day for a rental. One reader mentioned that he consistently rented bikes for half a day and inevitably brought them back late without being charged extra. While I don't encourage this, Tahitians may allow for "Tahitian time" in regards to rentals. Then again, they may not.

HITCHING With the exception of Tahiti, Moorea and Bora Bora, hitchhiking is fairly easy. As a rule, the less populated the island, the easier it is to hitchhike. Hitching is fairly safe in French Polynesia but always exercise common sense. Travelers may find it easier to get rides if they are not perceived as being French. The lesson here is, leave your berets at home.

PUBLIC TRANSIT On most of the Leeward islands there is a marvelous bus system consisting of owner-operators driving jitney-like vehicles known as *Le Truck*—a triumph of small-scale entrepreneurship. Many French Polynesians cannot afford cars, so *Le Truck* transports the majority of the population, especially on Tahiti where commuting to work in Papeete from the rural areas has become a way of life. Fares for *Le Truck* are always under 200 CFP around town but may be as much as 500 CFP for long-distance trips. Note that there is a surcharge for night trips and extra bags.

On the outer islands, where commuting is not as big a factor and the population density is much smaller, buses are less frequent. On these islands (such as Bora Bora, Huahine or Moorea) it definitely behooves you to rent a car, motorcycle or bicycle for the day's sightseeing rather than depend on public transportation. Taxis can be found everywhere, but tend to be very expensive.

I find Tahitian motorists have their own rules of the road, so when in doubt, drive defensively. Watch out for motorists who may insist on passing on blind curves, tailgating and turning without signaling. Beware also of children playing on the street, pedestrians who seem oblivious to traffic, dogs, and on the weekends, drunks—both in automobiles and on foot.

PHONES The phone service in Tahiti is quite good, and a number of public phones appear on the streets of Papeete and villages around French Polynesia—even in the most remote Tuamotu atolls. Nearly all of the phones are card-operated; very few accept coins.

If you want to make an international call and you don't have a telephone card nor want the expense of the hotel surcharges, you will need to go to a post office. International rates are now as low as 135 CFP per minute.

Telephone Calling Cards Pre-paid calling cards can be purchased at any post office, newspaper stand or shop with phone booths nearby.

There are three denominations of cards that purchase corresponding "call units"—5000 CFP, 2000 CFP, 1500 and 1000 CFP. If you plan to make a long-distance call, it's a good idea to pick up a 5000 CFP card.

One rule of thumb is to never, absolutely ever, make a long-distance call from a hotel unless you use a phone card from your home country. Rates in French Polynesia are astronomical enough and a hotel-placed call is likely to be double the rate of the local Office de Postes & Telecommunications—Polynesie Française.

You might want to take advantage of the new "call back" services available from U.S. vendors. These services get around the outrageous French Polynesia rates. You call the vendor in the U.S., who in turn calls the user back and connects them with the number you wish to call. This takes advantage of much lower U.S. phone rates and saves a lot of money. If you are not enrolled in a "call back" service and have an AT&T, MCI or similar long-distance calling card, you can still save money by using these long-distance carriers. To do so, you must go through the French Polynesian operator, who will process and verify your card through the AT&T or MCI operator.

To make a direct overseas call, dial the country code, the area code and the phone number. International codes are as follows: (0054) Argentina, (0043) Austria, (0061) Australia, (0032) Belgium, (0055) Brazil, (001) Canada, (0056) Chile, (0044) England, (16) France, (0049) Germany, (00852) Hong Kong, (0039) Italy, (0081) Japan, (0052) Mexico, (0064) New Zealand, (0063) Philippines, (0065) Singapore, (0034) Spain, (0046) Sweden, (0041) Switzerland, (0031) Netherlands and (001) U.S.

MONOI OIL

A locally grown product to bring back that is considerably less expensive than black pearls is *monoi* (mohn-oy) oil, soap, shampoo, body cream and other items derived from this indigenous product. Monoi is a blend of the extracts of two plants—the Nucifera coconut and the fragrant *tiare* flower *Gardenia tahitensis*. Tahitians (and other Pacific Islanders) have used the oil for centuries as a salve or moisturizer. The homemade version of the oil is readily available in the public markets. You can find the amber or olive-oil colored liquid in refilled gin bottles or medicine flasks. What may be more appealing to the folks back home are the fine, commercially developed Monoi de Tahiti products available in shops. The best places to purchase the commercial products are the large discount stores (see the section on markets north and south of Papeete in Chapter Four).

INTERNET ACCESS   You will find computers with internet access on nearly all of the Society Islands and some of the outlying islands as well. (French and Japanese keyboards can often make typing a challenge for English-speaking visitors). While some facilities are clearly marked as "internet cafés," others are nothing more than a single computer in the dim back room of a shop. The connection—through French Polynesia's main ISP, Mana, is generally reliable, if slow. The cost ranges from 250 CFP for 15 minutes on Tahiti to double that on Bora Bora. Look for island-specific details in each chapter.

MAIL   The French Polynesian postal system is generally very efficient. Due to the numerous flights in and out of Papeete, delivery time from the islands to the U.S., Australia and Europe is usually no longer than a week. The main post office in Papeete is a gleaming modern wonder.

In addition to the main post office on Boulevard Pomare, there is a branch at Faa'a Airport that is open weekdays from 6 to 10:30 a.m. and noon to 2 p.m. On Saturdays, the hours are 6 to 10 a.m. You can make international phone calls from this small office as well as purchase stamps. ~ Papeete; 41-42-42; www.opt.pf.

Most postal addresses given in this book include a BP (*boîte postale*), or post office box number. A lodging may have a BP number or address that's different from the actual location. For example, a pension in Moorea may be located in Haapiti but may have a mailing address in Pao Pao. It can be confusing.

Stamps from Polynesie Française are gorgeous and sought after by collectors. Sets are available in special philatelic windows. Look for a three-stamp series (25, 68 and 72 CFP) created by Moorea resident Dr. Michael Poole. An American marine biologist, Poole took the photos and wrote the philatelic circulars illustrating the life histories of the animals featured on the stamps.

The Philatelic Bureau even has its own website: www.tahiti-postoffice.com.

Sending and Receiving Mail   Foreigners wishing to receive mail may do so by asking at the *poste restante* (general delivery) window. Holders of American Express cards and/or traveler's checks may receive mail at the American Express office at Tahiti Tours, Rue Jeanne d'Arc. Telegrams, telexes and a fax service are also available at the post office. Hours are 7:30 a.m. to 5:00 p.m. on weekdays and 7:30 to 11:30 a.m. on Saturdays.

MEDIA   **Newspapers**   Kiosks and bookshops selling the *International Herald Tribune* (flown in regularly from Paris) and the Pacific edition of *Time* and *Newsweek* are scattered throughout Papeete. Other European publications are also available. (The kiosk at the Vaima Shopping Center on the waterfront is a convenient place to

Pearl Buying

Black pearls are less expensive in French Polynesia than anywhere else in the world. But import taxes on precious metals and labor costs add quite a bit to jewelry with elaborate settings. High-quality, pre-set black pearl jewelry may cost the same or more than you would pay in the U.S. If you want the most value for money, buy the best pearls you can afford and take them home to be set. An exception to this rule might be at the very high-priced boutiques and upscale shops.

Tourist offices and jewelry shops offer free brochures on selecting and pricing pearls by luster, symmetry (roundness), surface flaws, size and color. Rick Steger of Pai Moana Pearls has written a very informative black pearl guide.

For an excellent background on the history of the black pearl, as well as a "buyer's guide," check out www.tahiti-blackpearls.com, a site run by Perles de Tahiti, a Tahiti-based retailer. This is not necessarily where you want to purchase your pearls, but it is a good reference for starting your research.

If you do your homework, you can get excellent deals here on unset pearls. The more you see and price, the better your chances of getting a good price and of knowing a good deal when you see it. The circle (seldom seen in the U.S.A.) and less desirable baroque pearls are great bargains, if you like them. Note that sometimes hematite balls may be confused with black pearls. They are always perfectly proportioned—something that is rare in the natural world—and much heavier. Real pearls have a slightly gritty texture between your teeth.

The best deals on small quantities of unset pearls in 2002 were in Rangiroa; the farms are easily accessible there, and competition is hotter than on the smaller atolls. Be sure to get a detailed receipt and certificate of authenticity. U.S. Customs allows the first $400 free of duty, with a 10 percent duty on the next $1000 of value.

browse.) French Polynesia is served by two daily French-language newspapers, *Les Nouvelles* and *Le Dépêche de Tahiti*. The French-language weekly *Tahiti Pacifique Magazine* covers economics, politics and the environment. Of special interest to tourists is an English-language weekly, *Tahiti Beach Press*, which covers the local scene extensively (often better than the French press), and has excellent travel information on hotels, airlines and tourism in general. The paper also has news on museums and special events. This tabloid-style weekly is given away free at most hotels in French Polynesia. English-language papers such as the *International Herald Tribune*, as well as magazines from the U.S. and Australia, are available at the larger bookstores or at the kiosk at Vaima Center.

A local French-language general-interest magazine is *Fenuo-rama*, aimed at the women's market. Three English-language magazines circulating throughout the Pacific are *Pacific Islands Monthly* (PIM), *Pacific* and *Islands Business*. *PIM*, published in Fiji, is an excellent regional publication and a venerable institution in the Pacific, oriented mostly toward the old Anglo colonies. *Pacific*, published in Honolulu, is a younger upstart that also covers the Pacific basin, but has better coverage of former U.S. Trust Territories and current U.S. dependencies than its rival. *Islands Business* is a Fiji-based monthly magazine that attempts to cover business and political developments in the Pacific.

Radio and Television   The local radio station, France Region 3, also known as Radio Tahiti, broadcasts in French and Tahitian. Along with local news and international news from the national French network, it features a pop-music format with selections by French, U.S. and Tahitian artists. There are also privately owned radio stations, including Radio Tiare, which broadcasts in French and has mostly a pop-music format, as well as two smaller district stations in Papara and Papenoo.

There are several television channels (some originating in France) that broadcast drama, quiz shows, highbrow French programs and interviews. The local TV station, Telefenua, broadcasts 16 channels (via satellite) including news and footage from international correspondents in Tahitian and French. A government-owned TV station (Tahiti Nui Television) debuted in the new century, featuring local news and entertainment. CNN, ESPN, HBO and other English-language cable stations are available in most hotels, and can be seen in private homes with cable.

TRAVEL ETIQUETTE   Avoiding offense involves common sense and sensitivity to cultural nuance more than anything else. For example, if you are about to enter someone's home and you note that everyone takes off their shoes before they enter, it's probably a good idea to do the same. Some occasions, such as a *tama'ara'a* (a feast usually held

Traditional
Medicines

Two traditional Tahitian medicines have enjoyed a renewal of interest in recent years. They can now be found in market stalls, grocery stores and tourist shops on the larger islands. Several excellent books detailing their use and preparation may be found at bookstores in Papeete.

Tamanu oil is prepared from the nut of the Ati tree (*Calophyllum inophyllum*) and used primarily for symptomatic treatment of contact allergies, acne, psoriasis, herpes, hemorrhoids, dandruff, burns, insect bites, and coral cuts. A booklet generally sold with the oil explains its history, uses, and chemical makeup. The book discusses the alleged clinical results of various research projects involving burns and deep wounds; the "before and after" photos are very graphic. Tamanu oil is now available at health food stores in North America, but at double the Tahiti price. Look for it in tourist shops, marketplaces, and next to the *monoi* oils in pharmacies throughout French Polynesia. For more information, contact the Bora Bora Oil Company at 58-31-63 or write to them in Punaauia, PK 16.8, Papeete, Tahiti.

Nono fruit (*Morinda citrifolia*) is used in various ways by traditional healers, but most often a tonic is made from the knobby green fruit. This beverage is available commercially as "No'rinda." The label modestly claims it to be an analgesic and dietary supplement, but the credulous find it useful in the treatment of arthritis, cancer and other ailments. The potent aroma may put you off. The debate continues to rage over the medicinal value of this common tropical plant (known as *nono* in Tahiti and *noni* in the Marquesas). Found throughout the Pacific tropics, *Morinda citrifolia* reaches a height of 20 feet and bears edible potato-sized fruit year-round. In the mid-1990s, Morinda, Inc. imported *nono* juice to the U.S., touting it as a cure-all for everything from diabetes to depression. It quickly became a fad medical potion. By 1998, however, several states successfully sued the company for false claims. Today the U.S. Food and Drug Administration continues to threaten legal action against companies marketing the juice as a drug. Available in grocery stores and specialty shops.

outdoors), call for eating without utensils, so in this instance, you are expected to eat with your fingers as well. The word is derived from "tama'a" (eat) and "ra'a" (big).

Though French Polynesians as a whole seem to be a raucous lot, their table manners are impeccable. Unless you wish to be classified as a barbarian, adopting good manners is a must.

You will also notice that friends greet each other or say goodbye with a peck on each cheek—French style. If you feel familiar enough with someone, it's okay to do the same. If you are an American, you may wish to hug them, but resist. It's not done in this society unless you are on an intimate basis.

PHOTOS

Film and photographic accessories are readily available in Papeete's modern shops, but they will probably be 25 percent to 50 percent more expensive than you will be accustomed to. Color prints can be developed from Kodacolor in one hour at QSS in Papeete's Vaima Shopping Center. Another QSS is located in the Continent shopping center in Faa'a. Always take twice as much film or memory cards as you think you'll need.

Keep in mind that daylight is very intense in the tropics. When in doubt, underexpose. That is, if you really want that photo, shoot according to what your normal meter reading dictates and then shoot another at a third to one full stop under. It's always best to take photos at dawn or dusk for optimal lighting conditions. Inexpensive underwater film cameras—and housings for digital cameras—can open up a whole new visual world to travelers. Remember that water absorbs light, so the closer you are to your subject, the better the photo will look.

Always keep film dry and cool, and have your camera cleaned when you get home if it has been exposed to the elements—the humidity and salt air can ruin sensitive photo equipment in no time. If you plan to go through airport security frequently, it's advisable to buy a laminated lead pouch for film, available at most camera shops.

When taking photos of local people, smile and ask permission. Sharing a peek at a digital photo goes a long way in breaking the ice. Most of the time people will be glad to let you photograph them, but some locals may not want to be part of your slide show.

BARGAIN SHOPPING

One does not haggle or bargain when shopping in the public marketplaces in Tahiti. More often than not, the price you see is the price you get. Tahitians, though perhaps not the Chinese merchants, might find it rude to haggle over prices. If you try to dicker with a Polynesian, more than likely the seller will get angry and either inflate the price even more or decide not to deal with you at all. The only exception in the "bargaining rule" is when you are making a large purchase of black pearl jewelry. The margins on these items are very high and a merchant might well consider knocking off a percentage in order to make a sale.

DRESS

Dress in French Polynesia is as varied it is in Europe or North America. Contemporary, informal garb for both sexes is a pareu with a T-shirt or variations thereof. In town, perhaps because of the longstanding French influence, people are expected to dress with flair. Tahitian women take great pride in their dress and always exhibit impeccable grooming. On a night on the town or even an average workday, you will often see women wearing the latest Paris fashions, and they look drop-dead stunning.

> Once in French Polynesia you will realize that locals have their own concept of time, usually one to two hours behind what you had planned.

Many local designers have taken a cue from the cultural renaissance and have created a neo-Polynesian style. A great deal of influence in dress comes from Hawaii and California as well as France, and colorful surf wear, tank tops, spandex and athletic-style bikini tops are definitely in vogue.

Bikini tops and lots of exposed skin are not taboo in Tahiti, although unusual in town. Tahitians tend to be the least modest of all Pacific Islanders and can often be seen sunbathing topless on the beaches. However, be aware of local mores if you are traveling in more conservative island groups like the Gambiers. Missionary attitudes still endure in some communities. Given the local standards, the female visitor has a great deal more latitude in dress here when compared to the rest of the Pacific Island nations.

Are you a man doing business in French Polynesia? I advise you to wear a nice pair of slacks and a good short-sleeve shirt if you expect the locals to take you seriously. One can usually tell the difference between tourists and locals a mile away because of their appearance. (That is not meant to be a compliment!)

SAFETY

Papeete is very safe by U.S. big-city standards, but there are still occasional reports of robberies. Some Tahitians are very poor and occasionally youths may resort to crime. Even though this is rare, you are urged to keep an eye on your valuables, just as you would anywhere else in the world. Depositing jewelry or cash in a hotel safe is a good idea. Outside Papeete and on the outer islands, there are fewer problems—the worst you may encounter is petty theft and the perpetrator may well be another tourist rather than a local! It's also a good idea not to leave cameras or other items of value unattended at the beach. There's a chance they will have disappeared when you return.

MEDICAL INFO

French Polynesia is malaria-free and inoculations are not required, except for those arriving from an area infected with cholera or yel-

Text continued on page 80.

Underwater Photography

With so much breathtaking beauty above the waterline in French Polynesia, it's hardly surprising that the spectacular landscapes continue beneath the waves. And what better way to capture that beauty than with a little underwater photography? The only problem is that it requires expensive and complicated professional equipment. Right? Not necessarily.

Underwater photography has come a long way since Jacques Cousteau roamed the high seas with underwater camera systems that looked like (and probably cost as much as) small satellites. These days a novice diver can pick up a US$25 disposable underwater camera in most U.S. supermarkets—and in many resorts in French Polynesia.

Better yet, travelers can now convert their small point-and-shoot cameras into underwater rigs by purchasing a US$75–$150 plastic housing. These simple waterproof cases are fitted around your camera and sealed with a series of latches and O-rings. Together with a small digital camera that allows you to take hundreds of shots and validate your focus and exposure underwater, these inexpensive housings are opening up the world of underwater photography to amateurs.

But what if you do want to become the next Mauricio Handler and sell jaw-dropping images to *National Geographic*? In addition to having hundreds of dives under your weight belt, you'll need a fat wallet. The tally for a professional 35mm camera, housing, lens ports, strobes and arms can easily top US$8000.

Having the right equipment is really only part of the equation. Never forget you are a diver first and photographer second. Diving requires constant vigilance—monitor your depth gauges and air frequently. Know your limits and don't dive beyond them. Getting bent or worse isn't worth a photo opportunity that will probably come along again on your next dive.

Another safety consideration is whether or not to attach your camera to you. After all, you don't want to lose a piece of expensive gear into the abyss. While it's fine—and probably smart—to attach your small point-and-shoot to a wrist strap or your BCD weights, the same isn't true of your far more expensive 35mm-housed camera. In an emergency, the first thing you want to do is drop extra weight so it doesn't become a fatal anchor.

It's also important to remember to respect the reef and wildlife. Be careful not to flounder around the bottom, breaking off delicate coral and sponges with your fins while you try to get that shot of a nudibranch or octopus. Likewise, frantically finning after that manta ray or sea turtle will only scare them off and anger your fellow divers. Most animals, if given the chance, will be unable to control their curiosity and will eventually approach you. Wild dolphins, in particular, will often respond to playful behavior on your part like spinning, blowing bubbles and dancing.

Finally, remember what the pros say about getting close. Water absorbs a tremendous amount of light. If you want to capture color—and have a flash on your camera—shoot within the reach of your arms. If you don't have strobes and still want some color, shoot in the top 12 feet of water where the sunlight still penetrates.

Some of the best dive sites for underwater photography in French Polynesia are:

TAHITI **The Aquarium**, just off the airport near the overwater bunga-lows at the Beachcomber InterContinental Hotel, is a shallow dive site that boasts a number of small bommies (coral heads) alive with small fish and crustaceans. There is even a coral-encrusted Cessna sitting on the bottom.

MOOREA Easily accessibly from hotels on the northern coast, **Taotoi Pass** features schools of small, bright tropical fish along with several larger Napoleon wrasse and inquisitive moray eels. **Tiki** is the dive to do if you want plenty of gray reef and lemon sharks (even the occasional turtle) swirling around you. But beware, the dive is on the outside of the reef and surge and low visibility can sometimes challenge photographers.

HUAHINE The mellow **Fa'a Miti** dive site, only ten minutes from Fare, is a boon for divers wishing to concentrate on macro photography. Trevallies, trigger fish and butterfly fish flock to the area because of regular feedings.

BORA BORA **Anau** is tucked in the shallow, protected waters of the lagoon. This site is a great place to find the majestic black-and-white manta rays as they feed off the lip of a drop-off. Remember to turn your flash off (the cloudy water will create backscatter) and don't chase the mantas.

RANGIROA With some of the last great schools of sharks in the Pacific (up to 300 grays can be seen schooling in this current-scoured pass), Rangi is *the* shark-diving capital of the world and **Tiputa Pass** is its crown jewel. The strong current means this is a dive that should only be done by confident and experienced divers.

low fever. The water is generally safe and plentiful in most areas, but for the skittish, there is always bottled water, canned or bottled soda or beer. To date, I have never had problems with the drinking water anywhere in French Polynesia, but I have heard reports of visitors acquiring waterborne parasites in the outer islands. When in doubt, it might be prudent to drink the local bottled water.

There are modern clinics and hospitals in Tahiti, and many of the outer islands also have hospitals. These include: Moorea, Huahine, Raiatea, Bora Bora, Maupiti, Rangiroa, Tubuai, Hiva Oa, Ua Huka and Nuku Hiva. If there is no hospital on an island, there will at least be a clinic or a pharmacy.

If you must seek medical assistance, hospitals in Tahiti are open 24 hours a day. On the outer islands dispensaries are open from 7:30 a.m. to noon and 2 to 5:30 p.m. during the week. Saturday hours are 7:30 to 11:30 a.m.

The extreme changes in humidity, exotic food and other foreign conditions may tax your system. The best advice is to take it easy for the first few days until you have acclimatized. You would do well to be prepared and bring sunscreen, an ice bag, cornstarch powder, antacids, cold tablets and cough syrup. Here are some other useful items to pack:

- Antibiotics. You may want to take along your own antibiotics, especially if you are going to be on the outer islands where there is little in the way of medical care. They must be prescribed and you should carry the prescription with you. An antibiotic ointment such as Neosporin is also handy to have along. Antibiotics are critical in helping heal reef cuts.
- Antihistamine (such as Benadryl). These can be used as a decongestant for allergies and colds, though some may make you tired. Antihistamines also relieve the itch from insect bites or stings.
- Antiseptics such as Bactine. Bring antiseptics in swabs or ointment form for cuts and bites.
- Aspirin, Advil, Tylenol or a similar pain reliever.
- Bandages and Band-aids.
- Calamine lotion or Benadryl ointment. These relieve the discomfort from bites or stings.
- Medications for diarrhea such as Pepto-Bismol or Imodium AD. You might want to get a prescription for something stronger, such as Lomotil, if you are prone to digestive problems while traveling. It might be advisable to bring along a rehydration mixture as well for treatment of severe diarrhea. This is particularly important if you are traveling with children.

- Scissors, tweezers and a thermometer.
- Water purification tablets.

Butch Martin, a colleague from New York City, recommends two products that he picked up at a local health food store. The first is "PB8," a pro-biotic acidophilus in capsule form that can be taken daily to promote a healthy balance of intestinal flora. The second is called "Pro Seed," an extract of grapefruit, an effective treatment for intestinal disorders. The latter has a bitter taste but is palatable in tea.

Food   There is an old saying: "If you can cook it, boil it or peel it, you can eat it—otherwise forget it." Salads and fruit should be washed with purified water or peeled where possible. Ice cream is usually okay if it is a reputable brand name, but beware of ice cream that has melted and been refrozen. Thoroughly cooked food is the safest, but not if it has been left to cool or if it has been reheated. Shellfish such as mussels, oysters and clams should be avoided—steaming does not make shellfish safe for eating. Undercooked meat can also be a problem. Beef in particular is minimally cooked in French Polynesia (read: braised on the outside and raw inside) unless you make a point of ordering it otherwise.

> Coral cuts are extremely slow to heal because coral injects a weak venom into the wound. Avoid coral cuts by wearing reef shoes and clean any cut thoroughly with peroxide or an antiseptic.

If a place looks clean and well run and if the vendor also looks clean and healthy, then the food is probably safe. In general, places that are packed with travelers or locals will be fine, while empty restaurants are questionable. Busy restaurants mean the food is being cooked and eaten quite quickly with little standing around and is probably not being reheated.

Sunburn   No matter how cool it feels on a given day in the tropics, the sun's ultraviolet rays are less filtered by the atmosphere than in other latitudes. Damage can be done to your skin and eyes, so be careful. Use a sunscreen with at least 25 SPF—you'll still get a tan with sunscreen, it just takes longer. A hat provides added protection, and you should also use a barrier cream, such as zinc, for your nose and lips. Don't forget to put sunscreen on your feet. The skin on the top of your feet are very susceptible to burning! A bad sunburn can ruin a vacation and a severe burn requires medical attention. A minor burn can be treated with a cool bath or cold compresses, soothing cream or steroids. If your skin "bubbles" don't peel it away because it may become infected. An aspirin two or three times a day will help to ease the pain. Some people are allergic to ultraviolet light, and the result is redness, itching and pinpoint-sized blisters. Clothing is the only answer for them. Fair-skinned people have to be very careful in the tropics!

Diarrhea   A change of water, food or climate can cause an upset bowel; diarrhea caused by contaminated food or water is more serious. Despite all your precautions, you may still have a bout of mild diarrhea, but a few rushed trips to the toilet with no other symptoms does not indicate a serious problem. Moderate diarrhea, involving a half-dozen loose movements in a day, is more of a nuisance. Lomotil or Imodium can be used to relieve the symptoms, but they do not cure the problem. For children, Imodium is preferable, but fluid replacement is important to avoid dehydration.

In case of car accidents or medical emergencies, dial 15.

Sexually Transmitted Diseases   As in many other Pacific nations, there are a multitude of sexually transmitted diseases in French Polynesia. AIDS has been reported in Tahiti, but statistics on its prevalence are hard to come by. Given the sexual proclivities of Tahitians, the large bisexual population and the numbers of visitors from every corner of the globe, the presence of AIDS should not come as a surprise. Needless to say, it's a good idea to practice safe sex and use condoms. As my good friend Dr. Jim Mielke, an AIDS researcher, advises male travelers, "wrap it up" when having sexual relations.

Insect-borne Diseases   Health authorities have expressed concern about filariasis, an insect-borne disease that attacks the lymphatic system. Short-term visitors have little to be concerned about, but doctors advise you to avoid mosquito bites.

Outbreaks of dengue fever also appear from time to time. There is no prophylactic available for this mosquito-spread disease; the main preventive measure is to avoid mosquito bites. Dengue fever (a relative of yellow fever) comes in four strains; the worst can be fatal. A 12-year-old girl died of this malady in Moorea in 1997, and several backpackers fell ill with it there in early 2002. A sudden onset of fever, headaches and severe joint and muscle pains are the first signs of dengue fever. Then a rash starts on the trunk of the body and spreads to the limbs and face. The fever usually subsides after several days. Recovery time varies.

Here is how to avoid mosquito and *nono* (sandfly) bites:
• wear light-colored clothing
• wear light-weight long pants and long-sleeved shirts
• use mosquito repellent containing DEET on exposed areas
• avoid scented perfumes or aftershave lotion
• use a mosquito net—it may be worth taking your own

Cuts, Bites and Stings   Skin wounds can easily become infected in hot climates. Be certain to treat any cut with an antiseptic or antibiotic cream such as Neosporin. Avoid bandages that keep wounds wet.

Centipede stings are notoriously painful. Centipedes are usually found in damp areas, under rocks, and in buildings constructed from palm fronds. They often hide in shoes or clothing. If you are in an area where centipedes are found, always shake out your shoes and clothing before putting them on. Fortunately, however, the bite usually heals after a day or two.

Ciguatera   A word of warning about ciguatera, a form of poisoning from eating infected fish. It has been reported in French Polynesia and other areas such as Hawaii, Papua New Guinea and northern Australia, and was known to have infected Captain Cook's crew in 1774. The toxin that causes the poisoning is released by a microscopic marine organism living on or near coral reefs, particularly reefs that have been disturbed (for example by development). When fish eat the organism, the toxin becomes concentrated in the head, organs and roe of the fish. Symptoms of ciguatera include diarrhea; muscle pain; joint aches; numbness and tingling around the mouth, hands and feet; reversal of temperature sensation (cold objects feel hot and vice versa); nausea; vomiting; chills; itching; headache; sweating and dizziness. If you experience any of these symptoms after eating fish, contact a doctor immediately.

According to Dr. Yoshitsugi Hokama, a recognized ciguatera expert from the University of Hawaii, fish caught in the open sea, particularly large pelagics such as tuna, are safe. However, reef fish, particularly groupers, jacks, and snappers from the *Letjnus* genus, commonly known as *Bohar*, should be avoided, even in restaurants. Barracuda should also be avoided. (In addition to ciguatera, barracuda also tend to have worms.) Dr. Hokama notes that yachties or others who plan to fish for their food should test their catch to make sure it is safe. A test kit for detecting ciguatera poison in fish is available from Oceanit Test Systems of Hawaii. ~ 808-531-3017; www.cigua.com, e-mail cigua@oceanit.com.

In general, eating seafood in the restaurants in French Polynesia is as safe a proposition as anywhere in the world, but it is definitely a good idea to avoid reef fish such as snappers and the other species mentioned above. If you catch your own fish, be sure to test it or check with the local people before you cook it (cooking doesn't eliminate toxins). Don't eat fish that have come from a disturbed environment. Also, avoid eating the head, gonads, liver and viscera of fish.

Swimming and Snorkeling   Divers are likely to run into underwater hazards such as fire coral, sea anemones, crown-of-thorns starfish, scorpion fish and sharks. Shore-bound visitors may meet up with rays off a sandy beach or eels on the reef at low tide. Beware: never stick your hand in a crevice or cavity in the reef! I've seen eels in shallow water on the reef. The best advice is simply don't touch anything underwater.

OCEAN SAFETY

Avoid swimming, walking barefoot or collecting seafood from beaches or lagoons directly in front of settlements, river mouths and yacht moorings. Raw sewage is often dumped or piped into the nearest convenient outlet—i.e., the beach that forms the villagers' front yard. When bathing, watch where the locals go— that's where it's most likely safe to swim.

Swimming in the lagoons is a safe practice—shark attacks are rare. A few commonsense precautions are in order: don't swim in the ocean at night; don't wear bright jewelry when swimming or snorkeling; and don't swim in an area where fish have just been cleaned or fish remains have been thrown into the sea. Also avoid river mouths and murky water.

Aside from the (minimal) threat of sharks, every year there are tragic drownings. Always be aware of the currents in the area where you are swimming. As a general rule, if the locals are swimming in a particular area, it's probably safe for you.

When snorkeling, avoid contact with sea urchins. In case you weren't aware, their long black spines can inflict a painful wound. (If you come into contact with a sea urchin, a local remedy is to urinate on the wound.) Sea urchins are plentiful—I've seen them near beaches in Moorea, Huahine, Raiatea and elsewhere.

Fire coral should also be avoided. You can recognize it by its almost velvet-like surface and fawn or rust color with white fringes. Bathing a coral scrape with lime juice is a good treatment; applying the outermost bark of *tiari* (candlenut) is also effective. Regardless of how deep the wound is, be sure to immediately treat it with antibiotics until it is healed.

Swimmers or snorkelers may also run into jellyfish at certain times of the year. Local advice on swimming conditions is the best way of avoiding contact with these sea creatures and their stinging tentacles. The Medusa jellyfish (related to the Portuguese Man-of-War) is sometimes found in the waters of French Polynesia but fortunately is not common. The stings from most jellyfish vary from being simply painful to causing shock or even loss of consciousness. Dousing in vinegar will deactivate any stingers that have not "fired." Calamine lotion, antihistamines and analgesics may reduce the reaction and relieve the pain.

Up on the Reef   Rule number one around the reef is to always wear reef shoes! Certain cone shells found in French Polynesia sting and the venom can be fatal. To avoid a tragic mistake, don't pick up any cone-shaped shells. The stonefish, which resembles its namesake, is an insidious creature (about six inches long) that is found in shallow water. Their natural camouflage makes them almost impossible to see. Surfers are the usual victims of this sometimes deadly creature. Still, stonefish are rarely found on the barrier reef's outer slope, where surfers congregate. The fish prefer calmer water.

THREE

The Land and Outdoor Adventures

Tahiti and the five archipelagos lie at the very center of the Polynesian Triangle. The three points of the triangle—Hawaii to the north, New Zealand to the southwest and Easter Island to the southeast—are nearly equidistant from Tahiti. Not only is Tahiti separated from the rest of Polynesia but she is far from the nearest continents and cut off from the biotic mainstream. Tahiti's isolated location has everything to do with its natural history.

GEOLOGY More than 25 million years ago a fissure opened along the Pacific floor. Beneath tons of seawater molten lava poured from the rift. This liquid basalt, oozing from a hot spot in the earth's center, created a crater along the ocean bottom. As the tectonic plate that comprises the ocean floor drifted over the hot spot, numerous other craters appeared. Slowly, in the seemingly endless procession of geologic time, a chain of volcanic islands, stretching almost 2000 miles, emerged from the sea.

On the continents it was also a period of terrible upheaval. The Himalayas, Alps and Andes were rising, but these great chains would reach their peaks long before the Pacific mountains even touched sea level. Not until a few million years ago did these underwater volcanoes break the surface and become islands. By then, present-day plants and animals inhabited the earth, and apes were rapidly evolving into a new species.

For many millennia, the mountains continued to grow. The forces of erosion cut into them, creating knife-edged cliffs and deep valleys. Then plants began germinating: mosses and ferns, springing from windblown spores, were probably first, followed by seed plants carried by migrating birds and ocean currents. The steep-walled valleys provided natural greenhouses in which unique species evolved, while transoceanic winds swept insects and other life from the continents.

Tahiti is actually very young when compared to her sister islands of Polynesia. For instance, the Tuamotu, the oldest Polynesian islands, are coral atolls that date back 50 million years. Some of the Hawaiian islands date back 40 million years, and New Zealand, once part of an ancient continent, has been an island group for at least 135 million years. Just a glance at the sharp, cone-shaped profile of Tahiti offers a clue to her volcanic origins and the fact that the island is so young. (A geologically older island would be worn and rounded by the elements.)

Of High and Low Lands   We can divide the islands of French Polynesia geologically into two basic categories: atolls (or low islands) and high islands.

High islands can be either volcanic in origin or the result of an upheaval from the ocean floor. Their terrain can be smooth, rocky and barren, or incredibly steep and covered with lush rainforest. Unlike atolls, where drinking water must be collected in cisterns and a limited range of crops can be grown, high islands often have an abundance of water and have the soil to support a variety of fruits and vegetables. Examples of high islands are Tahiti or Nuku Hiva, which are precipitous, craggy and quite young in geological terms.

Geologists actually order Pacific islands into six different classifications that pertain to the specific evolutionary stages from a high island into an atoll.

Atolls are what Daniel Defoe had in mind when he wrote *Robinson Crusoe*—flat strips of coral with little more than scrub growth and coconut palms adhering to the thin soil. There is little diversity in the flora and fauna, in part because the flat terrain discourages the development of diverse ecosystems. The soil found on atolls is usually poor in nutrients, which also hinders biotic diversity. This is generally accompanied by a chronic shortage of water. In relative geological terms, atolls are much older than high islands—they are in fact the final cycle in an island's evolutionary process.

But let's start at the beginning. The life of a volcanic island begins in the depths of the sea with a mound or rise created on the bottom of the ocean by magma forcing its way upward from the bowels of the earth. Eventually, the magma breaks free through the earth's crust and becomes lava as it erupts from the mouth of a volcano. As long as the lava flows, the island grows. When it stops, the dynamic of wind, water and wave action fashion the surface of the island and eventually help to create a topsoil from which plant and animal life can gain hold. Simultaneously in tropical environments, coral communities begin to take shape on the periphery of the island and the growth of reef systems begins. As the island sinks and the mountains erode and subside, the growth of the reef system keeps pace with the submergence of the land mass. This results in the formation of nearly vertical coral walls on the island's fringes, often creating lagoons.

The culmination of the volcanic island's erosion and submergence, combined with the full development of the coral reef is the atoll. The sinking of the volcano leaves only the coral, which then surrounds a lagoon. Some atolls contain a circular or oblong reef, which may entirely enclose a lagoon, while other atolls have lagoons that are enclosed by segmented islets separated by passes. From a bird's eye view, these atolls appear to be a lush green series of segments in a necklace of islands punctuated by narrow slits of blue water. The long, thin islands or *motu* as they are called, may vary in length from several hundred yards to several miles long. Though narrow, utterly flat and proscribed by the confines of the sea, the dazzling intensity of an atoll can overwhelm the senses.

Primal colors abound. The lagoon radiates with primitive blues and greens—lapis lazuli, cobalt and turquoise. The ceaseless trade winds stir the palm fronds overhead but do little to quell the fierce heat of the tropical sun. The ocean laps or pounds interminably on the blinding white coral shore. Though strikingly beautiful from afar, most people find atolls difficult if not impossible to live on for any length of time.

Coral Reefs

French Polynesia has at least three reef types: fringing, patch and barrier. The barrier reefs we see today around each island were once fringing reefs attached to (fringing) the shoreline of the volcanoes. As the volcanoes sank, the fringing reefs became barrier reefs. Reefs may be hundreds of thousands of years old with new coral growth constantly occurring. The old and dead coral is cemented together with coralline algae and can be compressed by the massive weight above to form a kind of limestone. Some coral atolls are formed over undersea volcanic mountains that are slowly sinking. If the coral growth matches the rate of submergence, coral limestone hundreds of yards deep may accumulate. Charles Darwin was the first to come up with this theory and, with slight modification, it has withstood the test of time and modern scientific inquiry.

The reef itself is created by the combined efforts of billions of tiny marine organisms ranging from algae and protozoa to coral animals known as *coelenterates*. Many of the organisms remove calcium carbonates from the water and build calcareous structures that we collectively call coral. The coral you may pick up from the beach or purchase at the souvenir stand represents only the skeleton of a once-thriving colony of sea anemone–like creatures known as polyps.

The polyps live in small depressions in the coral and generally feed at night by extending tentacles—exactly like their biological cousins, the sea anemones. The tentacles contain stinging cells that inject poison into small animal prey. The victim is then transferred to the mouth by the tentacles and into the organism's digestive cavity. Most coral stings are too weak to be felt by humans although some species, such as fire corals, have a nasty sting.

Interestingly enough, scientists find that theoretically there is not enough food in a reef ecosystem to keep these billions of animals fed. However, coral communities continue to expand despite what scientific logic dictates. How can this be so? Most corals contain algal cells, known as *zooxanthellae*, embedded in their tissues. Scientists tell us that photosynthesis by *zooxanthellae* during the day provides the coral with energy. Coral, in essence, farm their own food. Coral, in return, provide homes for the *zooxanthellae* and so both benefit.

As with all plants, the *zooxanthellae* require light for photosynthesis and this restricts most coral to a depth of no more than

200 feet. Below this level there is insufficient light for the *zoox-anthellae* and not enough food for the polyp. Temperature also effects coral distribution; reef-forming corals flourish between temperatures of 68°F (20°C) and 86°F (30°C).

The coral reef ecosystem is one of the most diverse on the planet, and its high productivity is matched only by the tropical rainforest. Despite the robust appearance of a coral reef, it is quite fragile. A careless snorkeler can destroy 20 years' growth just by kicking corals or breaking them off with his fins.

REEF LIFE   The creatures of the shore and coral reef are accessible to just about everyone. Some of the more common species you are likely to contact in or around the reef are mollusks, echinoderms and a crustacean or two. Mollusks include clams, sea slugs, octopus, bivalves and the most common mollusk of the reef, the gastropod. Gastropods (many of which produce what are commonly known as seashells) generally possess a single spiraled shell. Nearly all have an obvious head, with eyes and tentacles. Gastropods feed on a wide spectrum of organisms ranging from algae to small fish. If you find a live gastropod on the reef, such as a cowry, it's tempting to pick it up and stick it in your pocket. Remember that this creature may look like it will make a great souvenir, but like all living things it will die and begin to deteriorate immediately. If you place it in this state in your suitcase, it will indeed leave an acute odiferous imprint upon your belongings.

Some mollusks, especially cone shells, are best left on the reef. For example, the *conus textile*, so named because of its clothlike pattern, is downright venomous. This species and others have developed a harpoon-like radula that is meant to immobilize or kill prey. One species of cone shell is lethal. The lesson here is that it's not a good practice to touch live cone shells. If you are a shell collector, your best bet is to collect shells whose host organisms have gone on to another world. If you do find a shell on the beach that appears to be dead, double-check to make sure it's not inhabited by a hermit crab.

Bivalves such as oysters and other clams are also common on the reef and their shells are often seen in profusion on the beach. Bivalves lack a head, although they may have eyes. They are usually filter feeders, taking water into the body with an inhalant siphon.

Crustaceans make up a varied class of creatures including crayfish, shrimp, prawns, crabs, barnacles, fish lice, water fleas and wood lice. Shrimp and prawn include a variety of forms living both in freshwater and saltwater. Large freshwater prawns provided an important source of protein in times past and are still a popular item in Tahitian cuisine. Crayfish, which will only be seen by divers, are a much sought-after delicacy and are found in great numbers in the Marquesas Islands. Unfortunately, they have become so desired as cuisine for tourists that there is an imminent danger of overfishing this resource.

The largest members of the *Coenobitadae* family are the coconut crabs, which resemble lobsters. They have extremely powerful chelae (pincers) that are capable of opening up, yes, a coconut. Evidently this creature will actually climb a tree, cut off the nut at the spathe, descend and eat the nut. Anyone who has tried to husk a coconut will no doubt be amazed by this feat. Although rare on Tahiti, they may be found in the Tuamotu and are a great delicacy.

In addition to the various crabs found on the reefs and boulders that line the shore, there are a variety of terrestrial crabs, or *tupa* as they are called by Tahitians. Land crabs can be found in great profusion in low-lying coastal areas. They often can be seen crossing roads at night in search of food—they eat just about anything organic they can scavenge. During the day they stay close to their lairs, ready to disappear down their chutes at the first vibration or shadow. Male fiddler crabs, characterized by their enormously enlarged chelae (which are used to attract females), are small and are found by the thousands in swampy ground. Ghost crabs can be seen on the beach running so fast they appear to glide along the sand.

Coral bleaching, another way of describing the massive dying off of coral communities, was first discovered in 1980 on Australia's Great Barrier Reef. Since then, this phenomenon has been observed in the reefs of Hawaii, the Maldives, East Africa, Indonesia and French Polynesia.

CORAL BLEACHING

STROLLING SEASHELLS

One of the stranger sights for the first-time island visitor is finding a seashell "strolling" down the beach. Upon closer inspection, you'll note that the shell is inhabited by a crab, a hermit crab to be specific. Hermit crabs can be found near the shore or on land rustling through the underbrush (though I once found one creeping along the floor of a Catholic church!). Hermit crabs take up residence in empty shells to protect their vulnerable soft abdomens. They have developed a tail fan that grips the inside of the shell and an oversized pincer to block the shell's opening, lest they be easily extracted from their adopted homes. As the crab grows in size, it must look for a larger shell to find refuge. More at home on the ground, they return to the sea to find new shells or to reproduce.

The bleaching process occurs when the coral expels *zooxan-thellae*. Without the algae living in symbiosis with the coral, it does not receive enough energy to survive. Coral expels the algae when under stress caused by excessive sunlight, temperatures outside the normal range or extreme changes in salinity. Only a few degrees above the optimum temperature range of 80 to 86°F (27 to 30°C) can cause problems. Some scientists believe the culprit in this worldwide phenomenon may be global warming.

In *The Snorkeller's Guide to the Coral Reef*, Paddy Ryan quotes Thomas Goreau, the president of the Global Coral Reef Alliance, who notes that "Coral reefs now appear to be the first major ecosystem seriously disrupted by climate change." While it's difficult to pin the blame of bleaching solely on global warming, it is certainly implicated. Goreau reported that every documented case of bleaching correlated to the highest water temperatures on record at the various study sites in Puerto Rico, Jamaica, Cayman, Cozumel, Florida and the Bahamas.

Given that the rise in temperature correlates with coral bleaching, a counterargument to global warming as the cause is that there is no hard evidence that the rise in water temperatures is caused by global warming. A shift in currents may be the cause of bleaching in certain instances. For example, several years ago in Tetiaroa, the manager of the resort showed me a portion of the reef that had been bleached. According to his data, the reason for the bleaching was El Niño, the mysterious current that has been blamed for a number of weather-related problems.

Flora and Fauna

The flora and fauna of the tropical Pacific were, with few exceptions, unknown to the Western world until Captain James Cook and others of his ilk explored the Pacific in the late 18th and early 19th centuries. When Cook's ship, the *Endeavour*, ventured to Tahiti and other islands, he found an entirely new universe of plants and animals. These included mollusks such as the golden cowry, fish such as the butterfly fish, birds such as honey-creepers and cultivated plants such as taro and breadfruit. Illustrating documentation of the "new" species was done by Sir Joseph Banks and Daniel Solander. Along with the illustrations, specimens of shells, preserved fish, bird skins and pressed plants were collected by seamen and naturalists. Bearing the label *Otaheite*, many of these items were placed in museums and herbaria. Others were sold as objects of curiosity to well-heeled Londoners. It wasn't until the mid-19th century that Tahiti and the Pacific islands were recognized as having their own distinct biota.

A MYSTERY How flora and fauna reached the distant islands of French Polynesia and the other Pacific isles is one of the world's great mysteries. Modern scientists are torn between two opposing views. One theory has it that the Pacific's distant islands were populated from seed and birds brought by wind and sea currents —dispersing by chance. The majority of plants and animals in the South Pacific are closely related to species in Southeast Asia. However, the prevailing currents and winds that may have aided in their dispersal flow from the opposite direction, from the Americas. If the Dispersal Theory is valid, why then are there so few species in the Pacific from the Americas?

The second view, the Vicariance Theory, postulates that flora and fauna populated islands across (now submerged) land bridges, or simply stayed put while the land moved under them. In other words, the present position of the islands of Oceania are not where they were millions of years ago. Thus, it would have been possible for groups of plants and animals to travel great distances simply by remaining where they were. Another factor in this equation is that the sea level has varied greatly over the years. A lower sea level would have exposed more land, making it possible to cross land bridges with ease.

The male ghost and fiddler crabs are among the few crustacea that use sound to attract females. They create noise by vibrating their big claw or by tapping the ground with their legs.

This brings us to the most important point to consider regarding the evolution of French Polynesia's natural history—its distance from Australasia, the main source of its flora and fauna. Being so far away from everything has put the islands out of the natural reach of most of the plants and animals that would otherwise have populated it. This is especially true with the Society Islands whose rich volcanic soil would be an ideal medium to support a variety of species. Compared to Asia or South America, French Polynesia's natural diversity is impoverished.

The paucity of bird life is a good example. Most of the Pacific's ancestral birds came from New Guinea. Even the most distant islands such as Pitcairn and Hawaii have birds originating from there. Their colonizing route across the Pacific appears to have taken them from New Guinea to the Bismarck Archipelago, on to the Solomons, Vanuatu and New Caledonia, to Fiji, Samoa, east to the Society Islands and lastly north to the Tuamotu and the Marquesas Group. The megapodes, cuckoo shrikes, fruit pigeons, kingfishers, weaver finches, white-eyes and honey eaters all followed this route. As one would expect, their numbers dwindled as they flew eastward. In Tahiti, there are just 12 species of land birds, while an island of similar size in the Solomons or Vanuatu supports perhaps 40 species.

In a similar distance-makes-all-the-difference theme, there are no native land mammals in French Polynesia. There are no amphibians and only four species of reptiles. Only insects and spiders, which can be carried great distances by the wind, are represented.

Likewise, there are several families of flora which bear windblown seeds, and plant species such as the coconut, which can travel enormous distances over the water.

Yet another issue to consider regarding the distribution patterns of organisms in French Polynesia is island type. Differences of development both in marine and terrestrial flora and fauna are dependent upon whether the island is a high island or atoll. A rule of thumb is that atolls and other low-lying islands will have less diverse fauna compared to high islands. Atolls tend to have few species, and those they do have are widely distributed.

HUMAN INTRODUCTIONS   When the original settlers of French Polynesia first arrived, the variety of vegetation was limited to the seeds and spores borne by wind, sea and the birds that happened to find their way to the islands. To provide food and materials for shelter, the Polynesians brought with them a variety of plants, such as taro, yams, coconuts, bananas and breadfruit.

To the bafflement of scientists, they also cultivated the South American sweet potato—a plant that does not exist in Asia. How the sweet potato, a native of the Andes, got there is still a mystery. It may be that the seeds were dispersed naturally, rafting on coconuts or other organic material or perhaps assisted by birds. According to Thor Heyerdhal's theory, which he attempted to prove with his voyage on the *Kon Tiki*, Polynesians may have had contact with South America.

Long after the Polynesians settled, the missionaries came and introduced corn, cotton, sugarcane, citrus fruits, figs, pineapples, guavas, tamarinds, coffee and other vegetables.

Tahiti also owes quite a bit of its present-day flora to Edouard Raoul, a pharmacist-botanist who in 1887 brought a cargo of 1500 varieties of plants to the islands and experimented with the cultivation of hundreds of types of fruit trees. He also brought *kauri* (from New Zealand), red cedar, eucalyptus, rubber, gum and jack. Ten years after his arrival, Raoul's plentiful gardens were donating about 150 species of plants to farmers to improve their stock.

In 1919 Harrison Smith, an American professor turned botanist, purchased 340 acres in Papeari and settled down to cultivate hundreds of plant varieties that he had imported from tropical regions throughout the world. Like Raoul, he helped local farmers by giving them seeds and cuttings to better their crops. (For more information on Smith, see Chapter Four.)

There can be a price to pay for bringing in new species. Indeed, the introduction of alien flora and fauna often represents a real threat to the ecological balance. An interesting case in point can be made from the lowly *Partula*, a bean-sized snail native to the Society Islands. The *Partula* of Moorea evolved into differ-

The Islanders' Staff of Life

The coconut palm has been the staff of life for islanders for thousands of years and continues to provide a source of income to those in French Polynesia who harvest copra—the flesh of the dried nut. The coconut husk, which acts as a cushion to protect the inner nut from its rapid descent to the ground as well as acting as a life raft at sea, is also extremely useful. In the old days, islanders used sennit (braided twine or rope made from coconut husk fibers) to make sandals that protected them while walking on the sharp reefs. On at least one island, Bora Bora, locals have found a unique use for the discarded husk—using it as a fuel to power an electrical generator.

A coconut takes about a year to mature from flower to ripe nut. After reaching full size, but long before ripening, the green or yellow nut is at the drinking stage. It is easily whacked open with a machete and its liquid contents consumed. The pint or so of clear coconut milk can be almost effervescent and is wonderfully refreshing, especially when cold. In the islands vendors of cold drinking nuts are very popular.

During the green or "drinking nut" phase of maturation, a thin translucent layer forms inside the shell and is quite tasty. The soft, whitish pulp can be scraped from the inside of the shell with a spoon or, lacking any utensil, your fingers. When finished drinking the juice, simply crack open the shell on a rock and start eating. As the nut ripens, the soft pulp turns hard and the sweet juice loses its taste. The raw flesh of the nut is still good to eat at this stage and is sometimes roasted, shaved and used as an appetizer. Locals use it in cooking with fish, vegetables and in desserts. The raw meat is grated, squeezed through a cloth and the result is a white, rich liquid. The final eating stage of the nut is prior to germination. At this point the meat has become spongy in texture and has totally absorbed the juice. The soft flesh still makes good eating and is worth trying.

For modern-day Polynesians the coconut's value is as copra, a vital source of income for rural islanders. Copra production entails harvesting the nuts, cracking them open and letting them dry in the hot tropical sun or in special dryers made from corrugated zinc sheets. The dried meat turns yellowish-brown, shrinks from the nut casing and is removed by hand. It is then placed in burlap bags for shipment. The rancid, pungent smell of copra is unforgettable and you will very likely see bags of copra being weighed on the dock. The processed copra provides an oil that has many uses as an ingredient in soaps, vegetable oil, margarine and even nitroglycerine.

ent species, originally separated by the valleys and serrated ridges of this emerald isle. The *Partula* makes excellent fodder for scientific inquiry into evolution for a number of reasons. It lived on isolated islands, it didn't travel far, it had a relatively short life cycle (about 17 years) and it could be bred easily. Genetically, the snails were extraordinarily varied. They were in fact the perfect subject for observation of speciation, as noted in 1932 by H. E. Crampton, the great mollusk collector of the South Pacific.

Note that the past tense is used. The snail no longer exists on Moorea. The history of its decline began in 1803. At that time the governor of Reunion wanted to please his mistress, who had a fondness for Madagascan snail soup. In that year he imported some very large snails from that island and they promptly escaped from his garden. The creatures became a sort of slimy locust destroying the island's crops. By 1847, the giant African land snail (as it is now known) reached the Indian subcontinent and by the 1930s made its way to the South Pacific where it was introduced as a gastronomical treat, *l'escargot*. Although Polynesians showed little appreciation for the huge mollusk, the snail was greatly enamored with local fruit crops and multiplied with gusto.

The colonial authorities had to find some way to control this new pest and by the 1970s they were in a desperate state. A biological control perhaps was in order. Why not introduce another alien creature to combat the current plague?

In Moorea farmers had learned of a predatory snail from the southeastern United States that had been used successfully elsewhere in the Pacific. In 1977 *Euglandina rosea* was introduced to Moorea. The effect was dramatic. *Euglandina* can sniff the chemical scent of its prey like a bloodhound. Unfortunately, the local *Partula* snails were much easier to catch than the introduced African Land Snail. The result was that the *Partula* were being gobbled up as *Euglandina* spread like wildfire throughout the forests of Moorea. By 1987 a survey determined that the native mollusk was extinct on the island. However, a live specimen was recently found in Moorea at the Kellum Stop, a popular tourist attraction. Maybe there is hope for the creature after all.

Outdoor Adventures

French Polynesia offers a wide array of outdoor and sporting activities for the visitor including snorkeling, scuba diving, surfing, windsurfing, hiking and horseback riding. The venues for these activities are listed in each island chapter. *Pirogue* (outrigger canoe) racing is the closest thing to a national sport in French Polynesia. The best time to see both regional and international competition is during the *Heiva* festival in July.

Visitors may join the locals, many of whom are sports fanatics, in more recreational activities such as golf, bicycle racing, tennis, basketball, track and field, soccer and swimming. It should be noted that in 1995 French Polynesia hosted the South Pacific Games, a regional, Olympics-like event featuring only South Pacific athletes.

If one could zero in on a specific sport that indisputably captures the spirit of Tahitian society, it would have to be outrigger canoe or *pirogue* racing. **OUTRIGGER CANOEING**

Racing *pirogues* or *va'a* are long, slender canoes around 25 feet (7 meters) long. All have one outrigger and are manned by six or more individuals. Racing canoes that partake in international class competition weigh no more than 400 pounds (181 kilos) and are made of fiberglass. There are also traditional canoes constructed from local hardwood. In the late afternoon, it's not unusual to see teams of paddlers practicing or racing in lagoons throughout French Polynesia.

Paddling clubs are not solely the domain of men. There are also women's and children's divisions. Races between different islands and clubs are highly charged and extremely competitive affairs. Canoe teams train rigorously throughout the year for races held during the *Tiurai* celebrations, the highlight of the racing season. Another important race is the Hawaiki Nui Va'a marathon contest, which is held over a three-day period among four of the Leeward Islands. Once a year at least one Tahitian team travels to Hawaii (where the sport is also popular) to compete in the 41-mile Oahu to Molokai race with clubs from Hawaii, other Pacific islands and the mainland U.S.

Who has not visualized dropping anchor in the calm waters of a lagoon and falling asleep to the gentle sound of trade winds rustling through palm fronds? The romantic idea of setting sail for **SAILING**

CANOE CRAZY

Spend any time gazing out at sea and you're liable to wonder if Tahitians aren't a little canoe crazy. A steady stream of outrigger canoes can always be seen parading offshore, especially at dusk. Canoeing is not only a favored form of exercise, it is also a concrete link with the past. The sleek fiberglass boats you see today are updated versions of the earlier wooden outriggers known as *tipairua*. These single- and double-hulled canoes reached lengths of over 100 feet and ferried the first settlers across the Polynesian archipelago. The pinnacle of canoe celebrations these days is the October and November Hawaiki Nui Va'a canoe race between Huahine, Raiatea, Tahaa and Bora Bora.

the palm-tree-studded shores of French Polynesia is perhaps a universal dream. Fortunately, the dream can become reality.

Ideal weather (both winter and summer), steady trade winds and an abundance of anchorages make French Polynesia one of the great cruising destinations of the seven seas. And there is no better way to explore the islands than by yacht. In fact, the scarcity of roads and airstrips on the more remote islands make sailing the only way to see them. Navigation is generally easy throughout the archipelagos.

Bring along your PADI (or equivalent) open-water certificate if you are an experienced diver. And note that if you answer "yes" to any medical condition on your dive waiver, you will not be permitted to dive without a letter from your doctor.

Although French Polynesia is expensive, groceries and supplies can generally be procured on all but the most remote islands. In some remote areas like the Marquesas, locals will trade produce for items of clothing or other imported products. Excellent charts of the area are available and telecommunications are first rate compared to other South Pacific destinations. (See Chapter Two for entry permit information and island chapters for anchorage information.)

DIVING

Most of the islands of French Polynesia are bounded by reefs where tropical fish of every color and description thrive. Snorkeling, easily learned, is safe and leads you to fascinating underwater worlds. Mask and fins (flippers) are readily available at most hotels. The best snorkeling is found on the outer islands, where marine resources have been less affected by humans.

Snorkelers are apt to see oysters or *pahua*, a large white clam that may be marinated in lime juice and eaten. In addition to having edible flesh, *pahua* shells make nifty soap dishes; you may see one in your hotel room.

Echinoderms may not sound like a household term, but you will undoubtedly see them while snorkeling or on a reef walk. Some of the familiar or recognizable echinoderms are sea cucumbers, sea urchins, starfish, brittle stars and feather-stars. Most are plankton feeding, and the sea cucumbers, which appear to just lie on the sand all day, actually perform a very important function to the lagoon community. By feeding on organic matter in the sand they plough up the sea bottom and are vital to the health of the ecosystem.

One echinoderm you do not want to get to know intimately is the sea urchin. Most are algal grazers and this important task allows corals to flourish. They do, however, have spines that can be very painful if stepped on, and some species have spines that are coated with toxin. They are often found on reefs and some grow in sandy-bottomed lagoons where swimmers might congregate. The only place I've seen this is on Temae Beach on Moorea.

Sharky Waters

Few fears trouble visitors to French Polynesia as much as sharks. And it is true: These are some of the sharkiest waters in the world. That's great news if you are one of the thousands of tourists who thrill at watching these apex predators patrol their domain. But it's bad news if the fear of winding up on the menu keeps you from enjoying the warm and welcoming lagoon waters.

Of the 375 known species of sharks, naturalists agree that only a handful are true man-eaters. The four species most associated with fatal attacks are great whites, tigers, bulls and oceanic white-tips. Great whites (of *Jaws* infamy) are rare in Polynesian waters, and oceanic white-tips forsake the coast for the open seas. Tiger and bull sharks are both found throughout French Polynesia.

The most commonly encountered sharks, though, are mellow black-tips (favored guests at shark feeds), white-tip reef sharks, nurse sharks and lemon sharks. Virtually every bite from these species falls under the "provoked" category. If you tug on the tail of that sleeping nurse shark, or try and catch a panicked black-tip shark, you probably deserve a good bite.

The other common species—the handsome gray reef shark—is a bit of a wild card. Thousands of divers seek them out at Tiputa Pass in the Tuamotus and the Tiki dive site off Moorea every year with nary a problem. Up to eight feet in length, these beautiful sharks are usually only seen by scuba divers outside the reefs, where deep water and passes draw schools of bait fish.

Like any wild predator, however, grays can become aggressive if competing for food (spear fishing) or territory. In summer 2004 a surfer was bitten off Huahine in a territorial dispute (the shark won and the surfer had a great story to tell). If you see agitated behavior—head-wagging, a hunched back and dropped pectoral fins—move away or leave the water.

Far more dangerous are tiger and bull sharks. Named for adolescent stripes that fade as the sharks mature, tiger sharks haunt deep reefs and the open water beyond the reefs. Bull sharks—a broad-headed species that can grow to 12 feet—prefer coastal areas, particularly estuaries.

The best way to stay safe is to always treat sharks with respect and check with locals before swimming in unknown waters. Other common-sense precautions include not swimming alone or at night.

Keep on eye on where the locals swim, or better yet, bring your snorkel mask to check out the lagoon for yourself.

DIVE SIGHTS   The undersea attractions of French Polynesia vary a great deal from archipelago to archipelago. The coral growth on the barrier reef of the Windward Islands (Tahiti and Moorea) is dense, according to scuba diving savant Carl Roessler, but "not terribly interesting."

Corals are low growing and do not reach much more than several feet in height above the reef mass. This lack of development may be explained by excessive freshwater runoff. Another possible explanation is that by remaining squat, the corals may be responding environmentally by protecting themselves from violent wave action during storms. It is also possible that the land masses themselves block nutrient-bearing currents from reaching the coral colonies.

The most complex coral colonies in the Society Group, and hence those best for viewing, are found in the quiet sheltered lagoons of Raiatea and Huahine, where the fragile coral communities are protected from the pounding surf.

The Tuamotu Group, which consists almost solely of atolls, offers a much different environment for coral, and is in fact better for coral viewing. There are no mountains and no freshwater runoff to limit coral development. The reef corals, while still low growing, are far more massive and geologically older communities. Here one finds huge tabular structures two to four yards in diameter. The squat coral growth is a response to intermittent wave action and fierce ocean currents, but food and nutrient supply is very rich, resulting in branching corals found in the quiet protection of the lagoons.

Unlike the high islands, fish life is generally more dense in the Tuamotu reef systems. The low-growing coral offers good protection against predators and multitudes of soldierfish, masked butterfly fish, Achilles tangs and parrot fish dart through the waters. Some of the schools of tangs seem so nonchalant that they flock around divers as if tame.

SURFING IN TAHITI

Tahitians love to surf almost as much as they love to canoe. For good reason. Tahiti, Moorea and Huahine all have famous breaks that can challenge both beginners and pros alike. Conflicts between tourists and locals aren't common, but it pays to ask permission and approach in the spirit of friendship. Local boys and girls aren't the only ones who can get territorial when it comes to sharing the waves. In the summer of 2004, a surfer was attacked and bitten by a gray reef shark that apparently felt his waters were getting a bit too crowded.

The reef shallows in the Tuamotu are often narrow. From the fringing *motu* or islets to the outer reef's drop-off may be only 30 feet. Being extremely close to deep water, these marine gardens are exposed to pelagics such as gray sharks or manta rays that often suddenly appear from the depths and, just as unexpectedly, disappear.

Undoubtedly the most popular island to dive is Rangiroa. Its most famous marine features are its two passes. A diver exploring the passes will witness the daily movement of a tremendous amount of tidal water. The deep channels are barren, with the exception of a few coral heads, and marine life tends to congregate on the shallower side walls of the passages.

Divers tend to visit "Rangi," as it's called, for one major reason—sharks. Large numbers tend to dwell in the passes and divers can sometimes see schools of more than 300 sharks. One survey estimated at least 1500 gray sharks inhabit this area at any given time. The creatures align themselves against the sides of the channel facing the current and hold their positions much like aqueous hawks holding stationary, waiting for the right moment to attack from on high. Divers who sweep through the channels at the same speed as the current are ignored by the sharks. This blasé attitude changes rapidly if a diver anchors himself to one of the scattered coral heads and spears a fish. At that point up to ten gray sharks might charge the diver, posing a very real threat.

In addition to sharks and reef fish, divers in French Polynesia are apt to run into manta rays, moray eels, barracuda and other pelagics such as tuna. The very lucky might get to see a great hammerhead or tiger shark.

You will see a flying fish or two when traveling any distance on a boat. If you are lucky you may also observe some dolphins at play, and if you're really lucky, a sea turtle, although they are still actively hunted by locals and are harder to spot.

SURFING

Tahiti has excellent surf—nearly in the same category as Hawaii's awesome rideable waves. For several years Tahiti has hosted the Tahiti Gotcha Pro Surf Competition in April/May at Teahupoo in Tahiti Iti. Teahupoo is famous for its "killer left." (Check out www.surf.pf.) Surfing has grown ever more popular in French Polynesia, specifically in Tahiti, Moorea, Raiatea and, particularly with Americans, in Huahine. The west coast of Huahine is the most common destination for those who visit the islands just to surf, although Raiatea (west coast), Moorea (north coast) and Tahiti (west coast) have some seasonally respectable breaks. Tahitian surfers have traditionally been friendly to *popa'a* (foreign) surfers, but this has changed somewhat, perhaps due to the influence of some visiting Hawaiians who sport a serious anti-*haole* (white) attitude. If you want to get along with the locals, don't arrive at surf spots as part of a large group. Local surfing etiquette calls for shaking hands with your Tahitian colleagues when you first paddle out to a lineup (even if you don't know any of them). Consider surfing off hours (early a.m.) and off days (weekdays), and catch the waves they don't. Most locals really don't want visitors around; they're often tight-lipped about good breaks. However, the offer of a beer, a T-shirt or a surf leash can loosen things up. With a proposal to leave a board or wetsuit behind, you'll have an instant escort!

There are two surf seasons: summer (from November to March) and winter (from April to October). The summer swells come from the north. That means if there are 15-foot waves breaking in Hawaii, chances are there will be eight-foot waves on the north coasts of the Society Islands a few days later. Moorea's north coast, with its reef breaks, is considered better than Tahiti's north coast, which has almost exclusively beach breaks. The northeast trade winds intensify after mid-morning during this season so it's best to surf early in the day. The best time for quality surf is actually in the winter, as the big winter storms from Antarctica and New Zealand provide plenty of swells to the Society Islands' southern shores. When the swells come out of deep water and break along the reefs, the result can be very powerful, hollow waves. Most of the breaks tend to be passes in the reef system and a long paddle is usually obligatory.

The main hazard for surfers is getting bashed up on the reefs. There have also been problems with stonefish and, to a lesser extent with sharks, crown-of-thorns starfish and sea urchins. Stonefish are exceptionally nasty, and I've heard several reports of encounters with these less-than-cuddly creatures. The best way to avoid them is to shuffle your feet instead of high stepping it across the water. Walking on one would seriously spoil your surfing holiday.

WHERE ARE THE NATURAL RESERVES?

Given the worldwide destruction of the natural environment and the specific threats imposed by development in French Polynesia, one might expect local government to have instituted a coherent environmental policy. This hasn't happened. Throughout the years there have been ad hoc environmental protections, but no cohesive plan has been implemented. Furthermore, there are no terrestrial reserves in the Society Islands. Moorea, the Marquesas Group and Rapa are all at risk for environmental degradation. The Marquesas do have four, albeit inadequate, reserves on Ei'ao, Hatutu, Ilot de Sable and Mohotani.

According to the *Surf Report*, use any board that works well in hollow waves up to eight feet—the best surf is in the six- to eight-foot range. It is recommended that you bring removable fins and spares as well as an extra leash. A wetsuit might be useful to prevent tit rash and to save your skin should you encounter the reef.

Shop Tahiti sells boards and accessories and has four locations on the island of Tahiti, including one in Vaima Center. Like everything else here, repairs and gear are expensive. ~ Papeete; 43-74-94. Maraamu Stock, on a small street off the mountainside of the Vaima Center, has an excellent selection of surfboards, boogie boards, wetsuits, bags and other accessories. ~ 10 Passage Cardella; 42-67-71.

For more detailed information on where to surf in French Polynesia, I recommend that you get a copy of *The Surf Report*, Vol. 6, #4. Send US$6 to P.O. Box 1028, Dana Point, CA 92629, USA; 714-496-7849.

WIND-SURFING

Windsurfing (or sailboarding) and kite sailing have become very popular in Tahiti over the last decade. There's no lack of warm water and gentle breezes in French Polynesia, so it is an excellent place for experts—neophytes may be another matter. Many of the hotels advertise windsurfing and kite sailing as an activity, but you may find the equipment dilapidated or green with algae from lack of use. Coral heads in shallower areas of the lagoons may present a hazard for beginners who are not able to traverse deeper waters.

FISHING

Deep-sea fishing has been a popular recreational activity for visitors to French Polynesia for generations. By my reckoning there are over 30 charter fishing boats in the islands. Gamefishing was a favorite pastime of American pulp western writer Zane Grey, who had his own fishing camp in Tahiti in the 1930s. Game fish include marlin, sailfish, barracuda and other pelagics. If you plan to eat the fish you catch, stick with pelagics—deep-water fish. (Some reef fish carry *Ciguatera,* a rather unpleasant disease.)

The world-renowned Tahiti Billfish Tournament draws big-name international competitors who vie for coveted trophy-size fish. For the recreational angler, fishing charters are regularly available on most of the islands. Look for island-specific information in the "Fishing" section of each chapter.

RIDING STABLES

There is no shortage of horseback riding opportunities on Tahiti, Moorea, Raiatea and in the Marquesas Islands. The horses are usually of Marquesan stock. Information on riding is provided island by island in this book. Figure on spending about 2500 CFP per hour.

HIKING

Hiking has become a popular activity in French Polynesia; however, it's primarily favored by visitors or French residents rather than locals. There are a few professionals who lead day trips on Tahiti, Moorea and Bora Bora, all of whom are listed in the "Hiking" sections found in the area chapters. Trails are numerous on all the islands, but are often not clearly marked, and some may be dangerous. Also be sure to check your pack and clothing for island centipedes, which can produce a bite as painful as a bee sting. It's not a smart idea to take off into the rainforest unless you have a reasonably accurate idea of where to go. Though the likelihood of being confronted by wild beasts is nil, every year a trekker or two gets lost.

BIKING

I don't recommend bringing your bike to French Polynesia unless you plan to spend most of your time on the more remote islands that are not overrun by automobiles. Riding a bicycle in Tahiti or Bora Bora can be hazardous. But despite the dangers, a rental bicycle is a handy way to explore a smaller island. Just be careful.

Take a hat, wear protective clothing and be sure to wear sunscreen. Make sure you ride with the traffic. Take plenty of water with you, too.

As a counterpoint to these cautionary notes, reader Jay Jacobson biked all of the major islands except Tahiti and tells us that neither traffic nor dogs were a problem, though in some of the islands he found it difficult to find a decent rental bike to ride.

Many of the larger hotels used to provide their guests with free bikes; they now rent them at exorbitant prices.

GOLF

The only golf course in Tahiti is Olivier Breaud International Golf Course, also known as Golf d'Atimaono, a par 72 located at Atimaono in the Papara district. The area was formerly a cotton plantation established during the American Civil War to provide Europe with the fiber that was in short supply. The course was designed by Bob Baldock & Son, a Costa Mesa, California, firm that has designed links throughout the U.S. and Mexico. It features expansive fairways, two artificial lakes and lush greens planted with hybrid Bermuda grass brought in from Hawaii.

The facility is a 45-minute drive from Papeete. The course is open daily from 7 a.m. to 6 p.m. year-round. It includes a clubhouse, restaurant, pro shop, pool, tennis courts and driving range. Green fees are 5000 CFP. Clubs can be rented for around 2500 CFP per day. ~ PK 41, Papara; 57-43-41.

For more than two decades, plans have been in the works to build a golf course on Moorea. One project after another fell through, but the dream may be closer to reality now than ever before. Pacific Golf and Resort Development Company is slated to turn 52.5 acres of swampy land near Tamae Airport into an international-class, 18-hole golf course. The project also includes a Polynesian-style five-star hotel and 60 guest houses built along the course. Construction is expected to begin in 2003.

Camping in French Polynesia is restricted to a few campgrounds on Tahiti, Moorea, Bora Bora, Huahine and Raiatea. These campgrounds are always private; there are no facilities in parks or areas such as wildlife refuges. Campground habitués are typically backpackers or students looking to save a few francs rather than Audubon Society members in search of rare birds. Developed campgrounds often charge almost as much for permission to pitch your tent as a dorm bed would cost. Most have kitchen facilities in addition to communal laundry and bathrooms. Some now rent tents.

For those interested in spending time camping in the wilderness, guides on Tahiti will take visitors on camping trips. With permission, overnight camping is sometimes also allowed on the *motu*. Always clear it with the proper authorities before heading out. A local pension operator will probably know whom to contact.

CAMPING

FOUR

Tahiti

It has been 200 years since Captain James Cook first anchored off its shores, yet the island of Tahiti still evokes a sense of the idyllic South Seas. The gardenia scent of the *tiare* blossoms, the swaying palm trees silhouetted by the tropical moon and all the other clichés that Hollywood and a thousand novels have foisted upon us, come to mind.

So what is Tahiti really like?

An island in French Polynesia, there are grains of truth in the romantic silver screen and pulp fiction portrayals of Tahiti. Though sometimes Tahiti is invoked to mean French Polynesia in its entirety, technically, this is incorrect.

Tahiti is actually the largest island in French Polynesia, with an area of 651 square miles (1432 square kilometers), and can best be visualized as a figure eight on its side. The larger section of the island (Tahiti Nui) is connected to the smaller section (Tahiti Iti) by the narrow Isthmus of Taravao. The island's rugged terrain, marked by numerous rivers and deep valleys, is dotted with precipitous green peaks. The highest points are Mt. Orohena at 7334 feet (2236 meters) and Mt. Aorai at 6783 feet (2068 meters). Both peaks are often obscured by wispy clouds. Given Tahiti's mountainous interior, it's no surprise that the vast majority of the 170,000 inhabitants live on the coastal plain or fringes of the island's perimeter.

Tahiti is surrounded by a barrier reef on nearly all sides, creating a tranquil lagoon protected from the pounding surf. The coastline that encircles the island is about 95 nautical miles. The average year-round temperature is a mild 78°F (25.9°C) and it can be humid—up to 98 percent to be precise.

One main road makes a 70-mile (113-kilometer) circuit of the larger section of the island (Tahiti Nui), and comes to a dead end in the outer reaches of the smaller part of the island (Tahiti Iti). PK (Point Kilométrique) markers start at zero in Papeete and progress around the island clockwise and counterclockwise. Resembling miniature tombstones, they are painted a two-tone red and white, and are easily recognized on the roadside. When circumnavigating the island, it's good idea to pay attention to them. There are few street signs outside of Papeete so residents use mileage (or kilometrage in this case) to pinpoint their location.

Upon reaching the opposite side of the island (PK 60) at the Isthmus of Tara-vao, motorists may either complete the circle or explore one of three dead-end roads in Tahiti Iti. The main road around Tahiti Nui, which follows the perimeter of the island, is well maintained but tends to be narrow and overcrowded, particularly during commute hours (8 a.m. and 5 p.m.).

Tahiti has a rich cover of volcanic soil that nourishes a verdant tropical rainforest. From the air the island appears to be carpeted with a luxuriant layer of vegetation. However, biologically, the island is impoverished compared to biotically diverse islands such as Papua New Guinea, the Solomon Islands or even Fiji. Why impoverished? Tahiti is far from Australasia, the main source of its flora and fauna. Simply put, Tahiti's location at the center of the Polynesian Triangle, far from the Asian landmass, made it a difficult journey for most plants and animals and out of the natural reach of most of the flora and fauna that would otherwise have populated the island.

The coconut palm, perhaps the one species of flora most associated with the tropics, is very prominent on the landscape, growing wild from the shoreline to all but the very highest mountains. Other trees such as kapok, *pandanus*, *mape* (Tahitian chestnut), ironwood and giant bamboo are also present—some wild and some planted in yards and villages throughout the island. There are numerous plants and trees introduced by Polynesians or Europeans, including mango, breadfruit, papaya, avocado, orange, lime passion fruit and *pamplemousse*, a delicious species of grapefruit. Flowering plants are everywhere, either growing wild or in the gardens of private homes and hotels. Some of the more common species include gardenia, hibiscus, oleander, frangipani, bird of paradise, poinsettia, bougainvillea and ginger. Only two of the more widespread flowers, the *tiare* (*Gardenia tahitiensis*), which seems to be tucked behind the ear of every Tahitian, and the *pua*, are native to Tahiti. A rare and endangered white gardenia, *Tiare apetahi*, is endemic to the island of Raiatea.

Land fauna is scant. The ubiquitous rat was first brought to Tahiti by Polynesians, as were dogs and pigs. Other than insects and lizards, birds represent the most numerous fauna. Though some birds such as herons, flycatchers and kingfishers are native to the island, many of the indigenous varieties were hunted to extinction or pushed out of their niches by introduced species such as the myna bird.

In pre-contact times (prior to European influence) Raiatea and Huahine were the most important islands in Eastern Polynesia. It was only after the Europeans arrived that Tahiti became the center of missionary activity and trade, and eventually the focus for colonization. This is probably why the name *Tahiti* translates as "far removed" or "at the periphery." Most likely, Tahiti was settled after Raiatea and may have been considered an outer province. Today, ironically, Tahiti is hardly a province—indeed, it is the most densely populated and the most developed island in all of French Polynesia.

According to the latest archaeological evidence, Tahiti was settled sometime after A.D. 500 (after the Marquesas and Cook Islands). There is speculation that it may have been populated earlier but solid evidence has not yet been found.

Though Samuel Wallis was the first European to arrive (in 1767) it was the three voyages made by Captain James Cook from 1776 to 1777 that really put

Tahiti on the map. Cook was the first to launch a full-fledged scientific expedition to Tahiti, complete with a botanist, astronomer and illustrator. The missionaries came on the heels of the explorers and Tahiti fell under the influence of both the Catholic and Protestant churches. Within decades, much of the native population was converted to one form of Christianity or another. Meanwhile, the French, who had been slowly consolidating their influence over the islands from the late 18th century, declared Tahiti their protectorate in 1842. By the time Paul Gauguin, Tahiti's most famous visitor, arrived in 1891 with the idea of creating art and seeing, in his words, "no one but savages," much of the pre-European religion and the cultural fabric of Polynesian life had been lost forever.

Life in modern-day Tahiti centers around its capital, Papeete, but this is only one of 20 municipalities or districts on the island. Still, of Tahiti's approximately 180,000 residents, most live in or around the capital. A bustling city with a preponderance of smoke-belching trucks, cars and rush-hour traffic, nothing could be further from the languid, storybook South Seas image of Tahiti than this minimetropolis. Everything you could possibly want is here—discos, restaurants, travel agencies, internet cafés, baguettes, Beaujolais and a sophisticated 21st-century populace eager to consume whatever pop culture from North America or Europe washes up on the beach.

Although traditional culture no longer sustains the population of contemporary French Polynesia, there are still glimmers of the old Polynesian ways, even on this seemingly tarnished isle of love. Take a rental car for an hour's drive down to Tautira on the easternmost edge of Tahiti Iti and you will enter a world far removed from the clogged streets of Papeete. The distant sounds of pounding surf on the barrier reef and the spectacle of towering green mountains are unchanged since Captain Cook's arrival. Here fishing nets dangle gently from sturdy racks on the water's edge and the tranquility is interrupted only by the hollow thud of a coconut that occasionally crashes to earth.

As one long-time resident of Tahiti told me, "This island has the best and worst of all things. It will take some persistence, but smart travelers with good will and some time on their hands can discover its secrets."

Papeete

The translation of Papeete is "water (from a) basket," which most likely means that it was once a place where Tahitians came to fetch water. Indeed, at the time of captains Wallis and Cook, Papeete was a marshland with a few scattered residents. The town didn't attract too much foreign attention until 1818 when Reverend Crook of the London Missionary Society settled in Papeete with his family.

Papeete began to grow in earnest when Queen Pomare made it her capital in the 1820s and sailing ships began to use the protected harbor, which was a much safer anchorage than Matavai Bay to the east. By the 1830s, it had become a regular port of call for New England whalers. A number of stores, billiard halls and makeshift bars appeared on the waterfront to handle the business. When the French made Tahiti a protectorate in 1842–1843,

Text continued on page 110.

Tahiti

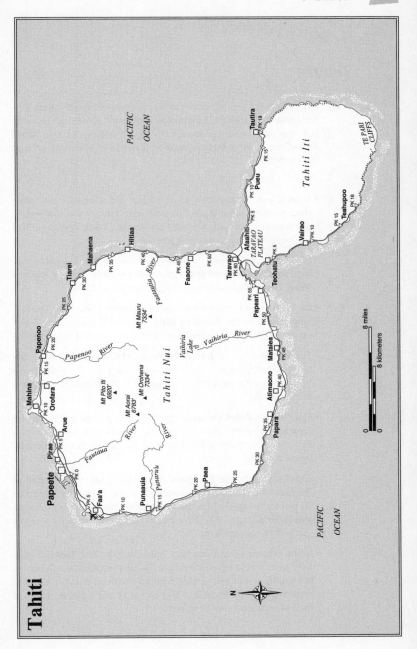

PACIFIC
OCEAN

Tautira
PK 18

PK 15

PK 10   Pueu

PK 5   *Tahiti Iti*

TE PARI
CLIFFS

Afaahiti

*TARAVAO
PLATEAU*   PK 5   Teahupoo
PK 18

PK 15   Vairao
PK 10

Taravao
PK 60   Teohatu
PK 55   PK 5

Papeari
PK 50

Mahaena   Hitiaa

Tiarei   PK 30   PK 35   PK 40

PK 25   *Fautaua River*   PK 45   Faaone   PK 50

Papenoo   PK 20

Mahina   PK 15   *Papenoo   River*

PK 10   Orofara

Arue   PK 5

Pirae

Papeete   PK 0   *Tahiti Nui*

Faa'a   PK 5

PK 10   Punaauia   *Mt Mauu
7334'*

PK 15   PK 20   Paea   *Mt Pito Iti
6920'*

PK 25   *Mt Aorai
6763'*   *Mt Orohena
7334'*

PK 30   *Vaihiria
Lake*   *Vaihiria   River*

Papara   PK 35

Atimaono   PK 40

Mataiea   PK 45

PACIFIC
OCEAN

*PACIFIC
OCEAN*

N

0   8 miles

0   8 kilometers

Tahiti

When visiting Tahiti, it's better to stay outside of town: Papeete traffic is onerous, parking is difficult and you'll want some fresh air without the noise and gas fumes. I'd suggest staying at the **Tahiti InterContinental Beachcomber** (page 153), which can arrange for car rentals.

Day 1

- Have a leisurely breakfast at your hotel and start your tour after the rush hour (after 8 a.m.) to avoid the traffic. If you can wait to eat breakfast until you get into Papeete, visit **Le Rétro** (page 120) for a cup of java and morning pastries.

- While in Papeete, check out **Marché Papeete** (the municipal market), stroll the **waterfront esplanade** and peek into the **Robert Wan Pearl Museum** (page 130) at the Vaima Center.

- Begin the day tour by moving clockwise around the island. The first stop should be the **Tomb of King Pomare V** (page 136). (A sign on the ocean side of the road marks the access road to the tomb.)

- The former home of **James Norman Hall** (co-author of *Mutiny on the Bounty*) (page 137) is the next stop. Look for Hall's green house after crossing a small bridge over the Vaipoopo River on the mountainside.

- Head for the **Point Venus** (page 138) picnic ground and swimming area. Several stores at a road junction (including the Venustar market) and a Poste sign are the clues to the correct turnoff that will be on the left-hand side.

- Continue on to the **Arahoho Blowhole** (page 140), located at the base of a steep cliff on the mountainside of the road. Another 90 meters on the right is the entrance to the three **Fa'aurumai Waterfalls** (page 140). Drive inland 1.3 kilometers. Bring a swimsuit and insect repellent.

- In the evening on the way back home, stop at **The Dahlia** (page 144), one of the better family-style Chinese restaurants in Tahiti. It's reasonably priced and located right off the main drag. Or, if you're returning to Papeete, grab a bite to eat at the *roulottes*, the local food service vans on the waterfront.

Day 2 • This will be a day devoted mostly to museums and parks. Jump on the freeway towards Paea (the opposite direction from yesterday) and turn off at the Musée de Tahiti et des Iles sign.

• Drive onwards (to Paea) to visit **Marae Arahurahu** (page 150). There's a sign on the main road at the turnoff. The rectangular pyramid is about the size of a tennis court and is completely reconstructed.

• Continue on and stop at the **Harrison W. Smith Botanical Garden** (page 162) and the **Paul Gauguin Museum** (page 162), located directly opposite the gardens. Have a snack at the museum's restaurant if you have time.

• If you didn't have a chance to visit the Paul Gauguin Museum's restaurant, on your way back to Papeete you can stop for a meal at the **Casablanca Restaurant** (page 156) at the Taina Marina in Punaauia. The cuisine is French and Tahitian; the atmosphere is lively and informal.

Day 3 • This is the outer-limits-of-Tahiti day—a journey to **Tahiti Iti**, the least visited area in the island. Prepare mentally for a full-day drive. Take the coastal road towards Paea, past the Paul Gauguin Museum, into the town of **Taravao** (page 160). Have lunch in Taravao at one of the better restaurants such as **Chez Myriam** (page 168) or **L'Escale** (page 168).

• Visit the spectacular vista point at **Afaahiti** (page 173), a half kilometer outside of Taravao on the east coast road. The Taravao Plateau sign is posted on your right, just before the school.

• Continue down the road another 18 kilometers to the village of **Tautira**. Just before the village you'll pass the Vaitepiha River, which empties into Vaitepiha Bay. This is as far as you can go on the east coast road.

• You now have a decision to make. If it's still early in the afternoon, go back to Taravao and explore the other coastal road leading to Teahupoo and head back to Papeete the way you came. Or simply return to Papeete taking the other coast road (via Mahina) all the way back to town.

the military came on the scene and in their footsteps came French Catholic priests and nuns.

In 1884, a fire destroyed almost half of Papeete, which resulted in an ordinance prohibiting the use of native building materials. Not much of consequence happened until 1906, when huge waves, the result of a cyclone, wiped out a number of homes and businesses. In 1914, two German men-of-war bombarded Papeete, sinking the only French naval vessel in the harbor.

Today, the population of greater Papeete is around 135,000. It is French Polynesia's capital and only real city, and continues to be a major South Pacific port of call for freighters, ocean liners and yachts. Papeete is *the* center of commerce and government. It is the site of the French High Commissioner's residence, the Territorial Assembly, the tourist bureau, the post office and telecommunications center, the banks, travel agencies, airlines, hospitals, and every other conceivable service.

Since the early 1960s, Papeete has undergone a construction boom necessary to support its rising population. Although growth was inevitable, much of it can be attributed to the growth of tourism infrastructure and France's erstwhile nuclear testing program.

The expansion has been at the expense of some of Papeete's beauty, but despite new apartments and offices, the town still has the provincial charm of a French colonial capital. There are whitewashed houses, buildings of painted wood with large verandas and corrugated tin roofs, narrow streets, parks, street vendors, an outdoor market and a profusion of odors ranging from pungent copra (dried coconut meat) to the aroma of frying steaks. When the breeze blows from the mountains you can catch the sweet fragrance of the *Tiare Tahiti*, the national flower.

Papeete is designed for walking. The sidewalks and avenues bordering the public market are lined with vendors selling shell necklaces, straw hats, sandwiches, sweet fried breads, pastries and candy. The aisles of the Chinese shops are crammed with cookware, rolls of brightly colored cloth, canned goods from New Zealand and the United States, mosquito coils and imports of every variety. You get the feeling that if you poke around long enough, you might discover a preserved 1000-year-old duck egg.

The best time to explore the narrow streets and browse through the stores is in the cool of the morning. Otherwise, fumes from cars and heat from the asphalt can be oppressive. A stroll through Papeete should be done in a leisurely manner, with several rest breaks at any of the many outdoor cafés and snack bars. There you can sit at tables shielded by canopies, sip a local Hinano beer or eat ice cream and watch the procession of tourists and locals go by. On Sunday mornings, activities cease and Papeete becomes a sleepy provincial town—it's also a good time to visit the municipal *marché*.

Unless you debark from a cruise ship, you will enter Papeete at Faa'a (yes, that is three vowels in row) Airport, 3.1 miles (5 kilometers) west of downtown. There is not much to see in Faa'a or its environs. The area near the airport is undeveloped, consisting of ramshackle homes inhabited mostly by the unemployed. There are, however, a few impressive hotels along the waterfront south of the airport, specifically the elegant InterContinental Beachcomber and the Maeva Beach. Heading south, away from Papeete, the area becomes more suburban in character, especially in the more affluent communities of Punaauia and Paea, which are 15 to 20 minutes by car from town. The stretch of road from Papeete to Punaauia is a freeway, or the closest thing that Tahiti has to a freeway. However, during weekday morning rush hour, after 7 a.m., the two-lane road is typically bumper-to-bumper with BMWs, Renaults and Volkswagens, which, when combined with the local buses or *Le Truck,* can make for a 45-minute commute

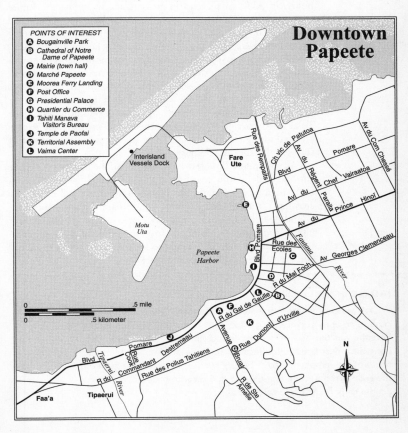

Downtown Papeete

POINTS OF INTEREST
- **A** Bougainville Park
- **B** Cathedral of Notre Dame of Papeete
- **C** Mairie (town hall)
- **D** Marché Papeete
- **E** Moorea Ferry Landing
- **F** Post Office
- **G** Presidential Palace
- **H** Quartier du Commerce
- **I** Tahiti Manava Visitor's Bureau
- **J** Temple de Paofai
- **K** Territorial Assembly
- **L** Vaima Center

on the 6.2-mile (10-kilometer) segment of road into town. The same procession begins in the opposite direction after 4 p.m.

The short four-lane "freeway" ends just short of downtown Papeete and drops motorists on the main drag, Boulevard Pomare, which runs along the waterfront. This is the main artery flowing through Papeete. Once an array of clapboard warehouses and run-down shacks, Boulevard Pomare is now dominated by sleek shops. Proceed on it and you'll pass the Tahiti Manava Visitor's Bureau and all the banks, airlines, nightclubs, boutiques and travel agencies you could ever hope for.

In August 1999, at the personal recommendation of former President Gaston Flosse, a third lane ("*la troisième voie*") was added to Boulevard Pomare. The lane begins in Faa'a and ends on Avenue Prince Hinoï, in downtown Papeete. Together with a new roundabout, the construction has helped ease the bumper-to-bumper traffic Tahitians suffer during morning and evening rush hours. In addition to road improvements, including the future construction of a large underground parking lot, Boulevard Pomare's entire seaside is undergoing a major facelift. At Fare Tauhiti, the *maison de la culture* (at the very beginning of Boulevard Pomare), a vast piece of land adjacent to the lagoon was created by landfill. On the site is a wonderful new waterfront promenade, grandstand seating for 5000, shops, restaurants and other facilities for the annual *Heiva* festival and other events. An esplanade connects the complex—known as Place To'ata—to Fare Manihini downtown and protects the yachts moored along the waterfront from the perpetual onslaught of traffic on Boulevard Pomare.

As you follow Boulevard Pomare north, the harbor is on your left-hand side. If you bear left on this road you'll follow the contours of the bay, passing the French naval base and eventually crossing a bridge. This will bring you to Fare Ute and Motu Uta, a landfill-created shipyard and dock area where the majority of inter-island vessels are berthed. From the air or on a map this resembles a huge mandible ready to shut its maw on all those expensive yachts and container ships.

JAILHOUSE BLUES

Church was not where you would find Herman Melville during his 19th-century sojourn in Tahiti. Long a foe of missionaries, Melville's Calabooza Beretani was the jail where Herman Melville was imprisoned in 1842. Long since destroyed, it was located on Boulevard Pomare, two blocks south of the Temple de Paofai. During his time here Melville gathered the grist for his second book, *Omoo*, and accurately described life during the early French colonial period.

When the wind blows from the direction of the docks, Papeete's air is filled with the pungent aroma of copra (dried coconut meat), one of the island's main exports. You will find the source of the smell in Fare Ute, where the copra boats are moored and where there is a coconut-oil processing plant. Here the vessels unload the crop they have picked up from the outer islands and exchange it for store-bought commodities. Watching the pallets containing beer, rice, drums of kerosene, sacks of flour, cases of canned butter and jugs of wine being loaded onto the rusty steamers gives you a feeling of the old days when all travel and trade were done by these boats.

Beyond the waterfront, Papeete has numerous neighborhoods with names like Patutoa, Orae, Mamao, Puea and other Tahitian monikers. These tend to be quiet, residential areas with perhaps a corner grocery store or a bakery. Located north from town (in the opposite direction from the airport) are the suburbs of Mahina and Arue.

SIGHTS

A good point of reference, and the best place to begin your tour of Papeete, is on Boulevard Pomare at Fare Manihini, which is home to the **Tahiti Manava Visitor's Bureau**. Situated on the waterfront, directly opposite the beginning of Rue Paul Gauguin, it consists of a cluster of brown buildings designed to resemble traditional Tahitian *fares* (homes). As you walk in the entrance there is an interactive map that shows the locations of shops, landmarks, airline offices and the like. Simply press the button on the board and look for the corresponding light of the shop, airline office or landmark to blink. Inside the office is an information desk staffed by English speakers who can field your questions. The walls are lined with racks of brochures, lists of hotels and pensions, ferry schedules and other data, including *Le Truck* schedules. There are often art exhibitions showing at Fare Manihini, as well. (There is also an information office at Faa'a Airport.) Closed Saturday and Sunday. ~ Boulevard Pomare; 50-57-12; www.tahiti-manava.com, e-mail infos@tahiti-manava.pf.

Next to Fare Manihini is a new reception area for cruise ships called **Vaiete Square**. In the evenings, colorful fountains of light illuminate the square and give it a carnival atmosphere. Many food vendors have *roulottes* (vans) with fancy neon signs. They gather here to set up barbecues and stools around their vans and open up mobile restaurants. The new square also features a bandstand where local entertainers often spontaneously perform as locals dance to the music and children zip about on roller skates. Clean new public restrooms and a building that *roulotte* vendors can use to wash dishes ensure good sanitation for the crowds that invariably gather.

If you walk north along the **waterfront esplanade** you will pass the local fishing fleet, the Moorea-bound ferries that deliver people and goods daily to Tahiti's closest island neighbor, the boats that journey to the outer Society Islands, and maybe a French naval vessel or two. In the late afternoon you may see the fishermen bring their catch ashore here.

Walk south from Fare Manihini along the waterfront and you'll see the many aforementioned yachts, as well as *pirogues* (racing canoes) stacked upside down under trees. Cross Boulevard Pomare just before Avenue Bruat and you'll find yourself at **Bougainville Park**, which was originally named Albert Park after the Belgian king and World War I hero. The name was later changed to Bougainville Park to honor the French explorer. On sunny days people usually occupy its concrete benches or enjoy the shade of its huge Indian almond tree. Of the two cannons prominently displayed, the one nearest the post office is off the *Seeadler*, the vessel skippered by the notorious World War I sea raider Count von Luckner, whose boat ran aground on Mopelia Atoll in the Leeward Islands. The other belonged to the *Zelee*, the French navy boat sunk during a German raid on Papeete in 1914. ~ Boulevard Pomare.

Adjacent to the park is the main **post office** cum telecommunications center, facing the harbor. Post office hours are: Monday through Thursday 7:30 a.m. to 3 p.m., Friday 7 a.m. to 2 p.m., and Saturday 8 a.m. to 10 a.m. ~ Boulevard Pomare; 41-42-42; www.opt.pf. The **philatelic department,** a big revenue earner for Tahiti, is on the ground level at the Boulevard Pomare entrance. ~ 41-43-35; www.tahiti-postoffice.com.

Vaima Center is a modern, four-level, block-square shopping center located directly across from the waterfront, about one block north of the post office. There are boutiques, banks, travel agencies, airline bureaus, book stores, restaurants and the like. If you find yourself at Vaima Center, you should not have to walk more than two or three blocks to take care of any of the above activities.

The Rue Lagarde, between the Vaima Center and the Fare Tony, is a pedestrian concourse. Many of the paving stones are laid out in a colorful mosaic fashion with patterns that include tropical fish. There's ample space for outdoor cafés, and benches have been placed strategically so that one may relax and observe the coming and going of locals and tourists. It's a great place to rest and soak up the ambience. On Saturday night you can often listen to live street musicians supported by the local vendors.

One block north of Vaima Center and a block from the waterfront is one of the most famous landmarks in Tahiti, the **Marché Papeete** (municipal market), which covers one square city block between Rue 22 September and Rue Francois Cardella. In 1986, the then 131-year-old market underwent a metamorphosis that changed it from a dark, crowded, seedy Casbah to a modern, well-lit, clean place of business. The old marketplace (a charming labyrinth of shabby, cramped stalls flavored by accumulated tropical filth) was one of the last true old-time South Pacific institutions left in Papeete. The new Marché Papeete is an airy, sunshine-filled, double-decked venue resembling something out of the 19th-century gaslight era in Paris or the French Quarter of New Orleans. The upstairs houses tourist souvenir vendors while the ground floor is devoted to fresh fish and produce.

Two blocks north of the market, across Boulevard Pomare, is Quartier du Commerce, a street that has become a haven for shoppers and pedestrians. The well-landscaped street forms an "H" and is graced by stores and cafés on both sides. This is Papeete's second pedestrian byway after Rue Lagarde. Note that the shops are open Saturday afternoon until 2 p.m. and until 5 p.m. most other days.

Just south of the Marché Papeete and across the street from the inland side of Vaima Center is the stately **Cathedral of Notre Dame of Papeete**, which literally rises above the din of honking automobiles and screeching motorbikes that circle around this imposing structure. Located in the very heart of Papeete, it is painted a genteel gray with a red-tiled spire and a red roof. Consecrated in 1875, the church was completely restored in 1987. The original stained glass dates from 1875 and a modern stained-glass window was added in 1988, designed by Deanna de Marigny.

The other major church in town is the Protestant **Temple de Paofai**, which is located on Boulevard Pomare about three blocks southwest of Bougainville Park. Constructed in 1873, this large, handsome structure is supported by two rows of six powerful old oak columns. The ceiling, painted sky blue, is adorned with three superb stained-glass windows. You may want to consider spending part of Sunday at a church in Tahiti, listening to the hymns and studying the women's hats. It's preferable to wear white if you do so. ~ Boulevard Pomare.

EASY MONEY

Behind the Socredo Bank (on the waterfront about 50 yards north of the tourist office) is a small booth with a money-changing facility (providing a lower exchange rate than a commercial bank but sans fee). Why would you need a money changer behind a bank? Convenience. It's open six days a week and is very handy for visitors who happen to be wandering around Papeete on a Saturday and are in need of cash. Closed Sunday.

Two blocks southwest of the cathedral is the **Territorial Assembly**. Constructed in the late 1960s as the chamber of the democratically elected representatives of the French Polynesian government, the modern Territorial Assembly building sits directly over the source of what once was the Papeete River. (The river has since been redirected to nearby Bougainville Park.) In this same area, Queen Pomare once had her home and eventually a royal palace, which, in typical governmental fashion, was not completed until after her death in 1877. Nearby was an exclusive clubhouse for high-ranking military officers and civil servants where Gauguin (while he was still accepted) used to drink absinthe. The clubhouse has long since disappeared. The other important building occupying these grounds is the High Commissioner's residence.

> Now a vacant lot and occasional parking lot, Place Tarahoi was once the home of a clubhouse where Paul Gauguin imbibed absinthe alongside high-ranking military officers and government officials.

Papeete's newest political landmark, situated at the corner of Avenue Bruat and Rue Dumont d'Urville one block east of the actual *Presidence*, is Gaston Flosse's **presidential palace**. The new building, which was completed in 2000, was built in the same style as the ancient military *caserne* that was razed.

Standing directly in front of the Territorial Assembly on Rue du Général de Gaulle is a monument depicting **Pouvanaa a Oopa**, considered one of the greatest contemporary Tahitian leaders. A decorated World War I hero and a courageous Tahitian nationalist, Pouvanaa served as a deputy in Paris for the Tahitian Territorial Assembly. He was later jailed on what many believe were trumped-up charges by the metropolitan French government and exiled from his beloved Tahiti from 1958 to 1969. After his release (at age 72) he served as an elected official until his death in 1978.

Five blocks north of Pouvanaa's memorial is the **Mairie** (town hall), which was inaugurated in May 1990 by the late French President Francois Mitterand. It is a two-story, 19th century–inspired veranda-style civic complex, reminiscent of colonial South Pacific architecture. Painted dark red, it has dormers and a turret on the roof, which add more eclectic features to this French-influenced edifice. There are also several abstract sculptures around the grounds of the *Mairie* done by Petero, an Easter Islander who resides in Tahiti. ~ Rue Paul Gauguin.

LODGING   Generally speaking, you will have little difficulty finding lodging around Papeete. For most visitors, Tahiti is merely a transit zone to the outer islands of French Polynesia. There are vacancies year-round, with one notable exception: During the *Heiva* celebrations (starting at the end of June and lasting until August) it is virtually impossible to find a hotel room in Papeete. Finding a hotel in late December can also be problematic. If you want to avoid crowds, these periods are not the time to come.

The accommodation possibilities in greater Papeete are divided into two general categories, those in town and those on the beaches of Papeete's suburbs. The major international-class hotels are actually south of the city limits.

While finding a room in Papeete may be easy, you won't get much value for your dollar—inexpensive rooms are scarce. They range from converted private homes with makeshift dorm rooms and communal bath/shower arrangements to spartan family-run hotels. There are also a few individuals with private homes that take in guests. Staying with families can be an inexpensive and often enriching alternative to hotels. Sometimes it affords you a chance to see a side of Tahiti you would otherwise never experience, but rates and services listed are more subject to change than are other types of accommodation.

To avoid surprises, travelers should be aware that the prices for backpacker and budget accommodations range from US$25 for a bed in a shared room to US$45–$60 for a private room with bath in a budget hotel. The least expensive mid-range hotel room in the Papeete area is around 10,000 CFP (around US$100)—and that will not amount to much in the way of amenities. The average mid-range accommodation in town (for example, the Royal Papeete, which is equivalent to an average motel room in the U.S.) will cost around US$125. Note that all hotels charge a 5 percent tourist tax on top of the 3 percent VAT.

One of the better budget accommodations in town is **Mahina Tea**, a no-frills, family-run hotel. There is no pretense of luxury about this two-story, aquamarine-colored concrete structure. It has 16 rooms, each with a private bath, as well as 15 studios with bathrooms and kitchens. The rooms are clean and very basic. The floors are threadbare linoleum and the bathrooms have aging tile. Some of the second-story units have small balconies. Hot water is available from 6 to 11 p.m. Mahina Tea represents a good value for budget travelers, though the roosters can be aggravatingly noisy in the early morning. Guests have noted that the owners are cost-conscious to the point of turning off the hot water in the morning and not permitting cooking at lunchtime. It's a family-owned hotel and it shows. The staff is cordial and in the lobby is a collection of photos and memorabilia. Visitors are as likely to be local students as budget tourists. To find it take Avenue Bruat (off of Boulevard Pomare) and bear right at the gendarmerie. For bookings, write to BP 17, Papeete. No credit cards. ~ Rue de Sainte Amelie; 42-00-97. BUDGET.

Another acceptable choice is the **Victoria Hotel**. The seven air-conditioned rooms are spacious and clean, and they feature nice wooden queen beds, armoires and refrigerators. The bathrooms are modern and fully tiled. The dorm with shared bath and cooking facilities is adequate but slightly overpriced. Recent guests report that this is a quiet spot and that management is friendly. ~ 10 Rue du Commandant Destremeau; 50-70-00, fax 43-27-28. BUDGET TO MODERATE.

Chez Myrna is a tidy private home on the southern fringes of Papeete very near the Faa'a district border. Owned by Walter and Myrna Dammeyer, a friendly middle-aged couple, it is a five-minute walk inland from Rue du Commandant Destremeau and about ten minutes from downtown Papeete. The Dammeyers have two clean, airy rooms with a shared bathroom. Meals are served on a small picnic table on the outside patio and food is reportedly very good. Chez Myrna comes recommended. The tariff includes breakfast. The minimum stay is two nights and a deposit is required. Weekly rates are available, but Chez Myrna does not accept credit cards. ~ Tipaerui Valley; phone/fax 42-64-11, cell 77-09-75; e-mail dammeyer.family@mail.pf. BUDGET.

Located across the street from the main post office, along the main waterfront thoroughfare (Boulevard Pomare), is the **Hotel Tiare Tahiti Noa Noa**. This is an excellent choice in the moderate range, with doubles as low as US$120 per night. The hotel, only five kilometers from the airport, has 38 rooms on five floors; some (the more expensive) have a panoramic view of Papeete's harbor. Large, clean and nicely furnished, the rooms offer air conditioning, TVs, telephones and private bathrooms. Most units have large tiled balconies with good views. Breakfast is available in a dining room downstairs. This is the place to stay in downtown Papeete. ~ 417 Boulevard Pomare, BP 2359; 50-01-00, fax 43-68-47. MODERATE TO DELUXE.

Prince Hinoï Noa Noa, located just off Boulevard Pomare in downtown Papeete, is a fragile 1960s-looking building. It has 72 air-conditioned rooms and the requisite cocktail bar. The rooms, done entirely in pastels, are on the small side but come with television and video. Perhaps the biggest plus is its downtown location, but traffic noise is a definite drawback. ~ Avenue du Prince Hinoï, BP 4545; 42-32-77, fax 42-33-66; e-mail hotelprince hinoi@mail.pf. MODERATE.

Hotel Le Mandarin, which opened in 1988, is one of the newer hotels in downtown Papeete. It has 37 air-conditioned rooms, average in size and quality, and six mini-suites. Among the amenities are television and direct international dialing. It is within walking distance of the Papeete town hall, the waterfront and the business district. Within the hotel complex is Le Plazza, one of the better Chinese restaurants in town. ~ 51 Rue Colette; 50-33-50, fax 42-16-32; e-mail chris.beaumont@mail.pf. MODERATE TO DELUXE.

The **Matavai Hotel, Resort and Sports Centre** in downtown Papeete offers 138 air-conditioned rooms, as well as a conference center, two swimming pools, a hot tub, a fitness center, miniature golf, tennis courts, squash courts and other amenities for those who want to keep active on their holiday. Diving and other activities are available for an additional fee. Two bars and two restaurants round out the offerings. ~ 42-67-67, fax 42-36-90; www.ho telmatavai.pf, e-mail matavai@mail.pf. DELUXE.

DINING

Papeete's eateries vary from inexpensive *roulottes* (vans converted into mini-eateries with collapsible shelves that serve as tables) to fine restaurants worthy of any Parisian's palette. Note that most restaurants in town are closed on Sunday.

Among the *roulottes*, I found **Vesuvio** to have excellent thincrust pizza. The seafood special was topped with mussels, calamari, fish, clams and cheese. **Chez Jimmy** (31 Rue des Écoles; 43-63-32), a Chinese-food specialist, features chow mein, curry beef, chicken and mixed vegetable dishes. Carnivores might want to sample **Chez Robert's** steak with herb butter as well as his own steak sauce. Dinner only. ~ BUDGET.

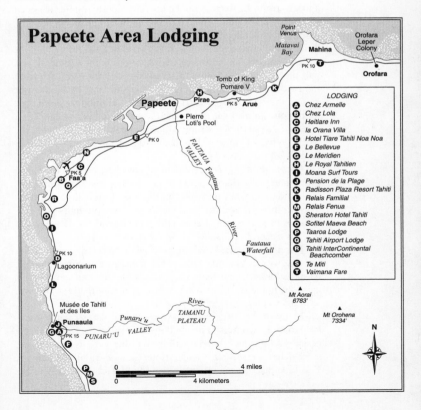

Papeete Area Lodging

LODGING
- Ⓐ Chez Armelle
- Ⓑ Chez Lola
- Ⓒ Heitiare Inn
- Ⓓ la Orana Villa
- Ⓔ Hotel Tiare Tahiti Noa Noa
- Ⓕ Le Bellevue
- Ⓖ Le Meridien
- Ⓗ Le Royal Tahitien
- Ⓘ Moana Surf Tours
- Ⓙ Pension de la Plage
- Ⓚ Radisson Plaza Resort Tahiti
- Ⓛ Relais Familial
- Ⓜ Relais Fenua
- Ⓝ Sheraton Hotel Tahiti
- Ⓞ Sofitel Maeva Beach
- Ⓟ Taaroa Lodge
- Ⓠ Tahiti Airport Lodge
- Ⓡ Tahiti InterContinental Beachcomber
- Ⓢ Te Miti
- Ⓣ Vaimana Fare

Perhaps the best *roulotte* in French Polynesia is **Tikipeue**. It has terrific meals including sashimi, steak with fries, chicken and fish. It is reputedly the only *roulotte* licensed to serve alcohol. Desserts are also first rate—don't miss the vanilla pie (some people actually reserve a slice upon entering, knowing how fast it disappears). Note that in addition to sitting outside the truck at a counter and a table, there's actually room for about six people to sit inside. There is also a tiny bar. ~ Vaiete Square. BUDGET.

Unless it is truly urgent, do not use the public restroom in the kiosk at Vaima Center. Instead, cross the street and use the clean new facilities at Vaiete Square where the cruise ships dock.

The Vaima Center, the popular downtown shopping center, has some good reasonably priced outdoor cafés, **Le Rétro** in particular—an extensive and popular open-air brasserie on the Boulevard Pomare–side of the complex. With two levels, an abundance of tables and glaring neon, this eating and meeting place includes everything from breakfast right through to a late-night coffee. It turns out complete meals, sandwiches, salads and ice cream. Le Rétro is one of the few Papeete restaurants open seven days a week and, open past midnight (it's probably the only place to go for a meal after everything else is shut down). ~ Boulevard Pomare; 42-86-83. BUDGET TO MODERATE.

On the backside of Vaima Center, opposite the cathedral, you will find **L'Oasis du Vaima**, a sprawling outdoor café with tasty sandwiches, pastries and ice cream. It is considered by locals to be among the best outdoor cafés in town. In addition to snack-type food, you can also get dishes such as chicken, beef or fish. It's a nice place to sit with a strong coffee or a cold beer and watch the world go by. ~ Corner of Rue Jeanne d'Arc and Avenue Maréchal Foch; 45-45-01. BUDGET.

Casse-croute, or French-bread sandwiches, are the best local eating bargain and are offered at **Le Motu**, a small takeout sandwich and ice cream eatery also on the side of the Vaima complex. The panini—pressed hot in a waffle iron as you wait—are fantastic even in the heat. I especially recommend the "Paysan." ~ Rue du Général de Gaulle; 41-33-59. BUDGET.

Just upstairs from Le Motu, perched on terraces on either sides of a stairway, is **Vitamine Glacier-Saladerie**. As the name indicates, its specialties are light snacks and salads. Be sure and sample their delicious home-style ice cream, which is among the best in town. ~ Vaima Center; 43-37-70. BUDGET.

Many of the better-value daytime eating places cater particularly to office workers at lunch. **Polyself**, next to the Bank of Polynesia, is a bustling cafeteria with local dishes such as *poisson cru*, sandwiches, soups, salads and various Chinese–Tahitian offerings. This little place has consistently good food. Get there early in the lunch hour or they will have sold out most of their fare. ~ Rue Paul Gauguin; 43-75-32. BUDGET.

Also well-visited by the lunch crowd is **Snack Jimmy** just opposite the town hall. On any given day this neon-lit greasy spoon is filled with locals scarfing up Tahitian and Chinese dishes. Fare includes sweet and sour soup, stir-fried veggies with pork, chicken and shrimp, chop suey, chow mein and other Chinese dishes. Sandwiches are also available. ~ Corner of Rue Colette and Rue des Ecoles; 43-63-32. BUDGET.

The market environs feature some of the least expensive restaurants and cafés in town. The cuisine is Chinese–Tahitian and generally the eateries offer the option of takeout food. These are prototypical blue-collar restaurants with no pretense of catering to the tourist trade. Typical of this category are **Waikiki** on Rue A. Leboucher ~ 42-95-27; **Te Hoa** on Rue du Mal Foch ~ 42-06-91; and **Restaurant Cathay** on Rue du Mal Foch ~ 42-99-67. The best item to order is a local mainstay called *maa tinito*, a mixture of red beans, pork, fresh vegetables and whatever else the chef feels like throwing in. These establishments also have chop suey, Chinese-style soups, and mixed vegetable dishes. ~ BUDGET.

◄ HIDDEN

Upstairs at the **Marché Papeete** is an open-air snack bar that serves hamburgers, sandwiches, *steak frites*, *poisson cru*, *maa tinito* and other Tahitian dishes for the budget-priced pocketbook. The food isn't great, but the eating area is breezy and some of the tables have canopies. Most of the clientele are local and it's an excellent spot for the weary shopper to have a meal. ~ BUDGET.

If you feel that a sandwich will do, one of the better specialists in this category is **Epi D'Or**, located right next to Restaurant Cathay. Typical fare is ham or cheese baguette sandwiches. ~ Rue du Mal Foch. BUDGET.

If you are in the mood for dessert, **La Marquisienne** is a fine neighborhood patisserie one block south of the Hotel Le Mandarin. It's a good place to stop for a coffee or some pastry when the blood sugar drops. ~ Rue Colette near the corner of Rue Paul Gauguin; 42-83-52. BUDGET.

◄ HIDDEN

Surf the web in the **Tiki Soft C@fe** while enjoying a delicious pie or a *croque monsieur*—a toasted sandwich with ham and gratined cheese—or a *croque madame*, the same but with a fried egg on top. In addition to snacks (and breakfast fare too), Tahiti's original Polynesian cyber café is a gathering place for Tahiti's young artistic subculture. It's a great place discover what's happening in the music and concert scene. There are also art exhibits and occasional live music, and the place stays open until 2 a.m. No breakfast on Sunday. ~ Pont de l'Est; 88-93-98, 77-44-34; www.tiki soft.pf, e-mail contact@tikisoft.pf. BUDGET TO MODERATE.

Next door to Tiki Soft is **Brasserie des Remparts**, which offers a slew of different beer, especially from Belgium. Run by the capable Bernard Procureur, who managed several restaurants in Moorea, it's open at 6 a.m. for breakfast. They also serve quick lunches as well as crêpes in the afternoon and dinner until 10 p.m. ~ Pont de l'Est; 42-80-00. MODERATE.

Aux Délices/Chez Louisette is located opposite the Vaima Center in the Passage Cardella. This tiny, gleaming white café offers a superb selection of coffee and pastry. It's run by the same people who operate Chez Hilaire, a popular café located near the Chinese temple in the Mamao Quartier. ~ Passage Cardella; 45-46-46. BUDGET TO MODERATE.

HIDDEN ► **Patisserie D. Hilaire** is a very famous café and *salon de thé* patronized mostly by local people. It's got the best French pastry you've ever imagined, including chocolate cake, pralines, apple pie and homemade ice cream. The store and café share the same floor. The café, with its splashy red decor, is reminiscent of a brightly lit American coffee shop. It's located in the next to Mamao hospital and the Chinese temple. ~ 4 Rue Commandant Chessé, Mamao; 43-65-85. BUDGET.

HIDDEN ► Sip the tea of your choice at **La Maison d'Eté**, which is one of the top small eateries in town and a *salon de thé* par excellence. Owners Marie-Claude, Agnes and Christophe serve you refined small snacks such as zucchini pie, fresh market salad and a wide variety of teas from throughout the world. La Maison can be found on Rue des Remparts, next to Europcar, in the same building as Boutique Elite. Open for lunch and afternoon tea. ~ Rue des Remparts; 42-53-78. BUDGET TO MODERATE.

HIDDEN ► Rest your world-weary body at **Café des Négociants**, a genuine Parisian bistro with year-round outdoor dining that those on the Continent can only dream about. Located on the cordoned-off pedestrian street in the Quartier du Commerce, this pleasant watering hole also offers jazz concerts once a week. ~ Quartier du Commerce; 48-08-48. MODERATE TO DELUXE.

HIDDEN ► Elbow your way through the locals and enjoy the great food at **Snack Mèmène**, located one block from the marketplace, next to La Marquisienne. The shrimp curry is unbeatable, but also check out the chow mein, sashimi and *poulet au citron*. Meals are especially enjoyable when consumed outdoors on the terrace. ~ 27 Rue Colette; 43-09-26. BUDGET TO MODERATE.

Painted a distinctive blue and white, **La Squadra Restaurant** is an Italian eatery that is very popular with locals and is usually packed at lunchtime. Service is good and it's a lively place—a good people-watching venue. There is a good selection of pastas, seafood and desserts—all of which are excellent. Closed Monday. ~ Passage Cardella; 41-32-14. MODERATE TO DELUXE.

◄ HIDDEN

Clearly the most popular pizzeria with locals is **Lou Pescadou**, located one block from the Vaima Center. It turns out a fine array of Italian food in general, but the specialty is pizza cooked in a wood-fired oven. The four seasons pizza is my favorite. Patrons come here just as much for the atmosphere as for the food. The walls are covered with movie posters and the noise level is a perpetual loud chatter. Definitely check this place out. ~ Rue Anne-Marie Javouhey; 43-74-26. BUDGET TO MODERATE.

Jack Lobster at Vaima Center has tasty food that is both reasonably priced and served in generous portions. Jack's is an informal setting with simple decor much like a pizzeria. Dishes offered here include seafood, meat, salads and several Tex-Mex–influenced dishes. And yes, they have lobster. ~ Vaima Center; 42-50-58. MODERATE.

The **Sushi Bar**, located just above Jack Lobster at the Vaima Center, is a cool little spot where the sushi float on tiny canoes along the counter until they are shanghaied by patrons. It's air conditioned and, thank goodness, a nonsmoking restaurant. Open for lunch Monday through Saturday and for dinner on Friday and Saturday. ~ Vaima Center; 45-35-25. MODERATE.

A good place to sample French cuisine or simply to have an after-dinner drink is **Morrison's Café** on the top floor of the Vaima Center. Named after Jim Morrison of the Doors, it's an indoor/outdoor café with a huge wooden terrace surrounding a swimming pool. Patrons dine at marble tables while sitting on plastic chairs. The Continental French menu includes dishes such as escargot, smoked salmon, seafood gratin, a large selection of salads and cold dishes such as carpaccio and sashimi. There is also a Tex-Mex

AUTHOR FAVORITE

Sometimes nothing hits the spot like a frothy beer; when that thirst catches up with me I head to **Les 3 Brasseurs**, Tahiti's first microbrewery bar/restaurant. Featuring indoor/outdoor dining, this hip watering hole sports decor that includes a paved stone floor and a copper bar. While inhaling its four varieties of brew (including pure malt and unpasteurized beers) you have a firsthand look at the vats and highly polished brewing *equipage*. When you sit down, the waitperson will hand you *La Gazette*, which is both a newspaper and menu. Be sure to try specialties such as *flammekueche* (sort of a non-tomato pizza) as well as sauerkraut, *entrecôte* and *poisson cru*. It's open daily from 8 a.m. until 1 a.m. ~ Boulevard Pomare, across from Moorea ferry; 50-60-25; www.les3 brasseurs.com, e-mail les3brasseurs@mail.pf. MODERATE.

Artists in Residence

Idyllic visions of the South Seas have lured artists and writers to Tahiti for more than a hundred years. Painter Paul Gauguin may be the most famous Western cast-away, but many others have followed their dreams to these lush island shores. Here are a few of the more notable visitors:

PAUL GAUGUIN   Paul Gauguin moved around Tahiti almost as much as he moved around the world. After a brief stay in Papeete in 1891, Gauguin settled in **Mataiea Village** (page 163). Here he lived with the locals and painted several of his dreamlike depictions of Tahitian life, including *Fatata te Miti* (By the Sea) and *Ia Orana Maria* (Ave Maria). In 1897 he relocated to **Punaauia** (page 148), where he produced around 60 paintings, including the masterwork, *Where do We Come From.* Later he moved to the Marquesas, where he died in 1903. More can be learned about Gauguin's life in the South Seas at the **Paul Gauguin Museum** (page 162).

ROBERT LOUIS STEVENSON   On assignment for a New York newspa-per, Stevenson spent two months in Tahiti in 1888. He stayed in **Tautira**

dinner where the menu boasts of the large quantities of meat. Morrison's Café is also open for lunch. The *plat du jour* is adver-tised on the chalkboard outside the elevator. Morrison's Café is the only establishment in French Polynesia that has a "scenic" ele-vator (built outside the restaurant with a fine view of the water-front). The clientele is young and hip and the owner, Pascha Allouch, is a bon vivant who will keep the jokes flowing at your table. There is a full American-style bar that's well stocked with tequila. Seventies-era rock music is played on the weekends—sometimes there is a cover charge. ~ Vaima Center; 42-78-61. MODERATE TO DELUXE.

Young and hip is the best way to describe the **Mana Rock Café**. It's a restaurant, a brasserie, a disco, a cyber café and a nightclub. Very popular among the young Tahitians (and those a bit older) the Mana Rock organizes concerts on weekends. On the menu are simple dishes like breakfast items, salads, grilled meat and fish, and ice cream. ~ Boulevard Pomare at Avenue du Prince Hinoï; 48-36-36, fax 48-36-37. BUDGET TO MODERATE.

La Romana has a great selection of pizza, a festive atmosphere and a reasonably priced menu. And it's one of the few places that features take-out meals. I recommend the Four Seasons pizza. ~ 3 (page 172), where he began work on *The Master of Ballantrae*, a novel with a Scottish setting. Homesick? Perhaps.

RUPERT BROOKE The saturated colors and alluring images of Gauguin's paintings inspired English poet Rupert Brooke to venture to Tahiti in 1913. Brooke spent three months in Mataiea, discovering love rather than lost art. His bungalow still stands (page 166).

JAMES NORMAN HALL With Charles Nordoff, Hall wrote *Mutiny on the Bounty* and several other books chronicling high adventure on the South Seas. The many Hollywood versions of *Mutiny* have made Hall's tale synonymous with Tahiti, where Hall himself lived from the early 1920s until his death in 1951. His residence has been rebuilt and converted into a museum (page 137).

ZANE GREY This prolific author of pulp Westerns (*Riders of the Purple Sage*) was also a passionate deep-sea fisherman. During the 1930s, he set several records for snaring enormous denizens of the deep. One of his favorite spots was just off Tahiti Iti at **Vairao** (page 173).

Commandant Rue Destremeau and Avenue Bruat; 41-33-64. BUDGET TO MODERATE.

L'apizerria also produces very good pizzas and although it may lack the chic atmosphere of Lou Pescadou, it does have the advantage of an outdoor dining area facing the waterfront. Try the pizza with capers, seafood and black olives. The food is just as good as at Lou Pescadou but the ambience is more subdued. There are entrances from Boulevard Pomare and from Rue du Commandant Destremeau. ~ Boulevard Pomare, Paofai; 42-98-30. MODERATE.

The Newport is a fine outdoor café under shady trees. It turns out tasty seafood, French cuisine and local dishes. The specialty of the house is sashimi prepared from locally caught tuna. Despite the prominent outdoor location on the waterfront, this is generally a local scene. ~ Corner of Avenue Bruat and Boulevard Pomare; 42-76-52. BUDGET TO MODERATE.

If Vietnamese food is in order, **Saigonnaise** is a reliable choice. The dining area is on the small side, which makes for a cozy atmosphere. If you want to keep the meal light, the seafood combination soup is a good bet. Closed Sunday. ~ Avenue du Prince Hinoï; 42-05-35. BUDGET TO MODERATE.

Le Parc Bougainville is a charming outdoor eatery set amongst the ponds and lush lawns of Bougainville Park. Open for breakfast, lunch and dinner, the menu includes omelettes, hamburgers, salads and other light offerings. Travelers with children will appreciate the restaurant's little playground—the adults can eat while the children entertain themselves. ~ Bougainville Park, Boulevard Pomare (near the post office). BUDGET TO MODERATE.

Le Snack Paofai near the huge Protestant church is a good bet for inexpensive snacks and sandwiches. Typical fare is *salade russe*, steak and *pomme frites*, fish and chow mein. ~ Located at the corner of Rue Cook and Rue du Commandant Destremeau; 42-95-76. BUDGET.

Le Café de la Gare, located on the same block of Rue du Général de Gaulle as the Big Burger, is a typical French bistro with marble tables and chairs fashioned from cast iron. The indoor ambience is definitely different from most places you'll find in Tahiti: it's a tiny, dark establishment with a green interior and a shiny brass bar. We think it's a great place to sit (indoors or outdoors) and let the world pass by. It also features live music on weekends. ~ Rue du Générale de Gaulle; 42-75-95. MODERATE.

Restaurant Le Janoko, located in Fare Tony just south of the Vaima Center, is always a busy lunch spot. It's a bit crowded sitting in the hallways of this minuscule shopping center but the *plats du jour* are worth waiting for. Some of our favorites include *couscous royale, tarte au chèvre* and a variety of great salads. ~ Fare Tony; 45-30-13. MODERATE.

DELUXE TO ULTRA-DELUXE DINING   For the well heeled, there is no shortage of expensive restaurants in Papeete. Varieties of cuisine include French, Chinese, Vietnamese and often a French–Tahitian fusion. In general, whatever the cuisine, the visitor will not go wrong ordering seafood in French Polynesia. When you

ROULOTTES—MEALS ON WHEELS

At Vaiete Square where the cruise ships dock, *roulottes* (vans), serve the best inexpensive food in town. Even if you are not planning to eat, just walking around these purveyors of meals on wheels is an obligatory part of the Papeete experience. Some of the owners have put a great deal of effort into ornately painting or affixing neon signs to the vans to advertise gastronomic themes ranging from pizzerias to crêperies. *Roulottes* dole out grilled chicken, steaks and fish piled high with *pommes frites*, omelettes, pizza and chop suey. There are also vans specializing in ice cream and several that serve crêpes. Most of the *roulottes* are open only in the evenings, although some are open during the lunch hour.

blend French culinary standards with locally caught seafood, the combination is difficult to improve upon.

Moana Iti, located beneath Club 106, has had the same owner for more than 20 years and features a traditional French menu. The atmosphere is elegant. The restaurant's reputation is very good and it's not unusual to see high government officials dining there during the lunch hour. Specialties include homemade pâté, duck fillet, rabbit and shellfish dishes such as Coquille St. Jacques. ~ Boulevard Pomare between Avenue Bruat and Rue Zelee; 42-65-24. ULTRA-DELUXE.

The intimate **La Corbeille d'Eau** to the west side of the Vaima Center is considered by many the best French restaurant in Papeete —a "restaurant *gastronomique*." The seafood dishes are first-rate, as are the traditional French dishes such as filet mignon and escargot. ~ Boulevard Pomare; 43-77-14. ULTRA-DELUXE.

Sip your favorite vintage at **Le Rubis**, Papeete's first wine bar. Here, you first choose the wine and then the food to complement it. Choose from over 120 different wines from all over the world. It will be tough to beat the excellent food and atmosphere of Le Rubis. ~ Rue Jeanne d'Arc, ground floor in Vaima Center; 43-25-55. DELUXE TO ULTRA-DELUXE.

◄ HIDDEN

Despite the Tahitian name, **Manava** has the typical decor of a French provincial restaurant. Management has revamped the menu and there are a variety of new dishes prepared by a new chef. These include minced tuna or salmon, oysters grilled in cheese, mahimahi with marinated shallots, and pork filet mignon with curry cream and pineapples. Try the lime crêpe for dessert— the specialty of the house. The art on the wall is courtesy of Christian, the owner's son. Manava is located opposite the government buildings complex on Avenue Bruat. ~ Avenue Bruat; 42-02-91. DELUXE TO ULTRA-DELUXE.

One of the newer and better restaurants in Papeete is **L'o a la Bouche**, which roughly translates as "salivating in the mouth"—an apt description for this gem of an establishment. The decor has a tasteful, understated elegance. The nouvelle French cuisine, mostly seafood, is superb. One dish we sampled, the Coquille St. Jacques with shrimp, was an original creation. It was fresh and prepared perfectly. Other dishes tasted were *feuilleté de saumon des dieux* (fish prepared with a pastry crust) and *salade de magret de canard* (smoked duck salad). This is a restaurant you do not want to miss. Closed Saturday at noon, and Sunday. ~ Passage Cardella; 45-29-76. DELUXE TO ULTRA-DELUXE.

◄ HIDDEN

One of the best Chinese restaurants is **Le Mandarin** at the Hotel Le Mandarin—one of the few restaurants in town open seven days a week. They have an excellent reputation and specialize in a Hong Kong–style cuisine (which means mostly seafood).

The chef, who is from Hong Kong, changes the menu on a weekly basis, and there is live music on Friday and Sunday nights. ~ 26 Rue des Ecoles; 50-33-90. DELUXE TO ULTRA-DELUXE.

The fine service and Cantonese-style cuisine at **Le Dragon D'Or** make it popular with locals and visitors. (Food served at Le Mandarin and Le Dragon D'Or is known locally as *chinoise rafinée*, which differentiates it from ordinary Chinese restaurants as a cut above or a "gourmet" restaurant.) Again, seafood is your best bet, but the menu also features pork, chicken and beef dishes. Located down the street from Le Mandarin, between Rue Paul Gauguin and Rue des Ecoles. Closed Monday. ~ Rue Colette; 42-96-12. DELUXE TO ULTRA-DELUXE.

GROCERIES There is no shortage of supermarkets as well as mom-and-pop grocery stores in Papeete to pick up a baguette, a wedge of cheese or a bottle of beer.

However, the mother of all markets in French Polynesia is the **Marché Papeete** (municipal market), which takes up a square block between Rue 22 September and Rue Francois Cardella. There you will find all manner of fresh fruits, vegetables, produce, fish and meat, as well as handicrafts and clothing. See "Shop 'til You Drop" in this chapter for more information.

For convenience, a visit to a supermarket or grocery store might make more sense. In Papeete, some of the stores to consider are **Magasin Louise Wong** on Cours de l'Union Sacrée ~ 42-08-98; **Supermarché Cecile** in the Fariipiti neighborhood ~ 42-79-30; and **Supermarché Casino** on Avenue Temple de Destremeau, behind the Paofai ~ 42-79-30.

SHOPPING Shopping in Papeete is a mixed bag—quality and selection are good but prices are very high. Here it's possible to purchase items from around French Polynesia: tie-dyed pareus from Moorea, wood carvings from Ua Huka, shell hatbands from Rangiroa, fine woven hats from Tubuai, tapa cloth from Fatu Hiva and black pearls from the Tuamotu Islands.

For the fashion-conscious, there are a number of boutiques with island-style and French clothing. Perhaps the best indigenous items to purchase are jewelry made from the famous Tahitian black pearl.

The upstairs section at the **Marché Papeete** is a good place to pick up handicrafts costing 2500 to 20,000 CFP. Despite the prices, very few of the carvings are quality items. Prices for typical items range from 1000 to 2000 CFP and up for pareus and starting at 1500 CFP for the least expensive hats. In general, the best time to buy crafts is during fairs or festivals. See "Shop 'til You Drop" on the facing page for more information.

Shop 'til You Drop

The "new and improved" **Marché Papeete** (municipal market), completely reorganized from the inside out, is much larger than its predecessor. Whereas in the old days fruit, flowers, watermelons and other produce would be sold on the sidewalk outside the perimeter of the market, today all selling goes on within the market's walls. The ground floor is reserved for flowers, taro, rootstalks and daily catches of fresh seafood. These are sold chiefly by Polynesians—an unwritten law here maintains that Tahitians may sell fish, taro, yams and other Polynesian foods; the Chinese sell vegetables; and Europeans and Chinese are the bakers and butchers. Downstairs, on the sidewalk, fruit and vegetables are displayed in the same traditional manner although the surroundings are aesthetically more sterile (and undoubtedly cleaner). You can still stroll through the aisles and find bananas, pineapples, starfruit, coconuts, oranges, papaya, limes, mangoes, avocados, cassava root, lettuce, tomatoes, onions, carrots, beans, potatoes, cabbage and even flower arrangements. The wary shoppers eyeing, squeezing, touching and scrutinizing the merchandise are still present.

An upstairs section, served by two escalators, is dedicated to handicrafts and is a good place to pick up inexpensive items such as woven *pandanus* hats, mats, bags, shell necklaces, pareus and other clothing. There are carved goods such as tikis, bowls and ukuleles as well. On the same floor is a café that serves hamburgers, sandwiches, *steak frites*, *poisson cru* and other budget dishes. The upper deck also provides an ideal place to take market photos without intruding on anyone's territory.

You'll find the best time to visit Marché Papeete is early Sunday morning when out-of-towners come to sell their goods, shop and attend church in Papeete. Don't be afraid to sample the exotic-looking fruits, vegetables and fish. The results will be very satisfying.

Unlike Asiatic countries, one does not haggle or bargain when shopping in the public market places in Tahiti. Tahitians, though not so much Chinese merchants, might find it rude to haggle over prices. If you try to dicker with a Polynesian, more than likely the seller will get angry and either inflate the price or decide not to deal with you altogether. The only exception in the "dickering rule" is when you are making a large purchase of black pearl jewelry. The margins on these items are very high and a merchant might well consider knocking off a percentage in order to make a sale.

Check out **Manuia Curios**, located in a row of shops facing the cathedral, for better-than-average quality carvings as well as shells, bags and other woven goods. This shop is also one of the few places where you can get traditional Tahitian dance costumes. ~ Place Notre Dame; 42-04-94.

Le Kiosque, a walk-in kiosk at the waterfront entrance to the Vaima Center, has a good selection of magazines and newspapers (including the *International Herald Tribune*, *USA Today*, *Time* and *Newsweek*).

Ganesha, located on the second floor of Vaima Center, has a superb selection of South Pacific handicrafts including *masi* (tapa cloth), mats, museum-quality carvings and other items from Fiji, the Solomon Islands and other areas. They also have small vials of sandalwood oil (the real thing) that has a sublime scent—a perfect gift for someone who enjoys fragrances. ~ Vaima Center; 43-04-18.

Tamara Curios is located a block south of Vaima Center in Fare Tony. One friend described it as a supermarket for tourists. There are T-shirts, *monoi* oil, postcards, key-ring holders and handicrafts. Nothing out of the ordinary, but Aline offers good prices (especially on T-shirts), plenty of selection and a handy location. ~ Centre Commerciale; 42-54-42.

On special occasions and during cruise ship visits, an outdoor handicrafts center comes to life in **Vaiete Square** on the waterfront. Vendors hawk pareus, T-shirts, carvings, shell leis and other souvenirs.

French Polynesia issues beautiful stamps, which are popular with philatelists around the world. Those interested should stop at the special sales area on the ground floor at the main **post office**. Phone cards, known as *telecartes*, adorned with various Tahitian themes and motifs have also become a collectible item and are available in any of the post office branches. ~ Boulevard Pomare; 41-43-35; www.tahiti-postoffice.com.

Black pearls are a product indigenous to French Polynesia and make a special gift or souvenir. To educate yourself on the origin and development of the black pearl, a good place to start is the **Robert Wan Pearl Museum**, downtown in the Vaima Center. The museum offers a general panorama of the pearl, from prehistoric to modern times. Themes germane to the black pearl such as history, science, art and mythology are developed in a rich and detailed exhibition. Not coincidentally, adjacent to the museum is Robert Wan's store, Tahiti Perles. Admission. ~ Rue Jeanne d'Arc at Vaima Center; 45-21-22, fax 42-13-39; www.tahitiperles.com.

In general, there are two main types of black pearl retailers: the large shops, such as Tahiti Perles, and the small artisans. Both have their place and bargains can be had in both types of shops. When you want to buy a black pearl look for the five criteria: luster, form, surface, size and color. The greater the radiance, the more symmetrical, the cleaner the surface, the larger the pearl and the rarer the color, the higher the value is. The Vaima Center has the largest concentration of black pearl shops. Other jewelry shops are located on Boulevard Pomare and in the pedestrian street of the Quartier du Commerce. Ground floor: **Tahiti Perles** ~ 45-05-05; **Frederic Missir** ~ 43-37-98; first floor: **Vaima Perles** ~ 42-55-57; **Tahiti Pearl Dream** ~ 45-48-15; Black Pearl Plaza: **Sibani Perles** ~ 54-24-30; and **World of Pearls** ~ 54-24-32.

While not exactly your average souvenir, you might want to bring home your own genuine Polynesian **tattoo**. (Polynesian tattoos utilize traditional Polynesian motifs, including geometric patterns and stylized animals such as birds or turtles.) Expect to pay around 15,000 CFP (around US$150) for a simple wrist or ankle tribal band tattoo. There are two popular places, both approved by the local public health authorities. **Jordi's Tattoo Shop** is behind the Prince Hinoï hotel. They promote the fact that they sterilize their equipment with an autoclave and always use new needles. ~ 43 Rue Leboucher; 42-45-00; www.jorditattoo.pf, e-mail jts@mail.pf. **Tattoo Maniac**, above Bar Taina, also has a good reputation among tattoo aficionados. ~ Corner of Boulevard Pomare and Rue Clappier.

> When buying pearls, if a deal seems too good to be true, hold off on your purchase. There have been reports of merchants who peddle artificially colored pearls, which is not what you want. Buyer beware.

If you enjoy browsing the newsstands or bookstores and are interested in a coffee-table book on French Polynesia to bring home, there are plenty to choose from in the shops. **Archipels** has a wide selection of books, principally in French but with a reasonable English section. There's an extensive section on Tahiti and the Pacific in English and French. Maps, however, are scarce here. ~ Rue des Remparts; 42-47-30.

The **Vaima Librairie**, which occupies space on the second and third stories of the Vaima Center, also has books in French and English. It has the best travel section in Papeete. One corner of the bookstore is reserved for books about the Pacific and Polynesia, in French and English (also secondhand books). If you have an interest in Pacific literature, this is a obligatory stop. Gilles Arthur, former curator of the Gauguin Museum, supervises the selection. ~ Vaima Center; 42-23-48.

The former Polygraph on Avenue Bruat has transformed into a cyber office known as **e-six**. Besides offering photocopies and small bindings, they rent a number of computers (PC and Macintosh) by the hour. Other services such as editing, printing and fax are available. They also send documents and parcels via FedEx. The book section has moved to Prince Hinoï Center, a large stationery shop on Avenue du Prince Hinoï. ~ Avenue Bruat; 42-80-47; www.e-six.pf.

INTERNET ACCESS

There are three reliable places to surf the web and check e-mail in downtown Papeete. Access at all of these places costs 250 CFP for 15 minutes.

Tiki Soft C@fe is Tahiti's original cyber café and is a gathering place for Tahiti's young artistic subculture. Besides a good internet connection, there are also art exhibits and occasional live music. They are open until 2 a.m. nightly. ~ Pont de l'Est; 88-93-98, 77-44-34; www.tikisoft.pf, e-mail contact@tikisoft.pf.

The **Mana Rock Café** on Boulevard Pomare at Avenue du Prince Hinoï is a restaurant, brasserie, disco, nightclub and cyber café. ~ 48-36-36.

e-six on Avenue Bruat is a "cyber office" that rents both Macs and PCs by the hour. Other services include printing, photocopies, fax, binding and editing. They also have a FedEx drop. ~ Avenue Bruat; 42-80-47; www.e-six.pf.

NIGHTLIFE

OUTDOOR CAFÉS & BARS   There is never a shortage of nightlife in Papeete, one of the liveliest ports in the South Pacific. The capital has a wide assortment of pubs, clubs and bars ranging from posh outdoor cafés and bars to sleazy servicemen's dives. Fortunately, Papeete is a small town, and most places are within several minutes' walking distance of each other, mostly along the waterfront or in the Vaima Center area. Wherever you go, be prepared to spend some cash—the cheapest beer in town is at least US$4 (400 CFP) and cocktails range from US$5 to US$7 (500 to 700 CFP). On weekend nights, most clubs have a cover charge of at least US$10 (1000 CFP), which includes a drink.

At the seedy northern end of Boulevard Pomare, opposite the Moorea ferry terminal, are the hangouts of the more colorful denizens of the night—soldiers, sailors, *Légionnaires*, prostitutes, transvestites, transsexuals, travel writers and even the odd tourist. Despite the relative seediness of this two-block area, you will feel safe. These are places for the more adventurous visitor to watch the world go by while sipping an espresso, a glass of wine or perhaps a Hinano. Typical of the bars in this category are **Le Zizou**, a disco bar that has a cover charge during the evening. At peak hours, it is chock-full of French military conscripts and their female and/or transvestite companions. ~ Quai Galliéni; 42-07-55.

In the same vicinity and category is **Le Manhattan**, located next to the Kon Tiki Hotel. Depending on entertainment, there may be a cover charge on the weekends. ~ Quai Galliéni; 42-17-53.

Morrison's Café, located at the top floor of the Vaima Center, is named after Jim Morrison (of the Doors) and decorated with 1960s and 1970s rock posters. A restaurant/outdoor café with a huge wooden terrace is where you can hear live '70s-era rock music on the weekends. There is a full American-style bar well stocked with tequila. Sometimes there is a cover charge. ~ Vaima Center; 42-78-61.

Rue Lagarde, the pedestrian street next to Vaima Center, sometimes offers outdoor music on Saturday night.

LOCAL BARS Undoubtedly the friendliest spots in town are the rollicking working-class bars where locals come to unwind with conversation and a few beers. They are noisy, crowded, smoke-filled dens that may have a trio or quartet strumming away on ukuleles and guitars. These places seem formidable at first because of the mass of people packed inside. As a visitor, once you're in and flash a few smiles, the locals will be quite amiable.

CLUBS For those interested in meeting locals, the club scene is a great way to make friends—if you know how to dance. Dance is a vital part of local culture and Tahitians appreciate a foreigner with the right moves. The flip side is, if you can't dance too well, don't make these venues a place to learn. A local might suffer through one spin on the dancefloor with a rank amateur, but never a second time. Would-be dancers interested in meeting Tahitians should practice their dips before they get to Papeete. Note that cover charges at dance halls apply only to men.

While in the building, you may want to peek into **Le Tamure Hut**, also inside the Royal Papeete Hotel. While more of a bar, with little room to dance, it has a live band that plays a range of music from local *kaina* flavor to rock-and-roll. There is a nice mix of Tahitians and tourists. It's perhaps a more comfortable place for visitors who just want to sip a beer and meet some locals rather than step out on the dancefloor. Admission is free if you're a guest at the hotel. Cover Wednesday through Saturday. ~ Boulevard Pomare; 42-01-29.

Le Grenier de Montmartre, founded in Paris during World War II, has been replicated lock, stock and barrel in Papeete. The original establishment in Paris had a long affiliation with Tahiti, because management often invited Tahitian musicians to enter-

◀ HIDDEN

DANCE TO A DIFFERENT BEAT

For the average Tahitian, the dance halls (as opposed to the discos) are the most popular places to go. For the visitor it's a great place to get some exposure to one of the most important elements of Tahitian culture—dance—and possibly rub shoulders with the natives. The dance halls have amplified sound systems and bands that play Tahitian waltzes, fox trots, rock-and-roll and music for the sensual *tamure*, the hip-shaking dance that has been known to cause palpitations in middle-aged men. In the background the thunder of drumbeats reverberates through the room. Originally an Eastern Polynesian (Tahitian and Cook Island) dance, the *tamure* has become a pan-Polynesian phenomenon and close to the national pastime in French Polynesia.

tain the guests. The Parisian incarnation of the club maintained this formula until 1997, when the venerable institution was transformed into a *crêperie*. Owner Maite Charlet, however, saved the interior of the old establishment, including the furniture, and shipped it to Tahiti. The restaurant was reconstituted right down to such minor details as the scads of paper money from throughout the world that hang from the ceiling. Live music is played on weekends and the atmosphere is incredible. ~ Avenue du Prince Hinoï; 45-47-77.

Club 106 is a popular place for the over-30 crowd. ~ Boulevard Pomare, next to Avenue Bruat; 42-72-92.

DISCOS Papeete's discos have a universal character—flashing lights, a pulsating beat and a high decibel level. In addition to the bars and discos that service the servicemen, there are also several clubs that have performances by transvestites or transsexuals. They are popular with visitors (gay and straight), French servicemen and locals alike.

The best place in town to see a bump-and-grind female impersonator is **Le Piano Bar**. The Piano Bar is the meeting place for *mahus* and features shows at least once an evening. It's a famous institution in Papeete and anyone who wishes to visit should do so. Visitors of any gender are welcome. You can spend the evening dancing or watching the assorted clientele drift in and out of the swinging doors. Cover. ~ Rue des Ecoles; 42-88-24.

Quite possibly the classiest disco in town is the **Ibiza** on the first floor of the Vaima Center. It's gone through several incarnations and now has the latest in laser lights, mirrors and shiny black furniture. The crowd is in their 20s and 30s and mostly *demi* (Tahitian half-castes) and Chinese. The clientele is always dressed to kill—here's where you'll see the single "beautiful people." Visitors are also welcomed. It's open Friday and Sunday for Tahitian nights mixed with disco; Thursday and Saturday are exclusively disco. Cover. ~ Boulevard Pomare; 43-41-42.

Perhaps the only bar with an Afro-Caribbean flavor is **Le Paradise**, opposite the harbor, across from the *roulottes*. The deejay plays a combination of zouk, reggae, calypso, Caribbean and

AUTHOR FAVORITE

Though I don't spend much time in nightclubs anymore, I make an exception for **Le Grenier de Montmartre**. Entering the club is like stepping into a Parisian hot spot—the interior (including furniture) was saved from the wrecking ball in Paris, transported to Tahiti and reassembled in its present location. *Très* cool. See page 133 for more information.

African music. It's a bit classier than the average military hang-out. The crowd is older, and there can be an interesting mix of French and Caribbean clientele. Once inside, you are required to order a drink. If you enjoy Afro–Caribbean music and a lively crowd sprinkled with servicemen and their Tahitian consorts, this is the place to go. ~ Quai Galliéni; 42-73-05.

Le Glamour on Avenue Bruat boasts a techno music format. The clientele is young and hip. ~ Avenue Bruat; 42-20-11.

GAMES   In Rue Lagarde, just one block behind the Vaima Center, City Games, a 400-square-meter center, provides video games as well as simulators for Formula One racing cars, jet skis, skateboards and motorcycles. A 13-member team helps gamers and surveys the crowd. ~ Rue Lagarde; 50-30-10.

North of Papeete

In order to orient ourselves geographically, imagine Papeete as the domain of a giant goddess sitting atop a throne. If she is facing the harbor, her backside is snug against the wall of Mt. Aorai, the highest peak of the verdant mountain range that towers above the city. Fanning out to our mythical goddess' right (north) are the districts of Pirae, Arue and Mahina. Formerly principalities or dominions run by local chiefs, the districts have evolved into bedroom communities of Papeete.

Over the past few decades, the migration of islanders from other parts of French Polynesia as well as of metropolitan French has swelled the population of these communities. Consequently, Pirae, Arue and Mahina have mushroomed into suburbs complete with grocery stores, schools, villas, slums, playgrounds and other familiar urban offerings.

For the visitor, it is now impossible to distinguish where Papeete ends and Greater Papeete begins. The suburb-like nature of these neighborhoods is clearly evident during rush-hour traffic (8 a.m. and 5 p.m.) when the coastal road is clogged with BMWs, Peugeots and Volkswagens creeping slowly, inexorably, to crowded parking lots in town or returning home.

The word "suburb" should not dissuade the visitor from seeing what lies beyond the city limits or even choosing a slightly out-of-town hotel or guest house. The ubiquitous *Le Truck* makes commuting into town for sightseeing or shopping (during non-rush hours) easy. The quietude of the suburbs is also a welcome relief from the noise and exhaust fumes of Papeete.

SIGHTS

One does not have to travel more than 1.5 kilometers from the edge of Papeete on Avenue du Prince Hinoï (which becomes Avenue du Général de Gaulle in Pirae) to enter Pirae, home of Tahiti's current president, Gaston Flosse, who also serves as Pirae's mayor. Pirae is headquarters for the infamous Centre du Expérimentation de la Pacifique (CEP), the agency that was responsible for nuclear testing. The complex of institutional buildings that comprise the CEP is on your left. This huge bureaucracy, which used to employ thousands of French Polynesians and metropolitan French, was being downsized even prior to the nuclear detonations of 1995. The testing facility has long been a key component of France's independent nuclear arsenal, *force de frappe*, which was developed during the days of Charles de Gaulle. French Polynesia was chosen as a venue to test nuclear weapons when Algeria (a former French colony that was once used as a testing range) became independent. ~ Avenue du Général de Gaulle, Pirae.

On a lighter note, if you travel another kilometer east, the road will cross the Fautaua River (PK 2.5, Pirae), which is the source for **Pierre Loti's Pool (Bain Loti)**. Pierre Loti was the pen name for Julien Viaud, the French merchant marine whose book *The Marriage of Loti* describes the love affair of a Frenchman and a native girl. The pool where he first saw the enchanting Rarahu (the novel's heroine) is several kilometers up the Fautaua River Valley. Unfortunately, this romantic spot on the river is now covered with concrete, but is marked by a bust of the author. Bain Loti is also the trailhead for a three-hour hike to the Fautaua Waterfall (see the "Hiking" section at the end of this chapter).

Perhaps the most famous manmade landmark in Tahiti is the **Tomb of King Pomare V**. A sign on the ocean side of the road marks the access road to the tomb. The Pomare line rose to power as a direct consequence of the European discovery of Tahiti. The first of the lineage, Pomare I, used ex-members of the *Bounty* crew, who were armed with guns, to defeat his enemies. His son and successor, Pomare II, was crowned at a temple just a few feet away from the site of the present-day tomb, where a Protestant church now stands. During the ceremony, a *Bounty* crew member, James Morrison, reported that three human sacrifices were made on behalf of the new king. ~ PK 4.7, Arue.

In 1812, Pomare II became the first Tahitian convert to Christianity and after three years managed to convince the populations of Moorea and Tahiti (with the use of arms where necessary) to follow his example. In his religious zeal, Pomare II constructed a temple in the shape of an oval hut. It was larger than King Solomon's temple and constructed from breadfruit tree pillars, palm fronds and other local materials. The Royal Mission Chapel, as it was called, was about 712 feet long (longer than St. Peter's in Rome), 54 feet wide and could hold 6000 people. Pomare II died in 1821 at the age of 40 from the effects of alcohol. Soon afterward, the Royal Mission chapel fell into disrepair. Today, a 12-sided chapel built in 1978 stands where the Royal Mission chapel once did.

The tomb itself was constructed in 1879 for Queen Pomare, who died in 1877 after a reign of 50 years. During this period, the country became a French colony. The Queen's remains were removed a few years later by her son King Pomare V who, feeling that his end was near, apparently wished to occupy the mausoleum by himself. Pomare V lived on a stipend supplied by the French government, and died in 1891 at the age of 52. In true Pomare tradition, he drank himself to death. An account of his funeral is given by Paul Gauguin in *Noa Noa*.

Local tradition has it that the object on the tomb's roof—which misinformed tour guides often say represents a liquor bottle (which would have been a fitting memorial to Pomare)—is actually a replica of a Greek urn.

Among the American literati who made their homes in French Polynesia, none did more to publicize Tahiti in the 20th century than James Norman Hall, whose **home** has been turned into a museum. The works of Hall and Charles Nordoff, authors of the *Bounty Trilogy, Hurricane* and *The Dark River*, will forever be synonymous with Tahiti. Hall died at his Arue home in 1951 and

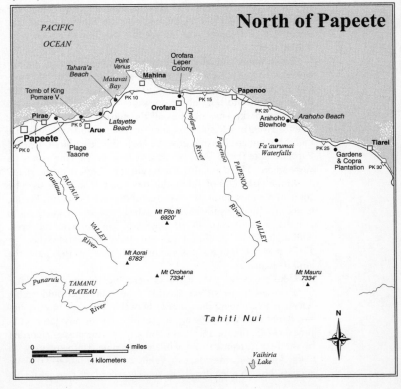

is buried on Herai Hill just above. To find the Hall residence from town, pass the primary school on the sea side of the road. Immediately after crossing a small bridge over the Vaipoopo River, look for Hall's green house on the mountain side, which is visible from the road. The Hall residence was completely rebuilt as a replica of the original. Inside, visitors can view artifacts from Hall's life, including his gramophone, personal papers and more than 3000 books spanning seven generations of American literature. A bilingual guide is available for tours, and conferences can be arranged with advance notice. Closed Sunday and Monday. ~ PK 5.5, Arue; 50-01-61, fax 50-01-60; www.james-normanhall.pf, e-mail jamesnormanhall@mail.pf.

On the ocean side of the road, the former Hyatt Regency Tahiti, which sits atop **One Tree Hill** in Mahina, affords a magnificent view of Moorea and Matavai Bay, where captains Samuel Wallis and James Cook once anchored. Wallis originally called this piece of real estate "Skirmish Hill" because he bombarded the Tahitians gathered here with cannonballs from his ship. Captain Cook eventually changed the name to One Tree Hill because of the solitary *atae* tree that grew here at the time. When the hotel was built in 1968 the owners kept the Tahitian name. The Hyatt Regency clings to the hillside like a scallop to a rock. ~ PK 8.1, Mahina.

Point Venus and **Matavai Bay** are of great historical significance and a fine place for a rest stop. Several stores at a road junction (including the Venustar) and a *Poste* sign are the clues to the Point Venus turnoff. It's about one kilometer from the coast road to the car park. This area has all the natural amenities—shady trees, a river, beach and exposure to cooling trade winds—that make a wonderful picnic ground. Near the beach area, toward Papeete, note that a local outrigger canoe racing club stores its vessels here. There are also a few souvenir shops near the road.

In the early days of Tahiti, this tiny point of land was used by some of the most important visitors of that era—captains Wallis, Cook and Bligh. Until the 1820s, when Papeete became a more popular port of call, all visiting ships anchored in the area. Although Wallis, Tahiti's European discoverer, landed here in 1767, it was Captain Cook's expedition in 1769 that gave the land its name.

Cook was sent by the Royal Geographical Society of England to record the transit of Venus, which, theoretically, would enable scientists to compute the distance between the earth and the sun —a figure that would be an invaluable tool for navigators. On June 3, 1769, the weather was good and the transit was recorded by the best instruments available at the time. Unfortunately, as Cook found out, the edges of Venus could not be seen sharply enough through telescopes to accurately record the transit and his measurements were for naught. However, his journey was still a success, because of the many new species of flora and fauna gathered by the other scientists on the trip.

During the *Bounty* episode in 1788, Lt. Bligh also landed at this spot, collecting breadfruit plants to use as a cheap source of food for the slave population in the West Indies. His landing became grist for Hollywood, which has come up with three different cinematic interpretations (1935, 1962 and 1983).

In 1969, captains Samuel Wallis, James Cook and Louis-Antoine de Bougainville were honored by wooden sculptures at Point Venus, but the monuments, along with the quaint Museum of Discovery, were swept away by a storm several years ago. Bligh, the third navigator to visit the area, was not remembered by any monument. Near where the sculptures once stood is an abstract monument, described by Danielsson as a "needle pointing to heaven," to commemorate the arrival of the first Christian missionaries on Point Venus in 1797. Dispatched by the London Missionary Society, they abandoned their mission in 1808 and did not re-establish themselves until 1817. Though they worked actively for the British annexation of the islands, the British missionaries were eased out of Tahiti after the French takeover in 1842. The missionary era came to an end in Tahiti in 1963 when an independent Protestant church run by Polynesians was formed.

About 150 yards (135 meters) northeast of the Missionary Society memorial sits a monument enclosed by an iron railing. According to the text on a bronze plaque (which has now disappeared), the column was erected by none other than Captain Cook in 1769 and refurbished in 1901. However, not only was the monument not built by Cook (it was a product of the local public works department), it is not on the spot where Cook made his astronomical observations (which took place between the river and the beach).

Finally, the most visible (existing) landmark on Point Venus is the **lighthouse**, constructed in 1868 (despite the 1867 date perhaps over-optimistically inscribed on the entrance). ~ PK 10, Mahina.

❖❖

MUTINY ON THE BOUNTY

During the shooting of the 1962 version of *Mutiny on the Bounty* with Trevor Howard and Marlon Brando, a sequence was filmed on Matavai Bay featuring thousands of Tahitian extras welcoming the visitors ashore. The director, wishing to portray the Tahitians in their former glory, had the Tahitian extras don long-haired wigs and false teeth before the filming to compensate for attributes most of them no longer possessed.

Though little remains today, the **Orofara Leper Colony** is still a poignant landmark in French Polynesia. Prior to WWI, victims of leprosy, what is now called Hansen's disease, were ostracized and chased into remote areas away from the general population. By government decree, in 1914 the Orofara Valley was set aside as a leper colony for all those in Tahiti who suffered from the disease. Until the development of sulphur drugs, there was little the French Protestant mission treating the patients here could do. Nowadays, it is possible to cure Hansen's disease. ~ PK 13.2, Mahina.

Cook anchored off Matavai Bay in 1773, 1774 and 1777, during his subsequent voyages of exploration.

Continuing along the eastern coastal road will bring you to the district of Papenoo and to **Papenoo Village and Valley**. There's a popular surf break just before Papenoo, a typical rural village of the type that has been rapidly disappearing since the end of World War II. Many of its homes are built in the old colonial style, with wide verandas. The Catholic and Protestant churches and *mairie* (town hall) rest along the highway. Past the village, a new bridge (the longest in Tahiti) spans the Papenoo River. The Papenoo Valley, the island's biggest, was formed by an ancient volcanic crater. The river's mouth (where the bridge is located) is the only hole in the crater wall. One can drive up the Papenoo Valley about one kilometer and continue on foot on a trail that leads across the island (see "Outdoor Adventures" at the end of this chapter). A few residents live at the entrance of the valley. The deeper reaches of this narrow valley are steep and unfit for agriculture or habitation. ~ PK 17.1, Papenoo.

In Tiarei, the next district down the coastal highway, is the ever-popular **Arahoho Blowhole**, one of Tahiti's biggest roadside attractions. It's unmarked, and located at the base of a steep cliff on a narrow shoulder on the mountain side of the road. Over countless years, battering surf has undercut the basalt shoreline and eroded a passage to the surface beneath the road. When waves crash against the rocks, the result is a geyser-like plume of sea water that showers onlookers. It's easy to miss the blowhole when coming from the direction of Papeete, so keep an eye open for the sign and the parking lot located on the ocean side of the road. Be careful crossing the road because the blowhole is on the shoulder of the road, at the crest of a hairpin turn. A few hundred yards from the blowhole, the small, crescent-shaped black-sand beach is a good spot to picnic and swim. There are also several vendors selling coconuts, *mape*, a delicious Tahitian chestnut, and, if it's the right season, *rambutan*, a wonderful lychee-like red-spined fruit native to Asia. ~ PK 22, Tiarei.

Another hundred yards (90 meters) down the coastal road is the entrance to the three **Fa'aurumai Waterfalls**. Take the inland turnoff where the waterfall sign is posted and drive inland 1.3 kilometers. The rainforest on both sides of this small valley is thick, nearly impenetrable and filled with *hutu* and *mape* trees. If you look carefully, you'll notice star fruit, guava and *mape* along the trail. From the parking lot, it's several hundred yards to Vaimahutu, the first fall, which cascades 100 feet to the earth and empties into a pool. Walk another 20 minutes down and you will reach the other two falls, Haamaremare iti and Haamaremare rahi. These are less dramatic but beautiful nonetheless. Bring a swimsuit if you want to stand under the falls and insect repellent to keep the mosquitoes away. A lot of work has gone into the waterfalls park—the access road has been paved, new bridges across the creek have been constructed and *Respectez la Nature* signs have been placed in the vicinity. ~ PK 22.3, Tiarei.

In the suburb of Pirae, **Le Royal Tahitien** is a sprawling complex of 40 rooms along the shoreline. The ocean view is good and there is a black-sand beach popular with residents, but which is not always clean. The crowd at the hotel is an unusual amalgam of French servicemen, Americans and Europeans. The rooms are fairly large by Tahitian standards, well maintained and clean. The expansive tropical grounds are well manicured. There is a good open-air restaurant on the premises frequented by locals. To find it, turn off at the *mairie* (town hall) sign approximately three kilometers from town on the ocean side of Avenue du Général de Gaulle. The location is a bit far from Papeete for walkers but *Le Truck* runs along Avenue du Prince Hinoï (which becomes Avenue du Général de Gaulle in Pirae) and it's easy to commute to town in this manner. ~ Pirae; 50-40-40, fax 50-40-41; e-mail royalres@mail.pf. MODERATE.

LODGING

The **Radisson Plaza Resort Tahiti** opened in June 2004. This full-service 165-room resort is beautifully set into the natural curve of exotic black-sand Lafayette Beach. The resort features a lagoon pool and outdoor jacuzzi, general store, souvenir market, health club and day spa. ~ PK 7, Arue; 48-88-88, fax 48-88-89; www.radisson.com/aruefrp. MODERATE TO DELUXE.

Vaimana Fare is the only budget place north of Papeete. It offers two bungalows with a double bed and a sofa, private bath and a self-contained kitchenette, living room and terrace. To get there, turn left off the main road at PK 10.5 and follow this road toward the sea for about 200 meters. The pension is just behind the *collège* of Mahina. (Note that *collège* in French means a secondary school, not a college.) ~ PK 10.5, Mahina; 48-07-17, fax 43-87-27. BUDGET.

One would think that the cool highlands of Tahiti would be a perfect place for a hotel and indeed in the pre-airplane era of tourism the mountains and Vaihiria Lake were an obligatory stop. Nowadays, **Le Relais de la Maroto** is the only mountain lodging in Tahiti. Located in the center of the island, high in the Papenoo Valley where the Vaituoru and Vainavenave rivers converge, it affords a splendid view of the valley and adjacent mountains. Relais, however, was never meant to be an alpine resort—it was erected as housing for construction workers for a nearby hydroelectric dam. However, of late its been completely renovated and can now truly be called a "hotel." The sturdy concrete structure has ten rooms with four bunks, a terrace and bathroom with hot water. There are also two suites with private jacuzzis and pools. A deposit is required for reservations, and transportation to and from the property via helicopter or four-wheel-drive vehicles can be arranged. The owner has an incredible wine collection—no doubt one of the best in the South Pacific. The best thing about the resort is that it makes a great base camp from which to explore the interior of the island. A number of hikes and excursions are available to archaeological sites and nature preserves. ~ Papenoo Valley; 57-90-29, fax 57-90-30; e-mail maroto@mail.pf. MODERATE TO DELUXE.

DINING

Most of the restaurants on Tahiti are concentrated in Papeete. However, there are a few in Papeete's bedroom communities worth checking out and rarely will you see a tourist in them.

Le Royal Tahitien has a large indoor-outdoor seafood restaurant covered with a tightly stitched *pandanus* leaf canopy. The dining area faces the sea (looking toward Moorea) and is often filled with local families on the weekends. We found the shrimp curry and the poached parrot fish with vanilla sauce very good. A wide range of salads and meat such as pepper steak and veal cutlets are also available. ~ Pirae; 50-40-40. MODERATE.

Le Lion d'Or, an excellent restaurant, is well known for its fresh seafood. It is located in the small commercial center in Pirae, behind the post office and the Banque de Tahiti. ~ PK 2, Pirae; 42-66-50. MODERATE.

In the same commercial center is another good restaurant, Le Vaitiare, whose specialties are fish soups, seafood, sauerkraut and couscous. ~ Avenue du Général de Gaulle, Pirae; 41-31-49. MODERATE.

Farther down the Avenue Général de Gaulle is the restaurant Apetahi. It serves classical Polynesian cuisine in a friendly atmosphere. This place is number one for karaoke evenings, especially on Saturday night. ~ PK 3, Avenue Général de Gaulle, Pirae; 42-70-88. MODERATE.

The restaurant with the highest elevation in all of French Polynesia is also located in the distrisct of Pirae: Le Belvédère. It is perched atop a 600-meter mountain with a stunning view of Papeete and Moorea. On a clear day you can also see Tetiaroa, the late Marlon Brando's atoll. At night the glittering lights of greater Papeete are a magnificent sight. The restaurant has its

Romeo & Juliet Tahitian Style

Once a beautiful 17-year-old girl named Fauai lived in Tiarei. Like all island girls, she loved to decorate her hair with flowers. Every morning, accompanied by her friends, she traveled through the nearby valleys gathering blossoms to make crowns of flowers. Her father, Chief Marurai, adored her with an obsession. Jealous and cruel, he wouldn't let any man approach her. As a result, two of his best warriors accompanied her during her strolls. One day, Fauai encountered Tua, a handsome young man. Not aware of the taboo, he snatched her crown of flowers, and ran away laughing. Without hesitation the guards chased Tua and killed him. Following the tragedy, Fauai took refuge with her ill mother. She later returned to the valley with her entourage, looking for medicinal plants to treat the old woman. They encountered Ivi, an emaciated boy who was seeking plants to treat his own malady. She pitied him and wanted to help, but there was the problem of the guards. What could she do?

She had an idea. She asked her friends to hide in the bush and begin screaming to distract the guards. Once the screams rang out, Fauai ordered the guards to see what the commotion was all about. She then joined Ivi. When he saw her he turned pale with fright and told Fauai to leave. She told him she wanted to help find herbs that might heal him. She took his hand and led him deeper into the forest. By this time the guards were alerted to her deception and began searching for the princess. They could be heard in the distance yelling her name. Ivi had to rest frequently to catch his breath and the calls from the guards drew closer. Realizing they would be found together, Ivi told the girl to return to her keepers and leave him alone to die. She refused, telling him that if he must die, she would die with him.

Ivi then revealed a secret to the princess. He was not a sick young boy but the forest spirit of the valley. He told her that in a few moments the two of them would be imprisoned forever in a waterfall. As soon as his words were complete both were stuck to the sheer wall of a rock face and Ivi was transformed into a handsome young man. A deafening noise filled the air and from high above the cliff two enormous masses of water poured down, entirely covering the two young people.

When the guards arrived, they discovered two magnificent falls cascading into two pools. From that day on, Ivi and Fauai remained hidden behind the falls. The warriors never returned to the village. On the way back, a third waterfall swallowed them up.

own *Le Truck* to pick up guests in the hotels or in Papeete (free). Or take the helicopter and combine a delicious lunch with a scenic flight over Tahiti. The cool air favors dishes as fondue and *raclette*, but French cuisine and Tahitian seafood are also on the menu. ~ Fare Rau Ape, Pirae; 43-73-44. MODERATE TO DELUXE.

The Dahlia is one of the best family-style Chinese restaurants in Tahiti. A cut or two above the neon-lit inexpensive Chinese eateries in town, the Dahlia offers the usual fare of chicken, shrimp and beef dishes, presented in a simple but tasty manner. The soups are particularly good. It's a local favorite and worth the few-minute journey out of town. ~ PK 4.2, Arue; 42-59-87. BUDGET.

GROCERIES   Numerous mom-and-pop local or small grocery stores line the highway and side streets of Pirae, Arue and Mahina. For serious shoppers and long-term residents, it's best to jump in a car or on *Le Truck* and visit one of the larger discount outlets such as **Tropic Import** in Pirae ~ 47-50-50, or **Continent** in Arue ~ 50-24-50 (known as a *hypermarché* or super store), which also has an outlet in Punaauia. These merchandisers are the least expensive places in French Polynesia to buy groceries, as well as other consumer goods such as audio tapes and CDs. Prices on these items are lower than at music stores. This is where the savvy locals go to shop.

Discount outlets or *hypermarchés* are the place to go for yachties or those who need to stock up on consumer items such as shampoo, canned goods, detergent, etc.

Some of the better grocery stores in the area are **Supermarché Hippo** at PK 4 on the corner of Avenue du Général de Gaulle at the Hippodrome (racetrack) turnoff in Pirae ~ 42-82-01, **Magasin Arue** at PK 6 in Arue ~ 42-71-13, **Supermarché Venustar**, at PK 10 in Mahina ~ 48-10-13, at the Point Venus turnoff, and **Magasin Jissang** at PK 17.5 in Papenoo ~ 48-16-69.

SHOPPING   On the main road in Pirae there is an open market area three kilometers from town where shell necklaces, jewelry, clothing and other souvenirs are sold at a small **pavilion** just off of Avenue du Général de Gaulle. The easiest way to find it is to drive along Avenue du Général de Gaulle until you see a small commercial center that includes the Pirue post office. The market is located directly across the road, on the seaside. *Le Truck* regularly makes stops, so it is quite accessible from Papeete.

NIGHTLIFE   The bar at **Le Royal Tahitian** is a lively dance spot on weekends. A Tahitian band plays Tahitian waltzes and fox trots as well as the traditional *tamure*. ~ Pirae; 50-40-40.

The restaurant **Apetahi** is *the* place in town for karaoke, especially on Saturday night. Given the natural gift Polynesians have for belting out a tune, it's a great pleasure to listen to them. ~ Avenue Général de Gaulle, Pirae; 42-70-88.

One naturally associates Tahiti with beaches, and there is no shortage of sand on this tropical island. Unfortunately, most of it is not the powdery white substance that many people who come to Tahiti expect. There are fine white-sand beaches in French Polynesia but not many on Tahiti. Most of the beaches in the Papeete vicinity are of the brown- or black-sand variety. They are of volcanic origin and finer in grain than white-sand beaches.

BEACHES & PARKS

PLAGE TAAONE ⚓ Located about five kilometers east of Papeete, this black-sand beach fronts Le Royal Tahitien hotel in Pirae and abuts a seawall. Named after the Taaone district, it stretches about a thousand yards. Offshore is a beautiful view of Moorea but the beach itself is not particularly picturesque. Plage Taaone is popular with locals and tends to be liberally sprinkled with soda cans and other litter. The amenities at the beach, which include restrooms and a restaurant, belong to the hotel. Le Royal Tahitien management prefers that only guests use the restrooms but if you buy a soda or a drink at the bar it's acceptable to use the facilities. I did see swimmers but the water looked murky and uninviting. Most of the Taaone denizens I saw were sun worshiping rather than swimming. Restrooms, restaurant. ~ Take Avenue du Prince Hinoï to Pirae, approximately three kilometers east of Papeete and turn left at the *mairie* (town hall) sign. The hotel and beach that front it are behind the Pirae town hall, just off the main drag.

LAFAYETTE BEACH This long stretch of black sand is in Arue at PK 7. Mostly used by locals and hotel guests at Le Royal Tahitien and the Radisson Plaza Resort Tahiti, it's easy to get to, as it lies at the edge of the coastal highway. There are shady trees along the periphery of the beach. As local beaches go it's not spectacular, but it is conveniently located. There is one outdoor shower but this is not a great swimming beach. ~ Take an Arue-bound *Le Truck* to PK 7 or pull off the road in your rental car at the small parking lot adjacent to the beach.

TAHARA'A BEACH ⚓ In Mahina at the foot of "One Tree Hill" is a crescent-shaped, black-sand beach, which has a dramatic view of Honu (Turtle) Point to the south. Standing on the beach, which is nestled snugly against the steep hillside, it seems as though you are at the bottom of a deep basin. Numerous shade trees line this beach, which is relatively close to town but feels much more isolated. I visited the beach on a Sunday and it wasn't very crowded. The swimming is excellent but beware of the undertow. ~ Take the coastal road north to the site of the former Hyatt Regency and take the hotel exit. Park outside the hotel lot near the perimeter of the park. The access to the beach is a narrow, black-top road, which is immediately to your left upon entering the former hotel grounds. PK 8.1, Mahina.

POINT VENUS 🏊 🏄 ⚓ Point Venus has a fine beach, but unlike the narrow crescent of sand at Tahara'a, it is wide open and more easily accessible. It's a good swimming beach and is popular with picnickers because of a shady grove of palm and ironwood trees. Surfers should know there is a hollow right reef break off the end of the point. It's intense—for experts only. A long paddle is required. This is also a choice windsurfing spot. Picnic tables, drinking water, showers and restrooms. ~ To find the turnoff to Point Venus, look for several stores on the ocean side of the road (including the Venustar) and a *Poste* (post office) sign at PK 10. Turn left and go another kilometer to the coast road until you see the parking lot. PK 10.1, Mahina.

HIDDEN ►

ARAHOHO BEACH 🏊 🏄 Across the highway and a few yards down the road from the Arahoho Blowhole is a small crescent-shaped black-sand beach. It's a terrific spot to picnic and boogie board the beach break. Swimming can be a touch dangerous—the currents are very strong. Take great caution. There is a short beach break that will only be of interest to boogie boarders. Just across the road may be several vendors selling coconuts, *mape*, Tahitian chestnut and, if it's the right season, *rambutan*, a lychee-like red-spined fruit native to Asia. Picnic tables, drinking water, restrooms. ~ Take the east coast road to the Arahoho Blowhole. If you are driving, watch out for blowhole spectators who may be standing on the highway. One of the blowholes is actually on the mountain side of the road. There is little if any room on the shoulder of the road (on the inside of a hairpin turn) to observe this phenomena, so curious visitors may be in harm's way. About 20 yards east of the blowhole on the ocean side of the road is a small parking lot. Pull in there. PK 22, Tiarei.

FA'AURUMAI WATERFALLS This is a series of three easily accessible waterfalls that has been turned into a park of sorts. The lowest fall is a ten-minute walk from the parking lot and plummets about 100 feet into a pool surrounded by boulders. This is an obligatory stop for most visitors to Tahiti and it's worth the effort to see it. Bring a swimsuit if you want to stand under the falls or take a dip in the pool below. (Don't forget insect repellent.) Restrooms, drinking water and picnic tables. ~ Just 100

AUTHOR FAVORITE

When I want to visit a beach with stunning views I check out **Tahara'a Beach** at Honu Point. Its black-sand beach is cleaner than the typical Papeete district bathing spots—and because it's off the beaten track, I can count on a bit of solitude. (Don't swim alone, however: the currents can be dangerous.) See page 145 for more information.

yards or so past the blowhole is the entrance to the 1.3-kilometer-long road leading to the three Fa'aurumai Waterfalls. From the parking lot it's several hundred yards to the first fall. The other falls are separated by 20-minute walks up a winding but well-maintained path.

PAPENOO ⚓ 🏄 There is a long stretch of black-sand beach along the shoreline of Papenoo Village. The beach is well known primarily because it faces one of the best surf breaks on the island. There are no shade trees near the beach but there are some on the shoulder of the road. It's easy to park on the side of the road and watch the action if the surf is "working." This is a very long beach break, and judging by the numbers of surfers out on a day when conditions are right, it's very popular. There's also a right-hand point break. At the Papenoo river mouth (on the east side of the point) are some excellent sandbar breaks—surfing at low tide here is best. If you are going to surf here don't come in large groups—the locals will not like it. When conditions are fine it can get quite crowded. ~ Take the coastal road to Papenoo about three kilometers past the waterfalls. Park along the shoulder of the road. To get to the river-mouth break take the first left (coming from Papeete) after the Papenoo River bridge. PK 25, Papenoo.

Scope out the official website for surfing in Tahiti and her islands. (We're talking surfing waves—not the internet!) The site provides info on breaks, upcoming international and local competitions, the latest ranking of local surfers, photos and video and, most importantly, weather forecasts. The site is in French, although an English version was under construction at press time: www.surfingtahiti.pf.

South of Papeete

Driving toward the airport from town (in a southerly direction) are the communities of Faa'a (where the airport lies), Punaauia and Paea. These districts have evolved into bedroom communities of Papeete. During rush-hour traffic in the morning and evening, the highway is as clogged as an L.A. freeway. Thankfully, a new road called **Route des Plaines** now connects the end of the four-lane freeway just outside of Papeete to the Punaruu Valley. This road eases congestion because it parallels the other road, on the foot of the hill. Of the three districts, Punaauia and Paea are the most prosperous and suburban in nature. Faa'a is a mixed bag—there are resorts, middle-class housing and slum areas. Faa'a is where many of the less fortunate islanders from throughout French Polynesia move in order to look for work in the big city. (It was said that many of the participants in the infamous riot that destroyed half the airport on September 5–8, 1995, were disenfranchised Polynesians living in Faa'a.)

SIGHTS　　Jumping on the short section of freeway south of Papeete or using the old coastal road, **Tahiti Faa'a International Airport** is the first landmark you will encounter. The airport is as modern as any in the world, but still has distinct Tahitian touches such as barefoot kids, rotund Tahitian women selling leis and perhaps an unattended dog sleeping near the ticket counter. ~ PK 5.5, Faa'a.

The **Tahiti InterContinental Beachcomber**, one of the top hotels on the island, is situated at **Tata'a Point**. In ancient Tahitian times, it was considered a holy place where the souls of the dead were said to depart to the netherworld. There may still be dead souls who inhabit the corridors of the hotel. ~ PK 7.2, Punaauia.

The **Sofitel Maeva Beach** is just beyond the highway entrance and is a popular local beach. From this point, motorists can either take the four-lane "freeway" and zoom back to Papeete, or take the old coastal highway north to town. ~ PK 8, Punaauia.

The **Lagoonarium** combines a good restaurant with an equally decent aquarium. There are large tanks with sharks and other pelagics as well as numerous exhibits of tropical reef fish. There is an entrance fee to the aquarium, but if you eat at the restaurant, entry to the aquarium is free. (Of special interest is the Polynesian dance reviews put on at the Lagoonarium.) Admission. ~ PK 11, Punaauia; 43-62-90.

If you take the road one and a half kilometers farther, you will see the **2+2=4 Primary School**. A 19th-century French landowner donated the land for this school and had the above mathematical equation inscribed at the entrance. According to historian Bengt Danielsson, the donor, dubious about the propriety of introducing the French educational system to Tahiti, figured that if nothing else the children would learn one thing of value. ~ PK 12.5, Punaauia.

Just south of the school, in an area now subdivided, is the site of a home where **Paul Gauguin** lived from 1897 to 1901 and where he produced about 60 paintings. Among these are *Where Do We Come From* (the Museum of Fine Arts, Boston), *Faa Iheihe* (Tate Gallery, London) and *Two Tahitian Women* (the Metropolitan Museum, New York). Note that this landmark is merely the site of Gauguin's former home—the structure is long gone.

Beyond the bridge at the entrance of the **Punaru'u Valley** was once a fortress built by the French during the Tahitian uprising of 1844 to 1846. The site is now used as a TV relay station. The road up the valley leads to a trail (see "Hiking" at the end of this chapter) to the Tamanu Plateau where oranges grow in profusion. ~ PK 14, Punaauia.

One of the obligatory stops on your visit to Tahiti should be at the **Musée de Tahiti et des Iles**. No visitor to Tahiti with an interest in the island's culture should miss the museum. The museum is difficult to find, but head to PK 15 in Punaauia and turn toward the coast at the *Musée* sign posted. From there it's about one kilometer. Coming from Papeete by public transport, a Punaauia *Le Truck* will take you close to the main road junction. The last truck back to Papeete departs in late afternoon.

Opened in 1978 on the site of a historic *marae*, the museum is an excellent introduction to Tahiti. Exhibits cover the gamut, from flora and fauna to Polynesian culture and history. Though damaged in a cyclone in 1983, it was later revamped and remains perhaps the finest and most modern museum of the South Pacific. Judged by international standards, a museum curator would find the displays lacking in sophisticated museum technology and signage, but the material is wonderful. It consists of four sections:

Natural Environment and Human Settlement—This area covers flora, fauna, geology and Polynesian migration. Many of the

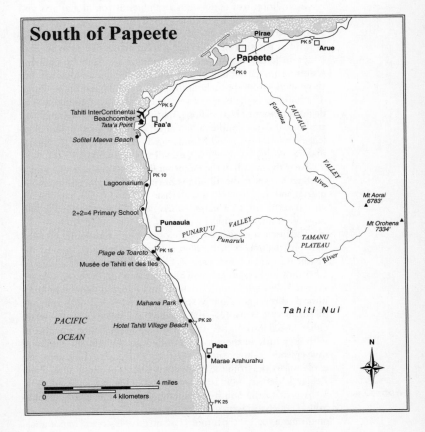

South of Papeete

Pirae
Papeete
PK S
Arue
PK 0

PK 5

Tahiti InterContinental
Beachcomber
Tata'a Point
Sofitel Maeva Beach
Faa'a

Fautaua

FAUTAUA

VALLEY

River

PK 10

Lagoonarium

Mt Aorai
6783'

2+2=4 Primary School

Punaauia

PUNARU'U   VALLEY

Punaru'u

Mt Orohena
7334'

TAMANU
PLATEAU

River

Plage de Toaroto
PK 15
Musée de Tahiti et des Îles

Mahana Park

Tahiti Nui

PACIFIC

Hotel Tahiti Village Beach
PK 20

OCEAN

Paea

Marae Arahurahu

N

0   4 miles
0   4 kilometers

PK 25

displays include sophisticated, electrically operated diagrams and instructional aides.

Traditional Polynesian culture—These exhibits examine pre-contact homes, costumes, religion, games, dances, musical instruments and ornaments.

Post-European era—The exploratory and missionary periods are extensively covered. The historical displays include figures illustrating captains James Cook, Louis-Antoine de Bougainville and Samuel Wallis, the Pomare dynasty, the missionary era and the history of the Chinese population.

Outdoor exhibits—A living natural-history section includes a botanical garden consisting of plants that Tahitians brought with them (such as taro, *ava*, yams and medicinal herbs). There is also a Canoe Room where traditional outrigger and dugout canoes are displayed.

In addition to the museum's exhibits of traditional arts and crafts, there is a wonderful collection of paintings and prints. Most of these are available for viewing in the **Exhibition Building**, which has rotating shows ranging from artists like John Webber (Captain James Cook's artist) to modern-day Tahitian painters, sculptors and potters. Exhibitions are not limited to local art, but show works from throughout the Pacific and the rest of the world. The building is the home of special events programming such as demonstrations of tapa-making, mat-weaving, instrument-making, traditional dances and exhibits illustrating the latest archaeological excavations. Closed Monday. Admission. ~ PK 15.1, Punaauia; 58-34-76, fax 58-43-00; e-mail musee@mail.pf.

Near the mouth of the **Punaru'u River** is a popular surf break. Surfing is a sport the Tahitians have practiced since time immemorial and they brought it with them to Hawaii. The same beach was also the site of a *marae* where in 1777 Captain Cook witnessed a human sacrifice.

This area was also the scene of an important battle in 1815 that pitted Pomare II, by then a Christian convert, against the heathen forces of the *Teva I Uta* clan. Pomare's well-armed Christian soldiers, aided by white mercenaries, overran their adversaries, but with true Christian mercy spared the enemy from unbridled revenge. Pomare spared human life but unfortunately all the artistic treasures—the wooden and stone carvings—were either tossed into the fire or destroyed, leaving future generations with very little in the way of Tahitian art. One of the results of this episode is that modern-day artisans carve tikis that are copies of works from the Marquesas Islands or those of the New Zealand Maoris. ~ PK 20, Paea.

HIDDEN ►

A visit to the South of Papeete sites ends at **Marae Arahu-rahu**. Danielsson writes that this particular *marae* (there's a sign on the main road at the turnoff) had no great historical importance, but provides a decent enough example of an ancient marae. It was restored in 1954 by the tourism authority under the supervision of the Société des Etudes Océaniennes. The rectangular pyramid is about the size of a tennis court and has a flat top. The *marae* is used occasionally during the Heiva festival in July as a stage for re-enactment of ancient rituals such as the "Crowning of a King" ceremony. The temple is in a lush valley bordered by steep cliffs. ~ PK 22.5, Paea.

LODGING

The **Sheraton Hotel Tahiti** sits on the large waterfront site of the old Hotel Tahiti, just at the Papeete/Faa'a border. A total of 200 rooms, including 10 suites, occupy a three-story structure. All rooms have waterfront views and there is a restaurant. ~ PK 2, Faa'a; 86-48-48, fax 86-48-40; www.sheratonsintahiti.pf, e-mail reservations.tahiti @sheraton.pf. ULTRA-DELUXE.

In the 19th century, Tahiti was a large exporter of oranges to New Zealand and—believe it or not—to California.

The **Heitiare Inn**, run by the congenial Mr. and Mrs. Tarahu, is directly across the street from the RIMAP military base, two minutes from the airport. It is a clean, wooden structure with six rooms, five of which are air-conditioned. Several of the rooms have a private bath and the rest have communal bath facilities. Communal kitchen facilities are available, as is a nearby swimming pool. The outdoor patio/deck is spacious and tiled. Rooms are clean and of adequate size. ~ PK 4.3, Faa'a; 83-33-52, fax 82-77-53. BUDGET TO MODERATE.

Chez Lola is located in the St. Hilaire area of Faa'a, five minutes from the airport. The house has two modest but comfortable rooms with a communal (hot water) bathroom and a TV. The owner, Lola Holozet, provides free airport transportation to her guests and will reduce the room price if you stay three nights or longer. No credit cards or traveler's checks accepted. ~ St. Hilaire, Faa'a; phone/fax 81-91-75. BUDGET.

Tahiti Airport Lodge is a budget accommodation only three minutes from the airport. A two-story, whitewashed structure, it has four rooms with shared bath facilities and two rooms with private baths. Breakfast is included and there is even a TV in the sitting room. Dinner is available for groups of ten or more. Backpackers report that this is the nicest dorm near the airport; it's certainly one of the better inexpensive facilities near town. It is best to book well in advance, as the facility frequently fills up on nights when international flights arrive. Airport transfers are free during the day but are charged after 10 p.m. The lodge is located on the mountain side of the road at Cite de l'Air. No credit cards. ~ PK 5.5, Faa'a; 79-30-84, fax 82-25-00. BUDGET.

The **Sofitel Maeva Beach** was one of the first upscale hotels constructed in Tahiti after the jet age brought mass tourism to the islands. A comfortable place with an ideal location for business or recreational use, it is approaching middle age—the international style of its 218 rooms seems dated—and is clearly second to the InterContinental in luxury. The parklike beachfront location and relaxed atmosphere are its biggest draws. Avoid the bottom-floor rooms as they can be more humid. Two restaurants and a beach snack bar are on the property. The Admiral de Bougainville Restaurant, overlooking the beach with a large outdoor dining area, is a very pleasant place to enjoy a meal or drink and always seems to be the center of activities. The best time to come is Sunday, when they offer a traditional Tahitian feast. The Sakura Japanese restaurant is also located inside the hotel. A tennis court and putting green are located on the grounds, and a wide range of recreational activities can be arranged. ~ PK 8, Punaauia; 86-66-66, fax 43-84-70, or 800-221-4542 in the U.S.; e-mail h0547@accor-ho tels.com. DELUXE.

Located in Punaauia, **Moana Surf Tours** has a dorm that will please surfers on a budget. With a communal hot-water bathroom and a kitchen, this is definitely a surfer's hangout. Moana sells a package that includes a bed, three meals and free transport to all surf spots for around US$100 per day. My hunch is that non-surfers are better off going elsewhere. No credit cards. ~ PK 8.3, Punaauia; phone/fax 43-70-70; e-mail moanasurftours@mail.pf. MODERATE.

Situated on the lagoon, **Ia Orana Villa** has done a great job of combining Polynesian style with modern comfort. Its 24 beach bungalows and 37 rooms are constructed in traditional style and fit nicely with the environment. The patio bar/nightclub is a perfect spot to cool off after a long day using the hotel's three tennis courts, swimming pool, boutiques and excursions/activities desk. Ia Orana Villa is reasonably priced and looks to be good value for the quality. Discounted weekly and monthly rates are available. ~ PK 10.5, Punaauia; 54-49-11, fax 54-49-14; e-mail iaoranavilla@ mail.pf. MODERATE TO DELUXE.

Relais Familial (Family House) in the district of Punaauia has two rooms with a shared kitchen, dining room, living room and terrace. ~ PK 12.3, Punaauia; 45-01-98, fax 54-30-03; e-mail relais. familial@mail.pf. BUDGET.

The upscale Polynesian-style **Le Meridien** resort, located in the Punaauia area, features 138 ocean-view rooms and 12 luxurious over-water bungalows, and two dining facilities. Recreational features include tennis courts, a sand-bottomed pool, outrigger canoeing, aqua-gym classes, scuba diving, massage and dolphin discovery. With the comforts of a tropical vacation, this hotel falls into the destination resort category, but if you suffer from mold allergies, go elsewhere. ~ PK 15, Punaauia; 47-07-07, fax 47-07-08; www.lemeridien-tahiti.com. ULTRA-DELUXE.

On the mountain side of the road is **Pension de la Plage**, the newest addition to the Punaauia-area lodgings. Built in a colonial style, la Plage offers nine double rooms with refrigerators and private hot-water baths. Some units have kitchenettes. There is a common lounge area for guests, as well as a shared dining room. Meal plans are available, and when it's hot you can dive into the swimming pool or cool off in the lagoon, just 300 feet away. ~ PK 15.4, Punaauia; 45-56-12, fax 82-85-48; www.pensiondela plage.com, e-mail laplage@mail.pf. BUDGET TO MODERATE.

Nearby **Chez Armelle** is an eight-unit complex on one of the island's coral beaches. The units are clean, basic and modern—all have private bath, fan and either a double bed or two singles. The eponymous Armelle has actually moved to Huahine, and the pension is now run by her two sons, Raimana and Heifara, who are friendly and helpful. They are also avid fishermen, and the day's catch will likely become the sashimi entrée or other fish specialty served at the pension's patio restaurant. One of the nice things about Chez Armelle is that it's close enough to town to take *Le Truck* without undue hassle. Surfers will appreciate that the pension is just 400 meters from the Sapinus reef break. Snorkeling gear, kayaks and bicycles are provided free of charge and the room price includes breakfast. To find it (coming from Papeete), go past Le Meridien hotel in Punaauia and take a right at the *Chez Armelle* sign posted on the highway. Follow the access road all the way to the end. To keep the noise down for the

◄ HIDDEN

AUTHOR FAVORITE

My all-time favorite luxury hotel in the Papeete area is the **Tahiti Inter-Continental Beachcomber**. Located two kilometers beyond Faa'a Airport and eight kilometers from Papeete (15 minutes with cooperative traffic conditions), the resort is a compromise between city and town—close enough to enjoy Papeete but far enough away to avoid the hustle.

The beachfront hotel's 233 standard rooms and 32 air-conditioned over-the-water bungalows are appointed with handpicked floral arrangements, and the bar/restaurant and conference hall have been totally revamped. The Intercontinental also has extensive water sports and an exotic freshwater pool that overflows into the sea near the lagoon bungalows. There are three restaurants, all of which are quite good. A nice touch is that you can also wash your clothes for free at washers and dryers in several locations, a welcome surprise in French Polynesia. ~ PK 7.2, Punaauia; 86-51-10, fax 86-51-30; www.tahiti. interconti.com, e-mail tahiti@interconti.com. ULTRA-DELUXE.

neighbors, guests are asked not to use the road before 8 a.m. ~ PK 15.5, Punaauia; 58-42-43, fax 58-42-81; www.pension-armelle.com, e-mail armelle@mail.pf. BUDGET TO MODERATE.

Le Bellevue is a well-maintained private home on the mountain side of the road. It has one very clean studio with a kitchenette and private bath. Minimum stay is one week. You must rent a car if you plan to stay here. The property is located three and a half kilometers from the shore in the residential area of Temaruata. ~ PK 16.5, Punaauia; 58-47-04. BUDGET TO MODERATE.

To the horror of the missionaries, Tahitian surfers practiced in the buff, prompting the prohibition of the sport during missionary years. It wasn't until the 1960s, after Tahitians had visited Hawaii by plane, that surfing made a comeback.

Taaroa Lodge consists of a large wooden bungalow with clean rooms near the beach. On the first floor is a dormitory that provides bunks for a maximum of eight people. On the ground floor are a shared bathroom, kitchen, dining room and a private room for two people that has a private bath. It's located behind the snack bar on the seaside. ~ PK 18, Punaauia; phone/fax 58-39-21; www.taaroalodge.com, e-mail taaroalodge@mail.pf. BUDGET.

The owner of Relais Familial also runs the **Relais Fenua**. Located only 200 yards from the white-sand beach in Punaauia, Relais Fenua offers six rooms and two suites, all with private facilities, air conditioning, TV and internet access. One room is wheelchair accessible. There is also a tropical garden, which has a swimming pool and a jacuzzi. Airport transfers are 2200 CFP. ~ PK 18.3, Punaauia; 45-01-98, 77-25-45, fax 45-01-98; e-mail relais-fenua@mail.pf MODERATE.

Te Miti is marked by a sign that announces "Bed and Breakfast." Located on the mountain side of the road, it consists of two homes on a quarter-acre of land loaded with banana, breadfruit, mango and papaya trees. There is both dorm-style accommodation with several beds to a room and good-sized private bedrooms—unusual for budget lodging in Tahiti. The rooms have fans and plenty of space for storing clothing and suitcases. The buildings are modern and have tiled floors, clean showers and toilets, and cooking facilities with a refrigerator where guests can store perishables. There is also a patio with space to lounge or read. The young managers are friendly and provide bicycles and breakfast as part of the package. (They will also cook guests lunch and dinner, but that is extra.) This is one of the best, if not *the* best, budget lodging on the island. It's also ideal for surfers because of the proximity to breaks on the south side of the island. Weekly and monthly rates are available. To get there, take the Paea bound *Le Truck* to PK 18.6 and walk 200 yards inland, up the street that has the *Te Miti* sign. It will be on your left. Management will provide transportation from the airport if you arrive at night and call them.

During the day you must take *Le Truck*, but note that it stops running after about 5:30 p.m., which means you can't get to and from Papeete at night (there are stores and restaurants in the area, however). This property is so popular that the bathroom situation gets tight at times, and the police occasionally stop by to check travel documents, searching for those who have overstayed their welcome. If your visa has expired, this is not the place to stay! ~ PK 18.6, Punaauia; phone/fax 58-48-61, 78-60-80; www.pension temiti.com, e-mail pensiontemiti@mail.pf. BUDGET.

Fare Opuhi Roti is a modest bungalow suitable for a couple or a small family. It's located in Paea on the mountain side of the road. There are several beds with mosquito nets, a fan and a small kitchen table. Run by the amiable Alain Lehartel, it has cooking facilities, a private hot-water bathroom, and even a TV. ~ PK 21.2, Paea; 53-20-26. BUDGET.

DINING

Coming from town about 1.5 kilometers before the airport on the ocean side, you will find **Le Grand Lac**, which offers good, inexpensive, Hong Kong– and Singapore-style Chinese food. Their specialty is seafood dishes and the menu has a litany of items ranging from a whole fish braised in a spicy black bean sauce to locally caught crabs. ~ PK 4.5, Faa'a; 83-18-18. MODERATE.

Though hotel dining is not always recommended in Tahiti, the restaurants at the **Tahiti InterContinental Beachcomber** are reasonably priced and quite good. Next to the pool is the **Lotus Restaurant**, an indoor/outdoor eatery on the patio that serves lunch and dinner (a sumptuous salad bar at a reasonable price or à la carte grilled food). The **Hibiscus**, which has uncharacteristically inexpensive prices (for French Polynesia), is also recommended for breakfast. For example, you can get a great omelette at a budget price. Along with à la carte items, one can also get a full breakfast—but this is quite a bit more expensive. Fish and grilled steak are available for lunch or dinner. ~ PK 7.2, Punaauia; 86-51-10. BUDGET TO DELUXE.

Farther down the road in Punaauia at **L'Auberge du Pacifique**, you can get first-class seafood as well as tourist menus. They also serve excellent drinks distilled from tropical fruit. ~ PK 11.2, Punaauia; 43-98-30. ULTRA-DELUXE.

Just minutes down the road you will find **Coco's**, which has a lovely view of the sea, good seafood and an American-style bar. ~ PK 13, Punaauia; 58-21-08. ULTRA-DELUXE.

The **Admiral de Bougainville Restaurant** at the Sofitel Maeva has long had the reputation of being one of the best on the island. Many of the dishes are a French–Tahitian fusion that utilizes fresh seafood combined with Polynesian ingredients such as coconut milk and local herbs. Bougainville Restaurant has breakfast and lunch buffets Monday through Saturday, nightly happy hours from 9 to 10 p.m., and buffet dinners on Friday and Saturday followed by a Tahitian dance show. There is also a Sunday Tahitian buffet lunch with a dance performance. ~ PK 8, Punaauia; 42-80-42. DELUXE TO ULTRA-DELUXE.

Casablanca Restaurant at the Taina Marina in Punaauia is a hip outdoor restaurant on the waterfront. The cuisine is French and Tahitian; the atmosphere is lively and informal. Typical dishes include couscous and *poisson cru*. Open seven days a week (with live music but no dancing on weekends), Casablanca is popular with locals but not well known to the tourist crowd. ~ Taina Marina, Punaauia; 43-91-35. MODERATE.

On the west coast of Tahiti you can find some reasonably priced restaurants, such as **Captain Bligh-Lagoonarium** ~ PK 11.4, Punaauia, 43-62-90; **Venezia**, a good pizzeria ~ PK 12.6, Punaauia, 41-30-56; **Tiare Anani**, good Chinese cuisine ~ PK 12.7, Punaauia, 43-45-06; **Fleur de Lotus**, a Chinese restaurant ~ PK 13, Punaauia, 41-97-20; **Chez Rémy**, French cuisine ~ Centre Tamanu, PK 15, Punaauia, 58-21-61; **L'Imperial**, Chinese cuisine and dim sum. ~ PK 15, across from Le Meridien, 45-19-18.

The restaurant **La Plantation** at Le Meridien is clearly one of the best in Tahiti. Be sure and check out the sumptuous buffets on weekends—a pleasure for the eyes and the palate. The brunch on Sunday is a terrific bargain. ~ PK 15, Punaauia; 47-07-07. ULTRA-DELUXE.

HIDDEN ►   **La Mangue Verte** also specializes in Tahitian and French cuisine. In its indoor/outdoor setting on the ocean side, one can sample a variety of seafood, fish, lobster and *poisson cru*. Extremely popular with locals, this eatery features Tahitian music and dancing on the weekends. It's a good place to meet locals. ~ PK 18.3, Punaauia; 48-19-99. MODERATE.

Chez Armelle is a budget accommodation that also has a small restaurant/snack bar with a shaded, outdoor patio that looks over the sea. Dishes range from sandwiches and burgers to steak and *frites*, pasta, and fresh-caught sashimi and grilled fish. The food is tasty and reasonably priced. Ambience on the beach is great. ~ PK 15.5, Punaauia; 58-42-43. BUDGET.

GROCERIES   Throughout Tahiti there are the ubiquitous grocery stores to buy bread and other everyday items. Volume shoppers or penny pinchers who don't mind trekking an extra kilometer for a bargain should definitely shop at **Carrefour**, a discount warehouse-style outlet (also called *hypermarché*). It's part of a huge shopping center called Moana Nui located just off the freeway. Though prices still pale in comparison to American-style merchandisers such as Costco or Sam's Club, all manner of food and consumer goods are less expensive at these stores than anywhere else in the country.

Competition in the retail area did not exist in Tahiti until the *hypermarché* was introduced in the early 1990s. (On the outer islands, especially Bora Bora, the gouging continues unabated.) ~ Moana Nui Shopping Center, PK 8.3, Punaauia; 46-08-08.

Some good local supermarkets include **Supermarché Faa'a** at PK 4.9 in Faa'a ~ 82-77-19, **Supermarché Marina Lotus** at PK 9.2 in Punaauia ~ 45-01-89, **Supermarché Tumanu** at PK 15 in Punaauia ~ 45-01-89 and **Supermarché Paea** at PK 19.5 in Paea ~ 53-26-65.

The big hotels put on island-night dance performances, often combined with a buffet dinner of Tahitian food. One of the best of these performances is the show at the **InterContinental Beachcomber** on Friday and Saturday evenings. Ringside seats come with the purchase of a buffet dinner, although you can watch the show for the price of a drink at the bar. ~ PK 7.2, Punaauia; 86-51-10.

NIGHTLIFE

> Prices at Carrefour are such comparative bargains that it is actually less expensive for residents of the outer islands to take a ferry (with car) to Tahiti, stock up on groceries and return to their home island, than to buy from a local grocer.

A Polynesian *spectacle* at the **Sofitel Maeva Beach** takes place in the Admiral de Bougainville Restaurant on Friday and Saturday nights at 8 p.m. ~ PK 8, Punaauia; 42-80-42.

The **Lagoonarium** dance performances are more than a cut above the ordinary and worth seeing if dance is an important part of your itinerary. Performances are scheduled Friday and Saturday evenings. Admission. ~ PK 11, Punaauia; 43-62-90.

On Friday night be sure and check out the **Hotel Le Meridien**, which has one of the best *Soirée Polynésienne* extravaganzas in town. A delicious buffet is served in a magnificent setting; the stage is a *motu* in the swimming pool facing the restaurant La Plantation. ~ PK 15, Punaauia; 47-07-07.

SOFITEL MAEVA BEACH This is the closest beach to town heading south. The sand is brown in color—a sort of hybrid of the black- and white-sand varieties. It's popular with locals on the weekends and swimming is very good—with one caveat. The Tahiti Tourist Board warned me that due to large amounts of effluent, it is sometimes not advisable to swim in this area, and some visitors have experienced rashes after doing so. Best to check with the tourist office regarding the (health) status of the water if you plan to swim. Midway between the beach and the barrier reef, which is about 200 yards offshore, is a pontoon anchored in nine feet of water. It makes for great sunbathing and a 360° panorama, but keep in mind there's no shade on the pontoon. For 500 CFP, a launch will take you out to the pontoon, where nude sunbathing is permitted.

BEACHES & PARKS

The beach here is public, but the restrooms and restaurant facilities belong to the hotel. There are a few canopies (no trees) to shade you on the beach and a multitude of beach chairs courtesy of the hotel.

HIDDEN ► **PLAGE DE TOAROTO (TOAROTO BEACH)** Plage de Toaroto is but one entry point to a long, fine white-sand beach in the Punaauia district that runs approximately from PK 15.5 down to PK 19. Even though this is a long stretch of beach front, it lies opposite a residential area and is accessible only at a few points. Usually not more than 50 feet wide, it is generally clean and uncrowded. The water is deep enough in most areas to make it fine for swimming. The snorkeling is also good. There are toilet facilities near the main road and Chez Armelle, a local pension, has a snack bar open to the public. ~ Take the main highway south to Punaauia. Keep an eye open for the Mobil Station (on the inland side of the road) and perhaps 50 yards after the station note the green *Plage de Toaroto* sign. Take a right and pull into the parking lot. From there, walk down to the easement to the beach.

HOTEL TAHITI VILLAGE BEACH Known also as Plage de Toaroto, this beach includes the former grounds of Hotel Tahiti Village (which has since been torn down). The beach is narrow, clean and generally not too crowded. Swimming is good, particularly if the tide is high. Snorkeling can also be done. There is a large pavilion with toilet and shower facilities (they were under construction when I last visited). ~ To find it, look for the large wooden sign on the ocean side of the road at PK 20 that announces you have just entered the district of Paea. Go through the large green wooden gate, which opens up to a huge parking lot.

MAHANA PARK The only beach in Tahiti that's also a park, Mahana features a beautiful white-sand beach and a play-

LIFE IN A LOCAL BAR

Someone will most likely buy you a beer and ask where you're from and whether you're married. Tahitians are extremely curious about one's marital status. If you have no spouse, they will shake their heads and say, "*Aita maitai* (no good). Maybe you'll find a nice Tahitian to marry." Expect to be chided a little if you go to working-class bars. Tahitians are generally polite, but often the visitor bears the brunt of their jokes. Laugh along. One evening at a local dive, several Americans were entertained by a drunken Tahitian comedian who told outrageous jokes. He was bringing the house down. The routine was entirely in Tahitian, and the Americans were the butt of every joke.

ground for children, as well as rental *pedalos*, kayaks and canoes. Nearby is the restaurant La Mangue Verte, where you can wet your whistle or take a freshwater shower and relax after a full day of outdoor activities. ~ PK 18.2, Paea.

Just 12.5 miles (20 kilometers) either side of Papeete takes you far from the center of commerce, beyond the suburbs

Outer Districts of Tahiti

into what locals call *les districts*—the outer reaches of the island. Here life is generally slower, the population density is lower, and the culture is more traditional. Though the Tahiti of Gauguin and Stevenson is long gone, a visitor may still glimpse something of the way things were. You may pass an old man peddling a bicycle with a fresh baguette tucked under his arm or see the family of a fisherman peddling the day's catch dangling from twine on the shoulder of road. Whatever you do, don't confine yourself to Papeete, thinking that you've seen it all.

Since we have already covered the attractions from Papeete to PK 22.1, in the North of Papeete section, let's begin the round-the-island tour in Tiarei at the next landmark, which is at PK 25, the Gardens and Copra Plantation. Likewise, since we have covered the area from Papeete southward to the Marae Arahurahu, PK 22.5, that is where the tour will end.

Gardens and Copra Plantation is a private reserve, but you can park and view the lily ponds and accompanying flora that thrive in the area from the main road. The coconut plantation here, one of many on Tahiti and its neighboring islands, was once an important source of cash for the average Tahitian. Although harvesting copra (dried coconut meat) continues to be a vital occupation for islanders outside Tahiti, it is of secondary importance in a Tahitian economy that now relies on tourism, black pearl cultivation and the governmental bureaucracy as sources of jobs. ~ PK 25, Tiarei.

SIGHTS

Though nothing more violent than a cockfight occurs here today, in another era this area was a **battlefield**. The annexation of Tahiti by France in 1843 sparked armed resistance among Tahitians, and guerrilla warfare continued until the rebellion was crushed in 1846. The most important battle of this war was fought at Mahaena on April 17, 1844. The battlefield stretched from the beach southward to the present-day church and city hall. Heeding the advice of British sailors and French Army deserters, Tahitians dug three parallel trenches and awaited their French adversaries. Two French warships appeared and a force of 441 men stormed the Tahitian position, which had approximately twice the defenders but lacked modern weapons. When the dust cleared, 102 Tahitians were dead and the French had lost only 15 men. After this blow the natives realized that guerrilla warfare was the only alternative and they continued to operate from bases in the bush until their main stronghold was captured in 1846. ~ PK 32.5, Mahaena.

In April 1768, less than 100 years before the battle, Captain Louis-Antoine de Bougainville anchored here. To find **Bougainville's Anchorage** look out to sea and note the two offshore islets, Variararu and Oputotara. The former has a few trees and the latter just brush. Just off Oputotara is where Bougainville anchored. Although cultured to the bone, Bougainville was not much of a sailor. His choice of this particular anchorage, which lacked the proper shelter and wind conditions, was not the best. He managed to lose six anchors in ten days and nearly lost the ships as well. Soon after this debacle some Tahitians actually salvaged one of the anchors and gave it to the King of Bora Bora as a gift. Captain Cook later took possession of it in 1777. ~ PK 37.6, Hitiaa.

To get a terrific **vista** of the peninsula, stop here. At this point you have a splendid view of Tahiti Iti, Tahiti's panhandle and the high, verdant peaks that tower over it. From here it's easy to see how Tahiti Iti (little Tahiti) is the smaller loop of this figure eight of an island. ~ PK 39, Hitiaa.

The **Fa'atautia River Bridge** is a good place to stop and view the Vaiharuru Falls in the distance. This site was chosen by U.S. filmmaker John Huston to make a cinematographic version of Herman Melville's *Typee*. Unfortunately, because his first attempt at a Melville movie, *Moby Dick*, was commercially unsuccessful, the scheme was abandoned. ~ PK 41.8, Hitiaa.

The Isthmus of Taravao marks the halfway point of your round-the-island tour. On the outskirts of the community of Taravao note the sentry at the gate marking the entrance to the **Military Base** on your right. Military and police installations have existed here since 1844 when the French guarded the isthmus to prevent marauding guerrillas from filtering down from the peninsula to the main part of the island. The old fort (within the army camp) still stands. Since then, the site has served as a *gendarmerie*, an internment camp for Germans unfortunate enough to be on the island during WWII and, most recently, a military base. ~ PK 60.5, Taravao.

Past the fort, on your left, is the junction to Tautira, which will take you to the north coast of Tahiti Iti. A kilometer down the north coast road is the junction to the inland road that straddles the Taravao Plateau.

Shortly after passing the junction you will see a few buildings and shops scattered alongside the road with little thought to aesthetics or planning. You are now in downtown **Taravao**. Though the backdrop of the community has drop-dead vistas of lush mountains and shoreline (which makes the drive to the island's end worthwhile), the town is not particularly attractive. Other

than the military base and a few very good restaurants (worth
checking out), there is not much to this community. Recently a
massive new dock was built near Taravao with the idea of bringing jobs and commerce to the area, but it has yet to be determined what will be shipped in and who will actually use the facility. At the south end of town on your left is the junction to the
southern coast, which will take you to Teahupoo, the village at
the end of the line. Note that the coastal roads on the periphery of the peninsula do not meet—rather they terminate before
reaching the far end of Tahiti Iti. To circumnavigate the island
you must hike.

Continuing on the loop around Tahiti Nui, look carefully
among the mango trees on the hill and you will see the former
home of English writer **Robert Keable**. Although not a household
name today, Keable produced two religious novels, *Simon Called
Peter* and *Recompense*, which sold a combined total of 600,000

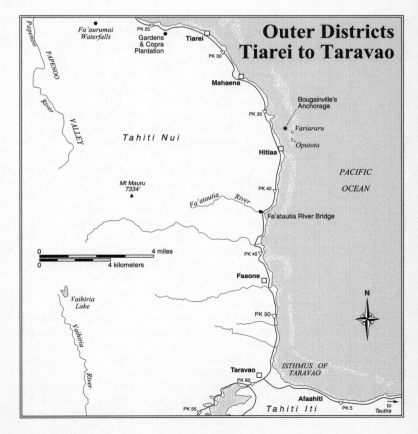

copies in the 1920s. Obsessed with the question of why Tahiti and Tahitian women held so much attraction for white men, he provided his own answers in two more books: *Tahiti, Isle of Dreams* and *Numerous Treasure*. Keable's well-maintained home is in its original 1920s condition, but it is not open to the public. ~ PK 55.5, Papeari.

The **Debarkation Point of Ancient Tahitians**, according to traditional accounts, was the first place where the ancient Polynesians settled over 1000 years ago. Because of this, families chiefly from this district have always been held in the highest prestige among their counterparts in the other districts of Tahiti. The present-day village is known for its beautiful gardens and roadside produce stands. The Papeari inlet has a number of oyster beds and fish traps. Around this area, and throughout the rural side of the island, you often see fishermen on the side of the road selling their fresh catch dangling from nylon cord strings. ~ PK 52, Papeari.

The **Harrison W. Smith Botanical Garden** was established in 1919 by Smith, a physics professor who left the Massachusetts Institute of Technology at age 37 to dedicate the rest of his life to botany in Tahiti. He introduced a range of tropical shrubs, trees and flowers to the islands from throughout the world, and some became important local products. My favorite among these is the huge, delectable grapefruit known as the *pamplemousse*, which originated in Borneo. Smith did not merely putter around in his own garden but generously gave seeds and cuttings to Tahitian farmers to help them improve their own crops. After his death in 1947 the garden was willed to another botanist and, through the help of U.S. philanthropist Cornelius Crane, was given to the public.

The massive gardens are laced with footpaths that wend their way through acres of well-tended palms, hibiscus, elephant ears, bamboo, bananas and many other species. There were also several Galapagos tortoises brought to Tahiti in the 1930s, which were given to author Charles Nordhoff's children.

The gardens, which you may find more interesting than the Gauguin Museum, were spruced up in 1990 for the visit of the late French president François Mitterand. Admission. ~ PK 51.2, Papeari; 57-11-07.

Opposite the garden grounds is a modern, Japanese-style structure—the **Paul Gauguin Museum**, with exhibits chronicling the life of Tahiti's most famous former resident. The walls are covered with documents and photographs from the Gauguin era, along with reproductions and—for the first time in years—some original Gauguin works, among them sketches, block prints and the original blocks. Sadly, there are no original Gauguin paintings. Though a century has passed since Gauguin put his brush to canvas, the perplexing moods of Tahitians that he captured are still displayed today on every street corner in Papeete.

There are also some original paintings by artist Constance Gordon Cummings, an Englishwoman who stayed in French Polynesia for six months in 1877. She painted some exquisite landscapes of Tahiti and Moorea. For sale at the gift shop are postcards, T-shirts, stationery and excellent reproductions of Gauguin's works, Cummings' paintings and the works of other artists who lived on the island. Bring along some insect repellent when you visit—the mosquitoes can sometimes be a nuisance. Note that there are separate entrances for the museum and the nearby beach park, both of which are open seven days a week. The Botanical Garden has a small and reasonably priced café. Admission. ~ PK 51.2, Papeari; 57-10-58, fax 57-10-42; e-mail museegauguin@mail.pf.

> Those taking Le Truck from Papeete to the Gauguin Museum should start early in the morning. The last Le Truck heading to town is at 1 p.m., and it's a long walk back.

Not far down the road is **Vaipahi Garden**, abloom with tropical flowers and plants such as hanging and upright heliconia, allamanda, ixora and bird of paradise. You can take a leisurely hike to a nearby waterfall, surrounded by red, pink and torch gingers. The garden, located on the seaside, is under the supervision of the tourist office. It's very well tended and has picnic facilities. ~ PK 49, Papeari.

The **Vaihiria River** originates from the lake of the same name —Tahiti's only lake. At 1500 feet (450 meters) above sea level, it is bounded on the north by 3000-foot (900-meter) cliffs, which make up the southern wall of the Papenoo crater. The lake is known among locals for its large eels and nearby plantations of *fe'i* (mountain bananas). It is accessible with the aid of a guide (see "Drive Tours" at the end of this chapter), but there are waterfalls visible from the road. ~ PK 48, Mataiea.

After living briefly in Papeete, Paul Gauguin moved to **Mataiea Village** in October 1891, where he lived until May 1893. He rented a bamboo hut, found a *vahine* and painted such masterpieces as *Hina Tefatou* (the Museum of Modern Art, New York), *Ia Orana Maria* (the Metropolitan Museum of Art, New York), *Fatata te Miti* (the National Gallery of Art, Washington, DC), *Manao Tupapau* (Albright-Knox Art Gallery, Buffalo), *Reverie* (the William Rockhill Nelson Gallery of Art, Kansas City) and *Under the Pandanus* (the Minneapolis Institute of Art).

Twenty-three years later, when Somerset Maugham came to the village culling information about Gauguin's life for his novel *The Moon and Sixpence*, he discovered three painted glass doors in the wooden bungalow belonging to Gauguin's landlord. These paintings by the great artist had never been discovered. Most of the paintings had been mutilated by children's play but Maugham picked the best one up for 200 francs and painstakingly shipped it back to Europe. Near the end of his life he sold the forgotten door at Sotheby's for a princely sum. ~ PK 46.5, Mataiea.

Although the fairways of the **Olivier Breaud International Golf Course** are trim and green now, in former times this area was white with cotton. The plantation that flourished here for a short time had a tremendous impact on Tahiti's population and history. The story begins not in Tahiti but in the United States, during the midst of the Civil War. The war made it impossible for Europeans to import cotton and created a tremendous demand for this commodity. Scottish wine merchant William Stewart, who made a living importing liquor to the South Pacific, responded by setting up a cotton plantation in Tahiti. He acquired land in Atimaono, the only area in Tahiti capable of large-scale agricultural development and, with the help of blackbirders (slave traders), he recruited labor. This did not work too well, so coolie labor from China was used and thus the seeds of the powerful Chinese community in Tahiti were planted. Working conditions were atrocious and violence tempered by the guillotine was the rule of the day. ~ PK 41, Atimaono.

By 1867, despite the awful circumstances, 2470 acres of high-grade cotton were planted and the harvest lived up to Stewart's dreams. In the meantime, he had built a huge villa and spent his evenings as the king of the roost, entertaining Tahitian high society. However, there was a catch. The Civil War had ended and with it the shortage of cotton from the South. There were also problems with the weather, which was not ideal for cultivation of cotton. Stewart could not compete with his American counterparts, who were geographically much closer to Europe, and he fell into bankruptcy. He died at the young age of 48. A number of the Chinese workers elected to stay and intermarried with the local population.

The access road to the ruins of **Marae Mahaiatea**, once a great temple, is posted on the highway. Today the *marae* is only a huge pile of boulders but early European visitors like Cook were astounded by its dimensions—270 feet (81 meters) long, 90 feet (27 meters) wide and 550 feet (165 meters) high—and its architecture. Not only did the builders need a considerable amount of skill to construct the temple, they had to build it without the benefit of iron tools. Danielsson claims it was once the most spectacular monument in Tahiti. The temple's fall into decay is not only the fault of nature—apparently the old temple was used by William Stewart as a source of stones for his building projects at the cotton plantation a few kilometers away. In the words of J. C. Beaglehole, the great biographer of Cook, "Nature and human stupidity combine as usual to wipe out the diverse signs of human glory." ~ PK 39.2, Papara.

In Papara, you will find a beige-colored Protestant church and a seashell museum. In the graveyard of this **Tahitian church** lie the remains of a former United States Consul and Yankee hero of the Civil War, Dorence Atwater. At age 16, Atwater joined the Union Army, was captured by rebel scouts and served time in three Confederate prisons until he was sent to a hospital where he ended up as a clerk recording the deaths of Federal prisoners. Fearing that the Confederates were not keeping accurate records, he copied the lists and escaped, bringing them to the attention of the federal government. In 1875, Atwater wed the beautiful Princess Moetia of the local chief's family, which had ruled the district for generations. (At one point his grave was marked, but it no longer can be identified.) ~ PK 36, Papara.

Across the street from the church is the **Musée des Coquillages** (Seashell Museum), housed in a white colonial-style building. The museum has a very extensive shell collection as well as some aquarium exhibits. It's also a good place to pick up quality sou-

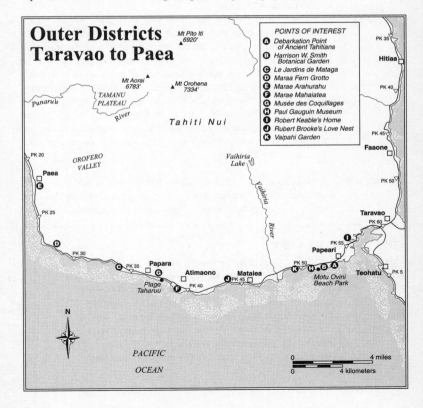

**Outer Districts
Taravao to Paea**

Mt Pito Iti
▲6920'

POINTS OF INTEREST

Ⓐ Debarkation Point
   of Ancient Tahitians
Ⓑ Harrison W. Smith
   Botanical Garden
Ⓒ Le Jardins de Mataga
Ⓓ Maraa Fern Grotto
Ⓔ Marae Arahurahu
Ⓕ Marae Mahaiatea
Ⓖ Musée des Coquillages
Ⓗ Paul Gauguin Museum
Ⓘ Robert Keable's Home
Ⓙ Rubert Brooke's Love Nest
Ⓚ Vaipahi Garden

PK 35

Hitiaa

PK 40

Mt Aorai
▲6783'

▲Mt Orohena
  7334'

TAMANU
PLATEAU

Punaru'u

River

Tahiti Nui

PK 20

OROFERO
VALLEY

Vaihiria
Lake

PK 45

Faaone

Paea

Ⓔ

PK 50

Vaihiria River

PK 25

Taravao
PK 60

Ⓓ

PK 30

PK 55

Ⓘ

PK 35

Papara

Ⓖ

Atimaono

Mataiea

PK 50

ⓀⒽⒷⒶ

Papeari

PK 5

Teohatu

Ⓒ

Ⓕ

Plage
Taharuu

PK 40

ⒿPK 45

Motu Ovini
Beach Park

N

PACIFIC
OCEAN

0   4 miles

0   4 kilometers

venirs such as woven pandanus hats, baskets and purses, which are sold in the gift shop. Admission. ~ PK 36, Papara; 57-45-22.

Also in Papara, **Mataoa Garden** has one of the most complete collections of tropical flowers and plants in Polynesia. Founded several years ago by a French couple (Alain and Jocelyne), Le Jardins de Mataga has guided tours (fee) where plant aficionados can learn more about the flora of French Polynesia. Adjacent to the garden is a boutique-like stand where locally made fruit juice and liquor can be tasted. Alain and Jocelyne are also owners of **Tahiti Fleurs**, a company that will ship tropical flowers and bouquets around the world. Closed weekends. ~ PK 34.5, Papara; 57-37-24, fax 57-36-49; www.tahiti-fleurs.com, e-mail info@tahiti-fleurs.com.

The border between the districts of **Papara** and **Paea** have the least amount of rainfall and are among the most desirable areas in Tahiti to live in. Note the fine homes on the coast (owned mostly by Europeans) and the quiet lagoon and beaches, sheltered by a barrier reef. ~ PK 29.

Just before Paea is the **Maraa Fern Grotto**, which always seems to be an obligatory stop on the visitor's itinerary. Actually there are three grottos, which are accessible from a trail that skirts the base of the rock face. The grottos are gaping holes in the cliff with shallow pools of water filled from water constantly seeping from the ceiling. Ferns dangle like stalactites and the vegetation around the grottos is lush. Its main significance is that it is an optical illusion—it seems to be smaller than it is. The area is, however, popular as a stop and has been improved to accommodate more cars and picnickers. It is a cool place to visit on a hot day. ~ PK 28.5, Paea.

LODGING   Almost all of the Tahiti accommodation possibilities are located either in downtown Papeete or close to town along the coast on either side of the city limits. There are a handful of possibilities

LOVE'S LABOR'S LOST

Shortly before World War I, poet Rupert Brooke jumped on a boat in San Francisco and headed for Tahiti "to hunt for lost Gauguins." He ended up in Mataiea, where he rented a bungalow, which became **Rupert Brooke's Love Nest**. Instead of discovering lost masterpieces, Brooke found his first and only true love. Mamua inspired one of his best poems, *Tiare Tahiti*. Brooke eventually left Tahiti with a heavy heart and several years later died on a hospital ship off Gallipoli, a casualty of the war. His beloved Mamua fell three years after that, a victim of Spanish influenza. ~ PK 44, Mataiea.

elsewhere on the island, for those who really want to get away from it all or who want to spend more than one day on an island circuit. They're found farther out around Tahiti Nui (the main part of the island), on Tahiti Iti (the smaller appendage) or up in the central mountains. See the Tahiti Iti section for accommodations on that peninsula.

Fare Nana'o remains one of the most popular, offbeat pensions in Tahiti. If you are going to stay on the far side of the island, this is *the* place to consider. Located on the water, it has six very original bungalows constructed from natural materials, mostly wood, stone and *pandanus* thatch. Rooms are large and airy. The owners, Monique and Jean-Claude Michel, emphasize that the shape of the walls, the support beams, the doors and the windows are determined by the natural shape and contours of the trees and stones. Even the outhouse is unusual—a fine ceramic toilet, complete with houseplant and floor lined with white coral belie the rustic exterior. You pay extra for food and activities such as sightseeing, sea tours and sailing. Transport to and from the airport is also an additional charge. Those with a taste for the unusual or the bohemian may find Fare Nana'o to their liking. It seems to be popular with Japanese visitors and comes highly recommended. No credit cards. ~ PK 52, Faaone; 57-18-14, fax 57-76-10; e-mail farenanao@mail.pf. MODERATE TO DELUXE.

◄ *HIDDEN*

Hiti Moana Villa, run by Auguste and Henriette Brotherson, offers four well-appointed bungalows suitable for surfers or golf fanatics, given its close proximity (about a ten-minute drive) to the Papara surf break and the Atimaono golf course. Motor boats, kayaks, *pirogues* and bicycles are available for rent. Minimum stay is three nights. ~ PK 36, Papara; 57-93-93, fax 57-94-44; e-mail hitimoanavilla@mail.pf. MODERATE TO DELUXE.

Papara Village is among the most interesting "district" accommodations. Situated on a hillside overlooking the sea, it has a swimming pool and two very comfortable thatch-roofed bungalows—one unit suitable for a couple, and one that can accommodate a much larger family. The small unit has a little fridge but no cooking facilities; the larger bungalow has kitchen facilities and a washing machine. Both have a private bathroom, terrace and TV. Dinner can be arranged ahead of time. Papara Village is handy for those interested in golfing (the course is only five minutes away), surfing, or visits to the Paul Gauguin Museum or nearby archaeological sites. Two-night minimum stay. PK 38.1, Papara; 57-41-41, 57-45-74, fax 57-79-00. BUDGET TO MODERATE.

Fare Ratere on the south coast near Mahaiatea beach is on the sea side in a peaceful locale with two local-style bungalows set in spacious, well-tended grounds. Each bungalow has two rooms, a mezzanine, living room with TV, kitchen and private bath. In addition is a unit containing three studios, each with

double bed, sofa, private bath, kitchenette and terrace. There is
a two-night minimum stay. ~ PK 39.5, Papara; 57-48-19, fax 57-
48-00; e-mail yannfareratere@mail.pf. DELUXE TO ULTRA-DELUXE.

DINING   Although most of Tahiti's restaurants are concentrated in Papeete, there are enough places scattered around the island to provide a selection of lunch stops for visitors making an island tour.
The following places are listed district by district in the same sequence as the round-the-island circuit.

Le Rouge et le Noir (The Red and Black), is located on the
site of the former Chez Bob Tardieu. The small eatery sports a
traditional Polynesian *fare pote'e* (a traditional meeting house)
that serves as a dining room. The owners are from the southwest
of France, a heritage that is reflected in the menu with specialties
such as *foie gras* and *canard maison* (home-style duck). Local
fish provide the substance of other specialties. Open for lunch
Tuesday through Sunday, for dinner on Friday and Saturday.
Once a month a musical event is presented. ~ PK 52, Faaone; 52-
19-00. MODERATE.

Baie Phaeton is an attractive white structure with a red-tile
roof. With a balcony overlooking Phaeton Bay, it has a splendid
view of the yachts moored just offshore and the rugged heights
of Tahiti Iti in the distance. Primarily a Chinese restaurant, it has
a rather large selection of seafood but poultry is also available.
There are also a number of salads, as well as sashimi and tuna.
Specialties are *fruit de mer* and curry shrimp. You can also get the
standard Chinese mainstays of chop suey and chow mein, along
with friendly service and nice surroundings. ~ PK 58.9, Taravao;
57-08-96. BUDGET TO MODERATE.

Snack restaurant **Chez Myriam**, located on the main drag in
Taravao, resembles an American fast-food restaurant from the
1950s. It is easily recognizable with a faded red awning. Myriam
will take your orders from a counter behind a window. The eatery
has outdoor and indoor seating and a fairly extensive menu posted
on a chalkboard. Myriam serves basic Tahitian fare such as steak
and fries, *poisson cru*, sandwiches and mahimahi. It's also a good
place to go for ice cream. If you are there on a Saturday try her
couscous. ~ PK 60, Taravao; 57-71-01. BUDGET TO MODERATE.

HIDDEN ►   **L'Escale** is also on Taravao's main street. From all accounts,
it is the hands-down favorite for French cuisine. Run by an amiable Frenchman named Claude, L'Escale is a fairly large restaurant by Taravao standards, with about a dozen tables on two levels and a bar that seats several patrons. It has a comprehensive
Continental menu including many salads (*salade nicoise* and
hearts of palm to name a couple) but the real specialty of the
house is fish and there is nearly always a reasonably priced
seafood *plat du jour*. Claude's recommendation is the mahimahi

in coconut cream and marinated tuna. Ice cream is the item to choose for dessert, including a great coconut, Kahlúa and vanilla. ~ PK 60, Taravao; 57-07-16. MODERATE TO DELUXE.

Restaurant Te Hana can be found in Taravao in the same parking lot as the Champion *hypermarché*. They serve inexpensive Chinese food, including duck and seafood dishes. ~ PK 60, Taravao; 57-21-84. BUDGET.

Ah Ky Vairua is a large outdoor pavilion on the main drag in Taravao. It's the kind of extremely rustic establishment you would expect to find in a developing country—simple, no frills and no thought of pretension. It has about half a dozen tables on a bare slab of concrete that screams "budget Chinese food." It is your basic greasy-spoon restaurant featuring chow mein, chop suey and a few mixed vegetable dishes. Strictly for those interested in spending as little money as possible. ~ PK 60, Taravao; 57-20-38. BUDGET.

Restaurant Pizzeria Chez Lola and Remy is a great place to ◄ HIDDEN stop for a cool Italian ice or ice cream. Of course, they also have pizza. Look for it on the first side street to your right as you take the road out of Taravao for Tahiti Iti. It's tucked behind the Fare Moana clothing shop. ~ PK 60, Taravao; 57-74-99. BUDGET.

Snack Musée Gauguin is located at the entrance of the botanical gardens. It's an unpretentious outdoor café where you can choose to sit under a pavilion or outside, shaded by trees, only several feet from the lagoon. The rustic surroundings give one the feeling of being on a picnic. What's more, the food is quite good and the service very cordial. The menu includes *poisson cru*, sashimi and stuffed mahimahi. ~ PK 51.5, Papeari. BUDGET TO MODERATE.

> One of the unconventional bungalows featured at Fare Nana'o is actually in a tree!

The **Restaurant-Bar Gauguin** is located on the water approximately one kilometer before the Paul Gauguin Museum. There is a wide selection of seafood and the restaurant has a solid reputation. It is a large structure, shaded by a huge tree, and has both indoor and outdoor dining. Next to the restaurant is a pier with several attached fish pens where you can gaze at what may be your dinner. Our recommendation is the stuffed mahimahi or the shrimp curry with coconut cream. ~ PK 50.5, Papeari; 57-13-80. MODERATE TO DELUXE.

The **Nuutere** combines French cuisine with what is available locally. Housed in an attractive white colonial-style building with blue awnings, it has an extensive seafood menu and serves meat dishes as well. ~ PK 32.5, Papara; 57-41-15. DELUXE TO ULTRA-DELUXE.

There are markets along the coastal road in every district. One of the better stores includes **Magasin Alice** at PK 37.5 in Papara ~ 57-42-80. In Taravao, there is a giant Champion *hypermarché*

GROCERIES

on the main drag that stocks just about anything you might want. ~ 57-16-76.

BEACHES & PARKS

MOTU OVINI BEACH PARK   This is part of the Smith Botanical Garden and Paul Gauguin Museum complex and is open seven days a week. The good news is that this is a particularly nice botanical garden—so nice that it has become another obligatory stop for the tour buses. The rocky, black-sand beach that fringes the park is thin and the water seemed murky. The bad news is that you must pay a fairly stiff entrance fee to get into the nearby museum and a separate one to enter the beach park cum botanical garden. It's an expensive proposition to do both, especially with a family in tow. Drinking water, toilets. ~ Simply take the coastal road south to PK 51 in Papeari. The signs for the museum/park complex are on the sea side of the road and are quite prominent.

PLAGE TAHARUU   One of the best surf spots on the south side of the island is the expansive beach break at Papara. The beach in question is of fine black sand and covers a swath of about half a mile. This is a beach break with lefts and rights that surfers and boogie boarders will enjoy. One can swim, but it's definitely a secondary activity on this beach. Some shade is available and there is plenty of parking space. There are a few makeshift shacks on the beach—perhaps club houses of sorts for the surfers. Wave-riding entrepreneurs rent gear by the hour or the day. ~ To get there, drive two miles out of Papara to PK 38. Cross the white bridge over the creek and note the sign designating the beach. Pull into the parking lot. Note that the creek bisects the beach and there is another parking lot (with more shade trees) on the opposite side.

At the halfway point on the island circuit, the community of Taravao has a number of small nack bars and restaurants. If you're looking for respite and a meal on your way around the island, then you've come to the right place.

MARAA FERN GROTTO   The grotto is a minor roadside attraction that ends up being an obligatory stop for the tour buses. There are actually three grottos, gaping holes in the cliff filled with shallow pools of water that seeps from the top of the caverns. The grottos are accessible from a trail that skirts the base of the rock cliff face. The grottos are a cool respite on a hot day and are a favorite of children who half expect a dinosaur to leap out of the shadows. Picnic tables and fresh water. ~ At PK 28.5, Paea; look for the turnoff on the mountain side of the road that resembles a freeway rest stop. Pull in and park.

Tahiti Iti

Tahiti is like a figure eight on its side with the smaller loop, Tahiti Iti, joined by the narrow isthmus at Taravao to the larger loop, Tahiti Nui. At the isthmus is a junction where two roads branch off and follow the contours down either side of the Tahiti Iti Peninsula. The road, however, does not completely circle Tahiti Iti. The easterly road runs 18 kilometers round the coast from Taravao to Tautira, while the southerly road also runs 18 kilometers along the south coast from Taravao to just beyond Teahupoo. The two roads do not meet. Walking trails continue some distance beyond the end of both roads but even to walk the complete coastline would be difficult. A third road straddles the middle of the Tahiti Iti peninsula to a viewpoint where it dead-ends. Along the two coast roads, the red-and-white kilometrage (PK) markers start at "0" from Taravao.

Tahiti Iti is verdant, wet and rugged. Thick rainforests blanket the mountains, which tower over the coastal roads. The Taravao plateau, which straddles both coasts, is carpeted with grassy mead-ows akin to an alpine setting sans the pine trees.

The largest community on Tahiti Iti is Tautira, a fishing vil-lage on the north coast. It was here in 1773 that Captain Cook's second expedition almost met its doom. One morning, the es-teemed navigator awoke to find his two ships drifting perilously close to the reef. (Apparently the crew had been too busy enter-taining Tahitian visitors the evening before to notice.) The ships eventually did run aground, but were saved by smaller boats that kedged the larger vessels off the reef. Cook lost several anchors in the confusion. In 1978, by sheer luck, one of the anchors was located and brought to the surface. The event was properly cel-ebrated by locals and the crew of movie producer David Lean, who was on location to promote a new version of the *Bounty* in-cident. Although the film was never made, the anchor can be seen at the Musée de Tahiti et des Iles.

This serene setting was also the scene of a confrontation be-tween the British and the Spanish over 200 years ago. Angered by the English presence in the Pacific (which the Spanish felt was theirs to plunder), the Viceroy of Peru was ordered by his king to send a ship to Tahiti. He promptly sent the *Aguila*, commanded by Boenecha, which after having the misfortune of striking a reef, anchored in a lagoon about three kilometers from Tautira Village and formally took possession of Tahiti for the King of Spain.

Less than a year later, on his second voyage of discovery, Cook wound up in the same vicinity and soon heard about the landing of the dastardly Spanish. In 1774, Boenecha returned to the area with two Franciscan priests in an effort to give the locals a little re-ligion. The mission failed miserably. Captain Boenecha soon died and the priests, scared witless by the Tahitians, erected a veritable fortress to keep the curious natives away. The *Aguila* returned at the end of 1775 with provisions, but the priests would have none of the missionary life and gladly sailed back to Peru.

Cook came back to Tautira in 1777 on his third voyage and found the padre's quarters still in good condition. The house was fitted with a crucifix, which bore the inscription *Christus vincit Carolus III imperat 1774*. On the reverse side of the cross, Cook ordered his carpenter to carve *Tertius Rex Annis 1767, 69, 73, 74, & 77*. By this time, historian Bengt Danielsson writes, "both England and Spain had realized that Tahiti was an economically as well as strategically worthless island and gave up their costly shows of force."

One hundred years later, Tautira was the temporary abode of Robert Louis Stevenson, who anchored the *Casco* here in 1888. He was taken in by local royalty and stayed for about two months, calling Tahiti a "Garden of Eden." Although on assignment for the *New York Sun* to write about the cruise, he spent his time in Tautira working on *The Master of Ballantrae*, a Scottish horror story. Upon Stevenson's return to England, his mother sent a silver communion service to the local Protestant church, where it can still be seen on display.

SIGHTS

TARAVAO TO TAUTIRA   The road winding from Taravao to Tautira often follows the base of steep verdant cliffs. This is, as the locals call it, *le district*—the countryside. About half a kilometer from the junction is a sign that marks the road to the Taravao Plateau, which meanders nine kilometers and dead-ends smack in the interior of Tahiti Iti. Several hundred yards from the road's end will take you to tiny Lake Vaiufaufa.

The coastal road continues to wind eastward, past homes with well-tended gardens. It's not unusual to pass a young man strumming a ukulele as he walks on the shoulder of the road. Near the end of the line, the Vaitepiha River, PK 16.5, empties into Vaitepiha Bay just on the outskirts of **Tautira**.

HIDDEN ►

Tautira really does feel like it's sitting on the edge of the island. Wedged between the towering green mountains of Tahiti Iti and the sea, this is as close as you'll get to a traditional village setting in 21st-century Tahiti. Romantics might be disappointed that it is not a fishing village out of *Mutiny on the Bounty* but it is nonetheless a bucolic backwater that merits a visit. There are no thatch-roofed bungalows (which is what you will find at the resorts). Rather, Tautira has cars, four-wheel-drive trucks and boat trailers parked in the front yards of comfortable modern homes divided by hedges of hibiscus. Built on a point of land, the village is bisected by a number of lanes that are shaded by breadfruit and mango trees. The paved streets are filled with teenagers on bicycles, children walking hand in hand with adults, and vehicles dodging potholes.

A beachfront road skirts a fringe of grass separating it from the rocky, black-sand beach. Planted firmly on the grassy strip are trees or rough-hewn racks from which blue nylon fishing nets hang limply. On the sandy shore, *pirogues* (outrigger canoes) sit beached. The locals, nearly all Polynesian, are friendly and smile at the occasional visitor as they go about their chores, raking leaves or mending fishing nets. ~ PK 18.

TARAVAO TO TEAHUPOO   About half a kilometer past the junction, there is an atmospheric **research station**, which was constructed during International Geophysical Year (1957–58) to study the ionosphere. ~ PK 0.5, Afaahiti.

Heading east down the coastal road you'll come to the former site of **Zane Grey's Fishing Camp**. Although the author of *Riders of the Purple Sage* and 60 other pulp Westerns spent his life cranking out stories about the old American West, his real passion in life was deep-sea fishing. From 1928 to 1933, he spent many months in Tahiti with his cronies catching marlin, mahimahi, sailfish and other sport fish. Like Melville's protagonist in *Moby Dick*, Grey dreamed of landing his own version of the white whale and on May 16, 1930, he finally did—a 12-foot, 1040-pound striped marlin that probably would have weighed 200 pounds more had not the sharks ripped off so much flesh. ~ PK 7.3, Vairao.

> Interested in hiking the coast of Tahiti Iti with a group? Contact any number of professional guides or ecological organizations that regularly lead groups into the area (see "Hiking" at the end of the chapter).

Almost three kilometers farther, you will see several ponds at the **IFREMER Research Station**. They are for breeding shrimp—one of the many ambitious projects of the Institute Française de Recherche Pour L'Exploitation de la Mer, a French government agency. ~ PK 10.4, Vairao.

The village of **Teahupoo** became suddenly famous in the surfing world several years ago after hosting the Gotcha Pro surf competition. Today it's an internationally known venue featuring the "the beast," so called by professional surfers. The biggest swells, by the way, occur in April and May.

The last **Refuge of the Nature Men** was well hidden at the end of the island. Years ago, the "nature men," as Danielsson called them, lived off the land, often as ascetics or beachcombers, and were a common fixture throughout Tahiti. As civilization marched on, this remote area became their last refuge. The best-known of these rugged individuals, who bore a strong resemblance to the R. Crumb's comic strip character "Mr. Natural," was Ernest Darling. Anticipating an entire generation perhaps half a century too early, Darling lived stark naked, slept on the ground with his head pointing north, and produced an endless stream of pamphlets extolling the virtues of nudism, vegetarianism, abstinence, pacifism, Christian Socialism and phonetic spelling. ~ PK 18, Teahupoo.

VISTA POINT   At **Afaahiti**, PK 0.6, just out of Taravao on the east-coast road, the Taravao Plateau is signposted on your right, just before the school. You will pass pastures with grazing cattle before you reach the dead end seven kilometers later. A short walk takes you a gorgeous panorama of the narrow Isthmus of Taravao with the mountains of Tahiti rising in the distance. The junction for a second, rather rougher and more potholed, road is just before the viewpoint car park, and ends up on the coast road to Tautira at PK 2.5. The two approaches can be combined to make a circuit route. Take care on the less-traveled, second road. During especially rainy weather it may not be passable.

LODGING **Chez Jeannine**, located in the Taravao district on the Route du Plateau, has four nice bungalows with private hot-water baths and kitchens as well as five rooms in a home, each with a double bed and private bath. There is a swimming pool on the premises. Weekly and monthly rates are available. ~ PK 4.4, Route du Plateau, Taravao; 57-07-49, 77-27-37, fax 57-07-49. BUDGET TO MODERATE.

Punatea Village, which opened in 2001, is the newest addition to Tahiti Iti's north coast. Located on the sea side, the property includes five bungalows and five rooms with either private or shared bath. There is also a restaurant and a swimming pool. Excursions on the lagoon or into the island's interior can be arranged. ~ PK 5, Afaahiti; phone/fax 57-71-00, 77-20-31; www.punatea-village.com, e-mail punatea-village@hotmail.com. BUDGET TO MODERATE.

Also on the north shore is **Fare Maithé**, a one-story building with two rooms for two to three people each, private baths and a communal kitchen and living room. Located on the waterfront, it is only a hundred yards away from a *motu* with a white-sand beach. The owners offer a discounted weekly rate. ~ PK 4.5, Afaahiti; 57-18-24; www.chez-maithe.com, e-mail rmo@tahitinui.net. BUDGET.

Meherio Iti comprises three seaside A-frame bungalows in Vairao, on the far southeast end of the island in the Tahiti Iti area. The units are modest affairs but have private hot-water baths

◆◆

NEW RIDERS OF THE PURPLE WAVES

In *Tales of Tahitian Waters*, Zane Grey details his deep-sea fishing adventures during his years in Tahiti. In one episode, Grey provides an insight into French colonial mentality. He relates that French officials had the local chief spy on the Americans because they thought the fishermen might actually be surveying the area for the U.S. government, which perhaps had designs on taking over Tahiti as a naval base. Said Grey, "The idea of white men visiting Tahiti for something besides French liquors, the native women, or to paint the tropical scenery had been exceedingly hard to assimilate."

and kitchenettes. Reports have been good but the place is quite far from stores and other amenities. Meal plans are available. ~ PK 11.9, Vairao; phone/fax 57-68-49. BUDGET.

Located on the sea, **Au Bonjouir** is tucked in a coconut grove surrounded by lush vegetation and the towering mountains of the Tahiti Iti peninsula. Accommodations include six bungalows and one studio with private baths and kitchens, and three dorms with 10, 14 and 16 bunks, in a home with communal hot-water bathrooms and a kitchen. Almost all the beds have mosquito nets—important in this part of the island. There is also a public sitting room with a TV. Camping is also available on the property—the only campsite on Tahiti. The owner, Annick Paofai, is helpful and friendly to guests, and he offers various excursions for an additional fee. This is a place to consider if you really want to get away from any trace of civilization on Tahiti. However, it is a good hour's ride from Papeete and a 15-minute boatride from Teahupoo. Call Annick for information on transfers. No credit cards. ~ Te Pari–Taiarapu; 77-89-69, fax 57-02-15; www. bonjouir.com, e-mail bonjouir@mail.pf. BUDGET TO MODERATE.

Te Pari Village, the other lodging on Tahiti Iti's south coast, is accessible only by boat. This family pension offers three bungalows with double beds and private facilities, communal dining and living rooms. The lodging price includes three meals, but excursions are offered separately. To get there, you must drive to the village of Teahupoo and arrange the ten-minute boat ride to this remote property. Call ahead to arrange a free boat transfer. ~ Te Pari–Taiarapu; phone/fax 42-59-12; e-mail teparivillage@yahoo.fr. BUDGET TO MODERATE.

DINING

◀ HIDDEN

L'Eurasienne (also known as Chez Jeannine), located on the heights of the plateau, is as good a small restaurant as you'd find anywhere in Tahiti. The owner is a petite woman of French and Vietnamese origin and her specialty is Vietnamese cuisine and *fruit de mer* (seafood). The menu features six different shrimp dishes alone. Nice—if simple—ambience and, judging by the number of local customers packed into her restaurant on a weekday afternoon, her food is well liked. It can be found on the premises of the pension Chez Jeannine. ~ PK 4.4, Route du Plateau, Taravao; 57-07-49, 77-27-37. MODERATE.

GROCERIES

When on the north coast, visit **Magasin Nico Star**. ~ Tautira; 57-19-32. On the south coast, there's **Magasin Teahupoo**. ~ PK 16.5, Teahupoo; 57-10-59.

BEACHES & PARKS

TAPUAEMAUI BEACH 🏊 This is a very slender strip of white sand several hundred yards long at PK 8.5 on the southern shore of Tahiti Iti. It's remarkable only in that it's the sole white-sand beach for perhaps 30 miles (50 kilometers). There are a few shade trees and some canopies to protect you from the sun. It's about a 50- to 75-yard swim from the shore to the reef. The water is very clean here (compared to the opposite side of the island) but not too deep, unless you are lucky enough to be there during high tide. A small store (Magasin Notehei) is on just the other side of the road from the beach and sells a few snack items. The proprietress is friendly and speaks English. Picnic tables, fresh tap water. ~ Take the southern coastal highway at Taravao past the Puunui turnoff in the direction of Teahupoo two kilometers or so past the marina.

AUTIRA BEACH At the terminus of Tahiti Iti's northern coastal highway is the community of Tautira, where a large black-sand beach fronts the village for about half a mile. It faces Captain Cook's old anchorage and is situated at the mouth of the Vaitepiha River. The primary reason to visit the area is the view from Tautira toward the rainforest-covered highlands of Tahiti Iti. On the shoreline is a grassy strip where the fishermen hang their nets from simple racks or coconut trees. The setting is bucolic and very serene. The swimming is good. ~ You can find the beach by driving to the end of the northern Tahiti Iti Road, PK 18. Bear to your left and follow the road along the shoreline.

Outdoor Adventures

CAMPING

Au Bonjouir is the only campsite on Tahiti. This is a place to consider if you really want to get away from civilization. It is a good hour's ride from Papeete and a 15-minute boat ride from Teahupoo. Call Annick Paofai for information on transfers. No credit cards. ~ Te Pari–Taiarapu; 77-89-69, fax 57-02-15. BUDGET.

DIVING & SNORKELING

Tahiti has a variety of sites for all levels of divers and is a good place to get certified. The west coast, in particular, because of its location lee of the prevailing trade winds means often flat-calm conditions on the surface of the lagoon. Given the availability of film processing in Papeete, it's also a good place to check out underwater photo equipment. If you have any qualms about your

THE TAHITIAN CREATION MYTH

Traditionally, Tahitian mythology dictated that the island came into being as a giant fish pulled out of the sea by Maui, one of the most powerful gods in the Polynesian pantheon. In this vision of creation, Tahiti Nui was the body of the fish and Mt. Orohena, the highest peak, was the dorsal fin. The tail lay in Punaauia, just south of Papeete, and the head of the fish was the smaller section of the island, Tahiti Iti, to the east.

gear, shooting a few rolls in the lagoon and getting them quickly developed in town is always an option.

There are a variety of dive sites in Tahiti, with subjects ranging from wrecks to sharks. Some of the better-known ones include:

The **Aquarium,** with a depth ranging from 9 to 36 feet (3 to 10 meters), is where one goes to feed fish by hand. It is the island's most popular (and crowded) dive site. Fish come in such abundance that it's sometimes difficult to see a few yards ahead. It's generally calm here, which makes it easy to shoot still camera or video and ideal for beginners. Just east of the Aquarium are **wrecks** of a *Catalina PBY* seaplane and interisland vessel that one can visit on the same dive. Both the ship and the plane are in a state of sufficient deterioration so that it's easy to dive into the interior of both vessels. The **Tahiti Wall** and **Shark Cave** are located on an outer reef where a sheer drop descends from a plateau of 12 feet (4 meters) to **Blue Infinity.** Along the cliff face are caves and crevices where one can feed white-tip sharks and moray eels. **La Source** entails a pinnacle about 90 feet (28.5 meters) off the reef, which is adjacent to a freshwater spring at about 25 feet (7.5 meters). The fresh water, which flows through the coral, is readily visible and resembles heat waves rising from pavement on a hot day. If a diver swims through the mass of fresh water rising to the surface, the image is blurred almost beyond recognition. The **Blue Hole,** located inside the lagoon, has a maximum depth of only 45 feet (16 meters). The site has eagle rays, nurse sharks and sting rays. The **Vavi Area** is characterized by a number of drop-offs and is rich in coral. There are a variety of soft coral, sea fans, Gorgonias and Alcynaceans. The Vaiau Cove is located about 1200 yards (360 meters) before Vaiau pass. The horseshoe-shaped cove is perhaps the best dive in the Peninsula area. One crosses the reef and enters a huge space full of grottos filled with red mullet and sweepers. **Les Failles d'Arue** is one of only a couple of dive sites on the east coast just off Matavai Bay. The site itself is a large submerged plateau covered in coral and split by faults *(failles).* Dive operators will only dive here when the seas are calm.

Tahiti Plongée, located between the InterContinental Beachcomber and the Sofitel Maeva Beach hotel, is headed by Henri Pouliquen. It is open seven days a week to divers of all levels. First-dive instruction and night diving are available; instruction is available in French or English. CMAS and PADI certification are available. ~ PK 7.5, Punaauia; 44-00-62, fax 42-26-06; e-mail plongee.tahiti@mail.pf.

Scubatek, located at the Tahiti Yacht Club, calls itself Tahiti's first diving school and has all equipment available, two dive boats, and a decompression chamber only three minutes by car from the premises. They offer bilingual instruction, night diving and diving outside the reef. CMAS and PADI certification are available. ~ PK 4, Arue; 42-23-55; www.chez.com/scubatek, e-mail plc.scuba tek@mail.pf.

Aquatica Dive Center, a five-star PADI center, is one of the best dive-teaching operations on Tahiti. Run by Didier Alpini, Aquatica caters primarily to local and French clientele. The center offers dive packages as well as snorkeling trips, glass-bottom-boat tours, and kayak, jet-ski and boat rentals. It has two fully equipped dive boats and can also cater to disabled divers. Located inside the InterContinental Beachcomber at Tataa Point. ~ PK 7, Punaauia; 53-34-96, fax 53-34-74; www.aquatica-dive.com, e-mail info@aquatica-dive.com.

Ocean World offers dives and certifications for all levels. Operated by Dominique Lestage, this outfit has gotten rave reviews for its dolphin-watch program. Getting there couldn't be easier: It's run right out of Hotel Le Meridien in the bay adjacent to the property. ~ Hotel Le Meridien, PK 15, Punaauia; 45-21-98, 47-07-07, fax 47-07-08; e-mail oceanworld@mail.pf.

Joshua Rouger and Nicholas Castel operate **Eleuthera Plongée**, located at Marina Taina. Once a month they organize a special excursion—a night dive, a shark feeding, a drift dive or a wreck dive. Their 28-foot boat takes clients to Moorea or Tetiaroa, or to one of the other 30 diving spots around Tahiti. They are open seven days a week and feature four dives a day. Full PADI/CMAS certification is available. ~ Marina Taina, Punaauia; 42-49-29, fax 48-04-04; www.dive-tahiti.com, e-mail info@dive-tahiti.com.

Iti Diving International offers an array of rarely visited diving spots and specializes in Tahiti's Peninsula area. It's operated by Gilles Jugel, who has installed moorings at seven dive sites so far, which means he is not dropping an anchor on the coral. Healthy and abundant hard coral is a big attraction in this region, as are wall dives. The walls start from about six meters and drop vertically into deep trenches. They're covered with golden gorgonians, black coral and soft coral, which are rare in this part of the South Pacific. In some places there are swim-through chimneys where you can observe white-tip reef sharks sleeping. Fish life here is rich and ranges from small colorful reef fish to giant barracuda, free-swimming moray eels and big Napoleon wrasses. Diving on the Peninsula is a no-miss proposition—one local friend describes it as the "real deal." ~ Marina Puunui, PK 6, Vairao; phone/fax 57-77-93; www.itidiving.pf, e-mail itidiving@mail.pf.

Ruahiti Tours, new to the island, offers lagoon visits, snorkeling excursions, fish feeding and dolphin- and whale-watching trips. ~ Papeete; 72-20-46, fax 72-20-46; e-mail ruahiti_tour@yahoo.fr.

Fluid, run by Yannis Saint-pe, handles small groups of two to six divers, and goes to sites between Tahiti and Moorea. He also does dolphin watching in Punaauia Bay. ~ Mahina; phone/fax 85-45-45; e-mail fluid@mail.pf.

The north coast of Tahiti offers good surfing—there are both beach breaks and reef breaks. The best time for quality surf is actually in the winter as the big winter storms from Antarctica and New Zealand provide plenty of swells to the Society Islands' southern shores. When the swells come out of deep water and break along the reefs, the result can be very powerful, hollow waves. On the southern coat of the island most of the breaks (with the exception of Papara) tend to be passes in the reef system and a long paddle is obligatory. Some of the popular reef breaks (going from west to east) are at **Taapuna Pass**, PK 10, just off of **Musée de Tahiti et des Iles**, PK 14.5 and off of **Paea** at the mouth of the Orofero River. There are also a number of breaks off of Tahiti Iti including **Tapuaeaha**, PK 9, **Ava iti**, PK 14, **Teahupoo**, PK 14.5 and **Vairao**, which is close to the most easterly tip of the island. **Moana Surf Tours** in Punaauia will provide guides or put together any combination of surfing, pension, boat and food packages for the islands of Moorea and Tahiti. (They also run a small pension catering primarily to surfers.) ~ Punaauia; phone/fax 43-70-70; e-mail moana surftours@mail.pf.

SURFING & WIND-SURFING

> All of the surfing passes necessitate transport on a boat—otherwise they are 20-minute paddles. Start making friends as soon as you get to the airport!

Tura'I Mata'are Surf School gives surfing and body board instruction at Papenoo and Papara beaches. Prices include boards, transportation and insurance. Classes are from 9 a.m. to noon and 2 p.m. to 5 p.m. ~ Papeete; 45-44-00, phone/fax 41-91-37; e-mail surfschool@mail.pf.

Moanareva offers introductory courses in surfing and body boarding. ~ Papeete; phone/fax 42-45-28; www.moanareva.com, e-mail moanareva@mail.pf.

Rentals   To rent boards try **Kelly Surf** ~ Centre Fare Tony, Papeete, 45-44-00; or **Local Style** ~ Point Venus, 48-07-16, 48-24-13.

Windsurfing is also catching on in Tahiti, but is not nearly as popular as surfing. It is nearly impossible to rent windsurfing equipment on the islands, so if you're experienced in the sport, make sure to bring your own gear. Some of the better breaks are off of Point Venus, Sofitel Maeva Beach, Musée de Tahiti et des Iles, off the Orofero River, and off of Vairao in Tahiti Iti.

One place that does rent windsurfing equipment and give lessons is **Arue Sailing School**, run by Cornette De Saint-Cyr. Hobie Cats and kayaks are also available. ~ PK 4, Arue; 42-23-54, fax 43-13-00; e-mail evatahiti@mail.pf.

Kayaking on the barrier reef around Tahiti is an absolute delight. The coral shoals and secret inlets are a magical playground for beginners and experienced kayakers alike. **Xkmer** in Teahupoo on Tahiti Iti can get you set up with gear as well as lessons if you need them. The company offers guided half- and full-day sea

SEA KAYAKING

kayaking trips that include reef exploration, a picnic and maybe some wave kayaking too. ~ PK 18, Teahupoo; 45-04-34, fax 45-04-34; e-mail xavierkmer@hotmail.com.

WATER-SKIING

Introductory and advanced waterskiing lessons are available from the **Ski Nautique Club** in Punaauia. Styles include wakeboard, ski-tubes, mono-ski and barefoot. While others are having a turn, you can sun yourself on the floating pontoon. Certified instructors are members of the French Federation of Water Skiing. ~ 77-22-62, fax 41-26-09; e-mail patou.nadou@mail.pf.

The **Waterskiing Club de Tahiti** is an official member of the French Federation of Waterskiing. They offer everything from introductory and advanced waterskiing to classes on wakeboards, mono skis and bare-foot skiing. ~ Pirae; 45-39-36, fax 41-26-09; e-mail patou.nadou@mail.pf.

FISHING

Sportfishing inside the reef is not particularly good because of problems with pollution and overfishing. Outside the barrier reef is another matter. There is an abundance of marlin, yellowfin tuna, mahimahi and other pelagics.

Every year, the world-renowned Tahiti International Billfish Tournament draws big-name competitors who vie for coveted trophy-size fish. The contest is a qualifying event for Bisbee's World Billfish Series. For information on joining a team, contact Mr. Alban Ellacott. ~ 43-19-00, fax 43-28-45; www.tahitisportfishing.com/tibt.htm, e-mail tibt@mail.pf.

There are several vessels that cater to deep-sea anglers, but a good place to start is Marina Taina in Punaauia. The majority of the sportfishing fleet is moored there and your best bet is to talk to the skippers right on the dock. ~ Marina Taina; 41-02-25.

Ruahiti Tours offers traditional open-sea fishing for mahimahi using drag lines. Both morning and afternoon half-day trips are available, as is a full-day excursion. There's a four-person minimum. The company also offers a sunset charter to catch flying fish. ~ 72-20-46, fax 72-20-46; e-mail ruahiti_tour@yahoo.fr.

LEARN TO FLY

Moanareva International Flysurf School offers training in the unique sport of flysurfing, in which participants skip a board along the water with the aid of a big kite attached to them by handles and a harness. Introductory and refresher courses and organized trips with a Zodiac escort are all offered. ~ Point Venus, Mahina; phone/fax 42-45-28; www.moanareva.com, e-mail moanareva@mail.pf.

Other deep-sea fishing vessels that run trips out of Marina Taina include:

Napuka, a 61-foot air-conditioned boat that holds a maximum of ten people. ~ 42-18-34, fax 42-18-35; e-mail moananui@mail.pf.

Tai San, a 54-foot Bertram run by Cathy Rossler. ~ 58-27-23, fax 58-37-93; e-mail kantoine@pbc.pf.

Heremana, an eight-person boat skippered by Eric Malmezac. ~ 50-48-00, fax 50-48-01; e-mail emalmezac@satnui.pf.

Ahavini, a 31-foot Bertram Sportfisherman that has room for four. ~ 77-13-06, fax 43-81-41.

Tohitika, a 58-foot trawler that can accommodate ten. ~ 77-82-25, fax 45-27-58; e-mail marina@mail.pf.

The **Haura Club of Tahiti** also has several boats equipped for deep-sea fishing. ~ Papeete; 42-37-14, fax 42-04-09.

Pedal boats and small fiberglass motorboats are available for half- or full-day rental from the **Tahiti Nautic Center** at Phaeton Bay in Taravao. ~ PK 56, Taravao; 57-20-70, fax 57-05-07; e-mail tahiti.sport@tahiti-sport.pf.

SAILING

The popularity of bareback charters in Tahiti has grown tremendously over the last decade. For complete information about sailing possibilities in the Society Islands, see the "Sailing" section in Chapter Three.

GOLF

At Atimaono in the Papara district, the **Olivier Breaud International Golf Course** is a 6944-yard, par 72.

The course is a 45-minute drive from Papeete and is open daily from 8 a.m. to 6 p.m. year-round. The course has recently undergone a 100-million CFP renovation that includes a new clubhouse, restaurant, pro shop, pool, tennis courts and driving range. Clubs can be rented. ~ Golf d'Atimoano, PK 41, Papara; 57-40-32; e-mail skiptahiti@yahoo.com.

Golfers can also contact Christian and Pierrot Savoie of **Golf Clinic** at the Sofitel Maeva Beach hotel. The pair specializes in technique training beginners to serious amateurs. Instruction is done on a 150-meter (300-yard) green. Closed Sunday and Monday. ~ Papeete; 86-66-27, fax 50-09-41; e-mail taurua@mail.pf.

TENNIS

Tennis fanatics can play at any number of hotels, as well as nine private clubs. Most will accept guests for a minimal fee. Try the following: **Fautaua Tennis Club** in Pirae ~ 42-00-59; **Fei Pi Sports Association** in Arue ~ 42-53-87; **Excelsior Club** in Papeete ~ 43-91-46; **Chon Wa Tennis Club** in Mamao ~ 42-01-31; **Club A. S. Dragon** in Papeete ~ 43-31-12; and **Club A S Phoenix** in Punaauia ~ 82-35-56.

There are also less-formal local clubs whose tennis facilities are available, including the **Pirae Tennis Club** behind Pater Stadium, **Tamarii Pater Tennis Club** also near the stadium near the Fautaua River, and the **J. T.** (Young Tahitian) **Tennis League** (Pirae; 45-13-14).

RIDING STABLES

Evidently, some residents of Tahiti have a love for horseback riding because there are several first-class facilities available. **Club Equestre de Tahiti** is on the road to the Hippodrome at the foot of the mountains. They teach novices on both horses and ponies. Closed Monday. ~ Pirae; 42-70-41, 77-18-25. **L'Eperon de Pirae** is also in Pirae near the Hippodrome. Closed Monday. ~ Pirae; 42-79-87. **Ranch Gauguin**, located in Papeari, has 20 horses and organizes half- or full-day tours along the beach or in the valley. ~ PK 53, Papeari; 57-51-00.

HIDDEN ►

On Tahiti Iti, you might want to try **L'Amour de la Nature a Cheval**. Located in the cool heights of the Taravao Rauvau Plateau, they offer private riding and training lessons. Open by reservation only. Contact Mrs. Rosa Castanet. ~ PK 2.5, Taravao Plateau, Tahiti Iti; 20-20-68, fax 43-50-79. **Poney Club le Centaure**, at the Pirae race track, is another training center. ~ Pirae; 45-02-61, 77-66-73, fax 45-02-61.

BIKING

It's not recommended that you bring your bike to Tahiti unless you plan to spend most of your time on the more remote islands that are not overrun by automobiles. Tahiti is definitely overrun by cars and it does not strike me as a bike-friendly environment. Because of traffic in the Papeete area, it's not recommended that you bicycle in or near town. I'm not aware of any bicycle rental agencies in town, but there are several sales and repair shops.

HIKING

Upon your arrival in Tahiti, the verdant hills beckon, but venturing into the bush can be a dangerous proposition unless you know what you are doing and where you are going. Torrential rain can swell streams into rivers and easy-to-find trails can be overgrown with vegetation in no time. It's always best for the serious hiker to be accompanied by a guide. In many instances, you may even need to rent a four-wheel-drive vehicle to get to the trailhead.

Despite the requirements, Tahiti has a variety of excellent trails and guides for hire. Here are six treks of varying difficulty. Most, but not all, require guides. Listed below are several individuals and ecologically oriented organizations (à la the Sierra Club) that organize treks into the bush. Generally these activities are scheduled during the weekends because nearly all the participants are locals.

Mataiea/Vaihiria Lake/Papenoo (18 miles/29 kilometers), a two-day hike across the island via Vaihiria Lake (Tahiti's only lake), begins on the south coast, traverses the island's ancient volcanic crater and ends in Papenoo on the north coast. Allow 45 minutes by four-wheel-drive vehicle to the Mataiea trailhead. Hikers should be in good physical condition and a guide is required.

The **Mt. Aorai** (20 miles/32 kilometers) trek begins at the end of the Belvedere restaurant road (near Papeete). This is a two-day hike. Small *fares* (huts) have been built for hikers along the trail.

The **Fautaua Waterfall** (4 miles/6.4 kilometers) hike is a day trip up the Fautaua Valley. To get there, take an ordinary car to Bain Loti (of Pierre Loti fame) and walk for three hours to the waterfall. A guide is not necessary, but permission is needed from the Service des Eaux et Forets.

The **One Thousand Springs** (4.2 miles/7 kilometers) hike is a comparatively easy jaunt and no guide is required. Take Mahina-rama Road (near the Hyatt Regency) to the end (about five kilometers) and walk for two hours to the springs. From this junction, it is possible to climb Mt. Orohena (Tahiti's highest), but a guide is required for such an undertaking. The short hike follows the Mahina Valley rift along the banks of the Tuauru River to the source of the springs. At the height of approximately 2000 feet (650 meters) is a magnificent 180-degree view of Mt. Orohena, Mt. Pito Iti and Mt. Pihaaiateta.

To get to the **Tamanu Plateau** (10 miles/16 kilometers), take a car to Punaauia (about 15 kilometers from Papeete) and enter the Punaru'u Valley road to the trailhead (one to two kilometers by car). Walk to Tamanu Plateau—an eight-hour hike. Trekkers should be in good shape and a guide is required.

The **Lava Tubes hike** (5 miles/8 kilometers) starts at PK 40 on the east coast and involves taking a four-wheel-drive vehicle for about eight kilometers. From there, it's an easy half-hour walk to the first lava tube, an hour to the second, and three hours to the third.

GUIDES The Tahiti Manava Visitors Bureau recommends several guides who regularly lead hikes to the hinterlands. Two of

BE PREPARED

If you plan to do extensive hiking, it is suggested that you bring a sleeping bag, backpack, gloves, utensils and food supplies. Hard-core trekkers may want to pick up an excellent guide (in French) to walks in Tahiti and Moorea called *Randonnées en Montagne* by Paule Laudon, published by Les Editions du Pacifique. It is available in Papeete bookstores.

these are Zena Angelien and Pierre Florentin. You may contact them by phone.

Zena Angelien of **Le Circuit Vert** leads a variety of different treks on the peninsula separating Tahiti Iti and Tahiti Nui. These entail one- to-three day hikes along the *sauvage* coastline of Tahiti Iti, including the mist-shrouded Te Pari Cliffs. You do not have to be a triathlete to participate but hikers should be in good physical condition. The scenery is breathtaking and sights include *marae* (ancient temples), burial caves, grottos and petroglyphs. Zena will take a minimum of five and a maximum of ten people. Those feeling a bit insecure will be relieved to know that Zena always takes her two-way radio, is insured and has medical training. Backpacks and tents are available. Zena will provide custom hikes for those with special needs or schedules. ~ Taravao; phone/fax 57-22-67.

Tiare Mato organizes four different types of outdoor adventures: hiking, overland tours with four-wheel-drive vehicles, mountaineering and the latest trend in eco-adventure—canyoneering. The longest trek is a three-day hike to Mount Pito Iti, one of the highest climbs in Tahiti. Two-day hikes include the Diademe, starting in the Fautaua Valley, and an ascent of Mount Aorai. Both have breathtaking views of the island. One should be in good shape for these trips. The trek on Mount Aorai includes a night in the Fare Ata refuge. Shorter excursions can be done at the waterfall in Fautaua Valley, Orofero Valley and the lava tubes. These tubes are underground caves with streams meandering through them. For the more experienced, the chief guide, Guillaume, offers climbs in the Papenoo Valley and the lava tubes region. Canyoneering involves rappelling into hidden canyons, sometimes abseiling right through waterfalls. ~ Mahina; phone/fax 43-92-76.

Polynesian Adventure is operated by Vincent Dubousquet, an amiable fellow who knows the backcountry of Tahiti and Moorea intimately. He offers trips or overnight camping for visitors of all fitness levels. Tahiti treks include Fautaua Valley, Mt. Marau, Aorai, Te Pari, Tipauerui Valley, Te Faaiti in Papenoo, Tamanu in Punaauia, Tuaaru Valley in Mahina, the Lava Tubes in Hitiaa, and Diademe Pass. In Moorea, he can take you to Vaiare/Paopao crossing, Three Coconuts Pass, Mt. Rotui and Mouaputa. Vincent suggests you bring a change of clothing, good hiking shoes, a hat, sunscreen, mosquito repellent and water. He supplies the food. ~ Tahiti; phone/fax 43-25-95 or 77-24-37; www.polynesianadv.com, e-mail polynesianadv@mail.pf.

Presqu'ile loisirs in Tautura organizes hiking tours in the Peninsula area. One of the favorite hikes crosses Tahiti Iti by walking along the magnificent Vaitapiha Valley. Mata, the guide, will show you petroglyphs along the way and point out different species of plants and birds. ~ Tautira; 57-00-57.

Tahiti Evasion, run by Eric Lenoble, offers extended hiking tours ranging from seven days to three weeks. The most impressive undertaking is the "Five Islands on Foot" tour, which includes extensive hikes on Tahiti, Moorea, Tetiaroa (the late Marlon Brando's island), Raiatea and Tahaa. The all-inclusive trip includes ascents of some of the most challenging peaks in the Society Islands: Mt. Aorai on Tahiti, Mt. Temehani on Raiatea, and Pierced Montain (Moaputa) and Vaiane breach on Moorea. The 21-day program is undeniably strenuous, but the operators have paid close attention to balancing the effort with reward. Besides the stunning views and awesome experiences of the hikes, the program includes snorkel stops, pearl-farm visits, *motu* picnics, a Polynesian show, 4x4 trips, shark and sting-ray discovery and *marae* visits. Tahiti Evasion orchestrates every last detail, from flights and ferries to lodging and dinner. Some nights are spent in small pensions or hotels; others are spent camping on mountains or beaches. For the outdoor adventurer who wants to know the heart of the land, this is the ticket. ~ Phone/fax 43-22-33; www.tahitievasion.com, e-mail tahitievasion@mail.pf.

Typical excursions with hiking guide Zena Angelien include walks through thick jungle, wading waist deep across untrammeled rivers and streams and hiking precipitous bluffs.

Transportation

AIR

Tahiti Faa'a International Airport is perhaps the only international airport in the world with three consecutive vowels. With its collection of pariah dogs, lei stands and blaring Tahitian music, the airport is as distinctly Tahitian as any institution on the island. The airport's runway was originally constructed by filling in a lagoon. Prior to its completion in 1961, Tahiti was served by a flotilla of passenger vessels and New Zealand TEAL flying boats.

Amenities at the airport include: two banks that open for an hour before international flights depart and for an hour after arrival; a post office that keeps regular business hours; a tourist information center that opens for arriving international flights; and a snack bar with restaurant. There is a *consign* (storage area for luggage) and shower facilities for transit passengers; three duty-free shops and two (non-duty-free) boutiques, which have fashions, souvenirs and a newsstand.

All incoming international flights to French Polynesia touch down at the Faa'a Airport. Tahiti is generally a stopover destination between Australia or New Zealand and the United States.

There are several car rental offices (including Hertz and Avis) and offices for Air New Zealand, Qantas, Lan Chile, AOM, Air France, Hawaiian Airlines and Air Tahiti. In separate buildings are offices for Heli Pacific, Heli Inter and Air Archipels, all charter carriers. Note that the office for Air Moorea is in a separate wing from the international and Air Tahiti offices and is adjacent to Tetiaroa's office.

Faa'a Airport is five-and-a-half kilometers from Papeete and getting there via *Le Truck* takes 15 minutes to town and costs 200 CFP during the day and 250 CFP at night. *Le Truck* runs to and from the airport until 1 a.m. To get to town from the airport, walk directly across the street and parking lot upon leaving customs, climb two flights of stairs up to road level and cross the road. Look for a good spot to wait for the next Papeete-bound truck.

CAR RENTALS

For the visitor spending any appreciable time in Tahiti, or wishing to do an around-the-island tour solo, renting a car is a necessity. Although the accident rate statistics are fairly appalling, Tahitian motorists are generally courteous compared with U.S. or Continental drivers. They do have their own idiosyncrasies, such as passing on blind curves, tailgating and turning without signaling. Beware also of children playing in the street, pedestrians who seem oblivious to traffic, as well as drunk drivers and numerous dogs. Be especially careful in rural districts like Tahiti Iti where there is less traffic and pedestrians often take little heed of vehicular traffic. Always drive very defensively. Prepare to pay around 140 CFP per liter of gas.

Car rental agencies in Tahiti are:

Daniel Rent-a-Car ~ Airport, 82-30-04

Europcar ~ Airport, 86-60-61; InterContinental Beachcomber, 86-51-10; Le Meridien, 47-07-07; Sheraton, 86-48-48

Hertz ~ Airport, 82-55-86; Tipaerui, 42-04-71

Avis/Pacificar ~ Papeete, Rue des Remparts, 54-10-10; Taravao, 57-70-70; Airport, 85-02-84

Robert Rent-a-Car ~ Papeete, Général de Gaulle Avenue; 42-97-20

Tahiti Auto Center ~ Papeete, 82-33-33

Tahiti Rent-a-Car ~ Airport, 81-94-00

PUBLIC TRANSIT

The local bus, known as *Le Truck*, is the most practical and widely used form of transport on the island. *Le Truck* is something between a jitney and a bus—usually a multi-colored truck or lorry with wooden benches that run the length of the vehicle. Seating, which is fairly low, is along the perimeter. The entrance/exit is generally, but not always, at the front, behind the driver's cab. The drivers are owner-operators who, like all independent truck drivers, must hustle to survive. They are often accompanied by their wives, girlfriends or children, who sit with them in the cab.

The trucks run on weekdays from the first light of dawn until about 5 p.m. Only *Le Truck* vehicles driving along the west coast to Faa'a, the airport, InterContinental Beachcomber and the Sofitel Maeva Beach operate until 10 p.m.—on Saturday until midnight or later. There is no service to the more distant destinations (such as the Gauguin Museum) on Sunday.

Drivers are usually paid after the trip is completed. The fares for adults/children range from 150 CFP if you're going from Papeete to the airport (just under six kilometers) to a maximum of 500 CFP to the other side of the island. Unlike taxis, a visitor won't have to fear being overcharged on *Le Truck*. The fare within a 20-kilometer radius of Papeete is 200 CFP or less. Rates do jump somewhat at night if you happen to catch a late-running truck.

After years of debate about the correct course of action, the entire *Le Truck* system was recently overhauled to help ease Papeete's horrendous traffic problem and improve the overall reliability of public transportation on the island. The newly organized service was inaugurated in April 2002.

> If you decide you can't uproot yourself from Polynesian soil and would like to stay longer, the airport has an office of Police de l'Air et des Frontieres—the place to go to extend your tourist visa.

The government voted in 1999 to replace *Le Trucks* with modern, air-conditioned vehicles, but truck operators—who own their own vehicles and often have long family histories in the trade—opposed the plan fiercely. After much negotiation, *Le Truck* owners were finally asked to form three autonomous, private companies. The result is the new Reseau de Transport Collectif (RTC), whose three arms represent the major service areas or lines: Orange, Red and Green.

The Red line serves greater Papeete, the Orange line serves the west coast, and the Green line serves Tahiti Iti and other east coast destinations. For the first time, there is a printed timetable for *Le Truck* service and—perhaps the most significant change—designated stops on all routes. In the past, *Le Truck* would allow on-and off-boarding wherever passengers wished. Now, it is allowed only at official stops. Although the stops are identified on the new route schedules, most have yet to be given signs, benches or shelters. This situation will improve over the next couple years. Make sure to ask if you have any doubt about where to get off.

Many *Le Truck* operators have already repainted their trucks to clearly reflect their new line colors and numbers, but many others still bear a colorful mishmash of hues, with only a cardboard placard announcing the new route number. Old destination names and numbers are frequently still prominent. To make things even more confusing, a blue, green and orange truck with red trim probably belongs to the Red line.

The lesson here is: *always confirm the destination with the driver when you board Le Truck.*

For better or worse, modern buses are being phased in to complement, and ultimately supplant, *Le Truck*. So far, there are 20 new buses on the road—mostly on long-haul routes.

Following are descriptions of *Le Truck* routes and the main stops in downtown Papeete. Some stops have a posted route schedule and service description; others do not.

Arrêt Banque de Tahiti is the main *Le Truck* station near the public market on Rue du Général de Gaulle. Many **Red line** trucks that serve greater Papeete stop here, including lines 20, 22 and 23, which visit the **Faa'a Airport**. The Arue-bound truck is the one to take to visit the **Pomare V tomb**. Theoretically, each of the 12 routes on the Red line has its own additional color for identification. Outbound Red line *Le Trucks* that stop here include: 20 Outumaoro–Arue (pink); 21 Outumaoro–Arue/express (pink); 22 Teroma (red); 23 St. Hilaire (dark blue); 24 Puurai (light green); 25 Pamatai (purple); Of note: several of these trucks stop at the hospital in Mamao. This is also the stop for three **outbound Orange** trucks: 3 Paea, 4 Taapuna, and 6 Zone Industrial Punaruu.

Hitchhiking is possible, with varying degrees of difficulty for foreigners. The idea is to be as conspicuously non-French as possible. Although Tahitians enjoy meeting foreigners, hitching isn't as easy in Tahiti as it used to be.

Other Red line routes board at **Gare de l'Hotel de Ville** beside the Town Hall and Hotel de Ville. Destinations include some of the more obscure residential areas in Papeete and Pirae, such as Mission. These trucks and buses also bear a secondary color for identification. They include: 26 Tipaerui–Motu Uta (light blue); 27 Tipaerui–Titioro (yellow); 28 Saint-Amelie–Mission (black); 29 Desserte Taunoa (gray); 30 Tenaho–Papeete (brown); and 31 Pater–Hamuta.

Arrêt Central du Front de Mer is on Boulevard Pomare at Fare Manihini, opposite the Tahiti Manava Visitor's Bureau. It the primary stop for **Green line** buses bound for the east coast. The buses and trucks heading east will likely be white with green trim. The routes include: 11 Tautira–Teahupoo; 12 Taravao; 13 Papenoo; 14 and 15 Mahina; 16 Erima; and 17 Tefaaroa–Continent Arue. Most of these trucks stop at the popular Cerrefour *hypermarché* along on the way.

On the lagoon side of the street near the Manava Visitor's Bureau is **Arrêt Fare Manihini,** the stop for long-haul buses bound for Tahiti Iti. The 10 Tautira departs from here and visits the airport on its way out of town. Two **outbound Orange** trucks also pick up passengers here: 1 Teahupoo, and 2 Taravao.

TAXIS

Local taxis, compared with cabs in other countries, are very expensive. The government regulates taxi fares, and has established rates from Papeete to virtually every hotel and restaurant. Computerized meters have recently been installed in every taxi. This may cut down on blatant rip-offs but they are still expensive.

Inside the greater Papeete area the taxi fare should not exceed 900 to 1000 CFP, so be suspicious of anything much more than that for a ride within town. The tariff from town to the airport or vice versa is around 1800 CFP, except after 8 p.m. when the price goes up 50 percent to 70 percent. All other fares double from 8 p.m. to 6 a.m., and on holidays and Sundays the minimum rate may go up by 25 percent. Got all that? Quantum mechanics is simple compared with calculating Tahiti taxi fares.

Any complaints should be directed to the Tahiti Tourist office. Although in theory taxi fares are regulated, some drivers may not adhere quite so strictly to the rules—especially if the passenger is a tourist.

AERIAL TOURS

There are two standard helicopter tours above Tahiti. A 35-minute flight cruises over Papeete, the lagoon above Faa'a, the major hotels and Matavai Bay to the north of town. The pilot then heads inland to point out Le Diademe, Mt. Orohena and the rainforests nestled in the deep cleft valleys. A 40-minute tour takes you around the island to the Tahiti Iti Peninsula and the Isthmus of Taravao. For more information, contact **Heli-Inter Polynesie**, 86-60-29. The company also has regularly scheduled tours to Moorea.

DRIVE TOURS

Tahiti's interior is one of the most beautiful (and seldom seen) attractions, making an inland tour a high priority.

Adventure Eagle Tours, run by William Leteeg, has a total of six tours, two of which are inland excursions—the "Morning Mountain Tour" and the "Mountain & Waterfall Tour." Both visit 4592-foot (1400-meter) Mt. Marau, which entails a climb in a jeep wagon to see what Mr. Leteeg calls "Tahiti's Grand Canyon where no big buses can go." The tour vans are air conditioned, and English is spoken. The Mountain & Waterfall Tour also takes in Vaimahutu Falls and is a half-day trip, whereas the Morning Mountain Tour takes only two hours. Mr. Leteeg's other excursions are variations on circle island tours that read like a menu in a Chinese restaurant. Each tour has a selection of landmarks and you can pick and choose the items you wish to visit. These include the Gauguin Museum, the Vaihpahi garden and waterfall, the Papenoo surfing beach, the Fern Grotto of Maraa, Point Venus, the Arahoho Blowhole and other points of interest. He also has a city tour of Papeete that includes visits to the Black Pearl Museum, Lagoonarium and the Musée de Tahiti et des Iles. ~ Papeete; 77-20-03.

Tahiti Safari Expedition also has a variety of land tours to remote sections of the island, including Vaihiria Lake, the Lava

◄ HIDDEN

Tubes and Tahiti Iti. The company offers both half- and full-day four-wheel-drive ecotourism expeditions. Contact Patrice Bordes for more information. Mr. Bordes also organizes half- and full-day four-wheel-drive overland expeditions to the Papenoo Valley, across the island with a lunch at the Maroto Hotel in the interior of Tahiti. You will enjoy a hidden world of lakes, high cliffs and waterfalls. If you have lepidopterist tendencies, he will organize a special butterfly tour. ~ Papeete; 42-14-15, fax 42-10-07; www.tahiti-safari.com, e-mail tahiti.safari@mail.pf.

D-Tour, run by Henri Eskenazy out of the InterContinental Beachcomber, offers private and group quad-bike tours into the rugged interior of the island. ~ Paea; 70-99-53, fax 82-97-76; e-mail he222@wanadoo.fr.

Natura Excursions offers half- and full-day four-wheel-drive trips into Papenoo Valley and a quest to "follow the tracks of *Bounty* mutineers." Knowledgeable guides have plenty of information to share about geography, geology, demography, wildlife, flora, archaeology and religion. French, English, Tahitian, Spanish and Portuguese are all spoken, and lunch is included on full-day expeditions. Special rates are available for photographers, scientists and large groups. ~ Tamanu; 43-03-83 or 79-31-21, fax 43-03-99; www.natura-exploration.com, e-mail natura. explo@mail.pf.

WALKING TOURS

Ron Sage and Nicolas Zukowa of **Papeete Adventure** offer daily full-day guided walking tours of Papeete. This is a good option for cruise ship visitors who would likely be charged more for a tour arranged by their ship. Tours depart every morning at 7:30 a.m. and return at 4:30 p.m. Six-person minimum. ~ Papeete; 56-42-43, fax 56-17-07; e-mail painapo@mail.pf.

Mato Nui Excursions, run by Mr. Hervé Maraetaata, also offers excellent hiking tours on Tahiti Nui and Tahiti Iti. He offers everything from easy half-day hikes to multiday treks, and along the way educates guests on the flora and fauna of the island and the local culture. ~ Arue; phone/fax 41-02-95 or 78-95-47.

ECO TOURS

Iaora Tahiti Eco Tours is one of the most interesting educational opportunities on the islands. Staffed by professional botanists, oceanographers, archaeologists and cultural historians, Eco Tours offers intensive natural history trips and cruises. Trips are based on themes, such as botany, island evolution, archaeology, geology, history, plants, birds or reef life. Possible destinations include all of the Society Islands as well as the Tuamotus and Marquesas. Programs range from day trips and lectures to multi-week educational journeys. Trips are all-inclusive, and if none of the company's offerings quite fit your interests, you can work with them to create your own custom itinerary. If you are serious

about the sciences, this is definitely worth checking out. ~ Faa'a;
phone/fax 41-04-20 and 77-09-96; www.iaora.com, e-mail eco-
tours@mail.pf.

▼▼▼▼▼▼▼▼▼▼▼▼▼▼▼▼▼▼▼▼▼▼

Addresses & Phone Numbers

In addition to the full telephone contacts listed below are emergency numbers such as police, fire department, etc., that can be
dialed by keying in only two digits.

Fire Department ~ 18
Hospital ~ Mamao Hospital, Mamao, Papeete; 46-62-62
Hospital ~ Taravao Hospital; 57-76-76
Medical Clinic ~ Clinic Cardella, Rue Anne-Marie Javouhey,
    Papeete; 46-04-25
Medical Clinic ~ Paofai Clinic, Boulevard Pomare, Papeete; 46-
    18-90
Pharmacy ~ Pharmacie de la Cathedrale, Place Notre Dame,
    Papeete; 42-02-24
Police emergency ~ 17
Police Station ~ Gendarmerie, Avenue Bruat, Papeete; 46-73-73
Post Office ~ Main Post Office, Boulevard Pomare, Papeete; 41-
    42-42; www.opt.pf
Visitor information ~ Tahiti Manava Visitor's Bureau (Fare
    Manihini), Boulevard Pomare, Papeete; 50-57-10, fax 45-16-
    78; www.tahiti-manava.pf
Airport ~ 86-10-10

FIVE

Moorea

After Tahiti, the second-most popular tourist attraction in French Polynesia is Moorea. And no wonder. The island is dramatically beautiful, with sharp serrated peaks that command deep cleft valleys, once centers for vanilla cultivation. When you imagine a South Pacific seascape, this is it.

Lying 12 miles (19 kilometers) west of Tahiti, Moorea is encircled by a lagoon of translucent green, fringed by an azure sea. The island is triangular in shape, one side punctuated by two large, deep bays (Cook's Bay and Opunohu). Covering an area of 80 square miles (200 square kilometers), and with a population of 12,000, it is the only other major island in the Windward group besides Tahiti.

Moorea (which is pronounced MOE-oh-ray-ah—or with the accent on the third syllable: moe-oh-RAY-ah—with a pause or glottal stop between the o's) means yellow lizard. The name was taken from a family of chiefs that eventually united with the Pomare dynasty of Tahiti. Archaeological evidence in the Opunohu Valley suggests that people were living on the island as early as A.D. 900, which corresponds with the oral history of the valley. At the time of Cook's return in 1774, there was internecine fighting among the islands' chiefs and warfare with tribes on neighboring Tahiti. The battles continued for many years and the arrival of the missionaries in 1805 actually helped the Pomare dynasty gain power in Tahiti by supplying arms and mercenaries in return for support. After Pomare I conquered Tahiti, Moorea (which had been his refuge) became no more than a province of the Tahitian kingdom. During the latter half of the 19th century, colonists arrived and cotton and coconut plantations began to spring up. Vanilla and coffee cultivation came later, in the 20th century.

Tourism is now by far the largest industry and the island's attraction for visitors is no mystery. The high peaks, deep green valleys, and white-sand beaches are generally still pristine. The island and the islanders retain their charm but not without a struggle. Several years ago locals fought off the planned development of a golf course in the verdant heart of the island that would have encroached upon archaeological treasures.

Moorea is quick and easy to reach from Tahiti—shuttle flights leave every 30 minutes from Faa'a Airport and ferries, a less-expensive and easier option, depart from Papeete throughout the day.

Once on Moorea, sightseeing can be easily accomplished via *Le Truck*, rental car or scooter. Naturally, the numerous tour companies, touted at every hotel, will be more than happy to show you around on their private *Le Truck* or minibus.

The complete circuit of the island is 36 miles (59 kilometers) and the coast road is marked by red-and-white PK (kilometer) markers at regular intervals. The highway markers begin at the airport at PK 0, and from there go round to PK 35 in a counterclockwise direction and PK 24 clockwise. (One would think it would be more logical and less confusing to go in one direction and just continue to count kilometerage consecutively until you reach the point where you started. However, this is not the way it works.) If you are confused, consult the map and remember this is not a big island. There is little chance of getting lost unless you hike into the bush.

For the ease of visitors who wish to do a circle island tour, our island circuit starts at the airport and proceeds counterclockwise around the island. The PK marker number is followed by the distance from the starting point. As a common courtesy, visitors should take care not to trespass on private land to take photos.

Vaiare Bay to Opunohu Bay

Visitors arrive on Moorea at the eastern corner of the island either at the airport (near Temae Village) or four kilometers south of the airport, at the ferry terminal at Vaiare Bay. Thus, if you can imagine Moorea as a three-toed hoof print, your point of entry would be on the right toe. From the Hotel Sofitel Ia Ora near the airport, it's easy to get around thanks to a service that taxi drivers lobbied against for years—a regularly scheduled bus system. The minibus service departs eight times a day from the Sofitel Ia Ora and goes as far as the Linareva Hotel, at the opposite (northwestern) end of the island. Most of the hotels, shops and indeed the majority of the population are concentrated along Moorea's northern coast.

SIGHTS

Cargo boats and daily ferries from Papeete (except the *Ono Ono*) dock in **Vaiare Bay**. A large pier can accommodate two ferries simultaneously, and a parking lot is where drivers of trucks, autos and motorcycles await their turn to drive up the ramp onto the vessels. Ancillary facilities such as warehouses, service stations and the island's largest supermarket are clustered in the area. As always, ubiquitous *roulottes* (food vans) are parked nearby to feed workers and passengers. The ferry-boat personnel manning the ramps are quite efficient and perhaps nothing in French Polynesia runs as smoothly as the loading and unloading of vehicles and cargo at the terminal. ~ PK 4.

The **Hotel Sofitel Ia Ora** is a good place to begin exploring the island. Located about a kilometer south of the airport, its numerous thatch-roofed and over-the-water bungalows are dispersed over a quarter-mile-long strip of beachfront. The hotel property basks in the shade of coconut trees that line the shore on the southern end of Temae Beach—which has the best public access of any beach on the island. Sofitel is one of several luxury resorts on Moorea, though it has seen better days and is currently undergoing renovations. You can get to the beach from the hotel but public access (north of the hotel) is a better idea. ~ PK 1.

Passing the Sofitel entrance and heading in the direction of Cook's Bay, the coastal road climbs the only significant grade along the perimeter of the island. At the top of the hill is **Toatea Lookout,** which offers a nice view down the coastline and across to Tahiti. Leaving the lookout point, at the bottom of the hill just past a bridge is the public access to **Temae Beach.** The sign is clearly marked and it's about one kilometer to the beach via a dirt road from the coastal highway. Temae is perfect for swimming. A long white-sand beach edging translucent blue water, Temae is shaded by great numbers of coconut palms. There's almost no coral around, which makes it ideal for wading in the water, though more often than not the beach is littered with beer bottles, plastic bags and other debris. Only a 50-meter section is public land, and the area between the public beach and the Hotel Sofitel is slated for development in the near future. Pacific Golf and Resort Development Company plans to turn the property into an international-class, 18-hole golf course. The project also includes a Polynesian-style five-star hotel and 60 guest houses built along the course. Construction is expected to begin in the near future. If you continue west, along the beach access road, you will eventually end up alongside the airport runway. ~ PK 0.

Temae Village was where, tradition has it, novelist Herman Melville persuaded the chief to have the *vahines* perform for him the erotic *Lory-Lory*, a dance forbidden by the missionaries. Melville came here after his release from jail in Tahiti, where he and other crew members of the *Lucy Ann* were punished for their participation in a mutiny. Temae Village is still famous for its dancing troupes, which perform regularly for the island's dance revues. However, other than a few shops and some residences, there is nothing that imparts to the visitor that this is a formal "village." ~ PK 1.

You will recognize you have arrived in **Maharepa Village** (pronounced MA-ha-ray-pa) by noting the brightly colored pareus strung between coconut trees along the road that mark the Lili Shop. Though the term "village" is used to describe Maharepa, it's little more than a cluster of shops and hotels along the roadside. Recently a shopping center with two dozen or so shops and restaurants has been built with Bank Socredo as the anchor tenant.

A little less than a kilometer from the Lili Shop is the former **Hotel Bali Hai Moorea,** one of the first hotels to be built at the

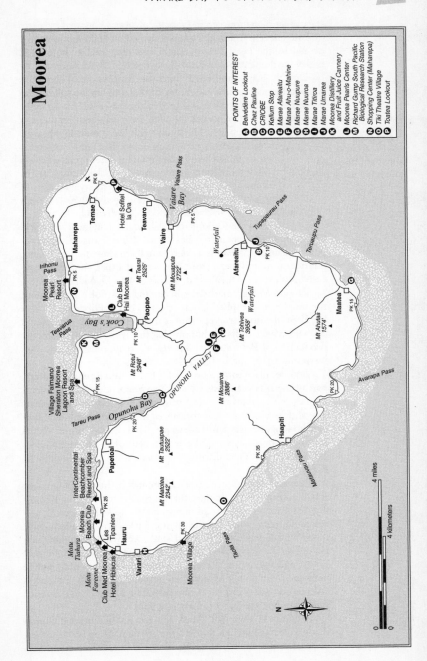

Moorea

POINTS OF INTEREST

Ⓐ Belvedere Lookout
Ⓑ Chez Pauline
Ⓒ CRIOBE
Ⓓ Kellum Stop
Ⓔ Marae Afareaitu
Ⓕ Marae Ahu-o-Mahine
Ⓖ Marae Nuupure
Ⓗ Marae Nuuroa
Ⓘ Marae Titiroa
Ⓙ Marae Umarea
Ⓚ Moorea Distillery and Fruit Juice Cannery
Ⓛ Moorea Pearls Center
Ⓜ Richard Gump South Pacific Biological Research Station
Ⓝ Shopping Center (Maharepa)
Ⓞ Tiki Theatre Village
Ⓟ Toatea Lookout

start of jet plane tourism in French Polynesia. Founded by a trio of American entrepreneurs known as the Bali Hai Boys, it is now owned by the Pearl Resorts chain and reopened in June 2002 under the name **Moorea Pearl Resort**. ~ PK 5.5, Maharepa.

Directly across the road from the Moorea Pearl Resort is **Maison Blanche**, a renovated turn-of-the-20th-century plantation house that is now a souvenir shop. During the vanilla boom in the latter part of the 19th and early 20th centuries, a number of homes like this were built in Moorea, but no other plantation house that I am aware of is in such excellent shape. (With a careful eye, you can still see other plantation houses tucked away in the bush or along the side of the road.) The style consists of clapboard construction, iron roofing and a veranda with white wooden fretwork. ~ PK 5.5, Maharepa.

> If you rent a scooter to tour the island, make sure to wear close-toed shoes if you have them.

Almost one kilometer past Maison Blanche you will find a **shopping center** that has a post office, bank, doctor's office, pharmacy, patisserie (where you'll find terrific ice cream), boutiques, a stationery store and several other shops. It's oriented both toward locals and visitors. ~ PK 6.3, Maharepa.

Paopao Village marks the beginning of **Cook's Bay**, one of the most photographed landmarks in French Polynesia. It also has the obligatory trinket shops, car and bike rental outlets and a wharf. Movie buffs might note that this was one of the sites for production of *Return of the Bounty*, although most of the scenes were shot in Opunohu Bay. ~ PK 7, Maharepa.

Another place to stop on Cook's Bay is **Aquariums of Pottery**, part of the **Moorea Pearls Center**. The brainchild of Teva, a local jeweler, this establishment was at one time a combination aquarium and jewelry store that specialized in black pearls. The aquarium no longer exists but the jewelry part is going full tilt. At the back of the building is a garden where, beneath a shade tree, Teva's assistants give a short discourse on black pearl cultivation. ~ PK 8; 56-30-00.

Paopao Village is the central community in the Cook's Bay area and is an important junction for the road leading to the island's interior. Paopao also has an important dock used by trading vessels and grocery stores. In the evenings, it's worth a walk or drive to see whether the mobile food stalls, known as *roulottes*, are parked on the wharf. If so, be sure to stop. The food is reasonably priced and very good. Paopao also has a small open-air **public market**, which is best visited early in the day. Finally, Paopao is where you turn off to get to the Belvédère Lookout and interior valleys and/or the Paopao-to-Vaiare walk. ~ PK 9.

A half-mile west of Paopao is a renovated **Catholic church** that's worth visiting. Here you'll find an altar inlaid with mother-of-pearl and a mural featuring brown-skinned Polynesian ver-

Moorea

You'll want a car in Moorea and have the option of picking it up at the airport (which may be less expensive) or simply setting up a rental at your hotel (which is more convenient). Renting a car is not cheap in French Polynesia but motorbikes are too dangerous. You could bike it but, unless you're in good shape, it's not a good idea.

• Starting clockwise from the airport, check out **Toatea Lookout**, with great views down along the coastline and across to Tahiti. Leaving the lookout point, at the bottom of the hill is the public access to **Temae Beach**, just past a bridge. The sign (that says Plage) is clearly marked and it's about one kilometer to the beach via dirt road from the coastal highway. If you're hungry, grab a bite at **Mahogany** (page 205) for local specialties.

• Continuing on, stop at the **Moorea Distillery and Fruit Juice Cannery** (page 198), which specializes in the island's agricultural products. You can also sample an excellent fruit liqueur, Eau de Vie, derived from local produce.

• Take another break at **Kellum Stop** (page 198), a historic homestead established by an American family in 1925. It resembles a large farmhouse, set in a spectacular location overlooking Opunohu Bay.

• From either Pao Pao or Opunohu take the road into the Opunohu Valley and follow it to the **Belvédère Lookout** (page 203), the vista point. Be sure to stop along the way and walk among the ancient *marae* (temples).

• Afterwards, stop over in **Papetoai Village** (page 211) for a few minutes to admire the refurbished **octagonal church**—the oldest building in French Polynesia.

• Continue rounding the island, and if you're hungry stop at **Chez Serge** (page 224) in the Petit Village Shopping Center, or further down the road at **Le Pitcairn** (page 223) or **Le Sunset Restaurant Pizzeria** (page 224) in the Haapiti area.

• In the evening catch the sunset and enjoy an outdoor cocktail at **Club Bali Hai** (page 210).

sions of St. Joseph, the Virgin Mary, the Archangel Gabriel and the infant Jesus. The landscape painted in the background depicts Moorea. ~ PK 10.

The **Richard Gump South Pacific Biological Research Station** was constructed on land donated by San Francisco jewelry magnate Richard Gump, in cooperation with the University of California at Berkeley. Here UC Berkeley has established a biological research facility for terrestrial and marine life. The station consists of two buildings, a dormitory, a lab and several boats. It is open to researchers from around the world, whose interests may range from insects to tropical fish. The facility welcomes guests, but you should correspond with the University of California ahead of time rather than simply show up. ~ PK 10.9.

Several hundred yards off the main highway (on the mountain side of the road) is the **Moorea Distillery and Fruit Juice Cannery**, which specializes in the island's agricultural products—pineapple, grapefruit, *pamplemousse* and papaya. A local greets you and gives a well-rehearsed monologue describing the various stages of the canning process. On the grounds is a small kiosk where visitors are served shots of Eau de Vie ("water of life"), an excellent fruit liqueur derived from local produce. Tasty *pamplemousse* fruit juice is available in liter cartons at any grocery store in French Polynesia, but freshly squeezed at a café or restaurant is even better. Oddly enough, you can taste samples of the Eau de Vie but samples of the fruit juice (sans alcohol) are not available. Closed Sunday. ~ PK 11; 56-11-33, fax 56-21-52; e-mail rotui@mail.pf.

Continuing west you will come to **Opunohu Bay**, Moorea's second dramatic inlet. Opunohu is less developed and therefore less touristy than Cook's Bay. It also has good snorkeling, but crown-of-thorns starfish and stonefish can pose a danger, so take heed. ~ PK 14.

HIDDEN ▶   While in the neighborhood, you would be remiss not to spend an hour or two at **Kellum Stop**. (See "Kellum's Legacy" in this chapter.) The Kellum home, which looks like a large farmhouse, is tucked among the coconut palms and mango trees. Open from 8 a.m. to 12 noon Tuesday to Saturday. Please respect Marimari Kellum's privacy and do not ask for a tour during off-hours. Admission. ~ PK 17.5, midway between the former Club Med and Club Bali Hai. Look for a small wooden sign on the mountain side of the road that marks the driveway to the estate. Park, walk to the gate on the opposite side of the road and ring the cowbell attached to it.

Drive west of the Kellum Stop and you'll come to the **Opunohu Valley Road**, which is the second access to the island's interior. The road eventually links up with the Paopao Valley Road and comes to a dead end at the Belvédère Lookout (see Scenic Drive on page 202). (Along the Paopao Valley Road look for vanilla plantations, which are readily identifiable by the vanilla vines that wind around posts.) Just prior to the road's junction on the main highway are several **prawn ponds.** ~ PK 18.

At the junction of the Opunohu Valley Road and the circle island road (opposite the prawn ponds) is a nondescript building with a sign that says **Centre de Recherches Insulaires et Observatoire de L'Environnement** (CRIOBE). This translates as "Island Research Center and Environmental Observatory." The facilities are owned by the Government of French Polynesia and operated by the University of Peripignon, a prestigious learning institution in France. CRIOBE is part of the French National Network of Marine Stations, but the outlook of the scientists who work here is decidedly global. CRIOBE welcomes students and researchers from around the world.

Dr. Michael Poole, an American researcher who lives on Moorea, is the director of CRIOBE's Marine Mammal Research Program. In 1998, he drafted a proposal to create a whale and dolphin sanctuary throughout all of French Polynesia's Exclusive Economic Zone (5 million square kilometers of ocean). After years of legal wrangling, the French government declared the official establishment of the sanctuary in April 2002, including the strict guidelines Dr. Poole created to protect the animals from hunting, harassment, boats, etc. Poole calls it "a wonderful victory for the environment and for our children's children." ~ Papetoai; 56-13-45, fax 56-28-15; e-mail criobe@mail.pf.

Dr. Poole also operates highly acclaimed dolphin- and whale-watching expeditions. See "Dolphins—Up Close and Personal" on page 229 for more information on his tours.

LODGING

On a white-sand beach facing Tahiti, two kilometers south of the airport, the **Hotel Sofitel Ia Ora** is one of several luxury hotels on Moorea. It has a dated feel about it, which will hopefully be remedied by the current renovations. There are two bars, two restaurants and all the amenities you could want: a boutique, outrigger canoes, tennis and water sports. Facing an expansive stretch of beach, the grounds are so big that when you check in, a *vahine* must drive you to your room in a golf cart. The 53 bungalows are

AUTHOR FAVORITE

When I travel to Moorea I never pass up **Kellum Stop**, a colonial homestead nestled among coconut palms and mango trees. What makes a trip here so special is host Marimari Kellum, granddaughter of the original owner, who graciously leads tours of the magnificent grounds. See page 198 for more information.

quaint and far enough apart to afford plenty of privacy; each has its own view of the sea. All have marble floors, air conditioning, overhead fans and huge bathrooms. The rooms are decorated in an attractive bamboo motif that includes rattan beds, coffee tables, chairs and trim. There are exceptional over-the-water bungalows as well, each with a stepladder that plunges right into the lagoon. ~ PK 1; 55-03-55, fax 56-12-91, or 800-221-4542 in the U.S.; www.sofitel.com, e-mail h0566-gm@accor-hotels.com. ULTRA-DELUXE.

Located at the entrance to Cook's Bay, about five kilometers from the airport, the Hotel Bali Hai Moorea was established by three Americans who came before the Tahiti tourist boom to run a vanilla plantation and wound up as hotel magnates. The hotel, now under new ownership and renamed the **Moorea Pearl Resort & Spa**, consists mainly of 95 bungalows that spread over a long narrow swath of land wedged between the main road and the lagoon. The rooms are all well appointed and include such creature comforts as a minibar and internet access. The 28 over-the-water bungalows have glass-bottom tables so you can watch reef life swim by. Many of the garden and over-the-water units also have jacuzzis. The hotel, which reopened in June 2002, also has a huge restaurant and bar, a little patch of beach, tennis and a pool. ~ PK 5.5; 50-84-52, fax 43-17-86; www.pearlresorts.com, e-mail maraea.temauri@spmhotels.pf. DELUXE.

Club Bali Hai Moorea primarily has time-share units but they also rent to walk-in guests. Fronting a small beach, this property is more intimate than its sister property, the Moorea Pearl Resort. Also located on Cook's Bay, the bungalows are surrounded by well-tended gardens and there is a dramatic view of Mt. Rotui. More than 44 rooms are available; they come in three configurations—over-the-water bungalows, garden bungalows and motel-like units (part of a large building). Even the most basic rooms (which go for around US$100) have tiled floors, plenty of space, a small refrigerator and large bathrooms. The garden bungalows each have small mezzanines that will sleep an extra person—a good deal for families. Kids are welcome. This property has also undergone a major upgrade that includes new room furnishings, roofs and a brand-new bricked deck area overlooking Cook's Bay. Club Bali Hai is famous for its Tuesday and Friday happy hours, with (usually) live local music (and equally lively locals) from 6 to 7 p.m. On Friday night, after happy hour, Club Bali Hai puts on a Tahitian dance show followed by disco dancing that lasts until 10:30 p.m. It's a good place to rub shoulders with the locals and the expats who live on the island. The bay view is nothing short of stunning. ~ PK 8.5; 56-13-68, fax 56-13-27; www.clubbalihai.com, e-mail reservations@clubbalihai.pf. MODERATE TO DELUXE.

Kellum's Legacy

On a magnificent stretch of Opunohu Bay, in the shadow of Mt. Rotui, rests the Kellum Estate—a solid, weatherworn bit of Americana nearly lost in the vastness of the South Seas. The small, hand-lettered sign that marks the Kellum Stop on PK 17.5 belies the impact that the Kellum clan had on Moorea.

The saga began in 1924 when Medford Kellum, Sr., a wealthy Miami businessman, and his family set out from Hawaii on the *Kaimiloa*, a four-masted schooner, to survey the lesser-visited islands of the South Pacific. Along with his crew, various members of the scientific community were invited to participate. Included were botanist Gerrit P. Wilder and Kenneth P. Emory, the most famous ethnologist and specialist in Polynesian studies of his time. (The story of Emory's life and ground-breaking studies on Polynesian culture and society are recounted in the book *Keneti*, by Bob Krauss, published by the University of Hawaii Press in 1988.)

When the *Kaimiloa* arrived in Moorea in January 1925, an enormous tract of land, some 3500 acres of lush tropical splendor held by a German company, was up for auction. The property comprised nearly the entire Opunohu Valley, including numerous archaeological sites, verdant meadows, streams and rugged cliffs. The Kellums purchased the land and Medford Kellum, Jr., along with his American wife, started a cattle, copra and vanilla plantation.

In 1962, the French government purchased most of the land from the Kellum clan with the proviso that they build an agricultural research facility, which still exists. Kellum, a sturdy Yankee with a down-to-earth demeanor, died in 1992 at the age of 90. With his passing, an enormous part of the island's recent history went with him. The Kellum home, however, remains the way Medford Kellum kept it, due largely to the efforts of his daughter, Marimari.

An accomplished archaeologist who studied in the U.S., Marimari has graciously opened the doors to the Kellums' Eden by giving private tours (in English or French) of the grounds. The one-hour tour includes a walk through the splendid garden where over 50 varieties of herbs and flowers grow. Here she explains how the local flora was used medicinally, cosmetically and in the construction of homes and utensils by the Polynesians of old. Of special note is a magnificent 65-year-old *tipanier* (plumeria) that was brought from Hawaii as a seedling. Also described in the tour is the Kellums' colonial-style home. Local artifacts are also on display, including the fabled tiki that the late Hugh Kelley (of Bali Hai fame) tracked down.

Paopao and Opunohu Valleys

The Opunohu Valley, with its reconstructed *marae* (temples), fine vistas and lush green meadows, is well worth a detour off the perimeter road. A round trip can be made by leaving the coast road at Paopao at the top of Cook's Bay and climbing up into the Paopao Valley to join the Opunohu Valley Road and return to the top of Opunohu Bay. Prior to European contact, these central valleys were teeming with people. Now they are largely deserted and devoted to agriculture.

OPUNOHU VALLEY The Opunohu Valley population declined in the early 19th century, soon after the abandonment of the traditional religion. More than 500 ancient structures have been identified here, including religious and secular stone buildings as well as agricultural terraces. The complexity of the remains indicates a highly developed social system. The chief remnants of these buildings are six *marae*, reconstructed in 1967. A council platform and two archery platforms have also been rebuilt. From the junction at Paopao, PK 9, it is several winding kilometers to the *marae*. All are an easy walk from the road. Before reaching the *marae,* you will drive through a pineapple plantation. Stop at the first hill, turn to the left and park. Walk across the road for a spectacular view of Cook's and Opunohu bays.

MARAE TITIROA The large Marae Titiroa is right by the car park and information board. This large temple complex was restored in 1969. The platform area or *ahu* is strictly reserved for the gods while the tablet-like stones protruding from the earth were backrests for chiefs or priests. This particular temple was used for animal sacrifices, which were placed here as offerings to the gods. A clear trail runs into the woods from here to the Council Platform, a smaller *marae* and the impressive Marae Ahu-o-Mahine. Another *marae* can easily be reached by rock hopping across the river from Marae Titiroa but the woods in the valley hide countless other traditional structures.

MARAE AHU-O-MAHINE The Marae Ahu-o-Mahine has the most elaborate form and features a three-stepped *ahu* (platform). It was once the

Motel Albert is on the inland side of the road about eight kilometers from the airport, across from Club Bali Hai. Along with a terrific views of Mt. Rotui and Cook's Bay, it is one of the best —if not *the* best—accommodations in the budget category. Nestled at the base of the mountains, it's a small, family-run affair with ten clean (albeit sterile-looking) cabin-like units, equipped with kitchenettes and small balconies. There are also four family-size community *marae* for the Opunohu Valley and was built some time after A.D 1780. Note that it is constructed with handcrafted, round dressed stones, similar to those of Marae Arahurahu in Paea, Tahiti. The intricacy of this particular temple is evidence of the highly developed society that existed in pre-contact times.

ARCHERY PLATFORMS   Archery was a sacred sport in ancient Tahiti, practiced only by people of high rank—chiefs' families and warriors. As is clearly visible from the map, archery platforms have distinct crescent forms at one end. Archers balanced on one knee to draw their bows and aimed for distance rather than accuracy. Of the three archery platforms in the Opunohu Valley, two have been restored. As in other parts of Polynesia, bows and arrows were not used as weapons of war. The tracks to the two archery platforms and the connecting Marae Afareaitu from Marae Titiroa are not easy to follow, and it's easier to drive around by road. Look for any small parting of the scrub between Marae Titiroa and the nearby parking area, and the Belvédère Lookout.

MARAE AFAREAITU   Between the two restored archery platforms is Marae Afareaitu, similar to Marae Titiroa farther down the trail. A small *ahu* near one end is the principal structure of the *marae*, which was reserved for the gods. On the perimeter of the *marae* are two small shrines, one attached and one detached from the main temple. Some of these independent shrines are associated with agricultural terraces and suggest that crop-fertility ceremonies were held there.

BELVÉDÈRE LOOKOUT   A few more kilometers up the road is Belvédère Lookout, the finest vista of the valley. Standing on the ridge of the caldera, the lookout point affords a great vista of Opunohu and Cook's bays. Belvédère Lookout was part of the setting for the latest film version of the *Bounty* story (*Return of the Bounty*) with Anthony Hopkins and Mel Gibson (which gave much-needed temporary employment to the locals). Continue back down the road, this time taking a left toward Opunohu Bay. On this route you will pass scenery that but for the coconut trees might belong to a Swiss valley—you'll see verdant pastures with fat, contented cattle grazing. Continue along and you are once more on the perimeter road that circles the island.

fare that are incredibly spacious and have full kitchens and two bedrooms. All have hot water. Stores and restaurants and a beach are within easy walking distance and you may rent a bike for about US$10 per day. The grounds are very spacious and well manicured, and Albert's staff may give you *pamplemousse* (grapefruit) or other edibles that fall from the trees. The two-person units are of higher quality than the other units—they include tiled floors, nice bathrooms with more than adequate kitchenettes but no ceiling fans. Guests must stay for a minimum of two nights to get the least expensive rates, but if occupancy is low you can bargain. Weekly and monthly rates are also available. No credit cards. ~ PK 8.5; 56-12-76, fax 56-58-58. BUDGET.

The M.U.S.T. **Lodging** is exclusively for divers using MUST. Located off a back road, it's not easy to find. It's a better idea to look for MUST's headquarters on the jetty near Cook's Bay Resort and have them take you there. Accommodations are in a simple, two-room home on a banana plantation. The house has one communal bathroom with hot water. Tariff includes three meals. Call Philippe Molle for more information. ~ Paopao Valley; 56-17-32, 56-15-83. BUDGET.

HIDDEN ►

Perhaps the best example of a family-run lodging can be found midway between Paopao and Papetoai, at the top of the point between Cook's Bay and Opunohu Bay. **Village Faimano** has six airy, thatch-roofed bungalows, each with kitchen facilities. The setting is very Polynesian and there is nothing presumptuous about Faimano, which makes it one of my favorite places to stay. There are lots of shady trees and fresh ocean breezes. The management is very laid-back (what else would you expect?) and leaves you to your own devices. Another plus is the proximity to a white-sand beach/swimming area on the property. All of the units have private bath, some with hot water. Garden bungalows sleep three or four, while the larger units sleep four to six. No credit cards are accepted, so don't forget to bring cash and be prepared to pay one night's deposit for a reservation. No towels are provided. The proprietress, Hinano Feildel, offers discounts for longer stays. Activities include canoeing, snorkeling gear and fishing in the lagoon. There is a two-night minimum stay. ~ PK 14; 56-10-20, fax 56-36-47; www.faimanovillage.com, e-mail faimanodenis@mail.pf. MODERATE TO DELUXE.

When touring the *marae*, be sure to bring along plenty of mosquito repellent.

The posh **Sheraton Moorea Lagoon Resort and Spa** lies roughly halfway between Opunohu Bay and Cook's Bay. The 106-room property, which opened in 2000, is the island's most expensive offering. The exclusive complex covers nearly three acres and includes 56 over-the-water bungalows and 50 garden and beach bungalows. Hotel amenities include a five-star restaurant, a cocktail lounge, a day spa, a swimming pool, an imported sand beach, an activities desk, a boat dock, two lighted 24-hour tennis courts and a fully equipped gym. During my stays here, the hotel suffered from maintenance issues and poor customer service. ~ PK 14; 55-11-11, fax 55-11-55; www.sheratonsintahiti.com, e-mail reservations.tahiti@sheraton.pf. ULTRA-DELUXE.

Close by, **Chez Francine** is a single home with two bedrooms and private bath with hot water. Rooms are spacious and have woven bamboo walls—a nice touch. One room has a kitchenette. Discounts are provided for long-term renters; the whole house can be rented for 13,500 CFP per night. The only problem with Chez Francine is its proximity to the main road, which makes things a bit noisy. ~ PK 14.5; 56-13-24. BUDGET TO MODERATE.

Fare Nani is located about 50 yards from the Sheraton. It has three thatch-roofed bungalows with wide trap-door windows that let the breeze through. There's a kitchen and cold-water bath. The setup is similar to Village Faimano, though slightly less traditional. The beach area (shared with Village Faimano) is just a few steps from the bungalows, and the gardens shaded by coconut palms are exquisite. You must provide your own towels, but outrigger canoes are available to guests. ~ PK 16; phone/fax 56-19-99. MODERATE TO DELUXE.

DINING

As on Tahiti, in the evenings be sure and check out the **roulottes** that park near the ferry stop in Vaiare, the wharf at Paopao at the head of Cook's Bay and at various other places on the island. The food at these mobile eateries is economically priced and generally quite good. The outdoor setting, on the waterfront beneath the stars, is wonderful.

Mahogany, next to Magasin Remy between Temae Beach and the Maharepa Shopping Center, is the first eatery you will pass driving along the north coast from the airport or the ferry terminal. In a large wooden structure akin to an old roadhouse, Mahogany offers reasonably priced Polynesian dishes including *poisson cru*, sandwiches, steak and *pomme frites*, and fresh fruit. The atmosphere is local, as is most of the clientele. ~ PK 4.3, Teavaro; 56-39-73. BUDGET.

Le Cocotier is a friendly, inexpensive restaurant that does a lively lunch trade. The food is tasty, and moderately priced by Tahitian standards. With about six small tables, the atmosphere is intimate. Fare includes *poisson cru*, sashimi, mahimahi and marinated tuna slices. At dinner, one can have steak and *pomme frites*, a cheese platter, wine and coffee for around US$25. ~ PK 4.5, Maharepa; 56-12-10. BUDGET TO MODERATE.

Just west of Le Cocotier, in the Maharepa Shopping Center, the **Patisserie Caramelire** serves Continental- and American-style breakfasts, pastries, ice cream, coffee and croissants, as well as more substantial fare such as pizza, crêpes and hamburgers. This small café is a good place to pop in for breakfast. ~ PK 4.5, Maharepa; 56-15-88. BUDGET.

Le Pêcheur ("The Fisherman") is a good roadside restaurant with indoor/outdoor seating. On the menu you will find *poisson*

Text continued on page 208.

Spas in French Polynesia

The islands of French Polynesia have often been called the world's largest outdoor spa—and with good reason. After all, you can soak your tired muscles in cool, clear mountain streams and soothe your skin with local monoi oil. In addition, the gentle afternoon rains will put the best Vichy shower to shame.

It therefore comes as a surprise to many visitors that up until recently, purpose-built spas were noticeably absent in the heart of the South Pacific. Not one to be left behind when it comes to travel trends, Tahiti has finally entered the spa market and several top hotels have recently added "and Spa" to their names. Here are the big five spa destinations in the islands:

Sheraton Hotel Tahiti's Mandara Spa, the smallest spa in the islands, is for many newly arrived tourists the most important. "Ninety percent of my clients have just arrived after a seven-hour flight from Los Angeles," says Francesca, a therapist. "They want to get over their jet lag and get out to see the Paul Gauguin Museum or take a four-wheel-drive tour." Her recommendation? "A coconut oil massage." Painted in warm earth tones, the two suites adjacent to the hotel gym have balconies and small gardens overlooking the ocean. There are twin massage tables and jacuzzis full of freshly cut jasmines. ~ Sheraton Hotel Tahiti, PK 2, Faa'a, Tahiti; 86-48-48, fax 86-48-40; www.sheratontahiti.com.

The **Sheraton Moorea Lagoon** also offers a Mandara Spa menu that is one-third Balinese, one-third European and one-third local. Indigenous treatments rely on native ingredients like coconut milk, ginger, vanilla beans, *tiare* flowers and grapefruit. The most popular treatment is the sunburn cooler, which starts with a lavender body wash and finishes with an aloe vera and tea tree oil wrap. Therapist Jezel says, "It's a hydrating treatment, perfect for people who were in the sun a little too long." ~ Sheraton Moorea Lagoon Resort and Spa, PK 14, Moorea; 55-11-11, fax 55-11-55; www.sheratonmoorea.com.

Set in a forested corner of the **InterContinental Beachcomber Resort**, Helene Spa is one of only two independent spas in the islands. The spa is a naturalist's delight—a rambling affair of palm-thatched *fares* (indigenous huts) and bamboo-ribbed walkways that seem to float across flower gardens. It is possible, in the space of a few footsteps, to find yourself lost in a magical labyrinth of shaded trees, dancing pools and creaking walkways. Owner Helen Sillinger combines European know-how with traditional treatments learned from local grandmothers. "They are the ones who massage the babies and take care of the sick," she says. "They always seem to know how to make you feel better." ~ InterContinental Beachcomber Resort and Spa, PK 24.5, Papetoai, Moorea; 55-19-19, fax 55-19-55; www.moorea.interconti.com.

It's hard not to feel better just walking inside the largest of the island spas, the Mandara Spa at the **Bora Bora Nui Resort**. The spa debuted on the island of the same name in 2003. The two-story center is perched on a ridge high above the resort, and overlooks both the sheer basalt face of Mt. Otemanu and the azure lagoon below. "The view is one of the things guests like most about the spa," says therapist Matahi. "One of the most popular requests is to have a sunset massage for two in the open-air pavilions." The spa houses a reception area and beauty salon on the top floor, and a gym, sauna and steam rooms below. Cobbled walkways lead to three open-air treatment villas, each with ocean views, twin massage tables and an indoor/outdoor jacuzzi. By far the most popular treatment is the Mandara massage—an 80-minute treatment where two therapists work their way through a combination of five styles—Japanese Shiatsu, Thai, Hawaiian Lomi Lomi, Swedish and Balinese. ~ Bora Bora Nui Resort and Spa, Motu Toopua; 86-48-48, fax 86-48-40; www.boraboranui.com.

The newest in the islands, **Bora Bora Lagoon Resort**'s Maru Spa is getting rave reviews from travelers, both for its unique architecture and broad menu. The highlight of the five-room spa (Polynesian for "soft and gentle") is a pair of treatment rooms suspended two stories off the ground in the majestic branches of Caoutchouc trees. The Maru Spa specializes in Balinese and local treatments. If you want a traditional monoi oil massage, this is the place to get it. ~ Bora Bora, Motu Toopua; 60-40-00, fax 60-40-01, or 800-860-4095 in the U.S.; www.borabora lagoonresort.com.

cru, mahimahi, mussels, curried shrimp, marinated tuna with fresh veggies and coconut milk, pepper steak and escargot. There is also a selection of salads and soups. ~ PK 6.2, Maharepa; 56-36-12. MODERATE TO DELUXE.

HIDDEN ►   **Allo Pizza** has become a favorite of locals. Located across from the Gendarmerie (on the mountain side of the road), Allo specializes in thin-crust pizza; you can really taste the ingredients. They have take-out service as well. Try the Hawaiian pizza. ~ PK 7.8, Cook's Bay; 56-18-22. BUDGET.

Alfredo's is a large, whitewashed, colonial-style building with green trim located just south of Club Bali Hai in Paopao. It has indoor/outdoor dining on a balcony with a view of the yachts moored in Cook's Bay and a mango tree in the front yard. On the menu are a variety of starters such as carpaccio, sushi and stuffed mussels. The specialties of the house are filet of tuna tartar, mahimahi sautéed with lemon and shrimp curry with coconut milk. Steak, pizza and pasta are also available. Unlike most restaurants on the island, Alfredo's has a full bar. Most everything I've heard about this establishment has been positive. ~ PK 5.5, Paopao; 56-17-71. BUDGET TO MODERATE.

L'Ananas Bleu ("Blue Pineapple") is owned by Charlie Hunter, a young Tahitian chef who specializes in seafood. It's a pleasant place to dine in an indoor/outdoor setting with a spacious dining area on the balcony. Charlie does serve crêpes, but other dishes to try include shrimp curry with coconut cream and the hamburgers. Savory *salée* include fried eggs, bacon and eggs, omelettes, ham and cheese and chicken/curry rice. Try your crêpes with *Cidre Brut*—partially fermented (dry) apple cider served in an ice-cold champagne bottle. It's located in the Club Bali Hai. ~ Paopao; 56-12-06. BUDGET.

Directly after Supermarche Are is **Snack Rotui**. With the usual array of French-bread sandwiches and soft drinks, it's little more than a few stools surrounding a fast food–style service counter. Snack Rotui is a good place to sit and meditate on the view of Cook's Bay. ~ Paopao. BUDGET.

GROCERIES   Starting from the direction of the airport and heading west, you will find **Magasin Remy** at PK 4.5 ~ 56-32-27, **Libre Service Maharepa** at PK 5.8 ~ 56-35-90, **Magasin Lee Hen Soi Louk** in Paopao ~ 56-15-02 and **Supermarche Are** in Paopao ~ 56-10-28. Paopao Village also has a small open-air public market, selling mostly produce, which is best visited early in the day.

SHOPPING   An art gallery located at the **Hotel Sofitel Ia Ora** has a fairly good selection of carvings and paintings from local artists. ~ PK 1; 55-03-55.

In Maharepa, shopping possibilities include **Maison Blanche,** a renovated turn-of-the-20th-century plantation house that is now a souvenir shop. They stock quality jewelry, pareus and other souvenirs. You may see many of the same things in the other shops, but these are the best prices I've found. Many of the items stocked here (and elsewhere) are from Indonesia, not Polynesia, so if this makes a difference to you, ask. It's located directly across the road from the Moorea Pearl Resort. ~ PK 5.5, Maharepa; 56-13-26.

> Expect to pay around 1000 CFP (US$10) or less for a meal at a *roulette*. The average entrée at a restaurant will be 1400 to 1800 CFP (US$14 to US$18).

The **Tahitian South Sea Pearl Company**'s Sofitel branch has a good selection of nicely set black pearls. ~ Temae; 56-11-85.

If you're looking for jewelry, consider visiting Ron Hall's **Island Fashions** near Cook's Bay. Hall came to Tahiti on a yacht in the 1970s with actor Peter Fonda and never looked back. ~ PK 6.9; 56-11-06.

Galerie Van Der Heyde has been on the island for years and has a selection of paintings and primitive art. They also have museum artifacts on display. ~ PK 7; 56-14-22.

The **Aquariums of Pottery**, despite its name, is a jewelry store run by Teva, a long-time resident and well-known jeweler specializing in black pearls. Teva is a large, blond-haired *demi* (part Tahitian) whose countenance always seems to bear a look of indifference. Admission. ~ Paopao; 56-24-00.

Also in Paopao, **Galerie Baie de Cook** has a variety of paintings, pottery and carvings from local artists. ~ 56-25-67.

INTERNET ACCESS

In Maharepa, pop in to **Maria@Tapas** and have a cold Hinano and a snack while you check your e-mail or surf the web. Located in the Kikipa Shopping Center. Open until 11 p.m. most nights, until 2 a.m. on Friday and Saturday. Closed Sunday. ~ Maharepa; 55-01-70.

In Paopao, you can check e-mail and browse the web at **Moorea Vision,** a small shop that also sells phone cards and trinkets. There are two computers in a back room and access costs 250 CFP for 15 minutes. It is located across the street from the Paopao elementary school. ~ Paopao; 55-01-75.

NIGHTLIFE

On Moorea it's best either to not expect too much nightlife or, better yet, bring your own. **Sofitel Ia Ora** puts on a big "Tour of the World" buffet each Tuesday night, followed by a Polynesian show and fire dance. A seafood buffet and show is held on Thursday, and on Saturday a grand Tahitian Tamaara'a buffet includes a Polynesian show and fire dance. ~ PK 1; 55-03-55, fax 56-12-91.

The **Cook's Bay Resort** also has regular island-night dance shows featuring the lively *tamure* on Tuesday, Thursday and Saturday. ~ PK 7, Maharepa; 56-13-68.

Club Bali Hai is famous for its Tuesday and Friday happy hours—check out the live local music (and equally lively locals) from 6 to 7 p.m. A public disco dance always follows on Friday. It's a good place to rub shoulders with the locals as well as the expats who live on the island. ~ PK 8.5; 56-13-68.

On Tuesday and Saturday nights, the **Sheraton Moorea Lagoon** puts on a buffet and Polynesian show that non-guests are welcome to enjoy (if they purchase dinner). The happy hour, from 5:30 to 6:30 p.m. Friday through Sunday, is also open to non-guests. ~ PK 14; 56-19-99, 82-79-37, 82-90-19.

BEACHES & PARKS

Beaches are all public property in French Polynesia, but getting to the beach may entail passing through a residence or hotel property. Fortunately, most of the hotels along the north coast do not mind you walking through their grounds.

TEMAE BEACH There are numerous small beaches along the northern coast of Moorea but Temae is clearly the most accessible. Unfortunately, Temae Beach is also one of the most littered. This white-sand beach begins near the Hotel Sofitel Ia Ora and stretches about a mile north to the airport. The water is clear and calm, which makes it popular for swimming and snorkeling. Unlike other beaches, it's easy to wade into deeper water without stepping on rocks or coral. The only downside here is the occasional sea urchin in the shallow areas. These are creatures you don't want to step on; their spines are hard to remove from your feet. If in doubt, watch where the locals swim so as to avoid these spiny animals. There are plenty of coconut palms and shade trees, which makes it popular with picnickers. Locals often go topless so it's a good place for visitors to do likewise if they are so inclined. The beach tends to be crowded on weekends and, on occasion (especially during holiday weekends), strewn with trash. Facilities include toilets and showers. Though you could enter from the Sofitel Ia Ora, the public access at the northern end of the beach is better. ~ To find this, look for the *Plage* (beach) sign just south of the airport. Take the rutted dirt road about one kilometer to the water and park in the small lot on your left. The shower and toilet areas will be on your right-hand side.

Few yachts are anchored in Opunohu Bay. Robinson's Cove, three kilometers down the road, is the more popular anchorage. ~ PK 17.

VILLAGE FAIMANO/MOOREA LAGOON BEACH
Village Faimano, the New Outrigger Hotel and several other pensions share this thin strip of white-sand beach located at the very center of the north coast between Cook's and Opunohu

bays. Shaded by trees and off the beaten track, this tranquil stretch of sand about half a mile in length is not generally visited by tourists. Swimming is excellent, it's easy to wade out without stepping on coral or rocks, and the water is deep. The facilities there belong to the hotels. If you are going to use the toilets or showers, you should ask permission. There is a restaurant/bar at the Sheraton Moorea Lagoon. Some of the best snorkeling on Moorea is just offshore. ~ Take the coast road to PK 14.5 between Cook's and Opunohu Bay. Look for the sign denoting the Moorea Lagoon Hotel and park in the lot.

Papetoai to Hauru Point

This section of the north coast road runs about nine kilometers from Papetoai Village at PK 22 to the Hauru Point area at PK 31. Here you'll find a high concentration of hotels, restaurants, shops and other attractions. Among the more well-known properties in this area are the huge—and now abandoned—Club Med complex and the InterContinental Beachcomber. In addition to the high-end accommodations, backpackers will be happy to know that some of the best campgrounds in French Polynesia are located on this short length of coastline.

SIGHTS

Papetoai Village was the seat of the Pomare I government and the scene of his conversion to Christianity. An **octagonal church** built by the London Missionary Society in 1822 (and reconstructed on several occasions) still stands and is the oldest European building in use in the South Pacific. In 1811, years before Moorea's importance as a vanilla-growing region was established, the island was the London Missionary Society's center for evangelical work for the entire Pacific. The church is built on the site of a former Polynesian shrine, but all that remains of the Polynesian temple is a slim monolith outside the octagonal church. Tall and austere, the church faces the lagoon and is surrounded by a thick, white-washed concrete wall. The black gate entrance is only ceremonial—if you want a closer look, it's easy to hop the retaining wall. Each side of the sanctuary has three large stained-glass windows. Behind the church is a cemetery and a solar energy panel. In front of the church is a large breadfruit tree and a detached bell tower resembling a fireman's ladder. (A century-late afterthought?) To find this edifice, look for the post office (the sign that says *Poste*) on the ocean side and turn inland about 100 yards (90 meters). ~ PK 22.

Hauru Village is the focal point of Moorea's hotel properties, which include the InterContinental Beachcomber Resort. Another noticeable landmark on the strip is Le Petit Village, which bills itself as "The Biggest Colonial-Style Shopping Center in Moorea." Quite a claim. It's a collection of shops, boutiques and restaurants catering to the numerous hotels in the area. (Note that there are several public phone booths in the shopping center, which are handy for international calls.)

An excellent place to garner information on any activity on the island is the **Moorea Visitors Bureau**, which is located in a kiosk at Le Petit Village. They have a collection of brochures and a very helpful staff. At most hotels you can obtain a one-page map/brochure of Moorea that also provides useful numbers of hotels, banks, ferries and other essentials on the back. There is also a tourist desk at the airport that is open 6 a.m. to 11 a.m. daily except Thursday and Sunday. Tours can be booked from this office, and chances are the advice you will receive will be accurate. (Representatives from the tourist board also distribute maps and brochures down at the dock at Vaiare every morning at 9:30 a.m. except Sunday.) Closed Sunday. ~ PK 28; 56-29-09; www.gomoorea.com, e-mail marc@gomoorea.com.

Offshore from Hauru are Motu Tiahura and Motu Fareone, two islets that offer good snorkeling. (Note that all the hotels in the area have snorkeling trips to the *motu*.)

Hauru marks the beginning of a three-mile stretch of sandy beach although finding your way to the *plage* is not always easy.

Varari is where the once *sauvage* side of Moorea emerges, with fewer people and a taste of what life is like on the outer islands of French Polynesia. Until just a few years ago, the paved surface ended on the main road. There are scattered copra plantations and the feeling is more rural. Driving on the road you may see locals on bicycles returning from the market cradling a fresh baguette, or women on the reef searching for shellfish along the shore at low tide. ~ PK 28.

Varari is also the site of **Marae Nuuroa**, a Polynesian temple used by the Marana royal family from which the Pomare dynasty originated. The *marae* is in a coconut grove at the mouth of a small creek and covers several acres. The surrounding walls of the temple and the *ahu*, or central platform, are made of coral. Much of the structure is intact, and work is currently under way to restore damaged portions.

Tiki Theatre Village is a Colonial Williamsburg of the South Pacific that purports to be a replica of a pre-European-contact Tahitian village. In actuality, Tiki Theatre Village is the home of a very accomplished dance troupe, which performs four times a week. This dance troupe has a dramatic, show-biz flair that differentiates them from other performers and are worth the price of admission. (Dustin Hoffman and his wife "re-married" at Tiki Theatre Village in a traditional Polynesian ceremony that is part of the troupe's repertoire.) You can also get a tattoo here from the resident artist if you are so inclined. There is a beach on the premises, though it's not particularly good for swimming.

Admission. ~ PK 31; 55-02-50, fax 56-10-86; www.tikivillage.pf, e-mail tikivillage@mail.pf.

For backpackers, some of the best camping and low-budget lodg- **LODGING** ings can be found in the Hauru Village area of Moorea. Camping prices are subject to change more than other types of accommo- dation because of the occasional price wars that break out be- tween the owners of rival campgrounds. In addition to budget lodging there is a fine selection of mid-range and upscale prop- erties in this area.

The most luxurious hotel on Moorea is the 150-room **InterContinental Beachcomber Resort and Spa**. The Polynesian- style bungalows (over-water, waterfront and garden) are charm- ing, airy and large, with thatched roofs and bright interiors. If you need air conditioning to sleep, conventional hotel rooms are available in a two-story building near the pool. Activities include boat and air excursions, snorkel trips, fishing, diving, parasailing, Dolphin Quest, submarine rides, waterskiing, canoeing, tennis and land tours. There is even a heliport and a botanical garden on the grounds. Many activities are free for hotel guests. White-sand beaches delineate the lagoon, but perhaps because the beach was "built" on an ancient swamp, the water is not very clear and the snorkeling isn't very good. Better to snorkel off the over-the-water bungalows on the other side of the hotel, or swim 50 meters or more east of the lagoon. The jewelry shop has an excellent selec- tion of black pearls and local artists set up handicraft tables in the lobby each day. There is live music in the bar at sunset, and large-scale Polynesian dance shows three nights a week. This prop- erty has all the creature comforts you expect of a hotel in this category, including a day spa called Helene, which non-guests are welcome to patronize. If you have the means this is a tropical theme park for all ages. ~ PK 24.5, Papetoai; 55-19-19, fax 55-19- 55; www.moorea.interconti.com, e-mail reservations@interconti. com. ULTRA-DELUXE.

Unarguably the top mid-range hotel on the island is **Les Tipaniers**, near the old Club Med. Shaded by a number of trees, there are 31 *fares* on a wide grassy area facing the lagoon. Some are brown with gingerbread trim, others have thatched roofs with woven bamboo walls. Many are equipped with kitchenettes that include refrigerators and four-burner stoves. Rooms are small- ish, but units are modern and well appointed with tile floors, overhead fan, spacious bathrooms and phones. In addition to the restaurant (a fixture on the island for years), a Tahitian-style thatch- roofed eatery on the property (next to the lagoon) serves break- fast and lunch. The Scubapiti dive center is located on the hotel grounds, as is a full array of other nautical activities. (Tipaniers also has an annex, about four kilometers east of the main hotel, consisting of five self-contained thatch-roofed bungalows on the water.) All things considered, Les Tipaniers is a terrific value for the price. ~ PK 25; 56-12-67, fax 56-29-25, or 800-521-7242 in the U.S.; www.lestipaniers.com, e-mail tipaniersresa@mail.pf. BUDGET TO MODERATE.

The **Hotel Hibiscus** has 29 thatch-roofed bungalows, packed rather closely together in a grassy, well-manicured garden, and 12 rooms. About half of the units have kitchenettes. The bungalows are on the small side, but all come equipped with private bath and hot water. The bungalows have recently been renovated, and with the folding of nearby Club Med, it is a much more tranquil locale. The property has a restaurant, snack bar, pool and beach. On the grounds of the hotel is Le Sunset Pizzeria, which has an outstanding outdoor setting and fine food. (Tariffs rise during holidays.) ~ PK 27; 56-12-20, fax 56-20-69; www.hotel-hibiscus.pf, e-mail hibiscus@mail.pf. MODERATE.

Nelson Camping sits on a broad swath of land, shaded by coconut trees and fringed by a thin strand of white-sand beach. One of three places on the island to camp, the facilities are clean and well appointed. Covered by a thatched roof, the cooking/dining area is large, airy and clean; the nine picnic tables, two refrigerators, two sets of burners and two sinks can accommodate the large number of backpackers staying here. The common bathing area/toilets are clean and modern with tile floors. There is also a snack bar in a structure near the water. Travelers can set up their tents, or stay in one of the barracks-like dorms or several spartan bungalows. There are also three first-rate bungalows with two bedrooms (a hundred yards along the road from the campsite), with kitchenette and private bath with hot water. On weekends, the better units are generally occupied by local tourists from

HOME VISITS

Some of the best values on the island are in the guesthouse category. These are run by entrepreneurial islanders who rent out rooms or homes, often with self-contained kitchen facilities. Neither hotels nor pensions, the great advantage of these properties is privacy. They are generally less expensive than hotels, but don't confuse less expensive with cheap. The style of accommodations range from comfortable to spartan. For visitors who like the feel of staying in someone's home rather than being another anonymous guest in a hotel, this might be the ticket. Many guesthouses require minimum stays of several days. They almost always provide bed linen, but no towels. It's advisable to check out a property personally before you plunk down your bags.

Papeete. There are free boats every day to the nearby *motu* for snorkeling, a service to the guests. There is a two-day minimum stay. ~ PK 27; phone/fax 56-15-18; www.camping-nelson.pf, e-mail campingnelson@mail.pf. BUDGET TO MODERATE.

Moorea Camping, located about a half-kilometer west of Nelson Camping, is also on the beach. The shower and kitchen facilities at this campground/budget lodging are quite respectable. The communal toilets, however, are frequently smelly and leave much to be desired. The cooking area is practically on the water and has picnic tables that face the sea. Lights at the communal area go off at 10 p.m. sharp. Although Moorea Camping is half the size of Nelson Camping, there is still room for a dozen or so tents in a shaded central quad that is ringed by the dorms and dining *fare*. The large, clean dorm unit has six small rooms, each with four bunks. There are several other thatch-roofed bungalows with a variety of sleeping configurations. These larger units are clean, well ventilated and some come with small refrigerators. By contrast, the single and double private rooms are small, rather cramped, and stuffy, but generally adequate. Snorkel gear and bicycles are available for rent on the premises. This facility costs slightly less than Nelson and the beach is nicer. The staff is friendly, too. In addition, Moorea Shark Tours anchors its boats here and runs two trips per day. Inquire at the Moorea Camping front desk. ~ PK 27.5; 56-14-47, fax 56-30-22; e-mail roemichel@hotmail.com. BUDGET TO MODERATE.

Fare Vai Moana, next door to Moorea Camping, is clean, modern, moderately priced and situated on a white-sand beach. It has 14 *fares* suitable for two to four persons. The thatch-roofed bungalows are decorated in a Polynesian motif, with sea shells and local hardwoods—maru maru, bamboo and *pandanus*. The hotel is in an old coconut grove with hibiscus and banana plants scattered around the manicured garden. It's far enough from the main road to offer quiet. The rooms are spacious and well appointed; each bungalow has a small deck. The bathroom I saw was very clean and certainly adequate for a small family. There's a restaurant with a small bar, used primarily by guests. ~ PK 27.5, Papetoai; phone/fax 56-17-14. MODERATE.

Just down the road from Moorea Camping is **Moorea Village**, also known as Fare Gendron. Facing a fine white-sand beach, Moorea Village has 80 very basic Tahitian-style bungalows (15 with kitchenettes), a bar, a restaurant, tennis and volleyball facilities and a large swimming pool. The self-contained bungalows represent good value, especially for families. All bungalows include a refrigerator and extra cots. Fairly large in scale compared with other properties on the island, the grounds are clean and well tended. Avoid the *fares* near the road as they tend be noisy. A barbecue with pareu show and fire dance is held every Saturday night. ~ PK 27.8; 56-10-02, fax 56-22-11; e-mail mooreavil lage@mail.pf. MODERATE TO DELUXE.

The **Club Med Moorea** at Hauru Point closed in 2000 due to lack of business, and there are no plans to reopen it in the foreseeable future. The shuttered property is now surrounded by a chain-link fence topped with barbed wire, a stark contrast to the paradise where it is situated. It is still, however, a noteworthy landmark, and you are likely to be given directions that include Club Med as a reference point. ~ PK 28, Hauru Point.

While staying at Moorea Camping, consider booking their shark-feeding tour, operated by the campground management and reputed to be the best on the island. Snorkeling trips to the *motu* across from the old Club Med are offered as part of the tour.

If you come looking for Billy, owner of **Chez Billy Ruta**, chances are you will find him underneath the chassis of a truck or some other vehicle. A genial guy, he is not only a full-time mechanic but a tour guide, dance impresario and hotelier. Billy's 12 A-frame–style bungalows are on the water but are small, spartan and unappealing—perhaps taking a back seat to the vehicles, tours and dance shows that occupy much of his time. Accommodations are adequate but overpriced. ~ PK 28; 56-12-54. BUDGET TO MODERATE.

On the water with plenty of beachfront, **Fare Matotea** has spacious, well-manicured grounds. There are nine thatch-roofed bungalows with kitchen and bath with hot water. Rooms are large and well maintained—some sleep up to six. The management is pleasant enough, but sometimes seem indifferent to the needs of guests. Renting a bungalow at Matotea would be good for a family or a group of friends, but it's almost mandatory to speak French if you want to communicate with the owners. Two nights is the minimum stay; prices go down for additional nights. Canoes are free of charge for guests. No credit cards. ~ PK 28.7; 56-14-36, fax 56-32-54; www.farematotea.com, e-mail mtt@mail.pf. MODERATE TO DELUXE.

Jeanne Salmon's **Fare Manuia**, located on Hauru Point, has six well-appointed and -maintained thatch-roofed bungalows in a wide grassy area near a fine beach. All are self-contained, with kitchens and private bath with hot water. Fare Manuia is a good bet for families or couples. There is plenty of room in the units, a grassy area for kids to play and a beach nearby. Extra mattresses are available. The minimum stay is two nights, you must provide your own towels, and no credit cards are accepted. A *pirogue* (canoe) is available free of charge and a three-person jet-ski can be rented on the premises. Ms. Salmon speaks excellent English. ~ PK 30; 56-26-17, fax 56-10-30. MODERATE TO DELUXE.

DINING   Overlooking the sea, the restaurant at the **InterContinental Beachcomber** is noted for its brunches and buffets. The tables are overloaded with fresh fruit, fish, cold cuts and desserts. The dinner menu is eclectic and has a large variety of meat and poultry, as well as seafood dishes—the chef's specialty. A vegetarian menu is available—hard to find in Tahiti. The friendly, alert staff offers a level of service rare in French Polynesia. The hotel's style is simple yet elegant. Cuisine here is very good, considering that it is "hotel fare," but it is generally more expensive than you'd pay in a good local restaurant. ~ PK 24; 56-19-19. ULTRA-DELUXE.

◄ HIDDEN

Les Tipaniers, near the shuttered Club Med, is a local institution that serves French, Italian and Tahitian specialties, including pizza. Their reputation for good food, especially the Italian cuisine, is well deserved. There are actually two restaurants on the property—the original building near the main road and a new thatch-roofed bungalow with an open-air dining room facing the lagoon. The new restaurant serves breakfast, lunch and evening drinks. The cuisine is lighter and somewhat less expensive than the older restaurant. Continental, Tahitian and American breakfast is served, and for lunch there are salads, burgers, sandwiches, *poisson cru* and lasagna. ~ BUDGET TO MODERATE. The older restaurant is *gastronomique* and has a more extensive menu. A large selection of salads are available as well as sashimi, tuna tartar, fish soup, pizza, pasta, mahimahi with vanilla sauce and broiled tuna. Try the duck, or, if you are a meat lover, the lamb sirloin with goat cheese. ~ PK 25; 56-12-67. MODERATE TO DELUXE.

Attached to Magasin Ami Réne (a grocery store), in between the campgrounds, is an inexpensive **café** with hamburgers and other basic fare. ~ Papetoai. BUDGET.

Magasin Ami Réne is a small store near the two Hauru Point campgrounds, which makes it convenient for backpackers. ~ PK 21, Papetoia; 56-12-56. There is also a grocery store in **Le Petit Village Shopping Center** that is small and overpriced, but conveniently located near the hotels. ~ PK 28.

GROCERIES

Arts Polynesiens in Le Petit Village has a nice selection of fine paintings, carvings and pareus. ~ PK 28; 56-39-42; e-mail artspoly nesiens@ifrance.com.

SHOPPING

Woody's Sculpture, just before the Hauru Point enclave, has wood carvings of bowls, abstract creations from artists on the island, jewelry and home-grown pearls. Woody has won several awards for his sculptures, including "best of show" at U.S. art shows. Woody also sells pearls in the shell. One can purchase a real mother-of-pearl oyster shell that is guaranteed to have a pearl inside. They are reasonably priced, the pearls are not bad and it's definitely a cool gift. ~ PK 24; 56-37-00.

Leilani is a boutique that sells T-shirts, pareus, black pearls and other souvenirs. The selection is excellent and readers report that the staff is friendly. Located between Le Petit Village and La Plantation Restaurant & Grill. ~ PK 26.8, Haapiti; 56-27-27.

The art selection at **Gallery Api**, next to the old Club Med, is tasteful and includes a fine array of carvings, sculptures and paintings. ~ PK 28; 56-13-57. **Galerie d'Art** features stone sculptures as well as works done in wood and on canvas by Guy Tihoti, a Tahitian artist. ~ PK 28; 56-30-30.

INTERNET ACCESS

There are two places in Le Petit Village shopping center where you can check e-mail and browse the web.

The tiny **Tiki@Net** has several computers, and access is just 20 CFP per minute. You can print and scan documents and burn CDs here too. Closed Sunday. ~ PK 28; e-mail tikinet@mail.pf.

L'Iguane Café has several computers at the back of the restaurant. They offer reliable connections, but the keyboards are programmed for French even though they are printed with the English keyboard layout. Confusing, but workable in a pinch. Open seven days a week until midnight. ~ PK 28; 56-17-16.

NIGHTLIFE

InterContinental Beachcomber has live entertainment open to the public. All shows start at 8:30 p.m. On Monday there's the Mamas of Moorea show; on Wednesday it's a Polynesian show; and on Saturday the Polynesian Revue on the beach is followed by a dance. You can see the show from the bar, but if you want the buffet dinner and a good table for the show, call for reservations. ~ PK 24; 55-19-19.

Tiki Theatre Village on the west side of the island has dance performances on Tuesday, Wednesday, Friday and Saturday evenings at 6 p.m. For those desiring a special moment, Tiki Theatre Village will arrange feasts for your wedding, anniversary or honeymoon. ~ PK 31; 56-10-86, 56-18-97.

BEACHES & PARKS

The hotel strip that runs from Les Tipaniers at PK 25 all the way down to Tiki Village at PK 30 sits on one almost continuous stretch of sand. (That's why the hotels were built there!) The only issue is beach access. There is no public easement or road to any of the beaches. One must either pass through a private residence (not a good idea) or through a private road running through a hotel property. My advice is to do the latter. Once at a beach adjacent to a hotel, please respect the fact that the amenities belong to the hotel and are not for the general public. Ask permission to use the facilities (toilet, changing room, etc.) if you need to do so. Most likely your requests will be granted.

INTERCONTINENTAL BEACHCOMBER ⚓ 🛥 🛎 🏊 Located opposite the hotel grounds, this is actually an "artificial" beach. All that white sand was brought in and a beach was created where none existed before. Artificial or not, the swimming is excellent. Unlike most of the lagoon beaches, the swimming area is deep (having been dredged out during the construction of the hotel). All the amenities that you would expect of a luxury hotel can be found at this superb strand—a first-class restaurant, a bar and a full array of nautical activities. Some of the activities are for guests only, whereas others, such as diving or parasailing, are open to visitors. ~ Coming from the direction of the airport, go two kilometers past Papetoai Village and look for the InterContinental Beachcomber sign on the road and pull in the parking lot.

For a sunset or after-dinner drink, the bar/restaurant on the lagoon at Les Tipaniers offers pleasant surroundings and a remarkable view. ~ PK 25; 56-12-67.

MOOREA BEACH CLUB BEACH ⚓ The Moorea Beach Club is not my favorite hotel on the island but the beach is generally underutilized and very clean. There is a nice stretch of white sand here along with some shade trees. A restaurant and toilets are available. ~ Look for the sign on the road at PK 25.5 and pull into the lot.

Haapiti to Afareaitu

The 12-mile length of road from Haapiti to the Ferry Terminal at Vaiare is sparsely populated and was the last section of the coastal road to be paved. If you are going to experience the "real" Moorea anywhere, it's going to be here, where the traffic is less frequent, the pace is slower and the landscape is less shaped by commercial interests.

SIGHTS

Haapiti Village is one of the villages least influenced by tourism or commercial interests on the island. There are approximately 1000 people living in the vicinity of the village—a collection of humble wooden homes dispersed along the side of the road. Many of the homes are surrounded by neatly trimmed hibiscus hedges that enclose front yards brimming with flowers. Haapiti boasts a soccer field, a Chinese store and two churches. The small gray-trimmed Protestant church in the center of the village is dwarfed by the huge, twin-towered Eglise de la Sainte Famille on the south side. The latter was formerly the center of the island's Catholic mission. ~ PK 24.

Along the roadside at **Atiha Bay**, one sees *pirogues* (canoes) set on blocks beneath the shade of ironwood trees. Fishing nets hang from poles. This bay has a double reef and sometimes young boys can be seen surfing from the inner reef on homemade plywood boards. One gets the reassuring feeling that traditional life for the Polynesian goes undisturbed in this nook of the island. A glance across the lagoon reveals a fine view of Tahiti. ~ PK 20.

Another six kilometers down the road is **Maatea Village**. Perhaps because of its rural setting, Maatea is a close-knit, friendly village with charming homes draped in flowers. To catch a glimpse of island life in one of the few traditional communities left on the island, turn inland from the coastal road at the center of the village. Meander down the shaded dirt road and soon you'll be in the Toto Valley. Among the breadfruit and mango trees you'll see modest homes and people going about their daily tasks—raking leaves, gathering fruit or perhaps hanging the wash. At the entrance of Maatea is a Chinese store, a school and one of the few movie theaters on the island.

Maatea is the site of **Marae Nuupure**, an ancient Polynesian temple that is on private land but is accessible from the beach. The shrine is on a small coral hillock constructed on the shore. ~ PK 14.

Continuing along the road you will reach **Afareaitu Village**. This is Moorea's administrative center. A tranquil village nestled along the coastal road, it has the typical jumble of small grocery stores, a few churches and a long yellow barrack-like hospital. Like the other Moorean communities of Papetoai, Haapiti and Maharepa, Afareaitu Village was built around ancient temples and chiefs' dwellings. ~ PK 10.

Chez Pauline, a family-style guesthouse, is worth stopping at. They have a wonderful collection of prehistoric stone tikis, no doubt imbued with ample *mana* (spirit). There are also other artifacts such as adzes and grinding stones and several wooden relics. All have been collected from around the village. ~ PK 9; 83-71-21 or 56-11-26, fax 83-71-21.

Down the road toward Maatea you'll come upon **Marae Umarea**, the oldest (A.D. 900) in Moorea. At the other end of Afareaitu, at PK 9, is an unpaved track leading to a waterfall (see the Afareaitu Waterfall Hike in "Hiking" later in this chapter).

LODGING

HIDDEN ►

The village of Haapiti is just beyond PK 35, where the road markers recommence and start counting down in the opposite direction. Just before the village is **Residence Linareva**, one of the most impressive lodgings in French Polynesia. The grounds are immaculate and the classic, thatch-roofed *fares* are truly elegant. Each one has a kitchenette (with a full complement of utensils), rattan furnishings, polished wooden floors and TVs. There are 12 units ranging from garden and ocean-shore bungalows to a large villa that sleeps up to seven. Occupants may use the canoes, bicycles, masks/snorkels, barbecue and raft free of charge. Unfortunately, recent visitors report that the swimming area is polluted by sewage flowing from a small creek about 50 feet from the dock. ~ PK 35; 55-05-65, fax 55-05-67 or fax 56-25-25; www.linareva.com, e-mail linareva@mail.pf. MODERATE TO DELUXE.

HIDDEN ►

The newest campground on the island is **Haapiti Camping**, which opened in 2002 just across from the renowned Haapiti surf break. The property, a huge grassy field backed by the dramatic peaks of the Belvédère's backside, is mostly undeveloped. So far there are small kitchen and bathroom facilities in addition to the

The Tale of Bali Hai

It is impossible to write about tourism on Moorea without mentioning the Bali Hai Boys: Jay Carlisle, Muk McCallum and Hugh Kelley (who died in 1999). After arriving in Moorea in 1961, the three invested in a rundown vanilla plantation and inadvertently became owners of a ramshackle hotel. Their timing was impeccable. Airlines were just beginning to land in Tahiti and, when a journalist discovered their dumpy but charming hotel, success was just around the next coconut tree. Since then, the "boys" have established hotels on Raiatea and Huahine (the former has since been sold) and turned the original plantation into an experimental farm. Although the Bali Hai Boys recently sold the original property and are no longer part of the hotel business on Moorea, they have left their mark on the island in many ways.

Lumbering Hugh Kelley was fond of telling the story of the return of Moorea's missing tikis. The two stone reliefs were in an ancient religious shrine on the vanilla plantation and were left undisturbed by the three Americans. A week after Kelley showed them to a wealthy Honolulu businessman, the tikis disappeared. Kelley denied rumors that he had sold the priceless artifacts and vowed to get them back somehow. Several years passed with no trace of the relics, until an American woman approached Kelley with some startling news. She had seen the tikis at the Honolulu home of the same businessman who was the last person to see them in Moorea. Apparently this man was an avid collector of Polynesian artifacts.

Kelley decided to take the matter into his own hands and flew to Honolulu to question the teenage son of the businessman about the tikis. The son insisted he knew nothing until Kelley blurted out a heart-rending tale of a dying Tahitian woman who supposedly owned the tikis. With mock anguish, Kelley claimed the woman was shivering on her deathbed because she thought the tikis were in a cold place. The boy broke down and assured Kelley the tikis were in a warm place—on the balcony of his father's apartment. That was all the wily Kelley had to know. He confronted the businessman and threatened to spread the word to the Honolulu papers if the man didn't return the tikis. Faced with an embarrassing situation, the businessman consented. Several months later, amid pomp, press coverage from Tahiti and Hawaii, and incantations by Moorea's *tahua* (shaman), the sacred tikis were returned to the island. (One of the tikis can now be found at the Kellum Stop in Moorea. If you take the tour, ask Marimari to show it to you.)

owner's quarters and his workshop. When we visited, two outdoor hot-water showers screened by tall tropical plants were functional and a dining *fare* was under construction. Mark Walker, the owner of the three-acre property, is an American woodworker who has lived on Moorea for 20 years. He will let you pitch your tent wherever you like and also has tents and bicycles for rent. The place caters primarily to surfers and backpackers, but Walker has plans for a village of bungalows, which he intends to build himself. ~ PK 23, Haapiti; phone/fax 56-43-02, cell 78-93-65; www.haapiti.com, e-mail tablesaw@mail.pf. BUDGET.

HIDDEN ►   **Tarariki Village** is on the ocean side of the road, just past Haapiti Camping. The little village of A-frame bungalows has recently been renovated by a new owner, whose artwork adorns many of the units. The five bungalows are clean and well kept, and each includes either a double bed or two singles, along with a private bath. Mosquito nets and coils are provided. Dorm lodging is also available, and there is a very nifty treehouse bungalow at the water's edge. Meals can be prepared in a common kitchen, and a barbeque grill is available for guests' use. *Pirogues* and kayaks are available to explore the lagoon, which unfortunately is not good for swimming. The shallow water is hot and brackish, and there is no coral or marine life to speak of. Still, Tarariki's quiet garden setting, laid-back vibe and reasonable prices make it worth stopping by for a night. Plus, it's close to the Haapiti surf break. No credit cards. ~ PK 23, Haapiti; phone/fax 55-21-05, cell 77-95-91; www.tahitilive.com, e-mail pension tarariki@mail.pf. BUDGET.

One of the few accommodations on the south coast of Moorea, **Chez Pauline** is about eight kilometers south of the airport. A quaint, colonial-style home surrounded by lush vegetation, it is the oldest family-run lodging on the island. Rooms are of average size and quality, but very clean. Chez Pauline could use some renovation, but it is one of the few places on the island where you can get authentic local ambience and a home-cooked meal. Pauline died in 1997 but her son continues to operate the hotel and restaurant. From all reports the food is still quite good. Visitors (guests or nonguests) interested in seeing the large collection of Tahitian

AUTHOR FAVORITE

My pick for the best place to stay in Moorea would have to be **Residence Linareva**. This family-run business, located right on the water, combines fantastic food with unpretentious lodging, a welcome change from the ubiquitous luxury hotels. See page 220 for more information.

artifacts Pauline acquired during her lifetime are welcome. Non-guests can also dine at Chez Pauline by reservation. ~ PK 9; phone/fax 83-71-21. BUDGET TO MODERATE.

Fare Manu is just north of Afareaitu, about four kilometers from the ferry dock at Vaiare. Best described as neo-Polynesian, it is built like a traditional *fare* with no walls, constructed almost completely from local materials such as ironwood, coconut wood and *pandanus*-thatch. Fare Manu is reminiscent of a tree house, utilizing sturdy ironwood limbs to support a roof and upper story (for sleeping). There are no right angles except a V-shaped, pitched roof. The floor is concrete, embedded with seashells and paved with ironwood flagstones. The unit is self-contained, with a shower/bath separate from the main building, and there are two rooms that sleep up to six. Located near shops, just a few yards from the shore and directly opposite a *motu*, Fare Manu is surrounded by a fragrant garden of *tiare tahiti* flowers. This place has a funky, bohemian feel about it that appeals to grownups and kids alike. Fare Manu is a bit difficult to find: Look for it on the seaside, adjacent to two white A-frame homes. Directly opposite the driveway is a large boulder. Call Ms. Heipua Bordes for more information. ~ PK 8.2; 57-26-54, 56-29-82. MODERATE TO DELUXE.

DINING

Moored directly off the Linareva Hotel grounds at PK 34.5 is a floating bar/restaurant known appropriately enough as **Le Bateau**. It is considered by locals to be one of the finest, if not *the* top, eating establishments in town. The interior of the vessel, formerly an inter-island boat, is all hardwood embellished with brass nautical antiques. A panoramic view of the reefs and the high peaks nearby add to your enjoyment. The best dishes are the seafood plates such as the shrimp or mahimahi. ~ PK 35; 56-15-35. MODERATE TO DELUXE.

At the end of the Hauru Point strip is **Daniel's Pizza**, which has a wood-fired oven in the garden. Daniel's is an informal restaurant where you sit at a bar on coconut tree logs. The pizza is excellent; Daniel will also take your orders for pizza over the phone and deliver. ~ Haapiti; 56-39-95. BUDGET TO MODERATE.

Restaurant Snack Tumoana, next door to Nelson and Josianne Camping, is a Chinese eatery that features grilled items and take-out dishes—chow mein, stir-fried veggies and the like. ~ PK 27, Haapiti; 56-37-60. BUDGET.

Painapo Beach has a great menu; curry tuna with banana is a local favorite. ~ Haapiti; 56-42-43. BUDGET.

Le Pitcairn, located a few hundred meters down the road from the Hotel Hibiscus, is a terrific little restaurant run by the same management as Honu-Iti, sporting a dozen tables, a sand floor and a thatched roof. Don't let the simplicity of this modest eatery

◄ HIDDEN

fool you—the food here is as good as just about any in French Polynesia. Serving mostly French cuisine, they also feature seafood dishes such as garlic shrimp, scallops, mahimahi, sashimi and some local specialties such as *poisson cru*. Service is friendly and professional and guests have time to ponder a large, movable chalkboard menu full of the day's specials. ~ PK 27, Haapiti; 56-55-46. BUDGET TO MODERATE.

Adjacent to Marae Umarea is a lovely coral garden ideal for snorkeling.

Le Sylesie II patisserie, adjacent to the Carol Boutique (near the Hotel Hibiscus), is a good place for coffee, a cold drink or ice cream, or for breakfast and other light meals. ~ PK 27, Haapiti; 56-15-88. BUDGET.

The open-air **Le Sunset Restaurant Pizzeria** resides on the grounds of the Hotel Hibiscus. Covered by a pavilion, it's a pleasant, breezy place with a terrific vista of the lagoon. The pizzas are worth trying. Salads, desserts, wine and espresso are also served. ~ PK 27, Haapiti; 56-26-00. BUDGET TO MODERATE.

La Plantation Restaurant & Grill, an indoor/outdoor eatery, serves Chinese and European cuisines. Located just past Club Med, the building has a distinctive colonial style, with lots of gingerbread fretwork. The menu includes chow mein, stir-fried vegetables and seafood combinations. ~ PK 28, Haapiti; 56-45-10. BUDGET TO MODERATE.

Across the road at Le Petit Village shopping center is the small, attractive **Chinese Café Restaurant**, which overlooks a garden. They serve stir-fry dishes, including mahimahi with a delicious black-bean sauce, chicken, duck and beef with vegetables. Sashimi, *poisson cru* and an array of local fresh fruit are also available. ~ PK 28, Haapiti; 56-39-41. BUDGET TO MODERATE.

L'Iguane Café, also at Le Petit Village, is a hip restaurant and nightspot that features a full bar and an extensive menu. Flashy tiger and zebra print tablecloths set the stage for dishes that include duck, chicken, brick-oven pizzas, fish and grilled lobster. L'Iguane also specializes in ice cream sensations. Try the "Coupe Iguane": pineapple, passion fruit and guava ice cream topped with pineapple pieces, chocolate sauce and whipped cream. If that doesn't appeal, the "Coupe Colonel"—green-lemon sorbet and vodka—is sure to set you right. Friday night entertainment includes local musicians as well as a fire-dance performance. Pool tables, internet access and a play area for children make L'Iguane a great place to hang out anytime. Free hotel pickup with phone reservation. ~ PK 28, Haapiti; 56-17-16. BUDGET TO MODERATE.

Chez Serge is a large white structure with an open-air deck located at Le Petit Village. Though now in a fancier setting than the simple A-frame hut where Serge first set up shop, there is nothing pretentious about this eatery. There's a very extensive seafood and Tahitian menu that includes sashimi, shrimp, lobster, steak and omelettes. The "ma'a Tahit" is particularly worth sampling. ~ PK 28, Haapiti; 56-13-17. BUDGET.

Chez Pauline is affiliated with the small, family-run hotel of the same name. You must call ahead to reserve a place. The restaurant offers old-fashioned hospitality and home-style cooking. There is no regular menu—you simply get what is cooked, whether it's seafood, chicken or beef. ~ PK 9, Afareaitu; phone/fax 83-71-21. BUDGET TO MODERATE.

GROCERIES

There are several basic local markets on the coastal road from Haapiti to Afareaitu. They include **Magasin Varari**, Haapiti, 56-15-64; **Magasin Soi Louk**, Haapiti, 56-51-04; and **Magasin Ivon**, Afareaitu, 56-11-54. **Toa Moorea Supermarket** has the largest selection of groceries and canned goods on the island. It's located opposite the ferry terminal. ~ Vaiare; 56-18-89.

NIGHTLIFE

This is definitely the quiet end of the island. The only thing remotely resembling nightlife takes place at **Le Bateau** on the grounds of the Hotel Linareva, where weekday happy hours are from noon to 2 p.m. and 4 to 6 p.m. ~ PK 35; 56-15-35.

BEACHES & PARKS

NUUROA BEACH 🏊 ⛵ 🎣 There is a short stretch of sand opposite the fire station. Since this is the least-visited side of the island, the beach denizens will most likely be locals and chances are it will not be crowded. This a good spot for a picnic, but shade is scarce. Swimming is fair, as the lagoon in this area tends to be shallow. Snorkeling is average. Being that this is the remote side of Moorea, there are no facilities here. ~ To get there, look for the fire station at PK 25 in Haapiti on the inland side of the road. The doors are generally open and you'll see the trucks parked inside. Access to the beach is across the road, opposite the fire station.

Outdoor Adventures

There are three campgrounds on Moorea—two located in the Hauru Point area on the northwest side of the island, the other near the Haapiti surf break.

CAMPING

At Haura Point, there are **Nelson Camping**, PK 27, Haapiti, 56-15-18; and a few hundred yards to the west, **Moorea Camping**, PK 27.5, 56-14-47. (See "Lodging" in the "Papetoai to Hauru Point" section for more information.)

Haapiti Camping, at PK 23, is on the mountain side of the road, across from the Haapiti break. The huge grassy property is mostly undeveloped, and the friendly owner caters to surfers. ~ PK 23, Haapiti; phone/fax 56-43-02, cell 78-93-65; e-mail table saw@mail.pf. BUDGET. (See "Lodging" in the "Haapiti to Afareatiu" section for more information.)

DIVING

According to Juan Pedro Duran, proprietor of Bathy's Club, Moorea has a variety of underwater attractions that will satisfy the veteran diver. It also is a good place for beginners because of the lack of strong currents. The most popular underwater activities are fish and shark feeding. Hereabouts, lemon sharks, Napoleon fish and moray eels are the primary species you'll encounter. A 10- or 20-minute boat ride provides the opportunity to see white-tip sharks, gray reef sharks, lemon sharks, nurse sharks and black tips. Some of the better-known dive sites include: **Le Tiki**, a 75-foot dive where you can see lemon sharks, black-tip reef sharks, gray reef sharks, schools of perch and Napoleon fish; **Taota Pass**, a drift dive where one can find schools of jackfish, leopard rays and nurse sharks; **Ray Corridor**, a site where it's possible to observe and swim with spotted eagle rays; **Napoleon Plateau**, the home of friendly 60-pound Napoleon fish; and the **Shark Dining Room**, a site dedicated to feeding both sharks and eels.

Pineapple has replaced vanilla as the biggest cash crop (although economically it is not as significant, by a long shot, as tourism).

There are several scuba operators on the island. M.U.S.T. **Topdive**, run by Nicolas Buray, has exploratory dives for experienced divers, night diving and facilities for teaching novices. The tariff includes equipment. Open-water certification is also available. They are located in the Sheraton Moorea Lagoon Resort. ~ Paopao; 56-17-32, fax 56-15-83; www.topdive.com, e-mail info@topdive.pf. **Scuba Piti**, run by Daniel Cailleux, operates out of Les Tipaniers. He teaches beginners the basics as well as taking out the experts. The price of a dive includes equipment and transportation to and from your resort. ~ Haapiti; 56-20-38, fax 56-47-79; www.scubapiti.com, e-mail scubapitidaniel@mail.pf.

Bathy's Club Moorea, based at the InterContinental Beachcomber, has a variety of dive trips that visit sites throughout the lagoon and beyond. They specialize in underwater photography and are fully equipped with photo gear, video cameras and underwater scooters. They also have a video center that allows you to edit your adventure. Juan Pedro, the owner, is a fine young divemaster with a keen awareness of the marine environment and is a local ecological activist on Moorea. ~ Haapiti; 56-31-44, cell 78-15-38, fax 56-38-10; e-mail bathys@mail.pf.

Moorea Fun Dive operates out of the Moorea Beach Club. Both CMAS and PADI certifications are offered. ~ Hotel Moorea Beach Club; 56-40-38, cell 78-92-10, fax 56-40-74; www.dive-moorea.com, e-mail fundive@mail.pf.

Ia Ora Diving is operated by Pascale Souquieres out of the Hotel Sofitel Ia Ora. In addition to recreational dives, she offers advanced open-water instruction and rescue diver training. "Imaging Tahiti" digital underwater photography is available to document your dive on CD-ROM. ~ Hotel Sofitel Ia Ora, Maharepa; 55-03-55, fax 56-12-91; www.iaoradiving.pf, e-mail iora diving@mail.pf.

Surfing on Moorea can be world-class. The best on the island is at **Haapiti**, a left-hander that averages a six- to ten-foot face but can churn up twenty-foot monster waves under the right circumstances. It's best to be taken there by boat. Otherwise, it's a half-hour, half-mile paddle. If you can find transportation, a local boat will cost you about 1000 CFP (US$10) roundtrip. There are no board rentals on Moorea, so come prepared if you plan to surf.

SURFING & WINDSURFING

Other breaks on the island, starting from the airport area and going counterclockwise, include **Airport** (midway between Faaupo Point and Aroa Point), **Teavarua Pass** (outside of Cook's Bay), **Tareu Pass** (outside of Opunohu Bay), **Taotai Pass** (outside the reef at the InterContinental Beachcomber), **Haapiti** (mentioned above), **Avarapa Pass** (outside of Atiha Bay on the southernmost point of Moorea) and **Tupapaurau Pass** (off of Afareaitu). Without exception, all of these spots are reef breaks that entail 10 to 30 minutes of paddling or, better yet, transportation via boat.

A discussion of the surfing scene on Moorea would not be complete without examining the state of affairs between local surfers and visitors. To be candid, as elsewhere in French Polynesia, Moorean surfers are not overjoyed at the sight of *popa'a* (foreigners) cavorting on their waves. Still, they are more tolerant than their counterparts on Huahine. Visitors to Moorea should be sensitive to this and make an effort to befriend their Polynesian brethren before getting wet. My impression is that a well-mannered, outgoing visitor will probably not have difficulties. But while an individual will generally be tolerated, a group of strangers is definitely problematic.

Sailboarding is practiced to some degree on Moorea but it's not as popular as surfing. The main reason is the cost of gear and transportation. Some of the best spots to windsurf, starting from the western side of the island and going counterclockwise, are just inside of **Motu Tiahura**, off of **Haapiti** (inside the lagoon), and the midpoint between Maatea and Haumi on the southeast side of the island, known as **Culina Point**. All of these sites are in the medium to expert range.

Fishing in Moorea, outside the lagoon, can be excellent. A variety of pelagics such as tuna, mahimahi, marlin and other species are snagged on a regular basis. Inside the lagoon, fish are not as plentiful due to overfishing and the hotel and population pressures on the environment.

FISHING

Half-day and full-day fishing trips are available with **Teanui** ("Great White") **Charters**, which has the 31-foot Bertram and is based in the InterContinental Beachcomber. ~ 56-15-08 and 56-35-95; e-mail teanuiservices@mail.pf.

Moorea Fishing Charters operates from Cook's Bay. Its 30-foot Riviera with flying bridge and crew is available for hire by the hour. Trip possibilities include half- and full-day deep-sea fishing as well as night trips. Closed Thursday. ~ Maharepa; 77-02-19, fax 43-77-44; e-mail halfon@mail.pf.

SAILING

A day trip outside the lagoon is one of the best ways to appreciate Moorea. In fact, the island is best admired from afar, particularly from the deck of a sailboat. Vessels can be chartered for day sails, sunset cruises or longer excursions to the outer islands.

In Opunohu Bay just before the Kellum Stop, on the mountain side of the road, is the office of **Archipels Croisieres**. This venerable company rents charter sailboats in the Society Islands as well as in the Marquesas Group. Look for the gorgeous schooner *Fetia Ura* (Red Star) anchored in Robinson's Cove opposite the Archipels office. It's available for day sails, sunset cruises and the like. ~ Papetoai; 56-58-41, fax 56-35-87; www.archipels. com, e-mail archimoo@mail.pf.

Tahiti Boats and Sea, based at Marina de Vaiare, rents monohull yachts and catamarans with or without crew for trips through the Society and Tuamotu islands. They also offer skippered charters, sailing lessons and special cruises on request. ~ Marina de Vaiare; 56-40-50, fax 56-40-60; e-mail tahiti.boats.sea@mail.pf.

HIDDEN ►

If you want to learn how to sail, **Ecole de Voile d'Arue** is a great place to get started. Alexandre de Vos opened the business in 2001 and offers lessons for both beginners and those who want to improve their existing skills. He has 13 Hobie Cats (10 are 13-footers and 3 are 15-footers), 11 kayaks and 15 "little sailing boats" for teaching children. The laid-back atmosphere, pristine bay setting, personalized attention and commitment to safety are why one recent student calls the place "a treasure." ~ PK 15; 56-55-11.

OTHER WATER SPORTS

Virtually all of the hotels, as well as the Moorea Visitors Bureau, book nautical day trips and other ocean sports activities. These include snorkeling trips to *motu*, day-long tours around the island via boat (that usually include a picnic), and the obligatory "sunset cruise." The companies vary in quality and style.

In addition, many of the hotels have expanded their nautical activities from merely offering snorkeling, diving or canoeing to include a whole new range of possibilities. Those interested in more information on local waterskiing, jet-skiing, "extreme" speedboating, helmet diving and semi-submersible submarine trips can contact the **Hotel Sofitel Ia Ora** ~ Temae, 55-03-55 ext. 4906,

Dolphins—
Up Close and Personal

The InterContinental Beachcomber is home to **Dolphin Quest**. Beginning with a dockside orientation, guests watch as trainers feed the animals and talk about the natural history and biology of the species. They are then invited to go to the shallow end of the lagoon to engage in hands-on interaction with these joyful creatures, while a photographer assiduously snaps pictures of each participant kissing and hugging the dolphins. The results of this photo-op are in turn offered for sale after the session. A second program option allows participants to snorkel and swim with the dolphins in the enclosure. Though this type of attraction has many visitors and animal activists up in arms, Dolphin Quest stresses that the animals are given a chance to frolic outside their pens at certain times of the day. Still, they are captive animals that many people feel are more appropriately observed in the wild. ~ Haapiti; 56-19-48, fax 56-16-67; e-mail dqmoorea@dolphinquest.org.

If you prefer meeting your dolphins in the big blue, there is an exceptional excursion called **Dolphin (and Whale) Watching Expeditions Tour**. American scientist Dr. Michael Poole takes visitors inside and outside Moorea's lagoon to observe these fascinating creatures. Dr. Poole is the director of the Marine Mammal Research program at the French Biological Research Station (CRIOBE) and a Research Associate with the National Oceanic Society based in California. His research and the tours have been featured on the Discovery Channel documentary "'The Ocean's Acrobats: Spinner Dolphins" as well as on Animal Planet.

Visitors accompany him on a speedy vessel that seeks dolphins in the lagoon and observes their playful behavior. Whales may also be sighted seasonally. While dolphins are found about 95 percent of the time, the tour offers a free second trip if none are sighted on the day you go out. Although this is a "wild" school of dolphins, participants may be invited to join them in the water, depending on water conditions and the dolphin's behavior on a given day. Though other people operate dolphin tours (some for a lesser price) I strongly suggest you stick with the original. Poole knows his animals (he's one of the world's top experts on dolphins) and how to find them. This half-day tour comes very highly recommended. It begins around 8 a.m. and finishes at noon. Fresh fruit and cold drinks are provided. Cost is 6900 CFP (approximately US$69; children 3-12 are half price). Book it through your hotel tour desk or contact Michael directly: 56-23-22, cell 77-50-07; e-mail criobe@mail.pf.

e-mail mooreablue@mail.pf or the **InterContinental Beach-comber**~ Haapiti, 55-19-03, 56-12-90.

Moorea Boat Tours is a day-tour operation run by Heifara Dutertre, a Moorea native, and his Hawaiian wife, Nani. They provide full- or half-day tours of Opunohu and Cook's bays aboard their 28- and 32-foot boats, with picnics on the *motu*, fish feeding, snorkeling and visits to culturally significant sites around the island. Nani told us they're not the least expensive tour operator but they wish to provide one-on-one service particularly to English-speaking guests. We found the two of them charming and especially enjoyed their stingray-feeding excursion, in which Heifara teaches you how to hand-feed the rays with raw chunks of fish. The couple also takes visitors on (seasonal) whale-watching tours just outside the reef. Both are knowledgeable about marine mammals and Nani, a University of Hawaii grad, did research on dolphins with marine biologist Dr. Michael Poole. We highly recommend their personalized offerings. ~ Haapiti; 78-68-86, fax 56-28-44; www.mooreaboattours.com, e-mail mooreaboat tours@mail.pf.

Another purveyor of nautical excursions is Hiro Kelley, who runs **What to Do Hiro's Tour.** Hiro, the son of "Bali Hai Boy" Hiro Kelley, has a variety of tours including glass-bottom-boat rides, *motu* picnic and snorkeling trips, sunset cruises and moonlight champagne rides. Though Hiro is half-Tahitian, he seems to have inherited his father's Irish charm and talent for putting his clients at ease. He will pick clients up at any hotel in Moorea. Boat tours are once daily and snorkeling tours leave twice daily. Kelley's prices are fair and competitive with other operations. ~ Maharepa; 56-57-64, cell 78-70-10, fax 56-13-27; www.whatto domoorea.com, e-mail wtdmoorea@mail.pf.

UNUSUAL ADVENTURES

One of the more offbeat (shall we say eccentric?) endeavors that came across our path was the **H.Q. of the Unusual** run by Douglas Pearson. Pearson (a.k.a. Tutara) will take you via foot or bicycle for a full- or half-day tour off the beaten track in search of the miraculous, the strange and the hidden side of Moorea. In addition he'll take you out at night to gaze at the stars, tell you stories and legends of the islands, or give you an archaeological *tour de force* courtesy of his time machine. From all reports, this is one guy you don't want to miss. You can find Douglas at his Ali Baba–style cavern, which he refers to as his office, workshop and den. He calls it a place of conviviality. It's located not far from the airport in Teavaro. ~ PK 1.4, Teavaro; 56-36-15.

Moana Lagoon Safari is also a Moorea institution that operates a budget hotel, a rental car agency and nautical tour activities. They offer a daily trip that entails visits to Cook's and Opunohu bays via outrigger canoe, snorkeling at one of the *motu*, and a barbecue. Hotel pickup is available. ~ Paopao; 56-13-53, cell 77-26-19, fax 56-40-58; e-mail alberttransport@mail.pf.

One of the most popular activities on the island is fish and shark feeding. This is offered by **Lagoon Excursions**, **Moorea Camping** and just about every tour operator. **Shark Tours**, the outfit based at Moorea Camping, reputedly has the best shark feed on the island, but they will not pick visitors up from other hotels. ~ PK 27.5; 56-14-47.

Mahana Parasail operates out of the InterContinental Beachcomber. For those who have always wanted to try parasailing (but were a bit intimidated), this is the place to do it. One is lifted from the deck of a boat like a feather and dropped gently back down on the deck when the tour is complete. The operation struck me as quite professional. The chute, which is launched from the boat like a kite, provides you with a spectacular view from as high as 450 feet above sea level. The experience is silent to the point of being eerie, yet thoroughly enjoyable. The vessel used is the *U'upa*, an immaculate, high-tech speedboat. Mahana Parasail also provides one-and-a-half-hour island tours, which include background information on the history, geology and culture of French Polynesia. You're apt to see fish, sea turtles and, if you're lucky, dolphins. Check it out. ~ Haapiti; 56-20-44, cell 79-66-77, fax 56-38-66; www.mooreama hanatour.com, e-mail ruta@mooreamahanatour.com.

RIDING STABLES

Horseback riding on Moorea is a pleasure. The trails are uncrowded and there is a variety of terrain ranging from beaches to rainforests. **Tiahura Ranch** is located near Moorea Village on the inland side of the road. They offer daily rides in the hills and on the beach. Closed Monday. ~ Papetoai; 56-28-55, cell 78-42-47.

BIKING

Bicycling is a better proposition on Moorea than on neighboring Tahiti, mostly because there is a lot less vehicular traffic. It is possible to see the entire island by bike in one day; however, it's a long haul—especially if your bike is substandard. Going up to Belvédère is especially taxing, even with a mountain bike, but people do it fairly regularly.

If you do decide to take your bike inland to the Opunohu Valley, be careful riding down the hills on the steep grades that are unpaved. Better yet, on dirt or gravel roads, dismount and walk your bike down.

Renting a bicycle is a good idea if you want to tour the portion of the coastal road that *Le Truck* does not service. You can rent bikes from **Albert's Rentals**, a family-owned business that has an outlet across the street from Club Bali Hai on Cook's Bay. ~ 56-13-53. **Moorea Vision** in Paopao also rents bikes as does **Europcar** at the Vaire ferry dock.

If you are more adventurous and want to tackle some of Moorea's unpaved back roads or the climb to the Belvédère, your best bet is a rental from **Rando-Cycles**. The new outfit rents full-suspension mountain bikes and organizes off-road mountain-bike trips into Moorea's interior for up to five participants. The experience is definitely worth a skinned knee or two. Ask for Patrick. ~ 56-51-99, cell 74-51-33; e-mail randocycle@mail.pf.

HIKING

Moorea has ample trekking possibilities if you are so inclined. In addition to going it alone, there is at least one organized tour. Below are some suggestions for those interested in making their way à pied:

Afareaitu Waterfall Hike (5 miles/8 kilometers) is a popular trek to the Afareaitu Waterfall that begins in a small, sauvage valley and ends where the Tevaiatiraa River falls from a sheer cliff. The trailhead is located at the turnoff just outside of Afareaitu Village. Several hundred yards inland you will come to a Vanilla Cooperative (where you can see how this valuable crop is cultivated and can purchase vanilla extract). Continue walking inland beneath a variety of trees including mango, miro and tou and past a host of flowers of every description such as orchids, Tahitian basil, and vanilla plants. Cross the wooden bridge and soon you'll reach a large open area filled with mango trees and a vista of the mountains. Continue straight ahead on the path staying on the right bank of the river. You should be able to see the waterfall from here. Note the well-preserved marae on your right. (At the end of the wall at the archaeological site is a footpath on the left that descends to the river and dead ends.) Instead of taking that path, continue on the main one where again you will pass mape trees. Cross the small tributary. Shortly you will arrive at the falls. The falls, or cascade in French, is about 60 feet high and, depending on the time of year, the volume of the water will vary. Likewise, depending on the volume of water, the pool at the bottom may or may not be deep enough to swim in. The water is cool and refreshing, so swim if you have the opportunity.

> The dense foliage around Afareaitu Waterfall, which includes numerous ferns and broad *mape* leaves, makes this a stunning setting.

To find the turnoff to the falls road, go to PK 8, look for the hospital in Afareaitu, and then head about 200 yards in the direction of the airport. Take a dirt road inland that begins opposite an A-frame house. You'll know it's the right road if after several hundred yards you run into the Vanilla Growing Coop building. A 200 CFP admission fee will be charged by the owner of the land. (Don't worry about finding him—he'll find you.)

Traversing **Vaiare to Paopao** (5 miles/8 kilometers) is a short and easy hike. Between Tearai, 2525 feet (770 meters), and Mouaputa, 2722 feet (830 meters), the ridge descends to a pass that is used to travel from the Vaiare Valley to the northeast section of the crater. Ascending the trail, the route passes through groves of *mape* and, on the way down, through a rugged basalt formation into a bamboo forest.

At the very beginning of the trailhead, look on your right for a large boulder, **ofai Tahinu**. Note the large cavity in the stone, which in the old days was used to make *monoi* oil for the queen. Five or six yards before the stone look for a track that leads from the left-hand side of the road and, within a few steps, look for a large, blocklike stone known as **ofai pahu** or drum stone. (It is partially hollowed out and when hit with a piece of wood has a deep resonant sound.) Continuing on the trail, take a left-hand cutoff that follows the riverbank.

Stick with this for another ten minutes and take a cutoff to the left, which climbs toward the pass. The trail should be marked by a sign that says *Paopao*. However, sometimes the sign is taken down or purposefully turned around to point in the wrong direction. To make sure you are headed the right way, look for the opening of the trail among the mango trees and for red marks on trees or on rocks. (If you miss the correct cutoff, you will come to a river. You may note other trails that ascend toward the ridge but none of them actually reach it. Therefore, you should turn back.)

Continuing on the track, you'll note that as you go through the mango grove the tree trunks are marked with red splotches of paint. This will continue up to the pass. As long as you see these, you are on the right trail. The track follows the right-hand side of the riverbank, climbing through an area dotted with coffee plants and *mape* groves. After about 45 minutes of walking, you should come upon a huge boulder on your right. About 15 minutes later you will reach the pass and will find a sign that reads *Oaa*. The view at this point is blocked, but if you follow the sign with an arrow pointing to the left and climb the ridge along the crater to the high point, you will find a wonderful vista of the valley below. In contrast to the somber forests you have passed through to reach this point, you will be able to hear the sounds of civilization, including tractor motors and other engines emanating from the agriculturally rich Opunohu and Paopao valleys.

You will then descend from the pass through a *mape* forest where you will see a jumble of basalt rocks and a bamboo grove. The track eventually reaches a dirt road that you can take past a home and then across a river. At the fork in the road, take a left leading toward the school and eventually to Paopao.

To get to the trailhead go to PK 4.5 in Vaiare, then take the road that leads to the Capo homestead (Mr. Capo is a horticulturist), climbing past the bridge along the Mouaputa River. At the fork of the road, take a right that leads you to the CJA youth center (*Centre pour Jeune Adolescent*). Park the car before the center, about 800 yards from a peripheral road.

Mt. Rotui from the north (5 miles/8 kilometers): Mt. Rotui, one of the most distinctive peaks on Moorea, has been compared to a fortress or castle, with its ramparts and gothic windows. In Polynesian mythology, it is traditionally known as a purgatory, where dead souls awaited their ascension to heaven at Mt. Temehani on Raiatea. In either case, the view at the summit that takes in the entire amphitheater of the ancient volcano may not be celestial, but it is certainly remarkable.

To get to the top it's a much easier proposition to approach Rotui from the north. The trek starts opposite the Village Faimano hotel. Look for a path on the right that heads directly toward the north face of Rotui. It's about a four-hour walk to the top and about three and a half hours on the way down. On the way you'll pass through a quiet grove of guava trees. However, there are a few wasps' nests in the grove so keep an eye out. Once you reach the ridge, hike along the crest until you mount the summit. At the top is a marvelous view of the caldera. On the way down, make sure you bear to the right in order to stay on the correct path.

Coming from Paopao, go to PK 14.2, after the Moorea Lagoon. Park opposite the Village Faimano and ask the charming proprietress (Hinano Feildel) for permission to use the trail (the beginning of which crosses her property).

There are several companies that run hiking tours in the Moorea mountains and interior.

Tropic Escape, run by Rémy Costa, offers half- and full-day guided hikes. The half-day option is an archaeological walk through the interior; the full day is a "sport ascent" of one of the island's peaks. Backpacks, raingear and water are provided, and lunch can be arranged. ~ Haapiti; phone/fax 56-42-49; www. mooreahiking.com.

Tahiti Evasion offers full-blown, 15-day adventures of trekking and rock climbing on Moorea and Tahiti. The company also runs longer trips that cover other islands on foot. Ask for Eric Lenoble. ~ Papetoai; 56-48-77, cell 74-67-13; www.tahitievasion. com, e-mail tahitievasion@mail.pf.

La Ferme Agricole du Mou'a Roa offers introductory climbing and rappelling training as part of its multi-day backcountry experiences. Trips include overnight hikes into the passes and a stopover at a nature cottage where a warm meal and a soft bed take the edge off those sore muscles. ~ Vaianae Valley; 56-58-62, cell 76-62-58, fax 56-40-47; e-mail ferme.mouaroa@mail.pf.

▼▼▼▼▼▼▼▼▼▼▼

Transportation

Air Moorea offers flights to Tahiti and Tetiaroa, and air tours of Moorea. ~ 55-06-01, fax 86-42-99.

AIR

There are regular connections via **Air Tahiti** between Moorea and Bora Bora, Huahine, Manihi, Maupiti, Raiatea and Rangiroa.

One company provides helicopter service between Moorea and Tahiti's Faa'a Airport, as well as aerial sightseeing tours. For more information, contact **Heli-Inter Polynesie** (86-60-29; www.heli.inter.fr, e-mail ops-helico@mail.pf).

FERRY

At least five vessels are available from Papeete for the 12-mile (20-kilometer) journey to Moorea. In Papeete, they dock on the quay several hundred yards north of the tourism office, Fare Manihini. I found taking the ferry preferable (as well as more economical) than the airplane. The short journey provides an opportunity to meet locals, see a slice of Tahitian life, and (if the seas are calm) enjoy a pleasurable travel experience. You also can't beat the enchanting view of the mountains of Moorea drawing closer and closer. While on the water it's possible to see flying fish propel themselves off the crests of the waves and dolphins swimming up to the bow. The ferries are crammed to the scuppers with men, women, children, animals, cars, cases of Hinano beer and every other provision imaginable. Depending on the size and speed of the vessel, crossings can take from 40 to 90 minutes.

All ferries—with the exception of the *Ono Ono*—stop at the terminal in Vaiare, four kilometers south of the airport. The *Ono Ono* docks at Cook's Bay.

Because of the frequency of service you need not worry about reservations. One-way tariff to Moorea is 1030 CFP. Note that *Le Truck* service is coordinated with the arrival and departure of boats so you must tack on another 200 CFP for transportation to or from the dock at Vaiare to your hotel.

◆◆

NIGHT-OWL ALERT!

Europcar offers a little-publicized deal on a car from 5 p.m. to 8 a.m. A 4000 CFP flat fee (about US$40) includes unlimited mileage, insurance and taxes. Perfect for shutterbugs who just want a car to chase the light at sunset and sunrise. The catch: the deal is subject to availability and you can't reserve ahead.

Schedules for all the boats are available at the Tahiti Manava Visitor's Bureau in Papeete, at the waterfront ticket offices or the Moorea pier. For more information, call the **Ferry Services** in Moorea. ~ 56-31-10.

For more information about the ships that ply the waters between Moorea and Tahiti, as well as selected timetables, see the "Travel between Islands" section of Chapter Two.

CAR, SCOOTER & MOTOR-CYCLE RENTALS

It is very difficult (if not impossible) to see the entire island on your own without a motorized vehicle. If you rent a car or scooter, be sure to check for such minor details as properly inflated tires, good brakes and headlights that work.

Avis/Pacificar is the largest car-rental agency on the island and has several locations on Moorea including the airport, ferry dock, Maharepa and Haapiti. They provide cars, scooters and bicycles. ~ 56-32-68, fax 56-32-62; www.avis-tahiti.com, e-mail avistahiti@mail.pf.

Europcar has locations at the airport, ferry dock, InterContinental Beachcomber, Sheraton and Sofitel Ia Ora. They rent both cars and scooters. ~ 56-34-00, cell 77-46-57, fax 56-35-05; www.europcar.fr, e-mail europcar-moorea@mail.pf.

Albert Rent-a-car, a much smaller, family-owned business, has three locations where they rent cars, scooters and motorcycles: on **Cook's Bay** ~ 56-19-28; in **Maharepa** ~ 56-30-58; and near the old Club Med in **Haapiti** ~ 56-33-75.

Teihotu Locations at the ferry dock has scooters at reasonable prices. Check the machines carefully before you head off; there have been problems with missing mirrors and broken headlights. ~ 56-37-24, cell 78-42-48, fax 56-40-58.

PUBLIC TRANSIT

If you arrive via ferry at the Vaiare dock, a bus or *Le Truck* will be there ready to transport hotel-bound passengers for 200 CFP, seven days a week. Unfortunately, *Le Truck* tends not to greet the *Ono Ono* when it arrives at Cook's Bay. If you come in on this vessel, make sure you arrange transportation to your hotel ahead of time. Hours for return trips on *Le Truck* and buses are posted in most hotels. They also appear on the widely available free tourist maps.

Shuttle services (akin to U.S. airport shuttles) have finally broken the monopoly that the taxis enjoyed. It's best to arrange pick-ups in advance as they may be busy. Cost is 300 CFP per person for two, 600 CFP for one person. Ask at your hotel desk for a shuttle rather than a taxi. Note that they operate roughly from the airport to Moorea Lagoon at PK 14 between Cook's and Opunohu bays. If you're bound for a remote part of the island, you may have to negotiate another price. Finally, if you must take a taxi, it is possible to bargain with them—at least on Moorea!

Taxis are inordinately expensive here. Even before you move a yard, the cab's meter is set at 800 CFP (about US$8). The 16-mile (25-kilometer), 20-minute trip from the airport to the Hauru Point hotel enclave can cost 5000 CFP (about US$50) or more. If you really *do* need a taxi, call 56-12-48.

TAXIS

Hitching is possible but not easy on Moorea. Perhaps because of the vast number of tourists, locals are less apt to pick up hitchhikers, although backpackers carrying a load will still likely get a lift. Minibus service on the north coast of the island has greatly reduced the need to hitchhike.

HITCHING

One way to explore Moorea is to take one of the four-wheel-drive tours. Several outfits offer expeditions into the island's interior to see a number of archaeological sites, pineapple plantations and stunning views. Each tour company essentially visits the same sightseeing places and one would be hard-pressed to say that one is better than another.

DRIVE TOURS

Ron's Adventure, run by veteran tour operator Ron Sage, specializes in four-wheel-drive, off-road visits in a sturdy Land Rover to the island's inaccessible interior. Called the Painapo Safari Adventure Tour, the itinerary includes a visit to various Polynesian archaeological sites, a swim in a river, a visit to a bamboo forest, and pineapple, vanilla and coffee plantations deep in the highlands. The trip is well worth it for those who wish to see beyond the fringes of Moorea. In addition to the standard tour, Sage offers a variation on the safari theme—an excursion to view the jungle by the light of the full moon, while sipping champagne. ~ Haapiti; 56-42-43, cell 79-59-09, fax 56-17-07; e-mail painapo@mail.pf.

In a similar vein, **Inner Island Safari Tours** has excursions twice daily (mornings and afternoons) aboard an air-conditioned Toyota (or one of three Land Rovers) to the inner reaches of Moorea. Contact Alex Roo Haamataerii for details. ~ Temae; 56-20-09, cell 72-84-87, fax 56-34-43; e-mail inner-saf@mail.pf.

Albert Safari Tours has a three-hour overland Jeep Safari Excursion. Albert's, like all the four-wheel-drive operations, visits the inland pineapple plantations, archaeological sites and vista points. They also feature (non-four-wheel-drive) island circuit tours and photo safaris. Albert's tours can be found opposite Club Bali Hai. ~ On Cook's Bay; 56-13-53, cell 78-46-60, fax 56-10-42; e-mail alberttransport@mail.pf.

Circle island tours, which can be booked at any of the island's hotels, are usually conducted in vans or buses. They are a standard fixture on Moorea and take about four hours. In addition to the obligatory stops at Cook's Bay and Opunohu Bay, they

generally include a visit to the archaeological sites at Le Belvédère. I can't recommend one tour company over another—they
all seem pretty much the same.

▼▼▼▼▼▼▼▼▼▼▼▼▼▼▼▼▼▼▼▼▼

Addresses & Phone Numbers

Bank ~ Banque de Polynesie Le Petit Village; 56-12-02

Bank ~ Banque de Polynesie Maharepa; 56-14-59

Bank ~ Banque Socredo Maharepa; 56-54-45 (ATM located at
Vaiare)

Bank ~ Bank of Tahiti Maharepa; 55-00-55

Dentist ~ Dr. Frederic Avet; 56-32-44 or Dr. Sztejnman; 56-
47-51

Ferry Boat Information ~ 56-31-10

Hospital ~ 56-23-23

Pharmacy ~ 56-10-51 in Paopao or 56-31-05 in Haapiti

Police Station ~ 56-13-44

Police Emergency ~ 17

Fire Emergency ~ 18

Post Office ~ 56-13-15 in Papetoai or 56-10-12 in Maharepa

Airport ~ 55-06-00

Visitor information ~ Moorea Visitors Bureau, PK 28, Haapiti;
56-29-09, 56-26-48

SIX

Bora Bora

Perhaps no island in the world, except Tahiti, is as synonymous with South Pacific paradise as is Bora Bora, located some 165 miles (264 kilometers) northwest of Tahiti. The popular myth of Bora Bora was primarily fueled by the writings of James Michener, who called it the most beautiful island in the world. Michener may well be correct. Bora Bora, which means "first born," possesses a captivating beauty. The center of the island is dominated by Pahia and Otemanu, two towering volcanic peaks of sheer black rock that look down on you wherever you are on the island. Sloping down from these peaks to the beaches and boat-filled bays are hillsides of lush tropical foliage.

However, Bora Bora's most alluring attractions start where the island stops. First there is a translucent lagoon tinged with myriad hues of blue. Open to the ocean by only one pass, the lagoon is enclosed to the east by *motu* and to the west by a reef. It is so well protected from the open ocean that swimming in its clear, calm water is like swimming in a resort pool. In fact, almost without exception, the hotels on Bora Bora—even the most upscale ones—don't have swimming pools. It would simply be redundant.

Bora Bora's lagoon offers everyone who visits the island, regardless of budget, something the best resort pools in the world can't offer at any price—the living ocean. Within the lagoon, and easily accessible to novice scuba divers and snorkelers, are all varieties of sea life: corals, tropical reef fish, clams, eels, rays of all types, barracuda, octopuses and, most popular of all, sharks.

The *motu* that protect and create Bora Bora's amazing lagoon are something to experience in and of themselves. No journey to paradise is complete until you escape to a *motu*. These miniature palm-covered islands take you away from the distractions of civilization. You won't find roads or cars and there isn't any shopping nor are there restaurants, but isn't that the whole idea? You can climb a stone stairway through the overgrown jungle to a sacred Polynesian site on Motu Toopua, or rest on a secluded stretch of beach on Motu Piti Aau. Most hotels will arrange a day trip to a *motu* for you. If you want to escape civilization for

239

longer than a day, there are also a small number of hotels that are located right on Bora Bora's *motu*. These hotels have the benefit of offering fine views of the island.

Known in ancient times as Vavau, Bora Bora was a haunt of Hiro, one of the most powerful gods in the Polynesian pantheon. Hiro's son, Ohatatamu, was supposed to have been the first king of the island.

The first European to visit the island was Captain James Cook, who came in 1777 after having previously sighted the island in 1769. Bora Bora remained with its own sovereign until 1888 when it was annexed by France. The last queen, Terii-Maevarua II, granddaughter of Queen Pomare IV of Tahiti, died in Tahiti in 1932.

In recent years Bora Bora has evolved into a mecca for well-heeled American, European and, increasingly, Japanese tourists. Much of her population of approximately 6000 are dependent upon tourism for their livelihood and have learned a thing or two about capitalism.

Bora Bora is a microcosm of the extremes that French Polynesia has to offer. No superlatives can adequately describe its spectacular beauty and no value can be placed on the opportunity of experiencing this for yourself. However, you should prepare to pay a premium, even by Tahitian standards, for this privilege. At the same time, you may find that many of the locals have a certain ambivalence toward tourists, no doubt because they have seen too many.

Bora Bora has undergone a great deal of tourism development over the past decade. Hotels are growing in size and number, and traffic—especially between Vaitape and Matira—is quite heavy when the island is at full capacity. Despite this, in a 1997 interview the mayor of Bora Bora stated that his island is still not yet overdeveloped! Many disagree, and fear what the island will become if development continues. While Bora Bora currently offers a good selection of hotels in all price ranges as well as many reasonably priced restaurants, the island is increasingly catering to well-heeled resort visitors.

A precipitous drop in tourism due to the negative publicity from the nuclear tests in the mid-1990s severely impacted the residents of Bora Bora. Hotel and tourism-related jobs disappeared and for the first time in many years, locals understood that they could not take visitors for granted. Whether that renewed attitude of hospitality will persist in light of the recent building boom and tourism revival remains to be seen.

When seen from a historical perspective, the ebb and flow of foreigners to the island is nothing new. During World War II, 4500 U.S. troops were stationed on the island. In 1977 the island was again occupied, this time by an army of Italian filmmakers shooting Dino De Laurentis' production of *Hurricane*. Again the economy boomed—local merchants turned a handsome profit and many of those hired by the moviemakers were riding new motorbikes or playing new cassette decks. When the Italians left, business as usual became the order of the day. Women returned to work in the hotels and men returned to their fishing boats. The islanders' flexibility is both admirable and a matter of survival.

So much of what you will discover on Bora Bora involves unusual twists on the traditional way of doing things. Even the process of flying to Bora Bora is unique. If you are arriving on an interisland flight from Tahiti, try to get a seat on the left-hand side of the plane so that you can see the breathtaking views of

Bora Bora

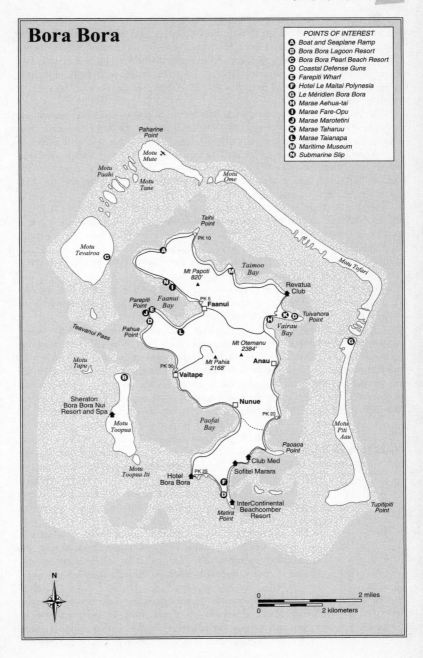

the island, lagoons and reefs of Moorea, Huahine, Raiatea, Tahaa and Bora Bora itself. When your plane lands at Bora Bora's airport, you will not walk down the steps onto the island of Bora Bora, but rather onto one of its many *motu*—Motu Mute. However, this is not an inconvenience; it's a free boat tour of Bora Bora's beautiful northeast coastline and lagoon. All plane tickets to Bora Bora include a free and very comfortable ferry ride from the airport to the dock at Vaitape, the main town on Bora Bora.

The dock at Vaitape is the central hub for the whole island. Most passengers arriving at the island disembark here. (Visitors staying at the *motu* properties usually go directly from the airport to their hotels.) Waiting for you at the dock is the visitor information center as well as free shuttles to the upscale hotels, and reasonably priced buses to all locales on the island. Vaitape is located on the west side of the island, and while there are some visitor facilities there, the vast majority of travelers head straight down to the Matira area.

Located at south end of the island between Raititi Point and Paoaoa Point, the Matira area has the best beaches on Bora Bora, almost all the hotels and a good number of its restaurants. The building boom continues here. An 80-room Paladien hotel is under construction on the waterfront just past Le Maitai. In addition, there are plans for a second five-star InterContinental Beachcomber Resort on a 22-acre parcel on Motu Piti Aau.

The entire north half of the island, including both west and east coasts, is pretty much ignored by travelers and is void of visitor facilities, but it is a nice area for a day trip when you want to escape the crowds.

Getting around Bora Bora is fairly easy. The coastal road around the island is 20 miles (32 kilometers) long and almost entirely level, with only one short unpaved section near Marae Aehua-tai. It's ideal to explore by bicycle, but keep an eye out for traffic, especially between Vaitape and Matira. A bicycle loop of the island can be completed in about two hours. (Cars and motor scooters can also be rented.) Along the route there are a number of ancient marae and several World War II coastal defense guns.

▼▼▼▼▼▼▼▼▼▼▼▼▼▼
Vaitape & Nunue Area

Vaitape is Bora Bora's main community, and the arrival point for passengers transferring by shuttle boat to and from the airport. The heart of town is only a few hundred yards long and is studded with shade trees. It's pleasant and easy to get around Vaitape. The pulse is slow, and groups of locals cluster around storefronts gossiping or trading jokes.

Despite the leisurely pace, taking care of chores in town is a snap. There is a complete array of shops in town, a gas station and several good, inexpensive restaurants. Most of the accommodations and formal eateries are concentrated in the Matira Beach area.

SIGHTS   The **Centre Artisanal de Bora Bora**, which also houses a **tourist office** directly opposite the wharf, is a good place to window-shop or purchase inexpensive souvenirs. If the tourism office is open, as it usually is during the arrival of passengers from the airstrip,

One-day Getaway

Bora Bora

Bora Bora is compact enough to do a circle island tour in a day. The best way to tour the island is with a car but it's expensive. You could rent a bike if you're adventurous—however the road can be hazardous. Be extremely careful if you decide to bike, and bring lots of water for the trip. Rent a car at your hotel for convenience's sake.

- Begin your day trip in **Vaitape**. Your first stop should be the **Centre Artisanal de Bora Bora** (page 242), which also houses a tourist office directly opposite the wharf. Stroll around town and window-shop or purchase inexpensive souvenirs. Grab a snack at **L'Appetisserie** (page 247), an air-conditioned local gathering spot.

- From Vaitape head southeast to the village of **Nunue** (page 244). Look for a road that begins next to a double-column telephone pole (near the shops) that will take you to a vista point. Park the car (or bike) and walk up the hill.

- Return to the main road and continue on a few more hundred meters to **Bloody Mary's** (page 244). Have a beer or just stop for a moment to peer in.

- Another few minutes down the road is **Matira Beach** (page 260)—the best on the island. You can also access a World War II coastal defense gun site by taking the path adjacent to Hotel Matira.

- Following the circle-island road four kilometers past Anau, where the road climbs the coastline as it crosses **Tuivahora Point** (page 261). Take the path up to another coastal defense installation with a great view. En route check out **Marae Aehua-tai** (Polynesian temple) on the right side of the road.

- If you're getting hungry by now consider stopping at **TOPdive Resort** (page 244), a Swiss-owned property with a great restaurant. Just prior to it is **Pahua Point** (page 244), where you can take yet another trail up to a coastal defense installation overlooking Teavanui Pass.

- In the evening enjoy a take-out meal from the **Croq'in Pizza** (page 247) or sit down at the inexpensive **Mahina View** (page 256).

it's a good source of information. ~ Vaitape; 67-76-36; e-mail info-bora-bora@mail.pf.

Near the tourism office, opposite the pier, is a granite slab **monument** dedicated to Alan Gerbault, who single-handedly sailed his yacht the *Firecrest* around the world from 1923 to 1929. There is also a *gendarmerie* across from the docks.

It's possible to hitchhike on Bora Bora—not easy, but possible.

Walking a mile (1.6 kilometers) north from Vaitape you will come to the remnants of the old **Club Med**, abandoned after one tropical storm too many. The Club Med crowd now enjoys the Coral Village on the other side of the island. Just past TOPdive Resort is Pahua Point. Keep an eye out for a marked path on the hillside that leads up the hill to what once was a battery of Mark II coastal defense guns constructed by the Seabees. It's a 10- to 15-minute walk up the steep hill to the **coastal defense gun emplacements** overlooking Teavanui Pass. From here you have a bird's-eye view of the boats coming and going through the island's only access to the open ocean.

HIDDEN ▶

Changing your orientation 180 degrees, heading south of Vaitape you pass through the village of **Nunue**, a spread-out collection of houses, shops and restaurants that edge Paofai Bay.

A few meters past Nunue, look for a road that begins next to a double-columned telephone pole. (Near the area is a cluster of boutiques and shops, so it is difficult to miss.) This road will take you uphill and eventually right across the island. At the crest of the hill is a magnificent panoramic view of Vaitape to the west, Motu Piti Aau and distant vistas of Raiatea and Tahaa to the east.

Near the cluster of shops, boutiques and the inland road leading to the TV tower you will see the intriguing-looking **Bamboo House Restaurant**.

Beyond the turnoff from the main road is **Bloody Mary's**, a Bora Bora institution. Outside is a huge double-boomed canoe with one boom longer than the other, for tacking against the wind. In addition to its fame as a watering hole, Bloody Mary's serves fine seafood. It's definitely worth putting on your evening's itinerary.

Continuing south on the coastal road you will come to the Hotel Bora Bora and the beginning of the Matira Beach area.

LODGING

There are few accommodations in Vaitape itself. Most affordable lodging lies just outside of town and south in Nunue.

If you're tooling around the lagoon and see a huge Swiss flag you'll know you've arrived at **TOPdive Resort**. Geared towards an upscale market, it combines luxurious accommodations and terrific food with great diving. Despite the Swiss overtones, the bungalows and restaurant are constructed in a Polynesian style using local materials such as hardwoods and *pandanus* thatch on the roof. The property consists of three over-water bungalows and six garden *fare*—each with a king-size bed and all the modern amenities. There are some nice touches, such as furniture designed exclusively for the resort. Cuisine is French with a local flavor, and it's delicious. The diving center provides daily dives in the Bora Bora lagoon or in a nearby atoll such as Tupai. The dive shop provides dive gear, T-shirts, polo shirts, black pearls and souvenirs. TOPdive Resort is located north of Vaitape, next to the decaying ruins of the former Club Med. ~ Vaitape; 60-50-50, cell 78-30-64, fax 60-50-51; www.topdive.com, e-mail info@topdive.pf. ULTRA-DELUXE.

South of Vaitape, the **Blue Lagoon** is a backpacker's hangout with five modest rooms equipped with fans and a communal bath between them. The place is on the shore but there's no beach. There is, however, a private pontoon. Despite the lack of beach, the managers Nathalie and Stephan are hospitable and do offer a great amenity—free internet access for guests. There is a small eatery graced with plastic chairs and pretty much bereft of ambience. Grilled fish and *poisson cru* can be had for budget prices. This is definitely the cheapest place in the whole island and it's only a five-minute bike ride south of Vaitape. ~ Vaitape; phone/fax 67-65-64. BUDGET.

Chez Ato is the closest thing to Shangri-la that exists in Bora Bora—at least when you're talking about altitude. Cooled by the trade winds, Chez Ato is an Eden-like setting on the mountainside, splashed with hibiscus, frangipani and other flora. Ato built a new house that consists of three rooms, each with a double bed, shared bath, kitchen and terrace. (The old hexagonal structure is rented out to a local resident.) A sturdily built Bora Boran, Ato is always a gracious host who plies you with the abundant fruit that grows on his estate. The property lies in the shadow of Mt. Otemanu, on a verdant hillside about a half kilometer from the main road, about two kilometers south of Vaitape. Ato also leads walking tours to see the petroglyphs in his valley. A sensitive man who likes to share his immense knowledge with others, he is by far the best tour guide on the whole island. ~ Nunue; phone/fax 67-77-27. BUDGET.

◄ HIDDEN

Moon B&B is located halfway between Vaitape and Matira Beach, next door to Gallerie Alain and Linda. There are two A-frame bungalows with private bath and kitchenette, and camping is available in a grassy area toward the back of the property. The shared kitchen appeared adequate, and though the toilets had no seats, the facilities were new and clean. The owners are clearly working to improve the property, which includes lagoon access, a picnic area and a good view of Mt. Otemanu. ~ Nunue; 67-74-36; e-mail moonbungalow@netcourrier.com. BUDGET.

◄ HIDDEN

HIDDEN ►   **Chez Rosina** is a local-style home with seven rooms, four with private baths, three with a communal bath. There are also a communal kitchen and a living room. Rooms are of average size, but are clean and well appointed, especially considering the low price. The house has a warm atmosphere thanks to Rosina, who is a convivial Tahitian. The private bathrooms make this one of the best values on the island. Tariff includes breakfast plus lunch or dinner. The only feature the property is missing is a nearby beach. Excursions are available. Payment is by cash only. Round-trip transfers to the airport are provided. Chez Rosina is located four kilometers south of Vaitape on Paofai Bay. ~ Nunue; phone/fax 67-70-91; e-mail adesaintpierre@mail.pf. BUDGET.

Just a kilometer north of Bloody Mary's is **Village Pauline**, which offers private bungalows, family *fare*, dorm beds and camping. The two bungalows and three *fare* have private bathrooms and kitchens. The communal bathroom for dorm and camping guests is quite adequate, and the shared kitchen/dining area has a television and a soda machine. Village Pauline also has a fantastic little restaurant on the premises. Manager Nir Shalev knows the island very well and is a good person to ask about local history, archaeology or where to find the petroglyphs. Those interested in exploring the island might consider visiting Bora Bora Kayak Rental Center (on Pauline's property) to view the island from its best perspective—the sea. The nearest beach is about one kilometer away, and grocery stores a ten-minute walk away. There's a pay phone on the property, and a food truck arrives each day at 7:00 a.m. and 2:30 p.m. so guests can purchase fresh baguettes, fruit and other foodstuffs. ~ PK 8, Pofai Bay; 67-72-16, fax 67-78-14; e-mail vpauline@mail.pf. BUDGET TO DELUXE.

DINING   **Bora Bora Pizza**, just north of Vaitape next to the pharmacy (look for the big green cross), not only offers tasty pizzas but great prices. Owner Laurent Mamode is super-friendly and even

AUTHOR FAVORITE

I'm always on the lookout for great restaurants, and the **TOPdive Resort**'s restaurant does not disappoint. Last time I was there, after sampling some of the *nouvelle cuisine* and fresh fish, I was not surprised to hear some locals praise it as one of the island's best dining establishments. As with all the restaurants in Bora, TOPdive offers free pick-up service for dinner to all hotel and pension guests. They are open for lunch from noon to 2 p.m. and for dinner from 7 to 9 p.m. ~ Vaitape; 60-50-55, fax 60-50-51. DELUXE TO ULTRA-DELUXE.

lets diners create their own pizzas. Pizzas start at 1000 CFP (US $10). ~ Vaitape; 67-54-81, cell 74-83-33.

At the Commercial Center is the air-conditioned **L'Appetis-serie**, a cozy little café that offers terrific cakes, ice cream and sherbets (all homemade) as well as croissants, quiche, pizza and a *plat du jour* that is usually a bargain. ~ Vaitape; 67-60-73. BUDGET.

Restaurant Au Cocotier features basic Chinese food. The ◄ HIDDEN specialty of the house is *poisson cru*, which is reportedly the best on the island and is reasonably priced. Restaurant Au Cocotier is located on the mountain side of the road between Chin Lee's market and the pharmacy. There is also a small arcade alongside the eatery where locals play video games or foosball. ~ Vaitape; 67-74-18. BUDGET.

Located next to the Restaurant Au Cocotier, **Croq'in Pizza** is a take-away pizzeria. Open for lunch and dinner, they got their start in Tahiti where they operate several eateries. ~ Vaitape. BUDGET TO MODERATE.

One of the most promising additions to the restaurant scene is the **Bamboo House**, three kilometers south of Vaitape. Looking like a cross between a Philippine *nipa* hut and a Tahitian *fare*, it has a small bar and an inviting outdoor terrace. Not only is the food good, but the menu has items for every pocketbook. Lunch offers hamburgers, steak or shrimp fettuccine. Dinner is much more expensive. The cuisine comes highly recommended. Entrées include pasta, stuffed jackfish, grilled salmon and lobster fricassee. Along with a tasty menu, the wine list has excellent selections from Bordeaux, Alsace and Beaujolais. As one local told me, "Service takes forever, it's very expensive, but the food is very good." There's a wooden sign that lists all the luminaries that have dined here. ~ Nunue; 67-76-24. MODERATE TO ULTRA-DELUXE.

Snack Sacha really should have a name that better reflects its ◄ HIDDEN character. Cleverly hidden behind an enclave of plants at the entrance to Village Pauline, Sacha's little restaurant might more appropriately be called Sacha's Secret Hideaway or, better, Sacha's Romantic Dinner Dream. With a sand floor, colored mood lighting, tangled vines and French jazz or rock, this little spot has got to be one of the better-kept secrets on the island. The menu changes frequently depending on what is available, and Sacha is the perfect host. His *poisson cru* is absolute heaven, and the Saturday night all-you-can-eat buffet might include barbecued steak and mahimahi and the biggest platter of tuna sashimi you are ever likely to see. Burgers and the like are also available. Best of all, Sacha's prices won't break the bank. ~ Village Pauline, Pofai Bay; 67-72-16, fax 67-78-14. BUDGET.

The sand floor, thatched roof and coconut tree–stump bar stools at **Bloody Mary's** are reminiscent of a set from "Gilligan's Island" and make this a don't-miss Bora Bora experience. The seafood, brought in by local fishermen, couldn't be fresher. Diners choose their own fish or lobster and the chef slaps it on the grill. The menu also offers barbecued chicken and steak. At lunch, Bloody Mary's has reasonably priced burgers (try their Jimmy Buffet cheeseburger) and tortillas with refried beans and salsa. There's a wooden sign at the entrance (Ten Commandments style) with the original list of names of the famous and not-so-famous who have crossed the threshold. You come here first for the fun atmosphere and then the food. Closed Sunday. ~ Near the Hotel Bora Bora, Nunue; 67-72-86. MODERATE TO ULTRA-DELUXE.

GROCERIES   When shopping for a quantity of groceries or any other major purchases, Vaitape is clearly the place to go. A good place to start is the new **Super To'a Amok**, the largest store on the island. ~ Just north of Vaitape; 67-70-75. In town itself, the well-stocked **Chin Lee** is likely to have what you need. ~ Vaitape; 67-73-86. **Magasin Nunue** also has a good selection of groceries. ~ Nunue; 67-70-02.

SHOPPING   Inveterate shoppers will be happy to know that things have picked up here. You can purchase items ranging from black pearls to T-shirts. One place to begin looking is **Le Pahia**, a small shopping center in Vaitape located opposite the Protestant Church. There you will find **Sibani Perles**, **Tahiti Perles** and **Paradise Perles**—all of which operate beautiful stores. If you're not ready to drop the bucks for a pearl, **Boutique Pacific Sud** and **Boutique Extreme Sud** sell T-shirts, pareu and handicrafts in the same complex. The **Boutique Anae** also sells painted pareu, clothes and swimming gear. It's located next to the pharmacy in town.

    Bora Bora Spirit, next door to Fare Piti Rental Car, sells good-quality T-shirts and the owners pride themselves on featuring designs not found elsewhere. They also embroider some of their own shirts. ~ Vaitape; 67-70-92; e-mail boraboraspirit@mail.pf.

    Several Vaitape general stores such as **Magasin Roger** and **Chin Lee** (67-73-86) also stock inexpensive T-shirts and pareus. ~ Vaitape.

HIDDEN ► North of town in Gallerie Helena, a new waterfront shopping center, is **La Vie Est Belle** ("Life is Beautiful"), which specializes in local handicrafts. Check out the little stones carved with traditional tattoo designs—a great way to take home a Polynesian tattoo without the commitment. ~ Vaitape; 67-76-97. In the same complex are a dozen or so little shops, ranging from pearl boutiques to surf apparel.

    About three kilometers from Vaitape, heading toward Matira, one can find a cluster of shops near the Bamboo House restaurant including **Boutique Gauguin**, which has a fine selection of expensive gifts. ~ Amanahune; 67-76-67.

Next door to Boutique Gauguin is OPEC, an upscale black pearl boutique. Next door to OPEC is **Art du Pacifique**, which carries a nice selection of carvings and other handicrafts from the Marquesas. ~ Amanahune; 67-63-85.

For a truly unusual souvenir from Bora Bora, keep an eye out for a CD-ROM by local photographer **Jean Luc Peley**. The disc contains 435 pictures from Bora Bora, including aerial scenics and images from the *Heiva* festivities, a submarine tour, fishing, traditional tattooing, etc. ~ Phone/fax 67-76-63; e-mail jeanluc peley@mail.pf.

Garrick Yrondi is a French painter who has resided in the islands since 1977. Not surprisingly he has succumbed to the beauty of the lagoons and the local *vahine*. He makes his own pigments and uses traditional techniques to reproduce the unbelievable colors of these tropical islands. The primary colors found in his works are what my colleague calls "tropical fireworks," not unlike the colors used by Paul Gauguin a century ago. Garrick Yrondi is perhaps best known to visitors as the artist who produced the "Fish Lady," a sculpture of Portuguese rose marble, which can be seen near the airport while heading for Vaitape on the shuttle boat. This was his gift to the island of Bora Bora. It is said the *vahine e i'a* protects all lovers who present her with a flower. Look for Garrick Yrondi's gallery located behind the Gauguin Center. ~ Amanahune; phone/fax 67-79-66.

Local photographer Jean Luc Peley is available to shoot weddings, celebrations and "charm photos" at local hotels.

Located in the same vicinity, the **Honeymoon Boutique** is a fine place to shop. They offer a nice collection of pareus and other clothing. The owners usually stock items of high quality and price them fairly. ~ Nunue; 67-78-19.

There are two places on Bora Bora where you can check e-mail and browse the web. Be prepared, however, to pay roughly double what you would on the other islands. The ice cream shop **L'appetisserie** in Vaitape offers a connection at 40 CFP per minute. ~ Vaitape; 67-78-88; e-mail zani@mail.pf. The **Blue Lagoon** pension just south of Vaitape charges 250 CFP for 15 minutes but requires a beverage or food purchase as well. ~ Vaitape; phone/fax 67-65-64.

INTERNET ACCESS

Bora Bora is a fairly quiet place. When you come here it's best to be prepared to entertain yourself. In the Vaitape area the only nightclub is **Le Recif**, Bora Bora's only disco and after-hours club. It's a working-class Tahitian nightclub—crowded, noisy, dark and smoke filled. Toward the end of the evening, a number of the patrons may be drunk. It's best to go when accompanied by a local. Open only on weekends. ~ Vaitape.

NIGHTLIFE

Bloody Mary's is always a good place to stop for a beer or two. Or better yet, try their famous mai tais. Tap beer is reasonably priced and there may be an informal Tahitian combo strumming away on guitars and ukuleles. ~ Nunue; 67-72-86.

Matira Beach Area

The Matira Beach area, which stretches from the end of Nunue Village to the area around the south tip of the island, is the focal point for tourism on Bora Bora. Most of the accommodations, as well as boutiques and restaurants, are clustered near Matira Beach—clearly the best and largest beach.

The beginning of the Matira Beach area brings you to the luxurious Hotel Bora Bora, at Raititi Point. The Hotel Bora Bora is characterized by the over-the-water bungalows so often depicted as the epitome of elegance and beauty in Tahiti travel brochures.

SIGHTS

Matira Point, a pin-shaped spit of land with an access road bisecting it, is the site of several hotels and the best public beach on Bora Bora. The beach is popular with locals on the weekends. Matira takes its name from the 490-ton British ship *Mathilda* wrecked on Moruroa Atoll in the Tuamotus in 1792. The crew managed to get back to Tahiti where they were robbed. King Pomare I of Tahiti responded by offering his protection to the seamen and punishing the thieves. Three of the survivors decided to remain in Tahiti and one, a Mr. O'Connor, married Pomare's cousin. Years later his granddaughter (named Mathilda, after the ship) settled in Bora Bora and married a local chief. They named their property "Matira," which is the Tahitian pronunciation of Mathilda.

The most accessible World War II **coastal defense guns** can be found in the Matira area. They are on an elevation that overlooks the southernmost point of the island. They can be reached by a path that runs up the hill from the mountain side of the Hotel Matira. It took 400 G.I.s to drag the two 13-ton guns up the hill.

FEEDING THE FISH

If you think you've done everything there is to do on the island, what about feeding the fish? Grab a stale loaf of French bread and walk out on the dock at the Hotel Bora Bora. Casting your bread anywhere will result in a feeding frenzy that will roil the waters. This is the place to cast your bread because it is a marine park and no fishing is allowed. Bring the kids and they will never stop talking about it. Note: Be sure to ask the hotel's permission before you embark on this fish-feeding expedition.

Even with the aid of blocks and tackle, it couldn't have been an easy task. The whole gun assembly weighed 51,000 pounds (38,100 kilograms) and the weight of each piece is stamped upon it. Note the graffiti inscribed on the cement: "Battleing (sic) Battery B-276C." If you have any trouble finding the trail, use the Hotel Matira as a landmark. The southernmost bungalow on the lagoon side of the property is directly across from the trail-head. (If in doubt ask at the hotel.)

The next several kilometers beyond the point are peppered with hotels, restaurants and local homes. One of the most significant properties in this area is the **Sofitel Marara**, which was built in 1977 by filmmaker Dino De Laurentis to house his film crew during the filming of *Hurricane* (which, by the way, bombed). The newest development in this area is the hotel Le Maitai Polynesia, which opened in 2001.

The coastal road climbs up as it passes Club Med and then drops down (past the Club Med tennis courts) to the coast again before arriving in the village of Anau.

LODGING

Travelers seeking lodging have a lot to choose from in the Matira area when it comes to price categories. In addition to the more pedestrian bungalows, virtually all of the high-end hotels have over-the-water bungalows, a style of lodging pioneered in Moorea by the Bali Hai Boys. The majority of the posh hotels are located within several minutes' walk of each other, making the Matira Point area truly a "Gold Coast."

Visitors who stay in the Matira area (and in other parts of Bora) should know that they will be confronted by something they've probably gone to Bora Bora to avoid—noise and traffic. Not only is there a great concentration of hotels in the area but there is little space—in some instances 100 meters or less between lagoon and the mountains. Because of the lack of real estate, guest rooms are often constructed very close to the road—the only road on the island. Traffic starts early in the morning and doesn't let up until late at night on weekends. Visitors who do not wish to contend with this should consider booking a hotel on an offshore *motu*.

Starting at Raititi Point, about five kilometers east of Vaitape, **Hotel Bora Bora** has one of the best locations on the island, with splendid views, a fine white-sand beach and excellent snorkeling. The feeling at Hotel Bora Bora is of a country club—quiet, reserved and one of the best honeymoon getaways in Tahiti. There are 54 impeccable *fares*, including 15 over-the-water units and several *fares* with private swimming pools. Even the most basic bungalows have separate bedroom and living room areas and an outside terrace. Rooms are exquisite, and the hotel is overflowing with amenities. In addition to a restaurant, there are two bars that overlook the sea, two swimming pools, a boutique and, of course, a complete array of water activities. (The diving concession is run by the Bora Diving Center—a top-notch operation.) The management, to its credit, has created a nature preserve around both the hotel grounds and the waters surrounding the property that is rigorously maintained. For over 20 years, guests have fed fish by hand so the creatures are quite tame. In the early evening, it's not unusual to see huge manta rays gliding gracefully around the pier under the lights. ~ Matira; 60-44-60, fax 60-44-66, or 800-421-1490 in the U.S.; www.amanresorts.com/bora_m.html, e-mail reservations@hotelborabora.pf. ULTRA-DELUXE.

Continuing south on the coastal road is **Hotel Matira**, set on a fine white-sand beach. It consists of a decent moderately priced Chinese restaurant and about 20 bungalows—four of them are over the water, four are on the beach (near the eatery) and the balance are 200 meters down the road. The thatch-roofed units are well constructed and are of average size. Some are located on the beach and others have a lagoon view in a garden. ~ Matira; 67-78-58, fax 67-77-02; www.hotelmatira.com, e-mail hotel.matira@mail.pf. ULTRA-DELUXE.

Located on the east side of Matira Point is the elegant **Inter-Continental Beachcomber Resort**, recognized as a perfect honeymoon hotel. All 50 of the over-the-water units have air conditioning. There are also 14 beachside bungalows, including two with the suite configuration, each with private terrace. The interiors and furnishings of all units have been completely redone, and a major facelift is taking place in the main hotel as well. The bar is being expanded into a full lounge, and an activities *fare* is being built near the pool area. Activities include the usual water sports and sunset cruises. The food at the resort is *nouvelle cuisine*. ~ Matira; 60-49-00, fax 60-49-99, or 800-835-7742 in the U.S.; www.borabora.interconti.com, e-mail borabora@interconti.com. ULTRA-DELUXE.

Farther down the InterContinental's access road, on the west side of Matira Point, is **Chez Nono**. It is perhaps the nicest mid-range accommodation on the island. A good sign is its popularity with local tourists as well as overseas visitors. Not only are the units clean and well appointed, but they are on the beach. There's a family atmosphere at Chez Nono. The property has ten units: a house with six rooms (that can be rented out individually) with shared kitchen and bath (all with hot water); and Polynesian-style *fare* with bathrooms. These include two twin bungalows and two round bungalows. The house also has a large sitting room with a television. Bicycles are available for rent and excursions can be arranged, including canoe trips that feature

Bora Bora and World War II

In January 1942 America was still shaken by the Japanese raid on Pearl Harbor. With much of its Pacific fleet out of commission, the Pentagon had to reappraise the perimeter that could be defended until a counteroffensive against Japan could be mounted. The arc 1987 miles south from Hawaii to the Free French Society Islands (now French Polynesia) and westward through Samoa and Fiji to New Zealand was believed to be defensible in those somber, early days of the war. Bora Bora, 3975 miles along the direct route from Panama to New Caledonia and Australia, was selected to be the first of a chain of refueling bases across the South Pacific. It was code-named Bobcat.

By January 21, 1942, the Bobcat convoy—four cargo vessels and two recently converted passenger ships—was being filled with disassembled seaplanes, spare parts, bombs, ammunition, trucks, bulldozers, pontoon barge sections, landing craft and prefab buildings, as well as military personnel. The six-ship convoy arrived in Bora Bora on February 17 without incident.

According to an article by Jack Roudebush and Donald I. Thomas, both U.S. Navy captains who were there, "The island was virtually unspoiled by civilization; no vehicles; no roads except coral paths for bicycles and pedestrians and coconut log bridges across streams; and no utilities except a minimal water supply. . . ."

Paradise was soon filled with some 4500 U.S. servicemen, a seaplane squadron, coast and anti-aircraft defense artillery, trucks, bulldozers, tents, prefab buildings and thousands of tons of other equipment and supplies.

The face of Bora Bora quickly changed. According to Roudebush and Thomas, "the din created by heavy trucks and bulldozers shattered its tranquillity, to the delight of the young natives who had never seen these mechanical monsters." All footpaths and bridges were destroyed by the vehicles and the Seabees set about construction of heavy-duty "American" roads.

As part of the island's defense, seven-inch guns were painstakingly unloaded and hauled up the hills. Three of the four original batteries can still be seen today, as can the remains of much of the other military paraphernalia. The guns were never fired in anger—the Battle of Midway eliminated any threat of hostility. In any case, they were of little military value—their range hardly went beyond the outer reef, and the considerable recoil from any prolonged use would literally have knocked the big guns off their bases!

By 1943, the Seabees had constructed an airstrip on the northern side of the island. This now serves as Bora Bora's commercial airport. The island was handed back to the French in June 1946.

picnics and snorkeling. Breakfast is available, but you're on your own for dinner. A deposit is needed to reserve a room. ~ Matira; 67-71-38, fax 67-74-27. BUDGET TO MODERATE.

Chez Robert et Tina rests at the tail end of Matira Point, a minute's stroll down the access the road from Chez Nono. Robert has two units: a house with three bedrooms, a living room, a kitchen, a terrace and a common bath; and a second house with five bedrooms, a kitchen and a bath. Both places are clean, but the rooms are small, spartan and dreary. Circle-island tours via outrigger or picnics on the beach are available on request. The location is good, but Robert's moodiness is often a bit much to deal with. Roundtrip transfers from the dock are provided. ~ Matira; 67-72-92, cell 79-22-73. BUDGET.

HIDDEN ►

Back on the main coastal road, just across from the Inter-Continental Beachcomber, is **Pension Pemanuata**, located behind the fine restaurant of the same name. Its eight very clean, comfortable and simple bungalows feature tile floors and have either double beds or two singles, as well as overhead fans; all have private baths and hot water. Two family-size *fare* that can accommodate up to five people are also available. Best of all, they are just a few meters from the water and close to one of the best beaches on the island. The ownership has recently changed hands and the pension is now run by Pauline Youssef of the Village Pauline and Le Maitai Polynesia hotel empire. ~ Matira; 67-75-61, fax 67-62-48. BUDGET.

Chez Maeva, a pension run by Rosine Temauri, was once home to artist Jean Masson. It still feels like a home, rather than the typical, nondescript, thrown-together-for-the-tourists shack that sometimes passes for low-end lodging in Tahiti. This two-story wooden structure, complete with a large and well-equipped communal kitchen, is clean and airy with a large dining room/salon area. The two (hot water) baths and showers, however, may not be enough for a full house. Rooms range from a loft-like sleeping area (known as the dorm) that accommodates up to four or five people, to separate rooms for individuals or couples. Chez Maeva is very hip, but overpriced for the backpacking crowd. ~ Matira; phone/fax 67-72-04. BUDGET.

Chez Maeva was the former abode of artist Jean Masson, and his works (some of them very good) still line the walls of this funky, slightly off-center, bohemian pension.

On the site of a former campground, you'll now find the impressive **Le Maitai Polynesia**, which features 19 over-water and 65 beach-and-garden bungalows. All rooms have similar furnishings such as a king-size bed, phone, TV, refrigerator and terrace. Some have air conditioning, while the rest have ceiling fans. The on-site Haere Mai restaurant specializes in international cuisine that combines French and Polynesian food. Pauline Youssef, who got her start hosting backpackers here, owns the land and hotel, which is managed by the Maitai hotel chain. She also owns Village Pauline on Paofi Bay and recently acquired the Pension Pemanuata on Matira Point. Pauline has done a commendable job building her empire—not an easy feat for a native Bora Boran who began with no capital. This hotel has a definite Polynesian look and feel and she can justifiably claim to have the only major "homegrown" hotel on the island. Her brochure claims that Bora Bora finally became affordable (though it certainly isn't cheap—the least expensive room is more than US$200). ~ Matira; 60-30-00, fax 67-66-03; www.hotelmaitai.com, e-mail info@bora.hotelmaitai.com. ULTRA-DELUXE.

Nearly opposite the Te Tiare Market you'll find the **Bora Bora Motel**. The attractive, modern and well-appointed thatch-roofed units are all cooled by overhead fans. There are four cozy studios decorated with white tile that accommodate up to three adults. Each has private bath, double bed, living room, dining area, terrace and kitchen with large refrigerator. There are also three apartments that will sleep up to four adults that come with a double bed, living room with sofa bed, dining room, terrace, kitchen and private bath. The beach is excellent for swimming. The management is friendly and accommodating, but I think it is a bit overpriced. The motel offers discounts to airline employees. ~ Matira; 67-78-21, fax 67-77-57. DELUXE.

The **Bora Bora Beach Resort**, the new kid on the block, boasts 80 rooms and a thatched-roof local Polynesian flavor. All rooms have balconies overlooking tropical gardens, and feature satellite TV and an internet connection to stay in touch with the outside world. But why would you? You'll be too busy taking advantage of all the activities on hand, from diving to late-night karaoke. ~ Matira; 60-59-52, fax 60-59-51; www.polynesian-resort-hotels.com, e-mail contact@polynesian-resort-hotels.com.

The **Sofitel Marara** was originally constructed by Dino De Laurentis to house his staff during the production of *Hurricane*. The hotel turned out to be a better investment than the movie. It has 64 units including 22 superb over-the-water bungalows and 11 high-end bungalows on a private *motu* just offshore. With white tile floors, thatched roofs, plaited *pandanus* walls and attractive rattan furniture, the rooms are spacious and well appointed, but not ostentatious. The spacious open-air dining area has a wonderful view of the lagoon. The beach is excellent and there is an extensive array of water sport activities such as snorkeling, diving and parasailing; tennis and excursions are also available. The Sofitel Marara has consistently good Tahitian dance revues that begin at 8 p.m. daily; no cover. The staff is friendly and the service quite good. ~ Matira; 60-55-00, fax 67-74-03, or 800-221-4542 in the U.S.; e-mail h0564@accor-hotels.com. ULTRA-DELUXE.

DINING   The biggest change in the restaurant scene on Bora Bora has been the proliferation of decent budget-priced eateries, especially in the Matira area.

Along Rofau Bay, just beyond the Hotel Bora Bora, you will come to **Snack Julie**, opposite the Chez Helene boutique. It has basic fare including hamburgers, chicken, soft drinks and the best *poisson cru* on the island. ~ Matira; 67-77-32. BUDGET.

Snack bar **Mahina View** is a great little eatery perched on the white sands of Matira Beach. Constructed entirely out of local materials, it beckons visitors with inexpensive dishes that include sandwiches, spaghetti, salads, *poisson cru* and steak. Dinner is also served, and meals consist mostly of fish and meat plates. The beach location is incredible. You can find it just prior to the extension of the Hotel Matira's bungalows. Closed Sunday. ~ Matira; 67-61-53. BUDGET.

Continuing down the road is **Ben's Place**, an open-air café on the island side of the road. Ben's has a wider (and more expensive) range of food than nearby restaurant, the Matira. Ben Teraitepo, an engaging native Bora Boran, and his American-born wife, Robin, enjoy shooting the breeze with their guests. They have the only menu I've seen in French Polynesia that is completely in English. In fact, there is no hint of a French influence here. Ben's has pizza, lasagna, steak (including salad and fries) and tuna steak. This is the kind of place that may be too expensive for the average backpacker, but provides an off-beat alternative to hotel cuisine. Closed Thursday. ~ Matira; 67-74-54. BUDGET TO MODERATE.

A few steps past Ben's is the **Matira**, which offers basic stir-fried Chinese fare. The food is average, but the restaurant is in a nice locale, on a patio overlooking the lagoon. The menu includes chop suey, seafood, fish and lobster. This is also a great place to take a break on your stroll around the point. ~ In the Hotel Matira, Matira; 67-70-51. BUDGET TO MODERATE.

HIDDEN ►   Along the road from the InterContinental Beachcomber is **Restaurant Temanuata**. The spiffy restaurant serves an array of excellent seafood, plus Chinese-style choices and Tahitian dishes such as *poisson cru*. Service is better than you're likely to find in many Papeete restaurants. ~ Matira; 67-62-47. BUDGET.

HIDDEN ►   **Snack La Bounty**, near the Bora Bora Motel, is a modest thatch-roofed, bungalow-style affair with an outdoor patio. It has French/Tahitian cuisine. Other dishes include fish, sashimi, shrimp, salads and the best pizza on the island. Snack La Bounty is popular with French visitors. ~ Matira; 67-70-43. BUDGET TO MODERATE.

Snack Patoti, located on the mountain side of the road just after the Sofitel, overlooks the lagoon. It's a pleasant spot to scarf down sandwiches, *poisson cru* and other simple meals. ~ Matira. BUDGET.

The **Le Tiare market** is a tidy shop located directly in front of the
Bora Bora Beach Club. It has a comprehensive selection and is
one of two markets on this side of town. ~ Matira; 67-61-38.

For those who don't fish, bonito can be purchased at roadside stands for about US$1 per pound.

Magasin Temerii, located opposite Restaurant Temanuata, is
a fairly large market with a good selection of groceries. ~ Matira;
67-70-00.

There is no shortage of souvenir shopping possibilities on Bora
Bora. Note that many of the items on sale come from Southeast
Asia or China, however. Balinese woodcarvers are obviously adept
at adding "Bora Bora" to their handicrafts.

Located a short distance north of Raititi Point is **Moana Arts**,
an establishment run by Erwin Christian, a famous Tahitian photographer. There is a superb selection of cards, posters and fashions shot by Mr. Christian. ~ Matira; 67-70-33.

A few hundred yards north of the Hotel Bora Bora is **Martine's Creations**, a small boutique that began as a roadside stand
and is now a chic shop selling black pearls and
tie-dyed and air-brushed T-shirts that are the   Turtles were sacred to
owner's own creation. It's a good place to start   the ancient Polynesians,
looking for souvenirs and is less expensive than hotel   and were only con-
gift shops. Martine's is one of Bora Bora's many bou-   sumed by chiefs and
tiques and family-run craft stands, an important cot-   priests.
tage industry on the island. ~ Matira; 67-70-69.

Along Rofau Bay look for a small vendor named **Chez
Helene**, opposite Snack Matira. Helene has good quality
pareus, which you can see her making. They're sold at competitive prices.

Logic will tell you that shopping for jewelry is foolish in a
tourist destination so thickly infested by the affluent. However,
those looking for black pearls might be in for a pleasant surprise
at **Matira Pearls and Fashions**. This modest shop sells black pearls
for every pocketbook and stocks a variety of island clothing. The
American owners will take their time and talk you through the
subtleties of pearl purchasing; they aren't in a hurry to sell you
anything. They claim that because they keep the overhead low and
buy smart they can save you money. As always, it's best to educate yourself by looking around. The shop is located on Matira
Point, around the corner from the Hotel Matira. ~ 67-79-14, fax
67-70-45; www.matirapearles.com.

Approximately six kilometers from Vaitape is Matira Point, most
of which is a white-sand beach. Unfortunately, it is occupied by

Text continued on page 260.

Motu Getaways

Accommodations on Bora Bora's outlying *motu* are one of the best ways to enjoy a holiday in French Polynesia, particularly if privacy and tranquillity are high on your list. Another upside: you will usually receive very personalized service (the smaller ones are often run by families). The downside is that to shop, send a telegram, sightsee, check out a restaurant or do anything connected with the outside world means jumping on a boat and going to the main island.

Motu Tane Dream Island is an oval dollop of an isle off the northern tip of Bora Bora, just a few minutes by boat from the airport. Studded with coconut palms and fringed by white sand, it does resemble someone's Robinson Crusoe fantasy. There are two villas on the beach, each with a kitchen, hot-water bathroom and private terrace. Amenities include canoes and snorkeling gear. Meal plans are provided; three-night minimum stay. ~ Motu Tane; 67-74-50. MODERATE TO DELUXE.

Le Paradis, located quite close to Motu Tane, is another dream island drenched in sunshine and shaded by coconut palms. Seven simple, thatch-roofed bungalows are just a few steps from the shore. The larger units have private cold-water bathrooms; the smaller *fares* share a bathroom. The accommodations are traditional Tahitian style, with an attractive coconut-motif exterior. Meal plans are available. No credit cards. ~ Motu Paahi; phone/fax 67-75-53, cell 78-27-87; www.haere-mai.com, e-mail haere-mai@mail.pf. MODERATE TO DELUXE.

Le Méridien Bora Bora is built on the northern point of the ten-kilometer-long Motu Piti Aau, east of the main island, opposite the village Anau. The 82 over-water bungalows and 17 beach bungalows share a private garden. Elegant and in harmony with the site, each bungalow has a large bedroom, a bathroom with a lagoon view and a terrace with direct access to the water. In the living room you can watch the underwater world through a large window in the floor. The Mikimiki Bar is built to replicate the prow of a boat and Le Tipanier Restaurant opens to a sheltered interior lagoon. You can enjoy lunch in rocking chairs right on the sand, next to the dark blue swimming pool that contrasts the turquoise water of the lagoon. Activities include outrigger canoeing, scuba diving, beach volleyball, etc. ~ Motu Piti Aau; 60-51-51, fax 60-51-52; www.le meridien-borabora.com, e-mail rez@lemeridien-tahiti.com. ULTRA-DELUXE.

Eden Beach Hotel opened in 2001 on the same *motu* as Le Méridien. With 16 beach and garden bungalows, this property is much more intimate than its *motu* mate. Billed as "the most environmentally friendly hotel project in French Polynesia," Eden Beach includes solar energy, recycling and its own desalination and wastewater treatment systems. The bungalows are made from natural local materials and have all of the conveniences you'd expect—except perhaps for one: there are no TVs. These people really get it. ~ Motu Piti Aau; 60-57-60, fax 67-69-76; www.borabora.tel.com, e-mail borabora@mail.pf. ULTRA-DELUXE.

The **Bora Bora Pearl Beach Resort** on the southern tip of Motu Tevairoa has 50 gorgeous over-water Polynesian-style bungalows whose presence blends well with the magnificent colors of the lagoon. Ten suites sit on the white sandy beach—all facing Otemanu, the monolith that dominates Bora Bora. The units have an incredible outdoor bathroom adorned with coral, shells, palms, bamboo and driftwood in a private garden. Add a jacuzzi and you've got quite a scene. Twenty additional pool *fare* suites open to a private tropical garden with a swimming pool/jacuzzi. The bungalows are equipped with ceiling fans and air conditioning. The shower is set in the back of the suite in a small garden. The restaurant offers good French cuisine and a once-weekly Polynesian buffet. Other activities include an 18-hole mini-golf course, a tennis court, a badminton court, and *petanque piste* (the French version of bocce ball) to keep clients busy. ~ Motu Tevairoa; 60-52-00, fax 60-52-22; www.pearlresorts. com, e-mail welcome@borapearlbeach.pf. ULTRA-DELUXE.

Mai Moana is a private island for the well-to-do traveler who desires the seclusion of a small offshore resort but doesn't want to share it with a hundred other guests. The three *fare*-style bungalows, near a white-sand beach, are well appointed, and come with a double bed, private bath and dressing room, not to mention a TV, video and phone. Windsurfing and other nautical activities are there for the sporting set. Unlike less expensive offshore opera- tions, Mai Moana has a small restaurant/bar on the premises. Located on Motu Iti, Mai Moana is five minutes by boat from the airport or ten minutes from the ferry dock. Roundtrip transfers are included in the tariff. ~ Motu Iti; 67-62-45, fax 67-62-39; www.mai-moana-island.com, e-mail stan@mail.pf. ULTRA-DELUXE.

Located on Motu Toopua, a small white-sand islet across from Vaitape, the luxurious **Bora Bora Lagoon Resort and Spa** offers 16 beach bungalows and 50 over-the-water bungalows, including two suites and two handicap units. The classic hotel is the new favorite of Hollywood celebrities and the *beau monde*. The posh units include wood floors, private lanais, TVs and phones. In addition to the bungalows, there are two restaurants on the property as well as a full complement of activities including tennis, volleyball, windsurfing, diving and other nautical activities. The treehouse spa offers a wonderfully natural way to experience relaxation. ~ Motu Toopua; 60-40-00, fax 60-40-01, or 800- 860-4095 in the U.S.; www.boraboralagoonresort.com, e-mail reservations@ bblr.pf. ULTRA-DELUXE.

Sheraton Bora Bora Nui Resort & Spa is the newest addition to the *motu*-hotels. Located on the backside of Motu Toopua, the massive develop- ment includes 84 over-water bungalows and suites and 36 lagoon-view bungalows and suites. The property also includes a restaurant, three bars, a conference center, a banquet room, a theater and its very own helicopter landing pad. Travelers, however, have complained of poor service. ~ Motu Toopua; 86- 48-48, fax 86-48-40; www.sheratonsintahiti.com, e-mail reserva tions.tahiti@sheraton.pf. ULTRA-DELUXE.

a number of hotel properties. But, as in all of French Polynesia, all beaches have a public access.

HIDDEN ▶ **MATIRA BEACH** 🏊 Perhaps the best-kept secret on the island is the sole public beach on Matira Point, a hidden local favorite. This long stretch of white sand is great for swimming or picnics and the crowd is almost always Tahitian. There is not much in the way of facilities but there are several mushroom-like canopies for shade, and a toilet. If you're lucky, you'll see manta rays skimming along the sandy bottom near the shore. A note of caution: It's not prudent to leave any valuables on the beach unattended. ~ The beach is located on Matira Point. To find it, look for the sign for InterContinental Beachcomber. This marks the small road that bisects Matira Point. Walk to the end of the road; the beach will be on your right-hand side.

Anau Village to Faanui

The beginning of Anau Village starts just over the hill from the new Club Med, which sits on its own bay. The old Club Med Coral Garden, on the other side of the island was smaller and prone to storm damage. The new Club Med is a much more ambitious development both in size and quality.

SIGHTS The first stop in the area is Club Med's own **belvédère** (lookout) atop the ridge above Mataorio Bay. The path to the lookout is accessed by Club Med's private tunnel under the road, but if you go just beyond the Hibiscus boutique toward Anau you can see where the steps emerge from under the road, and make your way up to the path. ~ Anau; 60-46-04, or 800-824-4844 in the U.S.

Anau extends another kilometer along the shoreline. Anau is the least adulterated, most typical Polynesian village on Bora Bora. This is because it is the most isolated settlement on the island. Until the construction of the new Club Med, there has never been a major hotel in the vicinity. Anau is strung out along a rocky stretch of coastline. It has churches, a school, a general store and rambling, tin-roofed homes with well-kept gardens. But despite the bucolic setting, it is not a terribly friendly place.

AUTHOR FAVORITE

It's hard to visualize nowadays, but during World War II Bora Bora was home to thousands of American servicemen. When I visit the island I never fail to hike the spectacular Tuivahora **coastal defense gun emplacements** and meditate on the dark days of our history. For more information see page 261.

Next to a vehicle maintenance shop is the start of a dirt road that traverses Bora Bora. This path rises sharply and affords a magnificent view of Motu Piti Aau and the islands of Raiatea and Tahaa. The road ends at Pofai Bay, near a cluster of boutiques and shops. The hike across the island can be done at a leisurely pace in under 30 minutes.

If you instead continue just past Anau, you are in the shadow of 2384-foot (727-meter) **Mt. Otemanu**, the highest point on the island. It has been said that the mountain has never been climbed because of the crumbling nature of the sheer rock walls below the summit. At the base of these walls, and not easily accessible, is the **Otemanu Cave**, formerly a burial site. Rumor has it that G.I.s added that well-known World War II graffiti "Kilroy was here" to the cave walls, but I haven't been able to verify that as the ascent to the cave is steep and dangerous. I don't recommend you try to either.

Four kilometers past Anau the road climbs the coastline as it crosses **Tuivahora Point**, then drops and rises again like a roller coaster. In between dips, on the sea side, is **Marae Aehua-tai**, one of several ancient Polynesian temples on Bora Bora. This *marae* is one of the best preserved on the island and appears to be a wall of black basalt slabs propped upright like giant tombstones. From the *marae* site there are fine views across the lagoon as you stand nearly in the shadow of Mt. Otemanu.

At Tuivahora Point the road bends sharply and there is an offshoot of a trail that descends to a private home. The trail continues behind the house out along the point to **Marae Taharuu**, a tall, natural obelisk that appears to still be used by Tahitians. The black thumb-like boulder juts up from the earth. There are marvelous views in both directions from this vantage point. If you do take the small trail to the *marae*, be respectful of the proprietor.

The Tuivahora Point area is also the locale for the most spectacular **coastal defense gun emplacements** on the island. To get there, take the first right at the bottom of the hill; a rutted jeep track follows the contours of the shoreline. Continue along this lonely road past a concrete platform that looks like a foundation for a home. Carry on to the second platform down the road, and after a few steps, stop. At this point, backtrack a few yards and follow the jeep track that goes straight up the hill. There's an outstanding view, but a newly created open-pit garbage dump makes visiting the guns hard on the nose. When the dump is not burning and smoke is not an issue, flies and the odor can be offensive. (Considering that this is one of the most beautiful views on the island, it was a rather unenlightened choice for a garbage dump. But according to the mayor, this was the only public land available on which to build it.)

From Tuivahora Point, the next few kilometers of the coast are virtually uninhabited, sprinkled only with a few houses and banana groves, coconut palms and taro patches.

As you continue along the road look for the colonial-style **Revatua Club** facing Taimoo Bay. This club has a beautiful swimming pool and clear ocean water for snorkeling. Revatua's **L'Espadon Restaurant** is a superb place to sit on the veranda and quench your thirst. ~ Anau.

HIDDEN ►

Two kilometers past Taimoo Bay is the minuscule **Maritime Museum**, run by Betrand Derasse, an architect who's constructed a number of traditional Polynesian-boat models and models of European ships with a historic connection to French Polynesia, such as Captain Cook's *Endeavour*. ~ Faanui; 67-75-24.

Another two kilometers brings you to **Taihi Point**, the northernmost spot on the island. From here you can trek up the hill to the top of Popoti Ridge, the site of a former U.S. Navy radar installation. (See "Hiking" later in this chapter.)

Various landmarks on Bora Bora carry the god Hiro's name, including the bell of Hiro on the very southern tip of Motu Toopua. It's actually a rock that, when struck, produces a bell-like ring.

Just past the point are the remnants of a Hyatt hotel. It was to be built on the hillside and over the lagoon. But when it was close to completion the developer ran out of money. The incomplete hotel is now slowly deteriorating under the tropical sun. Beyond the hotel site are the **Bora Bora Condos**, a collection of houses perched on stilts on the hillside. Some of them were owned by Jack Nicholson and Marlon Brando.

Strewn along the next five kilometers, which includes the Faanui Bay area, are a collection of relics and artifacts from both ancient Polynesians and the U.S. government. At the 25-kilometer point you can see a **boat pier** and **seaplane ramp**. The pier, still used today, was a World War II addition to the island. The concrete ramp sloping gently into the lagoon was used as a seaplane base. It was here that up to 12 OS2U single-engine float seaplanes could tie up. Just another kilometer down the road is an old **submarine slip**. Resembling a giant concrete vat, it was built to accommodate submarines, but over the years has seen more action as a swimming hole for village children.

You are now on the fringes of **Faanui Village**. Look for a "40 kilometer per hour" speed limit sign and you'll see **Marae FareOpu**, an ancient Polynesian temple on the sea side, squeezed between the road and the water's edge. Two of the slabs are clearly marked with turtle petroglyphs.

The Faanui Bay and Village section are where most of the U.S. servicemen were stationed during Operation Bobcat during World War II. Faanui Bay was chosen by the U.S. Navy as the most strategic place for a base. The location was protected on all sides by land, was directly opposite a *motu* and could only be seen from the air. The bay had to be extensively dredged to accommodate submarines and other vessels, and to this day it remains environmentally damaged from this endeavor. Visible in the area are pilings from a dock and several Quonset huts nestled in the bushes. They are found mostly along the mountain side of the road. Also visible is a massive ammunition bunker on the hillside.

From the Faanui church at the head of the bay, a road runs directly inland. It can be taken to the ridge above and then down to the other side of the island to Vairau Bay. (See "Hiking" later in this chapter.) Situated in a coconut plantation that overlooks a small field on the inland side of the road is **Marae Taianapa**. Associated with Mt. Pahia, the 2168-foot (661-meter) peak that towers over Vaitape, this *marae* is a fairly large temple with two small petroglyphs. (You've overshot the temple if you come to the Hinano Beer and Coca Cola depot, about 100 yards beyond the temple.) Right behind this depot is the Faanui Power Station, a steam generator powered by burning coconut husks.

Bora Bora's major freight unloading facility, **Farepiti Wharf**, is a sturdy dock built by the Seabees during the war. Interisland ships from Tahiti, including the popular *Vaeanu*, still dock here. Walk along the shoreline for about 100 yards beyond the dock and at the tip of the point lies **Marae Marotetini**, which historically was the most important temple on Bora Bora. It was restored in 1968 by Dr. Y. H. Sinoto, head archaeologist of Honolulu's Bishop Museum. According to the old religion, the *marae* is associated with Mt. Otemanu. Near the *marae* are two tombs built for the Bora Bora royal family during the 19th century.

LODGING

Club Med is located on a nice beach at the foot of Paopao Point, about 12 kilometers from Vaitape. There is nothing rundown or chintzy about this Club Med, and it comes highly recommended as a honeymoon getaway. The 150 twin-share bungalows are well spaced throughout the "village," and each one has a view of the sea. The interiors are modern and very comfortable, as are the posh bathrooms. All are cooled by overhead fans, and the rooms come with many amenities. An aesthetically debatable choice was made by the designer to paint the facility in pastel shades of yellow, mauve and chartreuse; some locals have complained that the pastel motif clashes with the traditional Polynesian-style thatched bungalows. The Club Med machine is in full force here, offering the usual battery of activities such as snorkeling, windsurfing, volleyball, tennis, aerobics classes, basketball, outrigger canoe rides, visits to a neighboring *motu*, and excursions of every kind. *And* the service and food are excellent. A full array of quality salads, seafood, meat dishes and desserts are available buffet-style. If you like the Club Med environment and the all-inclusive Club Med program, then Club Med is a bargain for top-end visitors. For more information on Club Med, it's best to contact your travel agent. ~ Anau; 60-46-04, fax 42-16-83; www.clubmed.com. ULTRA-DELUXE.

Pension Teipo consists of five well-constructed thatch-roofed bungalows located on the water (near a seawall rather than a beach). All include private cold-water bathrooms, kitchenettes and free airport transfers. Kayaks and bikes are available free to guests. The downside is that these attractive units are a bit hemmed in by neighbors and are far from stores, beaches and restaurants in the village of Anau. The closest diversion is Club Med. ~ Anau; 67-78-17, fax 67-73-24; e-mail teipobora@mail.pf. MODERATE TO DELUXE.

Pension Bora Lagoonarium is owned by the family that owns the Lagoonarium on the *motu* across the lagoon. There are three thatched-roof red bungalows that include a double bed, small table and private bath. A larger house built in the same style has small rooms with double beds and a shared bath and kitchen. There is also a dorm building that can sleep 16 people on sturdy wooden bunk beds. The kitchen facility is spare, but the picnic area overlooking the water makes for a nice atmosphere. If you stay here, you'll get a special rate on the popular Lagoonarium tour. A discounted monthly rate is also offered. You can find the place a few minutes' walk (about one kilometer) north of Club Med. ~ Anau; 67-71-34, cell 79-73-67, fax 67-60-29; www.bora boraisland.com, e-mail lagonarium@mail.pf. BUDGET TO MODERATE.

Past the Lagoonarium is the new incarnation of **Chez Henriette**. The popular backpackers' campground and dormitory

RESPECT THE *MARAE*

Stories abound of those who purposefully or inadvertently defiled sacred shrines and suffered grave consequences. One such story is about a laborer working near Marae Marotetini in 1973. He discovered a rusted biscuit tin containing what were believed to be the charred remnants of clothing worn by the last queen of Bora Bora. The tin was accidentally destroyed and not long afterward, despite the efforts of modern medicine, the worker died of a mysterious malady. According to author Milas Hinshaw's account of the incident in *Bora Bora E*, the worker's dead body "turned black—resembling a corpse that had been consumed by fire." Hinshaw and his son claim to have been cursed by this same *marae* when they picked up several human bones there and took them home as souvenirs. Not until five years later, after returning the bones to their resting place, did the author's spate of bad luck stop. Why it took him five years to figure this out, I do not know.

Bora Bora's highest point is 2384-foot Mt. Otemanu, a towering volcanic peak of sheer black rock that looks down on you wherever you are on the island.

Above: There's no lack of warm water and gentle breezes in French Polynesia, making the islands an excellent place for kite sailing.

Right: A bicycle is a handy way to explore a smaller island.

Below: Mellow black-tip sharks are favored guests at shark feeds.

Above: Out of every hundred black pearl oysters, only seven will eventually yield commercially acceptable pearls.

Below: A motu's white-sand beach, just a short boat ride from Bora Bora, is an ideal setting for a picnic.

Four-wheel-drive overland expeditions are a popular way to tour hidden backcountry.

Above: Haapiti is home to the huge, twin-towered Eglise de la Sainte Famille, formerly the center of Moorea's Catholic mission.

Below: Some of the most fascinating archaeological sites in French Polynesia, including the monument at Pa'eke, are found in Nuku Hiva's Taipivai Valley.

Above: Modern tattoo artists such as the talented Akitini Touatini create original designs based on traditional motifs.

Above right: A steady stream of outrigger canoes can always be seen parading offshore, especially at dusk.

Right: The lush Hanavave Valley is located on the western coast of Fatu Hiva, the most remote island of the inhabited Marquesas Group.

Above: Taioha'e, the administrative center of Nuku Hiva and the entire Marquesan archipelago, sits on the shores of Taioha'e Bay, a first port of call for many cruisers from the west coast of North America.

Above: The coral reef ecosystem is one of the most diverse on the planet, and its high productivity is matched only by the tropical rainforest.

Below: A vahine knocks a tree to call villagers to a local gathering.

moved from its long-time home in Anau in 2001 because of a land dispute. This new location north of the village has a lot of potential. A new spacious and modern dorm building has room for 15, and the tiled bath facilities are spotless. The kitchen has a new refrigerator and four-burner gas stove with oven. However, the campsite is up a steep hill toward the back of the property, which is a bit problematic. The owners plan to build toilet and kitchen facilities at the top, but for now campers must make the trek up and down the hill to use the dorm's facilities. Still, the view may just be worth the schlep. The camping area offers a powerful view of Mt. Otemanu, as well as a panorama of the water and a direct sightline to the Marae Taharuu obelisk. This will be a choice spot once the facilities are built. There is currently no sign for the campground. Look for a white building sitting perpendicular to the road on the mountain side, just after you pass the mountain's peak. Better yet, call ahead for a transfer. ~ North of Anau; phone/fax 67-71-32.

Also set far away from the teeming crowds (in fact, it's the only accommodation on this side of the island) is **Revatua Club,** on the eastern side of Bora Bora. There are 16 rooms, and a boutique and bar/restaurant are built on stilts over the water. There is also a pontoon into the lagoon that leads to a seawater swimming pool. The atmosphere is definitely barefoot, local and French, which I found comfortable. L'Espadon, the hotel restaurant, is the only eatery in town. The friendly bar is a good spot to meet local folks. There is excellent snorkeling nearby. Tours are also available. Located 12 kilometers from Vaitape, on the leeward side of the island. ~ Anau; 67-73-31, fax 67-76-59. MODERATE TO DELUXE.

Near the decaying Hyatt hotel at the north end of the island you'll find **Bora Bora Condos**. There are 12 bungalows on the mountain side and four over the water. Each bungalow has two bedrooms, a living room, dining room, bathroom and terrace, and accommodate five people. Though the bungalows are well maintained, the crumbling remnants of the old hotel nearby makes the area seem rather eerie and deserted. Not only is it far from any dining or tourist area, there is simply no compelling reason to stay here aside from the sunsets, which are magnificent from this spot. ~ Faanui; 67-71-33. DELUXE.

DINING

You don't have much choice out this way. There is only one real restaurant—**L'Espadon** at the Revatua Club. Luckily, the French and Tahitian food here is good. Specialties of the house are grilled seafood and *fruit du mer*. A pleasurable spot to dine, this indoor/outdoor restaurant overlooks the lagoon. ~ Anau; 67-71-67. MODERATE TO DELUXE.

Next door to L'Espadon is a snack bar called **Le Totara** that advertises "Polynesian BBQ." ~ BUDGET.

Non-guests are welcome to enjoy the nightly dinner buffet and show at **Club Med,** but prices are a bit steep. The tariff for the meal and show is 6000 CFP (US$60) for non-guests. Call ahead for reservations. ~ Anau; 60-46-04. ULTRA-DELUXE.

GROCERIES There are a couple of small markets in the village of Anau where you can purchase soft drinks and other small grocery items. The selection isn't as good as the bigger markets in Vaitape, but if you're staying on this side of the island and need just a few small things, it's a lot more convenient. One of the better stocked is **Magasin Anau.** ~ 67-65-43.

SHOPPING Occasionally a small vendor sets up a stand selling green (drinking) coconuts and shell leis a hundred yards or so past the Reva-tua Club.

Hibiscus is a souvenir shop/boutique located just beyond the entrance to Club Med on the mountain side of the road. Pareu, jewelry, T-shirts and the like may be had for very reasonable prices. They also rent bicycles at fair prices. ~ Anau; 67-72-43.

HIDDEN ► **Paarara Mountain Artist** is a small boutique where Emmanuel, the son of famed artist Jean Masson, and his wife sell their paintings and gorgeous painted pareu. This beautiful spot, in the cool heights and greenery of the mountains, is also the original site of Masson's *atelier*. The house is set in a splendid garden, and sometimes the family will share a meal of *kaveu* (coconut crabs) with clients. To find it, take the road at the Faanui Village church up the mountain about two kilometers. You can walk or take a taxi. ~ Faanui; 67-65-31.

NIGHTLIFE **Club Med** has a daily variety show that is always good for a few chuckles. There is also a Polynesian dance performance on Sunday and Thursday nights. Non-guests are welcome, but they must purchase Club Med's "bar book," a book of tickets to exchange for drinks, for about 2000 CFP. ~ Anau; 60-46-04.

▼▼▼▼▼▼▼▼▼▼▼▼▼▼
Outdoor Adventures

Chez Henriette north of Anau has a camping area with great views of the mountain, ocean and obelisk. The downside is that the campsite

CAMPING sits atop a steep hill and—for now anyway—the toilet and kitchen facilities are at the bottom. ~ Anau; phone/fax 67-71-32. BUDGET.

Camping is also available at **Moon B&B**, located halfway between Vaitape and Matira Beach, next door to Gallerie Alain and Linda. Noise from the road may be bothersome here. ~ Nunue; 67-74-36; e-mail moonbungalow@netcourrier.com. BUDGET.

Shark
Feeding

Shark feeding on Bora Bora was originated by resident photographer Erwin Christian. A tour leader takes you, snorkel and flippers in hand, to an area of the lagoon that has been roped off. Your guide stands in the roped-off section throwing bait in the water while a dozen or so black-tip reef sharks go into their patented feeding frenzy. The audience stands a safe distance away.

Is shark feeding necessarily a "good" thing to do? The jury is still out. From what I can determine, feeding sharks inside the lagoon is somewhat innocuous—the sharks are fed daily, and the participants are small reef sharks. There are some divers who feed sharks outside the reef and this can be dangerous if not properly handled. You not only attract larger, more aggressive species (i.e., hammerheads, grays and tiger sharks), but if these creatures get used to being fed on a regular basis and you don't happen to have food when you run into them, they instinctively look to your hands for something to eat and ... well, you get the picture. Michel Condesse, the capable owner of the Bora Diving Center, assured me he has not had problems with sharks biting divers. However, snorkelers or divers feeding moray eels have run into problems; morays are less circumspect about what they latch onto.

If you're interested in participating in this spectacle there are two outfitters to contact:

Franck Sachsse of **Moana Adventure Tours** has come recommended as a shark-feeding specialist inside the lagoon. ~ Matira; 67-61-41, fax 67-61-26.

Nono Leverd has a popular shark feed. Nono will actually pick small reef sharks, show them to tourists and then let the sharks go. It's not a recommended practice for visitors. ~ Matira; 67-71-38.

Village Pauline on Pofai Bay offers camping and has a common cooking area and shower/toilet facilities for campers. ~ Pofai Bay; 67-72-16, fax 67-78-14. BUDGET.

DIVING   There are popular dive sites both inside and outside the lagoon. Since there's only one pass, Teavanui, it can be a long trip to some of the outer-reef dive sites. Sites closer to the pass are well visited. Manta rays are often seen in the lagoon's shallow waters. Calypso Club does a manta ray dive daily in the waters between Anau Village and Motu Piti Aau, an area nicknamed **Manta Bay** or **Manta's Reef**. Manta rays are harmless plankton feeders. Their impressive size (up to 18 feet in length and weighing up to two tons!) and graceful appearance make them favorites with divers. Moray eels and turtles are also spotted, but it's the rays that are the big attraction. Because of blooming plankton, visibility is often poor. **Manta Ray Channel** or **Manta Ray Pit** is another lagoon dive site where the magnificent rays are regularly encountered. It's just south of Motu Toopua Iti, the smaller *motu* to the south of Motu Toopua. Eagle rays are also encountered in the lagoon, particularly in **Eagle Ray Channel** between Motu Toopua and the main island.

The **Aquarium** is a popular diving and snorkeling site. It's located between Motu Piti Aau and the inner edge of the outer reef near Tupitipiti Point, immediately offshore from Club Med, just south of their *motu* beach.

Outside the reef the **Tapu Dive** is popular, both for its proximity to Teavanui Pass and for the large numbers of moray eels that are seen. It's also a good spot to observe giant Napoleon fish and jackfish. The dive starts at about 75 feet, makes its way up almost to the surface as it approaches the outer edge of the reef, then turns and descends back to the dive boat's anchor line. Moray

UNDERWATER GARDENS & PARKS

Alas, snorkeling is not particularly good along the shore of Bora Bora, except for the areas around the Hotel Bora Bora and the Revatua Club. The reason given is that the island has been overfished. The waters around the **Hotel Bora Bora** are teeming with fish because the hotel has established an underwater "park" where fishing is strictly forbidden. The hotel grounds are not generally open to the public, but if you obtain permission, it's okay to snorkel. A more difficult area to reach, but an excellent spot, is known as the **Coral Garden**, offshore from the Sofitel on the south tip of Motu Roa. Many of the hotels and pensions feature this as part of their excursion program and will drop you off at the *motu*.

eels are encountered along the way. The **Teavanui Pass Entrance**, right at the mouth of the pass, is another popular outer-reef dive.

White Valley Dive, also known as **Muri Muri**, is a curving sandbar off Paharire Point, off Motu Mute, where the airport is located. Because of the strong currents, larger species are found here, in particular shoals of barracuda. It's not unusual to see up to 30 gray sharks, turtles and dolphins. Outside the reef at **Tupitipiti Point**, just the other side of the reef from the Aquarium lagoon dive, is an excellent dive site. The one drawback is the time it takes to get there. According to Michel Condesse of Bora Diving Center, it has the best coral wall in all of Polynesia as well as numerous caves. **South Point Dive** on the outer reef directly south of Matira Point, also a long haul to get to, is an above-average dive destination, with an emphasis on pelagics rather than the reef system. The lack of rich reef life here can be traced to the damage caused by dredging the lagoon during World War II and overfishing inside the lagoon.

Bora Diving Center is run by an engaging Frenchman, Michel Condesse. Located in a tidy bungalow just past the Hotel Bora Bora (coming from town), they serve both the general public and Hotel Bora Bora, Hotel Bora Lagoon Resort and Sofitel. Their staff consists of six bilingual instructors and they have four dive boats, four air compressors and dive gear for more than 30 people. Their equipment appears to be well maintained. They dive at over ten different sites, primarily outside the lagoon. They will take you to see a variety of undersea flora and fauna, including manta and eagle rays, turtles, Napoleon fish, shark, barracuda, dolphins and moray eels. Bora Diving Center is a PADI-certified facility and a Three-Star CMAS operation. ~ Matira; 67-71-84, 67-74-83, fax 67-74-83; www.boradive.com, e-mail boradiving@ mail.pf.

Nemo World is run by by long-time Bora Bora resident Vincent Soustreau. Four dive instructors, one of whom speaks Japanese, can take you to all the best sites in and out of the lagoon. In addition to dive site visits, they offer exploration dives and lessons for beginners. Nemo World can be found in the Bora Bora Beach Resort and Le Meridien. ~ Matira; 67-77-85; www.nemodivebora. com, e-mail mail@ nemoworld.pf.

Diveasy at Matira Point offers recreational dives and CMAS certifications. Owner Bernard Heriteau also offers dives using underwater communication systems. ~ Matira; 79-22-55, fax 67-69-36.

TOPdive, the diving club found at the resort of the same name, offers a two-tank dive (two bottles, two dives, two exceptional sites) every morning. Also offered every morning are the manta ray dive and the lagoon dives. In the afternoon, introductory dives for beginners are provided. The club has a fleet of three speedy boats with twin outboards. TOPdive is located just north of Vaitape. ~ Vaitape; 60-50-50, fax 60-50-51; www.top dive.com, e-mail info@topdive.pf.

The **Bora Bora Blue Nui** dive center, based out of the Bora Bora Pearl Beach Resort, is operated by seasoned pro Gilles Petre, who formerly ran Manihi Blue Nui in the Tuamotu Islands. ~ Motu Tevairoa; phone/fax 67-79-07, cell 79-22-72; www.blue nui.com, e-mail boraborabluenui@mail.pf.

SAILING   You can see Bora Bora by hiring a boat on the island or chartering a vessel from another point, such as Tahiti or Raiatea, and seeing Bora Bora as part of a larger island tour. For those interested in the latter, see the "Sailing" section of the individual island chapters. Most of the skippers on Bora Bora will do day trips or will be amenable to extended charters.

Blue Lagoon Charter based in Vaitape runs week-long catamaran trips through the Society and Tuamotu islands as well as day sails around Bora Bora and Tahaa. The boats are a Hippocampe II and a Privilege 45. Contact Michel Bordier. ~ Vaitape; 67-73-48; e-mail bluelagoonchart@mail.pf.

A catamaran can be hired through long-time French Polynesian resident **Rich Postma**, the dean of the cruise scene. His *Taravana*, a 50-foot catamaran, is affiliated with the Hotel Bora Bora but he will take anyone who wishes to come along and will also do private custom charters. Rich has a knack for making everyone feel very special on his cruises. He has a variety of trips, including sunset cruises and deep-sea fishing. The vessel is comfortable, very fast and inexpensive to charter for a couple. Eight-person maximum. ~ Matira; 67-77-79, fax 67-77-78; www.bora borasportfishing.com, e-mail taravana@mail.pf.

Bora Bora Voile operates *Taaroa III*, a large catamaran that provides sailing tours around the island. Pascal, the skipper, runs both circle island and sunset tours every day. He tries to avoid using the motor and relies on the wind as much as possible. The three-and-a-half-hour lagoon cruise is in the morning, with swimming stops in shallow waters (eight passengers maximum). Soft drinks and cocktails are included in the price. ~ Matira; phone/fax 67-64-30; e-mail boravoil@netcourrier.com.

Croisiéres O'hana Bora Bora is operated by Bernard Marmillon, who has a 20-meter catamaran set up for day trips in the lagoon. This beautiful vessel hosts up to 30 passengers and does so with Polynesian flair. Star of the show is Tino, a former Mister Bora Bora whose sparkling personality really adds to the mix. For the afternoon cruise the boat sails south to a coral garden for snorkeling. En route the crew explains the wonders of the lagoon along with a discourse on Polynesian navigation and friendly banter. A guitar and ukulele serenade accompanies the sunset. Morning or whole-day excursions are also offered and the boat is available for special charters. Croisiéres O'hana Bora Bora is based at Le Méridien hotel on Motu Piti Aau. ~ Phone/fax 60-51-03; e-mail spotconcept@mail.pf.

Small motorboats that hold four people can be rented without a license at **Rene and Maguy** in Matira. Rentals go by the hour or are available for half- or full-day excursions. ~ Phone/fax 67-60-61, cell 79-26-36.

Like his enterprising brother Dany, who runs Tupuna Mountain Expeditions, Nono Leverd has a day trip that has received good recommendations from visitors. **Teremoana Tours** provides motorized canoe trips that include shark feeding, snorkeling, a visit to the den of the leopard rays and a picnic on a *motu*. Teremoana, by the way, is the name of Nono's *pirogue*. ~ Matira; 67-71-38, fax 67-74-27.

A company called **Shark Boy of Bora Bora** runs similar motorized canoe trips on the lagoon and also has a 40-foot catamaran. Contact Evan Temarii. ~ Vaitape; 67-60-93, cell 78-27-42; e-mail sharkboy@mail.pf.

Moana Adventure Tours operates a glass-bottom boat for lagoon excursions. ~ Vaitape; 67-61-41, fax 67-61-26; www.moana tours.com, e-mail moanatours@maui.pf.

There are about a dozen other outfits that offer standard lagoon excursions. Most of the services are comparable, but shop around to get the best price.

Anne Condesse of the Bora Diving Center runs **Aqua Safari**. They'll set you up with a special helmet connected to an air supply piped in from a boat, so you're free of the usual diving gear and can delve into the depths to observe the stunning tropical fish in their natural setting—the lagoon. You can actually walk

**OTHER
WATER
SPORTS**

sights

AUTHOR FAVORITE

Bora Bora Exotic Lagoonarium offers half- or full-day excursions at their own Lagoonarium located off the small *motu* north of Le Méridien. Akin to a marine wildlife park, this is a place where you can swim with rays, sharks and turtles. The animals are accustomed to humans and it's possible to feed a shark or caress a stingray. A typical tour includes a picnic/barbecue and a coconut-husking demonstration. They will also show you how to grate and squeeze coconut milk. I recommend this tour. Closed Saturday. ~ Anau; 67-71-34, fax 67-60-29; www.borais land.com, e-mail lagoonarium@mail.pf.

on the sea floor. It's a fun, safe alternative to scuba diving that requires no certification. The Bora Diving Center is located next to the Hotel Bora Bora. ~ Matira; 67-71-84, cell 72-03-56; www.boradive.com, e-mail dan@mail.pf.

Aquascope represents yet another new technology that lets visitors explore places they've never been before. Tested in the Mediterranean, this nine-passenger, semi-submersible yellow submarine allows non-divers to admire Bora Bora's underwater world without getting wet. The sub is generally moored in the lagoon and you're transported to it on a fast shuttle boat. You transfer to *Aquascope*, where from your seat it's easy to watch the ballet of tropical fish, the corals and an occasional shark glide past the wide-view window. Roundtrip airport transfers are included. For information call Jean-Pierre or Sylviane Gonzalez. ~ Vaitape; phone/fax 67-61-92, cell 78-27-92; e-mail aquascopebora@mail.pf.

The moray eels in the Tapu area have become so familiar with divers that they often come up and make close-up, face-to-mask inspections.

Spirit of Pacific operates a full-fledged submarine and offers five dives daily to a depth of 50 meters (165 feet). Dives last about an hour, and the viewing window is advertised to be 360 degrees. ~ Vaitape; 67-64-00, fax 67-65-67; www.spiritofpacific.com.

Bora Bora Parasail gives you a fun way to admire the island from a bird's-eye perspective. This particular method of parasailing allows two people to fly together in a very safe manner. Sky riders are effortlessly launched and retrieved from a platform on the boat's rear deck and once airborne, the "passengers" can control the altitude they wish to fly to. This is soft "adventure travel" that even children or octogenarians can enjoy. It's based at the Bora Bora Hotel. ~ Matira; phone/fax 67-70-34, cell 78-27-10; e-mail parasail@mail.pf.

Several companies rent jet skis and wave runners. A guide to instruct visitors in the proper use of these controversial vehicles accompanies all tours. Try **Matira Jet Tours** (next to Chez Nono) ~ Matira, phone/fax 67-62-73, e-mail bborajet@maiul.pf; **Miki Miki Jet Tours** ~ Matira, 67-76-44, e-mail maeva@topdive.pf; or **Moanareva Tours** ~ Vaitape, 67-60-27.

FISHING

Sportfishing is quite good just outside Bora Bora's reef, where you can hook blue marlin, yellow fin tuna, sailfish, wahoo and mahimahi as well as bottom fish such as snapper and grouper. Inside the lagoon it is possible to snag some of the smaller reef fish, but because of *ciguatera* (a type of food poisoning), it's probably not a good idea to eat your catch.

Some of the other vessels available are the *Jessie L*, a 35-foot Luhrs, skippered by **Alain Loussan**. ~ Nunue; phone/fax 67-75-22; e-mail alainloussan@mail.pf. The *Hei Miki* is skippered by **Jean Bernard**. ~ 67-70-50. **Rich Postma** and his 50-foot catamaran *Taravana* are available for deep-sea fishing charters. ~ Matira; 67-77-79, fax 67-77-78; e-mail taravana@mail.pf.

The only show in town is **Reva Reva Ranch**, located on the same *motu* as Le Méridien. They offer guided rides along the beach at Motu Piti Aau as well as moonlight rides. ~ Motu Piti Aau; 67-63-63, cell 78-26-36, fax 67-63-64; e-mail ranchrevareva@hot mail.com.

RIDING STABLES

At one time the larger hotels provided free bicycles for their guests, but this practice has stopped. Most now charge for them. A bicycle is ideal for shopping or sightseeing and it's worth renting a bike for a round-the-island tour. One word of caution—traffic on the island, especially the corridor from Vaitape to the Matira area, has gotten quite heavy. A number of accidents involving tourists on bicycles have occurred. You should always ride defensively, and avoid riding at night.

BIKING

Bicycles can be rented at **Europcar**, located opposite the quay in Vaitape ~ 67-70-03 and 71-95-28, fax 67-79-95; and **Fare Piti Rent-a-Car**, opposite Fare Piti Wharf (prices are slightly better here) ~ 67-65-28, cell 78-60-28, fax 67-65-29. The **Hibiscus** boutique rents bikes as well. ~ Nunue; 67-72-43.

HIKING

VAITAPE AREA   The **Nunue to Anau** (1.5 miles/2 kilometers) hike will take you across the lower spine of Bora Bora. It can be easily traversed along a 20-minute track beginning at the **Television Transmission Tower**. The hike starts in the Nunue area, 1.5 miles (2 kilometers) from town heading toward Matira. Atop the crest of the steep hill, there is a magnificent panoramic view of Vaitape to the west and Motu Piti Aau and Raiatea and Tahaa to the east. (You will get into trouble if you're caught climbing the TV tower so suppress that urge.) At the top of the trail, turn left toward the TV tower (instead of to the right toward a private home). The overgrown footpath down the hill will take you to the village of Anau. Across the island it's only ten minutes up and ten minutes down, but it can be hot so bring water. If you are doing this on a bike, be sure to walk the bike down the hill. The terminus on the Anau side is at a truck maintenance shop. To find the trailhead on the Nunue side, look for a road that begins next to a double-columned telephone pole. (Near the area is a cluster of boutiques and shops so it is difficult to miss.)

The trek to 2168-foot-high (661-meter) **Mt. Pahia** (5 miles/9 kilometers) can be climbed with the aid of a guide or independently in half a day. The trail itself is very narrow and steep, but can be negotiated by those in good shape. Budget three hours up the mountain and three hours down. The vista at the top is well worth the hike, which passes through dense jungle. The trailhead is in downtown Vaitape. Just across the main street, opposite the pier, look for the basketball court that is adjacent to the *gendarmerie*. The road going toward the mountain that passes the court and Socredo Bank leads to the trail. Take three or four quarts of water per person for the hike and bring good shoes. (Be sure to tell someone of your plans lest you get lost!) If you want the guided tour, contact Ato, the proprietor of Chez Ato. ~ Nunue; 67-77-27.

ANAU VILLAGE TO VAITAPE   Another way to traverse the spine of Bora Bora can be accomplished by taking the track from **Faanui to Vairau Bay** (3 miles/6.4 kilometers) in 40 to 50 minutes. The scenery is spectacular and the trek can be done by people in average physical condition. I recommend that you start on the Faanui side as the trailhead is easier to find at the Faanui church. The easiest thing to do is follow the tire tracks made by the vehicles using the road. To find the trailhead on the Vairau side, look for the power line that crosses the island. Where the sealed road bends to the right, take the unsealed fork to the left. As it climbs up toward the ridge, more forks are encountered—continue to take the left fork. Eventually, the track comes to the ridge top and drops down the other side to Vairau Bay just south of Tuivahora Point. Don't forget to bring water and mosquito repellent.

A short but steep hike to 820-feet (249-meter) **Papoti Ridge** (1 mile/1.6 kilometers) will take you to the old U.S. military radar installation. The 20- to 30-minute trek to the top of the ridge affords a magnificent view of the island's northern end. This is the same horizon the U.S. Navy personnel scanned in search of enemy ships over 50 years ago. To get there, you must go to Taihi Point, the northernmost tip of the island. Look for the trailhead at the point where the coastal road winds up the hill.

▼▼▼▼▼▼▼▼▼▼

Transportation

AIR

The airstrip on Bora Bora is located on the northernmost offshore islet, Motu Mute. The field was constructed by the American military during World War II and necessitates taking a shuttle boat from the airport. There are **Air Tahiti** flights to Bora Bora from Papeete four to six times daily and once daily from Moorea. The flight time is about 50 minutes. Flights also connect Bora Bora with Raiatea, Huahine, Manihi, Maupiti and Rangiroa. There is a free boat service between the airport and the main dock in Vaitape. ~ Airport; 67-53-00.

SEA

Bora Bora is accessible from Papeete via the interisland vessels—the *Vaeanu* (Papeete; 41-25-35) and the *Hawaikinui* (Papeete; 45-23-24, fax 45-24-44). The journey on such a vessel takes roughly 16 hours from Papeete.

Maupiti Express has Tuesday, Wednesday and Friday boat service to Tahaa and Raiatea, leaving Vaitape at 7 a.m. and arriving in Tahaa at 8:15. Fare is 3000 CFP roundtrip. Roundtrip service to Maupiti is available on Thursday and Saturday. Vessels leave Vaitape at 8:30 a.m. and arrive in Maupiti at 10:30 a.m. ~ Phone/fax 67-66-69.

Fare Piti Rent-a-Car has friendly service and free pickup for clients at their hotels. The brochure states "rent a bike, scooter or car, wherever you are, at any time, whenever you want—one phone call away." They have better prices than the other places, but don't have a very large fleet of cars. ~ Vaitape; 67-65-28, fax 67-65-29.

All major hotels can arrange rentals; if you aren't staying at a large hotel, try Fare Piti, **Fredo & Fils Rent-a-Car** (67-70-31) or **Europcar** (67-70-03), both in Vaitape.

CAR RENTALS

Scooters are available in Vaitape at **Europcar** (67-70-03) or **Fare Piti** (67-65-28).

MOTOR SCOOTERS

Le Truck service on the island is sporadic, but trucks generally turn out to meet the arrival of ferries coming from the airport.

PUBLIC TRANSIT

All the hotels have some form of airport transfer service. A general **taxi** service is also available but it's extremely expensive. ~ Vaitape; 67-72-25.

TAXIS

Flightseeing over Bora Bora is possible via **Héli Inter Polynesie.** They will fly you to the top of Mt. Pahia and provide you with the option of hiking down on foot or returning back on the chopper. Héli Inter can also be chartered to fly you to other islands, transfer you to the airport or take you most anywhere else. For more information, call Philippe Morin. ~ Vaitape; phone/fax 67-62-59; e-mail helico-bora@mail.pf.

AERIAL TOURS

Tupuna Mountain Safari offers four-wheel-drive Land Rover tours of the island. It is owned and operated by Dany Leverd, a likeable local fellow who brings to his tour the personal view of a Bora Bora native. As a government surveyor for several years, he possesses an intimate knowledge of the flora and fauna as well as the culture and history of the island. The local angle makes a real difference. Another nice touch is a stopover at his family's estate, which was once a village with a population of 2000. Like Bora Safari, Dany's tour also takes in the old coastal defense gun emplacements, bunkers and other vestiges of the U.S. presence. The tour takes approximately three hours and is conducted both

JEEP TOURS

in the morning and afternoon. Definitely worthwhile, highly recommended. ~ Matira; phone/fax 67-75-06; www.safaribora.com, e-mail tupuna.bora@mail.pf.

Stellio Vaiho of Chez Henriette camping north of Anau runs **Bora 4WD Safari**. He has four vehicles that visit the coastal gun sites and bunkers as well as take in panoramic views of the lagoon and *motu*. ~ Vaitape; phone/fax 67-71-32, cell 21-34-57.

▼▼▼▼▼▼▼▼▼▼▼▼▼▼▼▼▼▼▼▼▼▼

Addresses & Phone Numbers

Doctors ~ Dr. Juen: 67-70-62, speaks English; Dr. Martina
   Roussanaly: 67-66-66
Hospital ~ 67-70-77
Pharmacy ~ 67-70-30
Police Station ~ 67-70-58
Post Office ~ 67-70-74
Town Hall ~ 67-75-19
Visitor information ~ Bora Bora Visitor's Bureau, Vaitape wharf;
   67-76-36; e-mail info-bora-bora@mail.pf

SEVEN

Huahine

One of the most picturesque and geographically diverse islands in the Society Group, Huahine has deep-cleft bays, rugged mountains and long white-sand beaches. Huahine is actually two islands: Huahine Iti and Huahine Nui (Little Huahine and Big Huahine). Although they are two islands, they are part of the same land mass and are connected by an underwater isthmus. (For the convenience of motorists, there's a bridge.)

The islands, located 109 miles northwest of Papeete, are verdant, rugged and scenic enough to make renting a car well worth the expense. The coastal road follows the terrain's steep contours, providing breathtaking views of Bourayne and Maroe bays. Maroe Bay, which is particularly spectacular, was once a volcanic basin and the high mountains framing it are remnants of the caldera wall.

The 5757 residents of Huahine have a long tradition of independence and pride in their Polynesian heritage. According to a Tahitian proverb, "Obstinacy is their diversion." To this day, their sense of dignity (and perhaps a bit of arrogance) is still manifest. The Tahitian independence movement is alive and well here, and you are likely to see the white and blue flag with gold stars that symbolizes Tahitian autonomy. Not surprisingly, you will also hear more Tahitian than French spoken on Huahine.

Perhaps this is why the island seems to entice the visitor who is more interested in absorbing culture than a tan. Huahine has also attracted about 30 long-term American residents, more per capita than anywhere else in French Polynesia.

Huahine is also a magnet for surfers. Although it does not have the type of waves that bring people to Hawaii or Australia, it does have some of the best and most consistent breaks in French Polynesia.

In June and July you may experience the *mara'amu*, a trade wind that blows with tremendous force, bringing downpours and gusts that can wash the sea over the road. During this time long-sleeve shirts or jackets may be necessary in the evening. With this in mind, I recommend staying in Fare and its environs during these months because it is sheltered from the stormy weather. Perhaps the biggest inconvenience on Huahine, from the visitor's standpoint, is the overall lack of public transportation. Occasional *Le Truck* service is available to far-flung communities such as Parea at the opposite end of the island. There are also taxis, but they are very expensive. Another option for travelers lacking an automobile is to stand on the side of the road with their thumbs out. Fortunately, hitchhikers are frequently picked up. Rental bikes are very handy, particularly if you are staying near—but not in—the main community of Fare. You can negotiate a discount on rentals of more than a few days. For a stay of two weeks or more, it may be cheaper to purchase a bicycle for as little as 15,000 CFP. You should have no trouble selling it when you leave. Keep in mind that it is exceptionally easy to get turned around when driving on Huahine. The roads are poorly marked—if they are marked at all. Pay close attention to your map when you come to a fork in the road, or you could end up somewhere other than intended.

Huahine Nui

Huahine's administrative center, maritime hub and largest settlement is Fare, pronounced "Far-ay." The pre-colonial name was *Fare nui atea* ("the great house far away"). Fare has been a port of call for Europeans since the 1830s when whaling ships stopped here following the northward whale migrations in May and June. Whalers regularly exchanged guns for pigs or perhaps traded a few yards of cloth for bananas, yams and sweet potatoes.

In the late 19th century, Fare was a temporary residence for the ruling Pomare family and was later settled by white traders who took Polynesian wives. In the 1920s, Chinese merchants established stores in the area and have remained a fixture ever since. Fronting the shoreline, Fare's main street has the usual complement of Chinese shops and a quay to accommodate copra boats and ferries.

There are several pension-style hotels shaded by huge trees and a number of good budget restaurants. It is a slow-moving town in the heat of the day, disturbed only by an occasional auto kicking up dust, or the sounds of giggling schoolchildren.

Besides fishing and copra production, the main activity on the island seems to be the ceaseless work of keeping the jungle from encroaching on the roads. Crews with weed-eaters can be regularly seen around the island performing this heavy labor.

SIGHTS

A good place to begin your visit of the island is at the main tourist office. Known as the **Manava Visitors' Bureau**, it's open six days a week (closed on Sunday) from 7:30 a.m. to 11:30 a.m. and is located in the same building as the pharmacy (on the south side of the Fare wharf). If the tourist office isn't open, information is available at the airport. ~ Fare; 68-78-81.

In 1997 a stone was placed on the wharf to commemorate the most rigorous canoe race in the South Pacific—the *Hawaiki Nui*.

Huahine

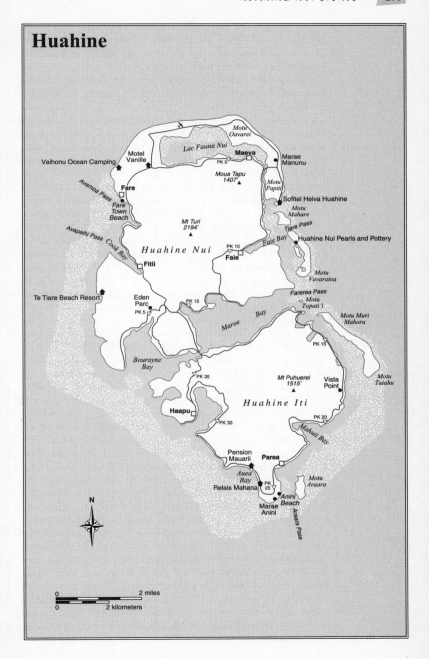

Motu Oavarei

Lac Fauna Nui

Motel Vanille

Vaihonu Ocean Camping

Maeva

Marae Manunu

PK 5

Avamoa Pass

Fare

Moua Tapu 1407'

Motu Papiti

Fare Town Beach

Sofitel Heiva Huahine

Avapeihi Pass   Cook Bay

Mt Turi 2194'

Motu Mahare

Tiare Pass

Huahine Nui

Faie Bay

PK 10

Faie

Huahine Nui Pearls and Pottery

Fitii

Te Tiare Beach Resort

Eden Parc

PK 5

Motu Vavaratea

Farerea Pass

Motu Topati'i

PK 15

Maroe

Bay

Motu Muri Mahora

PK 15

Bourayne Bay

Motu Taiahu

PK 35

Mt Puhuerei 1515'

Vista Point

Huahine Iti

Haapu

PK 30

PK 20

Mahuti Bay

Pension Mauarii

Parea

Auea Bay

PK 25

Motu Araara

Relais Mahana

Anini Beach

N

Marae Anini

Araara Pass

0   2 miles

0   2 kilometers

Every October, international teams gather in Huahine to participate in this three-day ordeal, which covers three segments—
Huahine to Raiatea, Raiatea to Tahaa and the home stretch between Tahaa and Bora Bora.

Another landmark is the **post office**, a bright white, colonial-
style edifice on the road heading out of Fare on the north end. ~
68-82-70.

Fare is separated from **Maeva**, the other major community on
Huahine Nui, by about six kilometers of road tracing the northern coast of the island. The road faces a bay known as **Lac Fauna
Nui**, which is enclosed by a huge *motu* the shape of an upside-down
salad bowl. Though Fauna Nui is called a lake, it's actually a bay
with an inlet so narrow you can toss a stone across it. (The mouth
of this inlet is opposite the Sofitel Heiva Huahine.) Unfortunately,
Lac Fauna Nui is heavily polluted due to pesticide runoff. Swimming is not recommended.

In ancient times, Huahine was a center of Polynesian culture
and ruled by a centralized government. This differed from the war-
ring tribes found on most of the other islands. Huahine is laden
with archaeological artifacts and is sometimes referred to as an
open-air museum. Most of the important archaeological sites on
the island are no more than five kilometers from Fare in the Maeva
area. In that community alone there are 16 restored *marae*. At the
end of 1999 some additional *marae* were restored by the archaeology department from Punaauia (in Tahiti). The majority are ancestral shrines of local chiefs. The stone slabs of these ancient temples jut out on the landscape, and are eerily reminiscent of the
ruins of Stonehenge. In the nearby lagoon, rich in crab and other
sea life, are nine ancient fish traps constructed from stone, some of
which have been rebuilt and are in use today. (See the "Hiking"
section at the end of this chapter for a description of these sites.)

HIDDEN ►   Above Maeva village on Matairea Hill is **Matairea-rahi**. This
is the second-most important temple in French Polynesia. Here
you can find foundations of priests' and chiefs' homes and a huge
fortification wall guarding the mountain sanctuary from sea
raiders. (See the "Hiking" section at the end of this chapter.) A
detailed map of the site is available at the Fare Pote'e museum.

Opposite Maeva, just across the bridge, is **Marae Manunu**, a
classic *marae* reconstructed originally by American archaeologist
Kenneth Emory in 1933. It is approximately 100 feet (30 meters)
in length, constructed in a rectangular manner resembling a shoe
box. Around the perimeter of the structure are huge basalt
tablets approximately eight feet (2.5 meters) tall and up to six feet
(almost two meters) wide, looking like gravestones. Unfortunately,
many of the slabs are now covered with graffiti. Near the old
temple is a **monument** to the 1846 Battle of Maeva. The monument is marked by seven cannons and commemorates the un-

equivocal French rule over Eastern Polynesia, even though con-
stitutionally the region was only a protectorate until formal annexation in 1880.

A cyclone destroyed one of the great landmarks of Maeva,
the old waterfront **Fare Pote'e** (meeting house), in 1998. It has
been rebuilt and opened in 2002 as the **Fare Pote'e museum and
interpretive center**. Fashioned after a traditional Polynesian king's
house, Fare Pote'e—which translates as "oval house"—is built
with massive beams of traditionally hewn wood and contains no
corners: The walls are rounded where they meet. Shoes are not
permitted inside, as the spacious floor is covered with traditional
matting woven from *pandanus* leaves. The self-serve center features artifacts, historical photographs, informational displays,
modern reconstructions and free maps of the nearby *marae* sites.

Flanking the Fare Pote'e museum and throughout the vicinity are numerous 16th-century **lakeside marae**. Here the individual chiefs worshiped their ancestors at their respective temples.
Heading south along the coastal road you will see stones piled in
a "V" shape inside the lagoon, an area particularly rich in fish,

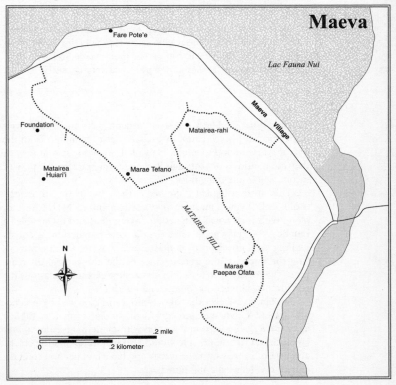

A Hike through the Past

In 1984, excavators found that Matairea Hill was occupied from A.D. 1450 to A.D. 1700. In efforts to uncover the past, they revealed a new historical trail that begins at the shore and goes to Marae Tefano: the Shoreline to Matairea Temple Complex trail (1.5 miles/2 kilometers). The trail begins at the fortification wall (built in 1846 when the French marines attacked Maeva) and continues up Te Ana hill. The trailhead is located a few minutes' walk west of Fare Pote'e in the direction of Fare.

ROYAL REMAINS   Just a few steps after the trail begins is a large stone-paved area that was part of a round-ended house foundation that most likely belonged to a supreme chief. Interestingly, the front terrace with the large paved area is oriented inland, facing the sacred mountain of Moua Tapu. The trail goes through the old fortification wall that protected residents from invaders from Bora Bora.

MATAIREA HUIARI'I COMPLEX   Just up the trail, the Matairea Huiari'i complex was created by families who occupied the entire inland slope of the hill. Each residential unit had one or more *marae*. To have a density of so many chiefly families in one place was very unusual.

crab and other sea life. These stone structures are ancient **fish weir traps** that have been rebuilt by archaeologist Dr. Sinoto from the Bishop Museum in Honolulu, Hawaii. They work as well now as they did hundreds of years ago. Fish enter the traps by the flow of incoming and outgoing tides.

This archaeological complex is the core of the historical/ecological "living" museum that was organized by Dr. Sinoto, along with the French Polynesian government and the people of Huahine. With the cooperation of the local population, scientists and the local government, a master plan has been created to ensure the integrity and maintenance of the archaeological treasures. The master plan also provides zoning recommendations for restaurants, hotels and commercial buildings.

Dr. Sinoto believes that agriculture can be revived by practicing age-old Polynesian ecology methodologies (such as taboos against overfishing) in combination with modern agricultural and aquacultural techniques. He would also like to rebuild the chiefs' and priests' houses near the *marae* and have families and caretakers occupy them on a full-time basis.

MARAE TEFANO   Nearby, Marae Tefano is an impressive sight. Its *ahu* is huge and the temple basks in the shade of a huge banyan tree, probably planted there around the time that the *marae* was constructed.

MATAIREA-RAHI   The most significant *marae* on the hill is Matairea-rahi, just a few minutes from Marae Tefano. It was the most important temple in the Society Islands prior to the building of Taputapuatea in Raiatea. According to oral tradition, when Taputapuatea was about to be built, stones from Matairea-rahi were transported to the building site to ensure that the new temple would retain the old temple's *mana* (power). Matairea-rahi consists of two structures: in the first, nine upright stones represent ten districts—the tenth stone is missing. There are also stone posts that serve as intermediaries to the gods. In the rear is an **ahu** (raised platform), which was a throne for the gods. Below the *ahu* is a lower platform where sacrifices—some human—were placed. On the other structure stood a house built on posts where the images of the gods were kept. The house was actually seen in 1818 by Reverend William Ellis, a missionary who saw a building perched on stilts guarded day and night by men to protect the holy images inside. It's a 45-minute walk back to Fare Pote'e from here. If you'd like to explore more archaeological sites in the area, see "Hiking."

An obligatory stop in Huahine, **Eden Parc** is found about five ◄ HIDDEN kilometers south on the road heading out of Fare. Owned by a Frenchman and his Tahitian wife, this is an organic farm where you will see taro, bananas and other Polynesian staples under cultivation. Take the self-guided botanical garden tour, where you'll find plants along with English-language descriptions of their use. The gift shop carries jams and fruit products—nice gifts to take home. You may take a short walk, weather permitting, up the hillside for beautiful views of the coastline. To find Eden Parc, head south out of Fare and look for the sign at a turnoff on the right. Its entry is about a kilometer down from the turnoff. Closed Sunday and during bad weather. Admission (unless you buy a juice—300 CFP—or something from the shop). ~ Fare; 68-86-58, fax 68-84-04; www.edenparc.org.

Just a few kilometers south of the Eden Parc turnoff is the road to the **Ariiura Paradise Garden of Revival and Conservation,** run by the same people who operate Ariiura Campground. They offer a tour, the emphasis of which is strictly ethnobotany— the traditional uses of plants as medicine. The garden is just northwest of the bridge connecting Huahine Nui and Huahine Iti. You won't see the sign coming from Fare, but if you make a U-turn just before crossing the bridge to Huahine Iti, you should see it. Take a right turn onto the dirt road just before the bridge. Open Sunday through Friday 9 a.m.–3 p.m. and Saturday 9 a.m.–noon. ~ Fare; 68-85-20.

LODGING

Le Petite Ferme, known primarily as a riding stable, has budget accommodations available. The facilities, run by a friendly French family, are simple and pleasant. In addition to basic rooms and dorm beds, there's a family bungalow with kitchen and private bath. Naturally, if you are a horse enthusiast this would be an ideal place to hunker down. Horseback excursions are offered to the beach, mountains and around the island. Rates are reduced if you stay more than one day, and breakfast is included in the price. It is located halfway between Fare and the airport and free airport transfers are available. ~ Fare; phone/fax 68-82-98; e-mail lapetiteferme@mail.pf. BUDGET.

HIDDEN ►

Motel Vanille is located at the intersection of the airport road with the main road north of Fare. There are six comfortable Polynesian-style bungalows, with baths and screens, and a pool. Rooms may be rented separately from meals; however, demi- and full *pension* are available with family-style meals. Breakfast is served on individual tables, and dinner on a large family-style table so that all the guests can dine together. There is some traffic on the nearby frontage road, but things quiet down in the evening. Bicycles and transfers are free for guests. Minimal English is spoken, so bring along your dictionary. Highly recommended. Two-night minimum stay. ~ Fare; phone/fax 68-71-77; www.motelvanille.com, e-mail yvesmotelvani@hotmail.com. MODERATE.

Most of the island's accommodations and archaeological sites are at the north end of Huahine Nui in the Fare and Maeva area. If you are staying at a Fare accommodation, it's easy to see the old Polynesian temples in the Maeva region on foot or by bicycle.

Vaihonu Ocean Camping rates a strong recommendation for backpackers wanting a dorm close to town. This lodging/camping facility is on the ocean and is an easy bike ride to Fare. In addition to the budget lodging, a large two-story waterfront house sleeps up to six people. It is comfortable and nicely decorated, with two bedroom areas, fans, TV, linens, full kitchen and lanai. The Tahitian owner, Etienne (who handily speaks English, Spanish and French), has created a place with local style. People have very mixed reactions to Etienne; he can be a bit condescending and sarcastic to visitors. The spacious six-bed dorm has fans and mosquito nets, linens, three bathrooms and a full kitchen. The camping area has shade trees and shares bathroom and kitchen facilities with the dorm. Prices are negotiable for longer stays; Etienne rents and lends bikes and operates four-wheel-drive tours around the island. Free airport transfers are provided. To find the place, turn left at the unpaved road just past La Petite Ferme, then left again at the end. ~ Fare; 68-87-33; fax 68-77-57; e-mail vaihonu@ mail.pf. BUDGET TO MODERATE.

Pension **Chez Mama Roro** offers two bungalows, each with a double bed and two singles. Each comes with a self-contained kitchen, private bath with hot water, ceiling fan and TV. Mama Roro offers free transfers and has bicycles for rent. ~ Located just behind Pension Vaihonu, Fare; phone/fax 68-84-82. BUDGET TO MODERATE.

Fare Maeva consists of ten modern bungalows, eight with double beds. Two *fare* have two rooms with one double bed each, a lounge, dining area, self-contained kitchen and (cold water) bath. Ten rooms with private baths are also available in a concrete structure. The back of the property overlooks the ocean and includes a swimming pool, covered patio and small restaurant. A good public beach is within walking distance at the (closed) Bali Hai Hotel. Fare Maeva is located just outside Fare. To get there, turn left at the unpaved road just past La Petite Ferme and continue to the ocean. ~ Fare; 68-75-53, fax 68-70-68; www.fare-maeva.com, e-mail faremaeva@mail.pf. MODERATE.

Chez Ella has two houses, each with two rooms, a lounge, kitchen, shared bath, terrace and TV. The houses can accommodate up to six people. Chez Ella also offers a cottage that can sleep up to ten people and features a large mezzanine. A lounge with a TV, a self-contained kitchen, bath, terrace and also a washing machine are included. No credit cards. ~ Located next to the Motel Vanille, Fare; phone/fax 68-73-07, cell 77-92-78; e-mail chezellahuahine@yahoo.fr. MODERATE.

Known for its fine cooking, **Pension Enite** has eight clean rooms surrounded by well-kept gardens. Rooms have fans, a common bathroom and hot water. There is also a living room with a television. Meals are served in an open-air restaurant/bar directly on the beach. The minimum stay is two nights. Guests must have a *demi*-pension—tariff includes breakfast and dinner. Food is excellent and, to quote a resident, it's "one of the best pensions on Huahine." Discounted rates are offered for children. Pension Enite is a few steps east of the dock on the sea side. ~ Fare; phone/fax 68-82-37, cell 73-05-07. MODERATE.

◄ HIDDEN

Highly recommended for backpackers and budget travelers, and also popular with locals, is **Chez Guynette**. Also known as Club Bed, this lodging has seven guest rooms, each with electric fan, private (cold water) bath, and a dorm with eight bunk beds and a communal bath. Rooms are decorated with colorful and whimsical designs of birds, animals and geometric shapes and each dorm guest gets one bunk for sleeping and one for storing belongings. There is a strict lights-off policy (the lights are on a timer) at 10 p.m. in the dorm and common areas. Screens on the bedroom windows translate into mosquito-free sleep. If you need anything that is not standard, such as a reading lamp, just ask the owners, Moe and Marty Tamahahe (he's from Huahine, she's from the U.S.), and they will provide it. If you stay more than one night, the rates go down. (BYO towels, but Chez Guynette provides sheets.) The owners have put a lot into renovations and the pension is impeccably clean, quiet and pleasant. The inexpensive restaurant is also first rate. You won't go wrong staying here, especially if you only have a few days to spend on the island. Chez Guynette is located on the waterfront downtown. ~ Fare; phone/ fax 68-83-75; www.iaorana-huahine.com, e-mail chezguynette@ mail.pf. BUDGET.

Chez Henriette, situated on a pebble-strewn beach, is a family-run business that has grown slowly and steadily. The six bungalows in a row on the beach create a picture of a small local business success. Each unit was built in consecutive order and the newest ones are bigger and more substantial than the previously built ones. They are also the best, though they are located behind the older ones and are closer to the road. The older units have recently been repaired, and all of the units now have metal roofs and window screens. The bungalows near the water are rustic, and the interiors are decorated with fabric curtains and Tahitian quilts on the beds. There are kitchenettes in each unit, but bathroom facilities are shared. The owners are friendly, and will be even more so if you make an effort to speak Tahitian. Chez Henriette is about four kilometers (a 20-minute walk) from Fare on the opposite side of the bay from town. No credit cards. ~ Fare; phone/ fax 68-83-71; www.iaorana-huahine.com. BUDGET TO MODERATE.

HIDDEN ►   **Pension Poetaina** is a clean, outrageously ornate, three-story pension with a pool. There are verandas on every floor of this bright, white edifice, and cement replicas of Greek urns adorn the ground floor. (The family that owns the property lives next door in a very modest Tahitian home.) The rooms are spacious and clean. Each floor has a large sitting area and a separate modern kitchen. All amenities in the kitchen and bathrooms feel Western. The price seems a bit on the high side for what you get. Some rooms include private (hot water) bath, while smaller rooms share a communal bath. However, if you want to be close to Fare, with all your creature comforts, it's an acceptable choice. Tours, picnics, fishing and other activities are available. A deposit is necessary for a reservation. Children under 12 years are half price. Pension Poetaina is located in the Fare district, one kilometer south of the dock and three kilometers south of the airport. ~ Fare; phone/fax 68-89-49, cell 78-86-39; e-mail pensionpoet aina@mail.pf. MODERATE.

Pouvanaa a Oopa—
Modern Tahitian Hero

Huahine is the birthplace of Pouvanaa a Oopa, the greatest 20th-century French Polynesian leader. A decorated World War I veteran, Pouvanaa was the son of a Danish sailor and a Polynesian woman. In 1947, he was jailed by the French for advocating Polynesian veterans' rights, and became the spokesperson for the Tahitian independence movement. Blessed with charismatic oratorical skills, and well versed in the Bible, Pouvanaa established himself as the most powerful politician in the French Polynesian Territorial Assembly. Known as Metua—"beloved father to the Tahitians"—he lambasted the colonial system for its treatment of Polynesians as second-class citizens and fought for legislative reforms that would grant Polynesians greater autonomy.

At the zenith of his power, Pouvanaa was convicted of conspiracy in a plot to burn down Papeete and was sent to the notorious Baumette Prison in Marseilles. At the age of 64 he was sentenced to eight years of solitary confinement and banished from Polynesia for another 15 years. Ten years later he was pardoned for the crime many felt he did not commit, and he returned to Tahiti. Eventually he went back into politics and again served in the Territorial Assembly. He died in 1976.

Pension Meri consists of three concrete houses somewhat akin to a condo in Hawaii or Florida. The pension includes a living room, television, kitchen, private (hot water) bath and a terrace. A washing machine is at your disposal, as are several canoes. With all the amenities, it is perhaps best suited for long-term guests. The whole house is available for rent as well. Pension Meri is also rather close to the road, which may make it noisy. I found it hard to find. It is located on the outskirts of Fare, near the sea, about two kilometers south of town. There is a three-day minimum stay required. ~ Fare; 68-82-44, 79-56-11, fax 68-85-96. MODERATE.

The **Bellevue**, situated on a bluff with a gorgeous view of the surrounding bays and hills, was one of the island's better mid-range hotels in its heyday. Sadly, it has fallen into decline and is now mostly bereft of ambiance. The halls and walls of the main building are completely bare; sitting areas lack furniture, and the restaurant—whose giant picture windows command a stunning view of the bay—showed no hint of guests in the huge, undecorated building. Each of the property's ten bungalows has screened windows, double bed, bathroom, terrace and private parking. There are also eight rooms with private baths and balconies located upstairs in a large building with tile floors. These rooms are basic and clean, if somewhat depressing. Meals are available on request, and the food is reported to be good. The Bellevue is five kilometers south of Fare. ~ Fare; 68-82-76, fax 68-85-35. MODERATE.

> If you need to launder clothing, a cleaner is located on Immeuble Rine, across the street from the Mobile station. Cost per load is determined by weight: ten pounds will cost you roughly 1000 CFP to wash, and another 1300 to dry.

Accessible only by boat and definitely off the beaten track, the luxurious **Te Tiare Beach Resort** epitomizes barefoot elegance. All 41 over-water, beach and garden bungalows are very spacious—among the largest we've seen. Each has a terrace with a sheltered space enclosing lounge chairs that invite you to relax, and an outside shower that beckons you to bathe beneath the stars. The Polynesian-style bungalows offer spacious bathrooms (some with jacuzzis), a walk-in closet, large living rooms and bedrooms, TV, minibar, fan and air conditioning. The main building, a combination restaurant/lobby/bar/boutique, is situated in a huge *fare pote'e* (traditional meetinghouse) with a spectacular roof. Other nice touches include direct access to the lagoon from the over-water bungalows and the fact that all the buildings face west so as to capture the spectacular sunsets. A small private beach is tucked away on the nearby lagoon. The food here is excellent—the hotel has one of the best chefs in the country. Free activities include snorkeling, canoeing and kayaking. The hotel offers free hourly transportation by boat to Fare, a ten-minute ride. Look for the transfer station next door to the *gendarmerie*. ~ Fare; 60-60-50, fax 60-60-51; www.pearlresorts.com, e-mail raina.plan tier@spmhotels.pf. ULTRA-DELUXE.

On the other side of Huahini Nui, in the village of Faie, is a new pension called **Te Nahe To'e To'e**. Built originally as a family home, To'e To'e is constructed entirely from rough-hewn coconut palms, *pandanus* leaves, bamboo and other local materials. The place has a magical feel to it, and the airy, informal construction makes it all the more welcoming. The bottom floor, covered in crushed coral, is supported by posts and has no interior walls or doors. Furniture and plants partition the space into separate areas for sitting, dining, cooking, etc. The whole house is decorated with keepsakes of the owners, Armelle and Philippe, making it feel cozy and familiar. Two upstairs lofts hold double beds with mosquito nets, bookshelves and fans. A third, larger loft has two double beds with three singles for dorm-style accommodations. Lying in bed under a peaked roof as rain falls on the *pandanus* thatch feels a lot like being in a treehouse. The bathroom has tropical plants, natural light and a hot-water shower, which drains into the coral floor (wear sandals!). Guests are free to use the kitchen, which includes a five-burner gas stove with oven. Baguettes, brewed coffee and chilled water are available anytime. Out the back, at the water's edge, is a covered patio with two giant slab tables—the perfect spot to unwind in the evening. To'e To'e is an authentic treasure. ~ Faie; 68-71-43; e-mail armellehua hine@yahoo.pf. BUDGET.

The **Sofitel Heiva Huahine** is not far from Maeva on the tip of Motu Papiti on the northeast corner of the island. This resort has one of the most spectacular settings in the Society Islands— surrounded by a white-sand beach with gorgeous views of the mountains and the lagoon. The property, which has a swimming pool, occupies several acres of manicured grounds filled with flowering plants and towering coconut palms. There are over-the-water bungalows, which command stunning vistas of the lagoon, and a number of thatch-roofed beachfront bungalows. Rooms are spacious, with verandas facing the sea. Snorkeling offshore is good, but be careful—there is a plethora of sea urchins and the current is often strong. Activities arranged through the hotel often involve a hefty commission that is tacked on to your charges. For example, a two-hour horseback ride will cost you 30 percent more if you have the hotel arrange it for you. Unfortunately, the hotel is isolated, making it difficult and expensive to get about. Roundtrip airport transfers are also pricey—something that isn't discussed before you step in the van. It's almost cheaper to rent a car. In general, this hotel is overpriced and no longer a luxury property, even though it's priced like one. ~ Maeva; 60-61-60, fax 68-85-25, or 800-221-4542 in the U.S.; www.sofi

tel.com, e-mail reservation_tahiti@accor-hotels.com. ULTRA-
DELUXE.

Those interested in renting a house should consider **Villas
Bougainville** on the north coast of Maroe Bay. Here Raphael
Matapo provides four villas and two bungalows. Three-room villas will accommodate up to six people, two-room units house up
to five people and the bungalows will take up to three. The houses
have self-contained kitchens and are equipped with amenities such
as TVs and washing machines. There's even a car and a boat at
your disposal. Villas Bougainville is ideal for a large party or a
family. A deposit is required on arrival. ~ Maroe Bay; phone/fax
68-81-59, cell 79-70-59; e-mail bougainville@mail.pf. DELUXE.

A similar set-up, also on Maroe Bay, is offered by Jean Rol-
land, who calls his place **Villas Standing**. You can rent any of the
three self-contained villas or the bungalow with or without use
of a car. The villas hold between four and six people each, while
the bungalow accommodates two. A deposit is required. Roundtrip transfers are included. ~ Maroe Bay; 82-49-65, cell 78-09-36,
fax 85-47-69; www.villas-standing.pf, e-mail jeanrolland@
mail.pf. DELUXE.

DINING   The restaurant situation in Fare is very good indeed. There's a
profusion of excellent inexpensive and mid-range eateries, and
good food can be found in most of the hotels as well.

Dining hours on the island may be erratic. People may suddenly close up shop for vacations or public holidays.

Consider stopping along the dock at one of the many **roulottes**
that appear at regular hours as well as when boats come in. Some
of these eateries on wheels are better than others. You can usually
tell which is the right one for you by sniffing the aromas as you
pass by. Two *roulottes* are usually on the wharf every night until
about 10 p.m. The white pastry truck that parks at the wharf every
morning serves tasty bakery items, delicious burgers and a potent
espresso. (If you don't like egg salad on your burger, tell them to
hold the egg.) They also serve homemade ice cream. **Café Titi'a**
is on the wharf every day for the lunch hour with notable hamburgers, cheeseburgers and fish burgers. There is also a *roulotte*
that sells crêpes, waffles and mouth-watering ice cream every
afternoon until sundown. The *roulottes* by the wharf are terrific
places to get inexpensive meals and enjoy the evening trade breezes.
You can always get your morning coffee along with an omelette
sandwich there, too.

HIDDEN ►   On the northern end of Fare is **Restaurant Tiare Tipanier**,
which has fine food, an extensive menu and good service.
Americans will be happy to see that hamburgers and pizza are
on the menu. Dinners include fish (considered their house specialty), chicken and beef. There is a fixed-price dinner (appetizer,

entrée, wine, dessert and coffee) at a reasonable cost. Ice cream and pastries are also served, and they are among the best on the island. The setting is pleasant—there are some tables outside—but unlike the other Fare eateries it is not on the water. Closed Sunday, and Monday until dinner. ~ Fare; 68-80-52. MODERATE.

Though not strictly a restaurant, **Pension Enite** will serve dinner *sur command*, even when you are not a guest. The home-style cuisine is a French/Tahitian blend that usually includes seafood. The food is first rate, though a bit pricey. ~ Fare; 68-82-37. DELUXE.

Te Marara, just down the street from Enite, has fine French and local food, good service and a cozy waterfront setting that's hard to beat. The tasty daily specials (which include grilled fish, chicken and steak) are worth trying, and the tuna sashimi is fantastic. A mix of tourists and locals provide an interesting ambience. ~ Fare; 68-70-81. MODERATE.

> If you have a rental car and would like to use the beach at the Sofitel Heiva Huahine but are not a guest, park in the lot next to bungalow number 37.

Chez Guynette offers items such as sandwiches and a wonderful chef's salad. (Full dinners are not served.) Drinks in the afternoon are accompanied by free popcorn. Along with the copious and inexpensive food, one of the best things about Chez Guynette is the camaraderie among the guests. This is no doubt fostered by the environment that the proprietors have created. The location, particularly the front terrace that faces the dock and sea, provides a leisurely atmosphere for guests and locals to sit and chat. What more can you ask for? ~ Fare; 68-83-75. BUDGET.

Snack Shop Salad is a fast-food eatery with take-away plates of standard fare including *poisson cru*. Gerard, the owner, also runs the only jewelry store in town, one block down the street. Snack Shop Salad is located next to the tourist office. ~ Fare; 68-71-09. BUDGET.

Les Dauphins specializes in seafood. They also sometimes feature live entertainment on the weekend. It's located next to the post office. ~ Fare; 68-78-54. BUDGET TO MODERATE.

Restaurant Tehina at the Fare Maeva pension is open for breakfast, lunch and dinner. The food is reportedly good. ~ Fare; 68-75-53. MODERATE.

◄ HIDDEN

Open daily, **Fare Pizza**'s wood-burning stove churns out excellent food with a local twist. The three-cheese pizza is a good vegetarian choice or you might sample the seafood combination. It's located just past the *gendarmerie* on the south side of town (look for the sign). ~ Fare; 60-60-01. BUDGET.

The restaurant at **Eden Parc** prepares meals with organic products from the farm. A good choice for a light meal would be the vegetarian Exotic Lunch, which consists of a large salad of the farm's produce, bananas flambé with coconut milk, and a vanilla coffee. The other choices offered include seafood. ~ Fare; 68-86-58. BUDGET.

In addition to Faie Glaces ice cream, the **Super Fare Nui** grocery store in the center of town also has baguette sandwiches and inexpensive pre-made plates of local food. Great when you're on the go. ~ Fare; 68-84-68. BUDGET.

The restaurant at the **Te Tiare Beach Resort** is only a ten-minute boat ride from Fare. A free hourly shuttle allows everybody to come and enjoy the spectacular French cuisine at this secluded hotel. The chef, Thierry (known as "Bocuse"), is famous locally for his seafood dishes. ~ 60-60-50. DELUXE TO ULTRA-DELUXE.

The **Sofitel Heiva Huahine** on the tip of Motu Papiti offers a luxurious setting for their fine cuisine. The lobby restaurant/bar utilizes local building materials and mimics traditional Polynesian motifs with ample displays of tapa cloth and sennit (coconut fiber), which is wrapped around beams and support structures. The restaurant area is a cavernous open-air structure. Its focal point, a central podium for dance performances, is surrounded by tables. Bird of paradise, ginger and hibiscus fill the restaurant with a sweet fragrance. The food is first class and I would highly recommend the seafood buffet. Be sure and try *tuai*, a small clam found in the immediate vicinity and prepared in broth. ~ Maeva; 60-61-60. DELUXE TO ULTRA-DELUXE.

Chez Piera, operated by a friendly local family, is located opposite Marae Manunu in Maeva. A small eatery with a delicious plate lunch, they serve *poulet citron* (lemon chicken), chow mein and *maa tinito* (a local concoction of beans, meat and vegetables) along with fresh cooled coconut juice to drink. You have the option of eating at nearby tables or taking the food to the beach. Closed Sunday. ~ Maeva. BUDGET.

HIDDEN ►   **Faie Glaces**, located several kilometers outside of Faie Village on the mountain side of the road, is marked by a sign. Here they serve wonderful homemade ice cream in a parlor setting. Many of the icy-sweet concoctions incorporate local fruit—banana, mango, soursop and coconut. Faie Glaces is an obligatory stop after feeding the eels or on a round-the-island car trip. Their ice cream is also available in the Super Fare Nui market in town. ~ Faie; 68-87-95. BUDGET.

GROCERIES   Bread is baked daily behind the Wing Kong Store on the waterfront—but don't go there to purchase bread because it's strictly where it's made, not sold. Fresh bread is, however, available at virtually all the grocery stores in town seven days a week. (In Fare you can buy bread at 6 a.m.) If you visit the markets early enough you'll also be able to pick up *pain au chocolat* and croissants. No alcohol is sold anywhere on the island on Sunday.

Food shopping is best done at **Super Fare Nui**, located in the center of town. This store is the island's hub of commercial activity. The store is open until about 10 a.m. on Sunday, and from 6 a.m. to 5 p.m. the rest of the week. It closes for lunch from noon to 2 p.m. daily. ~ Fare; 68-84-68.

The other large store in Fare, **Taahitini**, south of the main center of town just past the police station, has a friendly staff, but its shelves tend to be depressingly bare. It's open until 7 p.m. each evening, and on Sunday from 6 a.m. to noon and 4 p.m. to 7 p.m.—when other stores in Fare are closed. ~ Fare; 68-89-42.

I believe Huahine's adherence to Polynesian culture has attracted some of the best artists in French Polynesia. I would even venture to say there are more talented artists on this island than anywhere else in the South Pacific. This is obviously a good thing for those seeking gifts and souvenirs in the island's art galleries.

SHOPPING

Gallery Puvaivai, run by Joe and Frederique Perrone, is next door to Snack Bar Temarara. The gallery is adorned with original paintings and one-of-a-kind, hand-printed pareu on the walls. The owners also stock locally cultivated black pearls at bargain prices. Other interesting items are the locally crafted fishhooks. Although Joe and Frederique are from the U.S. and France, their art reflects the many years they have lived on Huahine, and the love and appreciation they have for Polynesian culture. They are exceptionally friendly and knowledgeable. ~ Fare; 68-70-09.

Across from the wharf, **Boutique Rima's Te Niu Tane** and **Boutique Vahine Mod** are next door to each other and have beautiful selections of local crafts, pottery, textiles and clothing, all at reasonable prices. ~ Fare.

Next door to the Banque de Tahiti is **Aux Trois Bonheur**, a clothing and fabric store with a wonderful selection of pareos at good prices.

Exotica has the best souvenirs in town with a fine selection of Gauguin prints, clothes, jewelry, handicrafts and pareos start-

AUTHOR FAVORITE

If you spend any time in Fare, you're likely to see a man who has the left side of his face and body completely tattooed. That's George, the friendly neighborhood tattoo artist who operates **Tihoti Tahtau**. George speaks impeccable English and is the one to seek if you're considering a lasting souvenir of your time on the islands. All his designs are originals, based on traditional Marquesan motifs. He has a steady and light hand, and he practices proper sterilization techniques. Besides his freehand masterpieces, he also does amazing cover-up work. Highly recommended. As his sign says: "*surrendez vous*." ~ Near the airport turnoff, Fare; 68-77-27; e-mail tihotitatau@yahoo.com.

ing at 500 CFP (US$50). ~ Fare; 68-72-86; e-mail exotic_pac@
yahoo.fr.

For information or to purchase film, postcards or a souvenir
be sure to visit Jojo located next to Chez Guynette on the waterfront. In addition to running his small souvenir store, Jojo rents
bicycles, offers e-mail and internet service, represents Europcar,
and is a knowledgeable source of information on the area. ~
Fare; 68-89-16.

Huahine Nui Pearls and Pottery is the only pearl farm in
Huahine, located in the lagoon adjacent to Motu Vavaratea, off
the east coast of Huahine Nui. They offer free tours (via boat) to
visit the farm for an informative lecture/demonstration on black
pearl cultivation. In the floating boutique a variety of black pearls
and handmade pottery (from famed local potter Peter Owens) are
for sale. Peter, considered perhaps the finest potter in French Polynesia, exhibits his wares twice a year at the posh Winkler Gallery
in Papeete. Closed Sunday. ~ Fare; 78-30-20; www.huahinepearl
farm.com.

Super Fare Nui, a grocery store, also sells the New Zealand
edition of *Time* magazine. ~ Fare; 68-84-68.

In the **thatch-roofed stalls** across the street from Super Fare
Nui, vendors sell fruit, vegetables, fish and handicrafts. Usually
open daily.

Boutique Blanche Bellais in Maeva has quality clothing and
locally made *tifaifai*-style quilts at reasonable prices. Across the
street from the shop is the studio where the *tifaifai* are made. ~
Maeva; 68-83-97.

Vanilla and locally made *monoi* oil scented with ylang-ylang,
a fragrant flower, are sold informally at small stands along the
road or in the front yards of homes in the Maeva area.

INTERNET
ACCESS

You can check e-mail and surf the web at **Ao Api–New World**,
located above Snack Shop Salad in downtown Fare. Access costs
30 CFP per minute. This is also the place to make photocopies,
send faxes, print documents and burn CDs. Access is by the stairs
at the back of the building. Closed weekends. ~ Fare; 68-70-99.

Internet access is also available at **Jojo** boutique. ~ Fare; 68-
89-16.

NIGHTLIFE

Local bands occasionally entertain on weekend nights at the
restaurant/bar **Les Dauphins** next to the post office in Fare. ~
Fare; 68-78-54.

Sofitel Heiva Huahine has regular happy hours from 5 to 6
p.m. and 9 to 10 p.m. Dance revues are performed here regularly
on weekend evenings. ~ Maeva; 60-61-60.

Fundraisers, which usually entail dancing and food, are typically advertised with placards posted on walls and bulletin

boards around town. They're a great way to meet locals. If you're looking for action at night, follow the sounds of music.

FARE TOWN BEACH 🏊 🛶 🚶 In Fare you can find a white-sand beach literally after stepping off the tarmac or dock. The shoreline near the pier is an excellent beach with adequate shade. It's a five-minute walk north of town along the shore, or ten minutes on the main road.

MOTU PAPITI BEACH On Motu Papiti, in the archaeological zone, is a long white-sand beach extending from Marae Manunu down to Sofitel Heiva Huahine. Shaded by coconut palms, it's perfect for a stroll and for beachcombing. However, the coral and shallow water make swimming or snorkeling iffy. Note that the farther you walk from the hotel the less people you will find. ~ Located five kilometers east of Fare.

SOFITEL BEACH 🏊 The long stretch of white-sand beach at the Sofitel Heiva Huahine is one of the choice spots on the island. The beach slopes gently into clear turquoise waters and is superb for swimming. It's open to the public, but don't use the hotel's beach chairs or other furniture. You can snorkel offshore but there are quite a few sea urchins in the area. ~ To get there simply walk or drive to Maeva, and cross the bridge that connects the *motu* with the mainland and continue south.

MOTU TOPATI'I 🏊 🛶 With an archetypal South Pacific setting of fine white-sand and coconut palms, Motu Topati'i is a wonderful place to laze the day away. Located at the foot of Maroe Bay, the swimming is wonderful. Bring your snorkeling equipment, for the water is clear and there are a number of reef fish to be spotted. The area is used by the Sofitel hotel for their *motu*

ARCHAEOLOGICAL SLEUTHS

Those interested in following up on the research in Huahine conducted by the venerable Yosihiko H. Sinoto of the Bishop Museum should look for:
- "Report on the Preliminary Excavation of an Early Habitation Site on Huahine, Society Islands" in *Journal de la Société des Oceanistes* XXXI (1974): 143–86.
- "Excavations on Huahine, French Polynesia" in *Pacific Studies* 3 (1979): 1.
- "The Huahine Excavation: Discovery of an Ancient Polynesian Canoe" in *Archeology* 36/2 (1983): 10–15.
- "Archeological Excavations of the Vaito'otia and Fa'ahia Sites on Huahine Island, French Polynesia" in *National Geographic Society Research Reports* 15 (1983): 583–99.

excursions so you might not be alone. ~ To get there you'll have to hire a local boat crew or go as part of an organized excursion with a hotel.

Huahine Iti

Huahine Iti lies to the south of Huahine Nui and is connected by an underwater isthmus (as well as a manmade bridge). Like the northern portion of the island (Huahine Nui), the southern (Huahine Iti) side is verdant and rugged. On the western side of the isthmus is Bourayne Bay. On the opposite side, you'll find Maroe Bay, which dominates the north coast. Both bays are spectacular dark blue bodies of water that shimmer in the tropical sun. Along the shoreline, where the sea is shallow, the color of water is light turquoise. These inlets are popular with sailboats and they can often be seen anchored offshore. Along the coastline there are also several striking inlets—Teapoa and Haapu on the western coast and Mahuti Bay on the southeast corner of Huahine Iti. Shallower than the other bays, they cleave deeply into the island and are surrounded by steep precipitous coastline. Vistas of the coastline are accessible from the road, and look for the many vanilla plantations taking root in the rich volcanic soil.

SIGHTS

The road around Huahine Iti may not always be in the best state of repair, but it is generally accessible with a standard automobile and is mostly paved. The southern side of the island lacks the number of Polynesian temples found on Huahine Nui, but there is at least one major archaeological site to visit, **Marae Anini**. Located on the southernmost tip of Huahine Iti, it once served the community as a place of worship of the deities Oro and Hiro. In 1818, the last priest of the temple told Reverend Ellis, an early missionary, that he was aware of 14 cases of human sacrifice at this shrine.

The principal feature of the *marae* is its **ahu** (platform). Sometimes the *ahu* are compared to altars, which is not correct. They

EEL SPOTTING

Along with archaeological sites at Maeva, the giant eels at Faie are the biggest attraction on Huahine. Some of the creatures are rumored to have grown to six feet long from the food, mostly canned fish, tossed at them by villagers and visitors alike. Eels can live up to 30 years. Mornings are best for eel watching; visitors can piggyback onto the Sofitel Heiva feeding tours that leave the hotel at 9:15 a.m. (Call to find out which days the tours operate.) Charlie, one of the local guides, speaks English and doesn't mind if you are not a guest at the hotel. All of the guides handle and hand-feed the eels.

are set aside for the gods Oro and Hiro. The **upright stones** are backrests for priests and chiefs, or memorials for deceased chiefs. A small *marae* was built when a royal family adopted a child of lower rank. A platform far out on the perimeter of the *marae* was where the house of Oro stood. Under each post of the house a human sacrifice was rendered.

After visiting Marae Anini you might want to take a picnic lunch, towel and good book and set yourself up on the lovely white-sand **Anini Beach** nearby. Shaded by ample coconut palms, its generally calm waters make it an enjoyable place for a swim.

On any circuit of the island, be sure and linger at the recently constructed **Vista Point** at PK 18 on the east coast road. Here the dividing line between the light turquoise of the lagoon and the deep blue of the ocean is striking. A few picnic tables have been added for your dining pleasure.

LODGING

Most (but not all) of the hotels that occupy Huahine Iti are up-scale properties. Because you are more isolated here, it is best to rent a car to tour the island.

◄ *HIDDEN*

Pension Mauarii is a small family-run pension operated by Breysse Vetea. The property has three garden bungalows—each with two double beds. One of the units has a self-contained kitchen. There is also a beach bungalow with a double bed, mosquito net and private bath. There is a separate sanitary building that includes five toilets and two showers, which all appear clean. In addition to the bungalows, a traditional Polynesian home on the beach is available; if you have a large group, this huge villa is something special. With a vast veranda, a ten-meter-long bar made of *marumaru* planks—a local hardwood—and a *pandanus* roof, the place has to be seen to be appreciated. On the ground floor are a bathroom and two bedrooms, each with a double bed, and upstairs on the mezzanine are three king-size beds dispersed over a huge floor. Typically, the whole house is rented, but individual rooms without kitchen access may be available. This pension is especially known for its fine cuisine, and internet access is available at the restaurant. ~ Parea; phone/fax 68-86-49, cell 70-48-30; www.mauarii.com, e-mail vetea@mail.pf. MODERATE TO DELUXE.

If you're looking for a property with an archetypal South Seas setting, go no further. Shaded by century-old *tamanu* and *auteraa* trees, the **Relais Mahana** is situated on an exquisite white-sand beach on a crystal turquoise-blue-and-green lagoon. It's on the quiet and remote south side of the island. (Rental cars are available at the property for those interested in exploring.) The Relais has 22 bungalows, some of which are twin units built side by side to accommodate large families. The simply designed units each contain a double and a single bed, a ceiling fan and a private bath. Cuisine is good and meals are served in a pleasant garden restaurant on the beach. Diving is available at the hotel and free activities include pedal boats, *petanque* (French bocce ball), kayak, canoe, tennis and ping-pong. When the sea is rough, guests can swim in the hotel's small sheltered swimming pool. We've heard only good things from people who have stayed here. Relais Mahana typically closes for a month during the winter holidays, so check ahead if you plan to visit in November or December. ~ Parea; 68-81-54, fax 68-85-08; www.relaismahana.pf, e-mail relaismahana@mail.pf. DELUXE.

HIDDEN ►   **Ariiura Camping** is one of the better campgrounds on the island. The property includes a secluded beach, and snorkeling in the quiet lagoon is good. In addition to a grassy field for tents, there are six "camping *fare*" with single or double beds and mosquito nets. The communal bathroom is rustic, and water is turned off at night. Although there are no doors and no security, there is seemingly little need for either. There is a kitchen for those who want to prepare their own food, and meals are taken in a traditional beachfront *fare* built by Hubert, the owner. Hubert is a botanist, and he will likely show you his garden of native and medicinal plants, which he has dubbed the "Magic Stone Garden of Fish." Snorkel gear and *pirogues* are available for rent. There's also a good snack bar next door. If you don't plan to buy food at the snack bar, be sure to get provisions in town before heading out. You'll need your own transportation to get there—or you can take the truck from Fare to Parea. The property is located off the road just before a monument to Gaston Flosse, near the *marae* at Parea. A sign on the road marks the property. ~ Parea; 68-85-20. BUDGET.

DINING

HIDDEN ►   **Fare Mauarii,** located just west of Parea on the beach, is a small restaurant that offers French and Tahitian dishes. Open daily, it is a pleasant respite for hungry visitors making their way around the island. The food is excellent and the peaceful setting and views of the sandy beach make it an obligatory stop. ~ Parea; 68-86-49. BUDGET TO MODERATE.

GROCERIES   There are a couple of small stores in Haapu and Parea. The one in Haapu is off the road and hard to see, and the store in Parea is open at odd hours. If they're open they're great places to buy

AUTHOR FAVORITE

After a busy day of sightseeing, there's nothing I need more than a nice relaxing dinner. **Fare Mauarii,** serving French and Tahitian dishes and set on a peaceful sandy beach, leaves me filled with excellent food and a buoyant mood. For more information, see above.

drinks after visiting Marae Anini. There are a few drinks-only roadside stands outside of the main population centers. These are marked by Hinano, Coca Cola or Fanta signs.

From Point Tereva on the southwest coast to the Huahine Beach Club on the southeast side is a stretch of white-sand beach that fringes the southern tip of the island. This stretch of beach is un-equaled in the Society Islands, except perhaps for the Matira area of Bora Bora. You can park virtually anywhere along this coast-line. Be respectful of private property, however.

BEACHES & PARKS

ANINI BEACH 🏖 🏄 This long strand of white sand bound by clear turquoise waters offers good swimming. There are two surf breaks close to the beach off a small *motu*—a clean right-hander and a sloppier left on the other side of the channel. If you are going to surf, it's best to go in the morning before the trades start blowing. Be sure to lock your car—unfortunately, the surfing crowd attracts people who rip off visitors. No facilities. ~ To get there look for the Marae Anini sign and park near the archaeo-logical site that is in walking distance of the beach.

◄ *HIDDEN*

RELAIS MAHANA 🐟 The Relais Mahana hotel on the south-west tip of Huahine Iti has some of the best snorkeling on the is-land. The reason—the hotel regularly feeds fish off the dock. ~ To get there take the coastal road and park at the hotel, which is clearly marked.

Chez Lovina is a budget accommodation on the fringes of Fare, about a 15-minute walk north of town. There is room for about 20 tents on the property. Communal toilet/bath facilities are available, and there is beach access. ~ Fare; phone/fax 68-88-06.

Outdoor Adventures

CAMPING

Ariiura Camping in the Parea area is also a good bet. Make sure to bring ample provisions; it's quite a haul back to Fare. ~ Parea; 68-85-20. (For more information, see "Lodging" in the Huahine Iti section.)

Camping is also available at **Chez Delord Vanaa**, on the road to the Sofitel. There are common bath and kitchen facilities. ~ Maeva; 68-89-51.

Huahine has a variety of sites for divers of all levels. The island is still fairly unknown as a dive destination, which means the sites you visit will not be overrun by humankind. Aquatic life is rich and includes the larger pelagics as well as standard reef fish. It's not unusual to see eagle rays, sharks, Napoleon fish, tuna, barracuda and turtles.

DIVING

Dive sites of note include **Avapeihi Pass.** Only five minutes by boat from Fare, it is known for its shark feeding and large schools of jack, barracuda and spade fish; **Sea Anemone Reef,** a large seabed laden with blue, violet, yellow and green coral as well as a rich variety of sea anemones; and **Bullfish Drop-off**, which has schools of bullfish, blood sea bass, unicorn fish and white-spotted pufferfish. **Safari Aquarium**, inside the reef, offers easy diving and fun snorkeling among pristine coral heads.

Dive Operators   **Pacific Blue Adventure** is located on the quay in Fare opposite the tourist office. It has operated on the island for more than seven years and has a reputation for being a well-run shop. They offer diving in the passes and outside the lagoon. There are two vessels, one of which holds up to 15 divers. There are two dives daily, at 9 a.m. and 2 p.m., supervised by English-speaking PADI instructors. Open-water and resort courses are available for beginners and there are a variety of dives for advanced aficionados. (They offer a 10 percent discount to guests of Chez Guynette.) If you are on a yacht and are willing to moor at their pier, Pacific Blue Adventure will fill up your water tanks. ~ Fare; 68-87-21, fax 68-80-71; www.divehuahine.com, e-mail pba@divehuahine.com.

Mahana Dive at the hotel Relais Mahana offers diving from motorized Zodiacs for up to seven people. ~ Fare; 68-76-32, cell 73-07-17, fax 68-76-63; e-mail kbi@mail.pf.

SURFING

There are excellent reef breaks throughout the Society Islands, but surfing seems to be the most popular with American and Australian visitors in Huahine. It's not the size of the waves that draws surfers, but their consistency and perfect shape. Of the four major breaks on the island, three are in the Fare area. They include **Fitii**, which has a good right peak and a great tube on south-southwest swells; **Fare**, which has an excellent left reef break and a long wall; and **Bali Hai**, a.k.a. "vahine" break, which walls up on north-northwest swells and is easier to deal with for less advanced surfers. Getting to the action on most of these breaks involves long paddles. The fourth site in **Parea** has two excellent breaks, including a fairly clean right on southeast swells. They are the best breaks on the south side of the island, but it's rather a long drive to get there.

> Visitors curious about how local bonito fishermen operate might be able to talk their way aboard a fishing vessel by donating a case of beer to the cause.

One caveat about the surf scene on Huahine: Locals are not enthusiastic about visiting surfers. If you feel bad vibes or indifference, it's probably not your imagination. The best way around this is to befriend a local and have him or her introduce you to the gang. Mind your etiquette, particularly on the south side of the island. The Parea (a.k.a. Anini Beach) break is very "local" and can get ugly if you don't know the crowd.

FISHING

Fishing in Huahine is above average. Tuna, mahimahi, marlin and other species can be snagged outside the reef on charter boats. Surf casting on Huahine is nonexistent because of the barrier reef that surrounds the islands.

Ruau II is a 36-foot fishing boat that offers up to six passengers half- or full-day fishing trips off the coast of Huahine or to Raiatea and Tahaa. Anglers regularly bag tuna, marlin, *wahoo* and mahimahi. The vessel can accommodate up to six people and the price includes water, soft drinks and beer. ~ 68-84-02, fax 68-80-30; e-mail huahine.mar.trans@mail.pf.

SAILING

Arriving yachties should always contact the harbor master for any questions about anchorage, water and the like. Fare's harbor is generally a popular place to moor because of the availability of water and provisions. Yachties should note that because of the establishment of pearl farms in the Huahine area, finding proper anchorage is no longer simply a matter of dropping an anchor. A vessel in the wrong place may inadvertently damage a pearl farm.

There are two charter companies that operate from Huahine. **Sailing Huahine Voile** has a 15-foot Eden Martin yacht that is available for trips to Raiatea, Tahaa, Bora Bora and the Tuamotu Group, as well as day sails around the Huahine lagoon. ~ Fare; 68-72-49; www.sailing-huahine.com.

BOAT TOURS

Poetaina Cruises, run by the pension of the same name, operates excursions on the lagoon. Activities include a visit to a pearl farm, snorkeling, and *motu* visits. ~ Fare; 68-89-49; e-mail pensionpoetaina@mail.pf.

Vaipua Cruises is another seven-hour cruise around Huahine with similar stops. Their picnic lunch is a barbecue that includes wine and beer. Children are half price, and there is a minimum of four people. Contact Colette or Henri. ~ Fare; phone/fax 68-86-42; e-mail here@mail.pf.

Huahine Discovery Tours provides four-wheel-drive tours of the island that include visits to archaeological sites, the famous eels of Faie and a vanilla plantation. In the afternoon you trade the jeep for a boat and they take you to the pearl farm, snorkeling at the reef and for a *motu* picnic. Our contacts tell us that Huahine Discovery Tours guarantee satisfaction. ~ Phone/fax 68-75-18; e-mail huahdisctour@mail.pf.

Marc Garnier offers glass-bottom-boat tours of the lagoon on the *Tepoe IV*. A snorkeling visit to the coral gardens is included. Twelve-person maximum. ~ Fare; 68-83-15; www.huahinenautique.com, e-mail huahinenautique@mail.pf.

Other boat tour companies include **Huahine Nautique** ~ Fare, 68-83-15; and **Vahine Api Cruises** ~ Fare, 68-84-02, fax 68-80-30.

Boat Rentals   **Huahine Lagoon** rents boats, kayaks and bikes. The boats come fully equipped with safety gear, masks, snorkels, cooler and a map of the lagoon. Kayaks come in one- or two-seat configurations and can be rented in half-day or full-day increments. Huahine Lagoon is located next to the Puvaivai gallery. ~ Fare; 68-70-00, fax 68-87-57.

JET SKIING

Huahine Nautique has eight three-seater jet skis available for guided lagoon tours that include a snorkel stop, ray visit and *motu* picnic. ~ Fare; 68-83-15, fax 68-82-15.

RIDING STABLES

La Petite Ferme Stable, located halfway between the airport and Fare, has 12 Marquesan horses trained in Western style. Able wranglers can take group camping tours of two days or more as well as shorter rides. There are a variety of excursions, including a one-hour beach ride and visit to a coconut grove, or a two-hour ride to Lac Fauna Nui and the beach. All-day rides plus picnics at the sea can be arranged. The operation will cater to your individual skills and needs. Six-day horse-riding programs with full board are available on request. ~ Fare; phone/fax 68-82-98; e-mail lapetiteferme@mail.pf.

BIKING

Biking around Huahine is a good option, especially if it means short trips from Fare to the market or short-distance sightseeing. Unlike Moorea or Tahiti, traffic is by no means overwhelming. Roads near the villages are generally in good shape, but in the outlying areas, especially on the periphery of Tahiti Iti, the roads may not be paved and in some instances not well maintained. A special caution when going to Maroe Bay—after Faie Village the road is unpaved and has a treacherous uphill grade. Don't even try it on a rental bike. If you have a good bike it's possible to see the entire island in a day. If you do attempt to see the whole island by bike, you'd better be in good shape. Naturally you should bring plenty of water.

Guided mountain-bike rides can be arranged through a company called **Bicycle Tours**. ~ Fare; 68-82-59, cell 73-64-63, fax 68-80-59.

Bike Rentals **Europcar** in town has bike rentals. ~ Fare; 68-88-03, fax 68-80-59. **Avis** also has bikes. ~ Fare; 68-73-34, fax 68-73-35. **Jojo** boutique also rents bikes. ~ Fare; 68-89-16.

Avis, with an office in town near the dock, also has bikes. ~ Fare; 68-73-34, fax 68-73-35.

HIKING

Huahine is akin to a giant outdoor museum. In many instances, the old temples and other archaeological remnants have been painstakingly restored. In conjunction with the restoration project, a series of trails have been constructed and are maintained for the benefit of the visitor. Those with an interest in the old relics will find delight in hiking these tracks that crisscross the old village complex. Throughout the archaeological region were vanilla plantations, marked by posts and covered with twisting vines. Most of these plantations now go largely untended.

Fare Pote'e to Marae Paepae Ofata (1.5 miles/2 kilometers): A few minutes' walk south of Fare Pote'e, along the coast road (opposite the Protestant church), is one of the trailheads for the many reconstructed *marae* on Matairea Hill. The trailhead is not obvious—it is set behind a house—so ask a local to show you. Keep in mind that the beginning of the trail is on private land, so be respectful of the plants growing on it. The ten-minute hike to the main section of the trail is a bit steep at the beginning. At the summit, the trail opens up and the area is covered with ferns and manioc patches. (At this point the mosquitoes begin to attack, so bring repellent along.) In former times, this was a vanilla plantation and you can still see the vines spiraling up the trees and bushes. It's worth taking the 25-minute hike to the top of the trail for a spectacular view from Marae Paepae Ofata overlooking the fish traps, the Sofitel Heiva Huahine and the narrow inlet that marks Faie Bay.

Walk ten minutes south of Fare Pote'e, cross the small bridge and continue to your left on the *motu* to another very impressive temple, **Marae Manunu**. This became the *marae* for the community of Huahine Nui after Matairea-rahi. Next to the low offering platform is the **grave** of Raiti, the last high priest of Maeva. When he died in 1915, one of the huge *marae* slabs fell. He was buried at the *marae* at his request.

A thorough tour of the *marae* near Maeva takes several hours and a bit of walking, so it is suggested you do it in the early morning. In the late afternoon you will have to deal with the mosquito population. Bring plenty of repellent whenever you go.

Moua Tapu Trail (3 miles/4.8 kilometers) leads to Moua Tapu, which towers above the northeast corner of the Huahine Nui. At 1407 feet (429 meters), it is not the highest peak, but it does offer a spectacular view of the Maeva environs. The summit affords a stunning vista of the coastline. ~ To get there take the road to the microwave tower that is accessible just west of Fare Pote'e and is distinguished by a barrier that crosses the entrance. Once at the tower, start climbing upwards following the ridgeline. The hike takes about one hour each way.

Transportation

There are air connections between Huahine and Tahiti, Bora Bora, Moorea and Raiatea. **Air Tahiti** has service from Papeete two to four times daily. Flight time is about 35 minutes. Most flights connect with Bora Bora and Raiatea as well. ~ Fare; 68-77-02.

AIR

Vaeanu (68-73-73, fax 41-24-34; e-mail torehiatetu@mail.pf) and *Hawaiknui* (45-23-24, fax 45-24-44) sail to Huahine regularly out of Papeete.

SEA

Aremiti Corsaire makes two voyages a week from Papeete. There is a snack bar onboard. Deck passage only. ~ Papeete; 42-88-88, fax 42-83-83; e-mail aremiticata@mail.pf.

CAR, JEEP & MOTOR SCOOTER RENTALS

All of the Fare-area rental agencies have desks at the airport or reps at the major hotels. The rates are getting more competitive all the time. You can usually get a good deal on the weekend rate (three days for the price of two); all agencies offer a weekend rate for rentals beginning Thursday or Friday. Guests at the local pensions receive 10 percent discounts from the agencies. Gasoline can be bought at the Faremiti or Mobil stations in Fare.

Europcar's vehicles include the minuscule Fiat Panda, Jeeps and motor scooters. There are Europcar outlets at the airport, in Fare and across from Fare Mauarii in Paraea. ~ Fare; 68-82-59, fax 68-80-59; e-mail kake@mail.pf.

Hertz also has an office here. ~ Fare; phone/fax 68-76-85.

From all reports, the best rental agency on the island is **Huahine Locations**. They provide Renault Twingos, scooters and bikes. ~ Fare; phone/fax 68-76-85; e-mail huahinelocations@voila.fr.

Avis also has outlets at the airport and in town. ~ Fare; 68-73-34, fax 68-73-35.

PUBLIC TRANSIT

One of the biggest problems about visiting Huahine is the dearth of public transportation. Each district on the island has its own *Le Truck* that leaves the villages in the morning to take locals into Fare. By 9 or 9:30 a.m. all *Le Trucks* have left Fare again to return to the villages for the day, where they stay until the next morning. Thus, the only solution (other than hitching) is to rent a car or scooter. Bikes are an option if you can find a good deal at a rental agency—or buy one and sell it when you leave. It's possible to bike the entire island in under six hours (including rest stops) if you have a good mountain bike and you can handle the sun exposure. Do not attempt to ride down the steep hill between Faie and Maroe Bay—a tourist died trying.

TAXIS

Taxi service is provided by **Taxi Enite**, with a mini-bus stationed at the airport for the arrival of each flight. If a hotel sends a taxi to meet you at the airport, you will be charged extra: your hotel will add a commission to the taxi fare. ~ Fare; 68-82-37.

HITCHING

Hitching around the island is quite good. Huahine is still enough off the beaten track that hitchhikers are somewhat of a novelty and locals will generally pick them up.

TOURS

Island Eco-Tours is the best option for those interested in natural history, archaeology and culture. Owner/guide Paul Atallah takes individuals and groups on half- and full-day four-wheeled-drive expeditions. A former anthropology graduate student,

Atallah knows his stuff and will take you where other tour operators can't. ~ Fare; 68-79-67; www.island-eco-tours.com, e-mail islandecotours@mail.pf.

Huahine Land Tours is the Huahine version of the overland four-wheel-drive tours that have become so popular on Bora Bora, Moorea and Tahiti over the last few years. They have departures twice daily for sites that include a vanilla plantation, *marae* and the eels. Children under 12 are half price. The brochure says "Let yourself be seduced by famous sunset trips and other ones on request." Why not? ~ Fare; 68-89-21, fax 68-86-84; www.huahineland.com.

Huahine Discovery Tour offers four-wheel-drive visits to scenic areas, archaeological sites and the least-visited places on the island. Expect to pay about US$75 for a full day. ~ Fare; 68-81-10, fax 68-75-18.

Huahine Explorer, based out of Vaihonu Ocean Camping and run by its owner, Etienne Faaeva, also offers a variety of excursions. ~ Fare; 68-87-33; e-mail vaihonu@mail.pf.

Quad Evasion, located near the airport turnoff, offers half-day guided ATV trips to explore Lake Maeva and environs, including a ride through a coconut plantation. ~ Fare; phone/fax 68-71-38; e-mail oa.oa@mail.pf.

▼▼▼▼▼▼▼▼▼▼▼▼▼▼▼▼▼▼▼▼▼▼

Addresses & Phone Numbers

Airport ~ 60-62-60
Doctor ~ Dr. Carbonnier and Dr. Motyka; 68-82-20
Hospital ~ 68-82-48
Police Station ~ 68-82-61
Post Office ~ 68-82-70
Visitor Information ~ tourist office; 68-75-30

EIGHT
Raiatea and Tahaa

As legend has it, Raiatea and Tahaa were originally one island until a giant eel swallowed a young girl. Possessed by her spirit, the enraged creature broke through the surface of the earth, causing the sea to gush. The impact of the water cut the island in two and Raiatea and Tahaa were created.

Raiatea is the bigger of the two islands, has a greater population and a well-developed infrastructure. These sister islands sit 122 miles (192 kilometers) northwest of Papeete, and 25 miles (40 kilometers) west of Huahine. The two islands share a common coral foundation and protected lagoon. Tahaa is slightly less than two miles northwest of Raiatea—about a 20-minute boat trip.

Raiatea, the largest of the Leeward Islands, was of seminal importance to Polynesian culture as a religious and cultural center. This was chiefly because the island was home to Marae Taputapuatea, the largest and most significant shrine in eastern Polynesia. Polynesians from as far away as New Zealand came to worship at the temple and tradition has it that any new temple constructed on neighboring islands had to include a stone from Taputapuatea. In addition, scientists have unearthed evidence pinpointing Raiatea as a jumping-off point for the ancient Polynesian mariners who populated other islands.

It was at Taputapuatea that Captain Cook first had a glimpse of Polynesian navigational acumen. In front of a *marae* dedicated to navigation, a local named Tupai drew a map of the neighbor islands in the dirt for the English explorer's benefit and gave him a discourse on navigational theory. Amazingly, Tupai knew the navigational specifics without ever having left Raiatea. Cook was impressed.

With an area of 105 square miles (170 square kilometers), the highest point on Raiatea is 3335-foot (1017-meter) Mount Tefatua. The island is totally surrounded by a reef, with several navigable passes. There are about 3568 residents on the island.

Raiatea has the only navigable river in French Polynesia—the Faaroa. Considered the original source of migration by the Maori (or *Maohi*, as the Tahitians call themselves) to the far reaches of Polynesia (Hawaii and New Zealand), the Faaroa has great historical significance to the Polynesians. Upon his arrival in Raiatea, Captain Cook noted that logs were floated down the river to build the numerous ships that were under construction.

Mount Temenani, another famous landmark, is supposedly the birthplace of Oro, one of the principal Polynesian gods and the home of the *tiare apetahi*, a white gardenia endemic to the mountain ecosystem. Legend has it that the blossom's five petals represent the five fingers of a young Tahitian maiden who fell in love with a Tahitian prince but was prohibited from marrying him because she was a commoner.

Raiatea receives plenty of rainfall to irrigate its fertile soil, and has a lagoon rich in sea life. Its main products are copra, vanilla and, in recent years, a burgeoning black pearl industry.

Raiatea

As a tourist destination, Raiatea hasn't changed dramatically over the last decade. The chief settlement, Uturoa, is still the sleepy provincial capital it always was, but it now has excellent markets in which to purchase provisions. Raiatea has never been much of a conventional tourist draw because of the absence of beaches on the main island. (Locals will emphatically point out to you that the beaches on the outlying *motu* are quite nice.) There are a number of excellent budget hotels catering to divers and those interested in the cultural aspects of the island, chiefly the Taputapuatea archaeological site. What *has* changed is the island's reputation as a yacht charter center.

Raiatea has just the right mix of modern conveniences and traditions to make it an excellent destination for the visitor who wants to see something of an unspoiled French Polynesia. One of the nicest things about the island is that it remains undiscovered. From the visitor's standpoint this is good because Raiateans are not inundated by tourists and are still relatively friendly.

SIGHTS

Uturoa, which translates from Tahitian as "long jaw" (which means "love of gossip"), is the island's capital and only port. It is both a commercial hub and the administrative headquarters for the Leeward Islands.

The second-largest town in French Polynesia, Uturoa consists of one main street, flanked by two-story cement structures interspersed with a few old-style clapboard buildings. The government administrative complex, **Tavana Hau,** is a row of *fare*-shaped buildings. Beginning with the mayor's office on the north side, the order of rank descends until you reach the lowly cesspool inspector's office.

One block from main street is a quay lined with ferry boats that ply the waters between Raiatea and Tahaa. Next to the quay is the dock for cruise vessels and interisland boats. Though hardly a metropolis, Uturoa does have an electrical power station, a hospital, a *gendarmerie*, a courthouse, supermarkets, restaurants and other amenities. An ice plant provides refrigeration for fish shipments to Papeete.

Uturoa is in the midst of a large-scale urban-renewal project that will continue over the next few years. The waterfront features a brand-new port and docking area for cruise ships, as well as a modern new two-story complex of fashionable boutiques and restaurants called **Gare Maritime d'Uturoa**. The complex is airy and inviting but strangely forlorn, perhaps because it was built for visitors who never materialized. The new facilities were constructed specifically to cater to passengers of the Renaissance cruise ship line, which declared bankruptcy and abruptly ceased operation in September 2001. Although several shops and restaurants have opened in the center, so far most of the new facilities have seen little use.

Commanding a beautiful view of the harbor, the **Raiatea Tourist Office** occupies the spacious ground floor of one commercial building—along with the empty counters of tour operators, built for the nonexistent rush of customers. Sadly, many small tour operators who invested heavily in new promotions and setting up shop in the center are now facing financial difficulties because they failed to recoup on their investment.

Nevertheless, there is an expectant feel to the place, and local tourism officials say there is hope another cruise line will decide to make calls here. In the meantime, visitors and locals alike enjoy the wonderful new waterfront promenade, which features wrought-iron lampposts and inlaid patterns of stone, for quiet evening strolls.

Also well received is the new handicraft area adjacent to the commercial buildings. The half a dozen little huts feature artisans at work making traditional crafts and, of course, all their wares are for sale. Just past the handicrafts area, situated in a lovely park with a lily pond, is an outdoor *fare* for concerts. Farther on are two massive, red-peaked buildings that are dedicated to cargo handling, warehousing and other heavy industry.

Subsequent phases of construction will include creating a pedestrian-only zone along the main street by rerouting cars along a new mountainside road, and a large park across from the new pier. This attempt at halting the typical strip development, a first in French Polynesia, is being hailed by urban planners throughout the South Pacific.

The old **Uturoa public market**, which has been closed since the end of 1999, will eventually be replaced with a new marketplace. In the meantime, a temporary wooden structure has been built just behind the town hall, towards the oceanfront, to host the various merchants who hawk food and souvenirs.

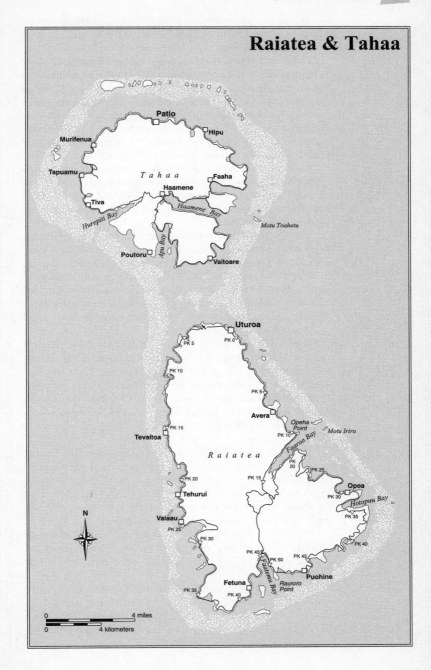

Raiatea & Tahaa

The other major edifice in town is the **Champion** supermarket, next to the Banque of Tahiti, opposite the harbor.

Along the **waterfront** area (Fisherman's Wharf) are several outdoor cafés that still evoke the old South Seas ambience. And, along with the traditional old businesses, a new block of stores has been constructed that includes everything from a travel agency to an electronics shop to an immaculate French-owned grocery store.

Branches of the four major **banks** are along both sides of Uturoa's main street. Bank of Tahiti and Socredo Bank have ATMs outside their buildings. Hours vary slightly; however, all the banks are open 7:45–11:30 a.m. and 1:30–3:45 p.m. Monday through Friday.

The **post office** is located along the northern limit of Uturoa's main strip (mountain side) and is open Monday through Thursday 7:30 a.m.–3 p.m., Friday 7 a.m.–2 p.m. and Saturday 8–10 a.m. There is also a post office on the second floor of the new Gare Maritime building.

Eight kilometers south of Uturoa, in the Avera district, is a large **community building** on the lagoon side that serves as a gymnasium and venue for large gatherings and theater performances.

About 1.5 kilometers north of Uturoa you will see a small sign for **Bleu des Isle**, pointing up a road toward the mountains. This drop-off laundry service is open Monday through Friday 8 a.m.–5 p.m. and Saturday 8–11 a.m. This service comes in handy! ~ Uturoa; 66-29-64.

One of the newer attractions on the island is the modern **Apooiti Marina complex**. The marina is home to the largest restaurant on the island, The Clubhouse, which has a large veranda that is a superb spot for sipping a beer on a balmy evening. It is also the base for Moorings Yacht Charters. The Apooiti Marina should not be confused with what is known locally as the Nouveau Marina, located about one kilometer from town. ~ Uturoa; 66-11-66.

Though Uturoa is the island's focal point, you will eventually want to visit some of the outlying communities. Getting around town with public transportation is not a problem but it can be troublesome in the outlying areas. Roads are well maintained but *Le Truck* tends to run infrequently to the far reaches of the island. Hitchhiking, however, is easily accomplished.

Raiatea has been hit by several cyclones over the last decade and has suffered a great deal of destruction. Four hundred and fifty new "cyclone-proof" houses have since been provided by the government.

Navettes (small commuter boats) to Tahaa leave from the small-boat pier in the center of town. There are several boats per day, with limited service on Saturday and none on Sunday. Tickets are purchased at the boats themselves; there is no ticket office. For more information, see the "Transportation" section in this chapter.

One of the best ways to explore Raiatea is to rent a vehicle and drive the 60-mile (96-kilometer) circumference of the island. Many of the rural roads vary in quality from fair to poor, depending on the weather. On the west side of the island the paved road ends just after Tevaitoa (although there is a short stretch again in Vaiaau). The road is also paved along the island's northeastern edge between Uturoa and Faaroa Bay. From Faaroa Bay there is a paved road that climbs over the saddle to Faatemu Bay where it joins the (unpaved) coastal road and provides access to the communities of Fetuna and Puohine. On the southerly road to Fetuna (about 45 kilometers from Uturoa) you can see gorgeous landscapes during the entire length of the journey. Give

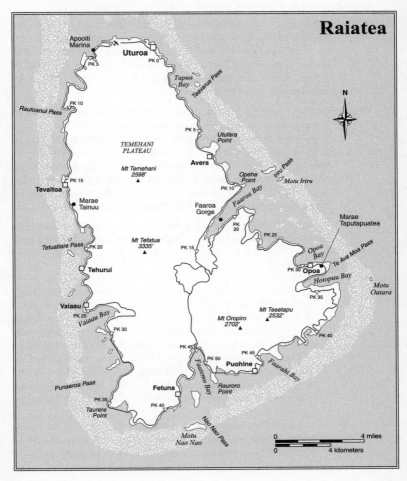

Taputapuatea Archaeological Area

The Taputapuatea archaeological area held great importance to ancient Polynesians. When constructing new *marae* on neighboring islands, a stone from Taputapuatea had to be used in the making of the new temple. Today, there are 19 *marae*, as well as one main oblong shrine that is 142 feet (43 meters) in length, within the Taputapuatea area. Plan on spending about two hours here if you go with a guide; on your own you will cover the area a bit faster.

MATAHIRATERAI   Marae Taputapuatea encompasses a large area on the flat, wide promontory named Matahiraterai, situated between Opoa and Hotopuu bays. Besides Marae Taputapuatea, there are five or six other shrines in the vicinity. They are found on a flat, sandy point, isolated by a ridge to the east called Matarepeta Hill, and a smaller hillock approaching the shore on the west.

VALLEY OF THE NIGHT   According to Kenneth P. Emory, an American archaeologist, the depression between the hills was sacred to the god Oro. It was called Te Po (the Night), while the rest of Raiatea was referred to as Te Ao (the Day). The exact boundaries of Te Po were marked in the west by a dikelike structure, Tuiamarafea, and in the east by a small basalt boulder in the water, Tupi-ofai. (Tupi-ofai also marks the boundary between the Opoa and Hotopuu districts.) Marae Taputapuatea occupies the central position in Te Po, and its *ahu* (altar) lies due north and south.

ORO'S SHRINE   The main shrine at Taputapuatea, an oblong-shaped temple, is considered the home of Oro, the god of war and an important

yourself an entire day to circumnavigate the island. (Note: There is no gasoline outside of Uturoa.)

In 1995 the black pearl industry gained a foothold in the lagoon that bridges Raiatea and Tahaa. The first harvests were promising and pearl farms have proliferated. Excursions to Tahaa inevitably include a visit to a pearl farm. As you travel around the island, you are likely to see what appear to be solitary over-water bungalows constructed in the middle of the lagoons. These are, in fact, small pearl production facilities. Oysters are hung into the water from them.

HIDDEN ►   Most of the lodging facilities organize excursions up the **Faaroa River**. The journey begins at the mouth of the river, a fjordlike inlet with steep, verdant cliffs on either side. As the boat travels up the tiny passage, the valley becomes a narrow gorge, passing through deity in the Polynesian pantheon. According to local lore, four men were buried alive in an upright position in the temple to guard Oro and keep him from straying. Unlike any other *marae*, Taputapuatea has a catacomb-like room (not accessible to the public). A great number of human sacrifices were performed at Taputapuatea. In 1969, approximately 5000 skulls were discovered on the temple site.

THE SACRIFICE STONE   Look for an obelisk-like basalt slab that stands about ten yards (nine meters) from the main temple. Known as **ofa'i tapu taata** (the sacrifice stone), this is where unfortunate victims met their fate in a particularly bloody ceremony. Here the right eye of the victim was removed for the priest, and the left eye was taken for Oro. If the priest deemed the ceremony unworthy, the poor victim was taken to a large upright slab of limestone (resembling an oversized gravestone) and was scraped against the rough surface of the stone until what was left of his body dripped with blood. There was a sacrifice held in Captain Cook's honor. Legend has it he was offered an eye to eat which he summarily swallowed. The last significant sacrifice was held in 1853 when 100 men were killed.

GETTING THERE   To get to the archaeological area, take the Opoa-bound truck from town. Only one truck per day visits the site and leaves Uturoa in the morning. ~ Faaroa; 66-23-64. If you want to get the full story on Taputapuatea, consider Bill Kolan's **Almost Paradise Tours**. Bill Kolan's tours are excellent, and he will customize them to your interests. ~ Faaroa; phone/fax 66-23-64.

a rainforest thick with foliage. The trip continues until the course becomes too shallow to navigate. Gliding up the river, you can easily imagine the ancient throngs of *va'a* (canoes) dwarfed by the steep walls of **Faaroa Gorge** heading westward into the great Pacific expanse.

Along with Huahine, Raiatea is an archaeologist's delight. There are a number of *marae* on this island, including **Marae Taputapuatea**, considered to be one of the most significant temples in all of Polynesia. Scientists have unearthed artifacts that have linked Raiatea to Hawaii, corroborating the locally held belief that Raiatea was a staging area for ancient Polynesian mariners. (If you look at a map you will note that the island's position is directly at the center of the Polynesian triangle.) An additional link to Hawaii is Raiatea's original name—Havai'i. For a hands-on look into this trans-Pacific link, visit the Taputapuatea Archaeological Area (see the "Walking Tour" in this chapter).

Marae Tainuu on the western side of Raiatea, just south of Tevaitoa, is one of the island's oldest *marae* and the only place where petroglyphs are easily seen. Look for them at the entry to the Protestant church's grounds. They are part of Chief Tevaitoa's former *fare* foundation stones. The lines on the turtle's back are said to refer to the Southern Cross—probably for use as a navigational aid. Another *marae* structure behind the church at the water's edge is a favorite playplace of local children. The church also has two interesting ship models on the altar, one of Cook's *Endeavor*, the other of Wilson's *Duff*. It's open for Sunday services at 10 a.m. and is an excellent place to listen to a Tahitian church choir. Tahitians love to sing and their harmonies are memorable. Lastly, the private *motu* owned by Diana Ross is the second (and largest) *motu* visible, just south of PK 20.

Next to the Protestant church are the graves of three missionary wives who accompanied their spouses to the South Pacific. They were recently honored by the erection of an upright stone monument organized by the church. In addition, the five Leeward Islands are also represented by stones.

LODGING Only one hotel, the Hinano, is located within Uturoa's city limits. Most of the accommodations are clustered within an eight-mile (12-kilometer) radius of town. Raiatea has a good selection of budget hotels and pensions; only two hotels on the island exceed US$100 per night for a double. Raiatea is more akin to a provincial capital, and does not have the stereotypical luxury beach hotels one might associate with Tahiti. Note that only the more upscale properties accept credit cards, so bring traveler's checks to Raiatea.

HIDDEN ▶ Located in a tranquil setting adjacent to the lagoon, the waterfront **Sunset Beach Motel** has 21 modern, self-contained bungalows with wooden floors. They are comfortable, clean and well maintained. Each bungalow comes with a picnic table, living room, TV and complete kitchen with large refrigerator and stove. Situated in an expansive grassy area that was formerly a copra plantation, the large, American-style cabins afford a great deal of privacy. The motel is ideal for families or couples who might want to cook for themselves. One bungalow can accommodate up to five people. There are also excellent camping facilities on the property with laundry and a first-class kitchen, but that are priced only slightly higher than other campgrounds. The office/reception area has a sitting room and library with a deck overlooking the sea and a view of Bora Bora and Tahaa. Contrary to the name of the property, there is no beach. Guests can swim off the pier. The English-speaking manager, Moana Boubee, is friendly, and often provides seasonal fruit to guests. Tours are available and the motel also provides free transportation for guests to and from town once a day for shopping. They also offer free airport transfer and kayaks. For those who need nocturnal action, The Clubhouse restaurant/bar is only one kilometer away. The Sunset Beach Motel is located two kilometers from the airport and five kilometers west of town. Credit cards are accepted. ~ PK 4, Uturoa; 66-33-47, cell 78-22-88, fax 66-33-08; www.raiatea.com/sunsetbeach, e-mail sunsetbeach@mail.pf. BUDGET TO MODERATE.

Hotel Hinano, upstairs from the California Shop on Uturoa's main street, offers ten clean rooms with tile floors, private hot-water baths, TVs and fans; four rooms have air conditioning. Its location in downtown Uturoa may be useful for early-morning boat departures/arrivals or for business travel. Bike rentals, breakfast and free airport or boat transfers are available. The friendly staff speaks English, and credit cards are accepted. ~ Uturoa; 66-13-13, fax 66-14-14. BUDGET TO MODERATE.

Raiatea Bellevue Bed & Breakfast is located just 1.5 kilometers north of Uturoa; it's aptly named, as the island views are lovely (and the air a little cooler) up there on the hill. Six small but clean and nicely appointed rooms with private baths overlook a garden and pool area. Rooms have mosquito nets, TVs, fans and refrigerators. The mostly European clientele recommends the Bellevue strongly. Breakfast is included, and is served on your own patio. Airport or dock transfers are free. This is a winner. No credit cards. ~ Uturoa; phone/fax 66-15-15. MODERATE.

The largest and most luxurious hotel on the island is the **Raiatea Hawaiki Nui Hotel.** Located on the ocean side, the hotel consists of eight garden bungalows, three lagoon bungalows, nine over-water bungalows and eight rooms. The over-water units feature fish-viewing panels in the floor, ladders into the ocean, TVs, safes, hairdryers, fridge and direct dial phones. The staff is exceptionally friendly and service oriented, and the small number of units makes for a quiet setting. Regular morning feedings off the pier bring in some big jack and other tropical fish. Friday and Saturday nights are a good time to meet locals: people stream in to hear music at the bar. With an outdoor terrace overlooking the pool and the ocean, the restaurant does a brisk business at

THE SPANISH CLAN

In 1863, a Chilean slave ship was wrecked near the village of Tiva. Before a rescue party arrived, several of the crew members disappeared. They hid in the village, married islanders and became the ancestors of Tahaa's Feti Panior—the Spanish clan. To this day their descendants live in Tiva and are renowned for their beauty.

lunch. A boutique is on the site, in addition to a bicycle, scooter and car-rental desk. The hotel offers *motu* visits and glass-bottom-boat rides, but can arrange other outside activities. Transfers to the airport or boat dock can be arranged. Credit cards are accepted. Special rates are available for children. ~ Uturoa; 60-05-00, fax 66-20-20; www.pearlresorts.com, e-mail h.raiateapearl@mail.pf. MODERATE TO DELUXE.

Pension Tepua is a homey mid-range accommodation that also provides budget-priced rooms and dorm facilities. There are four modern, spacious bungalows with tile floors, overhead fans, mosquito nets, private bathrooms, and mezzanines or lofts that sleep up to six. There is also a house with four rooms, two communal bathrooms (with solar-heated water), and a minimal kitchen. The dorm sleeps 12 on narrow bunk beds and feels rather cramped. A fine restaurant on the premises is open to the public. Amenities include a small swimming pool, pontoon, washer and dryers and bicycle rentals. Airport or boat transfers are available, as are moorings for visiting yachts. This is a good place for families. A wide variety of tours are available through the pension, and the friendly owner Joe speaks English, French, Italian, Portuguese and German. Located 2.5 kilometers southwest from the ferry dock in Uturoa (directly on Tupua Bay). ~ Uturoa; phone/fax 66-33-00; e-mail pension-tepua@mail.pf. BUDGET TO MODERATE.

The newest pension on Raiatea is **Pension Tiare Nui**, located behind the Europcar rental outlet a kilometer or so from the airport. The four new wooden bungalows are quite nice and include kitchens and private hot-water baths. Unfortunately, the tiny property is fenced on all sides and there is no water access, or even a view. The primary sightline is of a neighbor's rusted outbuilding. The owners did a commendable job with what they had, but it just doesn't outweigh the poor location. This would be a convenient choice as a transit hotel, however, and the management does offer a special package deal that includes lodging and car rental. ~ Uturoa; 66-34-06, cell 78-33-53, fax 66-16-06; e-mail europcar-loc@mail.pf. MODERATE.

Hotel Tenape is an expansive, two-story, white and light-blue colonial-style building reminiscent of an American Southern plantation house. It consists of 15 large rooms and one suite. Each comes with a double bed, private bath, terrace, TV, phone, air conditioner and teak furniture imported from Bali. There is also a suite with two bedrooms and a small living room that will accommodate up to four people. On the ground floor are the lobby, a bar and a restaurant, all open to the garden. The swimming pool features a pool bar for afternoon drinks. Tenape specializes in French cuisine and local fish specialties. This hotel is located about eight and a half kilometers north of Uturoa, on the

Omai, Friend of Captain Cook

Raiatea is the birthplace of Omai, one of the first Polynesians to visit Europe. The nephew of the king of Raiatea, Omai became an attendant to Huahine's king, Oree. When Captain James Cook arrived in Huahine on his second voyage in 1773, Omai made himself indispensable by procuring food for the crew and protecting the sailors from theft and threats of harm by a jealous chief.

Captain Furneaux, second in command in Captain Cook's party, invited Omai to accompany him on the return trip to England. So in 1774 the Polynesian set sail for England.

Omai soon became the darling of English society. Friendly and charming, he was dressed by his benefactors in velvet jackets and other finery. Over the next two years he dined in London's best homes, met the king, learned to shoot and skate and was a favorite with the ladies.

En route back to Tahiti, he served Captain Cook as a translator in the Society Islands and Tonga. He returned to Tahiti in 1776, bearing gifts of firearms, wine, tin soldiers, kitchenware and a globe of the world. But the hapless Omai was soon cheated out of many of his treasures by Tahitians.

Cook saw to it that Omai was moved to Huahine, where Cook's carpenters built him a house and supplied him with pigs, chickens and tools. Not long after the return home Omai died. Some of his souvenirs and artifacts from England were still around when the first missionaries arrived in 1797.

west side of Raiatea. ~ Tevaitoa; 60-01-00, fax 60-01-01; www.
raiatea.com/tenape, e-mail hoteltenape@mail.pf. DELUXE.

Pension Yolande is situated right on the water and claims a
tiny little white-sand beach shaded with palms. Yolande's four
"cabins" are all part of the same building. Each has a double
bed, kitchenette and private bath. While the walls are covered in
tacky paneling and the linoleum floor has seen better days, the
property is generally well cared for and clean. There are also two
larger family-size units—in better shape and with wooden floors—
that tend to be occupied by long-term tenants. The common
kitchen and dining area is pleasant and has a great view of Tahaa
and three *motu*. Meals are available and there is a washing machine. Yolande herself is friendly and forthright and has one heck
of a solid handshake. ~ PK 10, Avera; 66-35-28. MODERATE.

Pension Manava has four bungalows whose rooms overlook
a garden. Two units have private kitchen facilities; the other two
share a kitchen. Each unit has clean tile floors and airy bathrooms decorated with plants that give them a pleasant greenhouse
feel. There are also two rooms—one with a double bed and one
with a double and a single bed. They share a large, clean common
kitchen with a refrigerator and sink. There's also a common
shower and toilet. Proprietress Roselyne Brotherson sells her own
hand-painted pareu. Excursions are available to Mt. Temehani,
Tahaa and various *motu*. Airport and boat transfers are free.
Pension Manava is six kilometers south of Uturoa. Highly recommended. No credit cards. ~ PK 6, Avera; 66-28-26, fax 66-16-
66; www.manavapension.com, e-mail maraud@mail.pf. BUDGET.

Facing the sea, **Peter Brotherson's Camping** (a.k.a. Peter's
Place) is a combination dormitory and campground. There is a
single-row, dormitory-style barracks with eight spartan rooms
that sleep up to two, and a communal kitchen with three burners,
a refrigerator, an area to store food, and two picnic tables. The
four communal toilets and showers are fairly clean. The camping area is grassy and large enough to make you feel comfortable. This is the least expensive campground on the island and a
favorite of backpackers. Mosquitoes can be bothersome here, so
be sure to bring repellent and coils. Excursions are available at
competitive rates, and Peter himself has been known to take visitors into the bush with him to explore and look for fruit. Located next door to Pension Manava, six kilometers south of
Uturoa. ~ PK 6.5, Avera; 66-20-01. BUDGET.

Also in the Avera area is the **Kaoha Nui Ranch**, a pension and
riding stable. The ranch has two bungalows with private baths,
and four rooms with two single beds apiece, communal baths and
kitchen. The owners will rent beds in the rooms as dorm beds; they
cost a little more than Peter's Place, but they're quite a bit nicer.

Polynesian Navigators Revive Ancient Skills

The skills and heroic feats of ancient Polynesian navigators have not been lost on their modern-day descendants. In 1992, dubbed unofficially as the "Year of the Polynesian Canoe," Taputa-puatea became the site of a graduation ceremony for traditional navigators from throughout the Pacific who are relearning the art of steering by the stars and swells. The event attracted over 100 participants, including Hawaiians, Tahitians, Cook Islanders and New Zealand Maoris. It was reportedly the first time in 800 years that Polynesian navigators had come to one of the most sacred religious sites in eastern Polynesia.

On March 18, 1995, the shrine was again the venue for a Pan-Pacific gathering. A convocation of traditional double-hulled sailing canoes from Hawaii, the Cook Islands, New Zealand and Tahiti converged at Taputapuatea. In addition to the canoes, a reed raft constructed by Easter Islanders (living in Tahiti) was also there. The assembly not only revitalized ties between Polynesians from the three corners of the Polynesian triangle, but revived the importance of Taputapuatea as a Polynesian cultural center. The crews were welcomed with elaborate rituals, chants and speeches that brought new life to what many had thought was a dying culture.

Participating in this voyage of rediscovery were eight Polynesian canoes. They all retraced the 1500-year-old route from Tahiti to the Marquesas, and from the Marquesas to Hawaii.

Breakfast is available if you don't feel like cooking, and there's a small bar. The stables offer guided horseback rides of various durations, including a full-moon ride, on small Marquesan horses. They also offer half-day waterfall and Mt. Temehani hikes. The manager has a special interest in botany and medicinal uses of local plants; he will share his extensive knowledge with guests. Free airport and boat transfers. ~ PK 6, south of Uturoa, Avera; phone/fax 66-25-46, cell 74-37-13; www.tahitidecouvrir.com, e-mail kaoha.nui@mail.pf. BUDGET TO MODERATE.

> Although Raiatea is the last bastion of fire walking in French Polynesia, you'll rarely see it performed here. Raiatean fire walkers are generally seen in Tahiti during the *Heiva* festival.

Located on the waterfront at PK 8.8, **Coco Beach** offers six bungalows for long-term stays (one month or more) at 75,000 CFP per month for two. Amenities include carports, washing machines and hot water. This property is run by long-time Raiatea hotelier Marie-Isabelle. ~ Avera; 66-37-64. BUDGET.

Pension Rauvine is located on the lagoon side in the Avera district. The property boasts eight clean bungalows, each with a private bath, one large and one small bed and a fully equipped kitchen. A communal sitting area is perched on a pontoon over the water. The owners also run lagoon excursions with three large canoes, and 4X4 trips into the island's interior are available as well. Some English is spoken and they provide free pick-up from the airport. ~ PK 8, Avera; phone/fax 66-25-50; www.pensionrauvine.pf, e-mail pensionrauvine@mail.pf. BUDGET TO MODERATE.

Located near the Avera area at the foot of Faaroa Bay, **Raiatea Village** has ten bungalows, all with kitchenettes and private baths. Unfortunately, the place is looking quite run down these days: the bungalows need paint and the roofs of several structures were covered with blue tarps when we visited recently. Although the hotel is located on the water, I do not advise swimming here because of the presence of a particular type of algae that causes extreme itching. (The owners shrugged off the danger, which made me uneasy.) Bicycle, canoe and car rentals are available, and the hotel offers a full battery of excursions. ~ PK 10, Avera; 66-31-62, cell 78-23-53, fax 66-10-65; e-mail raiatea.village@mail.pf. MODERATE.

La Croix du Sud was constructed to accommodate guests from Stardust Marina, but other guests are certainly welcome. The property has three rooms on the mountain side of the road just across from the yacht center. From the hill you have a wonderful view of Faaroa Bay and the small yacht harbor. Another new pension, not affiliated with either La Croix or Stardust Marina, was under construction across the street in April 2002. ~ Faaroa Bay; 66-27-55. MODERATE.

Pension Te Maeva provides two bungalows, each with a double bed, private bath, fan, fridge and terrace. One of the best qualities Te Maeva offers is a terrific panoramic view. A swimming pool is also included in the amenities. Te Maeva is in the Taputapuatea district, 25 kilometers from Uturoa. ~ Taputapuatea; phone/fax 66-37-28; www.chez.com/temaeva, e-mail temaeva@mail.pf. MODERATE.

On Opua Bay, just past the Taputapuatea Marae, **Hotel Atiapiti** offers seven very nice detached bungalows set in a large manicured garden. Each bungalow accommodates up to five people and includes a living room, bath, covered terrace, tiled floor, air conditioning, TV and minibar. Some of the units have kitchenettes, but meal plans are available as well. This is a good choice if you have a special interest in the *marae* or just want to get away from it all. Inquire before going as the property closes occasionally for vacations. Contact Marie-Claude Rajaud—she speaks minimal English, but is very friendly. Roundtrip transfers from the airport or dock are 2000 CFP. ~ PK 30.5, Taputapuatea; phone/fax 66-16-65; e-mail atiapiti@mail.pf. MODERATE.

◀ HIDDEN

Starting from the northern tip of the island is **The Clubhouse**, facing the Apooiti Yacht Harbor. It is the largest and most formal restaurant in Raiatea. With a bamboo motif, The Clubhouse is shaded by a massive thatch-roofed canopy. The menu is reasonably priced and quite comprehensive. Some of the better dishes include *poisson cru*, chicken curry, mahimahi, grilled lobster and spaghetti with crab. The restaurant has a long bar and indoor/outdoor seating with a capacity of up to 200 guests. In addition to the food service, The Clubhouse is a fine place for a sunset cocktail or to catch the regular entertainment on the weekends. The downside is that the owner tends to be moody. A lot of locals don't care to eat there. ~ Apooiti Marina, Uturoa; 66-11-66. MODERATE TO DELUXE.

DINING

La Voile d'Or restaurant and snack bar is the bright blue building past The Clubhouse at the Apooiti Marina. With some tables set in the sand and a covered terrace overlooking the ocean, it has a true Tahitian ambience. Closed Monday. ~ Uturoa. MODERATE.

Just north of the Raiatea Marina where boats sit in dry-dock is **Patisserie Arnaud**. The little roadside stand sells a variety of home-baked breads as well as muffins, drinks and terrific-looking pies. Closed Sunday and Monday. ~ Uturoa; 66-14-32. BUDGET.

◀ HIDDEN

Located halfway between the airport and town is **Le Napoli**, which dishes up pizzas and other Italian fare. ~ Uturoa; 66-10-77. BUDGET.

There are several local bars and restaurants in Uturoa where you can take in the local scene and the gastronomical flavors of the island.

A good place to begin is **Sea Horse**, a Chinese restaurant in the Gare Maritime complex by the wharf. The menu includes the expected Chinese dishes as well as specialties such as shark fin or sea cucumber soup. ~ Uturoa; 66-16-34. BUDGET TO MODERATE. The **Quai des Pescheurs** ("Fisherman's Wharf") restaurant is also in the new complex. Not surprisingly, fish is the specialty, but French food is also served. The restaurant puts on "Le Spectacle," a Polynesian dance review, every Saturday night at 8:30. ~ Uturoa; 66-43-19. MODERATE.

The **Jade Garden** is a Chinese eatery on the main street. It has the standard litany of dishes, including chow mein and chop suey. ~ Uturoa; 66-34-40. BUDGET.

Michelle, at the rear of the Hotel Hinano, is an inexpensive indoor/outdoor restaurant that serves generous portions of French and Tahitian food such as fish, steak and pastries. It's popular with locals and the indoor/outdoor setting is very pleasant. Opens as early as 5 a.m. for breakfast. ~ Uturoa; 66-14-66. BUDGET.

Snack Chez Remy now occupies a spot in the new waterfront complex on the dock. It has good French/Tahitian food such as *maa tinito*. You can sip a local beer with the locals and drink in the terrific local color. Open only for breakfast and lunch. ~ Uturoa. BUDGET.

Raiatea Hawaiki Nui Hotel is the island's top-end accommodation—but it's popular with businessmen and resident families at lunch, and surprisingly economical given the quality of food, presentation and service, and the lovely setting. The daily lunch special is only around US$15, including dessert and coffee. Cuisine is mostly French; emphasis is on seafood. Breakfast, lunch and dinner. Don't miss the live local music on Friday and Saturday nights. ~ Uturoa; 60-05-00. MODERATE TO DELUXE.

South of Vaiaau on the island's southwestern shore, baguette sandwiches, fruit and drinks can be had at **Snack Punaeroa**. ~ PK 32.5, Punaeroa. BUDGET.

GROCERIES There are a host of markets and general stores in Uturoa. For volume shoppers or yachters the best bet for local produce, fish or poultry is the municipal market in town that opens at dawn

AUTHOR FAVORITE

Snack Moemoea, an outdoor café with a distinctive blue awning, is located on the waterfront. Here you'll find the best hamburgers in town. We also liked the grilled mahimahi on the lunch menu. The generous portion of chow mein is decent, too. Locals frequently gather here for evening beers and to greet passersby. This place opens early for breakfast and has a good, strong coffee that will start your day with a buzz. ~ Uturoa; 66-39-84. BUDGET.

every day. The savvy traveler should occasionally skip restaurant food and head here for a picnic of pâté, fresh fruit and wine.

For bulk goods, pharmacy items and the like, visit Uturoa's **Champion Store** downtown. Part of a European discount chain with outlets in Papeete, it also has a variety of everyday products as well as gourmet items such as exotic goat cheeses, pâté and duck confit. The prices are generally better than at the two main Chinese stores. ~ Uturoa.

For a more conventional supermarket, check out **Supermarche Leogite**, which has a virtual department store in its upstairs section. ~ Uturoa; 66-35-33. Likewise, **Supermarche Liaut** has all the basics including a nice array of wine, beer, pâté, cheese and other items for a picnic lunch. ~ Uturoa; 66-21-09.

SHOPPING

Librairie de Uturoa, the downtown bookstore, sells English-language newspapers and magazines. ~ Uturoa; 66-30-80. On the mountain side of Uturoa's main street, **La Palm d'Or** has a good selection of black pearl jewelry and locally made handicrafts. ~ Uturoa; 66-23-79.

Two galleries on the island have extensive selections of French Polynesian artwork and quality handicrafts. **Galerie Anuanua** (located on the main drag next door to La Palm d'Or) has art prints and local crafts made from gourds, pottery and shells. ~ Uturoa; 66-12-66; www.multimania.com/anuanua. **Galerie Arts Expo**, in the Apooiti Marina on the north side of the island, has a superb collection of original Polynesian paintings and prints (Deloffre, Campestro, Lux), as well as high-quality pareus, jewelry and handicrafts. ~ Uturoa; 66-11-83.

My Flower, in the Gare Maritime complex, has a nice selection of fine art, including paintings and wood carvings. They also feature local and imported flowers as well as local handicrafts. ~ Uturoa; phone/fax 66-19-19. **Sephora** is another boutique in the Gare Maritime complex that has high-quality merchandise. ~ Uturoa; 66-21-21.

For black pearls, visit one of several new pearl boutiques in the Gare Maritime commercial complex, or go directly to the source at the **Vairua Pearl Farm**. There are daily tours and demonstrations, as well as pearls for sale. There are shortened hours on Saturday; closed Sunday except by appointment. ~ PK 9, Avera; phone/fax 66-12-12; www.multimania.com/blackpearls.

◄ *HIDDEN*

Atettier du Marqouillat is a tiny jewelry workshop tucked behind Peter Brotherson's Camping in Avera. The little space is the creative space for C. Tremollieres, who works with black pearls, black coral, shells and mother-of-pearl with sterling silver or 18K gold. Open 9 to noon and 2 to 5; closed Tuesday. ~ PK 6.5, Avera.

INTERNET ACCESS

There are two places in Uturoa where you can check e-mail and browse the web. The **Europcar** office across from the wharf has a computer in the back room, and access costs 250 CFP for 15 minutes. ~ Uturoa.

North of town, **Phenix** computer store offers access for 15 CFP per minute, the cheapest rate I found in all of French Polynesia. The building has a big "Internet Cafe" sign, and sodas and coffee are available if you ask. This is also a good place to buy blank CDs, plug adapters and batteries if you need them. Open Monday through Friday 8 a.m. to noon and 2 p.m. to 5 p.m. ~ Uturoa; phone/fax 66-20-66.

NIGHTLIFE   The **Zenith** is a rollicking local disco, appealing to the younger crowd. Look for it upstairs from the Leogite Supermarket. Zenith features a good mix of live music and disco every Friday and Saturday night. ~ Uturoa; 66-27-49.

The bar/restaurant at the **Raiatea Hawaiki Nui Hotel** has live local music every Friday and Saturday night from about 8 p.m. until after midnight. It's a popular place with locals as well as visitors, and attracts a more upscale, middle-aged crowd. ~ Uturoa; 66-20-23.

Another fine venue for a sunset drink is **The Clubhouse** at the Apooiti Marina. It's a nice place to just sit outdoors and watch the sailboats come in. ~ Apooiti Marina, Uturoa; 66-11-66.

La Voile d'Or has a lovely terrace that makes a terrific setting for an evening drink. ~ Apooiti Marina, Uturoa.

Every Saturday night at 8:30, **Quai des Pescheurs**, a restaurant in the Gare Maritime complex, puts on "Le Spectacle," a Polynesian dance review. Make it a night out with dinner, or just stop by for a beer and enjoy the show. ~ Uturoa.

BEACHES   Alas, Raiatea is bereft of beaches on the main island. There are, however, a number of excellent beaches on the *motu* that dot the fringing reefs. You'll have to rent or hire a boat to get there. Most of the tour operators and hotels have picnic-at-the-beach options available.

AUTHOR FAVORITE

If you're looking for quality souvenirs, **Arii Boutique** has hand-painted T-shirts and pareus with Tahitian motifs. Located on the mountain side of Uturoa's main street, Arii purchases some of the best locally manufactured clothing from the factory next door. This is the best selection at the best prices you will find anywhere in French Polynesia for locally made men's, women's and children's shirts. The store also stocks a wide selection of Polynesian print fabric, if you'd like to sew your own. ~ Uturoa; 66-35-54.

MOTU NAO NAO 🐠 🐟 At the southern end of the island, just across from the village of Fetuna, is a large *motu* called Nao Nao that has a beautiful stretch of white sand and is good for picnics.

MOTU IRIRU 🐠 🐟 Another *motu* worth considering is Iriru, located off Opeha Point, near the mouth of Faaroa Bay. It has a fine white-sand beach and good snorkeling, as well as potable water, a shower, a barbecue and a small changing cabin. If you are in good shape and have a companion to help, it is possible to reach this *motu* by *pirogue* in about an hour and a half. Overnight camping is permitted here, but ask your pension to contact the proper authorities for permission before pitching your tent.

Only 20 minutes from Raiatea by boat is Tahaa, a drier, less fertile sister island sharing the same lagoon. Approximately 55 square miles (90 square kilometers) in area, Tahaa has nine villages and a population numbering around 4845. The island is surrounded by a reef with two passes. Long a poor relation to the more economically developed Raiatea, Tahaa offers the visitor an even more tranquil place to stop over—off the beaten track and friendlier than its neighbor.

Tahaa

Most people here live by subsistence farming, although vanilla and copra are produced commercially. In fact, Tahaa is the leading producer of vanilla in the Society Islands, giving it the nickname "The Vanilla Island." Livestock and chicken ranches are also important to the island's economy. Local crafts such as handwoven hats, baskets, place mats, bedspreads, shell necklaces and wood sculpture are cottage industries.

Although tourism is not Tahaa's mainstay, its importance to the island's economy is gaining. A five-star Pearl Resort—the first of its kind here and the most luxurious in all of French Polynesia—opened on one of Tahaa's *motu* in July 2002.

The largest community on Tahaa is **Patio** on the north coast. Patio has a lazy, backwater ambience, and is little more than a collection of concrete structures that include a *gendarmerie*, infirmary, post office and school. Perhaps the most noteworthy site is the sea-turtle park on the grounds of the Hibiscus hotel.

SIGHTS

Tahaa's road system is less developed than Raiatea's, making it a challenge to get around. Because there is no public transportation available, you will have to rent a car or walk if you want to explore the island on your own.

Tahaa is not stunning in the manner of Bora Bora or Huahine. It lacks the dramatic land- and seascapes of those islands. There isn't a major population center on Tahaa—rather, the island's inhabitants are scattered in a number of villages. There aren't any conspicuous gathering places in those communities, making it difficult for you to observe daily life. This characteristic, combined with a virtual absence of transportation, makes Tahaa difficult to get to know.

But its strength is as a port-of-call for yachts. Splendid sailing in the lagoon, the ease of finding protected moorage and lots of *motu* to explore make it an ideal setting for a sailboat. In addition, several hotels go out of their way to cater to the yachting trade.

If you are not a yachtie or a diver, the only other major activity on Tahaa is hiking. There are a number of trails and a coastal road that allow you to see most of the island by foot. If you have a mountain bike at your disposal, all the better.

Tahaa's terrain is rugged and rocky, covered with vegetation adapted to its relatively dry, tropical climate. There are coconut palms and much of the same flora that inhabit the rest of the Society Group, but Tahaa does not have Tahiti's lush cover of rainforest. There are, however, several strikingly beautiful bays on the island, the most attractive being **Haamene** and **Hurepiti**. Both are narrow, fjordlike passages that furrow deep into the body of the island. They are easily accessible on foot and offer stunning views.

Excursions to points of interest can be arranged with local guides, including visits to sites where the mythical Polynesian hero, appropriately named Hiro, left his mark. These **landmarks** include Hiro's bowl, left footprint, crest and boat. All of them are rather subtle and difficult to ferret out if you don't know what to look for. For example, Hiro's footprint is little more than an indentation on a rock. All of the sites are located on private property so it's best to go on a guided tour if you wish to see them.

LODGING   Despite the fact that the framework for tourism is in an embryonic stage on Tahaa, there is a good selection of mid-range accommodations. As in other isolated French Polynesian destinations, you should expect to pay with traveler's checks or cash—only a few resorts accept plastic.

Tupenu Village is a waterfront pension one kilometer from the Patio *navette* quay. They have one large *fare* with three rooms for rent. The rooms each have one double and one single bed. There's a communal bath, a self-contained kitchen, a dining room and even a small restaurant with a TV lounge. Transfers from Raiatea are available and island activities can be arranged. Two-night minimum stay. ~ Patio; 65-62-01. BUDGET.

HIDDEN ▶   **Hibiscus** has a large dock and other facilities for yachts. The large hotel houses a dining terrace, dining room, bar and salon. The grounds are well landscaped and tidy. Three very rustic rooms have private bath facilities while two spacious family-style bungalows have self-contained kitchens and private baths. The Hibiscus offers a unique blend of experiences: It is both a family stay in rural Polynesia and—at times—a sophisticated, cosmopolitan experience. Arriving by boat, one might hear the sounds of someone practicing ukulele, or the barnyard calls of roosters announcing the morning. But there's nightlife, too, with international visitors socializing in the bar, leisurely dining featuring Lolita's excellent cooking, and dance performances several times a week. Yachts are a very important source of income, so Leo and Lolita cater to them by offering free services in exchange for their patronage at the restaurant. I would recommend Hibiscus for someone who likes a gregarious crowd, as yachties tend to be when they hit shore. Yachties, take note: There are moorings for 14 boats. Hibiscus can be reached at VHF 68. Leo speaks English, German and French and will arrange for transfers from Raiatea. ~ Haamene Bay; 65-61-06, cell 79-28-81, fax 65-65-65; www. tahaa-tahiti.com, e-mail hibiscus@tahaa-tahiti.com. BUDGET.

One of the newer properties on the island, **Chez Patricia et Daniel Amaru** features four Polynesian-style bungalows set around a large central building with a pearl-jewelry shop, restaurant, communal kitchen and outdoor terrace for lounging or dining. The large bungalows are nicely decorated, and each has a private bath with hot water. This is a family effort and the owners are

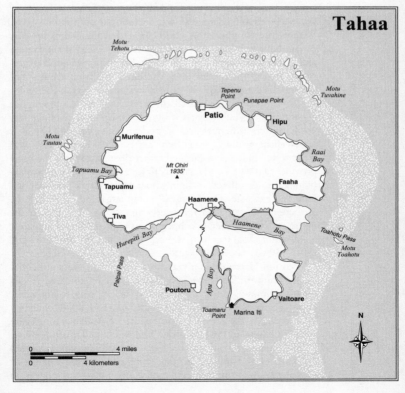

Tahaa

flexible and eager to please guests. The son (also Daniel) speaks English and they offer complimentary tours of the family pearl farm across the bay. Patricia specializes in Tahitian seafood; you may cook for yourself, or buy groceries and she will cook them for you, but why bother? Patricia is a terrific cook and the meal plans are among the least expensive on Tahaa. Patricia and Daniel will arrange for the usual excursions around Tahaa, and transfers from the airport or dock in Raiatea are very reasonable. This pension offers good value for the money; it's a good introduction to rural Polynesia with a pearl-farm tour thrown in. Reservations recommended. Credit cards are accepted. ~ Near the north mouth of Haamene Bay, Haamene; 78-67-68, fax 65-60-83; e-mail v.p@mail.pf. BUDGET TO MODERATE.

Pension Api in Vaitoare offers simple but clean rooms in a large *fare*, with or without private bath. Meals are also available, and the management runs a small lunch counter and take-out service. ~ Vaitoare; phone/fax 65-69-88; www.pensionapi.com, e-mail jjwatlp@mail.pf. BUDGET.

Marina Iti combines a nautical atmosphere with first-rate accommodations that have a decidedly European flavor. There are six nicely appointed bungalows, including a honeymoon suite. With privacy in mind, this unit is located at the end of the row of lagoon-side bungalows, and has a lovely view of the lagoon and Raiatea. All units have private baths and small outdoor terraces. Two of the newest ones also have laundry machines and are intended for longer stays. The restaurant has a chef from France and the cuisine is decidedly French. There is a beach, but it has a rather shallow shelf with a depth up to about three feet until you reach the reef edge—good for kids perhaps. This is is an excellent, well-run hotel that might appeal to someone who is interested in the conventional rather than the exotic. The hotel provides rental cars and transfers to Raiatea. Various nautical activities are also offered, including boat trips to Bora Bora or Huahine and excursions to Marae Taputapuatea and other Raiatea attractions. Located on the southernmost tip of Tahaa in the midst of a well-tended coconut plantation, the Marina Iti is just a ten-minute boat trip from Raiatea. ~ Toamaru Point; 65-61-01, cell 72-30-61, fax 65-63-87. MODERATE TO DELUXE.

Pension Herenui is only a short walk from the shuttleboat quay in Poutoru. The three bungalows, set in a manicured garden with a swimming pool, are clean and include private hot-water baths. Nearby is a communal open-sided *fare* with a fully equipped kitchen and TV for guest use. Meal plans are available, too. There are no kitchens in the bungalows and Madame Delort does not permit smoking or eating in the units. A small boutique is located at the entry and she will arrange for transfers from Raiatea or any of the usual tours or activities. Unfortunately, the ocean in this area is not suitable for swimming. ~ Poutoru; 65-62-60, fax 65-64-17; www.herenui.com, e-mail postmaster@herenui.com. BUDGET TO MODERATE.

Mareva Village, owned and managed by Yannick and Mareva Ebb, consists of six bungalows lined up like soldiers on the beachless shore. The quality of the accommodation is first rate: New Zealand lumber and fixtures were used in building the facility. Each bungalow is identical—a living room with a TV and a couch that converts to a bed, a ceiling fan, a kitchen with refrigerator and a well-appointed bathroom with a hot-water shower. A deck, large enough to dine on, at the front of each bungalow overlooks the lagoon toward Raiatea. The "village" has a restaurant with a deck that commands a stunning view of the lagoon, Raiatea and the open ocean. They serve a mix of French, Tahitian and Chinese cuisine. A variety of excursions are offered, including deep-sea fishing, snorkeling trips, a *motu* excursion and a land safari. Transfers are provided from Raiatea at an additional cost. ~ Poutoru; phone/fax 65-61-61. MODERATE.

Except for a Bank of Socredo agency in the village of Tapuamu, there is no banking on Tahaa. ~ Patio; 65-66-55.

If you seek a quiet respite, **Pension Vaihi** is the place to go. Though modest, it is a quality property, offering three *fare* constructed tastefully from bamboo and featuring tightly woven thatched roofs. Amenities include private (cold water) baths, two twin beds and a terrace. A private dock provides short transfer to the nearby Tapuamu quay. All meals are available and served in a communal dining room. ~ Hurepiti Bay; 65-62-02. BUDGET TO MODERATE.

Chez Louise, a popular restaurant in Tiva next to the lagoon, now offers dorm accommodations with shared kitchen and bath for up to eight people. ~ Tiva; 65-66-88. BUDGET.

Chez Pascal is clearly the budget traveler's choice for Tahaa. There are four bungalows with outdoor private (cold water) baths, and there's a house with two rooms available. The house is very clean and brightly decorated with colorful fabrics and the rooms are large and simply furnished. There are two private baths as well as cooking facilities. The electricity is solar powered. The tariff includes breakfast and dinner, or *pension complete* if you don't feel like cooking. A range of activities are offered at reasonable prices, including a trip to Motu Tautau, where the *Pêche aux Cailloux* (fishing festival) is held. The management is extremely friendly and generous—they also enjoy dining with guests. Chez Pascal is a good value compared to similarly priced accommodations. It is located in Tapuamu close to the quay. ~ Tapuamu; phone/fax 65-60-42. BUDGET TO MODERATE.

◄ HIDDEN

Au Phil du Temps in Murifenua on the west side of the island has two local-style *fare* on the lagoon facing Bora Bora. The bungalows each have double beds, TVs and minibars. Two private

◄ HIDDEN

bathrooms are separate from the bungalows but include actual bathtubs, practically unheard of here. There is a small restaurant and also a lounge for guests. Management offers free land and water activities if parties of two stay longer than three nights with full meal plans. Boat transfers are available from Raiatea; yachties will appreciate free moorings and the dinghy dock right in front of the pension. ~ Murifenua; 65-64-19; e-mail moutte. junior@mail.pf. MODERATE.

Located on secluded Motu Tautau off the western shore of Tahaa, **Le Tahaa Private Island & Spa** is not only the first five-star hotel on the island—it is the most luxurious resort in all of French Polynesia. The resort, which cost US$14 million to build, opened in July 2002. The accommodations include 48 over-water suites and 12 beach suites that are more than 300 square feet each. The beach suites each come with a private swimming pool and tropical garden. The public areas and lounges are built up in trees, giving guests a stunning view of Tahaa and Bora Bora. There are three restaurants, two bars, two boutiques, an Olympic-size swimming pool, a game room, a tennis court, a dive center, an activities desk, internet access and secretarial service. Can we stay forever? ~ Motu Tautau; 50-84-54, fax 43-17-86; www.pearlresorts.com. ULTRA-DELUXE.

HIDDEN ►   **Vahine Island** is a secluded *motu* accommodation a mile and a half off the northern tip of Tahaa. Six beach bungalows and three over-water units are situated on the private, ten-acre Motu Tuvahine. Each bungalow is fan-cooled and features one king or two twin beds. The location enjoys stunning views of Tahaa, Raiatea, Bora Bora and Huahine. The restaurant has a good reputation for seafood and French-fusion cuisine. A variety of activities and excursions are available, and a maximum of 16 guests is allowed on the island at a time. Their advertisements claim you'll "discover a perfect hideaway paradise." We're inclined to believe. ~ Motu Tuvahine; 65-67-38, fax 65-67-70; www.vahine-island.net, e-mail info@vahine-island.net. ULTRA-DELUXE.

DINING   The restaurant scene is mostly confined to the hotels. Not to worry—given the difficulty of getting around the island, you tend to eat where you reside.

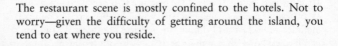

AUTHOR FAVORITE

My hands-down favorite for the best hotel is **Vahine Island**, located on a small *motu* off of Tahaa. Remote, but with just enough luxury to avoid being ostentatious, it's perfect for honeymooners. If you have the means, this is the place to stay not only on Tahaa but perhaps in all of French Polynesia. See above for more information.

Outside of the hotel scene you'll find **Restaurant/Bar Tissan** in Patio. Open for lunch and dinner on Friday and Saturday, it offers Chinese and Tahitian fare including *poisson cru* and chow mein. This is the place to go for local ambience. ~ Patio. BUDGET.

The island's newest non-hotel dining is the exclusive **Le Passage**, a *gastronomique* restaurant whose fixed-price menu of French cuisine changes regularly. Dining is only by reservation, which must be made at least a day in advance. Closed Sunday. ~ Faaha; 65-66-75. DELUXE.

◄ HIDDEN

Restaurant Hibiscus has good cuisine, including baked mahimahi, leg of lamb, calamari, salad and fresh fruit for dessert. Continental breakfast is offered in the morning—coffee, tea, hot chocolate, bread, butter and jam. You can probably get something more substantial if you ask for it. ~ Haamene Bay; 65-61-06. BUDGET TO MODERATE.

Pension Api runs a small lunch counter and take-out service. ~ Vaitoare; phone/fax 65-69-88. BUDGET.

The chef at **Marina Iti** is Guy, the highly regarded former chef of the Hotel Tenape and Chez Agnes et Guy on Raiatea. The excellent food and ambience here is enhanced by the fine lagoon views. Seafood is always a good bet; the restaurant will prepare a traditional feast, *tamaara'a*, baked in an underground oven upon request. ~ Toamaru Point; 65-61-01, fax 65-63-87. MODERATE TO DELUXE.

Chez Louise in Tiva is an open-air restaurant next to the lagoon. Their traditional "Marina Menu" features various seafood specialties tastefully served in bamboo. Popular with locals and tourists, this restaurant is one of the few eating places in Tahaa. It's open seven days a week from 8 a.m. to 10 p.m. ~ Tiva; 65-66-88. BUDGET TO MODERATE.

There are small stores in Patio, Poutoru, Tapuamu, Faaha and Haamene that have soft drinks, snacks and other basics. However, most locals rely on day trips to Uturoa on Raiatea to take care of serious grocery shopping.

GROCERIES

In Hurepiti, **Sophie Boutique** has a selection of pareus and shirts, as well as a limited selection of crafts. ~ Hurepiti; 65-62-56.

SHOPPING

There are also two well-regarded pearl boutiques that you might consider: **Motu Pearl Boutique** in Faa'aha Teuri (65-66-67) and **Vaipoe Pearl Boutique** in Hurepiti Bay (65-62-56).

Nightlife is minimal indeed, but the **Hibiscus** is often a meeting-place for yachts. When yachts are in town, the owners provide a wonderful evening's entertainment with good dining accompanied by local music. ~ Haamene Bay; 65-61-06.

NIGHTLIFE

BEACHES   Without exception, the best beaches are on the *motu* that fringe the barrier reef. Except for Vahine Island, a private resort, the beaches on the *motu* don't have any facilities. A boat ride to any of the *motu* can be arranged through the various resorts.

MOTU TAUTAU AND MOTU TEHOTU Motu Tautau and Motu Tehotu are small offshore islets accessible only by boat. Both have fine white-sand beaches and offer better than average snorkeling.

Outdoor Adventures

CAMPING   Situated on the edge of the lagoon, **Sunset Beach Motel Apooiti** has a spacious camping area for about 30 people. The management is quite hospitable. There are also excellent communal shower/bath facilities and a lounge area. Two kilometers from the airport and five kilometers west of town, it's slightly more expensive than the competition but well worth it. Free airport or boat transfers, snorkeling gear and canoes are available. It's clearly the best campground on the island. ~ Uturoa; 66-33-47. BUDGET.

Peter Brotherson's Camping (a.k.a. Peter's Place) is a combination dorm and very basic campground facing the sea. There is a small camping area set up for up to 10 tents; a communal kitchen with two sinks and a small stove, and communal bathrooms/ showers. It's located six kilometers from Uturoa. ~ PK 6.5, Avera; 66-20-01. BUDGET.

There are no campgrounds on Tahaa.

DIVING   The Raiatea–Tahaa lagoon offers excellent diving. There are a wide variety of both reef fish and pelagics. An unusual blue-and-purple colored coral can be found on the reef. Lagoon dive sites are numerous, and many are within a 10- to 20-minute range by boat from port. Fish feeding is practiced, attracting schools of Napoleon Wrasses, brown and white eels, Picasso triggerfish, yellow perches, red snappers, rainbow runners, silver jacks and plenty of white-tip, black-tip and grey sharks. Pelagic species include barracuda, surgeon fish, tuna and rays.

Some of the more interesting dive sites include **Avera Pass**, which has abundant coral, including black varieties; the **Coral Garden**,

PÊCHE AUX CAILLOUX

Pêche aux Cailloux is a local fishing festival held every year in October or November. It's a dramatic spectacle, involving the coordinated action of men in boats who drive fish into the lagoon toward the beach by pounding the water with stones attached to cords. On shore a large number of people wait with their nets. Call the Comité de Fetes de Tahaa at the Mairie (Town Hall) for information. ~ Patio; 60-80-80.

which has some terrific specimens of *agaricia* and *montipora*; and **Coral Caves**, where there are—you guessed it—coral caves.

There are several wreck dives in Avera Pass, including Coaler Wreck (an interisland vessel) and a Catalina seaplane. **Coaler Wreck** is at about 100 feet (30 meters) just off the Raiatea Pearl Resort. The vessel is an old German coaler that went down just before the turn of the 20th century. The bridge has since disappeared and it's easy to access the rather large hold. Inside is a great deal of immobile marine life, including sponges, gorgonians and black coral. When diving the wreck it's also possible to see alevins, shrimp and an old solitary barracuda who has established this as his hunting ground.

The **Three Masted Wreck** is one of the best wreck dives in French Polynesia and is great for night diving. **Japanese Garden**, which at a depth of ten feet (three meters), is perfect for beginners and has a plethora of triggerfish, sharks, Napoleon Wrasses and moray eels as well as coral. Other sites worth visiting are **Paipai Pass**, which offers cave dives; **Perch Ballet**, which often has schools of snappers, Napoleon Wrasses and black-tip sharks; **Toahotu Pass**, which is known for barracuda and platax; and **Octopus Grotto**, a deep dive renowned for legions of octopuses.

The **Catalina** belonged to an interisland airline company. It went down in February of 1958 about two kilometers southeast of Teavarua Pass on a beautiful day. Evidently, in making a turn over the lagoon, the plane's right wing clipped the water, causing the fuselage to split in half before sinking. Miraculously, all 11 passengers survived. The boat now rests at a depth of 100 feet (about 30 meters) in a sandbank and is remarkably intact. The plane is now home to thousands of striped sea bass, yellow-finned surgeon fish, one-spot sea bass, soldier fish and immobile marine life such as sponges and black coral.

Hemisphere Sub, operated by Hubert Clot and Floriane Voisin, provides equipment rentals, transportation and lessons for diving enthusiasts. The dive boat handles up to ten people inside or outside the lagoon. The two instructors provide open-water certification courses and two daily dives. Hemisphere Sub has some unusual excursions, including drift dives, shark feeding and Napoleon feeding. When I was there the Scuba Pro gear seemed to be well maintained. In addition to transporting you on their boat, for an extra charge they will bring your gear and rendezvous with your yacht at sea. A minimum of three people is needed for the special rendezvous service. Hemisphere will also rent gear to experienced divers who want to go it on their own. ~ Apooiti Marina; 66-12-49, fax 66-28-63; www.diveraiatea.com, e-mail hemis-subdiving@mail.pf.

Shark Dive Polynesia, based in Patio on Tahaa, offers daily dives in the ocean, passes and lagoon, as well as on the wrecks.

Le bapteme, night dives and two-tank dives are also available, as are advanced dive training and video. ~ Patio; 65-65-55, fax 65-65-50; e-mail shark@dive.pf.

Tahaa Pearl Beach Resort and Spa at Le Tahaa Private Island & Spa also offers diving. ~ Patio; 65-67-78 and 60-84-00; www.bluenui.com, e-mail tahaabluenui@mail.pf.

FISHING

Fishing is a way of life in the islands and the low population density in the area combined with a rich reef system makes it good sport. With a little luck it's possible to hook mahimahi, marlin, sailfish, jack and tuna.

On Tahaa, fishing expeditions can be inexpensively arranged though **Mareva Village**. ~ Tahaa; 65-61-61. **The Sakario**, a Bertram 28 with a capacity for four passengers, is one of the better local fishing boats available for half- or full-day charters. ~ Uturoa; 66-33-53. **Marina Iti** also charters vessels. ~ 65-61-01. **Te Manuata** is another possibility. ~ Uturoa; phone/fax 66-21-09.

West Coast Charters runs deep-sea and lagoon fishing trips. ~ Uturoa; 66-45-39, cell 79-28-78.

SAILING

Cruising is definitely the best way to see Raiatea and Tahaa. Public transportation and, often, road conditions, leave a lot to be desired on these islands. Consequently, if you have the time and money, touring Raiatea and Tahaa from the deck of a sailboat is the best way to explore the area. There are many good anchorages, plenty of fresh water is available and there are several uninhabited offshore *motu* accessible only by boat.

Just past the airport, at PK 6 on the north shore of Raiatea, is a central boatyard facility. **Raiatea Marine** (66-24-14) and **Raiatea Carenage** (66-22-96) offer haul-out facilities with a full range of surveying, storage and boatbuilding services. These operations can also be reached at CHF 68 or 72.

AUTHOR FAVORITE

When I want a cushy jaunt across some water I head out with **Faimanu Croisieres**. Louis, the seasoned skipper, built the exquisite catamaran himself and put 20 years of sailing experience into every inch of it. This is readily apparent when you step aboard the vessel, which is perfectly designed for the South Seas. The living areas are spacious, well engineered and very practical. The Faimanu Croisieres features three double cabins onboard and a single bunk. Louis' sailing skills, his understanding of the local waters and his intimate knowledge of life in Polynesia make his charters triply unforgettable experiences. His tours include the Leeward Islands, Tahiti and the Tuamotus, and goes out for day trips and longer journeys. ~ Apu Bay; 65-62-52, fax 65-69-08; e-mail faimanu@mail.pf.

For people requiring bonds for immigration, the Tresor-Public office is located just north of the post office in Uturoa. The bond required is the cost of a one-way airline ticket back to the country of origin. (For more information on requirements, see the "Sailing" section in Chapter Two.)

Among the yacht harbors on Raiatea, the **Apooiti Marina** is the premier facility. Constructed by Moorings Ltd., an internationally known purveyor of sailing vacations, it's one of the more exciting developments on the island. Apooiti has moorings for private vessels, as well as 30 of their own yachts that range in length from 38 to 52 feet (11.5 to 15.5 meters).

The Moorings offers two options for nautical adventurers: bareboating, for those who already have the skill to sail a yacht, and crewed yachts, where experienced sailors are provided (at a much greater cost, of course). In either case, the staff supplies all provisions from bread to drinks. Because of Raiatea's geographical position in the Society Islands, cruising to Bora Bora, Huahine and Maupiti is easy. Prices start at approximately US$490 per day or US$3430 per week for a Moorings 35, the least expensive yacht. Note that these prices are for high season, July 1 to September 1. ~ Uturoa; 66-35-93, fax 66-20-94, or 800-535-7289 in the U.S; www.moorings.com, e-mail moorings@mail.pf.

A smaller operation, **Tahiti Yacht Charter,** is located at the far end of Apooiti Marina. ~ Uturoa, 66-28-86; Tahiti, 45-04-00; www.vpm.fr, e-mail tyc@mail.pf.

Also at the marina, **Star Voyage Pacifique** operates two catamarans and two mono-hull boats that are available with or without crew. Contact them through The Moorings. ~ 66-35-93, fax 66-20-94; e-mail moorings@mail.pf.

Stardust Yacht Charters is in Faaroa Bay. Stardust has a flotilla of 20 boats, including catamarans. They will provide transportation from the airport and, like the Moorings, can outfit you for just about anything. Stardust also provides the option of bareboating or hiring a crew. Rates start at US$3300 per week for a Sun Dance 36 Jenneau (in low season). Vessels of up to 52 feet (15.5 meters) are also available. All Stardust boats have a minimum three-day hire. ~ Faaroa; 60-04-85, fax 66-23-19; www.stardustyc.com, e-mail stardustraiatea@mail.pf.

Danae IV and **Tetuanui** are cruising yachts located in Apooiti Harbor. They provide charters ranging from 3 to 18 days. Closed February and March. ~ For more information, contact Claude Goche, BP 251, Uturoa; 66-12-50, cell 78-38-07, fax 66-39-37; www.danaecruise-tahiti.com, e-mail claudine.danae@mail.pf.

If you prefer to sail on a mono-hulled boat and also seek a quality charter vessel, **Bisou Futé Charter** is your best bet. Ivan, a skilled seaman with decades of experience, mainly offers tours of the Leeward Islands. (Over the years I've come to prefer the personal services of individual charter boat owners such as Ivan and his friend Louis to the big charter companies.) ~ Apu Bay; 65-64-97, 65-69-08; e-mail jeanyvon@mail.pf.

There are several other boats available for charter. **Tane** is a 46-foot catamaran. ~ Uturoa; 66-16-87; e-mail charter.tane@lib ertysurf.fr. You could also try **Coup de Coeur**, sailed by Thierry and Luisa Jubin. ~ Raiatea; 79-19-57, fax 66-28-41; e-mail coup decoeur@mail.pf. **Atara Royal**, a 46-foot Europa motor yacht, is another option. ~ Raiatea; 66-17-74, fax 66-17-67; e-mail myc@ mail.pf. **Tataina**, a 51-foot Oceanus, is found at Faaroa Bay. ~ Raiatea; phone/fax 66-11-75; e-mail cruisepolynesia@mail.pf.

WIND-SURFING

Windsurfing in the Raiatea–Tahaa lagoon is quite good. It's possible to rent gear at the **Marina Iti**. ~ 65-61-01. Sailboarding gear is also available at the remote **Hotel Vahine Island**. ~ 65-67-38.

RIDING STABLES

If you prefer seeing Raiatea from the back of a horse, a visit to **Kaoha Nui Ranch** is in order. Located in Avera, the ranch offers a variety of trips ranging from a few hours to four-day camping trips. The rides traverse vanilla and pineapple plantations, bamboo forests, archaeological sites and other attractions. They also offer full-moon rides and lessons. Because the stable uses small Marquesan horses, a maximum weight limit applies to riders. Reservations are requested (at least a day prior to the ride). ~ PK 6, Avera; 66-25-46; e-mail kaoha.nui@mail.pf.

BIKING

Biking in and around Raiatea is a possibility, although a serious trip, such as from Uturoa to Taputapuatea, would necessitate a mountain bike and take a full day to complete. Traffic is not terribly heavy on this island, but the roads in the peripheral areas are unpaved, dusty and often in poor condition. In either Raiatea or Tahaa, the midday heat can be extreme; you will need some form of sun protection as well as plenty of water. If you take a few precautions, biking the back roads of Tahaa, visiting pearl farms, boutiques and vanilla plantations on your own, is fun— and cheaper than buying a tour.

Tahaa is a good island to explore by bike because there is so little traffic. On the other hand, the roads are usually in need of repair. It's possible to ride around the island by bike, but keep in mind the coastal road does not completely circle Tahaa. Do not attempt a long ride unless you have a sturdy mountain bike. Give yourself the whole day to do an extensive ride and check with a local who knows his or her way around before attempting to do so.

Bike Rentals   Almost all pensions and hotels either rent bicycles or lend them to guests. Check tires, brakes, seats, etc. before heading off. You can also try **Vaea Rent-a-Bike** at the wharf (79-16-61), or **Odile Locations** (66-33-47), based out of the Sunset Beach Motel in Uturoa.

Walking is still the basic form of transportation on these islands, and paths are well maintained.

HIKING

Mt. Temehani and the Temehani Plateau (2 miles/3.2 kilometers) affords marvelous views of the northern end of the island and the outlying *motu*. The area is home to the indigenous *tiare apetahi*, an endangered species of gardenia that is celebrated in local myth. There are two access trails, both of which take about two hours. On the eastern side of the island, the trailhead begins several hundred yards south of the Raiatea Hawaiki Nui Hotel. The trail follows a westerly direction for about one mile (1.6 kilometers) and then jogs south to the plateau. It is quite manageable in dry weather but after a rain it may be slick. On the west coast you can pick up the trail a few hundred yards south of the PK 10 marker. (See Chapter Four for an explanation of the PK system.) It follows a southeasterly course and is slightly shorter and more direct than the eastern track. This is a great summit from which to watch the sunset over Bora Bora.

> The sunsets and views of Bora Bora are stupendous from Tapuamu Bay.

Haamene to Hurepiti Bays (2.5 miles/4 kilometers): The saddle trail between Haamene and Hurepiti bays is a fairly easy trek that offers one of the most dramatic views on the island. The hike begins in the village of Haamene on the small main street and proceeds over the "hump," the geographic center of the island, in an westerly direction to Hurepiti Bay. At the summit you can see Bora Bora to the west and a magnificent view of Haamene Bay to the east. The trek can be done in a leisurely two hours. The track is quite good over the entire route and is not strenuous.

The walk between **Patio and Hipu** (1.5 miles/2 kilometers) is a leisurely stroll along several kilometers of the northern coast. It's not hard to find the right track. Basically the island has only one main road and it follows the coastline. Starting from Patio, walk east along the perimeter road and follow it until you reach the community of Hipu. The entire walk is only 45 minutes.

Transportation

Flights with **Air Tahiti** from Papeete to Raiatea are available seven days a week (at least three times daily). Flying time is 35 minutes. There are also regular flights to and from Bora Bora, Huahine, Maupiti, Moorea (through Papeete) and Rangiroa (from Bora). ~ Uturoa; 60-04-40.

CAR

Raiatea and Tahaa can be reached by interisland steamer from Papeete. The *Vaeanu* (41-25-35) and the *Hawaikinui* (45-23-24) take about nine hours. The *Aremiti Corsaire* (42-88-88), which can hold 350 passengers, makes two voyages a week from Papeete.

SEA

The *Maupiti Express* links Raiatea and Tahaa to Bora Bora and Maupiti twice a week (Wednesday and Friday). ~ Tahaa; 67-66-69, 65-67-10, fax 65-67-11.

Small commuter boats make several trips a day between Tahaa and Raiatea. There is limited service on Saturday; none on Sunday. There is no longer a ticket office for commuter trips across the lagoon. Tickets must be purchased at the boats themselves. **Tahaa Transport Services** has two boats, the *Uporu* and the *Iripau*. ~ Uturoa; phone/fax 65-61-33. **Tamarii Tahaa** makes daily trips. ~ Uturoa; 65-65-29. The **Taxi Boat Company** has two boats for *motu* rides and will make crossings to Tahaa on request. ~ Uturoa; 65-66-44, fax 65-62- 65; e-mail taxi-boat@mail.pf.

CAR & JEEP RENTALS

RAIATEA Car and scooter rentals are available at the airport or in town. They can also be arranged through most hotels and pensions. There are several car-rental agencies in the Uturoa area, two of which have airport offices—Avis/Pacificar and Europcar.

> All *Le Truck* vehicles are color coded, depending on the destination (and owners).

Europcar rents both cars and scooters. It has bureaus in town, at the Tahaa Pearl Beach Resort and at the airport. ~ Uturoa; 65-67-00 and 65-63-78, fax 65-68-08. **Location Guirouard** is located at the Motu Tapu Garage. ~ Uturoa; 66-33-09. **Tahiti Voyage** is situated right in the center of town. ~ Uturoa; 66-35-35.

Hertz also has an office in Uturoa. Look for it in the Raiatea Motors showroom in the south end of town. ~ Uturoa; 66-44-88, fax 66-44-89.

TAHAA The **Marina Iti** has some small passenger cars and two four-door pickup trucks for rent. The rates include fuel and 100 free kilometers (just enough to circle the island). The pickup trucks are an economical way for a large group to see the island. Reservations are essential. ~ Toamaru Point; 65-61-01, fax 65-63-87. **Europcar**, open seven days a week, has vehicles at the service station at Tapuamu dock. ~ Tapuamu; 65-67-00, fax 65-68-08. **Hibiscus** has both cars and trucks. ~ Haamene Bay; 65-61-06.

Location Monique is a modest, local car-rental agency. ~ Haamene; 65-62-48.

PUBLIC TRANSIT

Le Truck service is available to Raiatea's outlying districts between 5 a.m. and 6 p.m. Trucks regularly travel from Uturoa to Fetuna on the far end of the island at 9 a.m. daily. The trip takes about two hours and turns around at 12:30 p.m. for the return leg, arriving at Uturoa at 2:30 p.m. (The last truck to Fetuna departs at 3:30 p.m. from town, but does not return until the next morning.) The price is 250 CFP one way, and it's well worth taking the trip for the scenery and the local color.

Those wishing to visit Taputapuatea should take the Opoa bus. Figure that the ride from Uturoa to the archaeological site will take from one to one-and-a-half hours. From the bus stop it's an easy walk to the temple. The truck to Taputapuatea leaves from town Monday through Friday at 10 a.m. The roundtrip fare is 500 CFP. Check with the driver regarding the return leg so that you do not get stuck in Opoa for the evening. The bus terminal is located in downtown Uturoa, adjacent to the public market.

TAXIS

As throughout the rest of French Polynesia, taxis are very expensive in Raiatea. For instance, a taxi ride from Uturoa to Raiatea Village costs 2000 CFP and a one-way ride from town to a distant part of the island can be as much as 6000 CFP. All drivers carry a printed tariff card; ask to see it if you have a question. Taxi stands are located at the airport and at the rear of the Central Marketplace.

HITCHING

RAIATEA Perhaps because of the dearth of tourists, hitchhiking is quite acceptable on the island. In other words, if you stick your thumb out, chances are someone will pick you up.

TAHAA Hitching is possible, but given the scarcity of automobile traffic it's tough to find rides. Since there is no major commercial center, Tahaa is a pretty quiet place. I would be careful about heading to Marina Iti by boat and then trying to hitch from there as it is located in a very isolated part of the island.

BOAT TOURS & CRUISES

Mata Tours, a humorous lagoon-tour outfit run by Toimata Stephane, conducts half- and full-day tours that include ray and shark feeding. Toimata often takes rides on the backs of larger black-tip sharks! ~ Haamene; 60-89-01 or 74-11-43.

Manava Excursions offers half- and full-day excursions aboard their 12-passenger boat. Led by Andrew, a local guide, the half-day tour entails a visit to Raiatea's lagoon, the Taputapuatea *marae*, Faaroa Bay and up the famous river. The full-day tour visits the island of Tahaa, where you'll enjoy local food on a *motu* picnic. No excursions on Saturday. ~ 66-28-26; e-mail manava@free.fr.

Ofetaro Tours on Raiatea offers lagoon excursions that include fish feeding and a stop on a *motu* for snorkeling. Half-day trips include a picnic; full-day trips include a traditional Polynesian barbecue. Also available is a special dinner show that features the opening of a traditional Tahitian underground oven and a cultural presentation. ~ 66-34-46; e-mail polytrans@mail.pf.

Other lagoon tour operators based on Raiatea include: **Hinerani Tours** (66-25-75), **Manava Excursions** (66-28-26) and **Raiatea Discovery** (66-24-16).

Raiatea Jet Cruising is the only operator that rents wave runners. Christophe leads guided tours of the Raiatea and Tahaa lagoon. It's a good idea bring your own snorkeling gear. ~ Uturoa; 78-33-13, fax 66-16-06.

Bateau a Fond de Verre operates the only glass-bottom boat on the island. The *Hina IV* makes three-hour trips that include a *motu* visit, picnic and snorkeling. ~ Uturoa wharf; 73-76-37, 66-25-78; e-mail glassbottomboat@mail.pf.

West Coast Charters runs Faaroa River trips that include a visit to a botanical garden. West Coast also offers circle-island boat tours of Raiatea and Tahaa. All excursions include refreshments, and the friendly owners Marie and Tony speak great English. ~ Uturoa; 66-45-39, cell 79-28-78.

Tahaa Pearl Tours, based at the Apooiti Marina, offers full-day, circle island excursions on the lagoon aboard a motorized canoe. The trip includes a *motu* picnic. ~ Apooiti Marina; phone/fax 66-10-90, cell 78-33-28; e-mail tpt@mail.pf.

Other lagoon tour operators based on Tahaa include: **Tahaa Tours Excursions** (65-62-18), **Tahaa Discovery** (65-66-67), **Monique Cruise** (65-62-48) and **Atiniu Transport** (65-62-42).

The **Haumana** is a 110-foot-long cruise ship that offers trips between the islands of Huahine, Raiatea, Tahaa and Bora Bora. The boat provides four-star accommodations in 20 cabins. All rooms are air conditioned, have huge windows, queen-size beds, private baths, TV and video, and minibars. Onboard you'll also find a panoramic restaurant, an outdoor terrace, a lounge and a boutique. As this cruise ship is only made for a maximum of 40 people and has a shallow draft, cruising in the lagoon is no problem. Shore excursions are included in the fare. The three-day cruise visits the islands of Huahine and Raiatea; in the four-day cruise Tahaa is included. The Aquamarine and the Opal cruises take you to Bora Bora as well. ~ Papeete; 43-43-03, fax 45-10-65; www.boraborapearlcruises.com.

SAVE THE TURTLES

The **Foundation Hibiscus** is dedicated to protecting and caring for the local turtle population. The Foundation works through the World Wildlife Fund and similar agencies in Hawaii and Samoa on a project that involves purchasing turtles from local fisherman at the price of food value, then tagging and releasing them. Since 1992, over 700 turtles have been tagged and released, with some being tracked as far away as Papua New Guinea—an effort that has received international recognition. In order to fund this work, the Foundation Hibiscus allows individuals or groups to "adopt" a turtle, name it and participate in its formal release for a donation of 100,000 CFP. For more information contact the foundation's founders Leo and Lolita Morou (owners of the Hibiscus hotel on Tahaa's Haamene Bay) at 65-61-06 or fax 65-65-65; www.raiatea.com/seaturtle, e-mail hibiscus@tahaa-tahiti.com.

Almost Paradise Tours is run by Bill Kolans, an American who sailed to Raiatea in 1979 from his native Hawaii and has remained a fixture here ever since. He is an archaeologist, and is well versed in the history and culture of Polynesia. He is also the only English-speaking guide on the island. His tour to Marae Taputapuatea is quite popular with Americans and well worth the price. Bill's tour runs about two and a half hours, and includes transportation to Taputapuatea. Bill will also pick you up from your lodging. He will tailor custom tours for specific interest groups and will arrange visits to sites on other islands upon request. You can write to him at BP 290, Uturoa, Raiatea. ~ Faaroa; 66-23-64.

Patrick, the owner of **Kaoha Nui Ranch** in Avera on Raiatea, offers walking tours to the waterfalls and Mt. Temehani. He has a special interest in botany. ~ Avera; 66-25-46.

WALKING TOURS

◄ *HIDDEN*

Hinerani Tours organizes four-wheel-drive tours along the rugged east and south coasts of Raiatea. Highlights are the Taputapuatea *marae*, a botanical garden, and Faaroa Bay. If you book both a lagoon tour and a valley tour they will give you a special rate. ~ Uturoa; phone/fax 66-25-75; e-mail lysis@mail.pf.

Jeep Safari Raiatea organizes half- or full-day 4X4 excursions that include a visit to the Taputapuatea *marae* and a picnic. *Motu* visits are available on request for large groups. ~ Uturoa; phone/fax 66-15-73.

Trips with Raiatea 4X4 include exploration of the island's interior valleys and plantations, as well as a guided tour of the Taputapuatea *marae*. ~ Uturoa; phone/fax 66-24-16; www.raiatea discovery.fr.st, e-mail raidiscovery@mail.pf.

Rauvine Safari Tours, run by Josiah Bordes of Pension Rauvine, makes regular trips into the Faaroa crater, followed by stops at a coconut plantation and the Taputapuatea *marae*, and a trip to feed the river eels. A half-day trip is also available, which includes a snack and a pareu souvenir. Four-person minimum. ~ Uturoa; 66-25-50; www.pensionrauvine.pf, e-mail pensionrauvine@mail.pf.

Bernadette's Tours offers a variety of activities including deep-sea fishing, jeep safaris, pearl farm visits or snorkeling off a *motu*—just to name few. Bernadette isn't your typical tour operator. She has no phone but she can be found at the Uturoa wharf sitting among the *mamas* at the handicraft market. Everybody knows her and her American husband, Dick, who has lived here since the 1970s.

Vanilla Tours, located in Hurepiti, is owned and operated by Alain and Cristina Plantier. They can accommodate four to eight people seated in the back of a covered pick-up truck. This land safari has received good reviews from several different sources.

LAND TOURS

◄ *HIDDEN*

Vanilla Tours will meet visitors at Marina Iti, making a day trip possible from Raiatea. The tour focuses on the different aspects of local agriculture, including a stop at a taro garden. The Plantiers have their own vanilla plantation and bring the tour there for about 45 minutes for a demonstration of the "marrying of the male and female" vanilla plant. They provide descriptions of the economic and medicinal use of plants, as well as the obligatory scenic stops. The tour finishes at the Plantiers homestead, where guests are given a tour of the grounds and their traditional colonial-style home. ~ Haamene; 65-62-46, cell 23-84-87, fax 65-68-97; e-mail vanilla.tours@mail.pf.

Raiatea has its own Aeoroclub, a flying school that offers charter flights and aerial tours of the Society Islands. ~ Uturoa; 66-28-88.

Lolita Tours, operated by the Hibiscus, offers jeep safaris on the backroads of Tahaa. ~ Hurepiti; 65-61-06.

Other companies that offer similar tours include **Vaipoe Tours** (65-60-83), **Poerani Tours** (65-60-25) and **Tahaa Tours Excursions** (65-62-18).

Addresses & Phone Numbers

RAIATEA
Airport ~ 66-30-51
Dentist ~ Dr. Falieu; 66-35-95
Hospital ~ Uturoa Hospital; 66-35-03
Navettes (water taxis) ~ 65-66-44
Pharmacy ~ Uturoa Pharmacy; 66-15-56
Police ~ 66-31-07
Post Office ~ 66-35-50
Taxi Service ~ Municipal Market; 66-36-74
Visitor Information ~ Raiatea–Tahaa Visitor's Bureau; 66-07-77

TAHAA
Bank ~ Banque Socredo; 65-66-55
Doctor ~ Dr. Laurent Jereczek, 65-60-60; Dr. Evelyn Kerlau, 65-65-67
Police ~ Gendarmerie, Patio; 65-64-07
Post Office ~ Patio; 65-64-70
Visitor Information ~ Raiatea–Tahaa Visitor's Bureau; 66-07-77

NINE

Maupiti

Maupiti is still the unexploited gem of the Society Islands, despite its increasing popularity with travelers. Surrounded by small coral islets on the barrier reef, Maupiti is covered with lush vegetation. A variety of fruits, including mangoes, breadfruit and bananas, grow in profusion. In two hours or less, you can hike the five and a half miles (nine kilometers) around the island without seeing another soul.

With an area of 7 square miles (17 square kilometers), Maupiti is the smallest and most isolated island of the Leeward Group. It lies 23 miles (37 kilometers) west of Bora Bora and has about 1200 residents. There is only one pass—Onoiau—that leads into Maupiti and it is so narrow that the government boat that calls once a month can only enter the pass diagonally, and then only if the sea is calm.

The island is strikingly different from the other Leeward Islands because of its minuscule size, its isolation and the comparatively dense population of the villages. The population has doubled in the past decade or so and there are countless children and dogs running about. The three contiguous villages of Farauru, Vai'ea and Pauma together fill one long crowded strip along the eastern side of the island. Perhaps because of the population density, there seems to be never-ending, frenetic activity in the community.

If you stay at any of the pensions on the main island, you will be awakened at 5 a.m. by motor scooters en route to the bakery. The supply of bread usually runs out by 6 or 7 a.m. and people adjust their schedules around the opening of the bakery. Evenings in the village are also a beehive of activity. Walking from one end of the string of villages to the other, you will see people sitting, talking or occasionally strumming guitars and singing. The villagers with televisions tend to place them in the house near the door so that when something of interest is on (like the World Cup), neighbors can gather around the front porch and watch from there.

Maupitans appear to be a fairly industrious lot. They work hard at farming a variety of cash crops such as watermelon (*pastèque*), which is grown on the *motu*. The work is labor intensive as soil must be transported from the main island and each plant must be watered by hand. There is also a growing pearl industry here. About 50 people from Maupiti have temporary dwellings on the island of Mopelia (approximately 400 kilometers west of Tahiti), where they occasionally make trips to cultivate oysters. Copra, which is heavily subsidized by the government, is another source of income, and government boats are always filled with pungent brown sacks of the product.

Water is a significant problem on Maupiti, although it became considerably less so with the 1994 installation of a pipe that brought potable water into the homes.

Perhaps because of their isolation and independent streak, Maupitans have adopted a "no hotel" policy in order to preserve the island as it is. They have had several offers to build large, modern hotels, but the village elders have refused. Maupitans are well aware of the changes that have occurred on Bora Bora due to tourism and they don't like what they see.

Other than a post office (near the mayor's office) and a few tiny markets that are primarily adjuncts to people's homes, there is little in the way of amenities on the island. Banking is done whenever the bank representative flies into town for a couple of days. For visitors who expect to be entertained or need Club Med–style activities to keep them occupied, Maupiti is not an appropriate destination. As one travel writer, James Kay, described Maupiti two decades ago:

"There are no hotels, just a few no-star–rated boarding houses, no rental cars, bikes or motor scooters, no taxis or buses, no bars or restaurants, no bank, no credit cards, and nothing in the way of planned activities. I mean nothing."

I wouldn't agree that there is "nothing" on the island, although it is true that after more than two decades, there still hasn't been a lot of development. In my opinion, this is not a bad thing. However, activities are left to the individual, and the only tours that pensions undertake are day trips to nearby *motu*. One thing that anyone in town can do, however, is to wander down to the mayor's complex around noon for the daily spirited game of *boule*.

In November 1997, Cyclone Osea dealt a heavy blow to Maupiti by leveling 80 percent of all the tourist accommodations on the island as well as vital infrastructure such as the airstrip, roads and the dock. People's homes and the pensions were the first to be rebuilt. (The government provided special "anticyclone" bungalows that will resist winds of up to 200 kilometers per hour.) By February 2000 the small airport was repaired, along with the dock, the fuel depot and the cross-island road, which was inaugurated by President Gaston Flosse.

SIGHTS

HIDDEN ►

Maupiti is full of *marae* (about 60 in all) and one of the best is **Marae Vaiahu**, just beyond the south end of the village. According to the man who guided me around, Marae Vaiahu is the most important *marae* because of its historical significance. (It seems to be a standard comment that every island has *the* most important *marae*.) I was told that all of the kings from across Polynesia (including Hawaii) had to come to this particular *marae* to be crowned. Maupitans say that Marae Taputapuatea on Raiatea got its name from a place on Maupiti called Taputapuatea. (On Raiatea I was told that Taputapuatea means "very taboo far away place." On Maupiti the term refers to the cutting of the brother's umbilical cord and sending it far away. *Tapu* in Tahitian means taboo, but it also means "to cut.")

At Marae Vaiahu, look for two large **stone chairs** used by the kings. One is the old original chair and one is newer, constructed at the time of the missionaries. It was the king who presided over the people of the island and made all of the political decisions.

Also look for a rectangular pit in the ground with some magical stones in it. (These are not the original stones.) The pit was

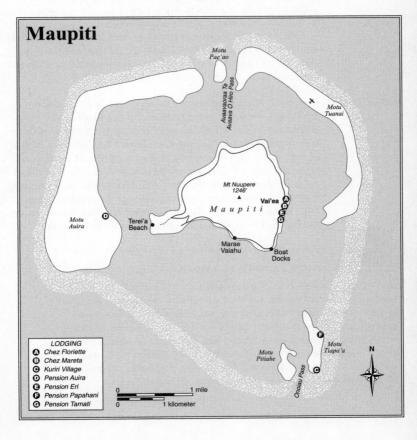

Maupiti

Motu Pae'ao

Avaavaoaa Te Avaava O Hiro Pass

Motu Tuanai

Mt Nuupere 1246'

Vai'ea

Maupiti

Motu Auira

Terei'a Beach

Marae Vaiahu

Boat Docks

Motu Tiapa'a

Motu Pitiahe

Onoiai Pass

N

LODGING
Ⓐ Chez Floriette
Ⓑ Chez Mareta
Ⓒ Kuriri Village
Ⓓ Pension Auira
Ⓔ Pension Eri
Ⓕ Pension Papahani
Ⓖ Pension Tamati

0   1 mile
0   1 kilometer

used with special stone charms to attract fish. In the old days, a woman (perhaps a priestess?) would take the stones (which were thought to be fish) and put them in the pit with their heads facing the mountain. The fish would respond by swimming in the lagoon from the sea toward the mountains. When enough fish were caught, the woman would turn the stones around, with the heads facing the sea, and the fish would swim out of the lagoon into the ocean.

Maupiti used to have two main villages, one on either side of the island, that fought each other. The one on the eastern side of the island was once adjacent to Marae Vaiahu. The original wharf was at the site of the *marae* as well, and you can still see the large stone that held up the pier.

Another interesting archaeological site on the island is the **Haranae Valley**, just north of the village, where wonderful petroglyphs of turtles and other figures can easily be seen if you walk about a half-kilometer up the dry stream bed. (Asking a local child to show you the way might be a good idea.)

There are also 16 ancient **graves** on Motu Pae'ao and several ninth-century graves on Motu Tuanai. To get there ask the proprietor at your lodging to arrange for a local boatman to take you there and point out the location of the graves.

LODGING   In general, Maupiti offers two categories of accommodation: in the village, which are in the midst of things and tend to be noisy; and on the *motu*, which are more isolated but where it is difficult to get transportation into the village. The choice is a matter of taste and style. Those who know a smattering of Tahitian and enjoy the local foods might prefer to stay in the thick of things *en ville*, sharing daily life with Maupitans who will respond warmly to anyone who makes an attempt at speaking Tahitian. Once a connection is made, English speakers will hear a lot more English in the village and communication becomes easier.

AUTHOR FAVORITE—LODGING

Soaking up the sun and the village ambiance are my first orders of business while staying at the **Pension Eri**. With a hospitable management and convenient location, all my needs are easily met. Pension Eri has four clean rooms, each containing a double bed. It also has a salon, kitchen, terrace with a *motu* view, and communal baths with cold water. Eri also offers airport transfers, *motu* picnics and auto tours of the island. Meals are available. It's located one kilometer from the old boat dock. ~ Vai'ea; 67-81-29 (between noon and 1 p.m. and after 6 p.m.). MODERATE.

Visitors to the outer islands should realize that accommodations at budget and even moderate resorts tend to be rustic. For example, in most of the pensions, especially on the *motu*, you will need to use a bucket to flush the toilet. Chances are you will be sharing the pension with a plethora of animals (dogs, chickens, etc.). Along with the animals are the insects. Many of the lodgings are riddled with mosquitos, so be sure to take your repellent. Mosquito coils, which can be purchased anywhere in French Polynesia, are also useful.

Visitors on the *motu* should also note that the physical isolation of the *motu* (and high cost of gasoline) means that, except for the occasional shopping trip, *motu* dwellers will be less apt to visit the village with great regularity. Also keep in mind that none of the lodgings on Maupiti accepts credit cards.

Chez Floriette is one of the older pensions on the island and has had a good reputation for many years. Unfortunately the property was leveled in the cyclone of 1997 but the owner has subsequently rebuilt. There are now two new bungalows—one of which accommodates three people and the other five. Visitors share communal baths (with cold water) and Floriette assures me that there are no problems with her water. Floriette is irrepressibly cheerful, an engaging host who runs a clean, quiet place—and who speaks better English than she thinks. Activities include *motu* picnic excursions and long walks. Tariff includes three meals and airport transport. The only downside is the racket caused by the marathon basketball games that go on directly outside the pension. Chez Floriette is not far from the old boat dock near the school. Children under six stay free. ~ Vai'ea; phone/fax 67-80-85. MODERATE.

Next door to Chez Floriette you'll find **Chez Mareta**. This pension is getting a bit haggard and is not the cleanest in town. It is, however, inexpensive. There are three rooms on the mezzanine floor, each with a double bed, and three rooms on the ground floor, each with two double beds. You will eat well here, but chances are you will eat the same thing until the food runs out. There is also a salon, terrace, kitchenette and common bath. Activities include trips to the *motu* and picnics. Children are 1000 CFP unless they don't eat much, in which case they stay free. Mareta only speaks Tahitian, but her daughter-in-law speaks French and some English. ~ Vai'ea; 67-82-32. BUDGET TO MODERATE.

Pension Tamati is a large building with nine rooms that include five doubles and four singles. All have private baths with cold water. This property is not well maintained and there are better places to go. Children under 12 are half price. Pension Tamati is just north of the old dock. Contact Mr. Ferdinand Tapuhiro. ~ Vai'ea; 67-80-10. MODERATE.

LODGING ON THE MOTU   Staying on a *motu* is a wonderful alternative to the typical "mainland"-style pensions. *Motu* are generally quiet, isolated and have a beachfront. Keep in mind that most of your time will be spent on a very small islet and getting off the island involves hiring a boat or perhaps hitching a ride with your hosts. All your meals will most likely be consumed at the pension where you reside.

HIDDEN ►

Located on a white-sand beach that's a 20-minute boat ride from the airport is **Pension Papahani**. Situated on Motu Tiapa'a close to the pass, this renovated lodging has had some very good recommendations. The owner, Mlle. Vilna Tuheiava (who has the most delightful giggle), is quite hospitable. There are five traditional bungalows with double beds and private baths. Vilna's son, Rudy, serves as a guide for boat tours of the lagoon or a hike up the mountain for 2000 CFP per person. Excursions and other activities are available. Swimming is excellent here. ~ Motu Tiapa'a; 67-81-58, cell 71-97-97. MODERATE.

Kuriri Village, which shares the same *motu* with Pension Papahani, has a white-sand beach with excellent swimming in a clear lagoon, amidst an undersea tropical garden. Reports have been very positive regarding the food and the setting. There are five bungalows set on the ocean side of the *motu* that afford a panoramic view of Bora Bora. The bungalows are constructed in traditional Polynesian style, each with a double bed, private (cold water) bath and mosquito net. There is also an auxiliary bathroom (with hot water) in the garden. Activities include canoeing, kayaking, snorkeling, fishing and guided hikes on the main island. Children under 12 are half price. Kuriri Village is situated on Motu Tiapa'a; a 20-minute boat ride from the airport is included. ~ Motu Tiapa'a; 74-54-54, fax 67-82-23; e-mail kuriri@mail.pf. DELUXE.

Pension Rose des Iles, also located on Motu Tiapa'a, offers one family-style *fare* on the beach. There is room for four people, and bathroom facilities are shared. Kayaks and snorkeling gear are available for guests. ~ Motu Tiapa'a; 70-50-70, fax 67-82-00. MODERATE.

Pension Auira (also called Chez/Pension Edna) is a rustic accommodation that has had good reviews. The people I spoke to raved about the food and the hospitality. Owner Edna Terai is a friendly woman who is prone to giving tourists an unsolicited ride when she spots them walking the main island. Her *motu* pension has four bungalows—two are on the beach. Two have one room with a double bed and a bath; the other two are family units with one double bed and four single beds, plus bath. At low tide you can walk directly across to Terei'a Beach on the main island. There is a restaurant/bar, a washing machine, fishing trips and tours of Maupiti. (And the tap water is potable.)

This lodging is charming, but may not be for everyone. There are numerous dogs living on the *motu* that tend to cluster around the bungalows and they bark and draw flies. The beach is fine, but garbage occasionally washes up. Activities can be organized through Maupiti Loisir. Airport transfer is 2000 CFP. Located 15 minutes by boat from the airport on isolated Motu Auira. Write to Mme. Edna Terai on Motu Auira, Maupiti for reservations. ~ Motu Auira; 67-80-26. MODERATE TO DELUXE.

DINING

For the most part, you are on your own when it comes to eating. There are a few snack bars but no restaurants in the villages. You will have to have all your meals in the facilities where you are staying, or when possible use the kitchens available.

Snack Tarona on the north end of the village dishes up tasty *poisson cru*, chow mein and other local favorites from 10:30 a.m. to 1:30 p.m. and from 6 p.m. to 8 p.m. Cold beers and sodas are also available, and meals are eaten on picnic tables on a covered patio. The owners are sticklers about their operating hours; don't be late or you'll go without. ~ 67-82-46. BUDGET.

GROCERIES

There is only one substantial market on Maupiti. Among other things, they stock canned goods, dairy products, soda, chips, beer and ice cream. Look for the white building on the mountain side, just north of the boat dock.

The are several tiny markets that are part of people's homes and provide basic items such as kerosene, mosquito coils, soap and the like. If you need these types of items, the best thing to do is ask somebody where to shop.

BEACHES

TEREI'A BEACH There is only one beach on this small island but it is pristine, perhaps one of the most beautiful small white-sand beaches in all of French Polynesia. Located on the western side of the island, it is a crescent-shaped expanse of coral

BURNING THE MIDNIGHT OIL

On Maupiti, as in many isolated communities, the residents have the curious habit of burning their lanterns all night. If you ask them why, they may or may not tell you that this is done to keep the *tupa'pau* (ghosts) away. According to the Maupitans, this island is a haven for every type of ghost, spirit and supernatural creature imaginable. There is even a semiannual beach party strictly for ghosts; every so often someone from the village passes the beach while these exclusive affairs happen to be going on. Maupitans say that from the empty beach—once the site of a village—the sounds of musical instruments and laughter are quite audible.

sand shaded by coconut palms. Snorkeling is good nearby. ~ If you are staying in the village, it is about a 45-minute walk to the beach. If you are staying on Motu Auira, you can walk the half-kilometer or so across the reef at low tide to the beach, but the water is waist-high. This can be a long walk so think twice before doing it.

Outdoor Adventures

DIVING

Snorkeling is particularly good in Maupiti. The ecosystem has not been adulterated or overfished the way it has been in Tahiti, Bora Bora and some of the other islands. Snorkeling is best off the *motu* or near Terei'a Beach. The coral formations are typical of the Society Islands—acpopora, pocillopora and fungia coral are common. The reef fish you will see include parrot fish, unicorn fish, labrida, triggerfish, red mullet and groupers.

BIKING

Exploring Maupiti by bicycle is ideal if you are only on the island for the day. Bikes can be rented at **Puanere Locations**. ~ Vai'ea; 67-81-68.

HIKING

You can hike around the island in an hour or two, depending on your mood. The main road basically circles the island. You can walk to the beach (where the road becomes a path) or better yet, take the route that bypasses the beach from the back side of the island and follow it over the mountain and into town. At the high point of the road, you'll come to a spot where the view of the surrounding lagoon will inspire most any photographer. Cars seem ill-adapted for the island and the road through the village functions as a children's playground as well as a resting spot for the numerous canine inhabitants.

If you can find a child to accompany you, ask him or her to show you the trail to the 400-foot cliffs that tower over the village. It's only a 10- to 15-minute hike and is not too strenuous, but local knowledge of the path is essential. Once on top, you are directly above the village. From this vantage point you can see the *motu*, the pass, and the church below.

Auguste Taurua of **Tefarerii Excursions** offers guided hikes to the top of Hotu Parata, the cliff that looms over Vai'ea village. ~ Vai'ea; phone/fax 67-81-83; e-mail nicolerichardo@mail.pf.

Transportation

AIR

Flights are available from **Air Tahiti**. Because of the limited number of flights to Maupiti, Air Tahiti is usually booked a month or so in advance. Air Tahiti has four flights a week, arriving from Papeete, Raiatea and Bora Bora.

Air Tahiti has a bureau next to the post office in the mayor's complex in the center of the village in Maupiti. Hours are Monday and Thursday from 8 to 11 a.m., and Friday 9:30 to 11 a.m. ~ 67-80-20.

The airport is located on a *motu*, so regardless of the carrier that gets you to Maupiti, you'll need to get from the *motu* to the mainland. All hotels and pensions pick up their guests; some do it for free and others charge as much as 2000 CFP. A launch from Vaie'a also meets each flight. Fares are 400 CFP for passengers and 200 CFP for large items like coolers and cartons. The launch will also take you to the *motu* to meet your departing flight. The launch's timetable is set up to coincide with Air Tahiti's schedule, allowing you to check in one hour and 45 minutes prior to departure.

Maupiti Express links the island to Bora Bora and Raiatea on Tuesday, Thursday and Saturday. It's the most frequent boat service to Maupiti. Travel time is a little under two hours and roundtrip fare is approximately 3500 CFP. On the return trip, don't be surprised if watermelons occupy more seats than humans do. The *Maupiti Express* is the main form of conveyance to get this local produce to market on other islands. ~ 67-66-69.

SEA

Maupiti Tou Ai'a departs Papeete, bound for Maupiti, at 3 p.m. each Wednesday and arrives Thursday at noon. Deck passage is available for 12 people; no food is available onboard. The boat departs Maupiti for the return trip to Papeete on Friday at 6 p.m. ~ Motu Uta, Papeete; 50-66-71, fax 43-32-70.

Government cargo boats, such as the *Meherio II* or *Te Aratai*, also make somewhat regular calls to Maupiti, and it may be possible to book passage on one of them. ~ 50-66-71, fax 43-32-70.

Maupiti Loisir, owned by Simone and Ui Teriihaunui, offers boat excursions on the lagoon with a *motu* picnic and snorkeling in the coral garden next to Motu Pa'eo. Ui also serves as a guide to the many archaeological sites of the island. ~ 67-80-95.

BOAT TOURS

Maupiti Poe Iti Tours offers lagoon tours in a flat-bottomed aluminum rowboat. A picnic lunch is available. Maximum 12 people. ~ Vai'ea; 67-83-14.

TEN

The Tuamotu Islands

According to Polynesian mythology, the Tuamotu Islands—the largest Polynesian archipelago—were formed when Tukerai, a Polynesian cross between Neptune and Hercules, tried to shake the sea one day. The result was a storm of biblical proportions from which chunks of earth were tossed to the surface, creating the land that became known as the Tuamotu chain.

Encompassing an area roughly half the size of western Europe, the Tuamotu Islands (sometimes called the Paumotu Group) consist of two parallel chains running northwest to southeast. Numbering 76 islands (only 41 of which are inhabited), they comprise the largest chain of atolls in the world. Despite the numerous islands and the vast area they cover, the total land mass of this group is only 300 square miles (777 square kilometers). And the entire population consists of a mere 12,000 souls.

The climate in these islands is generally hot year-round, but the period between May and October is the coolest and driest. Most of the rain falls during the hot season—stretching from December to February. Since the elevation of the islands ranges only from 6 to 20 feet, they are prone to severe damage from cyclones. In 1991 and 1993, the area was racked by devastating storms that destroyed the entire economy of several of the atolls.

The first European to sail through these shores was Ferdinand Magellan, who came in 1521 but only sighted one island—Pukapuka. Dutchmen Jacob Lemaire and Wilem Cornelisz van Schouten dubbed them the "Green Islands" when they sailed through in 1616. Captain James Cook briefly visited in 1767, while the early 19th century brought the missionaries.

No part of French Polynesia has undergone as radical an economic change as the Tuamotus. Agriculture (primarily the harvesting of coconuts) and fishing have been the mainstay of the area for generations. This has fundamentally changed in the last decade as the black pearl industry and, to some degree, tourism have expanded in these far-flung atolls. For all practical purposes, today copra is dead as a cash crop in the Tuamotu Islands. Perhaps this is an example of free-market economics in action. The copra farmers had been kept afloat only because of artificially high subsidies paid by the government to keep the population on the farm rather than crowding into Papeete looking for work. The emergence of pearl cultivation has not only provided work, but has also given locals an incentive to stay on the islands. There are now more than 250 pearl farms in the atolls.

Even commercial fishing, a seemingly logical business to undertake on an island, has taken a back seat to pearl cultivation. Commercial fishing is primarily confined to Arutua and Kaukura because of their proximity to Tahiti. (Given the great distances between many of the Tuamotu islands and Tahiti, the cost of shipping fresh fish is simply not viable.)

These traditional forms of employment have slowed down or died a natural death as pearl farming, a much more lucrative enterprise, has taken hold. Pearl farming has spread like wildfire throughout the archipelago, with about 30 islands involved. And for good reason. It has made a lot of Paumotu people better off economically.

Nowhere is this more evident than on Manihi, where the French Polynesian black pearl industry was born. Visit Manihi's main village of Turipaoa and you will find a supermarket (where a one-room market once stood) and stores stocked with any number of consumer goods. You will also see shiny new Nissan Pathfinders, Yamaha motorcycles and numerous scooters vying for space on the one kilometer or so of road. Even the residents of nearby Ahe, an island once considered the poor relative of Manihi, are now much better off materially because of black pearl–related businesses on the island.

Along with the march toward progress and materialism, budget and mid-range lodgings have sprung up on some of the outer Tuamotu islands that are not as caught up in the pearl industry. Some offer better bargains than the Society Islands, and they come with true Paumotu hospitality. A visitor in search of a genuine island experience should consider going directly to one of the more remote pensions. If you have a deserted island fantasy, the Tuamotus are the place to live it out. The primal sounds and colors of these atolls cast an unforgettable spell. However, be prepared to live on quantities of fish, rice, corned beef, stale French bread, *ipo* (a Tuamotan dumpling) and perhaps some turtle.

The actual settlements consist of little more than a church, a grocery store, a pier, a water tower or cistern and several rows of clapboard or fired-limestone homes with tin roofs. In the evening, the major pastime is playing guitar, listening to Radio Tahiti and watching television, which broadcasts news, music and messages to the outer islands. For young people, time is spent cooking, fishing, harvesting copra and planning liaisons with girlfriends or boyfriends.

Despite the higher standards of living, the trading schooners are the most important link with the outside world. When a boat arrives, the entire village flocks to watch the vessel being unloaded with staples from the mainland. Onboard there may be a store, run by the supercargo, that sells staples and luxury items such as cigarettes, hard liquor, chocolate and coffee.

There's an eerie solitude on these atolls that's not found on high islands. You notice it almost immediately. There is something elementally different, something you feel but is difficult to articulate. Perhaps it is because you are forced to look

Text continued on page 356.

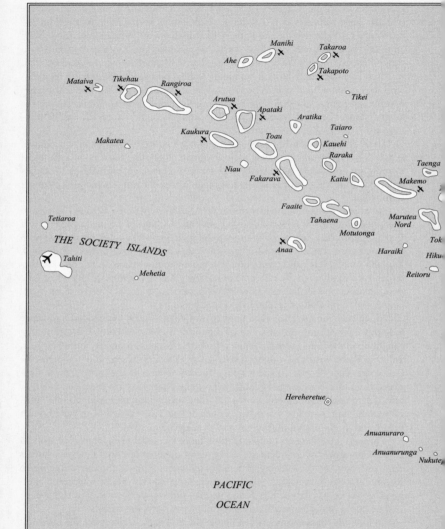

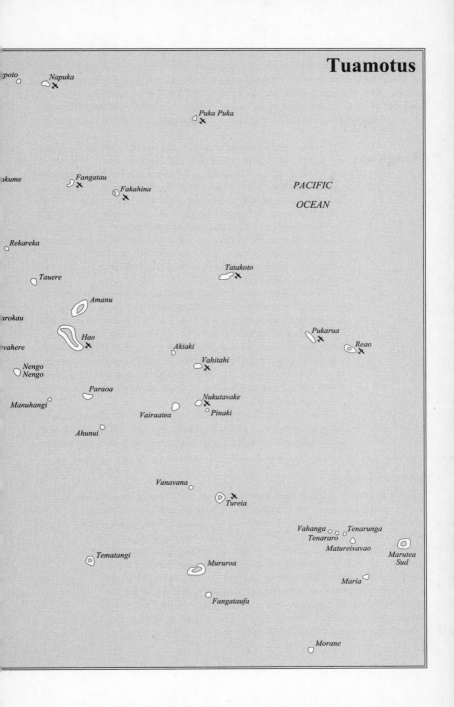

Tuamotus

poto

Napuka

Puka Puka

PACIFIC

OCEAN

kume

Fangatau

Fakahina

Rekareka

Tatakoto

Tauere

Amanu

rokau

Hao

vahere

Akiaki

Vahitahi

Pukarua

Reao

Nengo
Nengo

Paraoa

Nukutavake

Manuhangi

Vairaatea

Pinaki

Ahunui

Vanavana

Tureia

Vahanga

Tenarunga

Tenararo

Matureivavao

Marutea
Sud

Tematangi

Mururoa

Maria

Fangataufa

Morane

inward. There are no caves to hide in, no mountains to climb, no valleys to explore and nowhere to escape to. You become aware that you are on an insignificant speck of coral in the middle of an immense ocean. You feel stripped of all the familiar trappings of civilization while the mercilessly brilliant sun beats down upon you and the air is thick with humidity. There is only the endless chorus of lapping waves on the reef and the rustle of ceaseless trade winds through the palm fronds.

Rangiroa

Of all the Tuamotu islands, Rangiroa (Polynesian for "long sky") is the most popular with visitors—primarily divers and travelers seeking an atoll experience. Located 200 miles (322 kilometers) northwest of Papeete, Rangiroa is actually a series of islands around a lagoon, making it the largest atoll in Polynesia, and the second largest in the world. Indeed, it's 393-square-mile (1020-square-kilometer) lagoon is the star attraction. Marine life of every size and description, including gray reef sharks, manta rays, jack, surgeon fish, mullet, pompano, parrot fish, grouper, puffer fish, butterfly fish, trumpet fish and eels, live in its waters.

Most of the water flowing into and out of the immense lagoon is carried through two passes, which provide the only access for boats venturing in and out. The two towns, Avatoru and Tiputa, each sit on the eastern shore of a pass. The extraordinary tidal flow through the passes allows for exceptional scuba diving and snorkeling. Divers can observe a virtual freeway-traffic stream of marine life zipping by. The tremendous currents also mean divers should not attempt "pass dives" without proper training and local guidance.

This huge atoll has miles of empty white-sand beaches and silent groves of coconut palms. Rangiroa's lagoon is so wide that it is impossible to see the opposite shore when standing on one

SAFE PASSAGE

Visiting an atoll by yacht or small boat is no mean feat. Many of these islands, which consist of rings of coral, have only one boat passage into the lagoon. (Some may have no lagoon at all—such as Pukapuka and Nukutavake where the lagoon has become sealed off from the ocean and has dried up.) When the tide changes, the passes can become treacherous slip streams where currents run as fast as seven knots or more. These fast currents make navigating a boat through a narrow passage lined with razor-sharp reefs extremely difficult at best. According to Rodo Williams, one of the last old-time Polynesian navigators, a simple way to approximate when the water is slack is "when the moon is directly overhead, or directly beneath, the current should not be dangerous."

side looking for the other. I highly recommend you hire a boat and play Robinson Crusoe for a day.

Some of the local hotels specialize in diving, snorkeling and glass-bottom-boat excursions. From port it is possible to see local divers spear fish and then feed the unfortunate, wriggling creatures to the nearest shark.

Tourism has been an important factor in the island's economy for about two decades. In the days before tourism, Rangiroans depended mainly upon copra, fishing and the mother-of-pearl trade for their income. The mother-of-pearl industry disappeared when plastic buttons replaced pearl shell, but tourism, and lately black pearl cultivation, has reinvigorated the island economy.

Created in large part to meet the demand of tourists, *Le Truck* service began on the island in February 2002. The truck goes between the two ends of the main *motu*, Avatoru, twice a day, Monday through Friday.

SIGHTS

The bulk of the island's approximately 3071 people live in the villages of **Avatoru** and **Tiputa**, which are a 45-minute boat ride from each other on different *motu*. Avatoru is at the western end of a string of connected islands, separated only by channels. The Avatoru Pass separates this island chain from the next island to the west. Most of the hotels and pensions, shops, banks, the major resort hotel Kia Ora Rangiroa and the airport are on the Avatoru side.

Directly across the pass at the eastern end of the Avatoru chain, Tiputa separates the Avatoru chain from the next island. Various amenities and government agencies are more or less equally divided between Avatoru and Tiputa. However, of the two communities, Tiputa is the main administrative community, and has a town hall, post office, *gendarmerie* and infirmary. Avatoru has a small medical clinic, dentist's office, *gendarmerie* and a modern high school that serves all of Rangiroa's students.

You'll see many trees, stately walkways and even manicured lawns in the towns—a rarity on islands where fresh water and soil are precious commodities. During the island's heyday, soil was actually brought in by those who could afford it. Both towns have Mormon and Catholic churches that are worth visiting. (If you visit the cemetery in either community, note that the real estate is divided into two sections.)

In Avatoru, an open-air pavilion with basketball hoops and volleyball nets is a favorite gathering place for families and friends on weekend evenings. In addition to the informal court games, dozens of *petanque* courts are laid out with string in the sand surrounding the massive, roofed structure, and scores of people watch and enjoy beer or snacks as the matches are played.

Both towns have Mormon and Catholic churches that are worth visiting. (If you visit the cemetery in either community, note that the real estate is divided into two sections.)

The old **Catholic church** in the center of Tiputa is particularly attractive, as are the facades of many homes that hark back to a grander era. One of these old colonial homes has a dome-shaped **shrine** or chapel constructed of concrete. The structure is inlaid with stones and shells, and has a statue of the Virgin Mary. It's hard to miss.

In Avatoru it seems there's always a crowd hanging around the docks. (Perhaps there is not much else to do.) A boat crosses with reasonable frequency between the dock by Chez Glorine on the Avatoru side of Tiputa Pass to Tiputa Village. You can transfer via Kia Ora, which allows you a one-hour layover, for about 1000 CFP, or ask over at Chez Glorine for someone to suggest an impromptu water taxi that will take you across the pass for half the price.

There are several tiny islands within the lagoon that are important bird sanctuaries. **Paio** is the best known. Local boats will take you there for a minimal fee.

LODGING For those visitors needing creature comforts, life on a remote atoll can seem spartan. Rangiroa is an exception—here you can check into a luxury hotel and enjoy life on a faraway island at the same time. Apart from a couple of pensions in Tiputa, all of the local accommodations are on the Avatoru segment of the island. The following four Avatoru pensions—Pension Henriette, Rangiroa Lodge, Pension Herenui and Pension Hinanui—occupy a narrow piece of *motu* real estate. This puts them on the beach, but they are also adjacent to the road, which means more exposure to foot and vehicular traffic. For those who really want to get away from it all, there are lodging possibilities on the outer atolls. Almost all of the lodging facilities will organize bicycle rentals, picnic excursions to other *motu*, pearl-farm tours, glass-bottom-boat trips and fishing or snorkeling expeditions. The pensions and small hotels usually offer meal programs with the room tariff. These are referred to as *demi-pension* (two meals) or *pension complete* (three meals).

Perhaps due to competition, most budget accommodations on this island have similar prices. Lodgings usually cost about 6800 CFP for a *demi-pension* and 8800 CFP full *pension*. However, the differences in rooms can be dramatic. For the same price as a minuscule hut with no view, you can have a large, new oceanfront bungalow. Scrutinize the properties listed below, do some comparison shopping and make an advance reservation if you want value for your dollar. Note that Rangiroa has a bed tax that will be added to your bill: 150 CFP per person, per night.

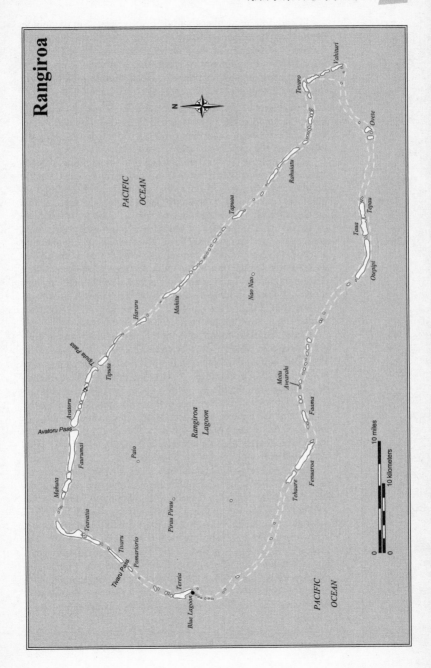

Rangiroa

N

PACIFIC OCEAN

Vahituri

Tevaro

Ovete

Rahitatu

Tapuaa

Tipau

Tuua

Otepipi

Nao Nao

Motu Avearahi

Faama

Tehaure

Fenuaroa

Harara

Mahiu

Tiputa

Tiputa Pass

Avatoru

Avatoru Pass

Fuarumai

Mahuta

Teavatia

Tivaru

Tiaru Pass

Pomariorio

Paio

Rangiroa Lagoon

Pirau Pirau

Tereia

Blue Lagoon

PACIFIC OCEAN

10 miles

10 kilometers

In addition, remember that just because you're in the middle of nowhere doesn't mean you should let down your guard. Unfortunately, lodgings in the Tuamotus have sporadic problems with theft and non-guests entering rooms. Always keep an eye on your belongings and make sure to lock your door before turning in for the night.

AVATORU AREA Avatoru's hotels and pensions are scattered along the lagoon side of the island. The descriptions that follow start at the western end at Avatoru Pass and move east along the island, past the airport to Tiputa Pass at the eastern end.

Starting at the west end of Avatoru you'll find **Pension Henriette**, which, unfortunately, has become rather rundown. The main building has an aging colonial-style veranda with boarded-up windows and "Pension Henriette" written in large faded letters on the awning. Two bungalows of various configurations have private baths. The largest unit has a living room with television, a dining room and a communal bath. The bungalows are in decline and the roofs of two units were covered with tarps when we visited recently. On the upside, the meals are very good—Henriette's dessert specialty is banana crêpes—and they come highly recommended. Located about five kilometers from the airport. Free transfers are provided, and kids under 12 stay for half price. No credit cards. ~ PK 5, Avatoru; phone/fax 96-84-68. BUDGET.

Chez Punua & Moana has a total of three thatch-roofed bungalows, two of which are rather tattered-looking beachside *fare*. Each one comes with one double bed and a communal bath. Punua also has two bungalows with one double and one single bed and a private bathroom. They also share six spartan bungalows listed with Chez Nanua's that are located 45 minutes by boat across the lagoon, where camping is also available. Punua's address is the same as Nanua's. It is located across the road from Chez Henriette on the western end of Avatoru. No credit cards. ~ PK 5, Avatoru; phone/fax 96-84-73. BUDGET.

Rangiroa Lodge may be the best place for backpackers seeking a dorm room. Located on the lagoon, the two dorm rooms each have three beds with linens; there's a communal kitchen and cold-water bathroom, and the tab will only run you about US$15 per night. Should you want privacy, there are four rooms for two, also with communal bath, for about US$5 more per person. The location provides easy access to the island's least expensive eating facilities, but meal plans are available and free transfers to the airport are provided. Make sure to lock your door at night; there are occasional problems with locals entering rooms to steal belongings and fondle female guests. ~ PK 4, Avatoru; 96-82-13. BUDGET.

A short distance to the east is friendly **Pension Herenui**, which has three thatch-roofed bungalows—all with private bath and terrace. The bungalows are practically sitting on the white-sand beach very close to the shore, and are shaded by coconut palms. Quite a few activities are offered here, including bicycling, drift snorkeling and waterskiing. Herenui is located about four kilometers from the airport. Free transfers are provided, and the room price includes breakfast. Contact Mme. Victorine Sanford. ~ PK 5, Avatoru; phone/fax 96-84-71. BUDGET.

Continuing east you'll come to **Pension Hinanui**. It has three well-constructed, white-washed, red-roofed bungalows, each with private (cold water) bath and terrace on the lagoon side. Tariff with two meals or *pension complete* is available. Good wine, fine food, nice management and excellent service distinguish Hinanui from many other pensions. The small shop on the premises is also handy. Breakfast is included and a meal plan is available. Children under 12 are half price and airport transfers are free. This pension also accepts credit cards (Visa and MasterCard), making it unusual among its competitors. ~ PK 4, Avatoru; 96-84-61. BUDGET.

Punua runs Sharky Parc excursions. He will take you fishing, snorkeling or on a picnic to one of the uninhabited *motu*. ~ 96-84-73, cell 79-24-66.

Miki Miki Village is located between the airport and Avatoru Village. It has five lagoon-front bungalows for one to three people; they are way upscale compared with most properties on this island. Units feature fans, refrigerators and hot water—a rarity in the Tuamotus. There are also two bungalows that each have a mezzanine for up to six people. The restaurant and bar are located in a large Polynesian-style building; it has a big dancefloor, with live music and dancing on Friday nights. The public is invited to dinner, but it's best to reserve your meals earlier in the day. The hotel offers boat tours of the Blue Lagoon and other popular destinations. Airport transfers are free. ~ PK 6, Avatoru; 96-83-83, fax 96-82-90. MODERATE TO DELUXE.

Continuing toward the airport, past Rangiroa Village is **Pension Nanua**, which has four very basic, small, turquoise-colored bungalows with thatched roofs. It's located behind Pareo Carole. There is also space for camping. Two of the bungalows have private bathrooms and two utilize communal facilities, which leave much to be desired. Some of the *fare* are located very near the shore of the lagoon so that the small ladder needed to get inside your unit is practically in the water. It's about as barebones as you can get, but the place does have a Polynesian spirit. And the meals are quite nice—copious and family-style. Kids under 12 stay for half price. ~ PK 4, Avatoru; 96-83-88. BUDGET.

You'll find **Pension Henri** on the ocean side of the atoll, across from Pareo Carole. Its four Polynesian-style bungalows are of average quality; all have private cold-water baths and small decks. You must take some type of meal plan; meals are served family-style in a central *fare*. Prices seemed steep, and the property is a long walk from any good swimming beach. Free airport transfers. Contact the David family for more information. No credit cards. ~ PK 4, Avatoru; 96-82-67 and 70-94-30; e-mail pensionhenri@ mail.pf. BUDGET.

Pension Loyna, one driveway past Pension Henri, is a large, two-story house with two rooms available. Located on the ocean side of the atoll (with no sign to identify the property), it lies just off the main road and does not have direct beach access. This pension is akin to a B&B accommodation—its guest rooms are inside the family home. The children sleep next door to the guests. The rooms have wooden floors, fans and screens with communal hot-water bath located downstairs. Although the meal plan prices are equivalent to what you can get with a detached bungalow elsewhere, activities and transfers (*motu* picnic, pass diving, fish park visit) are included in the price. A separate two-bedroom family bungalow in the rear has its own bath, tile floors, fan and TV. Children under 12 stay for half price. No credit cards. ~ PK 4, Avatoru; phone/fax 96-82-09; www.pensionloyna.fr.st, e-mail pensionloyna@mail.pf. BUDGET.

Pension Cécile has eight slender thatch-roofed bungalows, resembling an A-frame. Each has an attached bathroom with cold water and a small porch. The units are spotlessly clean and well maintained, and the food is very good. (Some of the units are newer and much better than the older accommodations. They are all the same price, so specify a newer one when you make the reservation.) You have the option of getting a room or *pension complete*. This is clearly one of the best quality pensions on the island. Cécile speaks English well, and both she and her husband Alban couldn't be more welcoming. It's located about midway between the Avatoru Pass end of the island and the airport (about five kilometers west of the airport). Transportation to the airport is free and two bikes are available. Cécile is reportedly a good cook. ~ PK 2, Avatoru; phone/fax 96-05-06 and 77-55-72. BUDGET.

HIDDEN ►

Pension Tuanake is about halfway between the airport and the town of Avatoru on the lagoon side. Its four Polynesian-style bungalows, two double units and two family bungalows with lofts, all have private cold-water baths, fans and patios. Tuanake also has one *fare* with two double beds, a kitchenette and a private bath. For warm-blooded types there is a small shower with hot water in the garden. The well-appointed common *fare* has a restaurant and a salon with TV, phone-card telephone and information board. The Terorotua family will arrange for excursions, provide free transfers and rent you a bike for very little. You can stay here with or without meal plan. We really liked the family atmosphere, which is typically Paumotu. English is spoken and the beach is terrific here. ~ PK 2.5, Avatoru; 96-04-45, fax 96-03-29; e-mail tuanake@mail.pf. BUDGET.

Tuamotan Practicalities

Virtually all the lodgings in the Tuamotus offer a *pension complete* plan, which means you pay an extra 2800 to 3800 CFP for three meals a day. This is usually advisable even when there are cooking facilities because on the remote islands there are few, if any, markets and no restaurants, except on Rangiroa.

Most guesthouses located more than ten minutes by boat from the airport will charge a transfer fee from 500 to 2000 CFP per person to pay for gasoline. And most of the pension-style accommodations in the Tuamotus discount their tariffs by 500 CFP per person per day for those staying more than three days.

Many of the pensions offer excursions (sometimes free) to a *motu* where you can swim, picnic and perhaps snorkel. You may be dropped off by a small boat while the owner is on the way to work. Be sure to bring your sunblock, water, a hat and a good book.

While in the Tuamotus, be prepared to conserve water, which is always a scarce commodity. At times it may be so scarce that people bathe in the sea rather than showering with fresh water. At a small pension you should not expect warm-water showers. Any water at all is a blessing and, besides, it's so hot a cold shower is refreshing.

Likewise, do not expect the electricity (if there is any) to be on more than a few hours a day. Many, but not all, of the pensions have generators, but fuel is expensive. All guests are provided with kerosene lamps, which work quite well and will add a romantic touch to your stay.

If you bring your American Express Card, don't expect to use it (or any other credit card) in the Tuamotus except at large resorts such as the Kia Ora Rangiroa or Manihi Pearl Beach Resort. And except for Rangiroa, there are no banks, so bring cash.

It goes without saying that the most visited islands in the Tuamotu Group, Rangiroa and Manihi, have the most amenities. The other islands have only started to develop tourism. Except for an airstrip, a few lodgings and perhaps a basic shop or two, there's little else on a typical atoll.

Finally, given the isolation of these islands, it's not a bad idea to call, write or fax before you drop in. A letter addressed to the pension, in care of the village and the name of the island, will get there. The postman will not have to ring twice.

Turiroa Village offers four bungalows and one *fare* on the lagoon side of the island. The bungalows are available with or without a kitchenette and there is a common lounge as well. Of special note, there is a laundry facility that guests may use. A visit to the owner's pearl farm is included in the price. No credit cards. ~ PK 1, Avatoru; phone/fax 96-04-27; e-mail pension.turiroa@mail.pf. BUDGET.

HIDDEN ▶   **Pension Raira Lagoon** has garnered kudos from many travelers. The ten traditional-style bungalows each have a sun deck and private bath and ceiling fans. The grounds are landscaped, and the service is excellent. The premises are regularly sprayed and, unlike other properties in the islands, are comparatively mosquito-free. There is a restaurant on the grounds that serves excellent, attractively presented food. *Pension complete* is available. Snorkeling is fairly good in the lagoon right off Raira Beach. Pension Raira Lagoon is located about two kilometers from the airport, near the Rangiroa Beach Club. Free airport transfers are provided, and credit cards are accepted. ~ PK 1.5, Avatoru; 93-12-30, fax 93-12-31; www.raira-lagoon.pf, e-mail rairalag@mail.pf. BUDGET.

A good value, **Pension Felix at Ariitini Village** offers nine traditional-style bungalows. Painted a distinctive chartreuse, the *fare* have thatched roofs and small porches. The two family bungalows have two (cold water) private baths; the others have one private bath. There is also an outside bath with hot water. Many of the bungalows are shaded from the sun by nearby trees. There is also a small restaurant and a guest salon that has a television. The management is helpful and friendly and the pension is clean. Kids under 12 stay for half price, and Visa cards are accepted. Ariitini Village is situated between Kia Ora Hotel and Chez Martine on the western side of Avatoru. ~ PK 1, Avatoru; phone/fax 96-04-41. BUDGET TO MODERATE.

Pension Martine provides five bungalows right on the beach. Three of the units have a double and a single bed, a private bath and a nice terrace. The water is suitable for bathing but is rather brackish and not potable. The units are solidly built on stilts and sport tiled floors and wooden roofs. The two older bungalows

AUTHOR FAVORITE

At **Kia Ora Sauvage**, a relaxing retreat that lies on a *motu* offshore Rangiroa's atoll, I can savor the ambience of being on the edge of the world while I'm pampered in luxury. It's set in a coconut grove, and looks rustic on the exterior, but everything inside is first class. For more information, see page 366.

have double beds and private baths. From all reports, the owners are very hospitable, and the property includes a small boutique also run by them. Pension Martine is located just on the beach, behind the restaurant Le Kaikai, across from the airport terminal. ~ PK 1, Avatoru; 96-02-53, fax 96-02-51. BUDGET.

Pension Hoka Nani opened in January 2000. The proprietress, Lovina, and her two sons built three Polynesian-style bungalows, which are constructed almost entirely from local materials: coconut fronds line the roof, walls are bamboo and terraces are made of *mikimiki* branches. Located in a coconut grove, facing the ocean side, each unit has a double bed, a small loft and a very nice private bath with cold water. For families, a house with two bedrooms and a lounge sleeps eight people. It has a large, airy dining area used to serve tasty breakfasts and dinners. Airport transfer is included in the rate and bicycles and scooters are available for rent. This is a great pension but unfortunately it's quite close to the main road. The view from the bungalows is of this road—not particularly appealing. Access to the property is by private path from the lagoon and the Kia Ora. Special group rates are available. ~ Avatoru; phone/fax 96-02-57. BUDGET.

Over-the-water bungalows are the main attraction at **Kia Ora Rangiroa**, one of the best high-end accommodations on this beautifully forlorn atoll. It's the largest hotel on the island, with 53 bungalows, 10 over-the-water bungalows, a restaurant and an over-the-water bar. The over-the-water bungalows come with glass-topped coffee tables that allow you to watch the underwater life while relaxing in your *fare*. And you have your own water-side deck besides. Rooms are spacious and nicely appointed, and the hotel appears to be well looked after. It's a very romantic environment whose clientele are mostly honeymooners. The setting is not as polished as one might find on Bora Bora but there is a rough-hewn charm to the property that is very fetching. The lagoon has a white-sand beach in this area and the swimming is good. So is the friendly, efficient staff. Nautical activities include snorkeling, windsurfing, sailing and fishing. Diving facilities at the Kia Ora are first class and the equipment is well maintained. The hotel is working toward a four-star rating; planned improvements include adding a swimming pool, installing air conditioning in all units and creating paved walkways. You can find the hotel close to the eastern end of the island, about three kilometers from the airport. Free airport greeting and transfer. ~ Avatoru; 96-02-22, fax 96-03-84; www.hotelkiaora.com, e-mail resa@kiaora.pf. ULTRA-DELUXE.

TIPUTA AREA   There are several accommodations in the Tiputa area, on either side of Tiputa Pass.

Pension Glorine is one of the better pensions on Rangiroa for several reasons: the food is good, the hospitality is generous, the service is above average and the location is stunning. There are six bungalows with various sleeping configurations, all with private bath. Children under 12 stay for half price. Unlike most accommodations, Glorine has a restaurant/bar facing the pass. Pension Glorine is adjacent to the dock, directly across from Tiputa Village on the Avatoru side (the eastern side) of Tiputa Pass. ~ PK 6, Avatoru; 96-04-05, fax 96-03-58; e-mail pensionglorine@mail.pf. BUDGET.

Pension Teina & Marie Guesthouse has seven thatch-roofed bungalows—two with private bath, four with shared bath and one family-style bungalow. The tariff per person is the same price with or without bath. You may rent rooms only or take demi/full *pension*. The food has had mixed reviews. This is a popular place with divers due to its location on the pass and proximity to two of the dive centers. There is also a payphone on the property. No credit cards. ~ PK 6, Avatoru; 96-03-94, fax 96-84-44. BUDGET.

Les Relais de Josephine is in a prime location with three traditional bungalows near the reef passage. All have private baths with hot water and there is a wonderful deck overlooking the channel. Meals are available. ~ PK 5, Avatoru; phone/fax 96-02-00; www.relaisjosephine.free.fr, e-mail relaisjosephine@mail.pf. MODERATE.

Crossing Tiputa Pass, **Chez Lucien** has three tree-shaded bungalows. Looking more like cottages with shake roofs and large porches than Polynesian *fare*, the bungalows have varied sleeping configurations, and all come with private baths. Chez Lucien's rooms are more spacious than the average accommodation and are well maintained. A deposit equaling one night's stay is required to secure reservations. It's located about a half-kilometer from the boat dock. ~ Tiputa; 96-73-55. BUDGET.

One of the best bargains on the island, **Pension Estall** has four simple thatch-roofed bungalows, each with one room and private bath. Estall has been in the hospitality business for a long time and her pension is a perennial favorite. A combination of comfortable accommodations, good food and nice management has earned high recommendations for Pension Estall. A deposit equaling one night's stay is required for reservations. Estall can be found a half-kilometer from the boat dock in Tiputa, situated between the ocean and the lagoon. ~ Tiputa; 96-73-16. BUDGET TO MODERATE.

OUTSIDE OF TIPUTA AND AVATORU   In addition to the hotels and pensions clustered around the communities of Avatoru and Tiputa, there are accommodations on *motu* located in other areas of this enormous atoll. Due to their extreme isolation, these places generally do not have phones.

If you want to fulfill your Robinson Crusoe fantasy in luxury, consider **Kia Ora Sauvage**, located on Motu Avearahi 30 kilometers—a one-hour boat ride—from Avatoru, on the oppo-

HIDDEN ►

site side of the lagoon. A sister property to Kia Ora Rangiroa, one might classify Kia Ora Sauvage as "ultra-deluxe primitive." The five bungalows have been completely reconstructed with local materials such as native woods and *pandanus* fronds from nearby trees. Comfortable and civilized, the *fare* have nifty semi-outdoor bathrooms with clamshell sinks. There is no electricity so kerosene lamps are used. There is also no pool, but with the crystal lagoon on your porch step, you'll hardly miss one. Despite the rustic nature, there is a restaurant and bar on the grounds. Prices, on the other hand, are not primitive—they are identical to those at the Kia Ora Rangiroa. Space permitting, guests at Kia Ora Rangiroa can switch over to this remote offshoot. There is a two-night minimum stay. ~ Motu Avearahi; 96-02-22, fax 96-02-20; www. hotelkiaora.com, e-mail resa@kiaora.pf. ULTRA-DELUXE.

DINING

Given its small size, there are a surprising number of restaurants on Rangiroa, mostly in the Avatoru area. Most visitors get meal plans with their lodging, however, because the population of this island is too small to sustain a large number of eateries.

The cheapest eating places for a hot sit-down meal are in Avatoru village. You can enjoy a full meal of fried fish, salad and potatoes at **Snack Mareta** for only 650 CFP—and it's good. Breakfast is served every day, too. ~ Avatoru. BUDGET.

Snack Chez Auguste has a much more extensive menu at similar prices. Look for the blue-green building with an open-air dining area off to the side; it's open for lunch and dinner. ~ Avatoru; 96-85-01. BUDGET.

Unpretentious and excellent, **Kai Kai** (which translates as "the meal") is run by Pierre and Dominique Seybald, the former managers of the closed Rangiroa Beach Club. Construction is very local. Up to 12 tables line a crushed-white-coral floor, and a thatched coconut-frond roof buttressed by shafts of bamboo protects clients from the elements. Service is friendly and the

AUTHOR FAVORITE

We think **Pizzeria Vaimario** serves the best pizza in town. In a deft move the owners, Serge Giroux and his wife, exchanged a parasailing business for a pizza oven. A special "fast" lunch menu includes salads, omelets, spaghetti, burgers, fish, steaks and of course, pizza. In the evenings chef Philippe serves fish and meat for dinner. A nice touch along with an inside dining room is the outside terrace with tables set on crushed coral. Serge also offers a pick-up service for his clients. Located on the ocean side next to the Beach Club. ~ Avatoru; phone/fax 96-05-96; e-mail resto.vaimario@mail.pf. BUDGET.

menu specializes in seafood. Specialties include *poisson cru*, sashimi, carpaccio, brochette, grilled fish, curried shrimp, beef tartare and steak. Kai Kai is located just across from the airport terminal, in front of Chez Martine. Roundtrip transfers from your pension are free with a reservation. Check it out. ~ Avatoru; 96-03-39. BUDGET TO MODERATE.

La Grignotte is a minuscule take-away that offers crêpes, panini, sandwiches, pizza, hamburgers and ice cream. Look for it at the entrance of the Raira Lagoon. ~ Avatoru. BUDGET.

Snack Manuragi is a great place for an inexpensive lunch. It's located next to Chez Punua and Moana and owned by the same people. Specialties include *poisson cru* and other seafood dishes. ~ Avatoru. BUDGET.

Ikimario serves pizza and local fare but specializes in Japanese dishes. A free transfer is provided from your pension with a reservation. ~ Avatoru; 96-65-96. BUDGET.

Pizza Filipo serves a variety of tasty pizzas as well as local dishes. The restaurant is located behind the Raie Manta Dive Center. ~ PK 4, Avatoru; 73-76-20. BUDGET.

Chez Beatrice is a good choice for Chinese food. It's got simple, rustic ambience and is popular with locals. It's located next to the pearl culture center. ~ Avatoru; 96-04-12. BUDGET.

You can find sandwiches and inexpensive dishes at Chez Henriette (96-04-68) and Chez Mareta. ~ Avatoru. BOTH BUDGET.

Chez Tauirarii at the Avatoru Marina has local-style food as well as superb fish. ~ Avatoru; 96-83-33. MODERATE.

Raira Lagoon offers home cooking in a simple, village-style outdoor setting that overlooks the sea. Traditional dishes such as *ipo* (Tuamotu-style dumplings) and *poisson cru* are sometimes served. ~ Avatoru; 96-04-23. BUDGET TO MODERATE.

Kia Ora Village is the best (and most expensive) restaurant on the island. Come for the very fresh—some come straight from the lagoon—seafood dishes such as tempting seafood brochettes and mahimahi. The restaurant bar is on the water, which makes for a very pleasant setting. It's the only place on the island where you can get espresso, and there is a wonderful dessert bar—for 1100 CFP you can pack down a great selection of homemade cakes, fruit salad, custard, tarts, etc. There is live local music during dinner several nights a week. ~ Avatoru; 96-04-06. DELUXE TO ULTRA-DELUXE.

Chez Glorine is an excellent local-style eatery that overlooks the sea. Traditional dishes such as *poisson cru*, grilled or fried fish, and *ipo* are often served, but Glorine's specialty is *langouste* (lobster). ~ PK 6, Avatoru; 96-04-05. BUDGET.

Good meals are also available at Miki Miki, a restaurant at the pension of the same name. ~ Avatoru; 96-83-83. MODERATE.

Riding a bicycle east on Rangiroa is more difficult because of the headwind. Bring plenty of water if you ride during the heat of the day.

GROCERIES

There are several small markets in Avatoru and Tiputa that stock a few basics, which tend to be expensive. If you are going to need much more than simple items (such as instant coffee, milk or cookies), purchase them in Papeete.

Magasin Daniel is a well-stocked little store where you can buy everything from canned goods and frozen foods to American cereals, diapers and imported beer. There is also a photocopy machine in the back office. ~ Avatoru; 96-04-98.

SHOPPING

Carole Pareo boutique sells pareus and handpainted T-shirts with fish motifs. (It also doubles as a bike/scooter-rental agency.) ~ Avatoru; 96-82-45.

Carolina, the owner of **Ocean Passion**, is a talented artist; her hand-painted pareus and T-shirts are a cut above the competition. Her shop is located between the hospital and Pareo Carole on the lagoon side. ~ Avatoru; 96-02-72.

There are dozens of places to purchase black pearls along the ten-kilometer stretch of road between Avatoru and Tiputa Pass. Some are farms giving technical demonstrations and tours, but most are just outlets. Some excellent deals can be found here, but do your homework before you buy. Refer to the notes on black pearl buying in Chapter Two.

Taaroa Bijoux, just past the Kia Ora Hotel, is a small shop that sells pearls in every price range. Unlike many other shops, the settings are handmade originals that are created on the premises. The high-quality work is classy and unique, definitely worth a look. ~ 96-03-04; www.taaroa-bijoux.com, e-mail fetia@taaroa-bijoux.com.

One of the largest local pearl farms on Rangiroa is **Gauguin's Pearl**. Besides selling pearls they offer visits with detailed lectures on the cultivation process. Gauguin's is located about one kilometer east of the airport. ~ 96-05-39; e-mail phcab@mail.pf.

In Tiputa, local arts and crafts such as shell leis, seashells and small carvings can be purchased at the artisan house in the main square.

INTERNET ACCESS

Amazing as it may seem in this far-flung place, you can check your e-mail and browse the web at **Taaroa Bijoux**, next to the Kia Ora Hotel. Fifteen minutes of access costs 350 CFP and two computers are available. ~ Avatoru; 96-03-04.

BEACHES

If you consider that almost the entire island is fringed by white sand and crushed coral, you'll understand why it's difficult to recommend a single beach. It seems just about every pension or hotel claims to have *the* beach in its front yard. In addition to the local beaches, there are day trips to *motu* around the lagoon provided by tour operators or various guest facilities.

L'ILE AUX RÉCIFS 🏊 🐟 L'Ile aux Récifs, or Reef Island, is a *motu* on the south side of the lagoon noted for its fossilized coral formations. Snorkeling here is excellent—perhaps the best accessible site in all of Rangiroa. ~ To get there you must take a boat. Any hotel or guesthouse can arrange a visit.

BLUE LAGOON MOTU 🏊 A popular trip to this *motu* is the Blue Lagoon cruise, a half-day affair offered by several tour operators. It includes a boat trip to a scenic *motu* area, and a picnic. Also included in the excursion is a shark feeding, probably the high point of the Blue Lagoon experience, which is otherwise a bit overhyped. Facilities exist, but they could use upgrading. ~ There are several tour companies that visit the lagoon. It's best to go in a covered boat such as Kia Ora's vessel because you will get soaked if the weather is not accommodating and a squall passes through. In fact, it's a good idea to take motion sickness tablets and a cushion—the slightest breeze rocks the boat wildly.

HIDDEN ► **TIPUTA VISTA POINT** If you are in the Tiputa area, one of the best things to do is check out the vista point that also serves as a modest picnic area on the Avatoru side of Tiputa Pass. An informal park, there are several circular benches with canopies where you can relax and watch the dolphins jumping in the pass or see the sun set. ~ It's located just as the road makes a right fork at the Paradive (scuba) shop. If in doubt, ask at Paradive.

MOTU NUHI-NUHI 🏊 🐟 In the Tiputa area there's good snorkeling and shallow diving at Motu Nuhi-Nuhi. You'll find a rich variety of marine life in the Nuhi-Nuhi Valley to the south of the *motu*. If you have the inclination, take a walk to the edge of the pass between 4 p.m. and dusk. With a little luck and a sharp eye you may see dolphins surfing the waves. ~ During low tide you can walk along the reef (with your reef shoes) or better yet, take a local boat. Walk to the edge of the pass from either the Tiputa or Avatoru side of the atoll. The *motu* is on the inner side of the pass. It's impossible to miss, it's the only small islet in the area.

Outdoor Adventures

DIVING

Only two passes take water to and from the island's lagoon (which is among the largest in the world). Tidal action causes the water to rush through the passes at an enormous rate; thus, dives in the area of the passes are almost always "drift dives," in which divers are taken to one end of a pass and the incoming or outgoing current tide carries them through to the opposite side.

Divers that take the plunge in "Rangi" will be well rewarded: white-tip reef sharks, black-tip sharks, the much larger gray sharks, silvertip sharks and hammerheads make their home in the passes. Manta rays are also numerous here; it's not unusual to see upward of 15 rays feeding in single file.

Motu Fara, the small *motu* at the southern end of the Avatoru Pass, divides the pass into two smaller channels. At average depths of less than 50 feet, **Tiny Pass** on the west side of the *motu* is a dramatic dive site, with its colorful coral and a countless assortment of smaller reef fish and larger species. The **Avatoru Pass Caves** are located on the wider and deeper pass that runs down to the east side of the *motu*. There are also superb dives, particularly for sharks and other pelagics, on the outer edge of the reef at the east and west side of the pass portal. July through November is a good time to spot manta rays.

Large swells sometimes run through the channel and dolphins are often seen playing in the waves or jumping the bows of passing ships in Tiputa Pass.

South of Avatoru Pass, beyond Motu Fara, the area known as **Mahuta** has coral formations and a rich variety of both lagoon and ocean fish, which meet in this intermediate zone. This is a great site for novice divers because of the weak currents and abundant marine life. The area from here back to Motu Fara is also excellent snorkeling territory. **Papiro Point,** south of Tiny Pass and farther into the lagoon, is also a prime snorkeling site.

Caves are found on the west side of the entrance to Tiputa Pass and in the center of the pass, before the area known as **The Valley**. The **Tiputa Caves** are also known as the **Shark Caves** or **Shark Point**, with good reason—large numbers of gray reef sharks can be observed here. It is French Polynesia's most famous dive site. Shark-feeding trips add to the excitement, but there are often so many sharks—upwards of 200—that any extra encouragement is scarcely necessary!

All of the Rangiroa dive operators are located on Avatoru. They offer lessons and lead dives to the lagoon, the passes and the open sea. Night dives are also possible.

Paradive is located next door to Chez Glorine and is operated by Bernard Blanc. Bernard is a charming, obliging chap. (If you want to see what a stonefish looks like, there's a preserved specimen in his office.) ~ Avatoru; 96-05-55, fax 96-05-50; www.chez.com/paradive, e-mail paradive@mail.pf.

The Six Passengers scuba outfit has a personal and competent staff that specializes in small groups. They provide free transportation to and from your hotel and will videotape your dive for a fee. ~ Avatoru; phone/fax 96-02-60; www.the6passengers.com, e-mail the6passengers@mail.pf.

Dream Dive is the dream start-up of three young dive instructors who have worked for other Rangiroa dive outfits. Their niche is diving in less-visited sites and at different times than their competitors. They cater to smaller groups (five divers maximum) and give classes in using underwater photography and video. They offer night dives and, unlike some other Rangiroa outfits, eschew shark feeding. Dream Dive is located next to Pension Tuanake. ~ Avatoru; 79-24-53, 96-03-72.

Yves Lefevre operates the **Raie Manta Club**, which was the only dive center on the island when it opened in 1985. The center has a second shop on Tikehau, and its multi-dive packages can be used there as well. A note of caution: instructors tend not to keep a close eye on divers. ~ Avatoru; 96-84-80, fax 96-85-60; raiemantaclub.free.pf, e-mail raiemantaclub@mail.pf.

TOPdive, which also runs dive centers on Bora Bora and Moorea, offers three dives daily. Their ten-dive pack can be used at any of the TOPdive facilities. ~ Avatoru; 72-39-55, fax 96-05-60; www.topdive.com, e-mail info@topdive.com.

Hotel Kia Ora dives are run by the **Blue Dolphins Diving Center**. Video is available. ~ Avatoru; phone/fax 96-03-01; www.bluedolphinsdiving.com, e-mail bluedolphins@mail.pf.

CAMPING **Chez Nanua** has one campsite but the ground is a bit rocky. It's advisable to bring your own tent. ~ Avatoru; 96-03-88.

FISHING Even though Rangiroa has one of the largest lagoons in the world, fishing is not a big draw. With a little luck, however, you can hook a marlin or a mahimahi. The vessels are available for charter work out of the **Kia Ora Hotel** and include the *Heikura Iti*, the *Parata*, the *Tutuke* and the *Ava*. ~ Avatoru; 96-03-34.

Deep-sea fishing on a 38-foot vessel can be arranged by calling **Hiria Arnoux**. ~ 96-02-88.

AUTHOR FAVORITE

For the ultimate Tuamotu diving experience, I book a live-aboard diving trip on the **Tahiti Agressor**, a 106-foot catamaran that can accommodate 16 passengers. Trips start in Rangiroa on Saturday and run through the following Saturday with five and a half days of diving. Because of the abundant—and largest—sharks, there are no night dives. Dives are made in the passes and around channel entrances of several Tuamotu atolls, including Rangiroa, Kaukara, Fakarava, Toau and Apataki. Nitrox, scuba gear and film processing are available onboard, and amenities include eight double staterooms each with private bath, a salon with entertainment center, a wet bar, a hot tub and a sun deck. A "pass flying," drift-diving certification course is mandatory and is included in the charter price, which is about US$2400. Whole- and half-boat bookings are available, and the boat is accessible for disabled divers. ~ 800-348-2628; www.aggressor.com, e-mail info@aggressor.com.

Peche a'Gras offers half- and full-day sportfishing trips. ~ Avatoru; 96-02-27, 23-69-52.

Pascal and Cosetta offer boat, canoe and jet-ski rentals as well as waterskiing trips. ~ Avatoru; 96-03-31.

Rangiroa Activities, based out of the Kia Ora Hotel, offers dolphin-encounter trips. Departure times are based on the daily tides. ~ Avatoru; phone/fax 96-03-31, cell 71-02-98; www.dol phin-watch.pf, e-mail p.rohde@mail.pf.

OTHER WATER SPORTS

Although snorkeling with the current through the pass is an easy activity, even for novices, you also have the option of viewing the underwater spectacle from the comfort of a glass-bottom boat. Local operators are available for independent or group excursions. If you wish to sail in the Blue Lagoon or to the bird sanctuary on Motu Paio, or want to check out the dolphins frolicking at Tiputa Pass or Site Ohutu in late afternoon, contact the following operators.

BOAT TOURS

Te Ono Ono is the tour boat that operates out of Kia Ora Rangiroa. It takes in both passes, with a pause for snorkeling at one of them and dolphin chasing in late afternoon. ~ Avatoru; 96-03-34.

C.A.N.A.R. (Centre d'Activités Nautiques et Aquatiques de Rangiroa) is operated by Serge Giroux, the owner of Vaimario Pizza. He has a variety of boats, Hobie cats and canoes for rent. He also offers snorkeling trips, pearl-farm visits, a dolphin tour, drift snorkeling, fishing expeditions and taxi boat service. Serge provides free pick-up for all his clients. C.A.N.A.R. is located between the Kia Ora hotel and the Six Passengers scuba club. ~ Avatoru; phone/fax 96-05-96, cell 79-24-79.

Pascal and Cosetta offer a two-hour snorkeling trip in Tiputa Pass. When the current permits, a snorkeling drift ride allows one to admire Rangiroa's fascinating flora and fauna. Pascal and Cosetta provide all the gear you'll need and a guide to help you do it. This is one of the most spectacular snorkeling trips you can take in French Polynesia. ~ Avatoru; 96-03-31.

Panua Tamaehu of Chez Punua has a tour boat and also operates a large catamaran that can take up to 20 passengers. Excursions out to the Blue Lagoon are available on a regular basis. ~ Avatoru; 96-84-73.

Matahi Tepa owns a glass-bottom boat and operates tours to a site known as the Aquarium, adjacent to Tiputa Pass. Snorkeling is possible from the boat. ~ Avatoru; 96-84-48.

Teheitapuarii Excursions offers half- and full-day trips to the Blue Lagoon and various *motu*. Lunch is available. ~ Avatoru; 96-84-68.

Vave'a Excursions, based at the Kia Ora hotel, has two motor-boats and offers regular trips. ~ Avatoru; phone/fax 96-05-87.

Ariitini Excursions has a 25-foot boat with fiberglass hull, as well as a 36-foot wooden boat available for guided excursions. ~ Avatoru; 96-04-41, fax 96-04-40.

Tane Tamaehu offers tours in a glass-bottomed boat. ~ 96-84-68. **Leon Revault** also offers boat trips. ~ 96-02-57.

HELI-COPTER TOURS

Two companies provide sightseeing tours over Rangiroa by heli-copter. Both are based out of Faa'a Airport on Tahiti, and both use five- or six-seater "Squirrel" helicopters: **Heli-Pacific** ~ Papeete, 85-68-00, fax 85-68-08, e-mail heli.pacific@mail.pf; and **Heli-Inter Polynesie** ~ Papeete, 86-60-29, fax 81-99-99, e-mail ops-helico@mail.pf.

BIKING

If you are not into water sports, there's not a lot to do on an atoll. Almost all the hotels and pensions rent or lend bikes to guests. Bikes are a perfect way to get around—the roads are flat and you'll never have far to go. There's only one road around the main islet and you can ride all the way from one end to the other and back again, a roundtrip of about 12.5 miles (20 kilometers), in a couple of hours. Landlubbers, or those just wishing to explore the island, might consider renting a bike at one of the following concessions: **Chez Nanua** ~ Avatoru, 96-03-88; **Raira Lagoon** ~ Avatoru, 96-04-23; **Pareo Carole** ~ Avatoru, 96-02-45; **Kia Ora Rangiroa** (guests only) ~ Avatoru, 96-03-84; **Chez Helene** ~ Avatoru, 96-82-84; or **Rangi Atelier** ~ Tiputa, 96-04-92.

Manihi

Enclosing a magnificent clear blue lagoon teeming with fish, Manihi is another classic atoll made up of an oblong string of flat *motu* located 322 miles (520 kilometers) northeast of Papeete. The population numbers approximately 1150; most people live in the village of Paeva. Like many of the other Tuamotu islands, commercial fishing takes a distant second to the cultured pearl business. Visitors with an interest in the cultivation of black pearls will definitely find Manihi of interest. And those pursuing underwater adventures will find diving conditions ideal. The plush Manihi Pearl Beach Resort features first-class diving.

When I first came to Manihi in the late 1970s, I found the inhabitants to be friendlier than those of Rangiroa, which at that time was the only other major tourism center in the Tuamotus. The people are still friendly, but tourism has declined with the growth of the black pearl industry. There are now more than 30 pearl farms on the island.

In the late 1970s, the presence of the hotel and the nascent cultured-pearl industry made the island a relatively prosperous community. (In those days prosperity meant owning Mercury outboards, Sony tape decks and clothing without holes.) What a difference a few decades make! Nowadays wealth on the island is not simply defined by who owns the newest outboard motor. Pearl farming has turned islanders into a Polynesian version of the Beverly Hillbillies. They drive up and down the half-mile or so of road in shiny new Toyota trucks while their children whiz along the atoll on motorcycles. There are even several two-story buildings that look totally out of place on this atoll. The truth is, Manihi today is a far cry from the little fishing community it once was.

Canoes, waterskis and jet skis are available for rent at Manihi Pearl Beach Resort. ~ Manihi; 96-42-73.

There are no banks on the island, so bring cash. The three lodging choices listed below all accept credit cards, as do the pearl farms. There are public phones (phone cards only) at the airport and in front of the pier in the village of Paeva. The post office is located near the big almond tree inside the town hall. It is open Monday–Thursday 7:30 a.m. to 3 p.m. and Friday 7:30 a.m. to 1 p.m. The notices of proposed marriages, court cases, weather alerts and upcoming community events posted on the town hall door give some insight into local life. There is also a small medical clinic in town—but any significant medical event, including childbirth, is passed on to Papeete.

SIGHTS

Entertainment in Manihi consists of watching Sunday soccer games, shooting pool, playing the local version of bocce ball and catching sharks off the pier. The latter is done at night with a handline attached to a giant hook baited with a chunk of moray eel. When participants land a shark, they slash its spinal cord with a machete and extract the shark's jaw for a souvenir. Considering the ecological implications of this practice, I would discourage it. Likewise, visitors should eschew purchasing items made from turtle shell, which of course is derived from an endangered and protected species.

Manihi's villagers take pride in their limestone and clapboard homes, which line the two main streets. Most homes have attractive front and back yards arranged with shells, shrubs and flowers. They are either fenced in or surrounded by curbs to discourage the bands of scrawny, marauding dogs that populate Polynesian villages. The village boasts one main concrete dock, a flagpole and a square where old people gossip under the shade of a huge tree.

The best thing to do is just enjoy the lagoon, whether swimming, snorkeling, diving or canoeing. The water is so clear you can see the fish from the docks.

LODGING

Only three places officially offer lodging (listed below); however, other places open and close seasonally. By the accounts of travelers and locals alike, the rooms offered in people's homes in town are not recommended. Our suggestion is not to arrive in Manihi without reservations. It's considered rude, and your odds of having a pleasant stay are not good. If you do arrive on the island without prearranged accommodations and you can't find a room, ask around at the airport or in town. Some residents will take you in if they are in the mood or have children away at school in Papeete.

Chez Jeanne is a small motel located on Motu Tangaraufara, a 20-minute boat ride from the airport and the village. There are two bungalows on the beach that will accommodate three people each and an over-water unit for two. All three have private baths, terraces and self-contained kitchens. No meals are available, but Jeanne has a small store for guests and she'll take you shopping with her when she goes to town. Activities include a visit to the family pearl farm, *motu* picnics, lagoon boat rides and snorkeling. Scuba diving is possible at Manihi Blue Nui, which is located next to the Manihi Pearl Beach Resort. Jeanne will transport guests to the dive center and back to the motel. ~ Motu Tangaraufara; 96-42-90, fax 96-42-91; e-mail motel.chez.jeanne@caramail.com. MODERATE.

Set on a white-sand beach, **Manihi Pearl Beach Resort** is a class act, with 19 over-the-water bungalows and 22 beach bungalows. The over-the-water units are big; they have king-size beds and glass-bottomed tables for viewing the lagoon waters below. The equally spacious beach bungalows have terraces that overlook the lagoon. These units have delightful indoor-outdoor bathrooms (where an occasional land crab might join you for company), telephones, overhead fans and minibars. The channel near the hotel has been dredged to allow small boats to enter a marina. There's an enormous swimming pool at the edge of the lagoon.

The property has the best (and the only) dive operation on the island, Manihi Blue Nui. Other water activities and tours are numerous and surprisingly inexpensive. They include lagoon fishing trips, drift snorkeling in the pass, and visits to a black pearl farm. All are offered at 2600 CFP per person or less. If you're interested in exploring the village, catch the employee boat that leaves the boat dock in the village of Turipaoa at 6:30 a.m. and returns at 4 p.m. each day; there's no charge if you eat or join an excursion.

The Manihi Pearl staff is very friendly, and there are lots of nice touches: a welcome orientation with drinks, hammocks, a video-viewing room, a billiard room, a miniature-golf course, a black pearl jewelry shop and boutique, and Tahitian shows three nights a week. ~ Turipaoa; 96-42-73, fax 96-42-72; www.pearl resorts.com, e-mail direction@manihipearlbeach.pf. In Papeete call 43-16-10. ULTRA-DELUXE.

Manihi's Pearl Industry

The island's 20-year-old cultured-pearl industry provides the fuel that powers Manihi's economy. Throughout the lagoon are buoys that mark the roughly 200-yard-long stations, with rows of pearl oysters dangling from lines stretched above the surface of the lagoon. Depending on the weather, water temperature or other conditions in the lagoon, these lines can be raised or lowered to provide optimal growth for the oysters. Lustrous black pearls with a silver sheen unique to French Polynesia are the result.

Every year tiny spheres of Mississippi River mussel shell (or a similar species) are implanted in the black pearl oysters collected from the lagoon by local divers. After three years, the oysters are harvested. Out of every hundred oysters, only seven will eventually yield commercially acceptable pearls.

Most of the hotels or pensions provide tours of the pearl facilities, which are ubiquitous on this island. Tours generally include a boat ride in the lagoon where a diver is sent to retrieve an oyster. The mature oyster is opened and the pearl is extracted and passed around the boat for inspection by the guests. Of course, there are no free samples.

The local hero who showed other Polynesians that they could succeed in the pearl farming business is known simply as Petero. When pearl farming was in its inception, the entrepreneurs were Japanese, Chinese or European businessmen. Polynesians did benefit from employment, but they were not the actual farmers or producers who profited directly. Petero showed them that it didn't have to be that way. He became the first Polynesian grafter (the technician who actually implants the seed within the oyster). Petero eventually started his own pearl farm and has prospered. His empire has grown from a pearl farm to a pool hall/curio shop/boutique that can be found on the ocean side of the atoll. (He reportedly sells good quality pearls at a substantially lower price than the pearls sold in Tahiti.) There are now approximately 30 pearl farms in Manihi alone. Most are family owned, and many are found on the more isolated *motu*.

HIDDEN ▶ Located on a private *motu*, ten kilometers by boat from the airport or village, **Pension Vainui Perles** is an honest-to-goodness pearl farm with guest accommodations. There's a standalone bungalow and six private rooms. Amenities include a white-sand beach, snorkeling, fishing, a jewelry showroom and a bar/restaurant (primarily for guests—don't show up for meals without reservations). They provide free airport greetings and boat transfers, technical demonstrations and a guided tour of the farm. All meals and activities, including fishing in the lagoon and a *motu* picnic, are included in the rates. Minimal English is spoken, so bring your French dictionary. Pension Vainui Perles has received high marks, and it's the only inexpensive property on Manihi. ~ 96-42-89, fax 96-43-30. BUDGET.

DINING Dining out will not require a big decision-making process. There's only one restaurant on the island, **Manihi Pearl Beach Resort**. The restaurant has a terrace that faces the beach and the pool. While generally catering to their own guests, they do accept visitors from other pensions. French cuisine and seafood are served—considering the quality and variety of fresh fish available, it's safe to say seafood is your best bet. However, what is served depends on what the fishermen have brought in. *Poisson cru* is consistently good and snapper is generally on the menu. Continental and American-style breakfast buffets are offered. Lunch entrées are an unexpected bargain: vanilla chicken with fries and vegetables, or (my favorite) sailfish brochette in lemon butter with rice and vegetables, cost only 1400 CFP. Dinner will set you back quite a bit more, but there's a good live Polynesian show three nights a week. Unless you're staying in the hotel, transportation can be a problem at night. ~ Turipaoa; 96-42-73. ULTRA-DELUXE.

If you go to the Manihi Pearl Beach Resort for lunch, ask about getting a return ride into the village on the boat that carries hotel employees.

GROCERIES There is a market in the village that sells bread, tinned fish, bottled water and other basics. Oranges were the only fresh fruit available when I visited. A bakery, on the inland street parallel to the marina, sells a sweet round bread. A few small stores inside people's homes will sell at off hours, but they are not obvious—there are no signs.

SHOPPING All of the lodgings in Manihi will either provide free pearl farm tours or arrange for a low-cost tour. You can make your own tour arrangements if you prefer, of course. The largest pearl farms are the **Brenaud family farm** on Korakoru Motu (96-43-41), and the **Tuamotu Pearl Company** (96-42-81) managed by the Bouche family on Takovea Motu. Both offer tours in English. While it is fun to visit the farms and prices are good for wholesale quantities, the price of set jewelry is comparable to Papeete and the selection is not as good. The best prices I found for small quantities of unset pearls were in Rangiroa, but you might get lucky if you know what you're buying.

The entire island is fringed by white-sand beaches, interspersed with coral. Be sure to bring insect repellent if you plan to use the beaches at dusk.

BEACHES

MANIHI PEARL BEACH RESORT Far from the village, the white-sand beach at Manihi Pearl Beach Resort provides excellent opportunities for swimming and snorkeling. For visitors staying on other parts of the atoll, it's not practical to use the facilities here on a regular basis, but if you are fortunate enough to stay at the resort, all manner of nautical and beach activities are available through the hotel. Nonguests can use the facilities with permission, but if you are staying elsewhere it's a long haul by watertaxi.

Manihi's weather patterns are consistently dry and the area has a large variety of species concentrated in shallow waters. This makes for good diving conditions. Unlike Rangiroa, the main passes in the Manihi area have milder currents, which make them less demanding for inexperienced divers.

Outdoor Adventures

DIVING

Dive sites are numerous. **Tairapa Pass** is a drift dive through the only pass in the atoll where you'll see plenty of pelagics, including schools of barracuda and tuna. Sometimes you'll even spot a turtle, eagle ray or manta ray, or you can visit with whitetip and nurse sharks in their **Shark Caves**.

The **Drop Off** is just that, a sheer wall located just outside the reef that descends over 5900 feet (1800 meters). Undersea life includes gray sharks, Napoleon fish, giant jack fish, schools of snappers and sea pike barracuda, tuna, marlin and other pelagics. Once a year thousands of groupers gather in this area to breed, which, according to local dive operator Gilles Petre, is an amazing sight.

The **Circus**, situated between the pass and the lagoon, is populated with Napoleon fish and black-tip reef sharks. Because its location keeps the water fairly murky with plankton, it's also a favorite refuge of manta rays and eagle rays, which can be observed year-round, alone or in groups, at an average depth of 30 feet (9 meters). The rays have become used to divers and are approachable.

West Point is on the ocean side of the reef and offers a magnificent coral garden that begins at a depth of 5 feet (1.5 meters) and descends another 90 feet (27 meters). Here you can find table coral, fire coral, antler coral and flower petal coral. On good days visibility is up to 200 feet (60 meters).

La Faille is another excellent dive site southwest of the atoll. The diving here is safe for novices and offers an opportunity to see moray eels and scorpionfish.

Manihi Blue Nui is a diving operation with four instructors on staff. Dive sites, most of which are outside the reef, are generally close to shore so drive time on the dive boats is minimal. ~ Manihi Pearl Resort, Manihi; phone/fax 96-42-17; e-mail manihi. blue.nui@mail.pf.

FISHING

Fishing trips where you can snag some tuna, mahimahi and jack can be arranged through **Manihi Pearl Beach Resort**. The boats used are the *Toohi II* and the *Arcoa*, a 30-foot fiberglass launch. ~ Manihi; 96-42-73; e-mail manihipearl.b@mail.pf. Other pensions will arrange trips as well.

BOAT TOURS

The *Toohi III* is a 24-foot, glass-bottom boat that makes trips to watch sharks at feeding time. Bookings can be made through the **Manihi Pearl Beach Resort**. ~ Manihi; 96-42-73; e-mail manihi pearl.b@mail.pf.

BIKING

There are unpaved roads and paths located around the atoll that make for interesting bike rides. A typical bike ride might take you along a lane pockmarked by land crab burrows and through shady groves of coconut palms. Bikes can be rented at **Manihi Pearl Beach Resort**. You might want to check with other lodging facilities as well. ~ Manihi; 96-42-73.

Tikehau

Tikehau comes close to the picture-postcard version of what paradise should look like. There is still quite a *sauvage*, or wild, quality to the place. You can walk along the beach or snorkel across the channels separating the *motu* without encountering another soul.

A little over 350 people inhabit Tikehau, which has a near-circular shape and a diameter of 16 miles (26 kilometers).

SIGHTS

The main village of **Tuherahera** is a tidy little island village. The streets are laid out in an orderly fashion and rubbish is less apt to be tossed about than in other Tuamotu communities. According to Arai, the proprietor of Panau Lagoon, the clean streets are due to his vigilance as the local *gendarme*. Another reason may be that the village was completely rebuilt after a devastating cyclone in 1983. There are four stores in town, but only one is obvious—the others are parts of people's homes.

When Jacques Cousteau's research group made a study of the Tuamotus in 1987, they found that Tikehau's lagoon contained one of the largest concentrations of fish in the entire archipelago, many of which are found in a number of fish parks. In actuality, these parks are nothing more than a bunch of poles connected with chicken wire that trap the fish. After being caught they are then air-freighted to Tahiti.

Among the points of interest on Tikehau is the deteriorating hull of an old wooden **shipwreck**, the *Mihimani*, which is lodged on the shore and lays keeled over to one side. Nearby, located very near the pass on the same side of the lagoon, is the fishing village of **Tuheiava**. (Note: The village has no store or food available.)

At the far east end of the atoll, away from the village, is a settlement called **Eden**. Founded by the Taiwanese New Testament Church religious organization, the residents of this group support themselves by growing fruit and vegetables. They also run a pearl farm and have an aquarium. Visitors are welcomed.

Tikehau's long, narrow islets are lined with paths that lead from one end to the other. A bike ride will take you through shady coconut groves to the edge of the reef. Some accommodations also offer bike rentals.

On a *motu* south of Eden are the **ruins** of an unfinished five-star Italian hotel that went bankrupt. The word is that construction of a new luxury hotel will pick up the pieces, although the timetable is uncertain.

The island's small *motu* are home to many bird colonies. Of particular note is the aptly named **Isle of Birds**, which is well known for its red-footed gannets and brown noddies.

LODGING

Large by Tuamotu standards, **Tikehau Pearl Beach Resort** is the first high-end lodging on the island. Situated right on the exquisite lagoon, it includes 16 over-the water bungalows—8 of them "premium" suites—as well as 14 beach bungalows. The facility has all the amenities you would expect, including lagoon-viewing panels in the floor of over-water units, a restaurant, bar and swimming pool. ~ Tuherahera; 96-23-00 fax 96-23-01; www.pearl resorts.com, e-mail welcome@tikehaupearlbeach.pf. DELUXE TO ULTRA-DELUXE.

Tikehau Village offers 11 bungalows. Each bungalow has a private (cold water) bath. There is a small restaurant/bar on the premises. Excursions are available to a *motu* (including free use of snorkeling gear) and to a fish reserve. The proprietors also offer an automobile tour of the island and visits to the village. Tikehau Village looked to be rather rundown and in need of repair, but if you can put that aside, it has a wonderful location on the beach with a view of the lagoon. Free roundtrip transfers are included, as are kayaks and bicycles. The small resort is situated one kilometer from the center of Tuherahera Village. ~ Tuherahera Village; phone/fax 96-22-86. MODERATE.

Panau Lagon features six bungalows—all of which have recently been renovated and feature private baths. Units vary in configuration to handle three to six guests. The A-frame–style bungalows (built in a mediocre fashion) are located on a broad beach with a splendid view of the lagoon. The owner, Arai, is amiable and will loan you the use of his bikes. The multitude of pigs and children contribute to an authentic Polynesian atmosphere here and his two sons will take you on excursions in the boat, including visits to the fish park and pearl farm, and picnics on a *motu*. The downside is the swampy ditch across from the facility, which seems to contribute to the mosquito problem. The accommodation here is comfortable, fairly priced and on the beach. Children under 12 are half price. No credit cards. ~ Tuherahera; phone/fax 96-22-99. MODERATE.

Typical activities on Tikehau include visits to the fishing village, picnicking on a *motu* or a visit to the bird sanctuary, a minuscule island located about 18 kilometers from the village that you can circumnavigate in minutes.

Aito Motel Colette, located in Tuherahera Village, consists of five bungalows on the beach and ten rooms in the "village." The buildings are modern concrete structures with tile floors, surrounded by manicured gardens. A shared kitchen is provided, and meal plans are also available. Day trips to the fish reserve, fishing excursions and picnics are offered. Aito Motel Colette is fairly priced and comfortable, but nothing out of the ordinary. Recent visitors report broken door locks, missing toilet seats and problems with luggage theft. ~ Tuherahera; phone/fax 96-22-47. MODERATE.

Pension Hotu offers three bungalows with shared bathroom facilities on the beach side of the island. Meal plans are available; meals are served in a common dining area. Roundtrip transfers are included. No credit cards. ~ Tuherahera; 96-22-89. BUDGET.

Pension Tematie is run by Nora Hoiore and offers three bungalows with private baths and a shared dining room. Two of the bungalows each have one double bed and one single; the other bungalow can sleep four, including one guest on a convertible sofa. Bicycles and kayaks are available for rent. Free roundtrip transfers, but no credit cards. ~ Tuherahera; phone/fax 96-22-65. BUDGET.

Pension Helene offers four guest rooms. One has a private bath; the rest share a common facility. This pension is not on the lagoon, but it's only a short walk away. ~ Tuherahera; 96-22-52. BUDGET.

The attractive **Chez Justine** is near the air strip in Tikehau. Though it is near a white-sand beach, it suffers from the same drainage ditch problem as Panau Lagon. However, the windows are screened, cutting down on the mosquito problem. Justine has two family-style bungalows, each with two double bedrooms, private bath, terrace and fan. A small restaurant is on the premises. The total capacity for all three units is eight people. All the usual activities are provided. Contact Mme. Justine Tetua for more information. ~ Tikehau; 96-22-87, fax 96-22-26; www.annuaire-tahiti.com. BUDGET TO MODERATE.

Kahaia Beach is a beachside resort on Motu Kahaia, near the village of Tuherahera. There are five thatch-roofed *fare* with private baths. Camping is possible on the *motu* for 1000 CFP. Meal plans are available; reviews have been good. The host, Pia, will reportedly take you on excursions. ~ Motu Kahaia; 96-22-77, fax 96-22-81. BUDGET.

Outdoor Adventures

DIVING

Raie Manta Club is the oldest dive operation on Tikehau. Yves Lefevre, a veteran dive instructor and underwater photographer, offers visits to one of the least-visited lagoons in the Tuamotu Group. The company has a second shop on Rangiroa, and its multi-dive packages can be used there as well. ~ Tuherahera; 96-22-53; raie mantaclub.free.pf, e-mail raiemantaclub@mail.pf.

Plongée Tikehau sets a very high standard for diving in the Tuamotus. In order to protect the environment on Tikehau, the director, Guy Genin, installed buoys on all dive sites so that boats have no need to drop anchor on the fragile coral reef. He also built a *fare* near the pass where clients can relax before and after their dives. Genin believes that Tikehau is an ideal locale for dive training because of the slow, predictable currents that occur over 300 days a year. Plongée Tikehau is located in the bustling heart of Tuherahera. ~ Tuherahera; phone/fax 96-22-32; e-mail plongee_tikehau@hotmail.com.

Tikehau Blue Nui is a well-regarded dive outfit that operates out of the Tikehau Pearl Beach Resort. ~ Tuherahera; 96-23-00, fax 96-22-40; www.bluenui.com, e-mail tikehaubluenui@mail.pf.

BOATING

Viti Viti Roa Excursions is a division of Plongée Tikehau, and the center for all things nautical on the island. Their dive boat, *Viti Viti Roa*, gets you there quickly (as one might expect from a boat whose name translates as "very, very fast") and safely. You also may want to check out their glass-bottom boat, the *Tiaki 2*, or any of the smaller boats, canoes or jet-ski rentals. Viti Viti offers lagoon trips and birdwatching excursions to the *motu*. A picnic lunch is available. ~ Tuherahera; phone/fax 96-22-32; e-mail plongee_tikehau@hotmail.com.

Mataiva

Located at the extreme northwest end of the Tuamotus (186 miles or 310 kilometers north of Papeete and 24 miles or 80 kilometers west of Rangiroa), Mataiva is a perfect place to experience the slow-moving life in a remote corner of the Tuamotus. You can hang out at the old wooden bridge, watch people fish and chat with the giggling village children. People here are patient, friendly and, like most Polynesians, somewhat shy.

However, Mataiva may not meet everyone's expectation of paradise. There is a somewhat brackish look about the island that one notices almost immediately upon landing. Mataiva is a rich source of phosphate. The atoll has within its lagoon about 70 phosphate-rich pools that were at one time commercially exploited.

There is only one—rather difficult—pass into the ten-square-mile (25-square-kilometer) lagoon, along with nine shallow channels or *hoas*. Mataiva is also a rich fishing ground, and the shallow lagoon has many fish traps, marked by vertical wooden poles that protrude in a number of areas.

There are enormous amounts of dark, almost black, coral (no doubt resulting from the phosphate) that give the land a surrealistic, moonscape quality. Some of the landscape is stained yellow, perhaps another legacy of the mining operation. Debris from a major cyclone that struck in the early 1980s may still be visible in some of the more isolated areas. In February 1998, Mataiva was hit very hard by a storm. Restoration of the island's infrastructure is still in progress.

SIGHTS

Pahua is the main village. (The village's name refers to a large mollusk or clam found in the reefs of Mataiva and throughout the South Pacific.) Almost all of Mataiva's population of about 200 live in Pahua, which is separated by a pass connected by a long, narrow, wooden-plank bridge. Despite the separation of the village by a body of water, locals still refer to both sides as Pahua. The village has a church on either side, but only one store (on the south side of the pass) with a narrow selection of items.

Sometimes it seems like the only thing that moves on Mataiva are the land crabs, which seem to be in plentiful supply. If you stand still and listen, there seems to be a constant rustling of these creatures in the brush. Mosquitos, too, are plentiful (which makes it hard to understand why some of the pensions don't have mosquito screens).

As one might expect, there isn't a lot to do on an atoll in the middle of nowhere. Riding a bike along the coconut palm–lined roads of Mataiva, however, is a must. The road goes most of the way around the island—about 20 miles (33 kilometers)—and is connected by narrow concrete bridges. One note: Apart from

FISHING LIKE THE LOCALS

Local-style fishing, usually with hand lines, can be arranged with Mataiva guesthouses. This means jumping on a *pirogue* (canoe) with the village children, baiting a hook with a live hermit crab and trying your luck on the reef. Be sure and bring a hat and your sunblock, as well as plenty of water.

mosquitoes and crabs, dogs also abound here, creating a potential problem for bicyclists. Riding a bike inevitably attracts these canine creatures and you don't want to be on a bicycle in the middle of a territorial dog fight. Cycle with caution. Bikes are available at **Super Mataiva Cool**. ~ Pahua; 96-32-53.

In addition to bike rides, excursions to the **swimming hole** at **Ponahara** (actually an inlet with a series of pools that connect the lagoon and the sea) and the coral beaches of **Pofai-Tounoa** and **Tenupa** are also worth your time.

Teaku is a bird sanctuary located inside the lagoon. It can be visited by boat for picnics or birdwatching.

A *marae* at **Papiro**, on the opposite side of the atoll from Pahua, is constructed from stone slabs. The *marae* is shaped in the form of an armchair, designed purportedly for King Tu, a legendary figure of Polynesia. It actually resembles a sofa, complete with backrest and armrests, and was rebuilt after the original was destroyed by a cyclone.

Another, perhaps more prosaic, attraction, located 100 yards (90 meters) behind the pension Super Mataiva Cool, is the fiberglass **wreck** of the *Cayuse*, an American boat that washed ashore in 1982. This was evidently the second American boat to meet its demise upon the shores of this phosphate atoll. The first belonged to the now-deceased author Jack Ferguson, who spent nine years in the Pacific and wrote a book about Mataiva entitled *Island of Nine Eyes*, which takes its name from the nine channels.

LODGING

◄ *HIDDEN*

Super Mataiva Cool may sound a bit presumptuous or even preposterous given how intense the sun gets in the Tuamotu Group, but one would be hard-pressed to improve on it. For starters, it's on a white-sand beach, with a magnificent view of the lagoon. The property consists of four new bungalows, each with a private (cold water) bath, terrace and fan. The bungalows are clean and offer relative comfort. The new units were constructed following the onslaught of Cyclone Veli in 1998. The electricity usually stays on until about midnight (which means you can run your fan until then). The owner, Aroma Huri, speaks a few words of English and does his best to make you feel at home. His sister, Taina, helps organize excursions and looks after guests. Boat trips to the surrounding *motu*, with picnic lunch, are available and there is a boat and several bicycles in fairly good shape for hire. Children under 12 are half price. Super Mataiva Cool is situated on the south side of the pass in Pahua. Free transfers. ~ Pahua, 96-32-53; in Tahiti, 43-18-84. BUDGET.

On Pahua's north side, closer to the lagoon, is **Mataiva Village**. The property has a manicured, orderly appearance and a better beach than Super Mataiva Cool. It consists of five attractive bungalows lined up along the shore. Small coconut trees have been planted in between the shoreline and the units, creating a pleasant shady front yard. Each of the bungalows has one bedroom with a double bed, a small terrace and a private bath. Some bungalows lack proper ventilation and mosquito screens. The food, on the other hand, is good. Camping is also available on the property. Free transfers. ~ Pahua; phone/fax 96-32-95. BUDGET.

Ava Hei occupies a wide sand beach on the south side of the atoll. Each of three traditional, thatch-roofed *fare* has a private bath and ceiling fan. All of the units have recently been renovated. This is one of the few places in the Tuamotus where camping is permitted. Visitors' reports have been good. ~ Tevahi; 96-32-39, 96-32-93. BUDGET.

In July 2001, Punua Tamaehu of Chez Punua opened a new pension named **Green Lagoon** on a small atoll called Papiro. Three traditional bungalows sit at the water's edge for a view that is nothing short of stunning. Each bungalow has a double bed, and there are shared bath and kitchen facilities. Punua also allows camping on the property. *Pension complete* is essential, as there are no amenities on the atoll. Snorkeling here is excellent and the crystal-clear water of the lagoon shimmers in striking hues of green, just as the name implies. Boat transfers to this remote lodging cost 1000 CFP. ~ Papiro; 96-04-98, cell 79-24-66, fax 96-84-73. BUDGET TO MODERATE.

GROCERIES   There is one modest store (on the south side of the pass) stocked with basics—mosquito coils, instant coffee and the like. (Like most stores on most of the atolls in French Polynesia, there's no fresh fruit or vegetables.)

BEACHES   **PONAHARA** 🏊 This swimming hole is actually an inlet between the ocean and the lagoon. If it were larger and deeper, it would be a pass. However, unlike a pass that can be filled with rushing water, Ponahara is shallow and calm. It's also filled with nooks and crannies, and pools of various depths that allow swimming and bathing. Facilities are minimal. There are a few simple benches, and a dilapidated shack sits near the swimming area. Paper from yesterday's picnic may litter the area. ~ Ponahara is located on the inside of the lagoon, approximately one quarter of the way around the island, about seven kilometers from the village heading south and then looping east. To get there, you could either ride a bike or hitch a ride.

POFAI-TOUNOA BEACHES 🏊 🤿 A classic white-sand (coral) beach shaded by coconut palms, Pofai-Tounoa is a perfect place to kick back. Swimming is good here. There are no facilities available. ~ It's about two to three kilometers from the village heading north. You can easily walk or bike it from the village.

The Outer Limits

The Moruroa and Fangataufa atolls are not open to visitors but are well known as nuclear testing sites. Testing began above ground in 1966, but was moved underground in 1975 and restricted to Moruroa. Total tests exceed 165 to date, including neutron tests, the publicly acknowledged hydrogen series and the well-publicized 1995 series. Although the base at Hao was built to provide logistic assistance for military, it is also an airfield used for civilian (Air Tahiti) flights, and visitors to some Tuamotu destinations may find themselves landing there.

From what has been written in the world press, after the experiments ended in 1996 Moruroa ceased to function as a test site. Presumably the military will either destroy or put much of the infrastructure in mothballs. The once-large civilian workforce, which numbered several thousand during Moruroa's heyday in the 1960s and 1970s, will never return.

These employees, mostly Tahitian, were paid well and pumped billions of francs into the economy. This supported a sizable portion of the population, but with the end of the Cold War and the tests, this workforce had to be let go. This has created unemployment and some of the social problems associated with joblessness.

Today only the military caretakers remain on the island. According to the local press, the atoll will most likely never be reactivated as a test site because of the emergence of electronic simulation as an alternative to nuclear detonations. The end of the Cold War and the anti-nuclear passions of other regional governments may also have had something to do with the cessation of testing.

TENUPA BEACH 🏊 ⛵ Tenupa is also a lovely white-sand beach on the ocean side of the island. There are no facilities here and only limited shade. ~ Located on the eastern end of the island, the opposite side from the village, about 15 kilometers away. It's possible to get there by bicycle, but it is much better to organize a boat trip with your pension and take in the nearby bird sanctuary at Teaku, a tiny island inside the lagoon, at the same time.

▼▼▼▼▼▼▼▼▼▼▼▼
Other Northern Tuamotu Islands

The Northern Tuamotus are among the least-visited islands of French Polynesia. Windblown atolls, with coral beaches parched white by the sun, they offer the visitor an opportunity to bask in a warm hospitality seldom experienced in the well-trodden Society Islands.

SIGHTS   **TAKAPOTO** Takapoto is a ten-mile-long island retreat. Come here to get away from any semblance of Western civilization and bask in Tuamotan hospitality. What you'll find in plenitude is solitude, beautiful white-sand beaches and plenty of fish to watch while snorkeling. What Takapoto doesn't have is a pass into the lagoon, but villagers get around this by landing whaleboats near the reef. It is said that when residents of the island return by boat, a double rainbow appears over the island.

Located 386 miles (624 kilometers) northeast of Papeete, there are about 465 people living here. Most dwell in the community of **Fakatopatere**, which is about one kilometer from the airport. The clapboard village stretches out along a narrow strip of land between the lagoon and the ocean. Nearby, the remains of Takai *marae* built of raised coral blocks are the main points of interest, along with visits to the numerous pearl farms that edge the lagoon. (The little atoll is almost entirely dedicated to pearl farming.)

Takapoto, and its neighbor Takaroa, were hammered by two very destructive cyclones in 1991 and 1993, which proved to be

◆◆

LOCAL HERO

The most famous man on Arutua is Arii Parker, who made a fortune as a pearl farmer. However, he will always be remembered more as a local hero rather than as a successful businessman. One windy day in 1993 a boatload of young French marines was crossing Arutua's pass. Inexperienced in handling the boat in a treacherous stretch of water, they capsized. Without a moment to spare, Parker sprang into action and single-handedly saved the lives of all 15 marines. For his valor and bravery, he was awarded the French Legion of Honor.

an unmitigated disaster for the island's nascent black pearl industry. Over the past few years several small pensions have sprouted up on this distant atoll but only two have survived. There's nothing in the way of luxury accommodations and amenities out this way, so bring a suitcase brimming with unread novels and leave your wristwatch at home.

TAKAROA Resembling a giant protozoan, this oblong atoll is about 14 miles long (24 kilometers) and 1 mile wide. The island is separated from Takapoto by only a little over eight kilometers of ocean and is home to about 400 people, most of whom live in the village of Teavaroa. Takaroa is one of the few remaining Tuamotu atolls with an existing *marae*.

The pass here is nine feet deep and anchorages are good in all parts of the lagoon. Like nearby Takapoto, Takaroa suffered extensively from cyclones in 1991 and 1993, which destroyed the local black pearl industry.

Takaroa more than any of the outer Tuamotus gives you the opportunity to experience Polynesian life with a local family. You will be able to share daily routines and learn something about life on an isolated atoll.

FAKARAVA The second-largest atoll in French Polynesia, Fakarava has an unusual rectangular shape measuring 37 miles by 15 miles (60 kilometers by 25 kilometers). It is located approximately 248 miles (400 kilometers) northeast of Tahiti.

Rotoava Village, located near **Garue Pass** (which measures three quarters of a mile wide), is home to most of the atoll's 248 inhabitants. There is also a small settlement in **Tetamanu Village** on the southern end of the atoll.

Local fishermen traditionally work Garue Pass by placing bottom lines, each attached to a buoy. When a fish strikes, the buoys bob furiously, attracting thousands of sea birds. The sight and sound of the birds circling overhead and squawking incessantly is a memorable spectacle.

Fakarava is the site of the oldest **Catholic mission** in the Tuamotus. The coral-fired limestone church was built by the followers of Pere Laval in the early 1850s. Laval was in the Gambiers 20 years earlier and had constructed the same type of buildings in Rikitea (in the Gambiers) during that period. The church is still in use today.

Black pearl cultivation has become an important source of income on Fakarava. The island hosts one of the business centers of black pearl king Robert Wan. It is not open to the public, but the numerous grids marking black pearl stations throughout the lagoon are visible to all.

KAUKURA There's not much to say about the oval-shaped Kaukura, which was discovered by Dutch navigator Roggeveen in

1722. Situated 201 miles (325 kilometers) northeast of Tahiti, it is 24 miles (40 kilometers) long and has a shallow lagoon with a narrow pass. The population numbers around 300, all of whom live in the village of **Raitahiti**. Local income is derived from pearl nursery production and fishing.

ARUTUA   Known for its abundance of fish and its talented musicians, the tiny island of Arutua is almost circular, with a circumference of approximately 17 miles. The abundance of fish can be attributed to a system of fish parks and pearl farms. Most of the nearly 300 inhabitants live in the village of **Rautini**. Pearl farming, pearl nurseries and fishing are the most important income earners, but tourism, in the form of small pensions, also exists.

APATAKI   Discovered by the Dutch navigator Jacob Roggeveen in 1722, Apataki is a rectangular-shaped atoll that lies just 12 miles (19 kilometers) from Arutua, which administers it. The main village is Niutahi, and the atoll has recently become a major center for pearl farm development.

AHE   Ahe, the most popular of the Tuamotus with the yachting community, can only be reached by launch from neighboring Manihi. In the old days, Ahe never reaped the benefits of the tourist trade and consequently it was isolated and poor. Whereas on Manihi even two decades ago most residents had modern water cisterns, slept on beds and washed their dishes under a freshwater tap, life on Ahe presented a different scenario. A cistern was apt to have been a rusty oil drum, children slept on a mat on the floor and the dishes were likely to be washed in the waters of the lagoon.

Thankfully, with the growth of the pearl industry, this way of life has become history. No longer the poor relative, Ahe has become immersed in the pearl business by acting as a shell nursery for Manihi's pearl farms. Money has also come to this once poor island community, but not in quite the same materialistic or organized fashion that is seen on Manihi.

Even with the change in lifestyles, residents haven't lost their friendliness toward yachters. The playful rivalry between Manihi and Ahe (where many families are related) is also still evident. Ahe residents would like the visitor to believe that wealth, which they say has changed Manihi residents, has left Ahe inhabitants unfazed.

MAKATEA   Makatea lies about 200 kilometers northeast of Tahiti and 100 kilometers southwest of Rangiroa. Discovered in 1722 by the Dutch navigator Jacob Roggeveen, Makatea differs from the other islands in the Tuamotus in that it is a high island: pancake-flat atolls make up most of this archipelago. With precipitous cliffs that jut 45 meters from sea level, this upthrust coral reef was once a prime source of phosphate rock.

In 1908, a British/French consortium built a dock at the village of **Temao** and began mining. For nearly half a century this tiny island was a crucial source of income for French Polynesia, but by the late 1960s the phosphate was gone and the mine closed.

About 60 people now live on Makatea. In Temao, you can still see the remnants of a little rail line that brought ore down to the ore ships, and the deepwater dock where they dropped anchor.

TAKAPOTO Only two pensions have survived the onslaught of hurricanes over the past few years. Since there are no restaurants on the island, both pensions provide *pension complete*—three meals a day—as part of the tariff.

LODGING

Temanuatea Pension, run by the namesake family, is located nine kilometers outside Fakatopatere on a pearl farm. They offer a clean beach bungalow with a meal plan and can provide guided activities, including *motu* picnics and sea kayaking. ~ 98 782 Takapoto; phone/fax 98-64-09. BUDGET.

Takapoto Village, run by Pimati and Marie Toti, is a single thatch-roofed bungalow on the white-sand shores of the lagoon. On the island's western side, near the airstrip and dock area, the unit has a terrace that overlooks the lagoon. They also operate a unit with a double bed and shared bath. Free airport transport is provided and all meals are included in the tariffs. Electricity is available from 7 a.m. until late in the evening. ~ Fakatopatere; 98-65-44, fax 98-64-81. BUDGET.

TAKAROA Accommodations on Takaroa are in or near the village of Teavaroa, which is located two kilometers from the airstrip. All guesthouses have electricity, and provide roundtrip transfers to and from the airport. As in most pensions on the outer islands, after the third day the price drops by 500 CFP per person.

Poerangi Village, run by Jean-Claude and his wife Patricia, is located on Motu Vaimaroro, on the southern end of the island. Its three whitewashed bungalows are right on the gleaming sand shores of the lagoon. Each has private bath, kitchen and small veranda. Here you'll get some of the best food we've ever sampled in the Tuamotus—superb meals offer a variety of both Caribbean and Polynesian seafood dishes. Jean-Claude provides a variety of activities including *motu* visits, picnics and snorkeling, and will even teach clients how to fish. A turtle and "shark park"

◄ HIDDEN

SHIPWRECKED ON RAROIA

It was on the reef of Raroia that Thor Heyerdahl's raft *Kon Tiki* was wrecked in 1947, and his crew of five Scandinavians was washed ashore. They were en route to Mangareva in the Gambier Islands to test Heyerdahl's theory, based on an Inca legend, that it was possible to sail from South America to Polynesia.

are located adjacent to the property. This is a winner. ~ Motu Vaimororo; 98-23-09, fax 98-22-65. BUDGET.

On the more basic side, **Chez Vahinerii Temanaha** is a concrete house with two rooms, each with a double bed. There is also a kitchen, living room and communal bath. Visits to a *motu* are provided. If you ask, other excursions, such as fishing trips, can be arranged. The scoop on Chez Vahinerii is that it's basically a nice place to stay, but leaves much to be desired in the way of service. A Tahitian friend told me that the owner, Vahinerii, pretty much abandons guests, and regards cooking for them an onerous chore. The house is near a beach and close to the airstrip. ~ Teavaroa; 98-23-59. BUDGET.

Designated the "Dangerous Archipelago" by Louis-Antoine de Bougainville in 1768, the Tuamotus have also been called "Labyrinth." There's no mystery to these grim monikers—the razor-sharp coral reefs are littered with the wrecks of many a vessel.

Another lodging possibility on Takaroa is **Pension Huti Huti**, which is a private home with rooms occasionally rented to visitors. ~ Teavaroa; 98-22-32. BUDGET.

FAKARAVA   Set next to a sparkling lagoon on a shoreline studded with palm trees, **Tetamanu Village** is pitched in an exquisite classic South Pacific setting if there ever was one. They offer seven bungalows on stilts, each bungalow with a double and a single bed. A (cold water) communal bathroom is available and an overwater *fare* accommodates a bar and a dining room. Sane Richmond, the charming owner, installed solar panels to provide limited electricity. Free transfers are provided to and from the airport and three meals a day are included in the rate. ~ Tetamanu; 43-92-40, fax 42-77-70; www.tetamanuvillage.pf, e-mail tetamanu village@mail.pf. BUDGET.

HIDDEN ►

Motu Aito Paradise is a small pension recently opened by Tila and Manihi Salmon, who have lived on their own private *motu* for more than 15 years. They built their own home as well as six traditional bungalows for guests, which each include a private bath. The pension is about 500 meters from Tetamanu pass, where the snorkeling is superb. The *motu* is reportedly free from mosquitoes and *nono*, and the friendly owners speak fluent English. Recent visitors report a very welcoming atmosphere and excellent food. Rates cover all meals and excursions, including fishing trips. Minimum three-night stay. ~ Motu Aito, Tetamanu; phone/fax 94-12-90; www.fakarava.org, e-mail motu-aito@mail.pf. MODERATE.

HIDDEN ►

Another recent addition to the Fakarava lodging scene is **Vahitu Dream** in Rotoava Village. Facing the pass (and the sunset) is a big house with five bedrooms that have fans and mosquito nets, and a living room with television and VCR. The dining room and bath are communal, and meal plans are available.

Free bowling, bicycles and parlor games are offered and excursions are available for a fee. ~ Rotoava; phone/fax 98-42-63. MODERATE.

Le Maitai Dream Fakarava, which opened in 2002, is Fakarava's first high-end lodging. Located on a pristine, white-sand beach on the lagoon side, it is the second Maitai built in French Polynesia; its sister hotel opened on Bora Bora in 2001. The Fakarava location offers just 30 beachside bungalows tailored for discriminating guests. Prices start at US$385 per night, and the well-appointed rooms feature private lanais with gorgeous views of the lagoon. The hotel boasts a *gastronomique* restaurant and a full bar, as well as a dive center. All-inclusive activities packages are available. ~ Rotoava; 98-43-00, fax 98-43-01; www.hotelmaitai.com, e-mail info@fakarava.hotelmaitai.com. ULTRA-DELUXE.

Pension Paparara, located ten kilometers from the airport, offers two *fare* and one bungalow on the lagoon side. Bathing and dining areas are shared, and meal plans are available. The owner, Corina Lenoir, can arrange lagoon excursions. ~ Rotoava; phone/fax 98-42-66, 74-69-10. BUDGET.

One of the best bargains in the Tuamotus, **Kiritia Village** has three thatch-roofed bungalows by the sea, each with a bedroom, terrace, living room and a communal bath shared by all guests. There's also a house on the property that has three bedrooms, each with double and single beds and a living room. One of the highlights of Kiritia Village are the excursions to a *motu*—complete with picnic, deep-sea fishing and net fishing. Or try the nighttime guided adventure to catch lobsters, which ends with a traditional Polynesian feast. Mme. Kachler, who runs the property, is an entertaining and informative host. Kiritia Village combines tasty food and local hospitality with a marvelous price. Mme. Kachler, by the way, speaks English. Kiritia Village is four kilometers from the airport. ~ Rotoava; 98-42-37. MODERATE.

Relais Marama is near the airport and the dock areas on the northern tip of Fakarava. There are three traditional bungalows and six rooms in a local-style home. All of the accommodations share a kitchen and bathroom. A food plan is available. The owner, Marama Teanuanua, is reportedly a good cook. ~ Rotoava; 98-42-25; tuamotu.plongee.free.fr/marama.htm. BUDGET.

Pension Havaiki has two local-style bungalows that are very informal. There is a shared dining room but private bath for each of the units. Meals are available and roundtrip transfers are included. ~ Rotoava; phone/fax 98-42-16. BUDGET.

KAUKURA Pension Rekareka has two locations. The village setting consists of a large home with six rooms located upstairs. Each room has a double bed and there is a spacious living room   ◄ *HIDDEN* with television, a dining room and communal bath. Rekareka "annex" has five small thatch-roofed *fare* on the private Motu Tahunapona, a 15-minute boat ride from the village. On the *motu* each bungalow (better described as a tiny cabin with a peaked roof) has one small room. There are also communal bath facilities. Mme. Claire Parker, the proprietor, takes care of her patrons by providing good food and clean accommodations at a fair price. She is also helpful and friendly. The pension is about two kilometers from the airstrip. ~ Raitahiti; 96-62-40, 96-62-39. BUDGET.

ARUTUA   All lodging on Arutua is found in or near the village of Rautini, which is a 30-minute boat ride from the airstrip.

Surrounded by a white picket fence and shaded by palm trees, **Pension Mairava** is located in a classic island setting. In the midst of Rautini Village, it has one house with six rooms and a communal bath. Rooms are of average size, and like most accommodations in the Tuamotu Islands, they are simple. The proprietor, Edouard Charles, a broad-shouldered Paumotu fisherman, will take you fishing or to visit the pearl farm in the lagoon. Write to the Charles family, c/o Rautini Village, Arutua, French Polynesia for reservations. ~ Rautini; 96-52-37. BUDGET TO MODERATE.

Also in the village, **Pension Pikui** is a house with communal bath and three rooms—two with double beds and one with three singles. The proprietors, the Tuteina family, also have a house on Motu Mutukiore, with two bedrooms. Activities include picnics, trolling in the lagoon or fishing off the reef for lobsters. The cost for these excursions varies. ~ Rautini; 96-52-34. BUDGET.

Another home to unpack your bags in is **Chez Nerii**. Here you will have two rooms with double beds, living rooms, dining rooms and a communal (cold water) bathroom. Excursions are provided to the fish park and a family-owned black pearl farm. ~ Rautini; 96-52-55. BUDGET.

APATAKI   **Chez Rosaline** has four bungalows by the sea as well as a restaurant that serves local-style meals. The bath and dining facilities are shared. Meal plans are available; excursions and bicycles are available for a fee. Free roundtrip transfers. ~ Niutahi; 96-12-22, 96-12-99, fax 96-12-00; www.chezrosalie.pf. BUDGET TO MODERATE.

AHE   **Coco Perle** is a modest pension that offers five bungalows on the lagoon side of the island, some with private baths. Lagoon excursions are available, as is roundtrip transfer by boat. Minimum stay is two nights. No credit cards. ~ Tenukupara. MODERATE.

Arrangements for lodgings at private homes on Ahe may be made from any of the pensions in Manihi.

There are approximately 20 dive sites in the Fakarava Lagoon area. The two main passes (located more than 50 kilometers apart) are the most popular haunts. **Garuae Pass**, with a depth of 15 to 45 meters, translates as "the big pass" and indeed is the largest pass in all of French Polynesia. Laden with pelagics like sharks, barracuda, tuna, dolphins and manta rays, there are also coral-covered canyons, which shelter numerous species of fish. **Tumakohua**, the large pass on the southern side of the atoll, is a 15- to 28-meter dive. This area is famous for its rich diversity of corals, unusual in the Tuamotu Islands. It's a great spot for underwater photographers. **Central Park** is best explored from 12 to 25 meters and is well known for *Montipora*, *Acropora* and *Millepora* as well as a rich mix of tropical fish. **Ohotu**, a 10- to 25-meter dive, is often a gathering spot for dolphins that come here to greet divers. You'll also find Napoleons, barracuda and shark. **Taupee Te Ava**, a 5- to 55-meter dive, has visibility often more than 60 meters. Here one can often find dolphins, sharks and manta rays.

Outdoor Adventures

DIVING

If you dive Garuae when the tide is coming into the lagoon, you'll often have visibility of up to 50 meters.

Eastern Tuamotu Islands

I loosely use the term "Eastern" Tuamotus to place the islands in a geographical setting. Two islands, Anaa and Nukutavake, offer accommodations. The military island of Hao and the atolls used in nuclear tests, Moruroa and Fangataufu, are also in this area.

SIGHTS

ANAA Anaa could be considered a model of the prototypical sun- and wind-scarred atoll. Located 271 miles (437 kilometers) east of Tahiti, it comprises 11 islets that enclose a shallow lagoon. Once the most populous atoll in the Tuamotu Group, it is now a quiet backwater of 700 inhabitants that sees few visitors.

There is no pass through the coral reef, but landing is easy on the lee side, where the reef slopes up to the shore. Several years ago the island was devastated by a cyclone, but has since been rebuilt. **Tuuhora** is the most important of the five villages. Unfortunately Anaa suffers from an abundance of mosquitos and pesky *nono*.

NUKUTAVAKE Nukutavake is located in the eastern region of the Tuamotu Archipelago, 675 miles (1125 kilometers) northeast of Tahiti. The atoll is oblong in shape, almost two miles long and 500 yards wide. There is a lagoon, but no navigable pass. The majority of the island's 142 residents live in the villages of **Mohitu** and **Terau**, at the northeast end of the island. Nukutavake is new to tourism and visitors are still a novelty.

HAO   The island of Hao earned its name from the French navigator Bougainville because it is roughly shaped like a harp. The atoll, which is just 34 miles (55 kilometers) long, is located some 572 miles (920 kilometers) from Tahiti. For many years it was primarily used by the French military, which built a base there to assist in nuclear testing on neighboring atolls (for more information, see "The Outer Limits" in this chapter). The base has an airfield now used by civilian flights. With the end of nuclear testing, Hao has begun a slow and uncertain evolution into a commercial deep-sea fishing port. The island has one of the longest lagoons in French Polynesia but only one reef passage at Kaki on the northern end of the atoll.

LODGING   **ANAA**   Sitting right beside the lagoon, **Te Maui Nui** is located in Anaa's Tuuhora Village, near the airstrip. Operated by François Mo'o, it has two very clean thatch-roofed bungalows—one with three bedrooms and the other with one bedroom. Both accommodations have communal (cold water) bath. They also have outdoor terraces for dining, covered with a thatched roof. François formerly lived in Papeete, where he ran a snack bar. ~ Tuuhora; 98-32-75. BUDGET TO MODERATE.

To'ku Kaiga has one traditional thatched *fare niau* and an A frame–style chalet. It is run by a charming couple, Joel and Romana Teaku, who serve excellent food. As one friend told me after staying there "they never stop smiling." The units have self-contained bathrooms (which is fairly unusual in the Tuamotus). The property is located a five-minute ride from the airport and a short walk from a wonderful white-sand beach. This is definitely one of the better places to stay in the Tuamotu Group. ~ Tuuhora; 98-32-69. BUDGET TO MODERATE.

Chez Louise, located near the lagoon in Tokerau, has two basic rooms. Bathroom facilities are shared, and meal plans are available. ~ Tokerau; phone/fax 98-32-69. BUDGET TO MODERATE.

MAKEMO

Makemo is the third atoll of French Polynesia in relation to Tahiti, which lies some 500 kilometers to the east. There are about 500 people who live in the village of Pouheva, which is situated near the atoll's two passes. Pearl farming, copra production and fishing are the atoll's main pursuits. Diving sites here are known for their diversity of species. Dives can be arranged through **Diving Center Makemo**, which is run by Ludovic Berne. ~ Pouheva; phone/fax 98-03-08; e-mail makemodive@hot mail.com.

NUKUTAVAKE There is only one place to stay on Nukutavake, but fortunately it is one of the better pensions in the Tuamotu Group. On the lagoon side of the atoll, **Pension Afou** is close to the docks on the sea side near a white-sand beach. There are three local-style bungalows, each with a double bed. The site has a dining room and shared bath facilities. The proprietors, the Teavai family, are pleasant and helpful hosts (who also run the local Air Tahiti office). The food is good, and the atmosphere is typically Paumotu. Pension Afou is located one kilometer from Tavavanui Village. Transportation to and from the airport is provided. Kids under 12 are half price. ~ Tavavanui; 98-72-53. MODERATE.

HAO **Tiare Paetahi** offers four basic rooms in Otepa Village, about three miles from the airport. The shared baths have hot water while private baths have just cold. There is a fully equipped kitchen and common dining area. Meal plans are available, and there is a washing machine on the premises. The minimum stay is two nights. Car rental is also available. No credit cards. ~ Otepa; phone/fax 97-02-14. BUDGET TO MODERATE.

▼▼▼▼▼▼▼▼▼▼▼
Transportation

AIR

RANGIROA There is no shortage of flights to Rangiroa. **Air Tahiti** services the island every day of the week from Papeete—the flight time is 60 minutes. The airport in Rangiroa is near Avatoru. There are also flights between Rangi and Bora Bora and from Rangi to Manihi three times a week. ~ Airport; 96-03-41.

MANIHI There are **Air Tahiti** flights to Manihi from Papeete ten times a week. The direct flight time from Papeete is one hour and 25 minutes, or one hour and 50 minutes with a stopover in Rangiroa. Rangiroa to Manihi flight time is 40 minutes. Flights to Manihi are also available Kaukura and Takaroa. ~ Airport; 96-42-71.

TIKEHAU Air service via **Air Tahiti** between Tikehau and Papeete is ten times weekly. Flying time is 55 minutes direct from Papeete or one hour 30 minutes via Rangiroa. ~ Airport; 96-22-66.

MATAIVA Flying time via **Air Tahiti** direct from Papeete is 55 minutes or one hour 35 minutes via Rangiroa. Service and to and from Papeete is twice weekly. ~ Airport; 96-32-48.

TAKAPOTO Air transportation is provided by **Air Tahiti**. There are flights from Papeete three times a week, with connections to Kaukura and Apataki. Flying time is one hour 30 minutes direct from Papeete. ~ Airport; 98-65-79.

TAKAROA Service via **Air Tahiti** from Papeete to Takaroa is three times weekly. Flight time from Papeete is two hours and ten minutes via Manihi or Takapoto. ~ Airport; 98-22-45.

FAKARAVA Service via **Air Tahiti** from Papeete is six times weekly and flying time direct from the capital is one hour 20 minutes (or two hours and 30 minutes via Rangiroa). No flights on Thursday. ~ Airport; 98-42-30.

KAUKURA   Flying time from Papeete via **Air Tahiti** is one hour direct or one hour 40 minutes via Rangiroa. Service (also on Air Tahiti) to and from the island is twice weekly from Papeete. ~ Airport; 96-62-52.

ARUTUA   Service to and from Arutua via **Air Tahiti** is two times weekly from Papeete. Flying time is one hour 15 minutes. ~ Airport; 96-62-52.

EASTERN TUAMOTUS   Flying time to Anaa direct from the capital via **Air Tahiti** is one hour ten minutes and service is twice weekly. Nukutavake has weekly air service with **Air Tahiti** but the price is steep—around US$600 roundtrip.

HAO   **Air Tahiti** offers three flights from Papeete to Hao each week, with a brief stopover on either Makemo or Anaa. There are return flights from Hao to Papeete every day except Friday and Saturday. Most Hao–Papeete flights are nonstop. Hao is also served once a week from the Gambier airport, but there is no return service on that route.

SEA   Boats that visit the Northern Tuamotus include:
  Rairoa Nui ~ 48-35-78, fax 48-22-86
  Dory II ~ phone/fax 42-30-55
  Vai Aito ~ 43-99-96, fax 43-53-04
  Mareva Nui ~ 42-25-53, fax 42-25-57
  St. Xavier Maris Stella ~ 42-23-58, fax 43-03-73; e-mail maris-stella@mail.pf
  Cobia II ~ phone/fax 43-36-43

RANGIROA   Interisland vessels frequently visit Rangiroa. At least five different vessels visit the island regularly from Papeete. The *Rairoa Nui* and *Dory II* arrive weekly. The *Vai Aito* comes two or three times a month; *Mareva Nui* and *St. Xavier Maris Stella* visit bi-weekly.

MANIHI   There are several interisland vessels sailing to Manihi regularly from Papeete including the *St. Xavier Maris Stella*, which departs every two weeks, *Dory II*, which makes weekly trips, and *Mareva Nui* and *Vai Aito*, which depart bi-monthly.

TIKEHAU   At least three different vessels visit the island regularly from Papeete, including the *Mareva Nui* every two weeks and the *Dory II*, which arrives weekly. The *St. Xavier Maris Stella* comes at least once a month.

MATAIVA   Interisland vessels that visit Mataiva from Papeete include the *Mareva Nui* on a weekly basis and the *St. Xavier Maris Stella* bi-weekly.

TAKAPOTO   Interisland vessels that visit Takapoto from Papeete include the *Mareva Nui*, the *Aranui III* and *St. Xavier Maris Stella* fortnightly.

TAKAROA   Interisland vessels that visit the island from Papeete are the *Mareva Nui* and the *St. Xavier Maris Stella*; both ships visit every fortnight.

FAKARAVA   Fakarava is visited twice a month by the *Mareva Nui*, the *Vai Aito* and *St. Xavier Maris Stella*.

KAUKURA   Interisland vessels that call on the island from Papeete include *Rairoa Nui* and *St. Xavier Maris Stella*, which come every two weeks, and the *Cobia* and *Dory II*, which visit on a weekly basis.

ARUTUA   Interisland vessels that visit the island from Papeete include the *Dory II*, *Cobia* and *Rairoa Nui*, all on a weekly basis; the *St. Xavier Maris Stella* visits bi-weekly.

AHE   There is a daily skiff from Manihi to Ahe. The island is also visited weekly by the *Dory II*, by the *St. Xavier Maris Stella* bi-weekly and by *Mareva Nui* and *Vai Aito* at least once a month.

EASTERN TUAMOTUS   Two ships visit the islands in the Eastern Tuamotus with regularity.

The *Kura Ora II* makes one voyage a month. The trip lasts 18 days and the route followed is: Papeete–Anaa–Faaite–Katiu–Makemo–Taenga–Nihiru–Hikueru–Marokau–Tauere–Amanu–Hao–Vahitahi–Nukutavake–Reao–Pukarua–Tatakoto–Fangata–Fakahina–Puka Puka–Napuka, Tepoto Nord–Takume–Raroia–Anaa–Haraiki–Papeete. ~ Contact Mrs. Vanina Paquier, Motu Uta, Papeete; 45-55-45, fax 45-55-44.

The *Kura Ora III* makes one 15-day trip per month. The itinerary is: Papeete–Anaa–Faaite–Katiu–Makemo–Taenga–Raroia–Takume–Marokau–Hikueru–Hao–Fakahina–Fangatau–Napuka–Puka Puka–Nukutavake–Reao–Tatakoto–Vairaatea–Pukarua–Papeete. ~ Contact Mr. Jean-Claude Paquier, Motu Uta, Papeete; 45-55-45, fax 45-55-44.

CAR & MOTOR SCOOTER RENTALS

RANGIROA   **Location Arenahio** rents cars, scooters and bicycles. ~ Avatoru; 96-82-45; e-mail carpom@mail.pf. **Rangi Rent-a-Car** rents cars and scooters. ~ Avatoru; phone/fax 96-03-28. **Avis Rangiroa** is another outlet. ~ Avatoru; 96-04-53, fax 96-03-33; www.avis-tahiti.com, e-mail avis.tahiti@mail.pf.

Chez Helene has three scooters that are available for rent for half or full days. They offer a discount for the second day. ~ Avatoru; 96-82-84.

Pareo Carole rents scooters and bikes. ~ Avatoru; 96-82-45. **Rangi Atelier** rents motor scooters. ~ Tiputa; 96-04-92. **Rangi**

Location (a branch of Europcar), rents scooters and is located about five kilometers from Tiputa Village. ~ 96-03-28.

PUBLIC TRANSIT

RANGIROA All transportation to and from the airport can be arranged through your hotel or guesthouse. Given the small area of land, there is little need for buses or taxis. However, in large part to meet the demand of tourists, *Le Truck* service began on the island in February 2002, connecting the two ends of the main islet. *Le Truck* departs the eastern end, known as Ohutu, at 8 a.m. and 1 p.m. traveling west, and Avatoru at 9:30 a.m. and 2:30 p.m. traveling east. Service is available Monday through Friday. Regular stops include the airport, hospital and old marina, although *Le Truck* will stop for you wherever you flag it down.

Getting around the atoll by boat is easy. A small watertaxi crosses frequently between the dock by Chez Glorine (on the Avatoru side of Tiputa Pass) to Tiputa Village. The best thing to do is ask at Chez Glorine for a recommendation for someone who will be able to take you across the pass. (Their prices will be less than what you would pay for transportation at the Kia Ora.)

ELEVEN

The Marquesas Islands

Whether seen from a sailing vessel or from the air, few sights
are as dramatic as landfall in the Marquesas Islands. The islands
rise like jagged spires from the sea. Volcanic in origin and geologically precocious, the Marquesas are rocky and precipitous.
They have no coastal plains, but are veined with deep, lush,
trenchlike valleys. The water surrounding the islands is indigo
blue and there are few reefs.

The Marquesas are comprised of ten main islands (six of which are inhabited)
and are located 875 miles (1400 kilometers) northeast of Tahiti. They are divided
into two groups: to the north is Nuku Hiva, Ua Huka and Ua Pou and in the south
is Hiva Oa, Tahuata and Fatu Hiva.

The climate in the Marquesas is, on average, similar to the rest of French Polynesia, but the seasons are reversed. The islands lie in the midst of a trade-wind
belt from the northern latitudes, bringing northeasterly winds most of the year. There
is no real rainy season, but rainfall is heavier in June and July. The mean year-
round temperature is a balmy 79°F (28°C).

Because of their proximity to the equator, the islands have been a backwater
of the Pacific. Although there is talk of building an international airport, the islands remain secluded. Most are accessible only by boat.

According to a theory held by University of California anthropologist Pat
Kirch, the six major islands of the Marquesas were settled around 2500 years ago
by Polynesian mariners from Samoa or Tonga. In 1595, the first European, Spanish
explorer Alvaro de Mendaña, "discovered" the Marquesas en route to establish-
ing a new colony in the Solomon Islands. Mendaña was a politically savvy man who
called them "Las Marquesas de Mendoza" in honor of his patron, the Marquis
de Mendoza y Cañete. After Mendaña's landing (in which natives in Fatu Hiva and
Tahuata were massacred), the islands remained undisturbed for almost 200 years
until Captain James Cook arrived. Cook's appearance was followed first by whalers,
and then, by 1862, slave ships.

Contact with the white man brought enslavement to some and disease to many. The slavers, known as "blackbirders," needed laborers for guano mining and South American plantations. Making promises of a better life, the blackbirders picked up their unfortunate victims, often with the help of other islanders, and sold them to the highest bidder. They plied their trade on most of the Marquesas, but principally sought their prey on the north coasts of Nuku Hiva and Hiva Oa.

While relatively few Marquesans ended up as slaves, the repercussions of this nefarious activity were enormous. When the French heard of the abductions, they took diplomatic action to secure the return of the Polynesians. However, before this could take place, a smallpox epidemic broke out in South America's coastal cities, and the repatriated Marquesans brought back the deadly virus with them to Nuku Hiva. This decimated the population and nearly destroyed Marquesan civilization.

When Cook first visited the islands, the inhabitants were thought to number at least 50,000. Some believe that the total population was as high as 100,000 before contact with outsiders. Regardless of what the pre-contact population was, 50 years after Cook visited, the number of inhabitants was down to about 30,000 and fell to 2000 before the numbers started to increase again. Today it stands at about 8000.

The first missionaries arrived on the scene in 1797, and in the following half-century various evangelistic sects zealously competed for the souls of the Marquesans. During this period of intense missionary activity, the American writer Herman Melville jumped ship from a whaler here. He later wrote *Typee*, based loosely on his experiences in the Marquesas. This rather embellished autobiographical account was the first South Seas romance, the earliest of a genre that brought many a white man to the shores of the Pacific Islands.

In 1804, a Russian exploratory mission commanded by Admiral de Krusenstern arrived at Nuku Hiva for ten very productive days. Aside from collecting ethnographic items (still in Russian collections), the voyage was illustrated and documented by scholars and artists. The Russian visit was also documented by two beachcombers living in the Marquesas. One was a Scotsman by the name of Edward Robarts, who lived on Tahuata, Hiva Oa and Nuku Hiva. (His journal has recently been published.) The other, Joseph Cabri, a Frenchman, lived on Nuku Hiva and published a short romantic narrative. Both men introduced the Russians to the tribes with whom they were allied.

In 1842, the French sent Admiral Dupetit-Thouars to colonize the Marquesas in order to establish a naval base, but the French found relatively little use for the islands. The French set themselves up on Tahuata, ostensibly to protect the local population from other European invaders. However, fighting soon broke out and the French carried out a successful war against the Marquesans on the island. Still, their presence was not seen as beneficial to either the locals or the Europeans, and after two years they withdrew their garrison to Nuku Hiva.

From the late 18th century through the 19th century, whalers from throughout the world converged here. The best sperm whale grounds ran along the equator, and the Marquesas were ideally positioned as "R&R" stops for whalers who plied the equatorial seas. In fact, it was the whaling trade that led to the discovery of the northern group of the Marquesas Islands. And it was this discovery that ultimately contributed to the depopulation of the archipelago—and the near destruction of the Marquesan culture. In all, the late 19th century was a time of darkness and death for the Marquesan people, marked by periods of savagery, killings and cannibalism. The French administration could do little more than preside over the death of a people.

Today, the islands remain an economic and social backwater. The main commercial products are copra and the *noni* fruit, and the government is encouraging the cultivation of vanilla. (They attempted to cultivate coffee in the 1920s but it never took off as a cash crop.)

The fishing grounds surrounding the Marquesas are rich with tuna and are fished by locals as well as large Korean vessels that pay the French Polynesian government a fee for the privilege of fishing in territorial waters. Much to their consternation, the Marquesans are not direct beneficiaries of these monies, and, lacking modern fishing vessels, it is difficult for Marquesan fishermen to capitalize on their rich off shore resources. Local commercial fishing is also hampered by the expense of shipping fresh seafood to Papeete and beyond because of the great distances involved.

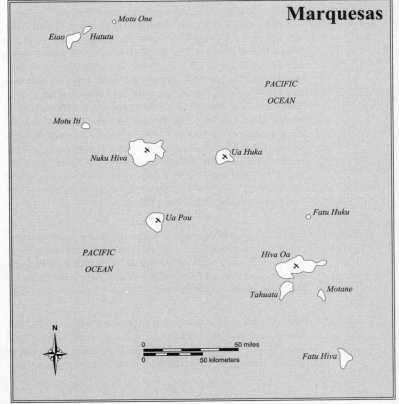

Text continued on page 406.

The Marquesas Islands

Getting in and around the Marquesas can be difficult: air service from Papeete is limited, and interisland travel takes planning (as well as a fistful of bank notes). Once on an island, there are few rental cars (travelers are usually better off hiring drivers). If you want to see the entire group, it will take a full month. But for those with limited time, a one-week trip to Nuku Hiva and Hiva Oa is convenient—there are regular flights from Papeete to both islands—and will give you a taste of the Marquesas.

Day 1
• Fly to Nuku Hiva from Papeete and check into the **Keikahanui Pearl Lodge** (page 414) or **Hotel Moana Nui** (page 414). Read Melville's *Typee* en route. Arrange your transportation for Days 2 and 3 after check in. Hire a driver for Day 2's trip to Taipivai Valley; you can do this through your hotel. For the boat charter to the Hakaui Falls trailhead on Day 3, talk to Rose Corser at the Keikahanui Pearl Lodge or ask at the local visitor's bureau for recommendations. You can now explore the small town of **Taioha'e** (page 409) on foot. This includes the new **museum** adjacent to Keikahanui Pearl Lodge, the old **fort and jail**, the **Cathedral of Notre Dame** and the **Piki Vehine** area that is full of modern stone sculptures. Be sure and see the restored **Tohua Koueva** archaeological site outside of town. Have a bite to eat at an inexpensive, no-name café on the waterfront. In the evening have dinner at the hotel and possibly a drink at the bar. Invite a couple of "cruisers" to join you and enjoy their blue-water tales of the downhill run from the U.S. West Coast.

Day 2
• Start at the crack of dawn and have your driver take you to the more remote archaeological areas of **Taipivai Valley** on Nuku Hiva's east coast. Visit the archaeological areas at **Pa'eke**, **Site Melville** and **Te Ivi o Hou** and visit **Anaho** village, **Tohua Hikokua** and **Kamuihei**. Lunch at **Chez Yvonne** (page 415) in Hatiheu village.

Day 3
• Pack a lunch and take your chartered boat to the Hakaui Falls trailhead. A two-hour hike (6.4 kilometers) brings you to **Hakaui Falls** (page 421), the highest waterfall in the South Pacific. This is a bit arduous but not too difficult for someone in good physical condition.

Day 4 • Fly from Nuku Hiva to Hiva Oa and check in at the **Hanakee Pearl Lodge** (page 438) or the less expensive **Pension Gauguin** (page 437). Hire a vehicle for Days 5 and 6, which you can arrange through your hotel. Now you can spend the day exploring **Atuona** (page 434). Visit the **Gauguin Museum**, **Gauguin** and **Brel's gravesites** and Brel's **Belvédère**, the site of the former singer's home. Dine at the **Restaurant Hoa Nui** (page 439) in town. In the evening have a drink over at the **Hanakee Pearl Lodge** (page 439).

Day 5 • It's very hot during the day so get an early start. Visit the **Taaoa Valley**'s *tohua* (ceremonial plaza) and other archaeological sites. The sites are located about 10 kilometers west of town. Hike inland at the marked trailhead near the phone booth. This is an all-day adventure and will require a car. In the evening have a meal at the **Hanakee Pearl Lodge** (page 439).

Day 6 • Get an early start if you're planning on seeing the *tiki* at **Puamau** (page 436)—the largest stone sculptures in the Marquesas. Figure on spending the entire day on this excursion and pack a lunch. Afterwards, take a swim at nearby **Puamau Beach** (page 440) if you have the time. Don't forget to pack insect repellent to ward off the ever-present *nonos*. The *tiki* in Puamau are a 40-minute trek beginning at the Puamau dock. In the evening dine at the **Hanakee Pearl Lodge**.

Day 7 • This will be your last full day in the Marquesas. If you've been hiking in the bush to see the *tiki* it's time to relax and enjoy the beauty of **Traitors Bay** (page 434). Take the 30-minute hike to the **Old Atuona Cemetery** (page 440) on the west end of town. It has terrific views of the coastline and there are several *paepae* (stone platforms).

IF YOU HAVE MORE TIME

If you have the luxury of time, see some of the lesser-visited islands such as **Ua Huka** and **Ua Pou**, both of which have air connections from Nuku Hiva. Give yourself at least a week between the two of these islands. Another option is to combine a visit of Hiva Oa with **Tahuata**, which is just a few miles south of the island but can only be accessed by boat. If you really want to get to beyond the pale, visit **Fatu Hiva**, which is also accessible via Hiva Oa. You'll really have to invest some time in visiting (unless you take the *Aranui* cruise vessel) because interisland transport is irregular at best.

In an effort to open up the islands, the French Polynesian government has approved a US$46 million renovation plan to convert the airstrip on Nuku Hiva into an international airport. President Temaru has said he would like to see direct flights to the islands from Hawaii. Whether it happens is another question altogether. If it is completed, it will give the local economy quite a boost and forever change the "paradise lost" charm of these remote islands.

Getting from island to island takes planning, and usually a fistful of bank notes. There is airline service between some of the Marquesas Group, but there are few regularly scheduled boats. To get from one island to another often requires chartering a boat—and that can be very costly.

Getting around an island can also be a chore. Even though maps depict "roads," they are rocky and generally not well maintained. During rainy days they may turn into rutted, muddy jeep trails. Roads are passable year-round, but tourist excursions may be limited if rainfall is unduly heavy. Driving the few roads that do exist requires a great deal of skill, especially during inclement weather. The plethora of precipices (roads are often cut from the sides of mountains) and the devil-may-care driving attitudes of locals make driving potentially hazardous to newcomers. There are few rental cars and travelers will most likely not be doing much driving on these islands. Hitching is an option, and sometimes it's possible to pick up rides in workers' trucks or carriers operated by local communities. (Women traveling alone should opt for a different method of transportation because of cultural mores.) Figure on spending 15,000 to 19,000 CFP (US$150 to US$190) per day for either rental vehicles or to hire a car with driver. If you don't want to spend the money, don't expect to do much sightseeing—unless you plan to walk a lot.

Like the cost of transportation, imported food is dear. Fortunately, Marquesans rely on traditional staples—breadfruit, taro, sweet potatoes, bananas and seafood—for the majority of their nutrition. Archaeological evidence indicates that this has long been the case. Ancient Marquesans consumed a wide variety of marine resources, including sting ray, porpoises and turtles. They also hunted land and sea birds, which resulted in the extermination of several species of birds such as rails and parrots.

The ancient Marquesans were a warlike lot who practiced human sacrifice as well as cannibalism. Various undertakings required victims to ensure the continued blessings of the gods. These practices had a specific place in their ceremonial life and warfare. Human flesh was generally eaten by males only.

Thankfully, these practices did not survive into the 20th century. However, Marquesans were also well known for their skills as tattoo artists and carvers of wood and stone, practices that continue to this day. Local artisans carry on these traditions in their woodcarvings and handcrafted ukuleles. Complex traditional design motifs are now imitated and applied in an almost cursive short-hand fashion. There are also ample remains of ancient temples and imposing stone *tiki* throughout the islands that illustrate the once-prolific talents of the ancient Marquesans.

The culinary spectrum of the Marquesas includes *ika te'e* (raw fish) as well as pork, goat and broiled lobster, which is in danger of being overharvested because of its popularity as fare for the few tourists that visit these remote islands. Baked breadfruit, as well as several varieties of fresh and fermented breadfruit pastes and puddings, are common. Taro, *manioc* (the starchy tapioca root) and bananas are also prevalent. While in the Marquesas you might be offered *popoi*, Marquesan-style poi made from breadfruit, which has a slightly sour, fermented taste. For dessert you'll no doubt try *poke*, a sweet, gelatinous mixture of pumpkin, banana or papaya and *amidon*. Naturally, there is always French bread, a variety of locally baked breads and a tasty biscuit-like treat, *kato*, made with coconut milk.

Nuku Hiva is the largest and most important island in the Marquesas—being the economic and governmental hub of the archipelago. One hundred and twenty-seven square miles (330 square kilometers) in area with a population of about 2100, its position as a center of civilization is nothing new. There are numerous vestiges of life before European contact. Here you will find *paepae*—the stone foundations on which the Marquesans constructed their homes, *pa*—fortifications, and *me'ae*—temples that testify to the once large population that the island supported.

Nuku Hiva

Nuku Hiva was the center of ancient stone architecture in the Marquesas and has the largest number of them remaining, particularly the large rectangular *tohua* (ceremonial complexes). These

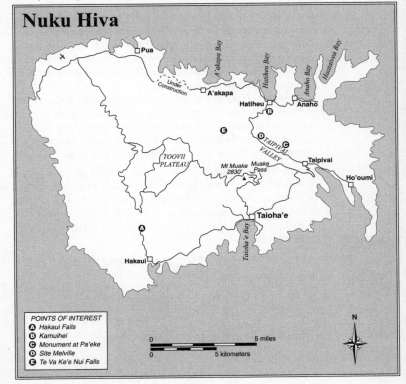

Nuku Hiva

POINTS OF INTEREST
- Ⓐ *Hakaui Falls*
- Ⓑ *Kamuihei*
- Ⓒ *Monument at Pa'eke*
- Ⓓ *Site Melville*
- Ⓔ *Te Va Ke'e Nui Falls*

0   5 miles
0   5 kilometers

often extended for 100 yards (90 meters) and were surrounded by huge stone platforms.

The manmade symmetry of Marquesan architecture is superseded only by the land's stunning majesty. Nuku Hiva is dramatically beautiful, with three major bays along the southern coast and equally breathtaking inlets on the northern coast. Taioha'e Bay, a cul de sac bounded by precipitous mountains, is located on the island's southern half and is the major port for the entire archipelago.

SIGHTS

Nuku Ataha, the Nuku Hiva airport, is located a few kilometers inland from the northwest coast. To reach the main settlement of Taioha'e you can either go overland by car via a winding, mountainous dirt road, which takes about two hours, or via helicopter, which involves a seven- or eight-minute vault over some incredible scenery. One of my friends described the helicopter flight as "seven or eight terror-filled minutes"—but I rather enjoyed it.

Coming from the airport you can also travel east, along the north coast past the village of Pua. There the road becomes an impassible track until the village of A'akapa, where once again a four-wheel-drive vehicle can negotiate the terrain. (Local government authorities told me that the impassible segment between A'akapa and Pua may be finished sometime in the near future, which would make life much easier for residents of the northeast side of the island who must drive a circuitous route to reach the airport. This remains a dream.)

Driving northeast from Taioha'e, you can travel overland by car to **Hatiheu** then to A'akapa and beyond. The road ends after another five kilometers or so. Motoring east and north from Taioha'e, you can travel to Taipivai and Ho'oumi. All roads are unpaved and extremely rough and/or muddy during the rainy season.

TOOVII PLATEAU AREA The central portion of the island is dominated by the **Toovii Plateau,** moor-like setting that you first glimpse on your drive in from the airport. Fertile and verdant, the hills above the plateau have been planted with Norfolk Pine. The tree-planting scheme is part of a government-established agricultural station.

AUTHOR FAVORITE

If I get out to the Marquesas, a hike through **Kamuihei** is mandatory. The restoration of this impressive temple complex is a collaborative effort, with work focusing on replanting indigenous gardens and building homes on their original foundations. For more information, see page 412.

Crossing Toovii Plateau in a southerly direction toward Taioha'e necessitates negotiating **Muake Pass**. From the summit there is a spectacular 360-degree view. The vista takes in the rugged coastline and Taioha'e Bay. On the distant horizon the island of Ua Pou rises like an apparition. A short taxi ride will take you to the overlook at 2830 feet (864 meters) above the bay.

In 1813, Muake Pass was the site of a major **fortification** of the Tei'i (Taioha'e) tribe when Commodore David Porter arrived. The entire ridgetop was enclosed by a log palisade. Trenches cut through the ridge, still visible today, were made by the Tei'i to prevent the neighboring Taipi warriors from reaching the fort along the crest. Although the area was greatly disturbed by reforestation projects, road construction and the erection of a radio tower, the remains of the fort can still be seen.

TAIOHA'E AREA Taioha'e, the administrative center of Nuku Hiva and the entire Marquesan archipelago, sits on the shores of **Taioha'e Bay**, the central bay on the southern coast. Bounded by high peaks, its calm, deep anchorage is a refuge for boats from the hurricane-prone southern reaches of French Polynesia and a first port of call for many cruisers from the west coast of North America. The main frontage road, studded here and there with shade trees, is lined with the requisite bank (Socredo), shops, post office, bakeries and government facilities.

Taioha'e is the undisputed shipping center for the Marquesan Group. On the *quai*, a freezer stores the catch of the local fishing co-op. Port facilities have been vastly improved in the past few years and a wharf has been constructed on the east side of the harbor.

An **old fort** and **jail** built for local troublemakers and political exiles stands just a stone's throw east of the Taioha'e town hall. Constructed in 1842, this relic is the oldest original European structure in French Polynesia. The old fort is the site of Commodore David Porter's Fort Madison, built by the American Navy in 1813. In 1814, the British took the fort over and by 1842 the same real estate was occupied by the French under Commandant Collet. It was eventually renamed Fort Collet, the name that stands today. Today, the jailhouse doubles as an urban planning office.

Be sure to visit the local **tourist office** located next to the town hall. The bureau is run by the very capable Sophie Le Naër. She knows everything that is going on in town, and is proficient in English. She also sells a variety of maps of the Marquesas. The office is open from 7:30 a.m. to 11:30 a.m. ~ Taioha'e; 92-03-73, fax 92-08-25; www.marquises.pf, e-mail tourisme@marquises.pf.

The **town hall** itself houses a substantial collection of rare books and manuscripts dealing with the entire archipelago. Visitors are welcome.

You might want to stop and see the **Cathedral of Notre Dame**, an interesting mix of traditional and Catholic symbolism. It was constructed in 1974, using stones from all the islands, and is the largest church in the Marquesas (able to hold 800 worshippers). The interior boasts locally carved wood sculptures. Be sure to take a look at the handsomely carved lectern with the figures of the twelve apostles. Mass is held every Sunday.

Adjacent to Keikahanui Pearl Lodge is a **museum** founded by longtime resident Rose Corser. Ms. Corser, a native Oklahoman who moved to Taioha'e decades ago, established the minuscule museum in concert with the local Catholic Mission. Many of the artifacts come from the Mission and Ms. Corser's private collection. Stored in an air-conditioned room (rare for the Marquesas Islands) are classic South Pacific artifacts including Marquesan war clubs, spears, *tiki*, whale tooth pendants, *tapa* (bark cloth), *penu* (stone pounders), stone adzes and ornamental items made of bone and human hair. Modern carvings are also for sale. A guided tour with Rose Corser, who has dedicated countless hours to the project, is a must for any visitor. ~ Taioha'e; 92-00-74.

The monument at Pa'eke was first reported and photographed by the German ethnographer Karl von den Steinen in 1897.

Tohua Koueva was restored for the Fifth Arts Festival of the Marquesas Islands, held in December 1999. Nearly everyone in town, including Nuku Hiva Mayor Lucien Kimitete, lent a hand to the restoration work, which was originally begun by French archaeologist Pierre Ottino. The large, platform-like *tohua* structures are ancient ceremonial sites where traditional Marquesan feasts and other rituals were performed. They consist of a rectangular flat dancing floor surrounded by elevated *paepae* that served as seats for the spectators. At one time traditional *tiki* were placed at various points but the ones here were stolen long ago and replaced by modern replicas that look every bit authentic. Shaded by massive banyan trees, the *tohua*'s stone platforms are now replete with traditional Marquesan *fares* and smaller thatched-roof meeting lodges. Though looking thoroughly Polynesian, the wide-open spaces and ample stone block construction give the area an almost Roman, plaza-like ambience. A restored paved path that begins at the stone quarry on the road to Taipivai/Hatiheu guides visitors to the site. You can either take the old track that begins at the seaside and meanders a bit or this half-mile uphill walk on the newer paved pathway.

On the waterfront it's hard to miss the newly restored *Piki Vehine*. The modern stone sculptures here are by artists from different islands, and a traditional *ha'e* (house) has been constructed. Be sure and see the monument erected in tribute to Herman Melville near the Pahatea Cemetery and the canoe house.

TAIPIVAI VALLEY AND NORTHEAST COAST   The east coast of
Nuku Hiva is high, rocky and dry. In parts, it is a formidable line
of sheer cliffs. Tucked away in the Taipivai Valley, just inland from
the coast, are many old temples, or *paepae* (pronounced "pie-
pie"), and large *tiki*.

Some of the most fascinating archaeological sites in French
Polynesia are found in this region, including the **monument at**   ◄ *HIDDEN*
Pa'eke. Here you'll find 11 *tiki*, probably representing the ancestral gods of the Taipi sub-tribes. Constructed around A.D. 1700,
they still stand at a ceremonial site located in what now appears
to be a cow pasture. The trail to the ruins leads uphill (as it seems
all treks in the Marquesas do) about one kilometer through a
shady coconut plantation. Exotic birdsongs can be heard in the
distance. The site is surrounded by lush palms, banana plants and
a plethora of *nono* and mosquitos. (Don't forget your repellent!)
You'll probably see a few horses grazing on the grounds as well.
~ The monument at Pa'eke is located high on the northern wall
of the valley (about four kilometers from where the valley begins).
It's a bit tough to find the trailhead (it's not marked) so have a
local guide you.

The famous **Site Melville** (Cite Melville) is where Herman Melville sojourned in 1842 after deserting his whaling ship. It's about
two kilometers past the Pa'eke monument on the lefthand side of
the road. **Te Ivi o Hou,** the *tohua* or ceremonial site, is located in
a remote part of the valley. In 1957, American archaeologist Robert
Suggs excavated the 300-yard-long area (274 meters) while sharing a house with Heiku'a Clark, a woman who claimed descent
from Melville's fabled Fayoway Peue. Those interested in more
details should get a copy of Suggs' *Hidden Worlds of Polynesia*.

The various bays and coves along the coast are accessible by
boat, and, in some cases, by four-wheel-drive vehicle. It's fairly easy
to get from the Taipivai Valley to one of the nicest bays, **Anaho,**
simply by continuing up the Taipivai Valley floor over the pass to
Hatiheu. Anaho Bay, with coconut palms edging its shoreline and
white-sand beach, is tucked between two rather high rocky promontories. (Note: Swimmers should keep an eye out for sharks.)

On the way up (before getting to the pass), ask the driver to
point out **Te Va Ke'e Nui Falls** on your left. The source of the
water is a large dam, which provides the electricity for much of the
island. (There is a good vista point near the top of the pass where
you can see the distant falls.) It's possible to drive nearly all the
way to the falls at the end of the valley by taking a new road that
runs parallel to the old Taipivai–Hatiheu road on the right bank
of the river.

The village of **Hatiheu,** also located on a sheltered bay, rests   ◄ *HIDDEN*
in the shadow of some spectacular peaks that tower over the landscape. The village has a secluded, restful feel to it, and there is a

fine pension (Chez Yvonne) where you can base your explorations of the region. The area is a mother lode of archaeological ruins. Of note are the **petroglyphs** and a well-restored ceremonial plaza, **Tohua Hikokua**, that displays both ancient and modern Marquesan sculpture. This site was reconstructed through the efforts of mayor Yvonne Katupa, the same disarmingly nice woman who runs the pension. A local dance troupe took its name from the Tohua Hikokua site, and they often perform for visitors on the actual plaza.

HIDDEN ▶

Continuing inland from Hatiheu, about 500 yards (450 meters) from the restored *tohua*, is an even larger ancient temple complex known as **Kamuihei**. This incredible jumble of ruins, including a *tohua* and petroglyphs, sits amidst a somber, dark jungle. It looks like a movie set from *Raiders of the Lost Ark*. Petroglyphs are relatively common in Hatiheu and A'akapa on the northern coast of Nuku Hiva. The Kamuihei ceremonial center was restored by French archaeologist Pierre Ottino, his wife Marie-Noëlle, and the population of Hatiheu. The site was also chosen for the Fifth Arts Festival of the Marquesas Islands, which occurred in December 1999. The restoration work includes replanting some of the indigenous gardens, building the houses on their original *paepae* (foundations) and repairing the fallen stone walls. The Kamuihei and Hikokua archaeological complexes are not far from the main road, but it's a good idea to have someone show you where to find both sites as they entail a short walk in the bush.

You can check e-mail and browse the web at the post office in Taiohae on Nuku Hiva. You will need to purchase a phone card for 1500 CFP. Get there early since there is almost always a long wait.

From the village it's a relatively easy hike to **Anaho Beach**. Many Marquesans regard Anaho Bay as the most picturesque in the Marquesas. The snorkeling is also good. Be prepared to lather yourself with *monoi* oil or insect repellent. *Nonos* can be a problem in many of the low-lying areas—even on the beach.

Along the northern stretch of coast between Anaho Bay and Pua, 20 kilometers east of the airport, is a journey worth taking. The scenery, which consists of a number of finger-like promontories jutting out to the sea, is spectacular. There are several white-sand beaches tucked along the shoreline, and you will be in the shadow of Nuku Hiva's highest mountains. However, the road stops shortly after the village of A'akapa and the best way to see this section of the coast is by boat. (The Pua area itself is still often regarded as *tapu*, off limits.)

As you near the airport area, the landscape sloping down from the plateau is volcanic and almost lunar in nature.

LODGING

HIDDEN ▶

TOOVII PLATEAU AREA For a unique Marquesan experience, consider staying at **La Ferme-Auberge de Toovii** (Toovii Farm), situated right in the center of the island at 800 meters (so it's re-

The Reality of Travel in the Marquesas

Visitors to the Marquesas Islands need to be independent, patient and able to rough it. Overland travel is nearly always by four-wheel drive. In some cases, boat, and even horseback, are used to get from one point to another.

Air service is not frequent and flights may be booked up weeks in advance during school holidays. The flight from Papeete is over three hours and the journey by copra boat may take a week or more depending on the schedule.

Getting to the Marquesas from Papeete is generally not cheap. Roundtrip air fare costs around US$500, which can be more than an air ticket from the West Coast of the U.S. to Tahiti.

Another option for getting to the Marquesas is via the *Aranui III*, a comfortable, regularly scheduled interisland vessel. This is the most intriguing option, but it comes at a price. The two-and-a-half week cruise costs between US$2000 and US$4000, including all meals and excursions. There are less expensive vessels, but their standards in terms of personnel, maintenance and accommodations are not high. Their schedules are also somewhat erratic.

One other note on things erratic. Prices in the Marquesas are subject to change. It's a good idea to get agreed-upon prices in writing.

freshingly cool). The working farm consists of 300 hectares of pastureland. It produces dairy products, meat, fruit and vegetables, all of which are sold in the local community. This is also a great place to get ice cream and is a favored (if out of the way) stop for newly arrived cruisers. The property includes four bungalows with queen beds and private baths, and a well-regarded restaurant, whose dishes are made from ingredients produced on the farm. The environmentally conscious management can arrange guided excursions on foot or by horseback, bicycle, horse-drawn cart or four-wheel-drive vehicle. ~ Toovii Plateau; 92-07-50, fax 92-00-04; e-mail ferme-auberge@mail.pf. BUDGET.

TAIOHA'E Chez Fetu is smack-dab in the center of Taioha'e village, west of the bakery and just inland from the waterfront road. It consists of one house with four rooms—two rooms have one double bed each, and two come with two single beds each. Bathrooms are communal and there is also a sitting room, a front porch and a nice kitchen with stove and refrigerator. Two bungalows with private bath are also available. The guest accommodations are very basic, but clean, airy and a good bet for travelers watching their pocketbooks. There are no mosquito screens on the windows so bring coils. Fetu and his family are personable and a pleasure to deal with, but the numerous children in the area can be noisy. ~ Taioha'e; 92-03-66. BUDGET.

Facing the sea, **Hotel Moana Nui** is a white, two-story building with a large veranda for its restaurant patrons. It has seven rooms, four of which have double beds and three with two single beds. The average-size rooms are clean and have private baths. There is also one bungalow with a private bath. The tariff includes breakfast. The hotel operates a restaurant downstairs that is *the* informal gathering place in town. Hotel Moana Nui is located midway between the east and west ends of Taioha'e Bay. ~ Taioha'e; 92-03-30, fax 92-00-02. BUDGET TO MODERATE.

At the western side of the bay you'll find the most luxurious hotel in the islands—the **Keikahanui Pearl Lodge**. Perched on a hill overlooking the sea and the town of Taioha'e, the hotel offers spectacular views from all of its 20 bungalows. Each bungalow was carved by a different local woodcarver and has a distinct flavor. All are air conditioned and equipped with minibar, telephone, TV, bathroom and a panoramic terrace. The restaurant and bar open toward a large terrace and to a dipping pool with a cascade. Some 50 steps lead down to the beach. Internet and e-mail service are available at the bar. ~ Taioha'e; 92-07-10, fax 92-07-11; www.pearlresorts.com, e-mail keikahanui@mail.pf. DELUXE.

Pension Pua has five bungalows situated in a garden about 100 feet from the water. Each of the units has a double bed, a private bath and a terrace. Three of the units have equipped kitchens. ~ Taioha'e; 92-06-87. BUDGET.

Andy's Dream provides two bungalows with kitchens and private cold-water bathrooms. ~ Taioha'e; phone/fax 92-00-80. BUDGET.

Nuku Hiva Village is a small hotel on the northern side of Taioha'e with six thatch-roofed bungalows spread over a large grassy area near the ocean. Each has a small private terrace and a hot-water bathroom. Meal plans are available. I found the place adequate but sterile. ~ Taioha'e; 92-01-94, fax 92-05-97; e-mail nukuvillage@mail.pf. MODERATE.

Mave Mai offers six rooms with a view of the bay. Bathrooms are private and have hot water. Three rooms have double beds; the other three have a double and a single as well as air conditioning. Meals are available in a shared dining area. The owners will arrange lagoon, four-wheel-drive and hiking excursions. ~ Taioha'e; phone/fax 92-08-10; e-mail pension-mavemai@mail.pf. BUDGET.

Also in Taioha'e is **Paahatea Nui**, which has six rooms with either private or shared bath. Three of the rooms have two single beds each, two have a double bed, and there is one "family-size" room with a double bed. There are also six self-contained bungalows that sleep three. Although on the mountain side, the pension has beach access and a view of the bay. Breakfast is included. ~ Taioha'e; phone/fax 92-00-97. BUDGET TO MODERATE.

TAIPIVAI VALLEY AND NORTHEAST COAST Chez Yvonne is ◀ HIDDEN
located right on the waterfront road facing the bay in downtown Hatiheu, approximately a one-hour drive from Taioha'e. Any way you look at it, you're in a remote corner of the universe. The accommodation consists of five spartan but clean bungalows—all equipped with double beds—set in a grassy field shaded by huge *pandanus* trees. The bungalows are a two-minute walk along the beachfront road from Yvonne's small restaurant. If you plan to stay in just one place in the Marquesas, this is a good property to consider. Just take plenty of insect repellent! ~ Hatiheu; 92-02-97, fax 92-01-28; e-mail hinakonui@mail.pf. BUDGET.

AUTHOR FAVORITE

When on Nuku Hiva, I never fail to book a table at **Chez Yvonne**. This waterfront eatery may be down-to-earth, but its food is out of this world—the deep-fried freshwater shrimp sends me to the land of ambrosia. The inexpensive lunches and dinners, combined with the homey ambience and Yvonne's pleasant disposition, make it an obligatory stop. It's on the waterfront road facing the bay. Reservations are mandatory! ~ Hatiheu; 92-02-97. BUDGET.

HIDDEN ▶   **Te Pua Hinano** (also known as Chez Juliette) is a big house
with two rooms, a dining room, a kitchen and a shared bathroom.
The basic but clean pension is situated in a spectacular setting near
the beach. The owners will take you free diving, fishing, swimming
and shell collecting. The informal Te Dua Hinaleo restaurant is
on the premises. ~ Anaho Bay; 92-04-14. BUDGET.

Also situated on beautiful Anaho Bay near the beach, **Ka'o
Tia'e** is the most luxurious property in the Anaho area. The tiny
resort is run by Raymond Vaianui and his wife, Maea. The five
bungalows, while not fancy, have tile floors and private baths;
the private terraces overlook a coconut plantation. The shower
is in the garden where you'll share facilities with the family
ducks! ~ Anaho; 92-00-08. BUDGET.

DINING   **TOOVII PLATEAU**   Meals served at **Auberge de Toovii** are made
from the meat, dairy products, vegetables and fruits grown right
on the property, which is a working farm. ~ Toovii Plateau; 92-07-
50, fax 92-00-04; e-mail ferme-auberge@mail.pf. MODERATE.

HIDDEN ▶   **TAIOHA'E**   Facing Taioha'e Bay is **Kovivi's Restaurant**, located
several minutes by foot east of the town hall. It is a brown chalet-
type structure with a small veranda. Chinese, French and Marquesan cuisine are served with a flair. Dishes are generally tasty, but
especially so when Bernard, the owner, cooks. Business hours are
sometimes irregular and reservations are needed. No breakfast Saturday. Closed Sunday. ~ Taioha'e; 92-03-85. MODERATE TO DELUXE.

HIDDEN ▶   The restaurant at the **Hotel Moana Nui** has a veranda facing
the sea where locals and visitors alike gather. They offer a wide-
ranging menu that includes fish, chicken and several varieties of
pizza. The pizza is made precisely as described in the menu—don't
even think about holding the anchovies or adding extra olives.
Changes are not permitted! The best way to order is to ask what
the cook would like to fix for you rather than what you want. The
atmosphere is quite pleasant and there is a colonial feel to the
place. Hotel Moana Nui is centrally located along the main street.
~ Taioha'e; 92-03-30. BUDGET TO MODERATE.

A small, whitewashed, cube-shaped eatery, **Te Ha'e Ma'ona** has
several benches with thatched canopies, and Michelin, who runs
the place, serves steak and fries, *poisson cru* and other local dishes.
Located just off the main street on the western end of town. ~
Taioha'e. BUDGET.

Snack Celine, located near the Catholic Mission, serves inexpensive local dishes. Snack Celine is the island's closest thing to
a fast-food restaurant. Fare includes such standards as hamburgers, steak and fries. ~ Taioha'e; 92-01-60. BUDGET.

HIDDEN ▶   The best budget restaurant in town is the small **eatery** tucked
in the back of the waterfront *marché*. It's so off the beaten path
it doesn't even have a name. This is not only the least expensive

restaurant in Taioha'e, it's perhaps the only place to get Marquesan dishes. To say the ambience is unpretentious is an understatement. Ripening banana bunches hang from the ceiling above the mismatched tables and chairs. Dishes include sashimi, *poisson cru*, steak and fish served with plantains. The sashimi is good, but the sauce served with it is a variation on a "thousand island" theme. (Don't expect wasabi or soy sauce here.) A nice local touch is the cold, green coconut juice served as a beverage. ~ Taioha'e. BUDGET.

If you're interested in collectibles, the best articles are wooden bowls, small wooden and stone *tikis* and the expensive but exquisitely carved coconut shells made in Fatu Hiva.

The chef at the **Keikahanui Pearl Lodge** prepares French cuisine with a local touch. His *tartare du thon* comes highly recommended. Fresh fish, crayfish and freshwater shrimp are also often on the menu, which changes regularly. Be sure and make time for happy hour and enjoy a spectacular sunset from the terrace of the hotel. ~ Taioha'e; 92-07-10. MODERATE TO DELUXE.

There are two **roulottes** (they don't have names) in town that serve inexpensive local fare along the beach road during the day.

TAIPIVAI VALLEY AND NORTHEAST COAST Te Pua Hinano (a.k.a. Chez Juliette) has a tiny restaurant/bar where fish with coconut milk and other basic local fare is served. The food is appetizing, but unless you are staying there, you must call ahead to let the manager know you're dropping in. ~ Anaho; 92-04-14. BUDGET.

TAIOHA'E Fresh bread is baked daily and is available at any of the general stores in Taioha'e. The stores are on or near the beachfront road and have a good selection of canned food, fish, cheese and sundries. They include **Magasin Kamake** ~ 92-03-22 and **Magasin Larson** ~ 92-03-31.

GROCERIES

TAIPIVAI VALLEY AND NORTHEAST COAST The small town **marketplace**, located next to the Taipivai Road junction, is open from 7:30 a.m. to noon. Local fruits, veggies, goat meat, fish and honey are available. **Magasin Bigot** is a do-it-yourself hardware store/garden center that carries many useful (non-food) items. ~ 91-00-10.

TAIOHA'E Carvings are one of the best things to bring back from the Marquesas. Good quality items can be purchased in Taioha'e because it is the commercial center where visitors are likely to congregate. Expect to pay 5000 CFP and up for a good carving. You can visit the carvers behind the Te Ha'e Ma'ona to start your window shopping.

SHOPPING

You can also contact one of the following craftsmen directly:
Pierrot Keuvahana ~ 92-06-14
Damien Haturau ~ 92-05-56

Jean-Baptiste, Raphael, Edmond or **Jonas Ah-Scha** ~ 92-02-46

Roti Teikitohe ~ 92-01-65

Mooroa and Philipe Utia ~ 92-01-68

Damas Taupotini ~ 92-02-42. You can watch Damas carving bone sculptures and amulets every day in front of the Piki Vehine archaeological site near the cathedral.

Also check out **Edgard and Benoit Tamarii**, a famous and talented family of sculptors who live behind the bakery, just off the frontage road. ~ 92-02-42.

Some local handicrafts are for sale at the **Kanahau Boutique**, next to the marketplace and in the hairdresser's at the shopping complex next to the town hall.

The age of the Kamuihei petroglyphs is unknown, but they are thought to be much older than most of the *tiki* in the Marquesas.

Shop Loisirs has an excellent choice of newspapers, magazines, books and stationery. Look for them at the town hall shopping center. ~ 92-05-06.

Veronica and Renaud Coquille run **La Galerie d'Art de Marquises**. They sell beautifully framed traditional bone, wood, shell and stone carvings. ~ 92-08-62; e-mail renaud.coquille@mail.pf.

Dried local bananas, a Marquesan specialty, are a lovely treat, but you'll have to ask around to find them. They are generally not sold in stores.

If a tattoo is on your wish list, ask the Keikahanui Pearl Lodge to put you in touch with the talented and soft-spoken **Akitini**. Or simply keep an eye out in town for a man with facial tattoos. Akitini does all original designs based on traditional motifs.

NIGHTLIFE Offering a splendid view, the Keikahanui Pearl Lodge is a good place to imbibe in the evening, particularly during happy hour from 4 to 6 p.m. When yachts are in town, the bar/restaurant is filled with Americans with adventurous sailing stories. On Friday, it's the only place in town with live music. The rest of the time Keikahanaui is pretty quiet. ~ Taioha'e; 92-07-10.

The **Hotel Moana Nui** is *the* place in town to sip coffee or a beer and watch the world go by. With the islands' only outdoor brick oven, this is the place for pizza. It's also a good spot to meet locals or other travelers. ~ Taioha'e; 92-03-30.

BEACHES **TAIOHA'E** Taioha'e Beach ~ Taioha'e Beach, fronting the eastern side of the village, is a long stretch of golden sand. On shore there are plenty of shade trees, while offshore the water is often abob with yachts. The beach is usually clean and is popular with locals, especially on weekends. However, if there are yachts around, keep an eye out for raw sewage and skip the swimming. ~ To find Taioha'e Beach, walk to the west end of town along the frontage road.

TAIPIVAI VALLEY AND NORTHEAST COAST Anaho Beach

≈ ⤚ This white-sand beach is one of the best in the Marquesas. Protected from the wind and offering plenty of shade, it is a crescent-shaped strand, approximately one and a quarter miles (two kilometers) long. Swimming is excellent. Snorkelers can take advantage of the coral reef and, with a bit of luck, spot a turtle or harmless white-tip reef shark (*moko*). Be prepared to cover up or protect yourself from *nonos*, which can be a problem. A freshwater tap is available here and it's possible to purchase beer or soft drinks at nearby Chez Juliette. ~ The access trail is an easy, two-kilometer trek over a 650-foot (200-meter) pass from the village of Hatiheu.

Xavier, the local dive operator, reckons that diving in the Marquesas is altogether an entirely different experience than you'll find elsewhere in French Polynesia. You don't have to dive as deeply—40 to 60 feet (12 to 18 meters) is the maximum you need to go—to see a multitude of undersea life, including pygmy orcas, tuna and scalloped hammerhead sharks. Xavier also does quite a bit of cave diving, including a visit to a cave that is packed with lobsters. Few people dive these waters, so the sealife is generally not frightened of humans.

Outdoor Adventures

DIVING

The biggest difference between diving here and in the rest of French Polynesia is that the Marquesas have no coral reefs or tranquil lagoons. This means divers should be prepared for strong swells and currents. The waters are also rich in plankton so visibility is considerably reduced (30 to 60 feet is the norm).

At **Sentinelle Aux Marteaux** (Sentinel of the Hammerheads), you can see spotted leopard rays, lion fish, groupers, black-tip reef sharks, and the occasional manta ray. The best time to see hammerheads is January through July.

Scuba diving in Taioha'e is available through **Centre Plongee Marquises**, which is the only dive operation in the Marquesas. Operated by Xavier Curvat (known locally as Pipapo), it offers dives to about 20 sites near Taioha'e. Xavier speaks English and has lived in the Marquesas for years. He offers package trips that include accommodation in Taioha'e as well as trips to Ua Pou. CMAS certification is also available. Make sure you call ahead and make reservations. As the islands' only dive center, boats are usually always booked several days ahead. ~ Taioha'e; 92-00-88; www.marquises.pf.

Hatiheu to Anaho (1.25 miles/2 kilometers) is one of the nicest short hikes on the island. You can easily do a day hike over to Anaho, enjoy the beach, then hike back. It only takes about an hour

HIKING

to 90 minutes (roundtrip). The Hatiheu side is steep, slippery and potentially muddy, so wear good hiking shoes or sandals. Along the way you'll see spectacular views of Anaho Bay and neighboring Haatuatua Bay. As you continue along the trail, the views only get better. One panorama offers a scene of Haatuatua and Anaho bays. If you are fortunate, a nice easterly breeze will cool you off. ~ To find the trailhead in Hatiheu, take the first road to the right of Yvonne's restaurant (where the town hall is located). This leads uphill and eventually becomes the trail to Anaho Bay. Keep going straight uphill (don't take the right turn).

Tohua Hikokua (1 mile/1.6 kilometers). There are two archaeological ruin sites near Hatiheu. One of them, a huge rock face with petroglyphs, is one of the best in the islands. Tohua Hikokua resembles a soccer field with stone bleachers. There are three ornate *tiki*, but they're new. Although they look weathered, they are not the authentic old stone variety. If you look closely, you'll note there are three old *tiki* in the wall of the platform. The *tohua* is still used by traditional dancers, who often perform for visitors. As you approach the *tohua* from the road, look for the large phallus sculpture on your left near the corner of the platform. It's at least 150 years old and is about three feet (one meter) in height. It is believed that if an infertile woman touches this rock it will help her become pregnant. ~ To get there, begin by facing the church. Take the beachfront road to the right. Continue along the road, which winds uphill to the left. From town, it's about a 15- to 20-minute walk up to Tohua Hikokua.

To reach **Kamuihei** (.75 mile/1 kilometer), a massive *tohua* site in the Hatiheu area, continue up the main road toward Taipivai about one kilometer and look for a massive banyan tree on your left-hand side. The tree is sacred and marks the trail to the petroglyphs. (Ask a local to take you because the petroglyphs are not

THE LAST SURVIVOR

Few travelers had ever seen—let alone heard of—the Marquesas Islands before the popular reality television show "Survivor" brought the island of Nuku Hiva into millions of living rooms in 2002. In countries where the show previously filmed, tourism was boosted tremendously, and Tahitian tourism officials hope for the same long-term result. Marquesas travel planners consciously market the "Survivor" angle, proudly displaying the "Survivor Marquesas" logo on their advertisements and websites.

"Survivor" fans considering a trip to Nuku Hiva should understand, however, that there is nothing show-related left to see. Even more disappointing is the fact that the remote beach where much of it was filmed is a stone's throw from an overlook off the road to Taipivai.

easy to spot.) The track is not clearly marked (there are several paths that meander back and forth across each other) and is covered with wet leaves and large mossy rocks. It can be quite slippery so take care. Streams trickle down alongside the trail and there are more banyan trees with long tangled roots along the way. The scene is quite eerie, in a beautiful way—exactly what a movie producer might come up with when filming Melville's *Typee*. The trail wanders past the banyans to a small grove. (It takes about ten minutes.) At this point look for a large rock (about six feet/ two meters high) with petroglyphs of turtles and fish. A rock cairn marks the site—the petroglyphs are on the other side of the rock from the trail.

Just beyond the petroglyph site at Kamuihei is a **tohua complex**, approximately 300 yards long. Located in the midst of dark jungle filled with the sounds of strange birds, it is a massive jumble of boulders and stone platforms. The site has been restored and gives you a clear idea of the enormity of the construction projects that took place in ancient times. You should not miss Kamuihei if you are in the neighborhood. ~ To find the Kamuihei *tohua* complex, walk up the main road from Hatiheu in the direction of Taipivai, about one kilometer, and look for the massive banyan tree on your left-hand side.

A visit to the **Hakaui Falls** (4 miles/6.4 kilometers) can be done ◄ HIDDEN
two ways, one quite simple, the other rather arduous. The recommended method is to charter a boat from Taioha'e for a 20-minute ride around the coast. You will then be let off at the trailhead to the falls. From there it's a two-hour walk (one way) through the jungle to the magnificent, 1148-foot (350-meter) falls, the highest in the Pacific Islands, and among the highest in the world. Someone from the boat will accompany you to the spot. The other way to reach Hakaui Falls is to trek from Taioha'e overland. It takes about four hours along precipitous coastal ridges to get to the falls' cutoff. After reaching the Hakaui trail, it's another two hours to reach the falls. The coastal trail has recently been improved by the government and although a guide is not necessary, it is recommended that you hire one. The roundtrip walk takes about 12 hours, not including a lunch break. That's a lot of walking for one day!

If you simply want to see some of the coastline, it might be better to walk part of the coastal trail and leave the falls for another time. Naturally, you will want to take a picnic lunch and plenty of water. ~ To get there by boat costs about 12,000 CFP for the charter. Check with Rose Corser (92-00-74) for charter information. It is probably a good idea to check with Sophie Le Naër at the Tourism Office (Taioha'e; 92-03-73; e-mail webmaster @marquises.pf) to find out what condition the trail is in before you set off.

FISHING   The waters off Nuku Hiva are rich in sealife and it's possible to hook mahimahi, tuna and other large fish.

If you want to charter a boat for a fishing trip, try the *Heetai*, a 40-foot tuna boat skippered by **Laurent Teiki Falchetto**. ~ Taioha'e wharf; 92-05-78.

SAILING   If you have several weeks of traveling time on your hands, a sailboat is the best way to truly see the Marquesas. Well-heeled visitors can charter a yacht in Papeete or Raiatea. Several companies have vessels that are available for trips to the Marquesas. See the "Sailing" sections at the end of the Tahiti and Raiatea chapters for detailed information on possibilities.

HANG GLIDING   The **Upe O Te henua Enana Club** will take visitors hang gliding from Muake, Vaioa or Pahatea Peaks (for experienced 'gliders or from smaller, less demanding heights for beginners). Contact Joseph Tauira or Roland Peley. ~ Taioha'e; 92-05-30; e-mail pelaygamnt@mail.pf.

RIDING STABLES   For horseback riding in Taioha'e, contact **Sabine Teikiteetini**. ~ 92-03-01, 21-24-15.

Le Ranch, operated by Patrice Tamarii, offers hourly horse rentals and guided trips of two days or more. ~ Taioha'e; 92-06-35.

ISLAND TOURS   Most tours in Nuku Hiva originate in Taioha'e. However, the term "tour" is misleading. If you don't speak French, a tour will be little more than a taxi ride to an archaeological site with no understandable commentary.

From Taioha'e there are three day trips that you should not miss: the Taipivi Valley and various archaeological sites; the village of Hatiheu and nearby Anaho; and Hakaui Falls.

Taipivai and its environs (including Hatiheu and Anaho) can be done in one day, but it will be a long day if you are to see everything. My advice would be to start early. Taipivai (sometimes referred to as Taipi) is a half-hour drive from Taioha'e over Muake Pass, past a commercial teak grove and into Taipivai Valley. (Upon your descent into the valley, apply insect repellent.) Cost for the tour (to hire the four-wheel-drive vehicle) is 15,000 CFP if you just go to Taipivai Valley or 20,000 CFP if you go on to Hatiheu, which is another half-hour or so down the rocky road. There are two major archaeological sites to visit in the narrow Taipivai Valley, including Site Melville, where author Herman Melville spent several months, and the Pa'eke area.

In order to truly see Taipivai you should book a room at a local pension. They can organize tours to archaeological sites and make sure that you get back to Taioha'e and/or the airport. (The perennial problem in the Marquesas is getting from Point A to Point B when you want to.)

A visit to Hatiheu with lunch at Chez Yvonne Katupa should be on your agenda. She is the mayor of Hatiheu and quite helpful at organizing local tours to the various archaeological sites— especially if you plan to stay at her pension. If you plan to have lunch with her in Hatiheu on a day trip, make a reservation. Be sure to stop by her office in the village to see artifacts from the famous Ha'atuatua archaeological digs. From Hatiheu you can take a 50-minute trek over the hill to Anaho Bay. Hatiheu also has three wonderful archaeological sites a short distance from the village that should be on your agenda. ~ Hatiheu; 92-02-97.

As a general rule, if pensions don't have their own e-mail address, messages sent to tour isme@marquises.pf will reach the lodging for which they are intended.

Mave Mai Tours, operated by the pension of the same name, offers three different trips on Nuku Hiva. The first involves a boat ride to Hakatea and a hike through the Hakaui Valley for a picnic lunch and a swim at the waterfall. The return hike is via the beach. The second option is a four-wheel-drive trip up the Taipivai, Houmi and Aakapa valleys, then a swing through Hatiheu and Anaho bays with lunch at Chez Yvonne. The third possibility is a trip to the Toovii Plateau and Muake Ridge, with lunch at the Toovii Farm. ~ Taioha'e; 92-08-10; e-mail pension-mavemai@mail.pf.

For those who want to really explore the terrain, **Jocelyn Henue Enana Tours** offers guided discovery trips of the Marquesas Islands lasting two to eight days. Jocelyn, a French woman, is a self-taught archaeologist. Trips may focus on Nuku Hiva only or may include multiple islands in either the southern or northern part of the group. All trips include roundtrip four-wheel-drive, boat and helicopter transfers as well as full board and lodging. Overland treks can also be arranged, as can single-day excursions. ~ Taioha'e; 92-08-32, fax 92-00-52; www.marquises voyages.com.pf, e-mail jocelyne@mail.pf.

Pua Excursions offers a three-day excursion that explores the Valley of the Kings, Hakaui Waterfall, Taipivai and Hatiheu valleys and Anaho Bay. An eight-day version adds visits to the royal Taiohae *marae* and cathedral, Mt. Muake, Aakapa, Anoho and Haatuatua Valley. There's also the opportunity to do some deep-sea and inshore line fishing. Helicopter and boat transfers are included. ~ Taiohae; 92-02-94, fax 92-01-35.

Heli-Inter provides helicopter tours around Nuku Hiva and neighboring islands. (One-way helicopter fare is 7500 CFP.) The office is in downtown Taioha'e, next to the town hall. ~ Taioha'e; 92-02-17, fax 92-08-40; e-mail helico-nuku@mail.pf.

Ua Huka

Ua Huka, 897 miles (1448 kilometers) northeast of Papeete, is around 50 square miles (129 square kilometers) in area and has a population of about 600. Much of inland and upland Ua Huka is arid, rocky grassland sprinkled with shrubs. It looks more like the Scottish Highlands than a tropical island. The desiccated nature of much of the island most likely has to do with the overgrazing caused by the ubiquitous wild horses and goats that roam the land. There is, however, dense vegetation in the Vaipae'e, Hane and Hokatu areas. The inland valleys are deep, well watered and bounded by steep cliffs. Ua Huka is the home of the blue lorikeet, a gorgeous bird called *pihiti* by locals. Off Ua Huka's southwest coast are small islands with extensive bird colonies.

Ua Huka is the flattest and driest of the Marquesas. The island was never popular with early traders because it lacked sandalwood and a protected anchorage, but today its tiny airstrip, located between Vaipae'e and Hane, is serviced three times a week (Sundays, Wednesdays and Fridays) by connections to other Marquesas islands and Tahiti.

Most early Polynesians steered clear of Ua Huka because of the scarcity of water. However, those who did set down roots found large quantities of nesting birds and manta rays, both good food sources. Today, people live in three friendly villages scattered along the southern coast. The tiny villages cling to the valley floors and feature tidy little homes. One small road connects the villages.

The main attraction in Ua Huka is the semi-wild horse population, which outnumbers the human population fourfold. The horses can often be seen on the road between Vaipae'e and Hane.

SIGHTS

The **Vaipae'e Archaeological Museum** is a must-see for visitors. It was designed and produced by Marquesan artisans along with cultural authorities and displays a collection of very unusual artifacts. They are grouped by specific areas within the workings of the ancient culture: food preparation, fishing, carving and handicrafts and funeral rites. The museum also contains some material excavated in the 1960s from the Hane Valley beach dune site. Joseph Vaatete, the curator of the museum and resident stone- and woodcarver, is a distinguished artist in his own right. Admission is free and the museum is open Monday through Friday from 8 a.m. to 3 p.m. A 20-minute walk inland from the boat landing, the museum is located in the town's center. ~ Vaipae'a; 92-60-74.

Over the years, Ua Huka has been deforested by wild horses and goats. In an attempt to "re-vegetate" the island, Leon Lichtle, the area's dynamic mayor, created the **Papuakeikaha Arboretum**, which makes an interesting stop. The nursery features more than 400 species of flora, including 144 varieties of citrus plants, the largest collection in the Pacific. There is no admission; the arboretum is open to the general public from 8 a.m. to 3 p.m. Monday through Friday. It's located between the villages of Vaipae'e and Hane on Ua Huka's main road. ~ Vaipae'e; 92-61-51

Leon Lichtle has also built a second museum in the village of Hane. Dubbed the **Hane Maritime Museum,** it is dedicated to the sea and has replicas of traditional canoes (constructed by Tehau Joseph Vaatete) as well as fishing gear and old fish hooks carved from mother-of-pearl. The artifacts, with detailed descriptions of archaeological excavations, make this spot well worth a visit. The museum is located next to the handicraft center in Hane and has the same phone number and operating hours as the Vaipae'e museum.

The highest point on the island, at 2903 feet (885 meters), is **Mt. Hitikau,** which overlooks Hane. For an eye-popping panorama, climb the mountain to see the *Aranui III* as it snakes its way into Vaipae'e Bay and turns around, with inches to spare.

Other sightseeing attractions on Ua Huka are the ruins located high in the Hane Valley, several with **ancient tiki.** This area is known as a *me'ae,* a sacred place where ancestors are buried. Among the more interesting *tiki* here is a second, miniature version of the famous "pregnant woman" *tiki* from Puamau on Hiva

◀ HIDDEN

Ua Huka

N

Haunanu
Point

Mt Hitikau
2903'
▲

Hane
☐

Vaipae'e ☐   Hokatu ☐
✕

*Vaipae'e
Bay*

Haavai
Bay

Teoho Ote
Papa Point

Tekeho
Point

Hemeni
Island

0   2 miles
0   2 kilometers

Oa. ~ The ruins are about 30 minutes by car from the airstrip. Ask a guide to take you; they are off the road and involve a short hike.

In the village of Hokatu is the **Hokatu Geological Museum**, which features objects made of stone, including old and new *tiki*, *poipoi* pounders, petroglyphs, and other traditional items. François Rollet, a former curator at the Museum of Tahiti in Papeete, made copies of the famous petroglyphs from Vaikivi Valley and other parts of the island that will also be exhibited in this museum. The museum is located in central Hokatu, next to the handicraft center. Open weekdays from 8 a.m. to 3 p.m. ~ Hokatu; 92-60-55.

When the *Aranui III* is in port, woodcarvings are sold in the small shack next to the pier. It's right behind the canoe house, on the beach.

Excursions to Vaikivi Valley and the Bird Islands near Haavai Bay on the southern coast are also worth checking out. Of particular interest in **Vaikivi Valley** is a major archaeological site with many examples of petroglyphs, located a one-and-a-half-hour walk from Vaipae'e. It is possible to reach the **Bird Islands**, rocky outcroppings, by boat. Once there, at a prudent distance, it's possible to observe the 20,000 terns nesting on the stony surface. Manta rays can sometimes be observed at the foot of these islands. (Warning: Climbing on these rocks can be very dangerous.)

LODGING

HIDDEN ►

Chez Alexis Scallamera is a two-room house. Guest rooms are large, airy and colorfully decorated with floral-print carpet and curtains; each has one double bed and one single. There is a communal bathroom. *Pension complete* is available. The cuisine here is first class, with a presentation equal to any good restaurant. Alexis is an excellent guide who provides excursions around the island and roundtrip transfers from the airport. The house is located seven kilometers east of the airport and two kilometers west of the dock. ~ Vaipae'e; 92-60-19, 92-61-16, fax 92-60-12. BUDGET.

Chez Christelle Fournier is a four-room home with shared cold-water bath and kitchen and a sitting room with a TV. The property is at the foot of a hill that offers a fine view of the village. Meal plans are available. ~ Vaipae'e; 92-60-34, 92-60-85. BUDGET.

Also in Vaipae'e, **Manatupuna Village** has three A-frame bungalows with private hot-water bathrooms. There are no cooking facilities for guests, but the owner will provide meals. ~ Vaipae'e; 92-60-08, phone/fax 92-61-01. BUDGET.

Auberge Hitikau is an inn-style accommodation consisting of a duplex home with three rooms, each with a double bed. There's a communal bath, a restaurant/bar and excursions to the valleys and to the Bird Islands off Haavai Bay. The Hane Valley *tiki* are a humid 25-minute uphill climb from here. The one report I have had about this lodging was not glowing. Located seven kilometers from the airport. ~ Hane; 92-61-74. BUDGET TO MODERATE.

◄ HIDDEN

Chez Maurice et Delphine offers two rooms with a double bed in his house with an equipped kitchen, two bathrooms with hot water, a salon with sofas and a terrace with mountain and ocean views. Three additional bungalows have been constructed on a small hill just outside the village of Hokatu. The view is terrific, the units are well appointed and the atmosphere is very calm. *Pension complete* is available. Roundtrip transfer to the airport is 2000 CFP. It's 12 kilometers from the airport. ~ Hokatu; phone/fax 92-60-55. BUDGET.

DINING

The dining scene here is limited to the meals provided at the pensions. The following three serve meals to nonguests as well. (Be sure to call ahead for reservations; never show up unannounced.)
Vaipae'e   Chez Alexis ~ 92-60-19 and **Manu Tupuna Village** ~ 92-61-01
Hane   Auberge Hitikau ~ 92-61-74
Hokatu   Chez Maurice et Delphine ~ 92-60-55

GROCERIES

Several small markets in Vaipae'e stock essentials such as matches, cigarettes and mosquito coils; sometimes fresh vegetables are also available. Try **Chez Maurice et Delphine Magasin** ~ 92-60-55.

SHOPPING

Woodcarving is still practiced in Ua Huka; each of the three main valleys has a carving exposition or display area with works from island artisans. If you plan to purchase carvings in the Marquesas, these outlets are worth checking out. The quality is often excellent and prices are reasonable. Expect to pay 5000 CFP or more for a good-quality bowl. ~ The expositions are in Vaipae'e (near the museum), Hane (near the post office) and Hokatu (near the beach).

Carvings may also be purchased from individual craftspeople. Ask at the small museum in Vaipae'e for names of artists. Stone and bone carving are also practiced here and are of good quality.

BEACHES

There are many small beaches reachable by horse or on foot. But they're infested with *nono*, making them quite unpleasant.

Outdoor Adventures

Captained vessels can be hired for sightseeing, interisland transfer or fishing trips (about 2000 CFP an hour), weather permitting. Try any of the following.

FISHING

Vaipae'e   Alexis Fournier ~ 92-60-05, **Nestor Ohu** ~ 92-60-18 or **Vanance Ah-Scha** ~ 92-61-54
Hane   Jean Tamarii ~ 92-60-07
Hokatu   Paul Teatiu ~ 92-60-88, **Paul Teikiteepupuni** ~ 92-60-48 or **Maurice Rootuehine** ~ 92-60-55

RIDING STABLES

Exploring the plateaus of Ua Huka on the back of a horse is a wonderful way to see this compact island. **Edmond Lichtle** provides mountain and seashore rides. ~ Vaipae'e; 92-60-87. **Alexis Fournier** (92-60-05). **Francois Brown** (92-61-31) and **Jonas Teiki huavanaka** (92-60-57) in Hane also offer horseback riding.

▼▼▼▼▼▼▼▼▼

Ua Pou

Ua Pou means "Two Posts" or "Two Peaks," which refers to the two massive volcanic spires—Pou Maka at 3264 feet (1043 meters) and Mount Oave at 4040 feet (1232 meters —that seem to brush the clouds. The two peaks accentuate the island's jagged, scarplike relief. Both mountains are plugs extruded from the throats of extinct volcanoes. There are six main valleys, most with lush green vegetation, bounded by exceedingly steep cliffs.

Where you arrive on Ua Pou will depend on your mode of transportation. The *Aranui III* stops at Hakahau and Hakahetau. Vessels from Nuku Hiva stop in Hakahau as do the taxi services from the airfield (which is located between Hakahau and Hakahetau). If you have a vehicle and a driver, it's possible to get just about anywhere. There's a dirt road that circles near the perimeter of the island.

SIGHTS

Hakahau, the principle village on the island, sits on the shore of a crescent beach. The community extends onto a large valley floor. While in the village you feel like you are in a natural cathedral— two tall spired peaks tower magnificently overhead.

A manmade cathedral, the local **Catholic church,** lies in the shadow of nature's sanctuary. Of particular interest in the church are the exquisite carvings decorating the interior. This is in keeping with island tradition—residents often fashion stone and wood carvings and weave hats and mats. The church is open to the public until noon.

Hakahau has a small administrative complex near the airport and the requisite shops, bank, hospital and post office. There is also a small **museum** with scattered maritime artifacts including ancient fish hooks and shark jaws. All signage is in French. There are no set operating hours so call ahead. ~ 92-52-11.

HIDDEN ►

The holiest ancient temple on Ua Pou is **Te Menaha Taka'oa.** The monument was sacred to the local god Te Atua Heato, who was said to be "white" (i.e., not tattooed). The site was considered quite *tapu* (forbidden) up to the late 1800s when it was visited by the German ethnologist Karl von den Steinen. You will need a guide to take you there. ~ Contact Tony Tereino; 92-53-19, 92-51-68.

Ua Pou is the only place in the world aside from Brazil where "flower stones" are found. Volcanic in origin, these curiosities are dark brown stones with yellow flower-like patterns. Ua Pou was also the source of gray-green *phonelite,* which was traded in pre-contact days throughout the Marquesas and was used to make flake tools for woodworking, for butchering animals and as weapons. Called *Klinksteine* in German, the moniker accurately refers to the bell-like ring when the stone is struck. You can find these stones all over Ua Pou.

Also of interest, just off the southern shore, is the islet **Motu Oa**, which is a sanctuary for thousands of nesting terns. This area is fragile ecologically, so visiting from a distance by boat is urged. Bring your binoculars. ~ Contact your pension for more information on transportation.

LODGING

Pension Pukue'e, located near the dock in Hakahau, is a seven-room property situated in the hills overlooking the sea. The setting is truly splendid, with great views of the bay and the towering peaks. Facilities include living room, TV, common kitchen and cold-water bathroom. Meals are available. ~ Hakahau; phone/fax 92-50-83; e-mail pukuee@mail.pf. BUDGET.

Located in the center of the village, **Pension Vehine** is run by the charming Claire Teikiehuupoko. The property has two rooms

with double beds and sports a communal bath with hot water, a living room and a terrace. Claire has recently opened two bungalows. Snack Vehine is nearby and is also owned by Claire. She and her husband Toti are members of the Motu Haka cultural association and are active as teachers to revive the Marquesan culture. Toti speaks English. ~ Hakahau; 92-50-63, phone/fax 92-53-21. BUDGET.

Chez Dora is another small pension with two rooms (with a double bed in each room), a communal bath with hot water, a living room area, a fully equipped kitchen and a dining room. Breakfast and dinner are available. ~ Hakahau; 92-53-69. BUDGET.

DINING

Vehine Hou at Hakahau is worth checking out, but not just for the Marquesan and French cuisine. The owner, Claire Teikiehuupoko, is the president of Motu Haka (the Society for the Preservation of Marquesan Culture) and is well versed in local lore. ~ Hakahau; 92-53-21. BUDGET TO MODERATE.

Vaitiare, a snack and bakery shop, is also worth visiting. The bread there is excellent. ~ Hakahau; 92-50-95. BUDGET.

Try **Tati Rosalie's** for traditional food like raw fish, octopus, pork rice and banana pudding. ~ Hakahau; 92-51-77. BUDGET

We've heard tell that **Chez Etienne Hokaupoko** makes great local food. ~ Hakahetu; 92-51-03. BUDGET.

GROCERIES

There are several grocery stores in Hakahau. Most are attached to homes. Basic items can be found at **Magasin Haeapa** ~ 92-51-77, **Magasin Mokohe** ~ 92-52-08, **Magasin Tereino Naha** ~ 92-51-68, **Magasin Marielle** ~ 92-54-49 and **Magasin Gueranger** ~ 92-51-49.

SHOPPING

Artisans **Christian and Catherine Kervella**, originally from France, have lived in Ua Pou since 1989. The couple have revived the old art of decorating bamboo. Traditionally bamboo flutes and tattoo implements were finely embellished with burnt-in designs. The Kervellas have become masters of this technique, and museums throughout the world order copies of ancient bamboo flutes from them. They also create very fine necklaces and pendants made only of bamboo and natural materials. The Kervellas live in Hakamoui Valley in a remote area near Hakahau. They can be contacted by e-mail or through Gilles Bert at the video store in Hakahau. ~ Phone/fax 92-55-23; e-mail gillesbert@mail.pf.

Ua Pou islanders are talented woodcarvers and weavers. Sales of their crafts are usually made at the individual's home. To locate a woodcarver or weaver, ask around.

BEACHES

ANAHOA BEACH This fine strand of white sand on Anahoa Bay occupies the equivalent of several city blocks. In the distance

To Swim
or Not to Swim
in the Marquesas

Going to the beach is not generally an option in the Marquesas Islands. I do not encourage you to swim there unless you are accompanied by a local resident. And you will rarely see a local swimming in the water. (This should tell you something!) Swimming is possible, but you need to be aware of the following:

Pollution
Swimming near a village or area where yachts are moored is definitely not a good idea. Cesspools empty into the sea and yachts release their effluents in the open water.

Currents
If the beach is not too infested with *nono* and is swimmable, the currents and rip tides can be very dangerous. Exercise caution.

Marine life
The waters off of the Marquesas are renowned for the variety (and number) of sharks—hammerhead, tiger, blue-, black- and white-tip, bronze whalers—and rays. There are also venomous jellyfish and stonefish lurking about. I recommend that only experienced divers attempt to explore these waters.

are sloping hills and close by you'll find shade trees. The big waves are tempting to bodysurf, but there is an undertow—swim with caution! There are no facilities. ~ The beach is a 40-minute walk north of Hakahau.

HOHOI BEACH The small beach at Hohoi is famous for its "flower stones." They are volcanic in origin and colored dark brown with yellow, flower-like patterns. Unfortunately, they are becoming more difficult to find because locals pick them to sell to tourists. ~ The beach is located about 12 kilometers south of the airport on the southeast coast of the island. You can walk, but it is easier to catch a ride with a local resident. (You can also find flower stones on the pebble beach at Hakahetau.)

Outdoor Adventures

FISHING

Fishing off the island is very good; one can hook tuna, mahimahi, or even marlin and sailfish. Expect to pay around US$350 for half a day. For boat charters in Hakatao Village, contact: **Francois Keuvahana** ~ 92-53-31, **Alain Ah Lo** ~ 92-52-80, or **Felix Toata** ~ 92-53-39.

RIDING STABLES

Horseback riding is a great way to get around the island, and guided tours can be organized. Horses and tours are available in Hakahau from **Tony Tereino** ~ 92-51-68. Other people to try include **Albert and Atere Kohumoetini** ~ 92-52-28, **Francis Aka** ~ 92-51-83, **Jules Hituputoka** ~ 92-53-33 and **Rosita Teikitutoua** ~ 92-53-36.

HIKING

Hakahau Vista (1.5 miles/2 kilometers). For one of the island's most spectacular views, follow the track to the cross on top of the hill overlooking the village. Here you'll have a crow's-nest view of the Hakahau Bay and Anahoa Beach, which fringes a secluded cove on the other side of the mountain.

For the adventurous, there is the **Hakahetau to Hakahau** (7.5 miles/12 kilometers) hike. Little shade is provided so it can be brutally hot in the mid-day sun. There is only one track—basically follow the road north, past the airport, up and down the ridge from Hakahetau to Hakahau along the coast. It takes three hours and offers some dramatic vistas.

GUIDED HIKING TOURS **Ua Pou Evasion**, run by Tony Tefeino, offers guided tours of the island's archaeological and historical sites as well as its flora and fauna. Tony offers circle island tours and half- and full-day excursions as well as longer trips. A three-day trip includes mountain trekking, fishing and arts and crafts. A six-day trek includes overnight accommodations in local homes. ~ Hakahetau; 92-53-19, 92-51-68, fax 92-52-66.

Georges Toti Teikiehuupoko is a school teacher and president of Motu Haka, the Society for the Preservation of Marquesan

Culture. He arranges trips to the most sacred temple on Ua Pou, Te Menaha Taka'oa. Georges imparts something of the old culture to visitors. ~ Hakahau; 92-53-21.

Hiva Oa

Hiva Oa is perhaps best known as the burial place of Paul Gauguin. The island was originally named *La Dominica* by Alvaro de Mendaña when he discovered it on a Sunday in 1595. Almost 300 years later, Robert Louis Stevenson said of the island, "I thought it the loveliest, and by far the most ominous spot on earth." To this day it still retains a paradox of wild beauty and somber bearing.

Very little of the island's 200 square miles (518 square kilometers) is flat. There are rocky, unpaved roads to most of the island's communities. Major routes run east to west along the spine of the island and also along the southern coast. The airstrip, which was built at the geographic center of Hiva Oa, is about five kilo-

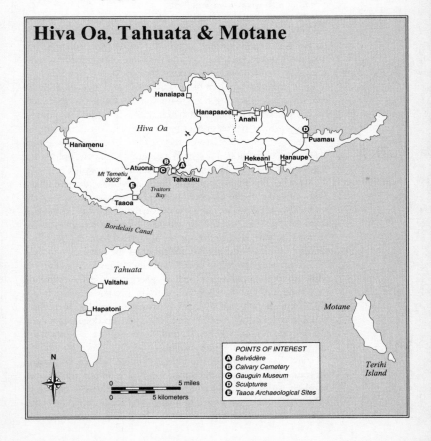

Hiva Oa, Tahuata & Motane

Hanaiapa

Hanapaaoa   Anahi

Hiva Oa

Hanamenu

Puamau

Atuona   Hekeani   Hanaupe

Mt Temetiu
3903'   Tahauku

*Traitors
Bay*

Taaoa

Bordelais Canal

Tahuata

Vaitahu

Hapatoni

Motane

*Terihi
Island*

N

POINTS OF INTEREST
Ⓐ *Belvédère*
Ⓑ *Calvary Cemetery*
Ⓒ *Gauguin Museum*
Ⓓ *Sculptures*
Ⓔ *Taaoa Archaeological Sites*

0   5 miles
0   5 kilometers

meters north of Atuona. Dirt tracks and horse trails provide access to the spectacular north coast.

SIGHTS

The main settlement on the island is **Atuona**, the second-largest town in the Marquesas. Towering 3903 feet (1190 meters) above Atuona is **Mt. Temetiu**, the island's highest peak. Atuona sits on the shores of **Traitors Bay**, which was created when the sea flooded a tremendous crater eons ago. The village is constructed on a slope at the base of a large valley. To the east, it is bounded by a very precipitous cliff—the highest on the island.

The largest building in town is the boarding school for girls, run by the sisters of St. Joseph of Cluny. There are about half a dozen stores, a hospital and dentist's office, one bank (Socredo), two restaurants and a variety of lodging possibilities. The **tourist office**, staffed by English-speaking Alanda and Solange, is right in front of the Gauguin Museum. Closed weekends. ~ 92-78-98; e-mail comtourismehiva@mail.pf.

The population of Atuona is about 1700, only a vestige of the large population the island once had. Many homes are built on the foundations of *paepae* (ancient stone platforms). At one time there were many large *tiki* on the island, but most have now been scattered to museums around the world.

The final resting place of Paul Gauguin and Jacques Brel, the well-known Belgian singer, are in the **Calvary Cemetery**. Brel spent his last years on Hiva Oa and died in 1978. Gauguin's monument is a simple stone marker and a small statue of a Polynesian woman known as "Oviri." Brel's tomb has a bas-relief of him, along with his female companion. ~ To get to their graves, take the uphill road that begins at the *gendarmerie*. It's a ten-minute walk.

HIDDEN ▶

Another landmark to visit is Brel's **Belvédère**, the site where Brel planned to build his home perched above the east side of the valley above Tahauku. The view of town and the bay is stunning from this vantage point. ~ To get there take the road to the airport. The path begins about 200 meters behind the Hotel Hanakee. If in doubt, ask for directions at the hotel.

To further explore the life of Paul Gauguin, visit the **Gauguin Museum**. Both attractive and well designed, it focuses, of course, on Paul Gauguin, who lived very close to the present museum building. There are copies of Gauguin paintings on display, and even a wax likeness of the artist himself. The museum documents Gauguin's work in French Polynesia and blends aspects of Marquesan culture with the Gauguin material.

Next door is a reproduction of Gauguin's residence, **La Maison du Jouir** (The House of Pleasure), a two-story affair with woven bamboo walls, thatched roof and a carved doorway and trim. Behind the museum it's hard to miss *JoJo*, Jacques Brel's airplane.

Paradise Nearly Lost

Resting midway between Australia and South America, the Marquesas are isolated as is no other landfall on earth. Given their detachment, one would think the ecosystems found on the islands have remained intact and unblemished. Not so. Over the years, horses and goats have rapidly chewed up native vegetation like hoofed locusts. Birds brought in to combat vermin now edge out rare native species. On every island, rats and cats introduced by Europeans have attacked indigenous birds, and have had few prey to control their own populations.

The onslaught of introduced flora and fauna started long ago when the original Polynesian settlers arrived bringing yams, taro, pigs and even their own species of rats to the islands. The "Polynesian" rat inevitably upset the indigenous ecosystem but probably did less damage than the larger, common European or Norwegian rat that arrived on European ships. The more aggressive European species preys on young birds and eggs and has been quite injurious to indigenous bird populations. Rats are the biggest threat to the beautiful ultramarine lorikeet found only in the Marquesas. Today, fortunately, on Fatu Hiva the lorikeet is being saved from extinction.

Unfortunately, things are not going as well for the Marquesas kingfisher, which is found only on Hiva Oa. The kingfishers' difficulties started when the great horned owl was introduced to combat the rat population. The owls developed a taste for the kingfishers as well as the rats. Consequently, the kingfisher is slowly dying out.

Europeans were not the only people to introduce predators of rare native flora and fauna. Polynesians bear just as much blame. On Nuku Hiva, the biggest threat to the indigenous Nuku Hiva pigeon is man. Once found in abundance, it has been hunted to near extinction by locals for food. Today, only about 100 pair exist and there is no legal protection for these birds. A similar threat stalks the spectacled gray-backed terns, found only in the tropical Pacific. On two tiny uninhabited islands, jointly known as Bird Island, thousands of sooty and spectacled gray-backed terns use the land to breed and can still be seen taking to the air in great numbers as boats pass. However, this sight may soon become just a memory. Over the last decade, the tern population has decreased from 80,000 to 20,000. Why? Locals scale Bird Islands' cliffs to collect eggs by the bucketful. Naturalists tell us this represents a clear danger for the spectacled gray-backed tern, and at present nothing is being done to remedy the situation.

TAAOA VALLEY ARCHAEOLOGICAL SITES The most interesting archaeological site to visit on the south central coast of Hiva
HIDDEN ► Oa is the immense restored **ceremonial center** at the head of **Taaoa Valley,** west of Atuona. The name of the Taaoa site is unknown, but it includes a large Nuku Hiva–style rectangular ceremonial plaza, or *tohua,* with many cut-stone facings. This type of fully enclosed *tohua,* constructed with extremely large stones, is very rare on Hiva Oa. Extending up the hill above the plaza, you'll find a series of temples with sacred banyan trees, and at least one **mortuary platform**, where the dead were exposed for preparation for burial. On one of the uppermost platforms stands a basalt column with traditional *tiki* features carved in low relief. This is said to represent the god Hu'upeke. According to legend, human sacrifices were killed on the *tohua* at the lower end of the complex and carried up and placed on top of this image. Another unusual feature of the complex is the wall that divides the site into units, each containing several structures. These were said to have marked the limits to which different castes were admitted during ritual ceremonies. Make sure you take your mosquito repellent while admiring these Marquesan handiworks. ~ To get there you must take a car or truck about ten kilometers west of Atuona on the coastal road. When you arrive at the phone booth, follow the trailhead inland to the archaeological sites.

PUAMAU The precipitous coastal road (heading west) between **Puamau** and the village of **Anahi** offers panoramas of an absolutely stunning coastline, akin to the rugged, fjordlike coast of Norway or Scotland. It consists of a series of fingerlike promontories jutting into the sea, all carpeted with lush green vegetation.

Just west of Anahi is the village of **Hanapaaoa**, another of those subtly eye-catching little Marquesan hamlets tucked beneath the island's craggy reaches.

On the northeast coast, near the village of Puamau, are the
HIDDEN ► largest **stone sculptures** in the Marquesas. These measure more than seven feet (2.5 meters). The **tiki** of Puamau, at Me'ae Te I'i Pona, are very late in origin, most likely A.D. 1700–1750. Some anthropologists consider them to be archaeological links to the *tiki* on Easter Island and those of Necker Island near Hawaii. The detached stone heads at Puamau are said to be representations of victims offered by leaders of the Naiki tribe, which formerly inhabited Puamau. Legend has it that the prone figure is that of Maki'i Tau'a Pepe, a priestess who died in childbirth in great agony. (Maki'i means "death agony.") Ancient Marquesans believed that women who died in childbirth became malevolent spirits that had to be appeased through worship. Admission. ~ To get there, hire a guide or get directions in Puamau village. The site is at the base of a large promontory on the east side of the valley.

The **Atuona Commune Bungalows** consist of three small units each with a double bed, shower, bathroom, electricity, refrigerator and hot plate. In addition, there are two larger double bungalows, each with two rooms, two double beds, shower, bathroom, gas stove and a veranda. These units, which are owned and managed by the local government, are pretty basic and are often rented to workers from Tahiti on a monthly basis. There is no meal program, so be prepared to cook your own food or patronize the local restaurants. Bring your mosquito net with you, as there will be plenty of these pests to greet you in the rooms. A room must be booked at the *mairie* (city hall) during office hours. Atuona Commune Bungalows are located in "downtown" Atuona. ~ Atuona; 92-73-32, fax 92-74-95. BUDGET.

LODGING

Offering a good value, **Temetiu Village** has five bungalows, four of which have a single room with both a double and single bed. The fifth bungalow has two rooms, one with a double bed and one with two singles. There is also a living room with a small library, television and video. All of the units have private baths and have recently been renovated. There is a good restaurant on the premises. Activities include visits to archaeological sites, snorkeling trips, mountain-bike rentals and picnics. The views are great and the owner, Gaby Heitaa, is a wonderful host, and plans to add a swimming pool to the property. Credit cards are accepted. Transfer from the airport and back is 3800 CFP. Temetiu Village is one kilometer from Atuona on the main road. ~ Atuona; 91-70-60, fax 91-70-61; e-mail heitaagabyfeli@mail.pf. MODERATE.

◀ HIDDEN

Pension Gauguin is a modest two-story building with six clean rooms, each with a double bed. Four of the rooms have private baths, and there are two communal baths with hot water, a salon and a large terrace upstairs with an ocean view. The owner, Andre Tessier, is a pleasant, well-informed guide and provides excursions around Hiva Oa and Tahuata, as well as visits to archaeological sites and fishing trips. The food served here is very good also. The house is on the main road, a five-minute walk east of Atuona. ~ Atuona; phone/fax 92-73-51; e-mail pens.gauguin@mail.pf. MODERATE.

◀ HIDDEN

AUTHOR FAVORITE

Hiva Oa's **Hanakee Pearl Lodge** gets my vote as the best hotel in the Marquesas. The panoramic views of the mountains and sea are incredible, the food is great and the accommodations, constructed with plaited *pandanus* and bamboo, are very unusual. For more information, see page 438.

Pension Ozanne, a family-style accommodation, has two large bungalows only 300 meters from the center of town. The units have two rooms (one double bed and one single), TV, hot-water bath, kitchen and mezzanine sleeping areas. There are also two rooms with double beds available in another building. The pension's best feature is its panoramic view of Atuona Bay. Meal plans are available, as is a four-wheel-drive vehicle for local tours. ~ Atuona; phone/fax 92-73-43. BUDGET.

The only hotel in Hiva Oa, the **Hanakee Pearl Lodge** is the sister property of the Keikahanui Pearl Lodge in Nuku Hiva. Constructed on the site of the old Hanakee Hotel on the slopes of Tahauku valley, the hotel has a panoramic view that takes in Traitors Bay, the island of Tahuata, the islet of Hanakee, Mount Temetiu and the blade-shaped mountain chain of the island. Hanakee Pearl Lodge provides eight deluxe bungalows, six family suites with ocean views and six mountain bungalows. (The deluxe bungalows have the best views.) The units are constructed with traditional materials, including plaited *pandanus*, bamboo walls and *tapa* cloth, and are festooned with intricate woodcarving. They are also equipped with air conditioning, TV and video, telephone, minibar and safe. The restaurant and bar have an incredible view while the outdoor terrace is wonderful for breakfast and lunch or for dinner beneath the stars. Internet and e-mail service is available at the bar. Activities and day trips of all sorts are offered by local guides—just ask the receptionist. The hotel is located 20 minutes by four-wheel drive from the airport and ten minutes from the village of Atuona. ~ Atuona; 92-75-87, fax 92-75-95; www.pearl resorts.com, e-mail hiva.oa.pearl@mail.pf. DELUXE.

The post office in Atuona on Hiva Oa has a computer where you can check e-mail and browse the web. You will need to buy a 1500 CFP phone card.

Pension Moehau is a big white house with a veranda, located at the entrance of the village of Atuona. It offers four rooms with two single beds, and four rooms with a double bed in each. All rooms are air conditioned and have private baths, televisions and in-house video channel. The bar, kitchen and dining room are communal. The view from the veranda is of Traitors Bay and Hanakee Rock. Gigi, the easygoing owner, is originally from the Tuamotu Islands and is married to a Marquesan. Credit cards are accepted, and kids under 12 are half price. ~ Atuona; 92-72-69, fax 92-77-62; e-mail moehaurelais@mail.pf. BUDGET.

In Puamau, **Chez Marie-Antoinette** is a house with two rooms, each with a double bed. There's electricity, a common bathroom and kitchen. The advantage of staying at Chez Marie-Antoinette is its proximity to the *tiki*, which are within easy walking distance. Meals are available and there is beach access. On the downside, the pension is extremely isolated, especially if you need to get to

Atuona. Transfers from the airport to the pension are a stiff 20,000 CFP. ~ Puamau; 92-72-27. BUDGET TO MODERATE.

DINING

Restaurant Hoa Nui (which means "big friend") blends Chinese and Marquesan cuisines. It is clearly the best eatery in town. Their specialty is freshwater shrimp, which is very good, as is the deep-fried breadfruit. You might also want to sample curried goat and chicken in taro. ~ Atuona; 92-73-63. BUDGET TO MODERATE.

The restaurant at the **Hanakee Pearl Lodge** offers French cuisine along with Polynesian favorites. The specialty of the chef is fresh fish and seafood, which of course is caught locally. The menu is presented on gorgeous carved wooden panels and the beverage list on similarly carved paddles. The restaurant is fabricated entirely with native hardwoods and features a marvelously ornate roof construction. On the terrace you can enjoy happy hour in a spectacular setting while listening to the music of Jacques Brel. Very romantic indeed. ~ Atuona; 92-75-87. MODERATE TO DELUXE.

At the hotel **Temetiu Village** you will find a seafood restaurant that specializes in lobster and shrimp. ~ Atuona; 92-73-02. MODERATE.

Several snack shops dot the town of Atuona. **Snack Kaupe** is located across the street from the post office and has basic local fare. **Snack MakeMake** specializes in Chinese food. Here you'll find both good quality and generous portions. Open for breakfast and lunch. ~ 92-74-26. BUDGET. **Snack Maire** serves Marquesan and Chinese dishes. It's located outside of Atuona, between Atuona and Taaoa. BUDGET.

Good meals are also available at **Chez Marie-Antoinette** ~ Puamau; 92-72-27, and **Pension Moehau** ~ Atuona; 92-72-69. Both BUDGET.

GROCERIES

There are several markets in Atuona where groceries and other necessities can be purchased. These include **Magasin Mowsang** ~ 92-73-49, **Magasin Naiki** ~ 92-73-48, **Magasin Chanson** ~ 92-74-65, and **Magasin Gauguin**.

SHOPPING

Those interested in purchasing sculptures or precious woods from Marquesan forests such as *tou*, sandalwood and *mi'o iu* (rosewood) can contact one of the following artisans: **Norbert Huhina** ~ 92-75-54, **Tuarae Gilbert Peterano** ~ 92-70-64 or **Gabriel Bonno** ~ 92-72-55.

For stone carvings, contact **Fernand Tetuaveroa** ~ 92-74-07 and **Otomimi Jean Marie** ~ 92-76-55.

Gauguin T-shirts are available at several of the shops on Atuona's main street. Next door to the museum is a **handicrafts shop** with fine wood carvings and reproductions of various Marquesan artifacts. There is also a **handicrafts center** located in the old marketplace, south of the museum. On display and for sale are hand-painted T-shirts, bags, sheets, bedcovers, *tapa*, jewelry made of local materials, and pareu. It's a terrific place to shop and is open only in the morning.

The **Gauguin Museum** has some great postcards. ~ Atuona.

BEACHES   **PUAMAU BEACH** 🏊 Just east of Puamau village is a long white-sand beach with shade trees that fringes the shores of Puamau Bay. The backdrop is the gently sloping hillside that frames a wide, expansive valley. Swimming here is terrific, but near the church is best. There is no undertow and you can bodysurf when the conditions are right. However, the pounding waves can be very strong so use caution. Fresh water is available and you can buy provisions in the nearby village, a 15-minute walk away. ~ The beach is located just off the road between the dock and Puamau village.

▼▼▼▼▼▼▼▼▼▼▼▼▼▼▼
Outdoor Adventures

As in all of the islands in the Marquesas Group, fishing is quite good. A variety of pelagic fish such as tuna and mahimahi can be snagged.

FISHING   Those interested should call **Leo Rohi** ~ Atuona, 92-76-57; **Mederic Kaimuko** ~ Atuona, 92-74-48; or **Gaby Heitaa** ~ 91-70-60.

HIKING   For a short excursion, take the **Old Atuona Cemetery and beyond** (1.5 miles/2 kilometers) hike. It is an older graveyard than the Calvary Cemetery where Gauguin is buried and is located on the west end of the village. There's a wonderful view of the village below and the rugged coastline. If you continue walking for several more minutes you'll reach an ancient *paepae* (stone platform). ~ To get there walk to the bridge past the public school at the end of Atuona and take the road to the right. After about a ten-minute walk take the road to the left—there's no sign pointing to the cemetery—for another 30 minutes, until you reach the site.

It is possible to visit the various archaeological sites around the island by foot on the **Atuona to Hanapaaoa** (10 miles/16 kilometers) trek. Some locations require guides and some don't. The trek from Atuona to Hanapaaoa through the center of the island is of medium difficulty, but I highly recommend that you take a guide. The length of the trek is about four hours (one way). ~ The trailhead is on the outskirts of Atuona, but it is best to ask a local for directions.

It's possible to see the archaeological sites near Taaoa on the **Taaoa Archaeological Sites** (1 mile/1.6 kilometers) hike. Taaoa is about five kilometers southeast of Atuona. However, in order to get there from Atuona, you must catch a ride about ten kilometers west, along the coastal road to the phone booth near Taaoa, which marks the beginning of the trailhead. The trail leads inland up the hill. After about one and a half kilometers you'll start seeing *tohua* and other ancient remains.

You can visit the **Tehueto Petroglyphs** (2 miles/3.2 kilometers one way) in the Tahauku Valley with relative ease. It's about a 40-minute walk. Take the airport road 50 yards (45 meters) to the left and look for the sign to the petroglyph site. Follow the road and after 20 minutes take the intersecting road to the left. Five minutes later you will cross an ankle-deep river. Continue to follow the road up the hill. You'll soon reach a small clearing, at which point you need to follow the small trail straight ahead and downhill until you reach the petroglyph. Here you'll find a series of double-outlined stick figures on a massive boulder. Backtrack to the clearing and continue on the trail to the right, uphill for another five minutes, traversing a banana and papaya plantation. Continue up the hill a bit more and look for a *tohua*. It has a paved dancefloor, and on the rear wall you'll see two *tiki* heads. This is a gorgeous spot that is worth spending some time in. ~ The trailhead begins near Snack Tahauku in Tahauku, near the intersection of the airport and dock roads. (Ask at the eatery for directions to the trailhead.)

The Marquesas kingfisher, found only on Hiva Oa, is in imminent danger of extinction.

Puamau Hike (1.5 miles/2 km). The *tiki* in Puamau are along a sweaty 40-minute trek that begins at the Puamau dock. From the waterfront take the road to the church, turn left after the soccer field and continue uphill. When you reach the paved portion of the road continue for 50 meters and take the right fork. Another five-minute walk and you'll see the *me'ae I'ipona* to your left-hand side. This is one of the greatest archaeological treasures in the Marquesas Islands. One of the tallest *tiki* of French Polynesia stands here, as does a temple with an ambience right out of an Indiana Jones flick. Surrounded by lush rainforest and drooping vines, it is a peaceful place, yet charged with what some of the Polynesians call *mana*, which roughly translates as "power."

On the way down the trail, turn left when the paved portion of the road begins. Note that the buildings in the left-hand corner belong to the mayor of the village, Vohi Heitaa. His structures are built on the dancefloor of an ancient *tohua*, a ceremonial place. There are some old graves on his property and on one of the *paepae* (old home foundations) is the burial site of the last ruler of the valley, Te Hu Moena. When she died in 1916, she was buried with her two bicycles, gifts of a French admiral. Next to her resting place is a small grave made of red stones and decorated with two small *tiki*. Vohi Heitaa claims this is the grave of Te Hau Moena, her father. However, there is still a controversy about who lies in which grave. After your hike is completed be sure and take a swim at Puma's golden-sand beach. (I can assure you, you'll need it.) There's great body surfing with no *nono* and no undertow. (There is an entrance fee to see the tiki at the *me'ae*.)

Local guides available for four-wheel-drive and walking tours include **Andre Tessier** of Pension Gauguin ~ 92-73-51, **Gaby Heitaa** ~ 92-73-02 and **Marie-Therese Deligny** ~ 92-71-59.

BOAT TOURS

Leo Rohi has island tours as well as interisland transfers. ~ Atuona; 92-76-57. Other boat tours in Atuona and transfers are available from **Gaby Heitaa** ~ 91-70-60 or **Mederic Kaimuko** ~ 92-74-48.

▼ ▼ ▼ ▼ ▼ ▼ ▼ ▼ ▼ ▼

Tahuata

Only 21 square miles (55 square kilometers) in area, Tahuata is positioned south of the Bordelais Canal, opposite Hiva Oa. The 550 people on the island live in the village of Vaitahu or in smaller villages scattered over the island. Like all the Marquesas, Tahuata is a craggy, precipitous volcanic island. The highest point on the island is the summit of Tumu Maea Ufu, at 1548 feet (472 meters). The inland valleys are covered with scrub and grassy vegetation. A number of beaches dot the perimeter of the island. Many look appealing, but are usually infested with *nono*.

SIGHTS

Tahuata is popular mainly with visiting yachts. (Boats provide the sole source of transportation to the island.) There are no true roads on Tahuata, making getting around problematic.

The main village is **Vaitahu**, which is backdropped by a massive, verdant cliff. A church, museum, post office, store and handful of wooden dwellings are all that make up the village. On the south side of Vaitahu beach is a small hill where a French fort was once located. On the north side of the valley is a sheer wall. A small river bisects the village.

Several locals provide horseback riding tours to the Hanatu'una Valley and to other archaeological sites around Tahuata. Contact Tahuata City Hall for information. ~ 92-92-19.

The **Catholic church** in Vaitahu is a relatively new affair, built in 1988 with funds from the Vatican. Made of round stones, it incorporates gracious carvings and an impressive stained-glass window depicting a brown-skinned Marquesan Madonna into its framework. Set against the rich green hillsides and towering peaks, this spectacular edifice is an aesthetic treat.

The tiny **Vaitahu Museum** next to the town hall is also of interest. It contains a great deal of information about a local archaeological site excavated in Hanamiai by professor Barry Rollet of the University of Hawaii. Rollet set up the first archaeological exhibit with Marquesan titles in the office of the mayor. There is a good illustration, accompanied by photos, of the layers of excavations showing the history of the island with artifacts such as shellfish hooks, soil samples and pork bones.

Open Monday through Thursday 8 a.m. to 4 p.m., Friday until 3 p.m. ~ 92-92-19.

Nicolas Barsinas can take you four-wheel driving. He doesn't have a phone so ask around to find him.

Vaitahu is the site of Spanish explorer Alvaro de Mendaña's only actual landing in the Marquesas. It was here that he came ashore, said Mass, raised crosses, planted a garden and allowed his soldiers to kill over 200 Marquesans. When Cook called at Vaitahu, nearly two centuries later, another Marquesan was killed. The village was also the site of much European-caused violence in the early 1800s. Home to many deserters, Vaitahu was frequently visited by Westerners who took advantage of Marquesan hospitality.

Monuments marking the fighting between the French and Marquesans are still visible in Vaihatu. They consist of the **ruins of the fort** on the hill overlooking the beach, and the **graves** of Frigate Captain Halley and Lieutenant Ladebat, who were killed when the Marquesans ambushed a French column moving up the valley at the start of the French-Marquesan war of 1842. ~ To see the ruins of the fort and a marvelous view as well, hike up the hill behind the cemetery, which takes about 20 minutes. To find the two graves, hike up the main valley road about one kilometer and look for an inconspicuous concrete terrace on the slope. This is the grave site. It was near here where Halley and Ladebat were ambushed.

There are **petroglyphs** in the Hanatu'una Valley. The *Tamanu*, a boat that sails from Vaitahu, can take you there. Or you can reach them on horseback from Hapatoni.

Hapatoni is a picturesque and friendly village by the sea, and is only 15 minutes by boat from Vaitahu. The seafront road in Hapatoni is made almost entirely from ancient paved stones. The road is shaded by *temanu* trees, which are often used in woodcarving.

LODGING

Pension Amatea offers five simple rooms with double beds. Bathroom facilities are shared, and there is a lounge and deck. Breakfast is included, as are roundtrip transfers. ~ Vaitahu; 92-92-84. BUDGET.

SHOPPING

One of the best bone carvers in the Marquesas Islands is **Teiki Barsinas**. His pendants, *tiki*, ear ornaments and other items are all made of bone and are beautifully decorated. Like the bamboo flutes of the Chervil's in Ua Pou, these items are museum pieces in there own right. ~ Vaitahu; 92-93-24.

Felix and Edwin Fii are also excellent carvers. However, their specialty is tattooing. The two brothers create new designs in a traditional manner and tattoo original motifs as well. They take great care of hygiene, wearing gloves and using new needles for each client. ~ Vaitahu; 92-93-04, 92-92-14.

There is a **handicrafts center** with first-rate woodcarvings in Hapatoni. It's open intermittently and the best thing to do is call Liliane Teikipupuni Hapatoni if you are looking to buy something. ~ Vaitahu; 92-92-46.

Another popular product of this island is scented **monoi oil**, which can be purchased from a dozen different women in Vaitahu and Hapatoni. Just ask around. For more information on this indigenous moisturizer, see page 71 in Chapter Two.

BEACHES   **TAHUATA BEACHES** ⬤ The north side of the island has several white-sand beaches. All have shade trees, but *nonos* may be a problem; bring *monoi* or repellent. Swimming is quite good from the reports I've had. ~ Because the beaches are so remote, they necessitate hiring a boat.

Outdoor Adventures

There aren't any organized outdoor adventures on the island, which is part of its appeal. Fishing trips and interisland transfers are possible on **Te Pua O Mioi**, a 42-foot fiberglass fishing boat. ~ Vaitahu; 92-92-19, fax 92-92-10. **Louis Timau** also does fishing charters. ~ 92-90-61.

FISHING

Fatu Hiva

Fatu Hiva, the most remote—and, many say, the most beautiful—island of the inhabited Marquesas Group, and only 80 square miles (130 square kilometers) in size, was the first island in the Marquesas to be discovered by Europeans. In July 1595, the Spanish, led by Don Alvaro Mendaña, wasted no time in showing their true colors. Apparently the Marquesans had come aboard the Spaniard's galleon and, perhaps, became too bold for the Europeans' sensibilities. The Marquesans were warned off by a few shots. They fled, but returned a barrage of rocks. The Spanish then opened fire on the canoes, killing several people, including a chief.

In the mid-19th century, Fatu Hiva was popular with whalers, despite the lack of good anchorages. This was most likely because it was well away from the authorities' eyes, and the seamen could raise Cain without paying a penalty.

Fatu Hiva was once famous for its talented tattoo artists. During the pre-contact days, an islander's body might have been completely covered by tattoos by the time he died. Of course, the artwork went to the grave with the body. (The only remnants of these artworks are now displayed in books or in museum archives.) Today, Marquesan tattooing is enjoying a renaissance and is exceedingly popular with most Marquesan men and, to a lesser extent, Marquesan women.

The island, also known as Fatu Iva, shares similar physical characteristics with the rest of the Marquesas Group. It is high, sheer, very rocky and carpeted with lush vegetation. Part of the island is the remnant of a volcanic rim. The highest point is Mt. Touaouoho, at 3149 feet (960 meters).

Today, Fatu Hiva is the only island in the Marquesas where *tapa* cloth, produced from the bark of mulberry, breadfruit or *hiapo* banyan trees, is made. Local artisans also carve wooden *tiki* and manufacture a local style of *monoi*, a perfumed coconut oil with fragrances derived from *tiare* blossoms and sandalwood. (The Marquesan word for coconut oil is *pani*.) The fragrant oil is used as a perfume for massages, to ward off mosquitoes or to attract a lover. *Pani* is a reasonable anti-*nono* protection (you drown them in it instead of killing them with poison), but it does not really stop the pests. You may also see local women wearing *umuhei*, a fragrant blend of herbs and flowers contained in a small packet suspended around the neck like a pendant—or, more commonly, in the hair.

There are two principal valleys—**Hanavave** and **Omoa**—on the western coast of Fatu Hiva, each with several **archaeological sites**.

SIGHTS

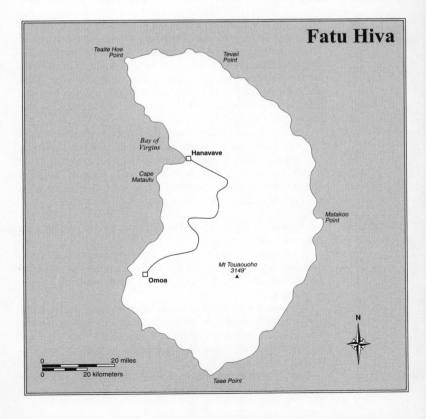

According to Marquesan legend, the cliffs of Hanavave are the remnants of a giant eel that came from Nuku Hiva. It visited the island at the request of a Fatu Hiva eel.

The stone structures in Fatu Hiva are not as large, nor are the complexes as extensive as those seen in Hiva Oa or in the northern group. There are still many sites to visit, however, and some interesting **petroglyphs** in Omoa feature huge fish and stick figures. It's possible to walk to these sites, but it's best to ask a local for directions and receive permission from the landowners.

One of the finest woodcarving collections in the Marquesas belonged to William Grelet who resided in a colonial-style home surrounded by a huge garden. His father, a Swiss-born businessman, migrated and built the home in the late 1800s. William, who died in early 1960s, settled in the village of Omoa and became its chief. Over the years, the family amassed a great collection of artifacts and furniture made of *tou*, one of the local hardwoods. Tutana, William's adopted Marquesan daughter, inherited the home and the collection that went along with it. (Some of Grelet's masterpieces are exhibited in the national museum in Papeete.) There is no shortage of wonderful museum-quality work on display in Omoa. These include giant *kokoa* (round wooden bowls for breadfruit dishes), war clubs, spears, and also stone adzes and *penu* (pounders). The **Grelet house** (admission) can be found behind the Catholic church in Omoa. Ask for Sarah Vaki to give you a tour. ~ 92-80-06.

Thor Heyerdahl (of *Kon Tiki* fame) spent most of 1936 on Fatu Hiva with his first wife and wrote a largely fictional book, *Fatu Hiva*, about his time there.

Another island locale to see is the **Bay of Virgins**, formed by two walls, one from the north and the other from the south, that nearly meet at the entrance of the bay. They form a gateway that towers over the bay with massive stone spires. While on Fatu Hiva keep an eye out for the beautiful aquamarine lorikeet, which is making a comeback after near extinction.

LODGING

Nearly every lodging on Fatu Hiva is spartan—don't expect a lot of creature comforts.

A four-person bungalow with a kitchenette and private bathroom is what you'll find at **Chez Lionel Cantois**. The owner of the property also hires himself and his Land Rover out for tours. ~ Omoa; 92-81-84. BUDGET.

The two rooms at **Chez Cecile Gilmore** have double beds; there's a common bath. At least one traveler I spoke to had a less than sanguine experience with Cecile so it might be best to look elsewhere. Roundtrip transfers are available from the dock. ~ Omoa; 92-80-54. BUDGET.

Chez Norma Ropati features a two-bedroom house; each room comes with a double bed. There's also a kitchen and communal bath. Norma's home is surrounded by a well-tended flower garden. *Pension complete* is offered. Roundtrip transfers are available from the dock. ~ Omoa; 92-80-13. BUDGET TO MODERATE.

Hanavave is beautiful, but overnight stays and/or shopping are not a good idea here. There are no pensions, but if you need a room, try contacting **Agnes Kamia** ~ 92-81-35 or the **Tevenino family** ~ 92-81-03.

In Omoa, **Restaurant Ropati** serves breakfast, lunch and dinner. **DINING**
The modest restaurant offers up seafood, when it is available, as well as chicken and pork dishes. ~ Omoa; 92-80-13. BUDGET.

Chez Mme. Bernadette Cantois has a snack bar that offers beef, chicken and seafood cuisine. ~ Omoa; 92-80-80. BUDGET.

There are several minuscule markets in Omoa and Hanavave that **GROCERIES**
sell the bare essentials.

The unique item indigenous to Fatu Hiva is *tapa* cloth, and Fatu **SHOPPING**
Hiva is one of the few places in French Polynesia where *tapa* cloth is still manufactured. Prices range from 500 to 5000 CFP depending on the size. The fabric is generally sold by individuals rather than purchased in stores, so ask around if you care to bring some home. This is also an excellent place to purchase stone and wood *tikis*. When the *Aranui* is in town, all the Omoa Village women display their handicrafts at the *fare artisanal* next to the town hall. The same sequence of events occurs when the vessel visits Hanavave. The handicrafts center is located right on the beach.

The beach situation in Fatu Hiva is pretty dismal. In Hanavave or **BEACHES**
Omoa you can swim from rocks along the shore. But always keep an eye out for sharks.

Omoa to Hanavave (10 miles/16 kilometers). ▼▼▼▼▼▼▼▼▼▼▼▼
Omoa Village is the starting point for a **Outdoor Adventures**
wonderful trek to Hanavave Village. This serpentine hike offers dizzying views and a majestic waterfall visi- **HIKING**
ble from the path deep inside Vaie'enui Valley. Take water and give yourself four or more hours for the journey. Better yet, plan a couple of days if you go into the valley. As you climb out of Hanavave, note the stone *tiki*-like formations and the intriguing "hole" in the top of the bluffs.

If you plan to spend time on Fatu Hiva you can go horseback **TOURS**
riding, hunt wild pig and visit the archaeological sites in Omoa and Hanavave. ~ Contact the Mairie (Town Hall) for information.

Horses are available in Omoa for tours around the island. For more information, contact **Roberto Maraetaata** ~ 92-80-23 or **Mr. Isidore Mose** ~ 92-80-28.

Motorized outrigger tours are available in Omoa from **Xavier Gilmore.** ~ 92-80-54.

There are several four-wheel-drive tour operators in Omoa: **Joseph Tetuanui** ~ 92-80-09, **Henri Tuieinui** ~ 92-80-23, **Didier Gilmore** ~92-80-86, **Roberto Maraetaata** ~ 92-80-23 or **Xavier Gilmore** ~ 92-80-54.

Transportation

Always reconfirm your tickets prior to the plane's departure. Bumping of (foreign) passengers is all too common in the Marquesas.

AIR

NUKU HIVA   Air Tahiti has a regularly scheduled service seven days a week from Papeete to Nuku Hiva, five days a week to Hiva Oa and once a week to Ua Pou. Flying time between Papeete and Nuku Hiva is about three and a half hours. From Nuku Hiva, which essentially is the hub for the other islands in the archipelago, there are flights to Hiva Oa, Ua Huka and Ua Pou. There are also direct flights from Tahiti to Hiva Oa and Ua Pou. Flights are also possible from Nuku Hiva to Rangiroa. ~ Taioha'e; 92-03-41.

UA HUKA   Air Tahiti connects Ua Huka from Nuku Hiva once a week. ~ Vaipae'e; 92-60-85.

UA POU   Air Tahiti has service from Nuku Hiva three times a week. ~ Hakahau; 92-53-41.

HIVA OA   Air Tahiti has regularly scheduled service six times a week to Hiva Oa from Papeete. Flying time between Papeete and Hiva Oa is about three and a half hours. ~ Atuona; 92-73-41.

SEA

Two boats make regular trips through the Marquesas. The cargo ship *Taporo VI* makes a trip every 15 days. The ship can handle a maximum of 12 deck passengers, and the roundtrip lasts 13 days. Meals are available. The route followed is: Papeete–Takapoto–

HEAL THYSELF

Traditionally Polynesia's main agricultural product has been copra. However, since 1996, the *noni,* a local fruit used as a medicine, has been finding favor in the United States. A Utah-based company exports ripe *noni* from the Marquesas Islands as well as other regions of French Polynesia and markets products based on the juice. The entire plant is used to combat a variety of ailments such as rashes, insect bites and even herpes. Advocates (including some scientists) claim that the plant supports the immune system, assists hormones that coordinate bodily functions and helps cells absorb nutrients.

Fatu Hiva–Tahuata–Hiva Oa–Oa Huka–Nuku Hiva–Ua Pou–Papeete. Contact **Morton Garbutt**. ~ Motu Uta, Papeete; 42-63-93, 43-79-72, fax 42-06-17; e-mail taporo@mail.pf.

A much more comfortable—and more expensive—option is a trip aboard the *Aranui III*. This working cargo/copra freighter has been specially outfitted to accommodate tourists on its 15-day swings through the Marquesas. The ship, which made its first voyage in summer 2002, replaces the beloved and storied *Aranui II* (now cruising the coast of Africa). The custom-built *Aranui III* features a 100-seat dining room, a business and conference center, a swimming pool, two bars, a fitness room and a video room with television and VCR. There is also a boutique and washing machines and dryers aboard, and an activities desk arranges fishing, snorkeling and diving from the ship. Four classes of accommodations are available: ten suites with balconies, five deluxe cabins, 63 regular cabins and 22 dormitory beds. Prices range from US$4000 for a suite to half that for a dorm bed. A bonus is that the ship stops at Rangiroa on the way back to Papeete, making it a good way to hop over to the Tuamotu Group. ~ Motu Uta, Papeete; 42-62-40, 43-76-60, fax 43-48-89; www.aranui.com, e-mail aranui@mail.pf.

The *Tahiti Nui* also travels on an irregular schedule between the islands. Contact **Leonard Puputouki**. ~ Motu Uta, Papeete; 50-66-71, fax 43-32-70.

NUKA HIVA **Xavier Curvat** of the Diving Center provides scheduled transportation between Nuku Hiva and Ua Pou on weekends. ~ Taioha'e; 92-00-88. Other boats that may be available for day trips or interisland charter include: *Nils I*, a 26-foot fiberglass motorboat ~ 92-08-32; *Ati Toka*, 26-foot polyester hull boat ~ 92-01-51; and *Prisca*, a 30-foot Bertram skippered by **Joseph Kavee** ~ 92-03-55.

UA HUKA Boats (with captains) are available for interisland transportation to Ua Huka. The voyage to Ua Huka takes two and a half hours from Ua Pou. In Vaipae'e, contact **Alexis Fournier** ~ 92-60-05, **Nestor Ohu** ~ 92-60-18 or **Vanance Ah-Scha** ~ 92-61-54. In Hane, try **Rataro Teikiteepupuni**. ~ 92-60-65. In Hokatu there's **Paul Teatiu** ~ 92-60-88, **Paul Teikiteepupuni** ~ 92-60-48 or **Maurice Rootuehine** ~ 92-60-55.

UA POU Several boat operators in Hakatao Village offer interisland transportation. Check with **Antoine Tata** ~ 92-54-87, **Rudla Klima** ~ 92-53-86 or **Francois Keuvahana** ~ 92-53-31. Hakatao's community boat can also be hired for island tours or interisland jaunts at cheaper prices.

HIVA OA For interisland transfers and fishing trips, contact **Andre Tessier** of Pension Gauguin ~ Atuona, 92-73-51; **Rohi** ~

Atuona, 92-76-57; **Mederic Kaimuko** ~ Atuona, 92-74-48; or **Gaby Heitaa** ~ 91-70-60.

Anchorage for yachts is far from ideal on Hiva Oa because the southeast tradewinds cause boats to roll during the April to October tradewind season. Yachts generally moor at nearby Taha-uku Bay, which has a fair yacht anchorage thanks to a recently built breakwater.

TAHUATA Interisland service on a 42-foot fishing boat is available from **Te Pua O Mioi** in Vaitahu. ~ 92-92-19, fax 92-92-10.

FATU HIVA Fatu Hiva is accessible by regular boat service from Hiva Oa. The trip takes about three and a half hours. The boat leaves on Tuesday mornings at around 4 a.m. and is supposed to return from Hiva Oa at 3 p.m. the following day.

Interisland transfers and fishing trips can be arranged on Fatu Hiva. The *Auona II*, a 51-foot catamaran, is available for charter with captain. ~ 92-80-23, fax 92-80-39. **Roberto Maraetaata** (92-80-23) and **Xavier Gilmore** (92-80-54) are also for hire along with their boats.

CAR RENTALS & TAXIS

Unless otherwise indicated, the only way to hire a car or truck on these islands is with a driver.

NUKA HIVA The main issue for non-French speakers in Nuka Hiva is that the drivers do not speak fluent English. **Jean-Pierre**, who can be hired through Rose Corser, speaks a smattering of English. ~ Taioha'e; 92-03-82.

Other possibilities include **Teiki Transports** ~ 92-03-47, **Nuku Hiva Transports** ~ 92-06-80, **Kimitete** ~ 92-05-22, **Rose-Marie** ~ 92-05-96, **Huki Tours** ~ 92-04-89 or **Heiatea Tours** ~ 92-08-22.

◆◆

THE NONO—SCOURGE OF THE MARQUESAS

The visitor's true initiation to the Marquesas is marked by the first brush with the *nono*. These nearly invisible creatures inhabit the seashore, valleys, streams and humid low-lying areas. Resembling a gnat, they are silent and insidious, attacking without the warning buzz of a mosquito. The tiny *nono* draws blood with the aid of an anticoagulant—the result being a red welt, localized swelling and acute itching. Scratching often introduces a staph infection. Welts typically take 12 to 24 hours to develop. To combat itching, apply lime or lemon juice to the bite. There are two species of *nono*: the black variety found only in Nuku Hiva and the white *nono*, found primarily on beaches throughout the Marquesas Islands. There are a few ways to deal with this minuscule pest—long sleeves and pants and/or copious amounts of *monoi* oil and insect repellent.

All of the guides will take visitors to the airport. Standard airport fare is 3500 CFP per person and it's a two-hour drive under optimal conditions.

Cars can be rented without drivers at the **Hotel Moana Nui Taioha'e.** ~ 92-03-30, fax 92-00-02. **Tapuama Location** also has vehicles. ~ Taioha'e; phone/fax 92-03-24.

UA HUKA Car (or truck) and driver in Vaipae'e can be hired from: **Hubert Fournier** ~ 92-61-24, **Alexis Scallamara** ~ 92-60-19, **Michael Teatiu** ~ 92-60-11 and **Isabelle Ohu** ~ 92-60-18. In Hane, try **Denis Fournier.** ~ 92-60-62. In Hokatu, there's **Paul Teatiu** ~ 92-60-88 or **Paul Teikiteepupuni** ~ 92-60-48.

UA POU Four-wheel-drive vehicles with a driver are available in Hakahau from **Jules Hituputoka** ~ 92-53-33, **Patricia Keavahana** ~ 92-51-49, **Helene Kautai** ~ 92-50-83, **Piri Kohumoetini** ~ 92-51-47, **Rudla Klima** ~ 92-53-86 or **Isidore Kohumoetini** ~ 92-50-16.

HIVA OA As far as I know, Hiva Oa and Nuku Hiva are the only islands in the Marquesas where it's possible to rent an automobile without the obligatory chauffeur, and make your own way around. (Drivers *are* available if you want one.)

David's Rent-a-Car is located several hundred yards beyond the cluster of buildings that include the Atuona post office. There are cars and two four-wheel-drive vehicles available for hire. ~ Atuona; 92-72-87. **Atuona Rentals** also has vehicles. ~ 92-76-07.

TAHUATA Vehicles with drivers can be rented in Vaitahu from **Marguerite Kokauani.** ~ 92-92-84. The **Tahuata City Hall** can also arrange transportation. ~ 92-92-19, fax 92-92-10.

HITCHING

Hitching in the Marquesas can be problematic. Many Marquesans derive their income by hiring themselves out as taxi drivers for tourists, making them reluctant to provide free transportation, especially if they have paying passengers onboard.

Also note: Women should never hitchhike without a male escort. Because of cultural differences, it will be misunderstood by the male Marquesan.

For the budget-minded, hitchhiking in Hiva Oa is an option, especially between Atuona and Taaoa because of the comparatively large amount of traffic between the two villages. However, hitching anywhere else on the island can be difficult.

TWELVE

The Austral Islands

Located about 372 miles (600 kilometers) south of Tahiti, the Austral Islands make up the southernmost chain of French Polynesia. Spanning a distance of 831 miles (1330 kilometers), the Australs are geologically part of the Austral Seamount Chain, which ranges from the Cook Islands in the northwest to the Australs in the southeast.

The Australs are made up of the uninhabited coral atoll Ile Maria (or Hull Island) and five high volcanic islands—Rimatara, Rurutu, Tubuai, Raivavae and Rapa. The elevations of the high volcanic islands escalate from northwest to southeast, culminating in the sharp peaks of Rapa. Not surprisingly, there are islands in both the Austral and Cook Island groups that share physical similarities. For example, both Tubuai in the Australs and Rarotonga in the Cooks have a fringing white-sand beach (an unusual feature for high islands in the other archipelagos of French Polynesia). Likewise, Mangaia in the Cooks and Rurutu and Rimatara in the Australs are all extremely rugged upthrust islands with limestone topography.

The climate in the Australs is decidedly more temperate and less rainy than Tahiti and the other islands of the Society and Tuamotu groups. The temperature is warm—the low average can dip to 64 degrees Fahrenheit (18 degrees Celsius)—and the seasons are well defined. The islands lie at the southern boundary of the southeast trade winds, which blow from November to March. In the cold season, from May to September, the winds are more variable and generally westerly, especially in Rapa. The Austral Islands represent the agricultural heart of French Polynesia. Typical "European" vegetables such as potatoes, carrots, onions and cabbage grow very well in its comparatively temperate climate. In addition to their agricultural produce, the Australs are famous for weaving *aeho* (the Austral reed) and *tifaifai* (patchwork) crafts, which have been passed down from generation to generation. Sumptuous, handwoven women's hats are a Sunday attraction at church services. *Tifaifai*, the very English tradition of making beautiful bedspreads, was originally brought to the Australs by 19th-century missionary wives who taught local women patchwork sewing skills. Today *tifaifai* bedspreads are a "traditional" wedding present in the Austral Islands. Most of them feature handsewn Polynesian motifs such as breadfruit, *tiare* flowers, fish and landscapes.

Rurutu has the only modern hotel in the entire region, but a number of pensions and small lodgings have opened up on Tubuai, as well as on the far-flung islands of Rapa, Rimatara and Raivavae. These obscure islands are now more easily accessible as well; Air Tahiti constructed an airstrip and began regularly scheduled service to Raivavae in June 2002.

Tubuai

At the core of the Austral Group is the high island of Tubuai, straddling the Tropic of Capricorn. It is composed of two submerged inactive volcanic mountains that create a landmass of 19 square miles (48 square kilometers). The largest of the Austral Islands, Tubuai is about three and a half miles (five and a half kilometers) wide and five and a half miles (nine kilometers) long. Most of the population of approximately 1400 live in the two major villages of Mataura and Taahueia, both of which are located on the north coast.

Getting around the island is easy. One road circles Tubuai and another bisects it. In some sections, the road is paved, but for the most part it is gravel or sand. Over the last two decades the roads have become filled with cars, trucks and motorcycles. It seems nowadays only children and visitors ride bicycles.

Physically, Tubuai is composed of three major features: two distinct clusters of mountains, their valleys and a littoral, or broad swath of land, which runs entirely around the island. The two groups of mountains, of which Taitaa (1308 feet/399 meters) and Tonorutu (1023 feet/312 meters) are the tallest, are joined by a low, broad plain. The high bluffs and broken terrain give way to the softer contours of hillocks, which are covered with tough grass and fern known as *anuhe*. The littoral is sandy, flat and sometimes swampy.

Tubuai is surrounded by a barrier reef and seven *motu*, some of which have excellent white-sand beaches. In addition to several shallow passes where small boats may enter or exit the lagoon, there are three main passes on the reef.

As in all the Australs, the weather on Tubuai is cool and mild compared to the Society Islands to the north. Tubuai lies near the limit of the Southeast trade winds and on occasion is hit by cyclones. The island was severely pummeled by Cyclone William in 1995, with damage estimated at US$1.5 million. To date, rebuilding is still going on.

If you're curious about local archaeology be sure and visit Larry Miller, the owner of the Sunset gas station in Mataura (95-05-42). This Canadian, a long-time resident of Tubuai, is a passionate amateur archaeologist who can discuss the numerous excavations in the area. Chief among these is the extensive project undertaken by Mark Eddowes of Tahiti's archaeological department. Eddowes actively excavated what has been called the Atiahara Site, located in the Mataura area, which was discovered in 1995 when house construction revealed buried deposits rich in archaeological material. Eddowes worked with local youths and discovered a treasure trove of artifacts—notably items made from pearl shell (such as fishhooks), coconut-shell scrapers and ornaments. The site attests to early human occupation of the Austral Islands.

In a scholarly paper, Dr. Patricia Vargas Casanova of the University of Chile stated that the artifacts found in the Atiahara area were directly comparable with others found in what are termed "early settlement sites" in other parts of French Polynesia including the Society, Gambier and Marquesas islands. The site has provided invaluable information about the evolution of a prehistoric fishing economy from first Polynesian occupation at around A.D. 700 up until the arrival of Fletcher Christian and the famous *Bounty* mutineers in 1789. Artifacts recovered at the site suggest that early interisland contact and exchange was conducted between Tubuai and Rurutu, Rimatara or the southern Cook Islands of Atiu or Mitiaro.

According to Dr. Vargas, the site at Atiahara reinforces the theory that Tubuai is an extension to the east of what are now called the Cook Islands. It stands in the logical trajectory of voyaging colonists coming from the west through the northern and southern Cook Island chain and then up into the Society, Tuamotu, Gambier and Marquesas islands. Atiahara provides an important link in the stages of Polynesian occupation of this part of Oceania in the early centuries.

The first written records pertaining to Tubuai were made by Captain James Cook, who sighted the island on August 8, 1777, during his third voyage in the Pacific en route to Tahiti from Tonga. Anchored offshore, Cook attempted to convince the crew of two Tubuain canoes to come aboard while the locals did their best to persuade the English sailor to come ashore. Cook stayed put and the Tubuains did not come aboard the boat. In 1789, Fletcher Christian and 24 crewmen took part in the famous mutiny on the HMS *Bounty* in the waters off Tonga. He then sailed to Tubuai intent on settling on the island that had been sighted but not yet explored by Europeans.

Their initial encounter with the natives was not promising. An offshore skirmish left 12 locals dead; the crew then sailed for Tahiti, where they loaded the vessel with livestock, food and companions. On June 23rd, the *Bounty* returned with their stores, and 28 companions. This time the Tubuain welcoming committee was more congenial. Christian organized trading with the local chiefs and began work on what was to be known as Fort George. Despite the initial warm reception, the presence of the *Bounty* crew exacerbated already existing rivalries between the islanders while at the same time alienating the local priests. These problems, along with dissension among the ranks of the *Bounty* crew, led to the eventual downfall of the settlers. Today, all that remains of Fort George is a rectangular ditch where the walls of the stockade used to be.

A few months after arriving on the island a second skirmish flared up, resulting in the death of 66 Tubuains. Following the battle, the *Bounty* crew took a vote and decided to return to Tahiti. Accompanied by a local chief and two commoners, the crew set sail for Tahiti after staying less than three months on Tubuai. Upon arrival, 16 crew members opted to settle in Tahiti while the rest, led by Fletcher Christian, ended up on Pitcairn Island. In 1842, the island became a French protectorate, and in 1880 was formally annexed by France.

SIGHTS

Currently, Tubuai is the administrative center for the Austral Group. Despite this, it is still a quiet tropical backwater. The two main villages on the island are **Mataura** and **Taahuaia**. There is very little in the way of commercial development. There is, however, extensive agricultural activity. Tubuai is responsible for supplying potatoes, carrots and cabbage for all of French Polynesia. Fishing is also an important activity. Over one half of the fami-

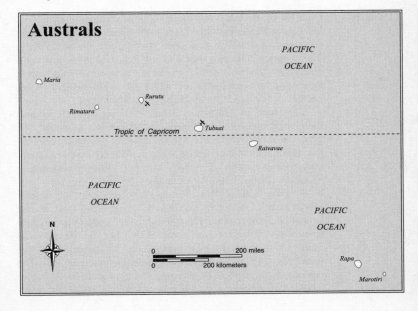

Australs

PACIFIC
OCEAN

Maria

Rurutu
X

Rimatara

Tropic of Capricorn — — — Tubuai

Raivavae

PACIFIC

OCEAN

PACIFIC

OCEAN

N

0   200 miles
0   200 kilometers

Rapa

Marotiri

lies have at least one adult member working for the government in jobs such as administrative positions and schoolteachers.

Tubuains are generally friendly to strangers but not effusive in their reception. Tourists are a rarity and somewhat of a curiosity. Though amiable, locals are relatively shy. It's up to you to make an effort to get acquainted with your hosts. The good news is that Tubuains do not look at visitors in terms of dollar signs. The bad news is that islanders are not anxious to take you on excursions to outlying *motu*, horseback riding or to participate in formal guided tours of the island. What's more, few people speak English. If you really want to get to know the people, and to have them show you around, have patience—plan to stick around for several weeks. Most importantly, take a French class before arriving. To break the ice, contact Melinda Bodin at the **Tubuai Visitor's Bureau.** ~ 98 754 Mataura; phone/fax 95-04-19; e-mail bodinm @mail.pf.

Tubuai is probably best known for the inhabitants' special manner of singing religious hymns, which is purposefully atonal. This haunting style of singing, which sounds strange to Western ears, is a vestige of the pre-contact culture. Interestingly enough, Tubuain singing must also sound strange to Tahitian ears. In a singing competition held in Tahiti a Tubuain choir was nearly disqualified by the judges. The reason? The Papeete judges did not know what to make of their Polynesian brethren's seemingly off-key singing.

LODGING   **Chez Karine & Tale** is run by an American woman married to a local man. The lodging consists of two bungalows with one guest room with a double bed, a salon, kitchen and hot-water bath. The property is located near a nice beach, and meals are available. Chez Karine is one of the better pensions on the island. Bicycles and cars are both available for rent. ~ Mataura; 95-04-76, phone/fax 95-04-52; e-mail charles@mail.pf. BUDGET.

Chez Sam & Yolande is a brightly whitewashed five-unit motel-style structure with shared bathrooms, hot water and TV. Meal plans are available. It's located on a white-sand beach on the seaside, on the outskirts of Mataura. Management can organize lagoon excursions. This pension is well worth considering. ~ Mataura; phone/fax 95-05-52. BUDGET.

Pension Vaitea Nui in Mataura also serves as the island's tourist board. Located in a quiet area off the main road, it consists of two white, rather squat-looking buildings. One structure houses the restaurant and terrace, the other the accommodations. The three rooms, all of which have private baths with hot water, have various configurations of double and twin beds. The restaurant provides all meals, specializing in seafood. Activities include lagoon tours with *motu* picnics, hiking in the hills, four-wheel-drive tours, fishing, scuba diving and horseback riding. Car and bike rentals are available. This pension is located off Tubuai's cross-island road, near the town hall, the post office and the stores. ~ Mataura; phone/fax 93-22-40; e-mail bodinm@mail.pf. BUDGET.

Pension Vaitea Nui in Mataura (95-04-19) and **Chez Sam & Yolande** in Mataura (95-05-52) serve meals only if you order in advance.

DINING

There are several minuscule grocery stores in Mataura where the most basic items, such as canned milk, mosquito coils and bread, may be purchased.

GROCERIES

For those in search of that special handmade souvenir—a woven mat or hat—seek out an individual artisan. Contact Mrs. Moro'ura Tanepau at the Federation Artisanale Tubuai Nui in Mataura, or through your pension.

SHOPPING

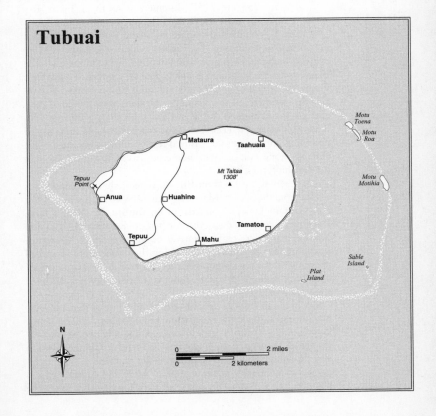

BEACHES   A barrier reef surrounds the island of Tubuai and the entire island is fringed by a white-sand beach. There are also beaches that line the outlying *motu* off the east coast of Tubuai that are accessible by small boats.

The best beaches are located between Mataura and the airport and along the west coast of the island.

Outdoor Adventures

RIDING STABLES

One of the best ways to explore Tubuai is on a horse—available by the hour or day from **Simon Viriamu**. He also organizes day trips and village visits on horseback. Simon's tours are highly recommended. ~ Mataura; 95-03-97.

BIKING   Bicycling is possible on the perimeter road that circles the island. Bikes can be rented in Mataura from **Tino Tahiata** ~ 95-07-54, **Chez Karine & Tale** ~ 95-04-52 and **Pension Vaitea Nui** ~ 95-04-19.

Rurutu

About 355 miles (572 kilometers) south of Tahiti, Rurutu, with a circumference of about 19 miles (30 kilometers), is an upthrust limestone island with steep cliffs that jut vertically into the sea. The highest peak on the island is Manureva, which reaches an elevation of 1263 feet (385 meters). The island is in the process of being pushed upward by geologic forces. What was once the outer lagoon is now a swamp well inside the perimeter of the island. In the same vein, the coral reefs that once surrounded the island are now sharp 300-foot (90-meter) bluffs that overlook the sea. Polynesians call these raised cliffs—or more precisely, raised-reef features—*makatea*. The cliffs are honeycombed with numerous caves. Rurutu is Tahitian for "gushing rock".

Archaeological finds on Rurutu suggest that the island was settled from the Society Islands in about A.D. 1050. It was in 1769 that Captain James Cook arrived on Rurutu. In 1821, a large Rurutuan canoe inadvertently drifted to Raiatea and London Missionary Society representatives provided the travelers return transportation to their island. Seizing the opportunity to spread their gospel, the representatives also sent two Polynesian missionaries back home with the Rurutuans. Christianity was adopted soon afterward.

In 1828, an English visitor to the island reported that a strange malady had ravaged the population, killing about 2500 residents, leaving only 350 inhabitants. It was said that only two people over the age of 25 survived the epidemic. The French established Rurutu as a protectorate in 1889 and annexed it in 1900.

Rurutu's interior is mountainous while the coastal strip is protected by a continuous coral reef that hugs the shoreline. The

The Illari Era

Expatriates have always been attracted to Tubuai. One of the best known was the Frenchman Noel Illari, the former president of the French Polynesian Territorial Assembly. In 1947, Illari sided with the Tahitian leader Pouvanaa and a group of Tahitian veterans protesting the hiring of French civil servants to fill jobs the veterans felt they were entitled to. Illari was sentenced to five months in prison by the French government.

Illari never forgave his homeland. He exiled himself on Tubuai and established the Ermitage St. Helene, named after Napoleon's place of asylum. He spent his time writing antigovernment newspaper articles and helped the local population fight monopolistic business practices of local merchants. In the early 1970s, Illari developed lip cancer and, feeling close to death, constructed his own tomb—a ten-foot-tall granite monument on his front lawn. He died several years *after* the tomb was constructed. The inscription reads:

> *In memory of Noel Illari*
> *Born in Rennese, France 11 September, 1897 died*
> *faithful to his God to family and to*
> *his ideals to his grateful country after long years of*
> *moral suffering within isolation*
> *and solitude at this place. Passersby, think*
> *and pray for him.*

Next to the tomb is a sign that says:

> *Interdite aux Chiens et aux Gaullists*
> *(Dogs and Gaullists forbidden)*

upper reaches of the island are carpeted with grass and fern, with dense vegetation, including hibiscus and casuarina, covering the ravines. The soil is not particularly fertile but islanders are able to grow taro, the preferred staple.

The island has a dry and temperate climate, especially in June, July and August. The outstanding physical features are the massive limestone cliffs and the many caves with grottos, stalactites and stalagmites. (Some of the caves are accessible—with a proper guide. Ask your host to provide a guide. Rurutu does not have a lagoon like the islands of the Society Group. However, the island is known for long, empty stretches of white-sand beach that invite swimming and snorkeling. From July through October, it's possible to see migrating humpback whales. Horseback rides or hikes to inland waterfalls are additional lures.

Rurutu is also known for a custom practiced twice a year (in January and July) called *amoraa ofai*. Young men and women from each village prove themselves with a show of strength. The object is to lift huge volcanic stones on their shoulders. The contest is followed by a traditional feast and dance celebration.

SIGHTS

Most of the island's 2104 inhabitants are clustered in the villages of Moerai, Avera and Hauti. **Moerai**, situated at the shore of a small bay on the northeast coast, is the principal settlement. **Hauti** is south of Moerai and **Avera** lies on the west coast of the island. Moerai and Avera are about five kilometers apart and it's easy to walk from one to the other on a well-trodden path that cuts through the center of the island. It is possible to circumnavigate the island's rutted peripheral road via four-wheel-drive vehicle, though such vehicles are not available to rent.

More than 20 **caves** (including underwater caverns) on Rurutu are accessible to tourists. Some require sophisticated equipment and guides to explore, so it's a good idea to contact someone like Yves Gentilhomme (see "Outdoor Adventures") before starting. Perhaps the best known cave on Rurutu is Ana Aeo or Grotte de Mitterand, which acquired the latter moniker from France's former president François Mitterand, who visited the island in 1990. The cave has served as a shelter for Rurutu residents for centuries and on January 2, 1995, nearly half of the population gathered here to seek refuge from Cyclone William. One of the cave's most striking features is a large chamber with an opening in the ceiling that serves as a marvelous hiding place. Inside, magnificent stalagmites and stalactites rise and hang like giant pillars from a baroque cathedral.

Stop by Moerai's **town hall** for a curious (though hardly unusual) bit of history: One of French Polynesia's most famous statues, the god A'a (according to legend the first colonizer of the island), was obtained by Britain in 1820 and brought to the British

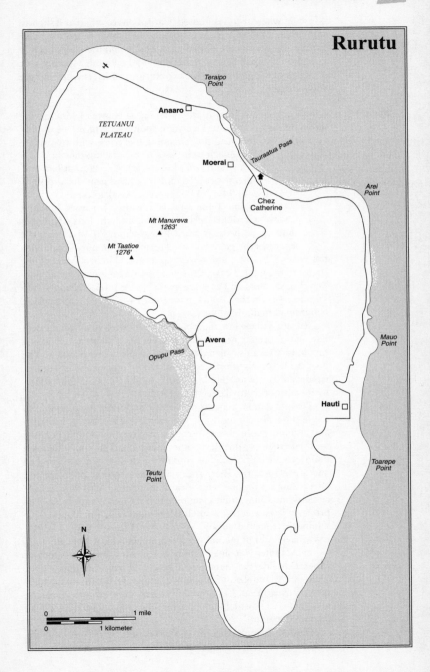

Museum where it still is housed. Carved out of wood and slightly more than a meter high, it is hollow, with room to store smaller statues. Both arms are placed on the belly and the whole body is covered with small figures. In May 1998, the British Museum sent a replica of the god-statue back to Rurutu, which is what you get to see here.

LODGING   **Chez Catherine** is a ten-room motel in the village of Moerai, situated on the oceanfront. Five guest rooms each have one double bed and the remaining five come with two single beds. Each unit has a terrace facing the sea and a private bath (with hot water). A restaurant/bar is on the premises of the motel. Located near the airport. ~ Moerai; 94-02-43. BUDGET TO MODERATE.

On Rurutu, the locals use bamboo poles to fish at the edge of the shore.

Pension Temarama is a white two-story building with six rooms with various configurations of double and single beds. A small living/reading room with a TV separates the guest rooms. There is a communal bath with hot water, a balcony, and a large communal kitchen. Meal plans, island tours, guided cave visits and other activities are available. Bicycles, scooters and cars are available for hire. ~ Anaaro, two kilometers from the airport; phone/fax 94-02-17; e-mail pension temarama@mail.pf. BUDGET.

Rurutu Village has eight bungalows nestled in a lush garden. Each has a private hot-water bath. There's a swimming pool—a rare luxury on this isolated island. Meal plans are available. The property is on the northern tip of the island, near the airport. Credit cards are accepted. ~ Unaa; 94-03-92, fax 94-05-01; e-mail pensionrurutuvillage@free.fr. BUDGET.

Pension Ariana consists of a house and three bungalows. On the house's floor level is a living room, a self-contained kitchen and a dining room. The two rooms (each with a double bed) are on the first floor; there's a communal bath. The bungalows are built into the cliff. Each has room for a double bed, a single bed and a private bath. There is a snack bar is on the premises and also a small boutique with local handicrafts. Activities include circle-island tours and hiking; bike rentals are also available. The property is located on a small white-sand beach in Vitaria, one kilometer from the airport. ~ Vitaria; 94-06-69, fax 94-07-14; www.haere-mai.pf, e-mail pensionariana@mail.pf. BUDGET.

Le Manotel is a small family hotel two kilometers south of Moerai, beside the lagoon and beach. It has four bungalows, each with a double and single bed, a private bathroom and terrace. Owner Yves Gentilhomme offers free airport transfers; meal plans are available. ~ Moerai; phone/fax 93-02-25; e-mail manotel@mail.pf.

Pension Teautamatea offers three rooms by the sea, near the island's royal archaeological site. Rooms are available with either private or shared bath. There is a lounge, deck and shared dining room, and meal plans are available. Management can organize lagoon and land excursions. Free roundtrip transfers. ~ Vitaria; 94-02-42; www.haere-mai.pf, e-mail pension.teautamatea@free.fr. BUDGET.

DINING

All of the pensions have small restaurants or snack bars. Meals may be taken at any of them, even if you are not staying there. Call ahead to make dining arrangements.

In addition, **Tiare Hinano** in Moerai serves Chinese food. ~ Moerai; 94-06-82. BUDGET.

Snacks may also be had at **Chez Paulette** (94-05-82) and **Chez Line Pihaatae**, both in Moerai. Both BUDGET.

GROCERIES

There are several small local markets in Moerai, the main village. Only the basics are sold here.

SHOPPING

Natives of Rurutu are known throughout French Polynesia for their fine woven hats and mats. Much of the exquisite plaitwork available in Tahiti is made by natives of Rurutu now living in Tahiti. However, it is possible to purchase mats, hats and fans from individual craftspeople on Rurutu. There is one shop at the airport that sells handicrafts—but it's only open when a plane arrives.

The *fare* **Taofe Tapiti**, Rurutu's only coffeehouse, is located next to the Rurutu Village bungalows. You can taste excellent homemade java, but also buy a jam made of squashes, the specialty of the island. Dried banana, vanilla beans, chili peppers and ground coffee beans are also for sale.

Mesutela Manuel of Avera specializes in sculpting *penu* (also known as pistils), the traditional Polynesian food pounder. This implement is still used by islanders today. Unlike the artisans on other French Polynesian islands, Manuel makes them out of white coral instead of basalt. The *penu* are generally used for poi—slightly fermented taro paste—a traditional staple of the Austral Islands (and Hawaii). ~ 94-02-07.

BEACHES

There are several white-sand beaches on the island. Swimming and snorkeling are possible.

Toatartara Beach, on the southern extreme of the island in the Naairoa district, is one of the most scenic spots in all of French Polynesia.

Outdoor Adventures

For the last several years, **Yves Lefevre** of the Raie Manta Club in Rangiroa and Eric Leborgne, also a dive instructor, have organized whale-watching tours to Rurutu. From July to October, humpback whales populate the waters off the Austral Islands. The area is favored by females who birth and nurse their young here until

WHALE WATCHING

they are strong enough to travel in the open sea. The surrounding waters are free from the whale's most aggressive predator— man. For more information contact Raie Manta Club at the Hotel Rurutu Village. ~ 94-03-92, fax 94-05-01; in Rangiroa: 96-84-80, fax 96-85-60; raiemantaclub.free.pf, e-mail raiemantaclub@mail.pf.

RIDING STABLES

Those interested in horseback excursions into the island's rugged interior can contact **Landry Chong**. ~ Moerai; 94-02-17.

Teuruarii Viriamu also has a variety of horseback tours. ~ Moerai; 94-02-42.

BOAT CHARTERS

For boat transportation from Avera, contact **Adrien Manuel** ~ 94-05-52, **Dominique Moeau** ~ 94-04-24 or **Pierre Harua** ~ 94-06-36. In Moerai, contact **Landry Chong**. ~ 94-02-17.

TOURS

M. and Mme. Iareta and **Madeline Moeau** have a vehicle with capacity for seven passengers for round-the-island tours. ~ Moerai; 94-03-92.

The absence of a surrounding coral reef makes Rurutu one of the best and most popular whale-watching spots in French Polynesia.

Manotour is run by Yves Gentilhomme, the president of the local tourist board. Yves knows his island well and offers perhaps the best tours in the Austral. He'll take you by four-wheel drive to see the best that the island has to offer in the way of natural history and manmade attractions. These include caves, farms, the local coffeehouse, the goat cheese factory and the local artisans. Yves also knows a great deal about the island's legends and its inhabitants. In addition to the land tour, he also offers lagoon tours in his boat. ~ Phone/fax 93-02-25; e-mail manotel@mail.pf.

Rimatara

One of the most isolated spots on the planet, Rimatara is the westernmost of the inhabited islands in the Australs. It lacks an airport and a sheltered harbor and is truly off the beaten path. Its three square miles (eight square kilometers) of land make it the smallest of the Australs. At the moment the only way to get there is still by boat, but the local citizens recently voted to construct an airport.

The island is primarily of volcanic origin, and rises to a height of only 272 feet (83 meters) at a hill known as Oromana. From the central slopes small brooks trickle into a series of swamps. The water eventually empties beneath an ancient elevated reef that occupies much of the island's fringe. This "reef" has formed a cliff 20 to 30 feet (8 to 12 meters) high surrounding the island in many places. Created from hard, white limestone, the formation has been eroded in many places and extends inland for several hundred yards. The island is also encircled by a coral reef that borders the shore, forming a lagoon near the village of Mutuaura. Here a 500-yard-long (480-meter) islet extends seaward from the main island. The lagoon has a curving, white-sand beach fringed by casuarina trees. The reef has three passes, two on the northern side and one on the east side.

The main village is **Amaru**, which is composed of a few shops, a post office, a *gendarmerie*, a town hall, an infirmary and a school. **Anapoto** and **Mutuaura** villages are connected by a few rutted dirt roads. Of interest to the visitor is an **old cemetery** near the dock. For its minuscule size, Rimatara has a rather large area of arable land with fertile soil that is used to grow taro, oranges, bananas and breadfruit.

SIGHTS

Although the island has electricity, there are few diversions. There are no car, bicycle or boat rentals. There aren't any restaurants or bars. (I was told that alcohol is not sold on the island.) However, a number of *marae* on the island are easy to visit and are quite impressive.

Situated near the quay of Taanini, you'll find **Rani Hiva**, named after a famous warrior of the island. It lies on the mountain side from the road between the beach and the limestone *makatea* uplift. A second *marae* is **Hare Ti'i**, which you can find by taking the inland road from Amaru Village to Motuaura at Vaitiare; it stands on a hill slope overlooking the taro plantation below. The largest chiefly *marae* that remains on the island is that of **Haera'i**, found on a hill slope in the island's interior, off the road from Amaru to Anapoto Village. Ask at the town hall of Amaru for directions or about a local guide who can accompany you to the sites. Rimatara is a very traditional island and the *marae* are respected, so visitors should follow some commonsense rules such as asking permission from a local before visiting the shrines, refraining from eating or from taking fruit, stones or anything as a souvenir.

Chez William Tematahotoa is in the main village of Amaru. This white wooden cottage with brown trim and a terrace has three rooms, two with double beds and one with two singles. The guest rooms have private bathrooms with hot water. You must bring your own food if you want to eat. It is located about 200 yards from the sea. ~ Amaru; 94-43-06; in Tahiti: 57-30-07, ask for Benjamin. BUDGET.

LODGING

Chez Paulette Tematahotoa is a two-bedroom home in the village of Mutuaura, located two kilometers west of the dock, just a few yards from the sea. Each of the bedrooms has a double bed. Other amenities include a kitchen, living room and a communal bath. Chez Paulette will rent you a room on a daily or monthly basis. The accommodation is acceptable, but food is not provided. Bring your own provisions. ~ Mutuaura; 94-42-27. BUDGET.

Chez Rita Hutia is the better place to stay in Mutuaura. It is located about 500 yards from the dock and is a short walk from the beach. The accommodation has three guest rooms, each with a double bed. There is also a cozy salon, kitchen and individual (cold water) baths. The proprietor, Rita, will cook for you. ~ Mutuaura; 94-43-09. BUDGET.

Umarere has two rooms in a private home on the seaside, with a cold-water bath and a small kitchenette. Meal plans are offered and discounted monthly rates are available. Umarere is about three kilometers east of Mutuaura on the southern end of the island. ~ Mutuaura; 83-25-84. BUDGET.

GROCERIES There are several tiny markets located in the villages of Mutuaura and Amaru. Keep in mind that only the basic necessities are available.

SHOPPING Local artisans produce finely woven hats, mats and fans. Crafts may be purchased from individual craftspeople. Inquire at your pension for information.

BEACHES There are several white-sand beaches on the island, including one near the village of Mutuaura.

Raivavae Until recently, Raivavae could only be reached by boat. Air Tahiti initiated flight service to the island with a new airstrip in 2002. The island sits 395 miles (692 kilometers) southeast of Tahiti—very, very far from the madding crowd. It is roughly double the size of Rimatara, six square miles (16 square kilometers), and has a rugged, verdant topography that is said to be one of the most beautiful in the Eastern Pacific. Con-

BIRDS OF A FEATHER

In 1993, 1994 and 1995 Rimatara and the western limits of the Austral Islands were subject to an intensive archaeological survey by Mark Eddowes of the Museum of Tahiti and Her Islands. Eddowes noted that the architecture of *marae* and ancient house sites he examined closely resembled that of the neighboring island of Mangaia in the southern Cook Islands. This suggested a close cultural affiliation and Eddowes determined that Rimatara was part of a region known as *te fenua ura* or "the red lands," and most likely a source of precious red feathers, highly valued in ritual exchange throughout East Polynesia. This geographic entity stretched from Atiu and nearby islands in the southern Cooks, to Rimatara where even today one can find an endemic multicolored parakeet known locally as *ura vaero* or *te 'ura*.

sisting of craggy, tree-lined hills, its highest peak is 1442-foot (437-meter) Mt. Hiro. The island is completely encircled by a barrier reef on which there are about two dozen wooded *motu*.

Raivavae was noted for its archaeological treasures, particularly large stone statues akin to those of Easter Island, though different in appearance. Two of these can be seen at the Gauguin Museum in Tahiti. (Unfortunately, most of the stone *tikis* have been taken from the island.) There are also several *marae* and the remnants of hill terraces on Raivavae, which have become popular visitor's attractions.

Raivavae is said to have been discovered by Captain Cook in 1777. However, Captain Thomas Gayangos of the Spanish frigate *Aguila* was the first European to set foot on the island, in 1775. In the early 19th century, several European ships called on Raivavae, seeking sandalwood. In 1819, Pomare II of Tahiti visited the island and the local chiefs formally ceded it to him. This led to Raivavae becoming a protectorate of Tahiti in 1842 when Tahiti and the other islands under its control came under French jurisdiction. The island was formally ceded to France in 1880 by Pomare V.

SIGHTS

There are four villages on Raivavae, which are home to about 1049 inhabitants. The most important settlement is **Rairua**, located on the western side of the island. Two of the other villages (**Mahanatoa** and **Anatonu**) lie on the north or west coasts, with the remaining community, **Vaiuru**, on the southern shore. The various settlements are linked by a coastal road that circles the island. There is also an overland road that connects Vaiuru with Mahanatoa and the northern communities.

Raivavae's cool climate and fertile soil are perfect for growing cabbage, carrots and potatoes as well as more tropical crops such as coffee and oranges. Despite the rich array of vegetables grown on the island, you should bring all the essentials you have room for, even a bicycle if you plan to stay a while. Plan a visit to Raivavae to enjoy its tranquility and bucolic landscape, which is unrivaled in this part of the Pacific.

Raivavae has numerous archaeological sights. Several *marae* have been restored, there are many petroglyphs in excellent shape and there are still *tiki* pending restoration. Most of the archaeological sites are quite remote so it's best to ask at your pension for directions or hire a guide to show you.

LODGING

Chez Annie Flores is conveniently located near the cargo boat landing. The home has two guest bedrooms, each with a double bed, private bath and kitchenette. It's easy to meet Mme. Flores. When the ship arrives she'll be selling fruit, fish and vegetables at her stand on the wharf. ~ Rairua; 95-43-28. BUDGET.

Rooms and meals are also available at **Pension Rau'uru**, run by Edmond Flores. ~ Rairua; 95-42-88. BUDGET.

Pension Ataha has two rooms available in a house near the beach. The shared bathroom has hot water, and the owner, Odile Tamaititahio, will arrange lagoon and walking tours. ~ Rairua; 95-43-69. BUDGET.

Chez Vaite is an attractive three-room home with a shared cold-water bathroom. Located on the seaside, it has a large terrace and a sitting room with a TV. Meal plans are available. ~ Mahanatoa; 95-42-85, fax 95-42-00. BUDGET.

Pension Moana is a two-room home with shared kitchen and private cold-water bathrooms. A TV is available for your viewing pleasure. The owner is said to be a great storyteller. ~ Mahanatoa; phone/fax 95-42-66. BUDGET.

Raivavae Tama Resort has four bungalows, each with one double and one single bed and an attached bathroom with hot water. Meal plans are available. ~ Vaiuru; phone/fax 95-42-52. BUDGET.

GROCERIES   There are small stores in each of the villages. Only the basics are sold here.

Rapa

With its nearest neighbor some 360 miles (600 kilometers) away, Rapa (the Polynesian word for "outside") is one of the most isolated islands in French Polynesia and not easily visited. The island's terrain is rugged and barren, its most distinctive features are the massive 1000-foot gray cliffs that tower over the sparsely covered landscape. The island is home to about 500-plus people and a plethora of goats.

Unlike other Polynesian islands, it is necessary to obtain permission to stay on Rapa. To do so contact the Subdivision Administration des Îles Australes. Visitors planning to travel to Rapa should keep in mind that there is no airport here and interisland vessels only visit this lonely destination every four to six weeks. So, if you plan to come, your stay will be at least one month in duration. ~ BP 115, Papeete, Tahiti; 46-86-76.

There are six peaks on the island—Mt. Perehau is the tallest, reaching over 2100 feet (650 meters). Rapa once had a volcano, but it collapsed at its center. The resulting bay is now home to the island's harbor. Rapa has many deep caves and valleys, some of which open to the sea and are, in effect, also bays. There is no fringing reef to protect the coastline.

Historically, Rapa has had a connection to Easter Island, Rapa Nui. The island has strong **fortifications** known as *pa*—dozens of terraces on steep cliffs supported by walls built with basalt blocks piled on top of each other, constructed by its an-

Eric de Bisschop—
Adventurer
Extraordinaire

Eric de Bisschop was an adventurer and an exceptional sailor. Born in 1891, he traveled to China in 1927 where he cut his teeth sailing junks. Later he built a double-hulled canoe, the *Kamiloa*, in Hawaii and sailed from there to France, arriving in Cannes on May 21, 1938. After the *Kontiki* (skippered by Thor Heyerdahl) successfully traversed the waters from South America to Polynesia, de Bisschop decided it would be possible to sail in the opposite direction, from Polynesia to the South American continent.

He built a bamboo raft, the *Tahiti Nui*, and in 1956, after a seven-month journey, nearly made it to Chile. His raft sunk next to the island of Juan Fernandez off the Chilean coast. Not quite satisfied with the results of his adventure, he built a second *Tahiti Nui* and departed Callao, Peru in 1958. The raft sailed across the Pacific but missed the Marquesas, the first landfall in French Polynesia. De Bisschop and his crew preferred to land in Rakahanga (Cook Islands) but had problems getting the craft into port. Unfortunately the raft violently collided with the coral reef in Rakahanga and de Bisschop died. His body was brought to Rurutu (where his wife hailed from) and was laid to rest on the island.

cient Polynesian residents. Discovered (but not claimed for Britain) in 1791 by explorer George Vancouver, carbon-14 dating indicates that there were approximately 2000 to 3000 inhabitants in the 18th century. Subsequent epidemics from the first European ships quickly decimated the local population.

France established Rapa as a protectorate in 1867 and annexed the island in 1881. Lengthy negotiations with Britain were inconclusive in resolving the issue of ownership, though New Zealand hoped that France would cede Rapa to Britain so that it could become an entrepôt between New Zealand and Panama.

These days international powers are not battling to control Rapa. In fact, its remote location makes it difficult to reach, and few boats call on the island. Perhaps because of the isolation, the local population has voted for the construction of an airstrip.

With its southerly location, the mid-winter climate is freezing by Polynesian standards, with temperatures dropping to 41°F (5°C). The soil is comparatively poor on Rapa, but a variety of produce is grown, including taro (the staple), peaches, pears, passion fruit, figs and superb coffee. (Despite the homegrown coffee, the islanders seem to prefer Nescafé—they ship their beans to Tahiti.)

There is abundant seafood in the waters and on the shoreline. The Rapans eat a lot of mussels, oysters, crab, shrimp, sea urchin and lobster. Goat rounds out their menu.

LODGING If you get to Rapa, **Chez Cerdan Faraire** is just about the only show in town. Located near the beach, it consists of one large home with three guest rooms, each with two single beds, a communal kitchen and bath with hot water. It's an acceptable accommodation, but, shall we say, quiet. Prepare to do your own cooking and bring your own food. It would be advisable to write to M. Cerdan Faraire at Ahurei Village well in advance to let him know of your plans. ~ Ahurei; 95-72-84. BUDGET.

A second option is **Chez Titaua**, a private house that rents one room with private bath to visitors. Kitchen privileges are included, and monthly rentals are available. Contact Miss Titaua Jean. ~ 98 751 Ahurei; 95-72-59, fax 95-72-60. BUDGET.

▼▼▼▼▼▼▼▼▼▼▼
Transportation

AIR

TUBUAI Air Tahiti serves the island five times a week from Papeete. Three of the flights visit Rurutu first; the other two are nonstop. Nonstop flight time is 1 hour 40 minutes from Papeete to Tubuai. ~ 95-04-76.

RURUTU Air Tahiti operates three nonstop flights per week to Rurutu from Papeete. An additional two flights are via Tubuai. The flight time is 2 hours and 40 minutes from Papeete to Rurutu (via Tubuai). ~ 93-02-50.

RAIVAVAE   Air Tahiti recently built an air strip and began regular service to Raivavae in 2002. Call Air Tahiti for schedule information. ~ Papeete; 47-44-00.

The Austral Islands are served by the 196-foot (60-meter) *Tuhaa Pae II* every two weeks. The itinerary is Papeete/Rimatara/Rurutu/Tubuai/Raivavae/Papeete and also Rapa (every two months). There are 44 berths available on deck, as well as 9 cabins. ~ Papeete; 50-96-09; e-mail snath@mail.pf.

The *Vaeanu II* makes three voyages a month and has room for 20 passengers. The itinerary is Rimatara/Rurutu/Tubuai/Raivavae/Rapa. Contact Wilfrid Tetuamanuhiri. ~ Motu Uta, Papeete; 41-25-35, fax 41-24-34; e-mail torehiatetu@mail.pf.

The administration ships *Tahiti Nui* and *Meherio II* also visit the islands on an irregular basis. Contact Leonard Puputouki. ~ Motu Uta, Papeete; 50-66-71.

The best anchorage is in Avera Bay, which is quite safe during the prevailing easterly winds. Moerai Bay, however, is *not* safe when there are strong trade winds. There are several passes for landing boats on the northeast, west and southeast sides.

There are two passes on the northern coast of Raivavae. Yachting enthusiasts should note that there are anchorages off the village of Mahanatoa (except during north or northwest winds) and at Rairua Bay, at the west end of the island. Rairua Bay has a jetty and offers safe mooring at all times.

SEA

TUBUAI   To rent a car, motor scooter or bicycle in Tubuai, inquire at your pension or in Mahu Village at **Bernard Le Guilloux**. ~ Phone/fax 95-06-01. **Tino Tahiata** also has bicycles. ~ 95-07-54.

RURUTU   **Rurutu Rent-a-Car** has four-wheel-drive vehicles and scooters. ~ Moerai; 94-02-17. Cars and bicycles are also available for rent by guests at Mataura's **Chez Karine & Tale** (95-04-52) and **Pension Vaitea Nui** (95-04-19).

**CAR, BIKE &
SCOOTER
RENTALS**

THIRTEEN

The Gambier Islands

The distant Gambier Islands (also known as the Mangareva Group) are located 1116 miles (1800 kilometers) southeast of Tahiti, seemingly the tail end of the Tuamotu archipelago. Unlike the flat atolls of the Tuamotus, however, the Gambier Islands are high and rugged. They are comprised of a few atolls and five inhabited high islands—Aukena, Akamaru, Taravai Kamaka and Mangareva—all formed from rims of extinct volcanic craters.

The islands are small and narrow, the largest being Mangareva with a length of four miles and a maximum width of one mile. The highest point in the group, Mt. Duff (1447 feet/441 meters), is also on Mangareva. The other high islands range from three-mile-long Taravai to one-mile-long uninhabited Makaroa.

A principle feature of the group is a barrier reef that encircles the islands. The reef lies several miles off the coast of the main islands, protecting them from the fury of the Pacific. Above water from the north to the southwest and about 19 miles long and 15 miles wide, the reef is dotted with coconut palm–covered *motu*. To the west and southwest the submerged reef completes a circle.

Located just north of the Tropic of Capricorn, you'll find the climate of the Gambiers in this southern latitude is much cooler than Tahiti and the Society Islands. The prevailing winds are easterly trades, which increase in velocity from March to August. The hottest season is from December to March, when the temperature ranges between 73° and 90°F (24° to 33°C). In June and July, by contrast, the temperature only climbs to 78°F (26°C) and can drop as low as 65°F (19°C). The dry and rainy seasons are not well defined—be prepared for rain anytime.

Though the land is not particularly fertile, crops such as cantaloupe, watermelon, lettuce, eggplant, oranges and coffee are cultivated. The grapefruit, in particular, is exquisite. Black pearls are also farmed on Aukena, providing jobs and income for those residents fortunate enough to be involved in the trade.

The Gambier Group was once an independent entity within French Polynesia, with its own flag. This independent status no longer exists. The population of the

Gambiers once numbered as many as 5000, but over the past 60 years, many of the inhabitants have migrated to Tahiti. Today, except for Mangareva, with a population of about 1097, the Gambier Islands are virtually uninhabited. Only a handful of people live on the outer islands, following agricultural and aquacultural pursuits.

Mangareva

Mangareva (Polynesian for "floating mountain"), the main island in the Gambier Group, is surrounded by small rocky islets. Like the other high islands in the archipelago, it is characterized by a high, razor-backed ridge, with tertiary ridges running from the spine to the coast and that end in steep promontories. In between are bays and flat land. There are several beaches (not particularly good for bathing) composed of gray sand bespeckled with black grains formed from seaworn lava.

The higher elevations have little vegetation, except for a thick growth of cane grass, which in the drier months can be swept by fires. There is little ecological diversity, but on some of the slopes you can find dense thickets of oranges, *hau*, breadfruit, mango and other tropical trees. Despite the paucity of natural life, the island is aesthetically pleasing, with gentle rolling hills and a Mediterranean climate and feel.

There are three passes through the barrier reef into the outer lagoon. The main port is Rikitea, which provides good shelter from the sea. It is the only port open to commerce in the Mangareva Group. However, anchorage is vulnerable to the southeast trade winds. Rikitea is a small settlement with five shops, a post office, a dispensary and a *gendarmerie*. Perhaps the most incongruous structure in this South Sea backwater is the huge covered sports stadium, and the large athletic field next to it.

The first settlers of Mangareva apparently drifted in small numbers from the Tuamotu Islands. Organized settlement, it is believed, began in the 14th century by people from the higher islands in the northwest. Rarotonga (part of the Cook Islands) is mentioned in the ancient traditions as the origin for some of the settlers, but local culture also shows an affinity to the Marquesans, who may also have been a colonizing source. In housing, clothing and general customs, Mangareva has much in common with Tahiti. (The dialect spoken in Mangareva resembles that of the Maori of New Zealand, the Cook Islands and the Tuamotu archipelago.)

Though the islands may have been sighted as early as 1687, credit for the European discovery of the Mangareva Group is given to Captain James Wilson of the *Duff*, who sighted the islands in 1797. In 1827, and in subsequent years, several vessels visited the group to obtain pearl shells.

In 1834, the Picpus fathers of France settled on Mangareva, and by 1836 the entire archipelago had been converted to Catholicism. Under the tyrannical leadership of Father Honoré Laval, a Belgian priest, the docile converts were taught to spin, weave, print, construct boats and, above all, erect buildings. Laval organized a native police force, ordered women to become nuns and men to become monks. He forced the islanders to work relentlessly to construct a city of coral and stone.

The centerpiece of this city was the St. Michel Cathedral, built on the ancient site of Marae Tangaroa. It is still the largest cathedral in French Polynesia—accommodating 2000 worshippers. In a similar neo-Gothic style, a school, triumphal arches, chapels, a convent, a monastery and a number of stone houses were also built at the behest of Laval. The massive construction projects took their toll on the health of the Mangarevans. A number of people suffered under the conditions of forced labor and servitude and in 1864 the new governor of Tahiti, Comte Emile de la Ronciere, visited the Gambiers to investigate the reports of this reign of terror, as well as Laval's purported trafficking in pearls and shell. When de la Ronciere ordered the prisons opened, he found two young boys in a dungeon (which was a large hole in the prison grounds, still visible today)—their cardinal sin had been to laugh during a mass. Laval's reign was finally brought to an end in 1871. You can read about Father Honoré Laval's strange saga in James Michener's collection of stories, *Return to Paradise*.

A testament to Laval's obsession with building are the more than 116 structures that still remain in the Gambiers. (A counterpoint to the injustices perpetrated by Laval is a development center to train youths in mechanics and carpentry that was opened in 1982 by the Freres of the Sacred Heart of Quebec.)

Today, Mangareva's main industry is the cultivation of black pearls, and to some degree, jewelry making, which involves cutting and grinding items out of mother-of-pearl. Robert Wan, the "Pearl King" of French Polynesia, has invested extensively on nearby Aukena, which today produces a number of high-quality pearls. Agriculture is also important and farmers grow grapefruit and coffee plants. Oddly enough, most of the farmers are Europeans.

Mangareva is another South Sea island so far removed from the rest of the world that you sometimes feel you are on another planet. You come here for the tranquility and the undeveloped nature of the island. Locals are shy, and like their cousins in the Austral Group, seldom see visitors. Perhaps it is the slow pace, but residents do not appear interested in going out of their way to show visitors around, even if you are willing to spend money for a tour. It's not that they are inhospitable, but as a friend of mine who visited noted, "They have no idea that tourists are interested in seeing the island." Locals also tend to be unreliable. For example, when asking directions for a particular guesthouse, five individuals will most likely give you five different responses, and if you are lucky, one of the answers may be correct. This could happen even if you speak perfect French. (Virtually none of the residents speak English.)

There are no restrictions on visiting the islands, but flying there is very expensive.

SIGHTS

In the main village of **Rikitea** you'll encounter a number of **ruins**, seemingly from a lost civilization, that include a convent, a triumphal arch, several watch towers, a prison and a court. These mostly tumble-down ruins have an eerie, dark feel about them, even in the light of day. Dominating the village is the **tomb** of Gregorio Maputeoa, the last king of Mangareva, who died in 1868 after having requested status as a French Protectorate for the island.

Not to be missed is **St. Michel of Rikitea**, the Catholic church built under the auspices of Father Honoré Laval. This neo-Gothic

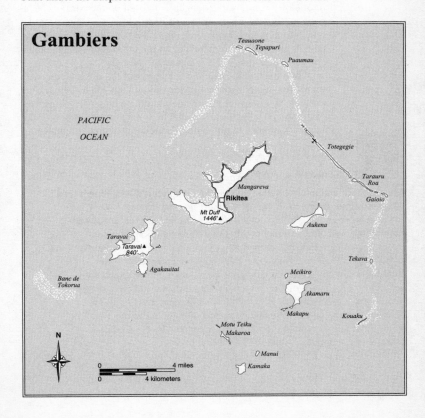

Gambiers

Teauaone
Tepapuri

Puaumau

PACIFIC
OCEAN

Totegegie

Tarauru
Roa

Mangareva

Rikitea

Gaioia

Mt Duff
1446'▲

Aukena

Taravai

Taravai ▲
840'

Tekava

Agakauitai

Meikiro

Banc de
Tokorua

Akamaru

Makapu

Kouaku

Motu Teiku
Makaroa

N

Manui

Kamaka

0   4 miles

0   4 kilometers

wonder of the South Seas was built of fired limestone, and incorporated mother-of-pearl inlay in its interior. Though in need of repair, it is still in use. Across the path from the church is the well-maintained 140-year-old **rectory**, occupied by the parish priest.

For more information about the town, contact Mrs. Bianca Urarii at **Comite du Tourisme des Gambier**. ~ 98 755 Rikitea; phone/fax 97-83-76; e-mail biancabenoit@mail.pf.

LODGING   **Chez Terii and Hélène Paeamara** is a two-bedroom home with living room, dining room, kitchen and (cold water) bath. Terii and Hélène are as hospitable as their kin down the street, Pierre and Mariette. The cuisine they provide is very tasty. Not surprisingly, Terii and Hélène have a similar list of excursions as Pierre and Mariette. They, too, make excellent guides. Water shortages are the only problems you might have to deal with. You can't go wrong staying with either family. ~ Rikitea; 97-82-80. MODERATE.

Chez Linda, operated by the gracious Henri Jacquot, consists of one very comfortable bungalow located on the edge of the lagoon in Rikitea. For the price of a night's lodging, Henri provides breakfast as well as free bicycles for his guests. If you stay a week, he will give you a free boat trip to the *motu* that fringes the lagoon. ~ Rikitea; 97-82-47. MODERATE TO DELUXE.

Chez Bianca & Benoit is a modern three-room home with shared hot-water bath and a living room with TV. Its best feature is the outdoor terrace where one can dine with a marvelous view of the sea. Meal plans are available. ~ Rikitea; phone/fax 97-83-76; www.tahitilive.com, e-mail biancabenoit@mail.pf. BUDGET.

AUTHOR FAVORITE

My choice for a comfortable stay while in the Gambiers is **Chez Pierre and Mariette Paeamara**. With two of the most hospitable hosts I know serving up tasty food and offering a plenitude of activities, my visits are always memorable ones. The property consists of a three-bedroom concrete home, complete with living room, dining room, kitchen and (cold water) bath facilities. The hosts, Pierre and Mariette, have a slew of activities available—a visit to a *motu* by outrigger speed canoe, fishing expeditions or a tour of the family-owned pearl farm. They also provide auto tours around the island as well as visits to historical sites or treks up to Mt. Duff. The food at Chez Pierre and Mariette Paeamara is also quite good. In fact, the only problem you might encounter here are occasional water shortages. ~ Rikitea; 97-82-87. MODERATE

Chez Jojo, run by Mrs. Jocelyn Mamatui, offers two rooms and a camping area in Rikitea. A communal hot-water bathroom and kitchen are provided; there is a TV, too. This is among the best bets for budget travelers on Mangareva. Meal plans are available. ~ Rikitea; phone/fax 97-84-69. BUDGET.

Chez Tara Etu Kura has one bungalow for rent at Teonekura ◄ HIDDEN
Point. The unit has a private bath, a hot-water shower and a refrigerator. The property is accessible only by boat, so make sure to contact the management ahead of time to make arrangements. ~ Teonekura Point; phone/fax 97-83-25. BUDGET.

There are no restaurants on Mangareva, but there is one minus- **DINING**
cule **snack bar** that theoretically opens for lunch. However, a colleague of mine was on the island for several weeks, and she saw neither proprietor nor customer during her entire stay. In other words, don't count on it being open!

There are several markets on the island and their stock gradually **GROCERIES**
decreases until the arrival of the next interisland freighter. Unfortunately, there's no bakery. Bread is brought in from Tahiti twice a month. So, unless you like stale bread, you are better off acquiring a taste for banana tarts, which are great, and are stocked in some of the shops. Oddly enough, despite the isolation, prices are more reasonable than on Bora Bora or Moorea.

A few local artisans (who can be located via the management of **SHOPPING**
your lodging facility) sell carved mother-of-pearl items. There are no other souvenirs to speak of, except a postcard of Mt. Duff.

AKAMARU AND TOTEGEGIE There are white-sand **BEACHES**
beaches on the outlying *motu* that fringe the lagoon. Coconut palms provide shade on both Akamaru and Totegegie, but there are no facilities. The swimming and snorkeling are quite good. Snorkeling is best on Akamaru. Here you'll find plenty of fish and coral gardens close to the shore. ~ The local pensions will provide transportation and picnic lunches to the beaches and *motu*.

The trek up Mt. Duff is hard work but worth the effort. The mountainside is filled with scrubby, overgrown vegetation and tall grass

Outdoor Adventures

that may hide the goat trails that meander up to the ridge. You **HIKING**
often have to get down on all fours to clamber through the bush (and sometimes mud) to navigate the hill. Getting to the base of Mt. Duff is easy—it is located directly behind the village of Rikitea. You simply follow the goat tracks that seem to dead-end every few feet. It is then up to you to decide which is the correct

route to follow. The hike takes about three hours to the peak, but the view of the island and lagoon is worth the effort.

▼▼▼▼▼▼▼▼▼▼▼
Transportation

AIR

The airport is built on the *motu* of Totegegie, across the lagoon from Rikitea, Mangareva's principal village. **Air Tahiti** visits Mangareva once a week from Tahiti. The flight time is five hours, sometimes with a stop at Hao. Upon arrival in the Gambiers, sea-shuttle service is provided between Totegegie (where the airport is located) and Rikitea, the main town on Mangareva. The crossing time is 30 minutes.

SEA

The 210-foot freighter *Nuku Hau* visits Rikitea every 25 days. ~ 45-23-24, fax 45-24-44. The *Taporo V* makes a trip every three weeks. ~ 42-63-93, 43-79-72, fax 42-06-17; e-mail taporo@mail.pf. The administration ship *Tahiti Nui* also makes occasional visits. ~ 50-66-71, fax 43-32-70.

Recommended Reading

A formidable number of books have been written about French Polynesia, some of them only readily available in the islands themselves.

CULTURE, ARCHAEOLOGY AND NATURAL HISTORY

The Art of Tahiti (Thames & Hudson, 1979) by Terence Barrow gives an overview of Polynesian art before European contact, with an emphasis on Tahiti.

Blue Latitudes (Picador, 2002) by Tony Horwitz is a *New York Times* bestseller. The subhead, "Boldly going where Captain Cook has gone before," says it all, though where Cook found innocence and wonder, Horwitz sees only the seedier, tainted side of paradise.

Coral Kingdoms (New York, Abradale Press, 1990) by Carl Roessler is a survey of the world's popular dive sites. Carl Roessler is a dive travel pioneer and a respected underwater photographer.

Diving and Snorkeling Tahiti and French Polynesia (Lonely Planet Pisces Book, 2001) is a diver's bible, covering dive sites and operators on every island. Pages are detailed with maps and color photographs.

Diving in Tahiti—a Divers' Guide to French Polynesia (Les Editions du Pacifique, 1991) by Thierry Zysman has an introduction to diving in French Polynesia plus a great many detailed descriptions of specific dive sites in Tahiti, Moorea, Huahine, Raiatea, Tahaa, Bora Bora, Rangiroa and Manihi. Well illustrated and full of color photos.

Exploring Tropical Islands and Seas—An Introduction for the Traveler and Amateur Naturalist (Prentice Hall, 1984) by Frederic Martini is not specifically on French Polynesia but is nonetheless a fine primer on the natural history of tropical islands. The title explains it all. Subjects covered include general island environment, coral reefs, marine life, geology and sharks.

A Fragile Paradise: Nature and Man in the Pacific (Collins, London, 1989) by Andrew Mitchell is for anyone interested in the natural history of the South Pacific, especially the interplay between man and nature. An important and fascinating work, it is both scholarly and yet eminently readable. *A Fragile Paradise* provides a comprehensive background on how the flora and fauna found their way to the Pacific Islands and how the presence of man has altered the ecological equation. A number of fine color prints are also included.

Hidden Worlds of Polynesia (Harcourt, Brace and World, New York, 1963) is by Robert Suggs, an American archaeologist who did seminal work in the Marquesas Group during the 1950s and 1960s in the areas of archaeology and anthropology. Probably the most popular of Suggs' works, *Hidden Worlds* is a narrative that chronicles the year the anthropologist spent on Nuku Hiva excavating for the American Museum of Natural History of New York. It is as much about the problems of living in Marquesan culture as it is about Marquesan archaeology. A must for would-be visitors and students of contemporary French Polynesia.

Hiva Oa, Glimpses of an Oceanic Memory (Departement Archeologie, 1991) by Pierre Ottino and Marie-Noele de Berge-Ottino is another fine book on the

Marquesas. Both Ottinos are archaeologists and their scholarly 50-page booklet is packed with fascinating historical information and maps on the region. For visitors to the Marquesas or armchair archaeologists, this is a must-read. Unfortunately, it is only available in Tahiti.

The Island Civilizations of Polynesia (New American Library, Mentor Books, New York, 1960) by Robert C. Suggs, was an attempt to summarize the results of stratigraphic excavations and other approaches to Polynesian pre-history. The book is dated now but is useful as a period piece representative of a certain stage in the development of thought on the topic of Polynesian pre-history.

Islands of Tahiti (Kea Editions, 1991) by Raymond Bagnis, with photos by Erwin Christian, is a coffee-table book on French Polynesia with some evocative images.

Keneti, South Seas Adventures of Kenneth Emory (University of Hawaii Press, 1988) by Bob Krauss is the fascinating biography of Kenneth P. Emory, perhaps the most influential 20th-century archaeologist to work in French Polynesia. Emory, a contemporary of Margaret Mead, inspired a generation of archaeologists. Bob Krauss refers to Emory as the "father" of dirt archaeology in Polynesia. Emory pioneered the study of Polynesian migration and was the first archaeologist in Polynesia to carbon date artifacts.

L' Archipel des Marquises (Les Editions Le Motu, Boulogne, 1994) by Paule Laudon, Franck Brouillet, Emmanuel Deschamps and Christian Ruhle, covers the Marquesas region.

Les Atolls des Tuamotu (Editions de l'Orstrom, 1994) by Jacques Bonuallot, Pierre Laboute, Francis Rougerie and Emmanuel Vigneron, is a wonderful source of photographs featuring the atolls of the Tuamotu archipelago.

Les Editions du Pacifique series (available in English) has a number of books on natural history that cover a wide variety of local flora and fauna. Typical titles include *Birds of Tahiti* by Jean-Claude Thibault and Claude Rivers, *Sharks of Polynesia* by R. H. Johnson, *Shells of Tahiti*, *Living Corals*, and other titles.

Little Worlds of the Pacific: An Essay on Pacific Basin Biogeography (University of Hawaii, 1980) by E. Alison Kay, is a 39-page academically oriented book that details the distribution of flora and fauna in the Pacific.

Man's Conquest of the Pacific (Oxford University Press, 1979) by Peter Bellwood and *The Prehistory of Polynesia* (Harvard University, 1979) edited by J.D. Jennings, are for readers interested in more hard-core Polynesian archaeology.

Marquesan Sexual Behavior (Harcourt, Brace and World, New York, 1966) by Robert C. Suggs is the result of joint research between Suggs and his wife. It is an attempt, in his words, "to correct some of the wacko psychoanalytic fantasies on this topic published in the late 1930s by Ralph Linton and Abram Kardiner." As a registered nurse, Suggs' wife worked almost exclusively with women while he interviewed men. Good bedside reading from one of the more knowledgeable people on Marquesan society.

Noa Noa by Paul Gauguin is an autobiographical account of his life in Tahiti. It paints a rather arrogant and troubled picture of the artist's final years.

The Snorkeller's Guide to the Coral Reef from the Red Sea to the Pacific Ocean (Exile Publishing, 1994) by Paddy Ryan is both a primer for neophytes that covers every conceivable aspect of snorkeling and a wonderful introduction to the flora and fauna of the coral reef. The book is tightly written and illustrated with glorious color photos of the creatures that inhabit the reef system and the aqueous environs of a tropical island. Paddy, a well-known New Zealand underwater photographer and naturalist, begins by covering the basics, such as what type of gear to buy and tips on first aid. He then looks at the marine flora and fauna found in the reefs. It is a valuable resource both for the serious snorkeler or the armchair traveler who has no intention of ever dipping a toe in the warm waters of a Tahitian lagoon.

The Société des Océanistes publishes a range of small booklets on specific subjects such as aviation in Tahiti, sacred sites, Pomare, Bougainville, etc., etc.

Tahiti from the Air (Les Editions du Pacifique, 1985) by Erwin Christian and Emmanuel Vigneron has wonderful aerial photos of French Polynesia, although the construction of new hotels has already made some of the shots look out of date.

The Tahiti Handbook (Editions Avant et Après, 1993) by Jean-Louis Saquet covers French Polynesia's geography, history and natural history with general information on marine life, plant life, canoe design, arts and crafts plus a great deal more. There are plenty of illustrations and it's very comprehensive, but a bit on the superficial side. (Available in English and French editions.)

Tahiti Romance & Reality (Millwood Press, Wellington, 1982) is a coffee-table book by the prolific James Siers, who specializes in South Pacific photography.

Tahiti, The Magic of the Black Pearl (Tahiti, 1986) by Paule Solomon is informative and has beautiful photographs. *Black Pearls of Tahiti* (Tahiti, 1987) by Jean Paul Lintilhac, is less glitzy than the Paule Solomon book but is more authoritative and factual. The photographs are also very good. Recommended for those with an interest in black pearls.

Tahitians—Mind & Experience in the Society Islands (1973) by Robert I. Levy is a tome-like work written by an anthropologist for anthropologists. It's a bit unwieldy but packed with all kinds of cultural information—a good reference book.

Tatau—Maohi Tattoo (Tupuna Productions, 1993) by Dominique Morvan, photographs by Claude Corault and Marie-Hélène Villierme, is a fascinating account of the resurgence of traditional tattooing in French Polynesia. Terrific black-and-white photos of all the tattoos anyone could hope to see.

Tuamotu (Les Editions du Pacifique, Papeete, 1986), a coffee-table book by Erwin Christian and Dominique Charnay, is a photo essay on the people, as well as the flora and fauna, of the Tuamotus.

HISTORY

The Fatal Impact by Alan Moorehead along with David Howarth's book (below) is the best available historical account of early Tahiti. It centers mainly around the three voyages of Captain Cook, portraying him as a humane commander but offering the premise that Polynesian contact with white civilization in general was to have horrible repercussions. Moorehead points out that within 80 years of Cook's visit to Tahiti the population on French Polynesia decreased from 40,000 to 9000, and the culture deteriorated because of disuse by the end of the 19th century.

Mutiny and Romance in the South Seas: A Companion to the Bounty Adventure (1989) by Sven Wahlroos is a must for *Bounty* enthusiasts. Wahlroos, a Finnish-born psychologist who practices in southern California, describes his book as one that "sets forth the known facts of the story and also points to those circumstances of which we cannot be sure." He feels strongly that Ian Ball's *Pitcairn: Children of Mutiny* is not an entirely reliable source on the subject.

Tahiti: a Paradise Lost (1984) by David Howarth is the best book I've encountered on the experience of the early explorers of French Polynesia—Wallis, Cook, Bougainville and company. It's fascinating and reads almost like a novel. A must for South Pacific addicts.

The Voyages of the Endeavour, 1768-1771 (1955) by Captain James Cook, is the classic edition of Cook's logbooks, edited by J.C. Beaglehole, four volumes.

MODERN ACCOUNTS

France and the South Pacific: A Contemporary History (University of Hawaii Press, 1992) by Stephen Hennigham is a comprehensive work that covers French Polynesia as well as other areas of French influence in the Pacific such as Vanuatu, Wallis and Futuna and New Caledonia. It is probably the most serious contemporary history of the region available in English. For students of issues such as nuclear testing, the Tahitian independence movement and the genesis of the current Tahitian political scene, this is the book to purchase.

The Happy Isles of Oceania (1992) by Paul Theroux is a chronicle of the kayaking adventures of one of America's best writers through the South Pacific. The ever-acerbic but oh-so-astute Theroux is a pleasure to read. The chapters devoted to French Polynesia recount his experiences on Tahiti and Moorea as well as a voyage to the Marquesas. His descriptions of the dysfunctional world of neocolonialism, *Heiva* in Papeete, and his search for a long-lost cousin are entertaining and insightful.

Home & Away (1994) by Ron Wright is a collection of essays by a man who has been called Canada's most renowned travel writer. And with good reason. Although the book covers a wide swath of turf (other than French Polynesia), Wright unerringly hones in on the Marquesas Islands, where he spent several weeks on the *Aranui*. Very few writers juggle and juxtapose travel, history and life in the late 20th century better than Ron Wright. Leave it to Mr. Wright to turn his vacation into a search for the literary ghost of Herman Melville. What's not surprising is that he tracks Melville down in the deepest jungles of Nuku Hiva. The book may only be available in Canada.

Kon-Tiki is a nonfiction classic describing the 1948 voyage of Thor Heyerdahl's crew of Europeans aboard a Polynesian-style raft sailing from the coast of South America to French Polynesia. The purpose of the voyage was to "prove" Heyerdahl's theory that Polynesians may have migrated from the South American continent instead of Asia. Whether or not you subscribe to Heyerdahl's theories, the book is a great adventure story.

Moruroa Mon Amour—the French Nuclear Tests in the Pacific (1977), by Bengt & Marie-Therese Danielsson, traces the history of the atomic bomb in French Polynesia and the socioeconomic effects it has had on Tahiti. Danielsson, who originally came to French Polynesia aboard the *Kon-Tiki*, has been the leading spokesperson against the nuclear testing program and at times a lonely voice of conscience. *Tahiti Blue and Other Modern Tales of the South Pacific* (Les Editions de Tahiti, Tahiti, 1990) by Alex du Prel is a collection of short stories reflecting the modern reality of French Polynesia as interpreted by Tahiti's number-one raconteur. Du Prel, who formerly managed Brando's resort, has been in the South Pacific for many years and is a veritable institution.

Tahiti, Forlorn Paradise (1978) by K.K. Stewart is a thinly veiled autobiographical novel by a former Oakland, California, writer. The plot centers around an expat writer who has become disenchanted with life in the U.S. Like his spiritual mentor (also from Oakland) Jack London, he seeks to find himself in the balmy South Seas. The not-so-hidden agenda of the protagonist and his equally randy sidekick, Chico Kidd, is to find the mythical little brown girl in the little grass shack. Both set sail for Tahiti full of great expectations. Written in the form of diary, the work chronicles their misadventures.

Tahiti, Island of Love by Robert Langdon is, as one of my esteemed colleagues says, one of the more popular accounts of Tahiti's history. Though most likely out of print, it's worth looking for.

Tin Roofs & Palm Trees (1977) by Robert Trumbull is a serious socioeconomic/political overview of the South Pacific nations with particular emphasis on their emergence into the 20th century. Trumbull is a former *New York Times* correspondent and writes with authority on the subject. This is a good primer on the background of the modern-day South Pacific.

A Writer's Notebook (1984) by W. Somerset Maugham is a well-known collection of notes, journals and character sketches, some of which Maugham later used in his short stories and novels. The collection covers the period from 1892 to 1944, with 40 pages devoted to his travels in the Pacific including Tahiti, Samoa, Fiji and Hawaii. For Maugham lovers, the reading is fascinating.

NOVELS AND ISLAND TALES

The Blue of Capricorn (1977) is Eugene Burdick's delightful collection of short stories and nonfiction essays about the South Pacific. Burdick, a master of the craft and coauthor of *The Ugly American*, explores white people's fascination with the tropics. It's one of the best collections of the South Pacific genre available.

South Seas Tales by Jack London is not London's most famous work but has a few good tales including *The House of Mapuhi*, the slanderous story of an avaricious pearl buyer. It's based on a real-life character with whom London had an axe to grind.

Typee: a Real Romance of the South Seas; Omoo: a Narrative of Adventures in the South Seas, a Sequel to Typee and Marquesas Islands by Herman Melville are all based on Melville's experiences on the islands.

Tahiti's Literati

Ever since its depiction as a Garden of Eden by 19th-century romantics, Tahiti has attracted not only missionaries and vagabonds, but artists and writers as well.

PAUL GAUGUIN AND TAHITI

"The reason why I am leaving is that I wish to live in peace and to avoid being influenced by our civilization. I only desire to create simple art. In order to achieve this, it is necessary for me to steep myself in virgin nature, to see no one but savages, to share their life and have as my sole occupation to render, just as children would do, the images of my own brain, using exclusively the means offered by primitive art, which are the only true and valid ones."

On April 1, 1891, Gauguin left Europe and 69 days later arrived in Papeete. No earthly paradise, Papeete in the late 19th century was a ramshackle, administrative center of a third-rate colony—a collection of brick buildings and clapboard houses with tin roofs. The local populace was equally disappointing. The noble savages he had envisioned were clothed in sarongs, white shirts and straw hats, while their female counterparts wore missionary-inspired ankle-length Mother Hubbard dresses. Local society, composed of French officials and their French or native wives, entertained each other with gossip and endless dinner parties.

Gauguin decided it would be better to spend his time with Tahitians and moved into a Tahitian-style hut. He worked feverishly and by 1893 sailed back to France with 66 paintings and a dozen wooden sculptures. There were numerous landscapes, portraits and scenes that depicted contemporary life in French Polynesia. These included Tahitians bathing in a stream, men inspecting their fishing nets, women weaving hats, and the like. Examples of these are *Under the Pandanus*, *The Burao Tree* and *Parau parau*. While the details are realistic and historically correct, as photos of the time confirm, Gauguin's eye is discriminating. He chose the most idyllic and aesthetically pleasing aspects of life on the island as his subjects. Other paintings were taken from themes found in Tahitian myth or religion.

With much fanfare, Gauguin organized a Paris exhibition on November 9, 1893. Unfortunately, no one in France seemed to recognize his genius, and his exhibition failed miserably. Although unsuccessful at selling his art, Gauguin did receive a small inheritance from an uncle, which provided enough money for him to carry on. He returned to Tahiti. So despondent was he that he even told a friend that he was giving up painting "apart from what I may do for my own amusement." In short, this was to be a voyage of no return. On September 9, 1895, he was back in Papeete.

Shortly after his return he sought a proper home. His declining health made him more dependent on being near a hospital, so he moved only eight miles from Papeete, in the Punaauia district. He decided to purchase his own plot, where he constructed a small plank house and studio. (The site is currently marked by a sign adjacent to a school in Punaauia.)

Even though Gauguin no longer had to pay rent, his cash-flow problems continued. He sold few paintings and lived almost solely on the credit granted to him by the local Chinese merchant. Ill health continued to plague him and at the end of 1897 he suffered from fainting fits and long bouts of insomnia, and was coughing up blood. He was ready to take his own life but before doing so he had to paint one last picture. Taking burlap used to make bags for copra as a canvas, Gauguin created his masterpiece: *Where do we come from? What are we? Where are we going?* He then swallowed an enormous dose of arsenic, but vomited up the poison and miraculously recovered.

In 1901, Gauguin received an unexpected offer from a Paris art dealer who agreed to pay him a salary for every picture he produced. With his chronic money problems out of the way, Gauguin, still in search of paradise or at least a primitive culture, decided to move to the isolated Marquesan island of Hiva Oa. His decision to move to the Marquesas was dictated primarily by the fine carvings he had seen in the Tahitian homes of civil servants who had been posted to those remote islands. Despite the exquisite bowls and other artifacts he had seen, Gauguin soon discovered the sad state of the Marquesan population, which had been decimated by disease, liquor and other endowments of Western civilization.

He settled in Atuona, the village and administrative center of Hiva Oa, which had a population of about 500 locals, a dozen European settlers and Chinese shopkeepers, a Protestant missionary and a small Catholic enclave. Gauguin found a vacant lot where he built himself a two-story structure that was the finest home in the Marquesas. Above the door in large letters a sign read *Maison du Jouir* (*House of Pleasure*). He soon acquired a companion, Marie-Rose, a 14-year-old *vahine*, who until then had been a resident of the Catholic mission school. She soon became pregnant, returned to her parents and gave birth to a daughter on September 14, 1902.

With plenty of money to spend, Gauguin became well known for his wild parties and quickly incurred the wrath of the local clergy and police. But, with some financial security, two servants, a home and Marie-Rose, he had the wherewithal to produce in just a few months over 20 splendid works. These included *Horsemen on the Beach*, *Et l'or or de leurs Corps* and *The Call*. In the final months of 1902 the artist's life came to a sad ending. His health declined, new enemies in the tiny community objected to his parties, his near abduction of Marie-Rose and his lifestyle.

On the morning of May 8, Gauguin sent for the Protestant pastor, with whom he shared some interests. He complained of pains and fainting spells. Later that morning a Marquesan neighbor found the artist lying on his bed with one leg hanging over the edge. The visitor was not certain that the painter was alive, so he resorted to a tried and true Marquesan tradition—a bite on the head—to determine Gauguin's state. He then sang an ancient death chant.

Gauguin lies buried in a cemetery on a hill above the village of Atuona. His "House of Pleasure" has been restored in 1958 by Pierre Bompard near its original location, next to a museum dedicated to the painter and Marquesan culture. Visitors regularly leave white plumeria blossoms on the grave in remembrance. (See Chapter Eleven for more information.)

HERMAN MELVILLE

In June 1842, the *Acushnet*, a Yankee whaler, dropped anchor off Nuku Hiva in the Marquesas. Aboard the vessel, 22-year-old Herman Melville couldn't wait to step ashore. He had already faced one and a half years of deprivation at sea and knew he wouldn't be returning home until all the whale oil barrels were filled, perhaps two, three or even four years later. He and a friend named Toby stuffed a few biscuits beneath their clothing and jumped ship. They hid in the deep, forested recesses of the island's interior, safe from the ship's crew that would surely come looking for them. They hiked for days on end with little food and no shelter. The fact that Melville's leg was burning with infection made the trek even more excruciating. The two young men accidentally stumbled into the Typee Valley, home of a tribe known for its ferocity.

Toby disappeared looking for medical aid for his friend and Melville was to spend the next four months with the Typees, an experience that would be the basis for his first book, *Typee*. He was treated well by the Marquesans, who gave him a servant and royal attention from Mehevi, the chief. However, Melville was never sure of the natives' intentions. Was he being treated as a distinguished visitor or simply being fattened for the kill? After all, these people were cannibals.

Fortunately for world literature, Melville survived his sojourn with the Typee, during which he was held in a sort of protective custody. He dwelt with the Marquesans neither in bliss nor in terror. He observed closely and made some startling revelations. "There were," said Melville, "none of the thousand sources of irritation that the ingenuity of civilized man has created to mar his own felicity." He noted that there were no debtors, no orphans, no destitute, no lovesick maidens, no grumpy bachelors, no melancholy youth, no spoiled brats and none of the root of all evil—money.

Melville adapted well, enjoying the company of a *vahine* named Fayaway and the companionship of the men. His foot, however, was still inflamed and spiritually he was isolated. He needed medical care but the Typees were unwilling to let him go. His situation was well known on the island and with the help of sympathetic natives and a captain who was hard up for crew members, he escaped by joining up with the Sydney whaler *Lucy Ann*, which sailed to Tahiti.

Apparently the conditions on the *Lucy Ann*—inedible food, cockroach and rat infestation and rotten rigging—were so god-awful that upon reaching Tahiti, Melville decided to join the crew members in a mutiny rather than continue. His fellow travelers—with such romantic names as Doctor Long Ghost (the ship's surgeon!), Bembo (a tattooed Maori harpooner), Jingling Joe, Long Jim, Black Dan, Bungs, Blunt Bill and Flash Jack—didn't need much persuading. When they refused to sail and complained to British Consul Charles Wilson in Papeete, Wilson decided against the mutineers and with the support of the French Admiral Dupetit Thouars, had them locked up. Melville was imprisoned in the *Calabooza Beretanee*, the local jail. After his release six weeks later, he went to the remote village of Temae on Moorea (now near the airport) and talked the chief into allowing the women to dance the *Lory-Lory* (the precursor of the *Tamure*), an erotic, passionate performance that the missionaries had forbidden, naturally.

Four years later Melville laboriously put together *Typee: a Peep at Polynesian Life*, which received immediate attention in America and Europe. Some critics hailed it, some doubted its authenticity, and others called it racy. The missionaries (who weren't treated too kindly in the book) found it appalling. Both *Typee* and *Omoo* were outspoken tirades against the ruination of the Pacific by Western civilization. Why, Melville asked, should the natives be forced to participate in an alien church, to kowtow to a foreign government, and to adopt strange and harmful ways of living? In *The Fatal Impact*, Alan Moorehead writes that although Melville was "possibly libelous and certainly scandalous in much that he wrote," his account of the "sleaziness and inertia that had overtaken life" in Papeete in 1842 is remarkably vivid. Perhaps Melville was accurate as well. Moorehead says that many of the Tahitians—by this time caught between the missionaries, the whalers and finally the French—had "lost the will to survive—the effort to adjust to the outside world had been too much."

PIERRE LOTT

Midshipman Louis Marie Julien Viaud, who later became known to the world as Pierre Loti, first came to Tahiti in the 1880s aboard a French naval vessel. His largely autobiographical book, *The Marriage of Loti*, brought him fame and is credited with influencing Paul Gauguin to come to Tahiti. In the book he describes his friendship with Queen Pomare IV and his all-consuming love affair with Rarahu, a young girl from Bora Bora.

Loti's book tells how he came upon Rarahu bathing in a pool (which still can be visited today) in the Fautaua Valley near Papeete. There he witnessed the girl accepting a length of red ribbon from an elderly Chinese man as payment for a kiss. Rarahu was poor and this type of behavior was not unusual for a girl of little means. Nevertheless, as a result of what the incensed Frenchman saw, the Chinese in Tahiti suffered for years following the 1881 publication of *The Marriage of Loti*. Despite Loti's virulently anti-Chinese propaganda, the book gave an accurate account of life in Tahiti during the late 19th century.

ROBERT LOUIS STEVENSON

Robert Louis Stevenson arrived in the Marquesas with his wife and mother in 1888, marking the first leg of his six-year voyage to the South Seas aboard the *Casco*. The South Pacific held him spellbound. In the Marquesas the health of the frail writer improved dramatically. He spent his days wading in the lagoon, searching for shells, or riding horses. The Stevenson clan was impressed by the generosity and kindness of the locals, so much that even Stevenson's mother, a staunch supporter of the missionaries, began to question whether forcing religion on the natives was actually beneficial.

From the Marquesas the *Casco* set sail for the Tuamotu atoll of Fakareva, where the Stevensons spent the balmy evenings trading tales with Donat Rimareau, the half-caste French governor of the island. The author's *The Isle of Voices* incorporated Rimareau's tales into his story.

Tahiti was the next stop on the *Casco's* itinerary. The travelers found Papeete to have a "half and halfness" between Western and Tahitian culture, which they disliked and they soon set sail for the other side of the island. There the Stevensons befriended a Tahitian princess (whom Pierre Loti had much admired) and a chief, who helped them. By this time Stevenson had become very ill, the family was short of money and the *Casco* needed extensive repairs. The generous Tahitians, who offered the wayfarers food, shelter and moral support, were a godsend. The long stopover allowed Stevenson time to work and recuperate. Stevenson's wife wrote that the clan sailed from Tahiti for Honolulu on Christmas Day of 1888 "in a very thankful frame of mind."

JACK LONDON

Perhaps the most controversial American writer of his day, Jack London first came to French Polynesia in 1906 on the ill-fated voyage of the *Snark*. He and his wife arrived in the Marquesas after nearly dying of thirst and sickness at sea because one of the crew members had inadvertently left the water tap open during a storm. The Londons stayed on Nuku Hiva for several weeks, renting the house where Robert Louis Stevenson had stayed. They also visited the Typee Valley, immortalized in Melville's *Typee*, one of London's favorite childhood books. London was, however, disappointed by what he saw. Melville's vision of 19th-century French Polynesia no longer existed, and London referred to the natives as "half-breeds," blaming the whites for the corrupting influence that decimated the Marquesan race both physically and spiritually. He spent his days feasting on tropical fruit, relaxing in the sun, collecting curios and trying to ward off huge wasps and *nonos*, vicious flies that inflict a nasty bite.

The next stop for the *Snark* was Tahiti, where London was greeted with the news that back home his checks had bounced. To make matters worse, he did not get along with some of the French officials, and thieves stole many items from his boat. Perhaps this is why the writer did not write about Tahiti in more flattering terms. In *The Cruise of the Snark* he wrote: "Tahiti is one of the most beautiful spots in the world," but for the most part was inhabited by "human vermin." He took a dislike to a well-known pearl buyer, Emile Levy, and in *South Sea Tales* unfairly depicted the Frenchman as an avaricious businessman who cheated a native out of a huge pearl and who met a horrible death. London did not bother to change Levy's name or physical description in the story, and the pearl buyer was furious. Even the other residents of Tahiti, who were not terribly fond of the hard-driving businessman, thought London had gone too far. In the end, Levy successfully sued London, who had long since returned to the United States, but who paid dearly in the end for his outpouring of venom.

RUPERT BROOKE

While visiting the west coast of the United States in 1913, Rupert Brooke, the great soldier/poet of the Edwardian age, suddenly decided to tour the South Seas. He came to Tahiti in January 1914, where he lingered until April, nursing an injury caused by bumping against coral. During this time he fell in love with a beautiful Tahitian woman named Taata (whom he called Mamua). It was here that he composed perhaps his three best poems, *The Great Lover*, *Retrospect* and *Tiare Tahiti*. According to biographer John Lehman, it was with Mamua that Brooke had the only "perfect and surely consummated love-affair of his life." Wrote Brooke in *Tiare Tahiti*:

> "Mamua when our laughter ends,
> And hearts and bodies, brown as white,
> Are dust about the doors of friends,
> Or scent a-blowing down the night,
> Then, oh! then the wise agree, Comes our immortality..."

On returning to San Francisco, Brooke's thoughts returned to Tahiti and his lover continued to haunt him. In 1915, on a hospital ship off Skyros, Brooke died of food poisoning at the tender age of 28. On his deathbed in the Aegean, he wrote these instructions to a friend: "Try to inform Taata of my death. Mlle. Taata, Hotel Tiare, Papeete, Tahiti. It might find her. Give her my love." Several years later, when Somerset Maugham came to Tahiti to research a book on Gauguin, Brooke's old friends still wept uncontrollably at the mention of his native name, Purpure, the only name they knew him by.

SOMERSET MAUGHAM

Among the works of the English writer Somerset Maugham is *The Moon and Sixpence*, a novel based on the life of Paul Gauguin. During World War I, when, according to Maugham, "the old South Seas characters were by necessity confined to the islands," he visited Tahiti to research the book. There he not only culled reminiscences of the painter from people who knew him, but also learned more of writers like Loti, Brooke, Robert Louis Stevenson and Jack London. Like those writers before him, Maugham was entranced with the magic of the South Seas. He spent his time interviewing everyone who knew Gauguin, including businessmen, a sea captain and a hotel proprietress. In Maugham's words, he wanted to make the protagonist of his novel as "credible as possible."

Despite Maugham's enchantment with Tahiti, most of his short stories about the South Pacific—including *Rain*, which immortalized the prostitute Sadie Thompson—took place in Samoa. Of this the author commented, "The really significant fiction of the world today involves a husband and wife relationship, the problems that lovers encounter and overcome, a cuckolded man, a jilted woman, an unrequited or pretended love for the other. From sexual conflicts we have our revenge and homicidal motives." However, Maugham observed that in a place like Tahiti, "where there are sexual licenses, excesses, the condoning attitude on infidelity, a tolerance of promiscuity, and an absence of sexual possessiveness, there does not exist the emotional tension that precipitates human drama. . . ." In addition, Maugham asserted "that Tahiti is a French possession, and the French with their *laissez faire* and *mènage-a-trois* tolerance of sexual philandering and indulgences don't really provide believable fictional protagonists for any human-triangle, story or play unless you want to make a comedy or farce out of the situation."

Paul Gauguin's case, however, falls into a different category. When the artist came to Tahiti, "the languor of this island, the Polynesian playfulness, the castrative sexuality that abounded there, could not save him from his ultimate and wretched fate. That of course was Gauguin's predetermined course of tragedy," Maugham said.

NORDHOFF AND HALL

James Norman Hall and Charles Nordhoff first met in the military service at the end of World War I when they were commissioned to write a history of the Lafayette Flying Corps. They were vastly different in temperament: Hall was shy, optimistic and romantic. Nordhoff, outwardly more confident, was pessimistic and skeptical. Hall was a native of Iowa. Nordoff had been raised in California. They distrusted each other at first, but their opposite natures were complementary and they eventually became the best of friends. Nordhoff convinced Hall that Tahiti was the place to go and write. When the *Atlantic* assigned them a piece on Tahiti and gave them an advance, they were on their way to the South Seas.

Years later, Tahiti had become their home. An outpouring of articles and books by the two ensued. They wrote some works separately, but continued to work well as a team, and after they collaborated on a boy's adventure, Nordhoff proposed doing another book in the same vein. Hall refused, but instead suggested an idea that was to become the most famous seagoing novel written in the 20th century—*Mutiny on the Bounty*.

During their initial research Nordhoff and Hall could scarcely believe that the most recent book on the *Bounty* incident had been published in 1831! No one had ventured to write a fictionalized account of the event even though it was the kind of story that begs to be transformed into literature. Based at the Aina Parè hotel in Papeete, the two writers plunged into their work. From the British Museum they procured accounts of the voyage, the mutiny, Bligh's open-sea voyage and the bloody Pitcairn experience, along with copies of the court martial proceedings and the Admiralty blueprints of the *Bounty*. Both immersed themselves in 19th-century prose, which helped to set a common style. The resulting narrative was divided into three sections: the *Mutiny On the Bounty*, *Men Against the Sea* (Bligh's open-sea voyage) and *Pitcairn Island* (the adventures of Fletcher Christian, his mutineer cohorts and the Tahitians who accompanied them). The trilogy was completed in 1934, after five years of work. Fifty years and three cinematic versions later, the story still hasn't lost its charm and fascination.

Hall is buried facing Matavai Bay where the *Bounty* dropped anchor and where he and Nordhoff used to sit discussing their work. A bronze plaque on the grave is inscribed with a poem he wrote as a young boy:

"Look to the Northward, stranger
Just over the hillside, there
Have you in your travels seen
A land more passing fair?"

Index

Lodging Index

Dining Index

HIDDEN GUIDES

Adventure travel or a relaxing vacation?—"Hidden" guidebooks are the only travel books in the business to provide detailed information on both. Aimed at environmentally aware travelers, our motto is "Where Vacations Meet Adventures." These books combine details on unique hotels, restaurants and sightseeing with information on camping, sports and hiking for the outdoor enthusiast.

THE NEW KEY GUIDES

Based on the concept of ecotourism, The New Key Guides are dedicated to the preservation of Central America's rare and endangered species, architecture and archaeology. Filled with helpful tips, they give travelers everything they need to know about these exotic destinations.

PARADISE FAMILY GUIDES

Ideal for families traveling with kids of any age—toddlers to teenagers—Paradise Family Guides offer a blend of travel information unlike any other guides to the Hawaiian islands. With vacation ideas and tropical adventures that are sure to satisfy both action-hungry youngsters and relaxation-seeking parents, these guides meet the specific needs of each and every family member.

Ulysses Press books are available at bookstores everywhere. If any of the following titles are unavailable at your local bookstore, ask the bookseller to order them.

You can also order books directly from Ulysses Press
P.O. Box 3440, Berkeley, CA 94703
800-377-2542 or 510-601-8301
fax: 510-601-8307
www.ulyssespress.com
e-mail: ulysses@ulyssespress.com

HIDDEN GUIDEBOOKS

____ Hidden Arizona, $16.95
____ Hidden Bahamas, $14.95
____ Hidden Baja, $14.95
____ Hidden Belize, $15.95
____ Hidden Big Island of Hawaii, $13.95
____ Hidden Boston & Cape Cod, $14.95
____ Hidden British Columbia, $18.95
____ Hidden Cancún & the Yucatán, $16.95
____ Hidden Carolinas, $17.95
____ Hidden Coast of California, $18.95
____ Hidden Colorado, $15.95
____ Hidden Disneyland, $13.95
____ Hidden Florida, $18.95
____ Hidden Florida Keys & Everglades,
        $13.95
____ Hidden Georgia, $16.95
____ Hidden Guatemala, $16.95
____ Hidden Hawaii, $18.95
____ Hidden Idaho, $14.95
____ Hidden Kauai, $13.95

____ Hidden Los Angeles, $14.95
____ Hidden Maui, $13.95
____ Hidden Montana, $15.95
____ Hidden New England, $18.95
____ Hidden New Mexico, $15.95
____ Hidden Oahu, $13.95
____ Hidden Oregon, $15.95
____ Hidden Pacific Northwest, $18.95
____ Hidden Salt Lake City, $14.95
____ Hidden San Francisco & Northern
        California, $18.95
____ Hidden Seattle, $13.95
____ Hidden Southern California, $18.95
____ Hidden Southwest, $19.95
____ Hidden Tahiti, $17.95
____ Hidden Tennessee, $16.95
____ Hidden Utah, $16.95
____ Hidden Walt Disney World, $13.95
____ Hidden Washington, $15.95
____ Hidden Wine Country, $13.95
____ Hidden Wyoming, $15.95

THE NEW KEY GUIDEBOOKS

____ The New Key to Costa Rica, $18.95

____ The New Key to Ecuador and the
        Galápagos, $17.95

PARADISE FAMILY GUIDES

____ Paradise Family Guides: Kaua'i, $16.95
____ Paradise Family Guides: Maui, $16.95

____ Paradise Family Guides: Big Island of
        Hawai'i, $16.95

Mark the book(s) you're ordering and enter the total cost here ⇨ [_____]

California residents add 8.25% sales tax here ⇨ [_____]

Shipping, check box for your preferred method and enter cost here ⇨ [_____]

☐ BOOK RATE   FREE! FREE! FREE!

☐ PRIORITY MAIL/UPS GROUND   cost of postage

☐ UPS OVERNIGHT OR 2-DAY AIR cost of postage   [_____]

Billing, enter total amount due here and check method of payment ⇨

☐ CHECK   ☐ MONEY ORDER

☐ VISA/MASTERCARD _____ EXP. DATE _____

NAME _____ PHONE _____

ADDRESS _____

CITY _____ STATE _____ ZIP _____

MONEY-BACK GUARANTEE ON DIRECT ORDERS PLACED THROUGH ULYSSES PRESS.